	Chapter 6—pages 129, 130, 131 [...]4, 146, 148, 149 Chapter 7—pages 159, 162, 174, 175 Chapter 9—pages 217, 224, 228 Chapter 10—pages 234, 244, 245 Chapter 11—pages 259, 260, 261
2b: Supporting and engaging families and communities through respectful, reciprocal relationships	Chapter 1—pages 4, 5, 12, 15, 17, 18, 19, 20, 21, 22, 23 Chapter 2—pages 32, 33, 34, 35, 38, 40, 44, 45, 46, 47, 48, 49, 50, 51, 52 Chapter 3—page 66 Chapter 4—pages 90, 94, 101 Chapter 5—pages 110, 111, 112, 123, 124 Chapter 6—pages 138, 139, 143, 146, 147 Chapter 7—pages 160, 161, 162, 163, 164, 165, 169, 170, 171, 172, 173, 174, 175, 176, 178, 180 Chapter 8—pages 187, 188, 189, 190, 191, 193, 194, 202, 203, 204, 206, 207, 208, 209 Chapter 10—pages 233, 236, 237, 242, 244, 245, 246, 247, 248, 249, 250, 251, 252, 253 Chapter 11—pages 265, 270, 272, 273
2c: Involving families and communities in young children's development and learning	Chapter 1—pages 15, 17, 18, 19, 20, 21, 22, 23 Chapter 2—pages 32, 40, 49, 50, 51, 52 Chapter 3—pages 66, 70 Chapter 6—page 140 Chapter 7—pages 161, 162, 163, 166, 168, 171, 172, 173 Chapter 9—pages 215, 220, 221, 222, 225, 226, 227, 228 Chapter 10—pages 242, 246, 247, 248, 249, 250, 251, 252, 253, 254 Chapter 11—pages 262, 263, 265
Standard 3. Observing, Documenting, and Assessing to Support Young Children and Families	**Chapters and Page Numbers**
3a: Understanding the goals, benefits, and uses of assessment—including its use in development of appropriate goals, curriculum, and teaching strategies for young children	Chapter 1—pages 17, 18, 20, 21
3b: Knowing about and using observation, documentation, and other appropriate assessment tools and approaches, including the use of *technology* in documentation, assessment and data collection	Chapter 1—pages 17, 20

Continued

3c: Understanding and practicing responsible assessment to promote positive outcomes for each child, including the use of assistive *technology* for children with disabilities	Chapter 1—pages 17, 18, 19, 20, 21 Chapter 11—page 265
3d: Knowing about assessment partnerships with families and with professional colleagues to build effective learning environments	Chapter 1—pages 17, 18, 19, 20, 21, 23 Chapter 2—pages 49, 50, 51, 52 Chapter 10—page 240

Families, Schools, and Communities

Together for Young Children

We dedicate this book to our families:
Clifford and Delores Stokum Couchenour
Bryan Maughan
Jay, Chelsea, and Christopher Couchenour
James and Martha Douglas Chrisman
Cindy Chrisman and
Kate Armstrong
and to the many families, schools, and communities
that added to our nurturing.

D.C. and K.C.

Families, Schools, and Communities

Together for Young Children

Fifth Edition

Donna Couchenour, Ph.D., C.F.L.E.
Kent Chrisman, Ed.D.

Shippensburg University

WADSWORTH
CENGAGE Learning·

Australia • Brazil • Japan • Korea • Mexico • Singapore • Spain • United Kingdom • United States

WADSWORTH
CENGAGE Learning·

Families, Schools, and Communities: Together for Young Children, **Fifth Edition**
Donna Couchenour, Ph.D., C.F.L.E. and Kent Chrisman, Ed.D.

Editor-in-Chief: Linda Ganster

Executive Editor: Mark Kerr

Assistant Editor: Joshua Taylor

Editorial Assistant: Greta Lindquist

Associate Media Editor: Renee Schaaf

Senior Marketing Development Manager: Kara Kindstrom

Art and Cover Direction, Production Management, and Composition: PreMediaGlobal

Manufacturing Planner: Doug Bertke

Rights Acquisitions Specialist: Don Schlotman

Cover Design: CMB Design Partners

Cover Illustration: Jeff Bane

For product information and technology assistance, contact us at
Cengage Learning Customer & Sales Support, 1-800-354-9706.

For permission to use material from this text or product, submit all requests online at **cengage.com/permissions.**
Further permissions questions can be emailed to
permissionrequest@cengage.com.

Library of Congress Control Number: 2012947567

Student Edition:

ISBN-13: 978-1-133-93894-1

ISBN-10: 1-133-93894-9

Advantage Edition:

ISBN-13: 978-1-133-94233-7

ISBN-10: 1-133-94233-4

Wadsworth
20 Davis Drive
Belmont, CA 94002-3098
USA

Cengage Learning is a leading provider of customized learning solutions with office locations around the globe, including Singapore, the United Kingdom, Australia, Mexico, Brazil, and Japan. Locate your local office at:
www.cengage.com/global

Cengage Learning products are represented in Canada by Nelson Education, Ltd.

To learn more about Wadsworth, visit **www.cengage.com/** Wadsworth

Purchase any of our products at your local college store or at our preferred online store **www.cengagebrain.com.**

Printed at CLDPC, USA, 12-18

CONTENTS

FOREWORD

Since Bronfenbrenner's seminal work, *The Ecology of Human Development and Learning* (1979), the early childhood education profession has been reconstructing itself in relation to creating environments and strategies that empower children, families, communities, and the profession itself. This process of renewal and transformation has been stimulated by the most rapid and dramatic social, economic, and technological changes ever to occur in human history. Our conceptions of what families, schools, and communities are like or should be like are experiencing revolutionary paradigm shifts. Several changes are powerful in their impact on how children and families learn and function: new work and family structures require more parent time, but society has actually reduced its support and resources; new technology and related educational advancements require more education for people to function effectively, but society has not responded with increased educational quality for all people; our knowledge of parenting and child/family development has improved, but too many early childhood professionals and too many parents and citizens lack this new knowledge and skills; and a self-centered and individualistic society requires more parent/family skills and bonding time, yet our society has busied parents and families with mostly isolated activities that contribute to continued economic and environmental abuses. Certainly there are exceptions to these stressors that are so real in all families, but one need only read the pages of Couchenour and Chrisman's book, *Families, Schools, and Communities: Together for Young Children*, to realize that the battle in the new millennium will be for a human competence that creates social decency and fosters spiritual and psychological relationships that empower everyone to be carers of each other.

Perhaps the most critical facet of Couchenour and Chrisman's work is their articulation of a theoretical construct that early childhood education professionals and concerned parents and citizens can use to develop strategies for having optimal conditions for everyone's learning and development. Their synthesis of the bioecological, contextualist, and family systems theory into a conceptual structure to use in addressing the many issues parents, children, families, schools, and communities experience is invaluable. The synthesis provides five important starting points for early

childhood education professionals to use in crafting their map for being truly high-quality family helpers.

1. The human development and learning process is the result of everyone's effort; that is, it is an interactive and renewing process that is influenced by all parts of the human community.

2. An empowering approach to working with the diverse and ever-changing needs and contexts of children and families must replace a deficit-oriented way of relating to children and families.

3. The power of parents and families to nurture healthy and proactive ways of living in children can occur within various forms and structures. The key is for families to have strong and nurturing relationships with each other and their supportive helpers.

4. Early childhood educators must create diverse and adaptive ways to support families in a world of constant change and stress.

5. Early childhood educators must lead the way for community transformation to create family-embracing ways of functioning. Each of these starting points for crafting a new vision and new paradigm for helping create powerful families is addressed by Couchenour and Chrisman.

Children's school and life success is indeed embedded within the multiple bioecological systems of person and environment relationships. Couchenour and Chrisman point to several examples within the multiple life systems that impact families: individual bioecological dynamics, social interactions, economic involvement, and cultural and societal events and experiences. Throughout history, families have needed nurturing and supportive relationships with the environment to thrive and contribute to the community. The need for a systems perspective of families is very critical in the complex and highly technological society in which parents and children now function. The prevailing belief that the individual can manage all of the factors that happen in life is myopic and distorted. As Couchenour and Chrisman so aptly describe, the challenges parents face in nurturing healthy and happy children are indeed great and require a total community structure to empower this critical child-nurturing function. Thus, the recognition that the human development and learning process is systemic requires us to approach parent, child, and family growth from an empowerment perspective. Engaging total families in the process of building on their strengths, identifying and addressing needs, and taking leadership in building strong communities are key strategies noted by Couchenour and Chrisman. This empowerment approach calls for the following:

- Understanding that families are the caring people who commit themselves to the child's lifelong well-being
- Nurturing children and adults in the family to reach their full potential and engaging them in activities in which they become the leaders in their communities
- Creating a sense of mutuality in families and in our professional and community relationships with families
- Validating parents and children—and their helpers—as the most important people in our communities
- Advocating and structuring schools and communities to be places in which parents, children, and families can renew and enrich their lives, thus empowering them to be the tremendously capable people they can be

Diversity in family and parenting forms and styles must be used as means to enrich and further develop family, child, and school-community strengths. If early childhood educators approach cultural and familial differences as sources of strength, so will parents, children, and other people in the community. As Couchenour and Chrisman suggest, the prevailing theme should be that of nurturing, caring relationships in all families by validating and valuing human differences as essential. This validating process can be achieved by early childhood professionals in several ways:

- Highlighting parent achievements across the diversity of family and cultural groups in and beyond the community
- Utilizing the diversity of parent and family talents as teaching resources for all children and teachers in the school
- Helping parents see the strengths present in themselves and their children, and then engaging parents and children in developing their strengths and talents
- Empowering everyone in the community to value and validate cultural diversity through needed social and economic changes

The only viable paradigm for developing successful family involvement in schools and communities is the partnership approach. This means crafting all facets of the family-school-community partnership together:

- Learning about each other in relation to strengths, skills, and talents that can be used to empower everyone
- Establishing equality in roles and relationships in family, school, and community, and in the transactions that occur between these groups
- Seeing, treating, and affirming parents as the key leaders in families, and as powerful leaders in the family-school-community triad
- Developing family-friendly strategies that invite parents and families to be actively engaged in school and community decisions
- Using diverse strategies that account for the varying work and family schedules, and situations that today's parents and families experience
- Valuing parents and family members as caring and capable people who are full members of the community team

Early childhood professionals can provide the needed leadership in stimulating community transformation toward becoming a family-centered place to live and grow.
As the authors note, several important starting points provide the foundation for this transformational process:

- Provide a model of family-centered functioning in the school and in relations with families and community members
- Engage members of the community in the total school program in ways that empower them to take ownership of creating the very best schools for children and families
- Educate the community on the key educational, social, and family needs that exist, and on strategies for addressing these needs
- Advocate for policy changes that will strengthen families in the community
- Participate in actions that help reshape the community toward being a positive force in the lives of families

Couchenour and Chrisman offer a wealth of ideas and information for building a new and stronger commitment to children and families. Most important, they provide a conceptual structure for crafting new strategies and approaches to engage families, schools, and communities in building healthy and positive places for children. Further, they connect this structure to the profession's standards of quality, to the urgent needs of families, and to our desire for a better future for all of our children. We owe the authors a big thanks for developing this powerful tool for reshaping our approach to supporting children and families. We can best thank them, however, by becoming active partners in our schools and communities in creating strong and nurturing environments and relationships for children and their families.

Kevin J. Swick
Professor of Education
University of South Carolina–Columbia

PREFACE

This book was written to meet a need for a textbook that included a theoretical and research foundation for early childhood educators' work with families, schools, and communities. As societal changes are mirrored in schools, the use of a contextualist model as a basis for family, school, and community partnerships makes sense. For early childhood educators, the current findings by neuroscientists about the importance of early interactions for optimal brain development point to the importance of supporting families to best meet children's needs. Further, early childhood educators are in a position of having knowledge that should be used by other professions and communities to enhance the lives of children and families.

New scientific information and current societal concerns about children's safety have led to a change in the charge of early childhood professionals. Teachers of young children must effectively involve families and communities in educating all of our children. Neglecting to do this at this critical time in history demonstrates both a lack of knowledge and a lack of caring about providing the best possible education for all children. We must meet the challenge of involving *all* families with their children's education, albeit that involvement must be individualized to best meet variations of diverse families.

The *Instructor's Guide* to accompany *Families, Schools, and Communities: Together for Young Children* provides the philosophy, a research base, and resources for early childhood teacher educators. Using the Harvard Family Research Project as a foundation, the authors provide a framework for both family involvement content and effective teaching strategies. This textbook addresses the Harvard framework for content in at least the following ways:

General family involvement: Chapters 1, 7, 8, 10, 11
General family knowledge: Chapters 2, 3, 4, 5, 6
Home-school communication: Chapters 7, 8, 9, 10
Family involvement in learning activities:
    Chapters 7, 9, 10
Families supporting schools: Chapters 1, 7, 9
Schools supporting families: All chapters
Families as change agents: Chapters 1, 7, 9, 10

Use of this textbook along with assigned, focused field experiences will provide both breadth and depth of knowledge for early childhood educators, future and present. Further, for each chapter of the textbook, the *Instructor's Guide* delineates knowledge, attitudes, and skills; a variety of instructional strategies; and reading lists for additional information. Resources include an updated list of suggested readings for further information about the content of each chapter. Videos related to each chapter are included with instructional strategies.

We are especially pleased with and proud of a valuable section of our *Instructor's Guide*. Dr. Rose Casement from the University of Michigan–Flint has compiled an annotated bibliography of children's literature to accompany many of the topics in this textbook. Rose's knowledge of high-quality children's literature and the significance of families in children's lives make this addition especially relevant. We believe that early childhood educators will find this resource to be beneficial in their work to support families and children.

It is our hope that this book will serve as one important tool in early childhood teacher education. In addition to the information in this book, teacher education must implement a variety of strategies for teaching both novice and experienced early educators about working effectively with families and communities. Both undergraduate and graduate students who study about working with families must have field experiences and field assignments so that they can practice skills and adopt attitudes such as compassion, empathy, and tolerance.

New to the Fifth Edition

While maintaining the previous strengths of a solid theoretical foundation and emphasis on creating mutual partnerships with families, the fifth edition of *Families, Schools, and Communities: Together for Young Children* has been expanded to include the following:

- In text call-outs for NAEYC teacher preparation standards
- In text call-outs indicating topics aligned with developmentally appropriate practice
- In text call-outs indicating diversity in practice

- Access to website video cases related to chapter topics
- Added content regarding technology and young children, including technology as a developmental issue for families of young children, as a topic for parenting support, social media, and new guidelines from NAEYC
- Added content regarding family roles in socialization of children, including a topic for parenting support
- Added child development knowledge in relation to chapter content including Erikson's and Piaget's stages
- Added content regarding children's approaches to learning
- Attention to a wider scope of parenting programs including federal cooperative extension and *The Incredible Years*
- Added content details for family involvement frameworks (Coleman, Cochran and Moll)
- Updated information regarding anti-bias education
- Understanding culture through the iceberg model
- Completely updated references, for both the research base and current practices
- Updated websites and web resources have been incorporated throughout each chapter. The web links can be retrieved directly through the companion website.

Supplements

Instructor's Manual

The instructor's resource manual (IRM) contains a variety of resources to aid instructors in preparing and presenting text material in a manner that meets their personal preferences and course needs. It presents chapter-by-chapter suggestions and resources to enhance and facilitate learning.

PowerPoint Presentation Slides

These vibrant, Microsoft PowerPoint lecture slides for each chapter assist you with your lecture, by providing concept coverage using images, figures, and tables directly from the textbook!

ExamView Test Bank

Available for download from the instructor website, ExamView® testing software includes all the test items from the printed Test Bank in electronic format, enabling you to create customized tests in print or online.

Education CourseMate

The Education CourseMate website offers access to TeachSource Videos including video cases, with exercises, transcripts, artifacts, and bonus videos. You'll also find other study tools and resources such as links to related websites for each chapter of the text, tutorial quizzes, glossary/flashcards, and more. Go to CengageBrain.com to register using your access code.

WebTutor(tm) on WebCT(tm) and Blackboard

Jumpstart your course with customizable, rich, text-specific content for use within your course management system. Whether you want to web-enable your class or put an entire course online, WebTutor (tm) delivers.

Acknowledgments

We wish to acknowledge those who so ably assisted with this writing project. We appreciate the many family members who have provided a voice to grandparents as parents, parenting a special needs child. Tamara Smith served as an invaluable graduate assistant and provided extensive new resources through searches of current literature. Her work as a graduate student is also reflected in the self-assessment instrument for parent conferences in Chapter 8.

We also appreciate our undergraduate and graduate students in early childhood courses who bring questions, ideas and suggestions in discussions about family engagement in early education.

Our families demonstrated patience with our work on this book as we missed visits and events as new due dates drive our schedules. We are grateful to many extended family members for their interest in this project. The staff at Cengage Learning who have worked with us including. Their continuing support for new editions of this textbook has increased the quality of this work. We are grateful for their varied ways of facilitating our work on this project.

The authors of this textbook began collaborating on professional projects in 1983. We worked together as friends and colleagues through 1994. Since then, we continue to collaborate in our work for children, families, and schools as spouses. Living together through the challenges and blessings of family life has influenced our understanding of the importance of family and community involvement in early education.

Donna Couchenour
Kent Chrisman

Reviewers

The authors are especially grateful to the following reviewers, enlisted by Cengage Learning, for their helpful suggestions, affirmation, and constructive criticism.

John Aiello
Editor and Publisher, *The Electric Review*

Audrey W. Beard
Albany State University

Carrine H. Bishop
Jackson State University

Marie Brand
SUNY Empire State College

Phyllis Gilbert
Stephen F. Austin State University

Barbara Nilsen
Broome Community College

Karen Ray
Wake Technical Community College

Barbie Underwood
Moberly Area Community College

Cynthia Waters
Upper Iowa University

Families, Schools, and Communities

Together for Young Children

UNDERSTANDING
FAMILIES

A Theory-Based Approach to Family Involvement in Early Childhood Education

OUTLINE

- **Objectives Aligned with NAEYC Standards**
- **Key Terms**
- **The Importance of Families and Communities in Children's Lives**
- **Perspectives on Family Involvement**
- **Contextualist Theories**
  Bronfenbrenner's Bioecological Theory
  Vygotsky's Sociocultural Theory
  Family Systems Theory
- **Implications for Practice in Early Childhood Education**
  Guidelines for Developmentally Appropriate Practice (DAP)
  Key Characteristics of Early Childhood Programs Practicing Inclusion

National Association for the Education of Young Children (NAEYC) Accreditation Performance Criteria
Division for Early Childhood (DEC) of the Council on Exceptional Children (CEC) Recommended Family-Based Practices
Family Support Movement

- **Summary and Conclusions**
- **Theory into Practice Suggestions (TIPS)**
- **Applications**
- **Questions for Reflection and Discussion**
- **Field Assignments**
- **References**

© Cengage Learning/ECE Photo Library.

OBJECTIVES ALIGNED WITH NAEYC STANDARDS

After reading and reflecting on this chapter, you should be able to:

- Apply each of three theoretical perspectives to relate the importance of families to young children's development **naeyc** 1

- Explain the scientific basis for including family involvement in early childhood education **naeyc** 2

- Consider the categories of internal and external developmental assets necessary for optimal child development **naeyc** 1

- Apply principles of developmentally appropriate practice (DAP) and the family support movement in meaningful ways **naeyc** 4

- Discuss the value of a national voluntary accreditation system for early childhood programs **naeyc** 6

Key Terms

accreditation
bioecological theory
chronosystem
circumplex model
cohesion
contextualist theories
developmental assets
developmental contextualism

developmentally appropriate
  practices (DAP)
exosystem
family life cycle approach
family support movement
family systems theory
flexibility
horizontal stressors

inclusion
irreducible needs
macrosystem
mesosystem
microsystem
sociocultural theory
vertical stressors
zone of proximal development

THE IMPORTANCE OF FAMILIES AND COMMUNITIES IN CHILDREN'S LIVES

❝ As we grow up in a family and in a broader social and cultural community, we all come to certain understandings about what our group considers appropriate, values, expects, admires. ❞

—Copple and Bredekamp

During the summer of 2005, divergent political philosophies echoed comments made nearly a decade earlier during the course of the 1996 U.S. presidential campaign. This ongoing political debate centers on whether it takes a village or a family to raise a child, pitting one against the other. Political philosophies differ in this regard, but the argument is found to be faulty when the evidence from child development research is considered. Researchers and practitioners are well aware that in order to reach their optimal levels of development, children need both families and communities. For this reason, schools must strive to support and partner with both families and communities.

DAP Partnership is a key to the establishment of successful relationships among families, schools, and communities. Partnership refers to equal rights for and responsibilities of all three entities. Further, partnerships imply that power bases are equal. Hierarchical models of family, school, and community will not lead to desired outcomes. That is to say, education professionals must work with families and communities through such mechanisms as two-way communication and shared decision making. **DAP**

Margaret Mead noted that children, of course, have needs, but that children also are needed by families and communities: "Of course we need children. Children are our vehicles for survival—for in them there is hope, and through them what has been, and what will be will not only be perpetuated, but also united." Thus, as Figure 1–1 demonstrates, children, families, and communities are entities that are interdependent with one another. In order for early childhood teachers to achieve the best results in their work with young children, this understanding must be practiced in every aspect of a child's education. It is the goal of this book to provide details of both the scientific evidence and the best educational practice regarding the formation of partnerships among families, schools, and communities.

Two key sources of evidence that inform early childhood educators about the essential need for partnerships among the significant adults in a child's life include the **developmental assets** work of the Search Institute (http://www.search-institute.org) and the work on the **irreducible needs** of children by Drs. T. Berry Brazelton and Stanley I. Greenspan.

naeyc 1 Recent research by associates of the Search Institute (http://www.search-institute.org) has led to the establishment of a framework of developmental assets, or critical factors, necessary for children's healthy development. Scholars continue to test and refine the details, but current child development understanding supports the framework. The list of assets includes 40 items for each period of development (infancy, toddlerhood, preschool age, elementary school age, and adolescence) and demonstrates

the importance that families, schools, and various community groups play in the lives of children. Each developmental level includes 20 external assets and 20 internal assets. These assets, in turn, are divided into the four subcategories, shown in Figure 1–2.

66 It takes a village to raise a child. 99

—African proverb

> **Do This**
>
> An examination of the four external asset categories (those that come from outside the child) shows that families and communities provide children with necessary care and love, safety, limits on expected behaviors, and a variety of healthy activities. As you consider these categories, list examples that you have experienced either from your own childhood or from a child you have known.

Similarly, an examination of the four internal assets (those that come from within the child) shows that children need the ongoing support from families and communities to build strong positive identities. When children have such support, they are able to commit

Figure 1–2	Categories for developmental assets.

FOUR EXTERNAL ASSETS

Support—Children need care and love from families, neighbors, and community groups.

Empowerment—Children are empowered when communities value them and keep them safe and secure.

Boundaries and Expectations—Children need to know what is expected of them. Limits should be clear, realistic, and responsive.

Constructive Use of Time—Children need to have opportunities to play safely. Choices should be provided with many varied activities. Both developmental level and individual differences should be considered.

FOUR INTERNAL ASSETS

Commitment to Learning—Families and communities encourage children to be lifelong learners.

Positive Values—Children are exposed to examples of caring, fairness, social justice, integrity, honesty, responsibility, and healthy life choices.

Social Competencies—Children have opportunities to learn how to get along with others, to celebrate similarities and differences, and to peacefully resolve conflicts.

Positive Identity—Children have positive role models and responsive nurturing so that they can develop a sense of self-worth and caring for others.

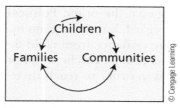

Figure 1–1   Children, families, and communities rely on each other.

© Cengage Learning

to being lifelong learners, exhibit positive values such as honesty and responsibility, learn social competence, and gain a positive sense of self. In order to develop these internal assets, young children are dependent on strong role models from both their families and communities.

Work on developmental assets has expanded on the viewpoint that families serve as primary socialization units for children. Inclusion of children's internal assets points to the understanding that children are active agents in their own development. The comprehensive listing of external assets necessary for healthy development indicate that parents and other family members maintain an essential role in interacting with and providing models for children. Child development is complex and is influenced by multiple internal and external determinants.

Brazelton and Greenspan (2000), both pediatric medical professionals, note that over the course of the twentieth century and into the twenty-first, families with young children have faced more and different kinds of stress than in the past. They emphasize young families' need for support from sources outside the immediate family in order to best nurture their children. Our society, they believe, is in grave danger of failing our children. When children do not get what they need for optimal development, society often pays the price. This cost includes the continuing presence of street gangs, drug and alcohol dependence, and ever-increasing prison populations.

The premise that all children have a right to sensitive nurturance and that no citizen has a right to ignore children's needs is a common thread throughout much of the work examining children's irreducible needs. This current and critical endeavor splendidly echoes the old African proverb "It takes a village to raise a child." The call for every citizen to care for children's needs is indicative that societal roles require all of us to be vigilant in meeting the needs of all children. This perspective supports the notion that children truly are the future of our society. Young children who have their needs met will grow into adults who can shoulder the heavy responsibilities of creating and maintaining healthy environments for all. **naeyc** 1

Figure 1–3   The irreducible needs of children.

All children must have the following needs met in order to grow and thrive:

- Ongoing nurturing relationships
- Physical protection, safety, and regulation
- Experiences that consider the individual differences of children
- Experiences that are developmentally appropriate
- Appropriate limits, predictable structure, and reasonable expectations
- A stable, supportive community
- Cultural continuity

© Cengage Learning

PERSPECTIVES ON FAMILY INVOLVEMENT

In this book, early childhood education is defined comprehensively as any program of care and education for children from birth through eight years of age. Early childhood educators—whether childcare staff, preschool teachers, kindergarten teachers, or primary teachers—are a critical part of a healthy community for young children and their families. Healthy communities rely on families to perform a variety of functions for their children. (Readers have noted that even though this textbook is geared toward educational programs for children through age eight, many of the principles and applications are relevant for programs for children through age 12, including programs that accommodate children with special needs.)

When families cannot or do not perform these functions, communities may operate interdependently with families for the good of the children. As society changes, the expected functions of families and communities shift. For example, many families today see a strong need to plan for their children's education beyond high school. It was only a few generations ago when it was more typical for families and other community members to educate for skills to earn a living—either through helping on a farm with household tasks or the care of plants and animals or by serving an apprenticeship to learn on the job. This change means an important family role of the past has been supplanted with formal postsecondary education programs.

The roles that children serve and the expectations that families hold for their children have evolved dramatically in the past 150 years. Moving from an agrarian society through the industrial revolution and into the information age has caused flux in all societal institutions. We have shifted from regarding children

Do This

Consider the developmental assets listed in Figure 1–2 and the irreducible needs of children noted in Figure 1–3. Examine overlaps. Discuss how these two sources provide evidence for the necessity of partnerships among families, schools, and communities.

as property of the father to perceiving them as individuals who have responsibility for themselves, from seeing them as miniature adults who have no rights to perceiving them as developing human beings who possess legal rights and who need societal safeguards (deMause 1974). Even as such change occurs, families remain a strong socialization force for their children. For many, though, these changes in the family, so much easier to observe and critique compared to changes in larger societal institutions, signal doom. Thus, some people deny the need for families to rely on the larger community for support.

In this latter perspective, the village becomes an enemy. This is faulty logic, however, and can harm young children as well as their families by denying children and their families needed sources of support. Expectations that any or all families can be strictly independent of others in the community is not only precarious, it is unrealistic. Whereas some families rely on extended family or kinship networks in a more private manner, others must count on more public forms of support. In all cases, healthy families benefit from strong communities and a caring society. In turn, healthy families are able to support their communities and the larger society in various ways.

> 66 Many things can wait. Children cannot. Today their bones are being formed, their blood is being made, and their senses are being developed. To them we cannot say tomorrow. Their name is today. 99

—Gabriela Mistral, Chilean poet

DAP Good early childhood teachers have always known that frequent, effective communication with families is imperative in the provision of quality care

Early childhood education teachers are a critical component of a community for both young children and their families

© Cengage Learning/ECE Photo Library.

and education for the youngest children. "The emphasis on parents in the settlement house movement of the 1880s, the nursery school movement of the 1920s, and the early intervention movement of the 1960s is exemplary of the parent participation tradition in early childhood education" (Powell 1989). Teachers have used traditional forms of communication, such as newsletters and conferences, when they are effective, but teachers also have created new and different strategies, such as interactive journals and portfolio parties, to adapt to individual circumstances.

Effective teachers also understand the essential role that families play in the socialization of children. As preschool age or younger children enter group care and education facilities, they will have already begun to establish a sense of self in relation to their families (Harter 2006; Brown, Mangelsdorf, Agathen, & Ho 2008). Supporting children within the culture of their families increases children's learning opportunities in early education settings. Teacher acceptance and respect for children's families ultimately leads to optimal child outcomes. **DAP**

The role of parents during the settlement house movement beginning in the 1880s has been documented. The focus of settlement houses throughout the early twentieth century was on urban poverty. "The old settlements taught adult education and Americanization classes, provided schooling for the children of immigrants, organized job clubs, offered after-school recreation, and initiated public health services.... Because of cultural diversity among immigrants, settlement workers had to come to their task with a certain humility. They had as much to learn from the immigrants as the new Americans did from them" (Blank 1998). Many of the settlement house programs provided to parents were intended to strengthen families for their lives in a new country. Involvement in their children's education was seen as a way to further economic success for the next generation while at the same time increase the quality of life for all.

The 1920s saw a nursery school movement with parents in essential roles. Growth in the field of psychology and a strong economy led to a zeitgeist of high optimism. Early education served a dual purpose of socialization for young children and a coping mechanism for mothers who felt isolated and burdened with child-rearing obligations. Having recently earned the right to vote, women were increasingly interested in roles outside of their homes. Katherine Whiteside Taylor, driven by these needs of the time, her own intellectual brilliance, and her love for her child, created a parent cooperative nursery. Taylor led mothers to understand child development and eventually the children's community was established with a trained professional supervisor of children, several mother-supervisors, and other staff. "Each mother worked for an entire day, once a week, assisting the director, the supervisor, and the cook in turn.... As new mothers joined, they were required to spend three days observing" (Byers 1972). A primary emphasis for family involvement during the nursery school movement revolved around mothers' study and application of child development principles.

In the 1960s, a key piece of legislation proposed by President Lyndon B. Johnson involved the creation of the comprehensive early childhood education program, Head Start. This program provided early education for preschool children, along with medical and social services for families. At the inception of the program, the belief that disadvantaged children needed a head start to compete indicated a deficit model of families. If children were provided with earlier education and families received social services and medical care, all would be prepared to meet challenges encountered upon children's formal school entry. Since that time, Head Start and other programs of early intervention have evolved and are more typically based on a systems model that emphasizes strengths rather than deficits of families. Even though most contemporary early education experts regard the early emphasis on needs rather than strengths as a weakened perspective, the focus on family involvement in this program was revolutionary.

Widely recognized as cofounders of Head Start, psychologists Edward Zigler and Urie Bronfenbrenner applied their strong vision about the importance of family involvement in education from the very beginning of this landmark program. These pioneers have contributed to our current understanding about the primacy of the family in children's development and learning. Continuing with his groundbreaking work in early education, Zigler's current efforts include Schools of the 21st Century. A major premise of this model is a commitment to building strong relationships with parents by providing a welcoming environment and a menu of services that can be accessed by each family to meet their perceived needs (www.yale.edu/21c).

Public school expectations for parents and families have evolved over time. In early colonial times, there was such an emphasis on parents as the primary educators of their own children that Massachusetts passed a law requiring parents to educate their children in reading, religion, and a trade. When this law was unsuccessful, another was passed to mandate localities to hire teachers to accomplish the stated goals. Over the next 200 years, schools became more and more bureaucratized, intending to provide basic skills to all so that everyone could serve as a productive member of a democratic society. However, with the increasing professionalization that accompanied this transformation, parents and families were regarded as having functions separate from their children's education. By the turn of the twentieth century, many forces led to broad support for universal public schools based on the concept that children from families across all economic statuses would be equally served. At the same time, many poor families chose to send their children to work rather than to school, often based on the family's economic need. In response to the concern that many children were not receiving an education in school, states passed compulsory attendance laws. Eventually, professional educators were often at odds with parents. A prevailing belief was that "education of children should be in the hands of the professional teacher and administrator, (and) parents did not possess the time, knowledge, or talents necessary for a child to meet the challenges of the emerging technology. Therefore the parent should turn over the process of education to professionals hired by the state" (Hiatt 1994).

The attitude that parents were ill equipped to be involved in their children's education continued and led to professionals with higher levels of education who were often removed from the school communities. Parents who had little education or were in a lower economic class often felt that schools belonged to those who possessed education and had greater wealth (Shipman 1987, as cited in Hiatt 1994).

Parallel to the revolution leading to rigid practices in public schools that disenfranchised families, a group of mothers formed the National Congress of Mothers, a precursor to the modern-day Parent Teacher Association (PTA). This group helped to connect families and schools despite the professional teacher-parent divide that was becoming institutionalized (Hiatt 1994).

Since the 1970s, when society saw an increase in the number of very young children in out-of-home care, a preponderance of early childhood literature supporting the need for family involvement has been written. In this same period, parents advocated more aggressively for children's education, as noted in the court cases related to desegregation, bilingual education, and education for children with disabilities. Educational researchers and policy specialists also increasingly employed evidence that partnerships with parents were necessary for the most positive outcomes. Many such policies were put into place in early childhood education, and gradually more models were encouraged for later elementary and secondary schools (Hiatt 1994).

The need for early education is even greater than it was three decades ago. The latest research on early brain development reinforces our intuitive notion about the importance of teacher-family partnerships, emphasizing again that parents are not only children's first teachers, but probably also their most important teachers.

DAP The concern about providing continuity in children's experiences is widely held as a rationale for positive and sustained relationships between early childhood teachers and family members (Powell 1989). Early childhood literature and practice have assumed that continuity is necessary and good for children. Though little research exists to document this as an absolute, some theories offer substantial support for the importance of continuity in young children's lives. In early childhood education, the best way to provide continuity is to develop strong family-school/childcare-community bonds. Descriptions of these contextualist theories follow. **DAP**

> 66 The reality is that learning does not begin when kids are age five. Learning begins well before they enter the schoolhouse. And what happens to children in their early years has profound impacts on the kind of entering students they will be. 99
>
> **—Sharon Lynn Kagan, Professor at Teachers College, Columbia University, and past president of NAEYC**

CONTEXTUALIST THEORIES

Three **contextualist theories**—bioecological, sociocultural, and family systems—demonstrate relationships among children, families, and communities that are crucial to effective family involvement in early childhood education. When early childhood teachers apply these theories, their family involvement practices will be more authentic and supportive.

Bronfenbrenner's Bioecological Theory

> 66 Understanding children's development requires viewing each child within the sociocultural context of that child's family, educational setting, and community as well as within the broader society. These various contexts are interrelated, and all powerfully influence the developing child. For example, even a child in a loving, supportive family within a strong, healthy community is affected by the biases of the larger society, such as racism or sexism, and may show some effects of its negative stereotyping and discrimination. 99
>
> **—Copple and Bredekamp**

Urie Bronfenbrenner's (1979) **bioecological theory** provides substantial support for upholding practices of involving families in early care and education. This theory emphasizes the developmental notion that biological predispositions and environmental influences interactively affect human growth.

A great deal of current information supports the understanding of the interaction of the forces of nature (biology) and nurture (environment). This view is in opposition to the age-old argument in psychology about nature *versus* nurture. "It is time to

reconceptualize nature and nurture in a way that emphasizes their inseparability and complementarity, not their distinctiveness…. [I]t is…nature *through* nurture…. [T]he coactivity of nature and nurture accounts for both stability and malleability in growth" (National Research Council and Institute of Medicine 2000). This and similar evidence led Bronfenbrenner to expand on his earlier ecological theory to one that acknowledges such a shift in thinking about the influences of nature and nurture to bioecological theory. A major impetus for Bronfenbrenner's development of this model was earlier research methods that produced narrow and inauthentic findings about human development from laboratory studies. He advocated for research methodologies that would make use of observational techniques in natural settings. The importance of studying children in their homes, schools, and communities undergirds this developmental theory.

Bronfenbrenner's model consists of five systems (which are graphically represented by concentric circles). Current understanding of the model, however, perhaps is best described as the Process-Person-Context-Time design (Bronfenbrenner 2001). Central to the model are the four concepts:

Process—The changing or dynamic relationship between the person and the context(s).

Person—The individual, including one's biological makeup and cognitive, emotional, and behavioral qualities. In the model, this concept is placed in the center of the nested circles.

Context—Environmental systems, each of which is identified in the concentric circle model in Figure 1–4.

Time—Viewed as multidimensional and including the historical period, the time in a family's life cycle, and the time in an individual's development. This concept is represented by the outermost circle of the model and labeled the **chronosystem**.

naeyc 1 Possibly the most celebrated of these concepts is context, often shown as concentric circles. Each of the levels of the environment is believed to actively interact with the individual. Understanding these systems can help early childhood teachers to also understand, in turn, that influences on children include the immediate environment (microsystem) as well as other environmental levels (**mesosystem, exosystem, macrosystem, and chronosystem**). The five environmental systems, including the dimension of time, are described in the following.

Urie Bronfenbrenner
www.human.cornell.edu/che/BLCC/About/People/urie.cfm
(accessed August 5, 2009)

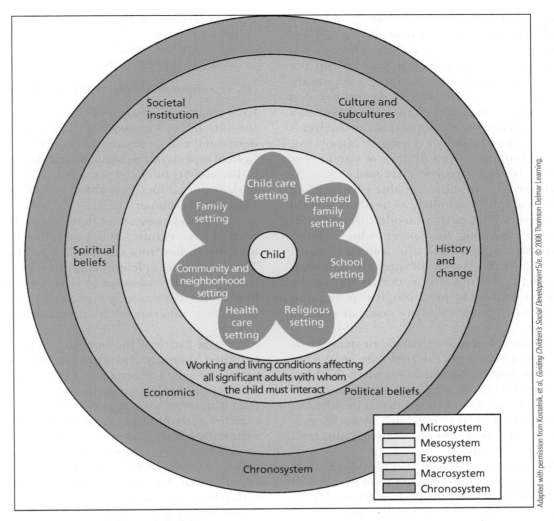

Figure 1–4   Concentric circle model of bioecological theory.

Bronfenbrenner poses five environmental systems:

1. **Microsystem** is the setting in which the individual lives, or the near environment. This includes the home, school, and community. Often, in a study of home-program relationships, only this system is considered.

2. **Mesosystem** is the relationships among contexts in the microsystem. The relationship or the connection between two forms of microsystems influences children's behavior and development. For example, a telephone call from the teacher regarding a child's difficulties at school may affect parental treatment of the child at home.

3. **Exosystem** is a system removed from direct access of the individual and has an indirect, rather than a direct, effect. Examples of exosystems include parental worksites, extended family, and mass media.

4. **Macrosystem** is the culture in which an individual lives. Values and beliefs of a culture or subculture affect children and families. Western culture is more individualistic, whereas many non-Western cultures are collectivistic.

5. **Chronosystem** is the time or the sociohistorical context. The era in which one lives affects behavior and development.

Taking each of these systems into account in the process of development indicates the complex nature of ecological effects on children. Many experts believe that when professionals understand the nature of such effects, more appropriate and effective strategies for optimizing children's development can be incorporated into early education practices, such as creating strong connections between children's families and early education programs.

These systems are most frequently understood as a series of concentric circles, with the individual at the innermost circle (Figure 1–4). Based on his theory, Bronfenbrenner has written frequently about what children need from their families and what families need from the larger society.

Although many early childhood teachers are capable of and committed to providing excellent educational climates for young children, they do not have responsibility for each child throughout the child's life. Thus, even when teachers' functions are similar to parents', a major difference exists between the two. This suggests that even though high-quality early education is extremely important for children's development, the family is even more important. For Bronfenbrenner, the importance of families for children goes beyond caregiving. He states unequivocally that parents are more capable of providing for the physical and psychological needs of a child when they have a third party who admires and loves them for their caregiving. So, a parent who has a loving relationship with another adult can more easily provide for children's needs. Bronfenbrenner summarizes human development as occurring "in the context of an escalating psychological ping pong game between two people who are crazy about each other" (1990).

The converse is that some single or unattached parents may not always get the fuel they need from other adults to provide optimally for their children. Multiple sources exist for single parents to feel loved and admired; any of these sources that is healthy can support that parent's caregiving. Such resources may include grandparents or other extended family, faith communities, or friendships.

Further, workplace policies affect family relationships. As the adults in more families than ever are all working outside the home, the effects of the workplace conditions are felt by children. Flexible hours, part-time positions with benefits, and availability of quality child care offer tremendous support for families with children. Such jobs, however, are not readily available for many workers in the current economy. Many jobs are part time, without benefits, and the hours change at the whim of the employer or manager rather than to meet family needs.

As a theorist, Bronfenbrenner is unusual in his advocacy for changing social policy in ways that will positively influence children's development. His recognition that the culture makes a difference in children's lives, as expressed in his definition of the macrosystem, has led him to call for national action in both public and private sectors to demonstrate our care for children and our support for their families.

Vygotsky's Sociocultural Theory

66 Families will want to know that what their children will learn in the early childhood program is in harmony with their values. Aiming for harmony between program and home can come about through culturally responsive practices. Cultural responsiveness can be compared to music, where notes that are harmonious aren't exactly the same notes, but they do go together. 99

—Gonzalez-Mena, in Copple and Bredekamp

Early childhood educators have increasingly looked to the work of Lev Vygotsky in their attempt to better understand the determinants of children's development. Certain aspects of this **sociocultural theory** are parallel to Bronfenbrenner's explanation of the importance of the external social world for a child's development (Tharp and Gallimore 1988).

Vygotsky postulated that human knowledge is derived from culture. This means that much of what we know comes from our families and larger society. The holidays we celebrate and the ways we celebrate them exemplify knowledge based on culture. The food we eat, the way we prepare and serve it, and even our table manners result from experiences within our culture.

DAP Much of the behavior of young children is rooted in family activities and expectations. Some four-year-olds, for instance, have learned at home that hitting back is an acceptable solution to problem situations with peers or siblings. It is important for early childhood teachers who are dealing with children who have learned that hitting is permitted to realize that not only must they teach the child a new set of rules for getting along with others at school, but also that they must communicate with parents and solicit their support for acceptable school behavior.

On the other hand, early childhood teachers sometimes must accept differences of behavior in children and accommodate these differences in the classroom. For example, teachers should support children's development of their home language. This practice demonstrates respect for a family's primary language and communicates that the early childhood staff values the family's culture. Further, children who speak more than one language have an asset that will serve them well in future endeavors.

Best practice in early childhood education points to viewing bilingual capabilities as an advantage for young children. In fact, the National Association for the Education of Young Children (NAEYC) (1996) recommends that teachers of young children "encourage and assist all parents in becoming knowledgeable about the cognitive value for children of knowing more than one language and provide them with strategies to support, maintain, and preserve home-language learning." Early childhood teachers must "honor and support" families in order to recognize the value of each of their cultural values and traditions. **DAP**

A child's development is dependent on both high-quality early education and the quality of family life.

Position Statement on Responding to Linguistic and Cultural Diversity

http://www.naeyc.org/
Click "Resources"; click "Position Statements"

English Language Learners: Partnering with Parents to Promote Oral Language and Early Literacy

Visit the Education CourseMate website at www.CengageBrain.com to view the Video Case, and then answer the following questions:

- What examples do you see in the video that relate to honoring and supporting a family's culture and home language?

- How does this video demonstrate the power of reciprocal relationships between teachers and families?

Lev Vygotsky's Theory

http://www.muskingum.edu/~psych/psycweb
/history/vygotsky.htm

Another premise from Vygotsky is that thinking is determined by social and historical assumptions. For example, social assumptions related to limited gender roles influence thinking, even when one claims to be logical or unbiased. Many couples find that before they had children, it was easier to maintain an egalitarian relationship. After having children, however, the added responsibilities seem to affect the degree of egalitarianism, and many fathers take traditional roles as breadwinners, whereas many mothers take traditional roles as homemakers.

Inaccurate historical assumptions also may cloud our thinking. An excellent example of this is the one so many practicing teachers were taught as students: Columbus discovered America. But, this assumption raises a logical question: could Columbus have discovered America when there were already people living here? We know now that there are more accurate ways of describing Columbus's explorations.

Of course, it is possible that our assumptions may also reflect greater accuracy than the previous examples illustrate. Accurate social and historical assumptions affect our thinking in useful and productive ways.

For Vygotsky, the **zone of proximal development (ZPD)** is the mechanism by which development occurs. This ZPD is technically the difference between what a learner can do independently and what can be done with the help of a more experienced or knowledgeable teacher. Note that for the purpose of cognitive development, a teacher might be a family member, classroom teacher, peer, or community member. This approach to understanding cognitive development emphasizes the collaboration between the learner and the teacher. The ZPD has four stages (Vygotsky 1962):

Stage 1: Performance is assisted by others who are more capable in the particular task.

Stage 2: Performance is assisted by the child herself as she moves toward self-regulation.

Stage 3: The child has internalized the task to a point that assistance would interrupt development. Performance is beyond both social and self-control; it is automatic and without self-consciousness.

Stage 4: Lifelong learning requires that the learner make recursive loops back to Stage 2 in order to improve or maintain skills. **naeyc** 1

An example of the first three stages of the ZPD is noted in the following anecdote.

Reflect on This

Chelsea, age 3, loves to sing and learns words to songs with ease. With this knowledge, her aunt sang a popular nonsense song to her one day: "Willaby, Wallaby, Wee, an elephant sat on me, Willaby, Wallaby, Woo, an elephant sat on you, Willaby, Wallaby, Welsea, an elephant sat on Chelsea." (stage 1)

The child responded at first by staring and smiling. Her aunt continued singing, using the names of other family members: Christopher, mommy, daddy, and Bryan. Soon, Chelsea started to sing the words that were familiar to her such as "an elephant sat on Christopher" (stage 2 begins), and later that day she was singing "Willaby, Wallaby, an elephant sat on mommy" (more stage 2). She did not use the unfamiliar words that rhyme with a name and begin with a "w," such as "wommy" or "waddy," but listened carefully when her aunt did.

Five days later, Chelsea visited her aunt again. At that point, she was singing the entire phrase and filling in names of her family (more stage 2). Several days later, Chelsea was singing the "Willaby, Wallaby" song without much effort or conscious thought as she played with blocks (stage 3).

It is too soon to tell whether Chelsea might engage in the recursive loop if she forgets the words at a later date.

DIVERSITY IN PRACTICE When early childhood teachers apply concepts from sociocultural theory, they demonstrate respect for all families' values and traditions. The understanding that knowledge is rooted in one's culture—or, as Vygotsky put it, that thinking is determined by social and historical assumptions—may help teachers analyze their own belief systems. For instance, some classroom or school-wide celebrations may be based on assumptions that come from the experiences or knowledge of the majority. Such events may cause some children or families to feel excluded or devalued. When this occurs, early childhood professionals must concern themselves with the ethical underpinnings of such celebrations.

Family Systems Theory

In addition to the developmental contextualist theory that has grown out of studies of human development across the life span, family sciences also have emphasized a systems approach: "In the **family systems theory**, everything that happens to any family member is seen as having an impact on everyone else in the family. This is because family members are interconnected and operate as a group, or system" (Olson and DeFrain 1994).

The following explanations of family systems theory include three models: developmental contextualism, circumplex, and family life cycle. All three of these models take a systems approach in that they view families as interactive systems in which children develop.

DAP *Developmental Contextualism* Supporting Bronfenbrenner's notion that children develop in context, Lerner notes "the family is not a context within which a child's ontogeny merely unfolds. Instead, the family is a dynamic context, one wherein a child is both transformer and is transformed. In addition, the child-family relation is reciprocally related to interactions with other key contexts of life, for example, the school and the peer group" (1989). This point of view, **developmental contextualism**, evolved from an effort to connect human developmental theories that espouse a strong biological foundation and family sociology theories that emphasize the family as the central social institution.

Similar to the bioecological model, in which individuals are actively interacting with their contexts, development is viewed as bidirectional and dynamic. Lerner emphasizes the need for researchers to include variables from biology, psychology, sociology, and history so that a pattern of variables might be more comprehensively understood. He believes that it is only through such comprehensive studies that human development will best be dependably described. Further, he posits the centrality of dynamic interactionism to explaining human development. This concept emphasizes the synthesis of variables influencing each other as well as the individual. Essentially, the developmental contextualist view does not emphasize either nature or nurture as more essential but rather supports the interaction of nature with nurture (or biology with context) as central to understanding influences on human development.

This view of human development is an optimistic one. The suggestion that people can acquire resources through various contexts in order to make the most of their own development can provide direction for many levels of education. In terms of early childhood education, it behooves us to work with children in their families and communities as well as at school or child care. Consideration for multiple levels of influence provides early education with information that can effectively support children's development and educational progress on such a variety of levels. **DAP**

naeyc 2 In addition to the developmental contextualist theory that has grown out of studies of human development across the life span, family sciences have also emphasized a *systems* approach. "In the family systems theory, everything that happens to any family member is seen as having an impact on everyone else in the family. This is because family members are interconnected and operate as a group or system" (Olson and DeFrain 1994).

Circumplex Model   Several family systems models have been developed. The **circumplex model**, created by Olson and others, is intended to demonstrate how all family members are interconnected. Following are three concepts that are critical to this model.

1. Cohesion or togetherness. **Cohesion** refers to the feelings family members have for one another as well as the amount and kind of time they spend together. A recent revision of this theory added another level of cohesiveness, making a total of five levels:

   - Disengaged/disconnected
   - Somewhat connected
   - Connected
   - Very connected
   - Enmeshed/overly connected (Olson and Gorall 2003)

The three middle levels are viewed as balanced, whereas the extremes (disengaged and enmeshed) are unbalanced.

2. Flexibility. **Flexibility** refers to the ability of family members to change roles and amounts of power they hold over time. This category looks at how families balance stability with change. The five levels of flexibility are:

   - Rigid/inflexible
   - Somewhat flexible
   - Flexible
   - Very flexible
   - Chaotic/overly flexible (Olson and Gorall 2003)

Just as with cohesion, the three middle levels are viewed as balanced, and the two extremes (rigid and chaotic) are unbalanced. Figure 1–5 demonstrates the relationships among various levels of cohesion and flexibility.

3. **Communication**. Family communication is a mechanism for establishing and maintaining

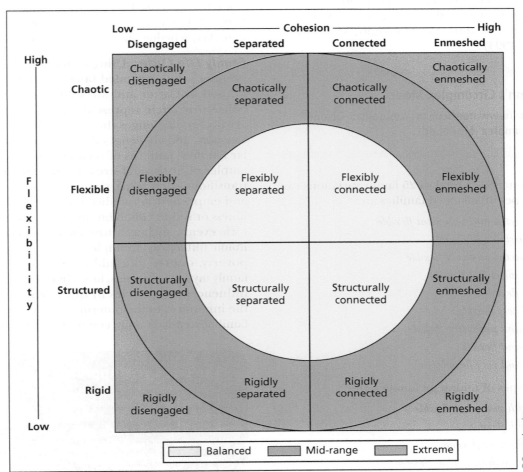

Figure 1–5   Flexibility and cohesion axes.

cohesiveness and for supporting families to be flexible over time in order to best meet family functions. Thus, this dimension is considered to be essential in order for families to change in relation to their levels of togetherness or flexibility. The following abilities are included in this domain: listening, speaking, clarity, respectfulness, concern for others, and self-disclosure.

In order to explain the processes involved in family communication, the circumplex model has recently been updated to include another graphic, a couple and family map, that features all five levels of cohesiveness and flexibility. Further, this updated version allows variations in characteristics of the family to be mapped over time.

Measures of these three dimensions can lead family scientists or therapists to classify a family in one of three ways:

1. Balanced families who have balance on both the cohesion and flexibility dimensions

2. Midrange families who are extreme on one dimension but balanced on the other

3. Extreme families who are extreme in both cohesion (either too close, enmeshed, or too far apart, disengaged) and flexibility (either too loose, chaotic, or not flexible enough, rigid) (Olson and DeFrain 1994)

Olson's Circumplex Model
http://www.noeticus.org/uploads/5-Olson-Circumplex_Model.pdf

From these concepts, a total of 25 family variations can occur. Nine types of balanced families are:

Somewhat connected and somewhat flexible
Somewhat connected and flexible
Somewhat connected and very flexible
Connected and somewhat flexible
Connected and flexible
Connected and very flexible
Very connected and somewhat flexible
Very connected and flexible
Very connected and very flexible

Twelve types of midrange families are:

Disconnected with somewhat flexible
Disconnected with flexible
Disconnected with very flexible
Overly connected with somewhat flexible
Overly connected with flexible
Overly connected with very flexible

Inflexible with somewhat connected
Inflexible with connected
Inflexible with very connected
Overly flexible with somewhat connected
Overly flexible with connected
Overly flexible with very connected

And, four types of extreme families are:

Overly connected overly flexible
Overly connected inflexible
Disconnected inflexible
Disconnected overly flexible (Olson and Gorall 2003)

Because families are dynamic, this family systems theory points to the importance of the family's ability to change over time. For example, family cohesion is often higher in young couples and in families with young children than in families with adolescents. The need for teens to separate from their parents and find their own identities often leads to less cohesiveness during this stage of family life. Not surprisingly, families with young children often find that they become less flexible than they were before the first child was born and then become more flexible when the children become adolescents (Olson and DeFrain 1994). Families with young children often have such tight daily schedules that flexibility lessens out of necessity.

Family Life Cycle   Using a model similar to Bronfenbrenner's, the expanded **family life cycle approach** espoused by Carter and McGoldrick (1999) employs a concentric circle representation with the addition of arrows for challenges that occur over time, **horizontal stressors**, and challenges that are embedded in particular families' patterns of relating, **vertical stressors**. Examples of horizontal stressors include developmental transitions, such as marriage, transition to parenthood, and empty nest; unpredictable events, such as chronic illness or sudden disability and unemployment; and historic events, such as hurricane disasters, war, and economic influences. Examples of vertical stressors include poverty, oppression, addictions, domestic violence, family myths and secrets, loss of leisure time, and genetic influences. The circles in this model represent from the innermost to the outermost: individual, immediate family, extended family, community, and larger society.

The Life Cycle Approach

The life cycle approach emphasizes that "families comprise people who have a shared history and a shared future. They encompass the entire emotional system of at least three, and frequently now four or even five, generations....Relationships with parents, siblings, and other family members go through transitions as they move along the life cycle" (Carter and McGoldrick 1999).

Do This

1. Draw a picture of your family at the time you were born.
2. Next, draw a picture of your family when you were a preschooler.
3. Draw your family when you were in elementary school.
4. Draw your family during your middle school or junior high years.
5. Draw your family as it was when you graduated from high school.
6. Draw your family as it is today.
7. Draw your family as you expect it to be five years from now.

Reflect on the following: How did your family change over time? How do you define family? On what did you base your expectations of your family in the future? Compare and contrast your drawings and reflections with others in your class.

Carter and McGoldrick also emphasize the importance of the family life cycle in order to best understand families. A family life cycle approach considers how families typically change over time. Relationships among family members take priority over family functions in this theory. Intergenerational relationships account for a great deal in how families move from one stage to another of the family life cycle process.

Most of the research and theory building done in this area is applicable to middle-class families in the United States. Families that differ culturally and economically from this group likely will not follow the same developmental cycle. This also may be true for families of various structures, such as single parent or blended family. It is important to understand that there is not a fixed sequence of life cycle stages for every family and that a flexible notion of predictable stages is helpful in understanding influences on individual development. For early childhood educators, the primary implication of this theory is that child development occurs within the context of the family life cycle.

Although there are several models of the family life cycle, some having as many as 24 phases, Carter and McGoldrick's work includes the following stages:

1. Leaving home: single young adults
2. Marriage: the new couple
3. Families with young children
4. Families with adolescents
5. Launching children
6. Families in later life

Because the emphasis in this text is on families with young children, this stage will be discussed further. Interestingly, Carter and McGoldrick refer to this stage as the pressure cooker phase of the family life cycle, which may help early childhood educators understand and work more effectively with families of the young children they teach.

The period when families have young children often requires immense adjustment by both parents. Each is moving, in terms of the family life cycle, from concern for the two of them as a couple to trying to balance child care, household responsibilities, and, increasingly, a full-time job. Caring for children is a primary effort during this stage, so when any part of this tenuous balancing act goes awry, it may cause the children's caregivers or teachers to feel the effects of the couple's apprehension.

Achieving a successful balance depends on many factors: well children, job security, quality and affordable child care, housing, working conditions of home appliances, and reliable transportation. When any one of the factors is out of the ordinary or unexpected, the balance is threatened. Thus, when an early childhood teacher requests a conference or a parent meeting, parents of young children often are immediately aware of how scheduling such an event may complicate their pressure cooker schedule. **naeyc** 2

DAP Further, when parents attend a conference or group family meeting, it is important that the time is planned carefully, that the starting time and ending time are communicated in advance, and that the time is well organized and used to benefit all concerned. In other words, educators must realize that a meeting might increase the pressure on families and, therefore, must be as useful and efficient as possible. **DAP**

Parents may have concerns about balancing full-time jobs and caring for their child.

© Cengage Learning/ECE Photo Library.

Because moving to the young children phase of the family life cycle requires so much adjustment for new parents and other family members, engaging in rituals is often seen as a way of supporting the family. Both extended family and community are often involved in such celebrations. Common secular rituals marking this phase include baby showers, newspaper announcements of births, handing out cigars, posting lawn signs announcing the baby's gender, sending birth announcements; other rituals, such as baptism, christening, and bris, are based on religious tradition.

A number of social changes over the past generation have affected tasks and responsibilities across the family life cycle in the United States. Important examples of such changes include a lower birth rate, longer life expectancy, the changing role of women, the relocation of young families for jobs or education, and the increasing divorce and remarriage rate. Divorce is now so common that many social scientists see it as a normative event.

naeyc 1 Specific implications for early childhood educators that can be culled from family systems theory include the following:

1. Teachers and caregivers need to remember the influence of all family members on children's behaviors. Influence may affect family members regardless of geographic distance or even after the death of some members. For example, one family member may insist to the parent that the child should have a structured reading program emphasizing phonics. This causes the parent or other primary caregiver to question the school's whole language reading program.

2. Each family member may play a role in a child's life that may remain consistent or may vary, depending on the family's situation. For example, a grandparent may become more actively involved if a parent dies, divorces, or changes jobs.

3. Stress in the family may change the child's role and his relationships with other family members. Parents may have concerns about balancing full-time jobs and caring for their child. Death of a parent or divorce may result in a child's greater role in providing emotional support for the remaining parent.

4. The function of myth may affect the child's behavior while she is at school. An example of one family myth, "We don't let anyone push us around," may influence the child so that she hits in response to conflict.

Do This
Changes in Families

To demonstrate recent changes in families, please do the following:

1. Write down the number of children your parents have, the number of children that were in each of your parents' families as they grew up, and the number of children in your grandparents' families as they grew up. Add the total for each of the three generations. What did you find?

2. Ask a relative about the ages at which your deceased relatives died. Note that current life expectancy for middle-class people in the United States is about 77 years. What did you find about earlier generations in your family?

3. What was your mother's role in the family in terms of working outside or inside the home? What were your grandmothers' roles? What roles do women in your own generation play? How have these changed over time? What are the reasons the roles have changed?

4. What was your father's role in the family in terms of working outside or inside the home? What were your grandfathers' roles? What roles do men in your own generation play? How have these changed over time? What are the reasons the roles have changed?

5. Has divorce or remarriage been an aspect of your immediate family? Your extended family? How has divorce or remarriage affected your family's life cycle process?

6. Do you live near your extended family? Have you ever moved with your immediate family? How does living near or far away from other family members affect relationships with grandparents, aunts, uncles, and cousins?

7. What is your family's philosophy regarding children? Speculate on how this philosophy might have changed over the generations.

Implications for Practice in Early Childhood Education

Multiple sources, including both professional literature and professional associations, point to the importance of early childhood educators understanding and practicing family and community involvement. Early childhood professionals not only must demonstrate an understanding or knowledge relating to families and communities, but also must apply their knowledge through allied attitudes and skills. **naeyc** 1

In terms of implications for practice, the following principles related to family and community involvement are offered: guidelines for developmentally appropriate practice (DAP); key characteristics of early childhood programs practicing **inclusion**;

Do This

As you examine principles in each of the categories of this section, note specific knowledge, skills, and attitudes that are implied in each of the items.

national program accreditation guidelines; Division for Early Childhood (DEC) of the Council on Exceptional Children (CEC) *Recommended Practices* in family-based practices; and the family support movement.

Guidelines for Developmentally Appropriate Practice (DAP)

66 Parents are the most important people in their child's life. 99

—Copple and Bredekamp

66 It is widely recognized that children vary on every measurable characteristic. Youngsters demonstrate individuality related to genetic, cultural, and contextual factors. Despite the rhetorical acceptance of such variability, conventional definitions of early development and learning have been more attentive to genetic and/or developmental variation than to cultural or contextual variation. Such a focus on genetic and developmental variability has had important and often negative consequences. 99

66 In some cases, access to differing educational opportunities has been determined by assessments that ignore cultural competence and that use majority-culture norms to determine competence on a single dimension.... 99

66 Developmental equivalencies are often not understood, and variation within cultures is often neglected. Individual, cultural, and contextual variables influence how children present themselves, understand the world, process information, and interpret experiences... 99

—Kagan, Moore, and Bredekamp

DAP Copple and Bredekamp, in the third edition of their book *Developmentally Appropriate Practice in Early Childhood Programs*, state that "developmentally appropriate practices derive from deep knowledge of child development principles and of the program's children in particular, as well as the context within which each of them is living. The younger the child, the more necessary it is for professionals to acquire this particular knowledge through relationships with children's families" (2009). Copple and Bredekamp identify seven guidelines to help professionals obtain this knowledge and establish reciprocal relationships with families of children in early education programs. These guidelines are as follows:

- In reciprocal relationships between practitioners and families, there is mutual respect, cooperation, shared responsibility, and negotiation of conflicts toward achievement of shared goals.

- Practitioners work in collaborative partnerships with families, establishing and maintaining regular, frequent, two-way communication with them. (With families who do not speak English, teachers should use the language of the home if they are able or try to enlist the help of bilingual volunteers.)

- Family members are welcome in the setting, and there are multiple opportunities for family participation. Families participate in program decisions about their children's care and education.

- Teachers acknowledge a family's choices and goals for the child and respond with sensitivity and respect to those preferences and concerns, but without abdicating the responsibility that early childhood practitioners have to support children's learning and development through **developmentally appropriate practices**.

- Teachers and the family share with each other their knowledge of the particular child and understanding of child development and learning as part of day-to-day communication and in planned conferences. Teachers support families in ways that maximally promote family decision-making capabilities and competence.

- Practitioners involve families as a source of information about the child (before program entry and on an ongoing basis) and engage them in the planning for their child.

- The program links families with a range of services based on identified resources, priorities, and concerns.

The DAP guidelines form the basis for excellence as early educators design programs for family involvement. Each program's leaders will, of course, develop unique ways of implementing the guidelines. Generally, however, using these guidelines can help ensure that program staff, when faced with the inevitable questions and decisions that arise when a new program is implemented, acknowledges the importance of, and makes decisions that reinforce, reciprocal relationships with families.

Position Statement on Developmentally Appropriate Practice

http://www.naeyc.org/
Click "Resources"; click "Position Statements"

Key Characteristics of Early Childhood Programs Practicing Inclusion

DIVERSITY IN PRACTICE   Nearly all early childhood education programs practice some form of inclusion, whether in a way that has been planned or unplanned. In this context, inclusion refers to programs that enroll both typically developing children and children with identified disabilities. It is not uncommon for young children to arrive at their early educational setting, whether it is child care, preschool, kindergarten, or the primary grades, without having been identified as having a particular disability. Further, legislation regarding special education requires that children with identified disabilities be included in regular educational experiences. The following guidelines (Schwartz, Sandall, Odom, Horn, and Beckman 2002) are provided as minimal requirements for providing all children with a high-quality inclusive educational experience.

- *Inclusive early childhood programs enroll typically developing children and children with identified disabilities.* In addition, early childhood programs commonly enroll children with disabilities that have not yet been identified.
- *Staff members are well trained and competent in providing a high-quality early childhood program.* Teachers who are highly qualified in early childhood or special education must be prepared to extend their expertise as necessary to provide the most effective program for all children in it. Thus, early childhood educators must understand the individual needs of atypically developing children, and special educators must understand typical developmental milestones and behaviors.
- *The same daily schedule is available to all children.* Children must not be excluded from any activity. Early childhood educators must work with families and other professionals to accommodate any special needs.
- *The curriculum is developmentally appropriate and meets the needs of individual children.* The very term *developmentally appropriate* indicates that early childhood teachers are required to plan and implement educational experiences for the entire group of children that take fully into account children's individual differences and needs. Accommodating special needs must be practiced routinely.
- *All children have the support they need to participate actively in the program.* This support may take the form of technological adaptations, physical adaptations, or an extra set of adult hands to help as needed.
- *Adaptations and modifications are provided for individual needs. Specialized services are provided as needed.* Early childhood and special education teachers must have current knowledge regarding child development as well as mechanisms for accessing available services and accommodations.
- *All children are supported to engage in successful peer interactions.* All children need the support of their early childhood teachers to learn to get along with others. Teachers should be prepared to provide various levels of support as well as to accommodate individual needs as necessary so that all children have sufficient opportunities to interact with peers.
- *Family members are active participants in various ways.* Application of all of the previously mentioned family and community partnership guidelines from DAP will be important for teachers to consider in inclusive early childhood programs. Teachers must interact with all families with respect and sensitivity.
- *Staff members and families collaborate to provide the best educational program for each young child.* The early childhood teacher's collaboration with families of children with special needs is necessary to ensure that each child's learning outcomes might be optimal.

National Association for the Education of Young Children (NAEYC) Accreditation Performance Criteria

NAEYC has devised a system of early childhood program standards and performance criteria that is administered by their Academy for Early Childhood Program Accreditation. Programs serving infants through kindergarten, under any auspices, are eligible to apply for this national, voluntary accreditation. This program began in 1985 and has recently been reinvented in order to increase the accountability of all systems serving young children and their families. The primary pur-

Consider This

More than 10,000 programs serving more than 850,000 children and their families are now accredited.

pose of this accreditation system is to encourage early childhood programs to participate in a structured approach to program improvement that considers all of the evidence-based components of high-quality early education. These components are organized by focus areas and performance categories. See Figure 1–6 for more information. DAP

Figure 1–6	NAEYC Early Childhood Program standards.

Focus Area: Children

Performance categories: relationships; curriculum; teaching; assessment of child progress; health

Focus Area: Teaching Staff

Performance category: teachers

Focus Area: Partnerships

Performance categories: families; community relationships

Focus Area: Leadership and Administration

Performance categories: physical environment; leadership and management

© Cengage Learning

naeyc 6 Four steps are involved in the process of accreditation. First, staff of early childhood programs enrolls in extensive self-study in order to assess strengths and areas needing work. After completing the self-study and undergoing a check to ensure that eligibility requirements are met, program staff submits a self-assessment report and officially applies for accreditation. The program then receives candidate status, and NAEYC begins the process of scheduling a site visit. During the site visit, the program staff must demonstrate that it meets all 10 program standards. More information is available at www.naeyc.org/accreditation/academyasp. **naeyc** 6

Most of the 10 program standards relate, in various ways, to family and community involvement, but we focus on the two standards specific to these topics: program standard 7 (families) and program standard 8 (community involvement). The families standard contains three categories:

- Knowing and understanding the program's families
- Sharing information between staff and families
- Nurturing families as advocates for their children

See Figure 1–7 for a list of the performance criteria for each of the categories in standard 7.

The community involvement standard incorporates the following categories:

- Linking with the community
- Accessing community resources
- Acting as a citizen in the neighborhood and the early childhood community

NAEYC Accreditation

http://www.naeyc.org.
Click "Accreditation"; click "Programs for Young Children (Academy)"

See Figure 1–8 for listing of performance criteria for each of the categories in standard 8.

66 The purpose of the National Academy of Early Childhood Programs is to improve the quality of care and education provided for young children in group programs in the United States. The Academy achieves its purpose by developing training resources, disseminating public information about high quality programs, and administering a national, voluntary accreditation system for early childhood programs. 99

—Accreditation Criteria and Procedures

Division for Early Childhood (DEC) of the Council on Exceptional Children (CEC) Recommended Family-Based Practices

DIVERSITY IN PRACTICE   In *DEC Recommended Practices*, Trivette and Dunst (2000) discuss two key features for early intervention (children with disabilities and children under age three) and early childhood special education (children with disabilities and children ages three through five) that family-based practices must include. The first feature is based on "resources and supports" and indicates that professionals must ensure that families have the necessary resources to engage in optimal child-rearing activities. The second feature relates to "family-centered help giving" and states that it is not only what is done with families that matters, but also how it is done. Ultimately, the goal is that "professionals must strengthen families' abilities to support the development of their children, in a manner that increases families' sense of parenting competence and not families' sense of dependency on professionals or professional systems."

66 Respect for all children and families is a fundamental value supported by DEC. All children and families means all—including children with disabilities, children at-risk for school failure, children who live in poverty, children who are non-English speaking, children with gifts and talents, and all of their families. 99

—Sandall, McLean, and Smith

Seventeen recommended family-based practices, organized into four categories, are as follows:

1. Families and professionals share responsibility and work collaboratively.
   - *Family members and professionals jointly develop appropriate family-identified outcomes.*
   - *Family members and professionals work together and share information routinely and collaboratively to achieve family-identified outcomes.*

- *Professionals fully and appropriately provide relevant information so parents can make informed choices and decisions.*
- *Professionals use helping styles that promote shared family/professional responsibility in achieving family-identified outcomes.*
- *Family/professionals' relationship building is accomplished in ways that are responsive to cultural, language, and other family characteristics.*

2. Practices strengthen family functioning.
   - *Practices, supports, and resources provide families with participatory experiences and opportunities promoting choice and decision making.*
   - *Practices, supports, and resources support family participation in obtaining desired resources and supports to strengthen parenting competence and confidence.*
   - *Disseminating public information about high quality programs, and administering a national, voluntary accreditation system for early childhood programs.*
   - *Intrafamily, informal, community, and formal supports and resources (e.g., respite care) are used to achieve desired outcomes.*
   - *Supports and resources provide families with information, competency-enhancing experiences, and participatory opportunities to strengthen family functioning and promote parenting knowledge and skills.*

- *Supports and resources are mobilized in ways that are supportive and do not disrupt family and community life.*

3. Practices are individualized and flexible.
   - *Resources and supports are provided in ways that are flexible, individualized, and tailored to the child's and family's preferences and styles and promote well-being.*
   - *Resources and supports match each family member's identified priorities and preferences (e.g., mother's and father's may be different).*
   - *Practices, supports, and resources are responsive to the cultural, ethnic, racial, language, and socioeconomic characteristics and preferences of families and their communities.*
   - *Practices, supports, and resources incorporate family beliefs and values into decisions, intervention plans, and resources and support mobilization.*

4. Practices are strengths and assets based.
   - *Family and child strengths and assets are used as a basis for engaging families in participatory experiences supporting parenting competence and confidence.*
   - *Practices, supports, and resources build on existing parenting competence and confidence.*
   - *Practices, supports, and resources promote the family's and professional's acquisition of new knowledge and skills to strengthen competence and confidence.*

Figure 1–7 Categories and accreditation performance criteria for program standard 7—families.

KNOWING AND UNDERSTANDING THE PROGRAM'S FAMILIES

New and existing program staff develop skills and knowledge to work effectively with diverse families as a part of orientation and ongoing staff development.

Program staff use a variety of formal and informal strategies (including conversations) to become acquainted with and learn from families about their family structure; their preferred child-rearing practices; and their socioeconomic, linguistic, racial, religious, and cultural backgrounds.

Program staff actively use information about families to adapt the environment, curriculum, and teaching methods to the families they serve.

To better understand the cultural backgrounds of children, families, and the community, program staff (as a part of program activities or as individuals) participate in community cultural events, concerts, storytelling activities, or other events and performances geared to children and their families.

Program staff provides support and information to family members legally responsible for the care and well-being of a child.

Program staff establishes intentional practices from the first contact with families designed to foster strong reciprocal relationships and maintain them over time.

Program staff ensures that all families, regardless of family structure; socioeconomic, racial, religious, and cultural backgrounds; gender; abilities; or preferred language, are included in all aspects of the program, including volunteer opportunities. These opportunities consider families' interests and skills and the needs of program staff.

Program staff engages with families to learn from their knowledge of their child's interests, approaches to learning, and the child's developmental needs, and to learn about their concerns and goals for their children. This information is incorporated into ongoing classroom planning.

Program staff uses a variety of formal and informal methods to communicate with families about the program philosophy and curriculum objectives, including educational goals and

Figure 1–7	*(Continued)*

effective strategies that can be used by families to promote their children's learning. The staff implements a variety of methods, such as new family orientations, small group meetings, individual conversations, and written questionnaires, for getting input from families about curriculum activities throughout the year.

The program works with families on shared child-caregiving issues, including routine separations, special needs, the food being served and consumed, and daily care matters.

Families may visit any area of the facility at any time during the program's regular hours of operation as specified by the procedures of the facility.

The program facilitates opportunities for families to meet with each other on a formal and informal basis, work together on projects to support the program, and learn from and provide support for each other.

The program's governing or advisory groups include families as members and active participants. Family members are mentored into leadership roles by staff or other families in the program.

Program staff and families work together to plan events. Families' schedules and availability are considered as part of this planning.

SHARING INFORMATION BETWEEN STAFF AND FAMILIES

Program staff uses a variety of mechanisms, such as family conferences or home visits, to promote dialogue with families. Program staff asks adults to translate or interpret communications as needed.

Program staff communicates with families on at least a weekly basis regarding children's activities and developmental milestones, shared caregiving issues, and other information that affects the well-being and development of their children. Where in-person communication is not possible, alternative communication practices are in place.

Program staff communicates with families on a daily basis regarding infants' and toddlers'/twos' activities and developmental milestones, shared caregiving issues, and other information that affects the well-being and development of their children. Where in-person communication is not possible, alternative communication practices are in place.

The staff compiles and provides information about the program to families in a language the family can understand. This information includes program policies and operating procedures.

Program staff informs families about its systems for formally and informally assessing children's progress. This includes the purposes of the assessment, the procedures used for assessment, procedures for gaining family input and information, the timing of assessments, the way assessment results or information will be shared with families, and ways the program will use the information.

When program staff suspects that a child has a developmental delay or other special need, this possibility is communicated to families in a sensitive, supportive, and confidential manner, with documentation and explanation for the concern, suggested next steps, and information about resources for assessment.

NURTURING FAMILIES AS ADVOCATES FOR THEIR CHILDREN

Program staff encourages families to regularly contribute to decisions about goals for their child and plans for activities and services.

Program staff encourages families to raise concerns and work collaboratively to find mutually satisfying solutions that staff then incorporates into classroom practice.

Program staff encourages and supports families to make the primary decisions about services that their children need, and it encourages families to advocate to obtain needed services.

Program staff uses a variety of techniques to negotiate difficulties that arise in interactions with family members. Program staff makes arrangements to use these techniques in a language the family can understand.

Program staff provides families with information about programs and services from other organizations. Staff supports and encourages families' efforts to negotiate health, mental health, assessment, and educational services for the children.

Program staff uses established linkages with other early education programs and local elementary schools to help families prepare for and manage their children's transitions between programs, including special education programs. Staff provides information to families that can assist them in communicating with other programs.

To help families with their transitions to other programs or schools, staff provides basic general information on enrollment procedures and practices, visiting opportunities, and program options. Prior to sharing information with other relevant providers, agencies, or other programs, staff obtains written consent from the family.

Figure 1–8	Categories and accreditation performance criteria for program standard 8—community relationships.

LINKING WITH THE COMMUNITY

Program staff maintains a current list of child and family support services available in the community based on the pattern of needs the staff observes among families and based on what families request (e.g., health, mental health, oral health, nutrition, child welfare, parenting programs, early intervention/special education screening and assessment services, and basic needs, such as housing and child care subsidies). They share the list with families and

assist them in locating, contacting, and using community resources that support children's and families' well-being and development.

Program staff develops partnerships and professional relationships with agencies, consultants, and organizations in the community that further the program's capacity to meet the needs and interests of the children and families that are served.

Continues

Figure 1–8 *(Continued)*

Program staff is familiar with family support services and specialized consultants who are able to provide culturally and linguistically appropriate services. The staff uses this knowledge to suggest and guide families to these services as appropriate.

Program staff encourages continuity of services for children by communicating with other agencies and programs to achieve mutually desired outcomes for children, and guides collaborative work.

Program staff identifies and establishes relationships with specialized consultants who can assist all children's and families' full participation in the program. This includes support for children with disabilities, behavioral challenges, or other special needs.

Program staff advocates for the program and its families by creating awareness of the program's needs among community councils, service agencies, and local governmental entities.

Program staff includes information gathered from stakeholders in planning for continuous improvement, building stakeholder involvement in the program, and broadening community support for the program.

ACCESSING COMMUNITY RESOURCES

Program staff usesits knowledge of the community and the families served as an integral part of the curriculum and children's learning experiences.

Program staff connects with and uses its community's urban, suburban, rural, and tribal cultural resources.

Program staff informs families about community events sponsored by local organizations, such as museum exhibits, concerts, storytelling, and theater geared to children.

Program staff invites members of the performing and visual arts community, such as musical performers, traveling museum exhibits, local artists, and community residents, to share their interests and talents with the children.

The program engages with other community organizations and groups to cosponsor or participate in cultural events to enrich the experience of children and families in the program.

ACTING AS A CITIZEN IN THE NEIGHBORHOOD AND THE EARLY CHILDHOOD COMMUNITY

Program staff is encouraged to participate in local, state, or national early childhood education organizations by joining and attending meetings and conferences. Program staff is also encouraged to participate regularly in local, state, or regional public-awareness activities related to early care and education.

The program encourages staff to participate in joint and collaborative training activities or events with neighboring early childhood programs and other community service agencies.

The program encourages staff and families to work together to support and participate in community improvement or advocacy projects.

Program leadership builds mutual relationships and communicates regularly with close neighbors, informing them about the program, seeking out their perspectives, involving them in the program as appropriate, and cooperating with them on neighborhood interests and needs.

Program staff is encouraged and given the opportunity to participate in community or statewide interagency councils or service integration efforts.

Program leadership is knowledgeable about how policy changes at local, state, tribal, or national levels affect the services and resources available for children and their families.

The Division for Early Childhood of the Council on Exceptional Children

http://www.dec-sped.org/

Family Support Movement

Since the mid-1970s, the interdisciplinary **family support movement** has evolved from emphasizing program development to providing principles for national efforts in work with families. The essence of this movement constitutes "a fundamental change in the traditional belief systems, reflecting a change from assuming that the role of government is to be a resource for families in crisis to recognizing the responsibility of our society to promote the well-being of all families" (Weissbourd 1994). This movement clearly is an application of Bronfenbrenner's theory, emphasizing the importance of various systems as they relate to children and families.

At the heart of family support is community building. The best way to improve the lives of children and families is through caring communities. This movement sees such community support for all families as an "inherent responsibility of a democracy" (Weissbourd 1994).

> Family support is about investing in the promotion of the positive things that families want for their children. In the long term, family support is a societal investment in the creation of happy, healthy, productive citizens. This investment not only has an impact on the families who participate in services, it has a secondary impact on us all.
>
> —Family Support America (http://www.familysupportamerica.org/, accessed October 7, 2005.)

Family Support America outlined seven evidence-based premises (http://www.familysupportamerica.org/, accessed October 7, 2005, but note that this organization is no longer active) on which programs of family support must be based:

- *Primary responsibility for the development and well-being of children lies within the family, and all segments of society must support families as they rear their children.* Teachers of early childhood education have a unique role in that they have been specially trained to understand and teach young children. Forming partnerships with families of these young children is the best way that early childhood professionals can support families in rearing of their children.

- *Assuring the well-being of all families is the cornerstone of a healthy society and requires universal access to support programs and services.* Early childhood teachers must advocate for such universal access to all programs of early education, including child care, Head Start, and other quality preschool systems, early intervention, early childhood special education, full-day kindergarten, and developmentally appropriate primary grade education.

- *Children and families exist as part of an ecological system.* An understanding of Bronfenbrenner's bio-ecological theory leads early childhood teachers to view the complexity of influences on children and families. This knowledge provides for individualized responses to children and families.

- *Child-rearing patterns are influenced by parents' understandings of child development and of their child's unique characteristics, personal sense of competence, and cultural and community traditions and mores.* Early childhood teachers have a responsibility to share accurate information about child development as a way to support child-rearing competence and confidence. In doing this, teachers must respect and honor individual and cultural differences.

- *Enabling families to build on their own strengths and capacities promotes the healthy development of children.* Affirming the strengths of each family is an effective way to advance healthy development of children.

- *The developmental processes that make up parenthood and family life create needs that are unique at each stage in the life span.* An understanding of contemporary issues facing families with young children will provide a strong basis for supporting those families. Further, providing specific resources and supports to those who need them can aid successful navigation through such challenges and joys.

- *Families are empowered when they have access to information and other resources and take action to improve the well-being of children, families, and communities.*

Early childhood teachers and programs can provide ongoing information about community events, helping agencies, and current issues.

This perspective recognizes "that families are responsible for their children's development, and that no family can function alone" (Kagan and Weissbourd 1994). Family support points to children and families' absolutely critical need for continuity between home and school. The family support movement believes that early childhood educators must become advocates not only for young children but also for the families and communities from which those children come.

A child gains her identity and sense of self from her family. When families' strengths are recognized and their needs are met through the community, they do better and children do better. Bowman (1994) explains how the family support movement changes our paradigm "from a prevention to a promotion model." This means we have evolved from defining families primarily as having deficits and thus defining our task as intervening to prevent problems, to seeing families essentially as having strengths and thus perceiving our task as providing resources to support and augment those strengths and thus promote families' well-being.

Family Focus

http://www.family-focus.org

National Dropout Prevention Center/ Network

http://www.dropoutprevention.org/effstrat /family_engagement/overview.htm

A child gains her identity and sense of self from her family.

Summary and Conclusions

❝ Teacher-parent communication is important in achieving a degree of consistency in the ways that the significant adults in the child's life guide and relate to that child. And young children feel more secure when they see that the adults who care about them share trust and respect. ❞

—Copple and Bredekamp

The information about theory and best practices in this chapter indicates that children do not arrive at early childhood programs having had the same experiences or coming from families who value the same experiences. This contextualist framework permits early childhood professionals to understand concepts related to building supportive partnerships with families, and then to apply those ideas to their work with young children and their families.

Young children do not enter educational programs on a level playing field. As members of families and communities, they come to us with all of the positive, negative, and neutral experiences of their families' lives and effects of plentiful or sparse community resources. Children have learned much about what to expect in their own social world before we see them in early childhood education programs. It is an increasingly important responsibility of early childhood educators to understand the significance of families and communities in children's lives. Further, educators and schools must include suitable components from all families' lives and community customs in early education. Throughout later chapters in this book the work of Robert Pianta (2003) and others are highlighted to give very specific ways to connect children, families, schools, and communities with each other.

Theory into Practice Suggestions (TIPS)

- Think about the meaning of theory for yourself as a teacher of young children. Reflect on ways that theories can impact your classroom practice.

- To understand the context of children's lives, make home visits to children's homes to get to know them and their families in a different context.

- To better understand children's neighborhoods or communities, visit grocery stores, parks, and libraries.

- Work with community agencies to understand services that they provide to families and children {Easter Seals, homeless shelters, food banks, etc.}.

- Visit with libraries to understand what programs they offer for families and children.

- Contact local chambers of commerce, United Way agencies, and other relevant group to find out what initiatives they may have that support families and children.

- Contact hospitals and clinics to find out the services they offer for children and families.

- Contact law enforcement agencies to find out typical services for families and children offered through schools or early education centers.

- Survey faith-based agencies to investigate programs, services, and initiatives that they sponsor for young children and families.

- Encourage families to become involved in young children's education.

- Be sensitive to children's responses to various family and community situations.

- Support community efforts to provide healthy activities for young children and their families.

- Advocate to local, state, and federal agencies for policies that support young children's education and family well-being.

- Take time to celebrate diverse cultures. Consider those that are represented in your school or center as well as others in the community.

- Emphasize the key role that families play in creating developmentally appropriate education for young children.

- Provide support that will lead to strengthening families.

- Increase your understanding of the effects of various types of stressors on families at different points in their lives.

- Communicate to a variety of organizations the importance of internal and external assets to children's optimal development.

- Observe and visit with staff of a NAEYC accredited early education program.

- Observe and visit with staff of an inclusive early education program.

- Observe and visit with staff of a Head Start or Early Head Start program.

- Interview family members whose young children are enrolled in an accredited, inclusive or Head Start program.

- Volunteer for an agency that supports children, families or early education.

- Search local newspapers for information about services for families and young children.

Applications

1. Using information from at least one theory discussed in this chapter, respond to the following comments from early childhood teachers or administrators:

   a. "My job is to teach the children, not to provide a shoulder for parents to cry on."

   b. "There are not enough hours in the day to plan, implement, and evaluate a family involvement program for my classroom."

   c. "I enjoy working with children, but not adults. That's why I wanted to teach."

   d. "How can I include a child with special needs in my center?"

   e. "If parents cared more about their children, teachers would be able to teach instead of discipline all day long."

   f. "I love to have parent volunteers in my classroom. They are so helpful when I need to have patterns and bulletin board cut outs prepared."

   g. "Families need to take care of their own children and not rely on others for help."

2. Using information from at least one theory discussed in this chapter, respond to the following comments from family members who have children enrolled in early childhood programs:

   a. "I send my child to preschool so that he can learn. The teacher's job is to make sure he does. I resent being asked to volunteer in the classroom."

   b. "I did not like school when I was a student. I am not comfortable being in the classroom."

   c. "I don't want those teachers at my daughter's child care center telling me how to raise my children. I won't go to any of the parent meetings as long as they're telling me what to do."

   d. "School is school, and home is home."

   e. "Children learn to read at school. I'm not a teacher; how can I help my child to learn?"

3. Using information from at least one theory discussed in this chapter, respond to the following comments from community members who do not have young children:

   a. "I don't want my tax money going to support preschool programs in the schools. Parents should take care of their own children."

   b. "Good parents don't put their kids in child care. I will never do that to my children."

   c. "Families don't care about children like they used to. They want the community to build parks and to provide recreation so they can send their kids out of the house and ignore them."

   d. "I stayed home with my children when they were young. It's a mother's responsibility to care for their young ones."

Questions for Reflection and Discussion

1. When you think about teaching young children, how do you envision your role with families? How have your expectations changed since reading and reflecting on this chapter?

2. When you think about teaching young children, what do you think about the community's involvement or influences on children? How have your ideas changed since reading and reflecting on this chapter?

3. What roles do families and communities have in relation to young children's developmental assets and irreducible needs? How might schools provide support to families and communities in these respective roles?

4. What is your understanding of the role of each of the following theories in developing exemplary family involvement programs in early childhood education?

   a. Bioecological

   b. Contextualist

   c. Family systems

5. Using each of the three theories explained in this chapter, critique the guidelines for developmentally appropriate practice, national accreditation, and family support.

Field Assignments

1. Interview several early childhood teachers or administrators about the role families and community members have in their programs. Consider interviewing early childhood professionals in the following types of programs: Head Start, child care, public school, family center, and early intervention. Compare and contrast family involvement in each kind of program.

2. Interview some parents or other family members about their involvement in their young children's educational program. Consider interviewing family members who have children enrolled in various types of programs as mentioned in Assignment 1. What similarities and differences did you find?

Additional resources for this chapter, including TeachSource videos, can be found on the Education CourseMate. Go to CengageBrain.com.

References

Blank, B.T. 1998. Settlement houses: Old idea in new form builds communities. *The New Social Worker* (Summer): 4–7.

Bowman, B. 1994. Home and school: The unresolved relationship. In *Putting families first: America's family support movement and the challenge of change*, ed. S. L. Kagan and B. Weissbourd. San Francisco: Jossey-Bass.

Brazelton, T.B., and S.I. Greenspan. 2000. *The irreducible needs of children: What every child must have to grow, learn and flourish.* Cambridge, MA: Perseus.

Bronfenbrenner, U. 1979. *The ecology of human development: Experiments by nature and design.* Cambridge, MA: Harvard University Press.

Bronfenbrenner, U. 1990. Discovering what families do. In *Rebuilding the nest: A new commitment to the American family,* ed. D. Blankenhorn, S. Bayme, and J. B. Elshtain. Milwaukee, WI: Family Service America.

Bronfenbrenner, U. 2001. The bioecological theory of human development. In Vol. 10 of *International encyclopedia of the social and behavioral sciences,* ed. N. J. Smelser and P. B. Baltes, 6963–6970. New York: Elsevier.

Brown, G.L., Mangelsdorf, S.C., Agathen, J. M., & Ho, R.M. (2008). Young children's psychological selves: Convergence with maternal reports of child personality. *Social Development, 17,* 162–181.

Byers, L. October 1972. Origins and Early History of the Parent Cooperative Nursery School Movement in America. ED 091 063.

Carter, B., and M. McGoldrick, eds. 1999. *The expanded family life cycle: Individual, family, and social perspectives,* 3rd ed. Boston: Allyn and Bacon.

Copple, C., and S. Bredekamp, eds. 2009. *Developmentally appropriate practice in early childhood programs serving children from birth through age 8,* 3rd ed. Washington, DC: National Association for the Education of Young Children.

deMause, L., ed. 1974. *The history of childhood.* New York: Psychohistory Press.

Family Support America. 2005. http://www.familysupportamerica.org (accessed October 7, 2005).

Harter, S. 2006. The self. In N. Eisenberg (Ed.), *Handbook of child psychology: vol. 3. social, emotional, and personality development (6th ed., pp. 505–570). Hoboken, NJ: Wiley.*

Hiatt, D. B. 1994. Parent involvement in American public schools: An historical perspective (Fall/Winter): 1642–1994.

Kagan, S. L., E. Moore, and S. Bredekamp, eds. 1995. *Reconsidering children's early development and learning: Toward common views and vocabulary.* Washington, DC: National Education Goals Panel.

Kagan, S. L., and B. Weissbourd. 1994. *Putting families first: America's family support movement and the challenge of change.* San Francisco: Jossey-Bass.

Lerner, R. M. 1989. Individual development and the family system: A life-span perspective. In *Family systems and life-span development,* eds. K. Kreppner and R. M. Lerner. Hillsdale, NJ: Lawrence Erlbaum Associates.

Lerner, R. M. n.d. A developmental contextual view of human development. http://gator.uhd.edu/~williams/child/Lerner.htm (accessed January 5, 2005).

National Academy of Early Childhood Programs. 1991. *Accreditation criteria & procedures.* Washington, DC: National Association for the Education of Young Children.

National Association for the Education of Young Children. 1996. Linguistic and cultural diversity—building on America's strengths. http://www.naeyc.org/ece/1996/03.asp.

National Research Council & Institute of Medicine. 2000. *From neurons to neighborhoods: The science of early childhood development.* Committee on Integrating the Science of Early Childhood Development. Jack P. Shonkoff and Deborah A. Phillips, eds. Board on Children, Youth, and Families, Commission on Behavior and Social Sciences and Education. Washington, DC: National Academy Press.

Olson, D. H., and J. DeFrain. 1994. *Marriage and the family: Diversity and strengths.* Mountain View, CA: Mayfield.

Olson, D. H., and D. M. Gorall. 2003. Circumplex model of marital and family systems. In *Normal family processes,* ed. F. Walsh, 3rd ed., 514–547. New York: Guilford.

Pianta, R. C., and M. Kraft-Sayre. 2003. *Successful kindergarten transition: Your guide to connecting children, families, & schools.* Baltimore, MD: Brookes Publishing.

Powell, D. 1989. *Families and early childhood education.* Washington, DC: National Association for the Education of Young Children.

Sandall, S., M. E. McLean, and B. J. Smith. 2000. *DEC recommended practices in early intervention/early childhood special education.* Longmont, CO: Sopris West.

Schwartz, I. S., S. R. Sandall, S. L. Odom, E. Horn, and P. J. Beckman. 2002. "I know it when I see it": In search of a common definition of inclusion. In *Widening the circle: Including children with disabilities in preschool programs,* ed. S. L. Odom. New York: Teachers College Press.

Tharp, R. G., and R. Gallimore. 1988. *Rousing minds to life.* New York: Cambridge University Press.

Trivette, C., and C. Dunst. 2000. Recommended practices in family-based practices. *In DEC recommended practices in early intervention/early childhood special education,* ed. S. Sandall, M. E. McLean, and B. J. Smith, 39–46. Longmont, CO: Sopris West.

Vygotsky, L. 1962. *Thought and language.* Cambridge, MA: MIT Press.

Weissbourd, B. 1994. The evolution of the family resource movement. In *Putting families first: America's family support movement and the challenge of change,* ed. S. L. Kagan and B. Weissbourd. San Francisco: Jossey-Bass.

Understanding Family Diversity

OUTLINE

OBJECTIVES ALIGNED WITH NAEYC STANDARDS

After reading and reflecting on this chapter, you should be able to:

- Discuss ways in which the three guiding theories view family differences **naeyc** 2

- Relate ways in which families differ in terms of ethnicity, race, and culture; language; economics; gender roles; religiosity; and geographic region **naeyc** 2

- Reflect on implications related to family differences for early childhood educators **naeyc** 6

- Describe strategies for honoring family diversity in early childhood settings **naeyc** 2

Key Terms

culture	inclusiveness	Temporary Assistance for Needy
ethnicity	principles	Families (TANF)
gender role	race	
ideals	religiosity	

CONTEXTUALIST THEORIES AND FAMILY DIFFERENCES

naeyc 1 Bioecological theory (Bronfenbrenner 1979) informs teachers that differences in children's microsystems will account for differences in children's behaviors and development. The social environment provided to children by their families is directly driven by the family's identification with race, **culture**, and ethnicity. Other factors that influence the microsystem include language, economics, gender, religion, and geographical region of residence.

In terms of financial influences, it is clear that the macrosystem, or the societal philosophy and practices of economics, affect microsystems (Garbarino and Ganzel 2000). For example, families who are impoverished for reasons related to an inability to compete for employment in a capitalist society (e.g., disabilities, addictions, prejudice) often live in impoverished microsystems. Impoverished families often live in situations that are associated with early risk factors in children. Such risk factors include unsafe communities, malnutrition, lack of appropriate medical care, low-quality child care, and poor schools.

Vygotsky's sociocultural theory emphasizes the notion that knowledge derives from culture. Teachers observe differences in behaviors of children and their family members based on their culture's view of what is appropriate. Such knowledge cannot be disputed in favor of a teacher's or other dominant view. Children's very definition, and thus knowledge, of family is rooted in their particular culture.

Cultural differences, thus, lead to differences in understanding, knowing, and behaving. Children acquire their knowledge by interacting with others who are important in their lives, especially parents or other primary caregivers. These daily, often ordinary interactions with one another provide children with the shared knowledge of the family's culture. Examples of this knowledge include selections of clothing, expected behaviors, choices of foods and how food is prepared, celebrations and rituals, and gender and other social roles. For example, the concept of respect is embodied through cultural differences in behavior: in some cultures, it is respectful to make eye contact, and in others it is not; in some cultures, it is respectful to refer to elders as "ma'am" or "sir," and in others it is not. Similarly, in some cultures it is expected that pork will not be served, and in others it is expected at various occasions; in some cultures men and women have distinct roles in families, and in others roles are more flexible.

A child's knowledge of family is rooted in her culture.

African American Web Resources
University of California CLNet

http://clnet.ucr.edu/
Type in "Afro"; click "African American Internet Links"

Asian American Web Resources
Center for Educational Telecommunications

http://www.cetel.org/
Click "Resources"

Native American Web Resources
http://www.hanksville.org/
Click "Index of Native American Resources on the Internet"

Latino Web Resources
Latino Web

http://latino.sscnet.ucla.edu

Multicultural Web Resources
Multicultural Pavilion

http://www.edchange.org/multicultural
Click "Centers"; click "Multicultural Pavilion"

New American Studies Web Resources
Georgetown University, Center for New Designs in Learning & Scholarship

http://lumen.georgetown.edu/

Family systems theory (McGoldrick 1989) places strong emphasis on ethnicity and culture as factors in a family's beliefs, practices, and values. Further, family income levels are likely to influence many aspects of decisions and behaviors. For example, many professional women who become parents celebrate the arrival of their first child at about the same age (31 to 35 years) that some lower-income women celebrate their first grandchild. Females and males are likely to experience family quite differently, from everyday behaviors to rituals and celebrations. "Religion also modifies or reinforces certain cultural values. Families....whose religion reinforces ethnic values, are likely to maintain their ethnicity longer." Families who live in close proximity to others of the same ethnic, racial, and cultural backgrounds are more likely to maintain the same norms; those who move away may become more homogenized into or more influenced by a dominant culture. **naeyc** 1

Recent research with same-sex couples leads to new questions about the usefulness of a family life cycle model that might apply to all families (Johnson and Colucci 1999). Findings indicate that lesbian and gay definitions of family often include close friends and other "families of choice." It is still unusual for families of lesbian and gay couples to have typical family rituals—for example, wedding ceremonies and wedding or baby showers—thus ignoring or denying such marker events with typical family rituals. Further, family titles do not exist for in-laws of the life partners of gay men or lesbians (Johnson and Colucci 1999).

WAYS IN WHICH FAMILIES ARE DIFFERENT

Families define themselves as a family. Membership in a family can be decided only by each member of that family. Thus, while it is the role of early childhood educators to be aware of who constitutes each child's family, it is never their role to define children's families for them. *Teachers should not attempt to alter a particular family's view about membership in that family.* Factors that make families different from one another include ethnicity, race, culture, language, economics, **gender roles**, religiosity, and geographic regionalism.

DAP We must consider these differences if we are to best serve *all* children and *all* families in early childhood programs. It is commonly said that we should honor the humanity in everyone by celebrating our similarities, but it is also important to understand the multiple differences that exist among individuals and families. It is often just such a lack of understanding that leads to stereotypes, prejudices, and exclusion. As we address family differences, we cannot ignore the often immeasurable effects of poverty and discrimination on individuals and families. **DAP**

Reflect on This

When we hear or read the word *family*, each of us tends to reflect on our own familial experiences, ignoring differences. Therefore, it is important to give thoughtful attention to the topics of family diversity addressed in this chapter.

ETHNICITY, RACE, AND CULTURE

Ethnicity "**Ethnicity** refers to a concept of a group's "peoplehood" based on a combination of race, religion, and cultural history, whether or not members realize their commonalities with each other. It describes a commonality transmitted by the family over generations.... [I]t is more than race, religion, or national and geographic origin....It involves conscious and unconscious processes that fulfill a deep psychological need for identity and historical continuity" (McGoldrick 1989).

Family ethnicity is sustained through "unique family customs, proverbs and stories, celebrations, foods, and religious ceremonies" (McGoldrick 1989). Although they are intertwined, differences have been noted between the notions of self-concept and ethnic identity. Families who value ethnic pride often find it difficult to instill related beliefs in their children in our

pluralistic society (Stauss 1995, citing Harriett McAdoo). Further, the effects of racism affect beliefs and practices in non-majority ethnic groups (McDade 1995).

It is the deep psychological need for identity that must be taken into account by early childhood professionals. The degree to which ethnicity is important to a given family, and thus to a given child, varies. Understanding these varying degrees will help early childhood teachers view each family's individuality as a strength and support children's sense of connection to their ethnic group. For instance, consider the following descriptions of three different families.

Chelsea is a three-year-old daughter of European-American parents. Her family portrait includes a picture of her mother, Stacey; her father, Jay; herself; and her five-month-old brother, Christopher. These family members live together in the same home in a small town in eastern Ohio. Living nearby, her paternal grandmother has almost daily contact with Chelsea's family. Her maternal grandparents live about 15 miles away and enjoy weekly visits with Chelsea's family.

Jamal is the five-year-old son of Janice. They live in St. Louis with Janice's mother, Dianne, and her long-time partner, Samuel. Jamal's family portrait includes his mother; his grandmother; Samuel; and Samuel's teenage daughter, Jalisa. Jamal calls his grandmother "Mamma" and his mother "Janice." Frequent family visitors include Dianne's mother and father who live in the same city, and Samuel's mother who travels from Chicago twice a year for a month-long stay.

Robin, seven years old, is the youngest child in her Japanese-American family. She lives in Seattle with her parents, her maternal grandfather, and two older brothers. Her family portrait includes her mother, Marcia; her father, Paul; her grandfather, Ito; and 13-year-old twin brothers, Rodger and Raymond. Last year, Robin's family traveled to Kyoto, Japan, to visit her paternal grandparents.

Understanding ethnic differences will help early childhood teachers support children's sense of connection to their ethnic group.

© Cengage Learning/ECE Photo Library.

" The first thing to remember about the American family is that it doesn't exist. Families exist. All kinds of families in all kinds of economic and marital situations, as all of us can see…. The American family? Just which American family did you have in mind? Black or white, large or small, wealthy or poor, or somewhere in between? Did you mean a father-headed, mother-headed, or childless family? First or second time around? Happy or miserable? Your family or mine? "

—**Louise Kapp Howe, 1972**

DAP For family events in early childhood programs, teachers and other staff should plan for and be prepared to include a variety of family members, not only parents and siblings. Early childhood educators must go beyond traditional parent-involvement work to a more timely approach that emphasizes whole-family involvement. Welcoming grandparents, aunts and uncles, and family members who have no official title based on bloodline can be a critical factor in building successful family-school relationships.

Teachers too often talk of children who come from good homes and those who have troublesome families. Often, "good home" means one whose family structure is synonymous with the teacher's own, and a less-than-good home is defined as one whose structure differs from that of the teacher's. Thus, knowledge about cultural differences is a key to changing teachers' perspectives and increasing their understanding about diverse families. DAP

Is the idea of family values one that is reasonable? Mellman, Lazarus, and Rivlin (1990) found in their research a high degree of consensus on love and emotional support, respect for others, and taking responsibility for actions. Perhaps these are the characteristics we should look for when we want to label a family as providing a "good home."

Race Ethnic differences go beyond race. The term **race**, based on physical differences, is often noted to be scientific in nature as opposed to the sociocultural nature of ethnicity. In this regard, most sources tell us that three races of humans exist in the world: Negroid, Mongoloid, and Caucasoid. Each of these is defined by specific characteristics, such as skin tone, facial structure, and geographic origin. However, in authentic

work with children and families, early childhood educators often realize that emphasizing race alone is not very helpful. This is seen most clearly in children of interracial families. The question "What race are you?" often is both confusing and irrelevant in the United States today. It is more helpful for early childhood educators to understand individuals within the diversity of families.

Wardle (1987) notes that we know little about interracial families. However, one point made strongly is that children from interracial families cannot choose to identify with the race of one parent over that of the other. This misconception is an oversimplified, misguided attempt to understand the unique difficulty that interracial children have with their need for identity. Wardle suggests that teachers work closely with parents (or other family members) to "feature cultural customs of both (or all) races represented in each interracial child, as well as create ongoing experiences for all children in which multicultural diversity is celebrated."

What Is Culture?
http://www.wsu.edu
Type in "culture"; click "learning commons—what is culture?"

Culture **Culture** refers to the unique experiences and history of various ethnic groups. Cultural differences often indicate differences in views on the family and the community, differences in expectations of children, differences in child-rearing, and differences in the value placed on education.

Carol Brunson Phillips (1995) notes that early educators need to have an understanding about both how culture is transmitted and how it is not transmitted. She has formulated six concepts to help with this understanding.

1. *Culture is learned.* Culture is not biological; teachers cannot identify a family's culture by how the family members look. Instead, each individual learns his culture's rules through daily living. Examples include table manners, interpersonal interactions, and ways of demonstrating respect.

2. *Culture is characteristic of groups.* An individual's characteristics are both cultural and individual. Unique personality traits are not culturally based. Cultural behaviors are rooted in groups. Some cultures may place greater emphasis on individuality or conformity than others.

3. *Culture is a set of rules for behavior.* "The essence of culture is in the rules that produce the behaviors, not the behaviors themselves" (Phillips 1995). So, culture is an influence on behavior, often a sweeping

influence, but the behaviors alone are not culture. Behaviors commonly influenced by culture include types of clothing and flavors in foods.

4. *Individuals are embedded to different degrees within a culture.* Some families and individuals place more emphasis on cultural traditions than do others. Some Irish families may act more Irish than others; some Vietnamese families may act more Vietnamese than others; some Kenyan families may act more Kenyan than others. These are individual variations within cultures. Teachers should not expect all people of one culture to be equally involved with their cultural rules. Understanding of both cultural rules and individual differences in people of the same or similar culture is essential in respect for diversity.

5. *Cultures borrow and share rules.* Over time, cultures have influenced one another. Culture is not stagnant. As people from two or more cultures interact, cultures are affected and may undergo transformations. One example can be seen in wedding rituals. A small town in western Pennsylvania was settled in the 1800s by various ethnic groups, including those from Ireland, Italy, Germany, Yugoslavia, and Poland. Over the years, as family members attended wedding celebrations of their neighbors and friends, traditions melded so that by the middle of the twentieth century, food, music, and celebrations became more similar in this geographic region.

6. *Members of a cultural group may be proficient in cultural behavior but unable to describe the rules.* Because young children begin to learn their culture in their own home environments, behaviors seem natural to them. Not only can they not tell you why they engage in these behaviors, it is also likely they are not conscious of all of the behaviors they have learned from their culture. When one Northerner spent her first Thanksgiving in the Deep South, she asked the cook, "Why do you put boiled eggs in the gravy?" Certain that there must be some interesting story or superstition related to this practice, she was surprised at the cook's response: "I don't know. That's the way my mother did it."

In their work to include families, teachers of young children may find it more advantageous to consider not only a child's race but also her ethnicity and culture. It is more likely that knowledge of sociocultural factors would provide greater understanding to teachers than information about physical differences noted in definitions of race. Thus, including understanding of racial differences is most useful in the context of cultural and ethnic differences as well.

One example for understanding how culture influences behavior and expectations can be observed within Latin American or Latino families. Even though Latinos have various geographic origins: South

Consider This

Consider each of the six concepts for understanding culture. Share an example of a behavior or expectation in your culture that relates to each concept. Reflect on how your actions or thoughts may be culturally based.

America, Central America and the Caribbean, four common cultural characteristics that have been derived from both their Spanish and Indian heritages have been noted by Fernandez Diaz (Olson, Skogrand, and DuPree n.d.). The four characteristics are:

- *Familismo.* Families are a source of joy and pride, taking precedence over individual choices and needs.
- *Personalismo.* Relationships with others, inside and outside the family, are emphasized through caring and concern.
- *Individualismo.* A person's uniqueness is valued and shared through cooperative rather than competitive means.
- *Fatalismo.* Happenings are not easily controlled by people, but rather a greater power governs the world (Fernandez Diaz 2006).

naeyc 1 According to contextualist theories, nuclear families, extended families, and communities play varied roles in children's lives. One important factor in these variations is related to culture and ethnicity. It is frequently noted that in the United States, ethnic groups that are not dominant in the culture are more strongly influenced by their extended families, while majority groups are more influenced by the larger society (McDade 1995). Further, the macrosystem and chronosystem for cultural groups differ. Figure 2–1 illustrates differences in parenting characteristics and in the value placed on education among a variety of cultural groups. **naeyc** 1

Hidalgo (1993) discusses culture as having three levels: the concrete, the behavioral, and the symbolic. The concrete level consists of those aspects of culture that are most visible to those outside of the culture. Cultural artifacts, music, and foods are often perceived as the essence of a culture when, in fact, they may lead to stereotypical representations based on observation from a holiday or historical image. Such examples can be observed in education settings when teachers and administrators have attempted to address issues of multiculturalism without efforts at increasing their own cultural competence. At Thanksgiving, it is not uncommon to see stereotypes of Native American headbands and tomahawks, even though historical accuracy is questionable.

The second level of culture includes behavior such as language (both verbal and nonverbal) and

Figure 2–1	Variations in parenting and educational values.

AFRICAN-AMERICANS

Parenting: Discipline often appears to be severe and punitive. Many parents emphasize high achievement and a strong work ethic. Boys and girls are socialized similarly, with emphasis on adaptive coping ability and emotional strength necessary for dealing with hostile environments (McDade 1995).

Education: Traditional educational strategies may not meet the needs of some children in this culture. Research suggests that some males are particularly not well-served through the feminine orientation of most elementary classrooms (Hale 1986). Many African-American parents emphasize education as the way to greater economic success.

ASIAN-AMERICANS/PACIFIC ISLANDER-AMERICANS

Parenting: Typically, children are encouraged to be independent and to respect authority. It is expected that they will be unquestionably obedient to their parents, and often they are expected to put the needs of their parents before their own. Parents desire children to be emotionally controlled, self-disciplined, and logical thinkers (McDade 1995).

Education: These families typically emphasize education and high levels of achievement in their children (Hamner and Turner 1996). The emphasis on the value of conformity may help children to adapt to expectations in U.S. schools.

HISPANIC/LATINO AMERICANS

Parenting: The family may take precedence over individuals and the expectation is for the family to be self-reliant. Individual achievement or responsibility is not valued in some families, but social skills are given a high priority.

Education: Hispanics as a group are increasing their educational achievement. Mexican-Americans are less likely to complete high school, however, than other Hispanic populations, with 56 percent of Mexican-Americans having less than a high school education (Hamner and Turner 1996).

NATIVE AMERICANS

Parenting: Although there are differences by tribe, some common values are found related to parenting. Children are generally valued by adults, and this is shown in their inclusion in all social events as well as in parents' gentle styles of discipline. Important characteristics to foster in children include loyalty, humility, respect for elders, reticence, and diminished emphasis on personal gain and private ownership (McDade 1995).

Education: Few Anglo teachers seem to understand tribal culture, while Native American children and families often feel a lack of cultural relevance in schools. Because silence is valued in tribes, children are comfortable with not answering questions in class, especially avoiding the risk of an incorrect answer and taunting by classmates. There is some movement toward having education under tribal control (Hamner and Turner 1996).

© Cengage Learning

roles ascribed to individuals based on gender or age. Behaviors are based on cultural values. As values shift, behaviors also shift. Cultural changes can be observed over time or through historical study. Perspectives on diversity in the United States have changed to move away from the melting pot paradigm, where we would all become one, to more of a tossed salad where we bring our uniqueness together to form a healthy blend of flavors. This allows each one to maintain cultural uniqueness and still be a committed citizen.

The third and deepest level of culture, the symbolic, is difficult to detect for those outside of the culture and implicit in the practices and values of those inside the culture. It is this level, that although is difficult to explain, drives much of our understanding about what is appropriate and expected behavior in various contexts. Parenting practices, including feeding practices and child care decisions, are often influenced by this level of culture. Farver and Howes (2004) found differences between the way that mothers in the United States and Mexico interact with their toddlers during pretend play. U.S. mothers are more likely to join the child's activities, whereas Mexican children join the mother's activities. Further, U.S. children learned through their mothers' teaching efforts during

their play and Mexican children learned through observation and imitation of adult behavior as they work.

One way that this multilevel view of culture has been represented is through an iceberg model. The smaller part of an iceberg is visible above the water, serving as an image for the concrete aspects of culture. The piece of the iceberg that is just beneath the water is indicative of behavioral aspects of culture and the deepest, least visible chunk of the iceberg corresponds to the symbolic level of culture. See Figure 2–2 for this representation.

In most complex societies, a dominant culture exists along with several subcultures or variations of the dominant culture. It is important to understand that a dominant culture is not necessarily of the majority of people, but of the power base of those who hold political and/or economic power. In the United States, the dominant culture has historically derived from those who have come from western European countries. As other immigrant groups arrive in the United States, some assimilation with the dominant culture typically occurs even as each group maintains variations of their culture of origin (Derman-Sparks and Edwards 2010).

Teachers sometimes unintentionally emphasize differences among groups of people, and the effect of

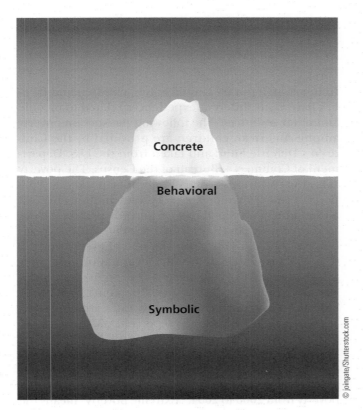

© joingate/Shutterstock.com

Figure 2–2 The iceberg model for understanding multiple levels of culture.

this emphasis is assaultive rather than respectful toward diversity. One way to avoid such an assaultive approach with preschool-age children is to "focus on the people in the child's world of today, not a historical world. *The goal with preschoolers is not to teach history, but to inoculate them against racism*" (Clark, DeWolf, and Clark 1992).

James A. Banks (1997) also reminds us that "an individual's identity with his or her ethnic group varies significantly with the times in his or her life, with economic and social status, and with the situations and/or setting." This statement should guide us as we work with families to focus on who they are right now; and that, in turn, will help us focus on children's needs and interests. In application of this principle to early education settings, Trawick-Smith (1997) states, "Only through a full understanding of parental beliefs, socialization practices, and family relationships can teachers meet the unique needs of individual children."

LANGUAGE DIFFERENCES AMONG FAMILIES

A "shared, rule-governed system of symbolic communication, language is a social tool for communication among the members of a culture, and it both reflects

and guides the experience of the people who produced it" (Papalia, Gross, and Feldman 2003). One source reports that at least 2,796 world languages exist along with nonverbal languages of Braille and sign language (Internet Public Library 2008).

In the United States, English is the primary spoken and written language. The Modern Language Association provides a map and data from the U.S. Census Bureau indicating the 33 most common languages spoken in homes in the United States. English is spoken by 82 percent of the population, with Spanish as the second most common home language at 10 percent. All other languages make up the remaining 8 percent with Chinese, French, and German being most common (Modern Language Association 2006).

DAP Home language refers to families' first language that they use most commonly at home. When home language differs from the majority culture language (English in the case of the United States), young children attending early childhood programs are capable of learning and speaking more than one language at a time. Best practice in early education indicates that teachers should share with families the importance of children maintaining home language even as they are learning English. Effective language-learning environments are of greater worth than the specific language that is being spoken. Maintaining relationships with family members and others of the child's home culture requires an ability to speak the language (Prieto 2009). DAP

In the recent past, it was a commonly held belief that when young children were required to speak two or more languages, developmental delays resulted. Current information dispels this idea as myth. "Learning, speaking, and using two languages may affect fundamental aspects of cognitive and neural development" (Yoshida 2008). Although explanations are not yet complete, bilingual children show executive function or self-control beyond their monolingual age-mates. Further study of cognition and immigrant children's learning will shed greater light on the positive aspects of bilingual speakers (Yoshida 2008).

Based on our current understanding of language acquisition, the National Center for Family Literacy (NCFL) has compiled a series of bilingual workshops "to promote the importance of parent involvement and literacy support at home" (Hasson and Price 2008, p. 2). These workshops include information for parents about the benefits of involvement in the classroom and at home, the use of two languages to build literacy skills, and reading strategies for the classroom and at home.

When teachers are aware that "for many English language learner parents, children's education in their home country may have been the sole responsibility of the teacher" (Hasson and Price 2008, p. 6), it helps them to recognize parents' past expectations with their children's teachers. "Parents' interaction with the teacher may have been minimal. Their role in their children's education could have been limited to providing guidance on social behavior and work ethic. The idea of active participation in their child's school, creating a relationship with a teacher and actually providing learning experiences for their child, is a new one— not one they had experienced in their home country" (Hasson and Price 2008, p. 6).

66 This does not mean these parents do not want to be involved; it only means they don't know they are supposed to be involved or how they can become involved. 99

—Hasson and Price 2008, p. 6

Although much remains to be understood in relation to bilingualism and English language learning for non-native English speakers, current best practices and guidelines for early childhood education provide a strong basis for both respecting diversity and optimizing children's learning. The National Association for the Education of Young Children (NAEYC) has delineated recommendations for working with both families and children in order to respect linguistic diversity.

naeyc 2 Guidelines for working with families are:

- Actively involve families in the early learning program.

- Help all families to understand cognitive advantages to children knowing more than one language.

- Provide strategies to help families to support, maintain, and preserve home language learning.

- Assure families that their home language and culture is honored.

Guidelines for teaching children:

- Ensure that children remain cognitively, linguistically, and emotionally connected to home language and culture.

- Encourage home language and literacy development to increase child's English language proficiency.

- Help to develop basic concepts in child's first language and within their particular cultural context.

- Develop creative strategies to promote all children's learning and participation.

- Plan and implement multiple modes for children to show what they know and what they can do (Many Languages 2005). **naeyc** 2

Culturally and Linguistically Appropriate Services (CLAS)

http://clas.uiuc.edu/links.html

ECONOMIC DIFFERENCES AMONG FAMILIES

In the contemporary United States, children and families have vastly different experiences related to income and other resources. The following statistics on poverty among American children are provided by the Children's Defense Fund and taken from the U.S. Department of Commerce, Bureau of the Census. The poverty rates for children six years and under peaked at 25.6 percent (more than one of every four children) in 1993 and gradually declined to 17.8 percent (still very close to one of every five children) in 2000, but had risen by 2004 to 19.9 percent (nearly one of every five children). These rates are not uniform nationwide: they are lowest in New Hampshire (9.7 percent), Connecticut (10.5 percent), Alaska (11.2 percent), and Maryland (11.4 percent); child poverty rates are highest in the District of Columbia (33.9 percent), Mississippi (31 percent), Louisiana (30 percent), and Arkansas (25.9 percent).

Differences in rates of poverty are also obvious among ethnic groups. Figure 2–3 shows increases in child poverty from 2000 to 2004. "Extreme poverty" means the families are living below one-half of the poverty level, or on about $7,610 a year or less (Children's Defense Fund, *State of America's Children*, 2005). (Note that the large increase in numbers of poor and extremely poor Latino children is related to an increase in the number of Latinos in the United States.) For various ethnic groups, this proportion is even higher (see Figure 2–3).

In 1996, federal legislation was passed that included time limits for which adults could receive governmental financial aid. Under this policy, the

Figure 2–3	Comparison of children in poverty from 2000–2004.		
	2000	**2004**	**% Increase**
Children in Poverty			
White, Non-Hispanic	4,018,000	4,507,000	12.2
Black	3,581,000	3,780,000	5.6
Latino	3,522,000	4,102,000	16.5
ALL	11,587,000	13,027,000	12.4
Children in Extreme Poverty			
White, Non-Hispanic	1,650,000	1,923,000	16.5
Black	1,581,000	1,908,000	20.7
Latino	1,168,000	1,459,000	24.9
ALL	4,634,000	5,561,000	20.0

© Cengage Learning

Temporary Assistance for Needy Families (TANF), parents must go to work after receiving welfare for a maximum of two years, and families are limited to a lifetime total of five years' cash assistance. States may exempt up to 20 percent of their cases from the five-year limit. Because this legislation gave states the responsibility of implementing the mandates, a variety of designs has been put into place. Marian Wright Edelman, president and founder of the Children's Defense Fund, notes that Minnesota stands out as a state that has "made it a goal to move families with children not just off welfare but out of poverty" (CDF Reports 1997). Further, Edelman writes, "There is no mystery about how to help families off welfare and out of poverty. States must provide the education, training, and work experience that parents need to compete for jobs with decent wages. States also need to remove the obstacles that often prevent parents from leaving welfare for work: lack of health care, transportation and child care."

Nearly a decade after the passing of TANF legislation, research continues to show that jobs alone are not enough to keep families out of poverty. Education and specialized training continue to be critical to the path out of poverty (Children's Defense Fund, *State of America's Children,* 2005). Regrettably, it continues to be difficult for low-wage workers to participate in any kind of training or education that might help to lift them from poverty. The resources needed for child care, transportation, and tuition or fees are often serious barriers.

naeyc 6 Early childhood teachers often take on the role of advocating for children and families with young children. Early childhood professional standards note that early childhood teachers must be "informed advocates for sound educational practices and policies" (Hyson 2003). Such practices and policies are related not only to children's immediate environments or microsystems, but also to the societal level or macrosystem. Early childhood teachers play an important role in being knowledgeable about and taking action for all levels of children's needs. Advocates understand that families must be able to earn a living wage; have access to health care; have reliable transportation; and have access to affordable, quality care for their children during the hours that they are required to work. At the macrosystem level, this involves contacting state and federal policymakers to provide information about the needs of young children and their families. **naeyc** 6

Frequently, educators' understanding of diversity does not include differences by family income or, to use the traditional term, social class. Yet financial resources have a tremendous impact on families, their practices, and their values. All parents are aware that poverty is a threat to children. Families living with scarce resources have had to learn the importance of meeting children's most basic needs.

Do This

The U.S. Census Bureau (2000) reported that the poverty line for a family of three was below $13,290 per year in 1999, or less than $1,108 per month. Investigate costs in your locality for housing, food, health care, transportation, and other necessities. Comment on your findings.

Cheal (1996) notes that as a society, we have several reasons for concern about families and their risk for poverty. He highlights three reasons:

1. The risk of poverty is highest in early childhood.
2. Families with children do not reap enough benefits from government redistribution of income.
3. Current political views about the role of government do not allow for assisting poor families in meaningful ways.

Even after President Johnson's "War on Poverty" during the 1960s, and into the 1980s and 1990s, young children continued to have the highest risk of living in poverty. This has been especially true for those children living in families headed by women. The economic picture for these families remains bleak. Even when women are employed, they typically do not make enough money to provide reliable transportation to their jobs, pay for high-quality child care for their children, and maintain a safe and healthy home environment. "The risk of poverty among women has often depended heavily on the nature of their relationships with men" (Cheal 1996). Further, traditional gender roles have been discarded for these single mothers. Often, mothers have not been expected to be employed, but rather it has been socially desirable for them to stay home and raise their children. This belief is no longer held in regard to women on welfare (Cheal 1996).

Consider This

Consider your opinion about maternal employment and child-rearing. What do you believe is the prevailing attitude about this in contemporary society? Is there a double standard for poor and affluent mothers? Should there be?

The American dream for modern times included the notion that children should not have to rely on the luck of the draw; that is, children's happiness and productivity should not rely simply on being born into a family at one economic level versus a family at another. With this view came the political notion that government would make an attempt to redistribute societal resources so that all children might benefit from them. (However, from 1978 to 1987, government expenditures on children decreased by 4 percent while those for the elderly increased by 52 percent [Danziger and Weinberg, as cited in Cheal 1996].) Public school was one way of attempting to even out children's lives. The presumption was that all children would have equal access to good, effective education, and this would equalize opportunities for poor children (Cheal 1996). One issue that faces education today involves seeking strategies for parity to those school districts having fewer resources.

Unlike the perspective of past decades, however, the predominant contemporary political view of poor families is that they must be moved from welfare to work, and for the most part they must achieve this on their own. Individual responsibility is now valued and expected. However, in the 1930s, at the time of the Great Depression, it was understood that poverty was not the result of individual failings, but rather that the economic structure of society played a very large part in family financial losses. Few policy makers today are willing to include societal explanations or responsibilities in their views on assisting the poor (Cheal 1996). Some child and family advocates believe that these political views contain racist and sexist elements. Because many poor families are composed of women and children, and because the huge majority of policy makers are white and male, this is a very real possibility. In his extensive analysis about systemic causes of poverty, David Cheal (1996) notes that "the poverty of children is not accidental. It is the fixed position of children in a carefully graded system, in which the youngest children have the highest risk of poverty." He accurately refers to this planned system as "perverse."

Do This

Research school funding for your state of residence. Are all schools/districts/counties funded equally; that is, are all children provided with equitable education resources? How are schools funded? What are the policy issues related to school funding for which early childhood professionals might advocate?

Consider This

Consider the political views explained by Cheal (1996). Using bioecological theory, discuss how the views are related to the various systems. Create an action plan for child and family advocates that could address these perspectives from each of the systems.

Children's Defense Fund
http://www.childrensdefense.org

National Center for Children in Poverty
http://www.nccp.org

National Center for Policy Analysis: Welfare
http://www.ncpa.org/
Click "policy issues"; click "welfare"

University Research on Families
http://www.childwelfare.com/

U.S. Census Bureau—Poverty
http://www.census.gov/
Click "poverty"

A review of research on low-income family involvement in children's education notes that while such families "strive to support their children's education, their overall levels of involvement are lower than those of families who do not live in poverty" (Boethel 2003). In addition to obvious barriers such as language differences and the lack of time, transportation, and child care, other barriers include cultural beliefs in which some families view the institution of school as the only source of education, a lack of understanding about the roles of family members at school, a lack of knowledge about subject matter that children are learning, and experiences of exclusion and discrimination (Boethel 2003).

Early childhood professionals often criticize families for not being interested in their children's education or for their reluctance to volunteer in the education programs. A complete understanding or appreciation of the minute-to-minute stresses of families living in poverty may not be possible. However, teachers must strive to accept each family. Further, early childhood educators must support all families at the place they are. Wishing away family stress caused by a lack of resources does not work. Helping to meet their pressing needs is the first step to forming partnerships with some families. Sometimes, teachers of young children feel frustration when families do not send money or notes back to school as the teacher requested. Rather than assuming that the parents or responsible family members are apathetic or hostile, it is helpful to keep in mind that the family may be dealing with other needs that were more pressing, such as keeping the heat turned on or a medical appointment. In such instances, teachers must call on their own compassion and understanding. Use of gentle reminders and a call of concern will be much more fruitful than accusations.

naeyc 1 A multitude of studies show that economic hardship puts many children at very high risk in the United States. Negative outcomes for children include difficult peer relationships, school problems, and low self-esteem (Bolger, Patterson, and Thompson 1995; Brooks-Gunn, Klebanov, and Duncan 1996). The stress of poverty makes parenting more difficult. The threat of violence in immediate neighborhoods is increasing in some communities. Involvement in their children's lives seems an impossible goal for some parents living in such desperate circumstances. **naeyc** 1

Families who live in poverty are often called on to pool their resources throughout their extended families and neighborhoods. Their very survival may depend on sharing child care arrangements and meals, as well as lending money. The addresses of poor families may change frequently as families move out of one home to live temporarily with others, and then, when finances get a little better, attempt to move back into a place of their own. In this need for mutual support seen in poor communities, some people rely on friendship networks for help as much as they do on extended family (Zinn and Eitzen 1987).

Prejudice against families who receive welfare abounds. "For most Americans, the words *welfare recipient* evoke the image of a good-for-nothing freeloader who drives a Cadillac, uses food stamps to buy sirloin steak, or watches soap operas all day. It is a classic icon of American culture, routinely projected upon all who are receiving public assistance" (Rank 1994). In an effort to describe the lives of welfare recipients, including their strengths and their problems, Rank's research includes information from interviews with people about their lives. What he found is that, like most families, the parents in his sample want what is best for their children. "Their frustration," he notes, "comes from not being able to provide it."

Planning for the future is not something that poor families can do easily, whether the reference is to the immediate future or to a time months or years from now. Unplanned or unexpected events such as illness, unreliable transportation, or requests from children's school for field trip money often have serious consequences on a family's financial plans. Working-class families often rely heavily on extended family for help. Siblings, parents, aunts, uncles, and cousins make up the primary social network in working-class families (Zinn and Eitzen 1987). When adults in these families have economic stability, their lifestyles may appear much more like those of the middle class; however, when jobs are not stable, these families teeter on the brink of poverty. Many of these families are one or two paychecks away from the welfare rolls. A married mother of two children relates her feelings about applying for welfare.

66 We felt like it was a shameful thing to be doing, basically. And I remember when the in-take worker was going over our form and wanted to know what our income had been for the previous month, and we said, it was something like two hundred and fifty dollars. And she looked at us and she said, 'Uhh, this can't be right, you couldn't live on this.' And we said, 'That's right, that's why we're here!' (Laughter.) I think we felt grateful that it was there. But it was a real blow to our pride. We had all kinds of …I mean…the way the public generally views welfare people, we had a lot of those same views. And it was really a hard thing for our pride to put ourselves in that position, and join that category of people. 99

—Rank, 1994

Working class people who are most likely to be affected by poverty are adults of childbearing age (25 to 44 years), the elderly (65 years and over), and children, especially under one year of age. The following percentages relate the likelihood that various age groups in the working class are living in poverty (Cheal 1996):

Children, under 1 year	53 percent
Children, 1–4 years	50 percent
Elderly, 65+ years	48 percent
Adults, 25–44 years	29 percent
Young adults, 15–24 years	24 percent
Middle-aged adults, 45–64 years	21 percent

At the other end of the spectrum, affluent, professional, or middle-class families with young children may have little or no problem meeting their children's basic needs and amenities. But these families, too, may fall prey to situations that may be harmful to their young children. Concern for their progeny's success entangles some parents in the "superkid syndrome." David Elkind (1987) has written about "the hurried child" and those who are "miseducated." "Parents today believe that they can make a difference in their children's lives, that they can give them an edge that will make them brighter and abler than the competition." Families with this goal for children pose another kind of challenge to early childhood teachers, who try to plan developmentally appropriate educational experiences for children but are often confronted with parental requests to move their child up a grade or place them in accelerated groups.

It is critical to note that the risks children in poverty face are unmatched by any other single variable. Still, children from affluent families often contend with undue pressure related to expectations that are not consistent with early development. All children must live in environments that provide the developmental assets (www.search-institute.org) described in Chapter 1. In review, these assets include:

- Support from families and communities
- Empowerment through families and communities valuing them as children
- Responsive boundaries and expectations
- Opportunities to play constructively
- Encouragement to be lifelong learners
- Exposure to positive values that include fairness, caring, honesty, and responsibility
- Opportunities to learn how to get along well with others
- Experiences that help to develop a positive sense of self-worth and caring for others

naeyc 6 Effective early childhood teachers can best help all families and communities by helping them understand that all of these assets are needed for healthy child development. When only two or three are emphasized, the necessary balance is overlooked and children may be stressed, neglected, or overcome with a sense of failure. **naeyc** 6

GENDER ROLE IDENTITY

66 Women have always played a central role in families, but the idea that they have a life cycle apart from their roles as wife and mother is a relatively recent one, and still is not widely accepted in our culture. The expectation for women has been that they would take care of the needs of others: first men, then children, then the elderly. Until very recently, 'human development' referred to male development and women's development was defined by the men in their lives.

They went from being daughter, to wife, to mother, with their status defined by the male in the relationship.... 99

—Monica McGoldrick, 1989

An individual's gender role is "a set of expectations that prescribe how females or males should think, act, and feel" (Santrock 1994). People's understanding of themselves as male or female, and what that means in their particular environment, is influenced by biological, social, and cognitive factors. Within any given family, the roles specified for males and females may be rigid or fluid. Families with rigid stereotypes are likely to view males as independent, aggressive, and power oriented, whereas females are seen as dependent, nurturant, and uninterested in power. Research regarding the interaction of ethnicity and gender on traditional gender roles has shown that expectations for males and females vary according to ethnicity (McGoldrick 1989).

The pluralistic culture of the United States contains many variations on gender roles. A feminist perspective on gender indicates that women and girls are competent in their own right. This conflicts with the traditional view of female existence as important only in relation to males.

Because early childhood teachers work with both female and male family members, it is important that teachers are aware of their own views about gender roles. Teachers may find it challenging to accept and support the role, whether traditional or feminist, that a particular parent has taken. For example, how would you react to the following situations, noting your own biases and preferences?

- In Suzanne's (age four years) family, Mr. Jaworski stays home with Suzanne and her younger brother, Tucker. Suzanne's mother, Dr. Stoner, who kept her maiden name, has built a successful career and travels on business at least six times a year.
- In Peter's (age seven years) family, Mrs. Jordan is a full-time homemaker. Peter and his two older brothers are enrolled in the elementary school in which you teach. Mr. Jordan has been in danger of losing his job because of cutbacks at his corporation.
- Debra's (age two-and-a-half years) mother, Ms. Meyer, is employed as an administrative staff member on a local university campus. She has insisted that you call her "Ms. Meyer," not "Mrs. Meyer." Debra and her mother live with Ms. Kennedy, who works on the grounds crew at the same campus.

Mother-headed families often have very different needs than father-headed, single-parent families do. First of all, there are many more of them. It is estimated that as many as one-half of all children will spend some of their childhood years in a family headed by a single woman (Garfinkel and McLanahan 1989). Single-parent families headed by women are much more likely to be poor than are those headed by men. Reasons for this include little or no support from fathers, the limited earning capacity of mothers, and the difficulties that come with trying to juggle the roles of sole breadwinner and sole caregiver (Burns and Scott 1994).

Gender Development
http://www.psy.pdx.edu/PsiCafe/
Click "Areas"; click "Developmental Psychology"; click "gender development"

Sexual Orientation and Gender Identity
http://www.aclu.org/
Click "Lesbian and Gay Rights"

As the social and economic climates have changed during the latter half of the twentieth century, women have been increasingly able to obtain employment that pays a reasonable wage. But comparisons with a number of other countries, most notably Sweden, show that in addition to access to employment that pays a living wage, mothers must also have access to affordable, high-quality child care and other family support services, and must be able to collect child support from the noncustodial parent (Burns and Scott 1994). One mother who attempted to leave public assistance noted how crucial good child care is:

66 Well, I had two little bitty babies. And I was working at the time I got pregnant. So I tried going back to work when Stacy was about, say, two months old. And the lady that I got to baby-sit for me just didn't come up to par for me. And with me having the two babies, one was just walking and one was an arm baby, I made the decision that it's best for me to try to be here with them. And I know they were taken care of like I would have wanted them to be taken care of. So that's when I applied for aid. 99

—**Rank, 1994**

Another topic related to gender identity centers on same-sex unions. Many educators have concerns about children of lesbian families. However, existing literature does not support the prejudice that children in lesbian families are worse off than other children (Burns and Scott 1994). Figure 2–4 delineates myths and facts about gay, lesbian, bisexual, and transgendered parents. The common view that children suffer from the lack of a father's presence, for instance, is not substantiated when children have relationships with multiple adults who have somewhat of a parenting role: friends, grandparents, or the biological father. When lesbian mothers have social, economic, and personal resources, "chosen, father-free parenthood" can meet children's needs (McGuire and Alexander 1985). Further, comparisons of characteristics of lesbian mothers with women in general show the following for lesbian mothers:

- Higher levels of education and professional training
- Scored as more normal on psychological tests
- Had more support and practical help from cohabiting partners than wives receive from husbands
- Mother-child relationships were closer
- Cognitive and social competence was normal or high
- Sex role behavior was normal
- Daughters chose more prestigious/traditionally masculine careers
- Daughters reported higher popularity (McGuire and Alexander 1985)

Figure 2–5 provides additional commentary.

Some beliefs about lesbian mothers that are shown to be empirically unfounded include that lesbian mothers have higher incidences of mental illness, are less maternal than heterosexual women, leave little time for parent-child interactions, and are generally unfit to be parents. Further, there is no research evidence to support the notion that children will be hindered in sexual identity development, that they are less psychologically healthy, or that they experience greater difficulties in social relationships than peers from heterosexual families. Actually, "children of lesbian mothers develop patterns of gender-role behavior that are much like those of other children" (Patterson 1995).

It is important to realize that just as heterosexual-parent families differ from one another, great diversity also exists among gay and lesbian parent families (Patterson 1995). Some gay and lesbian parents have biological children; others have adopted or foster children. Some have custody of their children; some have limited visitation with their children. Some are single-parent families; some are two-parent families. Some live in communities where their gay or lesbian identity is accepted; others live in communities that are not so accepting.

Concern about lack of father involvement in families or specifically with their very young children does not exist only when fathers are living out of the home. A British study by Jane Ribbens (1994) shows that contemporary child-rearing remains in the domain of women:

Issues of childcare, presumptions about the needs of children, and decision-making about how to deal with and relate to children are major preoccupations in women's everyday lives. Furthermore, a consideration of how women perceive, understand and resolve some of these issues around childrearing is essential to any analysis of gender relationships, divisions of labour and distributions of resources within households.

Further, Ribbens notes that it is generally the responsibility of the mother to create "the family." In this task, two processes are involved: (1) work on internal cohesion, making certain that the family members form a meaningful unit; and (2) work on external boundaries, making certain that there are clear separations of the family from other social units.

66 Within the apparently "conventional" families in my own study, images of family togetherness did not always correspond to how things worked out in everyday interactions. While the women living with their husbands were quick to tell me their good qualities as fathers, in the details of their accounts strains could also become apparent in constructing "the family" with an involved father. Much of the care of preschool children occurs in women's worlds, either within or outside the home, and men are marginal to these worlds. 99

—**Ribbens, 1994**

From C. Ray Drew and Kate Kendall, Family Pride Coalition.

Figure 2–4	Myths and facts about gay, lesbian, bisexual, and transgendered parents.

MYTH

Lesbians and gay men do not have children.

FACT

Lesbian, gay, and bisexual parents have biological children. They also have children through domestic and international adoption, artificial and donor insemination, foster care, and surrogacy.

MYTH

Gay men and lesbians have unstable relationships.

FACT

Gay men and lesbians often have committed, loving relationships. Sometimes these relationships are not open or obvious to others because of societal discrimination.

MYTH

Gay men and lesbians prey on children to recruit them to their "lifestyle."

FACT

Research indicates that children reared by gay or lesbian parents are no more likely to become gay or lesbian than children who grow up with heterosexual parents.

MYTH

Children who are in contact with gay men or lesbians face increased risk of being sexually abused.

FACT

Sexual abuse is caused by pedophilia, not sexual orientation. Ninety percent of sexual abuse cases involve a heterosexual male.

MYTH

Children raised by gay men and lesbians will be exposed to an "immoral" environment.

FACT

Morality is subjective. If all people were eliminated from the possibility of parenthood because of what someone believed to be immoral, there would be no parents left. In the United States, parents have primacy in decisions about providing a moral environment for their children.

MYTH

Families with gay or lesbian parents are not "real" families.

FACT

Lesbian and gay parents "cook dinners, change diapers, and take time off of work to care for children, help with homework, negotiate TV time, drive children to soccer practice, worry about child care, clean house, and read bedtime stories." Families define themselves.

MYTH

Gay men cannot be nurturing parents.

FACT

Research has shown gay fathers to be responsive to and supportive of their children.

MYTH

Discussing a gay or lesbian family member means you must talk about sex.

FACT

"As responsible parents, we are charged with speaking about sexuality to our children in accurate, appropriate and age sensitive ways. We want our children to have correct information and an understanding about how to interpret information that is congruent with our beliefs. However, to think that in order to discuss a *l*esbian, *g*ay, *b*isexual, or *t*ransgendered (LGBT or GLBT) family member means one must automatically speak about sex is wrong. When speaking of an LGBT relative, a responsible and caring parent can and should discuss such important issues as love, understanding, acceptance, diversity, and discrimination. To speak with young children about LGBT family members is to speak about what they understand most, family. For a child not to be able to talk about his or her family is not only discrimination, it is wrong."

MYTH

It is safer for children of lesbians and gay men not to talk about their families.

FACT

Strong schools will include information about all children's families in education programs. Strong schools must also provide an emotionally safe climate for all children through support for *all* families.

MYTH

Children raised by a gay or lesbian couple will not have proper male and female role models.

FACT

"Research suggests that our children are exposed to more people of the opposite sex than many kids of straight parents and even when our kids are not, there is no evidence to suggest that they are harmed."

After analyzing the information provided by the mothers in her study, Ribbens goes on to say that much of the mother-child time together did not occur within families at all, but rather in variations of networks of other women and their children. This finding brought Ribbens to the conclusion that observational studies are needed of mothers and their young children as they participate in "semipublic" settings such as playgroups.

Fathers play very different roles within families than those of mothers. Only since the mid-1970s has

Figure 2–5 Commentary on lesbian and gay parenting.

MOTHER'S DAY GUEST COMMENTARY
by C. Ray Drew and Kate Kendell

Until just recently, the existence of lesbian and gay parents went almost unrecognized in our culture. Much of our society simply believed that being a gay or lesbian parent was a contradiction in terms, and numerous negative myths promulgated that position. Heterosexist laws denied the possibility of parenting for openly gay/lesbian people, and penalized anyone with children from a prior heterosexual relationship with loss of visitation or custody.

The last 10 years have changed this landscape dramatically. We now find ourselves in the middle of a "gayby boom" as countless thousands of lesbians and gay men choose to become parents. We have countered the Radical Right's argument that a family consists only of a heterosexual father, mother and children, with our community's family values of love, diversity, respect, caring and pride. We have proudly stated to the world that "love makes a family."

But is love enough? What happens when the "love" between a lesbian couple fades or sours? In recent years we have experienced a threat to our community's families as alarming as the Radical Right's hate campaign. In surging numbers, we have seen an insidious increase in the number of custody battles within the community involving lesbian couples, as biological mothers deny visitation to their former partners.

No one is at their best when a couple splits up. It is a time of serious emotional crisis. It is a time when it is easy to rationalize that a former partner's behavior is a reflection of a poor parenting bond with the child. Friends and family may feel protective and support the biological mom in her dismissal of her former partner. In the absence of laws to the contrary, it is tempting to redraw the family construction around heterosexist laws, take the child and cut the partner out of the family picture forever.

But can we use the heterosexist, anti-gay laws to assure that a former partner is denied the right to see her child and simultaneously demand that others recognize our family commitments? While together, a couple may have lamented the fact that their family was discriminated against by IRS laws, insurance regulations, social security policies and numerous laws that denied the legal recognition of their family. Sadly, after dissolution of the relationship, the biological mother can use those very laws to deny that the other parent was EVER a "real" parent.

In the legal world of non-gay married couples, an elaborate court system is ready to decide custody and visitation issues when the parents cannot do so. Even if one parent was only marginally involved the court nevertheless recognizes their status as parent. In the absence of identified harm to the child, even the less involved or marginal parent is granted some visitation.

The community and court standards reflect the parental rights and obligations of both parents.

When a lesbian couple breaks up, without a legally sanctioned relationship or legal recognition of their family, who decides what is in a child's best interests? Couples, who had a clear, unambiguous agreement that they would be equal parents to this child, suddenly become very unequal in the face of divorce. The biological mother has absolute power in these cases to determine the fate of the child and the privileges of the non-biological mother. In case after case, the biological mother has denied that her former partner is even a parent. Some courts have agreed, denying the non-biological mother's right to her day in court to seek any legal redress, much less be granted visitation with her child.

Are legal protections important? Of course they are. We need the protection for our families that legally sanctioned marriage provides. We need the protection of second-parent adoptions in the absence of marriage.

But more important than these legal protections we need to honor our agreements and our intentions with one another. Family is a social construction as much as a legal entity. If we are to truly have permanent parental and family relationships, we need a social ethic that says they are permanent. We need a consistent community value, which says that a commitment to parenting is lifelong. If we want our children to grow up secure in who they are and who their family is, they need to see a community with a strong sense of family, a community that maintains that standard even when couples break up.

Does love make a family? You bet. And when love doesn't last forever, the "family" still does. It is our commitment that will signal to society and our children just how seriously we take our own families.

---

much research been done on fathering. Contemporary society sees fathers essentially in one of two ways: either as increasing their involvement with their children, or as absent and having little emotional or financial responsibility for their children. Furstenberg (1988) refers to this as the "two faces of fatherhood." Early childhood teachers may observe these vast differences in the fathers of children in their care. Sometimes, fathers are so removed from the family that children have not met them or barely know them. Adults are often under the mistaken assumption, then, that the children's closeness to another adult male, grandfather, or uncle simply replaces their relationship with fathers.

Erna Furman (1992) writes about young children who have been "deeply affected by the loss of their father through death or family breakup." She notes that the loss of a father may cause long-term hardship for a child, but that those children who never had relationships with their fathers should also be of concern to educators. She tells of two such children. Felicity, at three-and-a-half years, had never met her father. Her mother never talked about him and was certain that Felicity at this young age did not even think about her father. Felicity exhibited behaviors such as thumb-sucking and unceasing demands, however, that were determined by a therapist to be related to her desire to know her father. With this information, Felicity's mother tried to prepare her for possible disappointment and contacted her father to let him know of their daughter's wishes. In this case, the father responded and began to spend some time with his daughter. Even though contact between Felicity and her father was sporadic, the trust that the process generated between mother and daughter was a positive outcome to this situation.

In the second scenario, Ben also had not met his father. When Ben's toddler class planned visits by their fathers, his mother asked the teacher if Ben's beloved grandfather might come with him instead. When the teacher suggested that the mom ask Ben his opinion, the mom was surprised—and when she asked Ben, she was surprised again. Ben initially refused to have his grandfather go to school with him. Because he had never mentioned his absent father, Ben's mother assumed that meant he never thought about who his father might be. Once it was revealed that Ben did have questions about his own dad, his mother was able to explain that he lived far away and could not visit. Having this information and a new understanding, Ben was then willing to have grandfather accompany him to school.

DAP So many teachers assume that because it is now common for children to live in homes without their fathers, that children simply accept or do not even notice the absence. Furman (1992) points out that when teachers observe carefully, however, they report situations with children that contradict this viewpoint. She says, "There are no easy answers to these human dilemmas, but respecting our children's thoughts and feelings has much to do with respecting ourselves and with building a community in which we all learn to respect one another. Respect, like charity, begins at home." DAP

In his review of the research literature related to fathers and families, Parke (1995) notes that a great deal of research supports the fact that fathers spend less time with their children than do mothers. This is true from infancy through adolescence. Other consistent findings from research are that fathers are competent caregivers of their children when they need to be, and fathers interact in qualitatively different ways with children than do mothers. Whereas mothers are more verbal and directed and use toys in their interactions, fathers are more physical and tactile with children. It seems reasonable to believe that both styles of interaction stimulate children and that children benefit from such differences.

Dads and Daughters
http://www.thedadman.com
Click "Research agenda"

Family Support and Father Involvement
http://www.fcps.net/
Click "Research in Parent Involvement"; click "A Call to Commitment...."

What determines how involved fathers are in their children's lives? A variety of factors have been shown to contribute to any given father's interaction with his children. Parke (1995) uses empirical data to demonstrate that the following considerations are related to father involvement. It is evident that father involvement is based on a complex system of in-home and out-of-home variations.

- *Fathers' relationships with their own parents.* Those men who had positive interactions with their own fathers may model those with their children. However, there is also some evidence that men who view their relationships with their fathers as negative

Fathers can be competent caregivers of children.

© Cengage Learning/ECE Photo Library.

sometimes make an effort with their own children to increase positive feelings and interactions.

- *Fathers' belief systems about the roles of mothers and fathers.* Some men have more stereotypic ideas about what each parent should do with children. Others are more willing to be flexible in meeting their children's needs.

- *Attitudes of the mother.* Some mothers believe that they are the more important and competent parent, and restrict father involvement in various ways. As mothers are in the workforce full time, they may be increasingly willing to encourage a greater level of father involvement with their children.

- *Marital relationships.* When mothers provide support to fathers in their caregiving roles, fathers gain competence and confidence in relating to their children.

- *Timing of fatherhood.* Males who become fathers when they are adolescents tend not to be highly involved in their children's lives. Some of these fathers rarely even visit their children. Men who become fathers later in their lives often appreciate their children more and have greater self-confidence in their parenting. On the other hand, men who became fathers at more typical ages were more likely than older fathers to be physical with their children.

- *Family employment patterns.* Fathers typically spend a greater amount of time with their children when mothers are employed outside the home. It also may be that the quality of father-child relationships changes when mothers are employed outside the home.

- *Work quality.* Difficult or stressful work conditions may cause fathers to be more disengaged with their children when they are at home. It is also believed that positive workplaces can enhance the quality of the father-child relationship.

Those who advocate for higher levels of father involvement do so in part because they believe it results in positive outcomes for children. Parke (1995) also discusses the research related to this area of interest. Following are some of the findings related to children whose fathers do not live with them:

- Little effect of father contact on well-being of children 11 to 16 years

- No relation between father contact and children's social and cognitive development for children 5 to 9 years

These findings are somewhat surprising in light of the emphasis on father involvement in children's lives. One explanation, however, is that father presence during the first three years may be the most important

time. Several studies seem to support this point of view. Further, quality of interaction, versus just quantity of time spent together, seems to be important to father-child relationships.

Two aspects of the definition of *quality* are fathers' physical play and positive affect with their children. Young children whose fathers exhibit these two characteristics have been found to be more popular and have a higher degree of social acceptance from other children (Parke 1995).

As with mothers, individuals in our society typically assume that all fathers are heterosexual. This is obviously not true. It is difficult to obtain an accurate count of the number of gay fathers in the United States today. The primary reason for this is that the prejudice and discrimination against these fathers threaten their relationships with their children. It is believed that the largest group of children of gay fathers today is composed of those who were born in heterosexual relationships of their biological parents before one or the other parent had identified themselves as lesbian or gay. Gay fathers commonly do not have custody of their children, nor do they often live in the same home as their children. This is partially a result of the legal system's bias against gay fathers. This bias is so pronounced that not only do courts rarely grant custody to gay fathers, they may even deny these fathers visitation rights based on the notion that gay fathers are negative influences on their children (Patterson 1995).

Research on gay fathers is sparse. Patterson (1995), in her review of the literature on gay fathers, notes that they report differences in their parenting in comparison to heterosexual fathers. Gay fathers reported both greater warmth and responsiveness to their children and more limit-setting. The few studies that have compared gay fathers and gay men who are not fathers have found that these fathers reported higher levels of self-esteem and fewer negative attitudes about homosexuality than did the nonfathers.

One of our culture's concerns about the effects of gay fathers on their children is whether having gay parents will affect the sexual identity of gay fathers' children. At this time, no research supports the notion that children of gay fathers will be homosexual in their orientation (Patterson 1995).

As early childhood educators, our greatest concern for children from gay or lesbian families may be for their psychological and physical safety. However, this concern stems not from the dynamics within the family, but rather from the bigotry and hate that these families may receive from society.

DAP Early childhood teachers may find themselves in situations where colleagues, students, parents, or people in the community are openly discriminatory toward *g*ay-, *l*esbian-, *b*isexual-, or *t*ransgendered-parent (GLBT or LGBT) families. It must be the early childhood professional's first responsibility to do no harm to children and families. Further, because it is known that families compose the most important relationship for all children, teachers must respect and support a child's parents and the relationships that children have with their parents. DAP

FAMILIES AND RELIGIOSITY

Due in part to the constitutional separation of church and state, education has been silenced about religion. This can make it difficult for early childhood educators to explore the role that it plays, if any, in children's families. Nonetheless, understanding the importance of **religiosity** in families is as critical as understanding a family's culture or economic status. Some teachers and schools, of course, do place religion within a family's culture, but, generally, because there has been so little attention given to family and individual differences related to religion in education, we have chosen to discuss it here.

The term *religiosity* refers to the degree of emphasis families place on religion in their lives. This may not be immediately evident to early childhood professionals, both because of the variety of religious practices and because of the tremendous differences in degree of practice from family to family. Some families may discuss their religion with teachers in the context of specific classroom practices, such as holiday celebrations. Others may have unexpressed concerns, and still others may have no need to be open with their child's teacher about their religious views.

Black churches have historically provided a great deal of family support. Because members of these churches were often denied access to other forms of family support in the United States, church members intervened to assist with survival. Caldwell, Greene, and Billingsley (1994) note that black churches have had a social service role since their inception in the late 1700s. During the civil rights movement of the 1960s, black churches took on a political activist role. In the 1980s, when drastic cuts were made in public funding for social programs, these churches once again reached out to their communities to provide support to families. It is believed that family and church are "strong interactive institutions that are mutually enhancing in their influence on African American communities." Further, "Black churches are mediators that buffer and enhance the relationship between the family's informal social network and the larger formal societal network." One aspect of this "larger formal societal network" is the educational institution.

Religiosity
http://www.wikipedia.com
Type in "Religion"

Whether or not families discuss their religion with teachers, teachers must be aware that religious belief or practice may affect a child's behavior. For instance, Janice Hale (1986), a scholar in the area of African-American child development, speaks about the differences in black churches and Anglo churches. She notes that from very early ages, African-American children are active during church services. The expectation is *not* that they should sit still and be quiet, as so often is the case in Anglo churches. Imagine the shock, then, when these children come to school where they are expected to be still and quiet!

DAP Variations in religious beliefs and practices must be respected by early childhood teachers, just as teachers respect differences in culture, ethnicity, gender, and abilities. One source that helps to explain the differences is *How To Be a Perfect Stranger: A Guide to Etiquette in Other People's Religious Ceremonies* (Magida 1996). Knowledge about these differences is often the first step in helping teachers understand families' beliefs and, thus, is part of the foundation for building family-school partnerships. DAP (Figure 2–6 provides additional commentary.)

> A nation that does not stand up for its children does not stand for anything and will not stand strong in the twenty-first century....We must believe we can save all of our children and then do it!

—**Marian Wright Edelman, 1996**

There are several additional sources that early childhood teachers can turn to for help with this subject. Two are accessible through the Children's Defense Fund (CDF), the group that organized a rally at the Lincoln Memorial in Washington, D.C., on June 1, 1996, attended by more than 250,000 child and family advocates. The rally was a call to *all* communities of faith to come together to "Stand for Children." Continuing the rally's momentum, CDF created a religious-action branch, including the Interfaith Child Advocacy Network and Congregations to Leave No Child Behind. The mission statement for the Interfaith Child Advocacy Network indicates that the network will "provide opportunities for educating congregations and the public about the needs of children, the solutions, and our common responsibility for addressing those needs" (http://www.childrensdefense.org/religiousaction/). Congregations to Leave No Child Behind pledge to educate about the needs and concerns of children, to provide outreach for children, to practice spiritual disciplines, and to advocate for children and families. With these movements, CDF has made a clear connection between advocating for children and families and religiosity.

From "All Faiths Should Be Treated Fairly in Schools," by Charles C. Haynes, as published in PUBLIC OPINION (Chambersburg, PA). Reprinted by permission of the author.

Figure 2–6	All faiths should be fairly treated in schools.

Forget the home-run race. Litigation has now surpassed baseball as America's favorite national pastime.

The latest example of how quick we are to "call a lawyer" comes from Ohio, where a school district may face a lawsuit for closing school on Rosh Hashana and Yom Kippur (Sept. 21 and Sept. 30, respectively).

School officials argue that absenteeism is too high on those days to hold classes in any meaningful way. Some 15 percent of the students in the district are Jewish and most of them stay home or attend synagogue for two of Judaism's most significant holy days. In some schools, absences ran as high as 21 percent.

A group of parents—with the ironic name of Parents for Fairness—objects, claiming that closing the schools these two days would favor the Jewish faith over other faiths in violation of the First Amendment.

Who's right?

It's true that the First Amendment's establishment clause requires that public school officials be neutral among religions and between religion and nonreligion. The school board can't close the schools on Jewish holy days because it wants to favor Judaism.

But school officials have a good civic (or secular) purpose for their action: too many students would be absent those days to conduct a normal school day. The closings are meant to serve the educational needs of all the students, not to advance a particular religion. Just because the policy also benefits Jewish kids doesn't make it unconstitutional.

It would be different if the district had a much smaller Jewish population. In that case, the best approach would be to allow Jewish students to be excused for services and require them to make up the missed work.

Beyond the legal issues, Parents for Fairness might want to think more about what they mean by "fairness." After all, the school calendar already favors the majority faith since no classes are held on Sunday and Christmas is a national holiday. Most Christians don't need to worry about the school schedule.

By contrast, minority faiths have to work around the existing calendar. Jews who observe the Sabbath have a problem participating in Friday night ball games and Saturday activities. Muslim students who wish to attend community prayer midday on Fridays sometimes have a hard time getting released from school.

This built-in advantage should be all the more reason for school officials to be sensitive to the religious needs of students from minority faiths. Of course, that rarely means closing school. But it does mean finding ways to accommodate requests where possible.

Rosh Hashana, by the way, is the Jewish New Year, a time of celebration but also of judgment. According to Jewish tradition, during the 10 days following Rosh Hashana, God examines the deeds of the people. For Jews, this is a time of profound self-examination and repentance.

At the end of this period, on Yom Kippur—the Day of Atonement—God makes a final judgment and forgives those who have truly repented. Many Jews fast for 25 hours and spend much of the day in the synagogue, praying for forgiveness.

Repentance, judgment, forgiveness. Nowadays a little time off for these things seems like a very good idea.

GEOGRAPHIC REGION

Geographic location affects what it means to be an American family just as other factors do. Perhaps those who have relocated to other geographic regions can understand best the differences among families that geographic placement creates, even among families of otherwise similar ethnicity, culture, economic class, and religiosity. Regional differences even affect gender role expectations.

Geographic differences are the result of the confluence of many factors, including climate, terrain, proximity to waterways, economy, industry, and history. Figure 2–7 demonstrates that all of the components discussed in this chapter interact to impact individual families.

As Figure 2–7 indicates, one of the elements affected by geography is poverty levels. Poverty rates for the nine census geographic divisions for 1994 demonstrate regional differences (Triest 1997). The highest rate, 15.8 percent, existed in the west south-central region. Other areas whose rates were higher than the national average of 11.6 percent include east south-central, California, and New York. The lowest family poverty rate was in New England—8.2 percent—while the rates for the North Central, Middle Atlantic, South Atlantic, Mountain, and Pacific regions fall below the national average.

Consider This

Consider some of the notions you have about the people from one or two of the following regions: the Northeast, Southeast, Midwest, Southwest, Northwest, and Pacific. On what are your ideas based? What experiences have you had with people from regions other than your own?

Various stereotypes exist about people from different regions of the United States. Terms such as "salty New Englander," "Southern belle" and "Southern gentleman," "hillbilly," "farmer's daughter," and so on reflect images held by many living in other parts

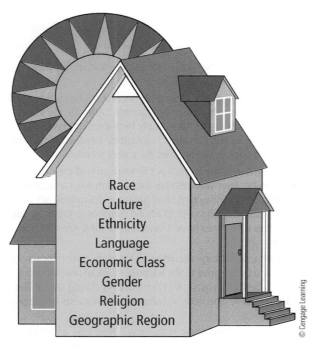

Race
Culture
Ethnicity
Language
Economic Class
Gender
Religion
Geographic Region

© Cengage Learning

Figure 2–7 All of these characteristics interact to create individuality.

of the country. As with all stereotypes, a small part of these may be based in reality, but the ensuing pictures are far too narrow to be accurate or useful, and they limit our understanding of differences among people.

Sometimes, differences in dialect, slang, or variations in manners will lead to degrading others. Understanding expectations from various regional groups can foster positive interactions with them. For example, a child whose family moved from the northeastern part of the country to the South soon learned that his teachers expected him not to reply to them with "Yes" or "No," but with "Yes, ma'am" or "No, sir." The child explained that this was difficult for him to learn because typically, when "ma'am" or "sir" was added to his speech in the past, it was not considered a sign of good manners, but, quite differently, a sign of sarcasm. Certainly, teachers should respectfully engage with students and expect respectful interaction in return, but it is important for teachers to understand how regional differences affect a child's understanding of what *respectful* means.

Alliance for Full Acceptance

http://www.affa-sc.org

Erase the Hate

http://www.ethonline.org/

Facing History and Ourselves

http://www.facinghistory.org

Museum of Tolerance

http://www.wiesenthal.com/
Select "Museum of Tolerance" from the drop-down menu at top of page

Teaching Tolerance

http://www.Tolerance.org

Tufts University Child and Family Web Guide

http://www.cfw.tufts.edu

50 Multicultural Books Every Child Should Know

http://www.soemadison.wisc.edu/
Type in "50 Multicultural Books"

naeyc 1 Another regional difference that teachers must be aware of is that priorities—the emphasis within a family of things that are of greater or lesser importance—may shift tremendously from region to region. In examining characteristics of Appalachian mountain families, for instance, Klein (1995) noted that connections between generations are critical for these families. Furthermore, most Appalachians emphasize the importance of spirituality over that of financial success. The consequent emphasis on humility among people of the Appalachians is often viewed by outsiders as making them "dull" and lacking self-esteem. After studying a number of characteristics that set this group apart from others, the author notes that educators must consider not only racial and ethnic differences but also those related to community and cultural heritage. **naeyc** 1

APPLICATION TO EARLY CHILDHOOD EDUCATION PROGRAMS

Celebrating Diversity

Celebrations and rituals are an important part of the human experience, but people celebrate for many different reasons and in many different ways. For instance, families may celebrate the same holiday but do it quite differently from one another. Other families may celebrate completely different holidays. One way to share information about the differences in the ways we celebrate is to have families come to early childhood programs to share their particular ways of celebrating.

In an effort to move to anti-bias approaches, some early childhood educators and institutions have done away with all celebrations. This is not necessary and may not even be desirable. Instead, it may be preferable to be sensitive to all ways of celebrating and to create celebrations unique to your classroom for special events such as new siblings, lost teeth, and other common developmental occurrences in families with young children. (See the information provided in the box with selected Web sites about various religious celebrations and traditions, and see Figure 2–8.)

Inclusiveness

The ultimate goal for understanding diversity in early childhood education is to provide an *inclusive* environment. **Inclusiveness** means that each child and family can feel a sense of belonging, regardless of the commonalities or differences that exist between them and others in the group. This is a lofty goal, and because of many societal factors, may not be easily achieved.

As teachers plan class lessons and activities, and as they set classroom rules and policies, they must examine each lesson, activity, rule, and policy to ensure that it is inclusive. Even the most sensitive and knowledgeable teacher may err in this process. What is important, however, is not that we err, but rather what we do to correct the error when we realize that our classrooms are not inclusive. Compassionate, effective early childhood teachers collect information, ask for guidance, and change their classrooms so that inclusiveness prevails.

Figure 2–8	Key terms for understanding Kwanzaa.

KWANZAA

Kwanzaa is celebrated by many African-Americans between December 26 and January 1. For African-American people who keep this African harvest holiday, it is a time of reaffirming themselves by focusing on their ancestors and culture. Traditions include the following:

Nguzo Saba: The seven principles

Kinara: Candleholder for seven candles

Mkeka: Straw or cloth placemat

Vibunzi: Ears of corn, one for each child in the family

One of Kwanzaa's guiding principles is applied to each of the seven days of celebration:

Umoja (oo-MO-jah): Unity of family and community

Kujichagulia (KOO-gee-cha-GOO-lee-yah): Self-determination

Ujima (oo-GEE-mah): Collective work and responsibility

Ujamaa (oo-JAH-mah): Cooperative economics

Nia (NEE-yah): Purpose (to set personal goals to benefit community)

Kuumba (koo-OOM-bah): Creativity

Imani (ee-MAH-nee): Faith

Kwanzaa Information Center at http://www.melanet.com/, click "Kwanzaa Info Center"

naeyc 2 A review of research has led to the following recommendations of sources that can help early childhood teachers understand specific ways to support diverse families' involvement in their children's education. As stated in Chapter 1, inclusiveness is the key to strong family-school relationships, and "relationships are the foundation of parent involvement in schools" (Johnstone and Hiatt, as cited in Boethel 2003). Considering the importance of relationships as well as the existing empirical evidence, Boethel recommends the following practices for fostering an inclusive environment so that all families can participate:

- Be sure that all family involvement policies focus on including all areas of diversity. Such policies will relate to (1) frequent two-way communication with families; (2) adapting all family involvement components to meet diverse backgrounds, languages, and circumstances; (3) involving representative families in planning and decision-making efforts; (4) providing effective professional development opportunities for teachers to work sensitively with all families; and (5) suggesting and supporting possibilities for families to build their own capacities in order to effectively be involved in their children's education.

- The school principal plays a critical role in meaningful family involvement. Active support from a principal includes: (1) frequent communication, with translation or in-home language; (2) informal meetings to check in with families about their interests, concerns, and questions as well as to update families on broad school concerns; (3) having a strong presence and active involvement at all school events; (4) prioritizing policies relating to family involvement; and (5) emphasizing the priority of family involvement with staff and families.

- Provide active support and respect that all families have high aspirations for their children. Demonstrate appreciation for the efforts of parents and other family members.

- In order to best honor diversity, both similarities and differences must be acknowledged. "It is important for schools and community organizations not to simply ignore issues related to diversity or to act as if differences don't exist" (Boethel 2003). Acknowledgement of differences must include not only festive, lighthearted celebrations of food and customs, but also making a place for everyone at the decision-making table. In order for diversity to be truly honored, all voices must be heard.

- Teacher preparation programs and ongoing professional development must include in-depth content in the area of working with families, including those families who may be different from the teachers' own.

- Schools must help immigrant families understand the system. Inform all families through ways that they can understand what is expected of them and of their children in their student roles.

- Go the extra mile to support families in their involvement with children's education both at home and at school. Some recognized ways to do this include: (1) make communication substantive by using families' home languages. (2) Make it doable for immigrant families to participate in various ways. Be sure that someone from the parent organization is carrying out the charge to welcome all new families. Some of the ways to involve families is to increase their comfort level by requesting that they provide something from their culture, such as fundraisers that involve selling or auctioning food or other cultural products. (3) Get into the community through home visits or involvement of school personnel in civic events.

- Trust is crucial, but it does not happen overnight. Keep in mind that each person has had past experiences, and, for some, past experiences with schools have not always been positive. In addition to all of the previous points in this list, it may take time for teachers, principals, and school communities to demonstrate that they can be trusted by families. **naeyc** 2

66 Understanding that 'family involvement' may mean different things to different people can help both teachers and family members avoid misunderstandings and negative or stereotyped assumptions. 99

—**Boethel, 2003**

66 When we make choices about what to celebrate, let us be very conscious of who we are doing it for.... If we are doing it for the children, let us be conscious of all the subtle messages inherent in what we do and choose things to celebrate that are meaningful, developmentally appropriate, and healthy for them. 99

—**Bonnie Neugebauer, 1990**

SELECTED WEB SITES ABOUT VARIOUS RELIGIOUS CELEBRATIONS AND TRADITIONS

Various Faiths and Practices

Information about atheism, Buddhism, Christianity, Hinduism, Humanism, Islam, Native American religions, New Age, Shinto, Taoism, Wicca, and more

http://dir.yahoo.com/Society_and_Culture/ Religion_and_Spirituality/Faiths_and_ Practices
Click "Society and Culture"; click "Religion and Spirituality"; click "Faiths and Practices"

Jewish Holidays

http://www.aish.com
Click "Holidays"

Jehovah's Witness

http://www.watchtower.org

Latter Day Saints (Mormon)

http://www.lds.org

Orthodox Church in America

http://www.oca.org

Scientology
http://www.scientology.org

ETHICAL CONSIDERATIONS

Relating Diversity to Developmentally Appropriate Practice

DAP Bredekamp and Copple's (1997) handbook on developmentally appropriate practice (DAP) includes the two primary components for appropriate practices in forming reciprocal relationships with families:

- *Caregivers form partnerships with parents through: daily communication; building mutual trust; working to understand parents' preferences; and respecting cultural and family differences.* It must be noted that practices and attitudes work together to form such partnerships. Daily communications can build trust only when they are respectful, two-way, and objective. It is possible for teachers to communicate frequently and to be ineffective or assaultive if they are not sensitive to families' preferences or differences.

- *Members of each child's family are encouraged to be involved in ways in which they feel comfortable.* It is important for teachers to consider comfort level when they encourage families to be involved in their children's education. It is possible that a grandparent or cousin may be more comfortable volunteering in the classroom than a parent. In these cases, such family members often share relevant information with the parents. Early childhood teachers

"Communicating with Parents: Tips and Strategies for Future Teachers"

Visit the Education CourseMate website at www.CengageBrain.com to view the video case, and then respond to the following items:

- Discuss ways that the tips and strategies in this video case address relationships with diverse families.

- What tips or strategies for building relationships with diverse families might you add to those included in this video case?

can look to various members of children's families for various kinds of involvement and then find ways to support those activities. DAP

Relating Diversity to Programs for Children with Special Needs

DIVERSITY IN PRACTICE The mission statement of the Division for Early Childhood (DEC) of the Council on Exceptional Children (CEC) includes "promoting policies and practices that support families" (http://www.dec-sped.org).

The DEC goals include:

- *Respecting families' diverse values, culture, and linguistic background.* When early childhood professionals are working with young children with disabilities, it is crucial to be sensitive to families' feelings and ways of working through the information that their child has a disability or multiple disabilities. In order to be sensitive to all families, diversity in value systems, cultural expectations, and beliefs must be considered. Using the families' home language is absolutely necessary so that the family can best understand the child's needs and care.

- *Promoting parent-professional collaboration.* The first consideration in building partnerships is the relationship between or among parents or other appropriate family members and professionals. Professionals must demonstrate respect for families as well as knowledge about their children's education. Creating positive relationships between families and professionals is one of the best ways to ensure that children can get all of their special needs met. Families and professionals need to communicate information about a child's disabilities that may be unique to their particular environment.

Relating Diversity to NAEYC Accreditation Guidelines

naeyc 2 Guidelines from the National Association for the Education of Young Children (NAEYC) for early childhood program accreditation provide specific ideas for application that are based on the research evidence. Criteria from the accreditation guidelines compiled by the National Academy of Early Childhood Programs that relate to the "Families" program standard (http://www.naeyc.org/accreditation/academy.asp) and to diversity are:

- New and existing program staff members develop skills and knowledge to work effectively with diverse families as a part of orientation and ongoing staff development.

- Program staff uses a variety of formal and informal strategies (including conversations) to become acquainted with and learn from families about their family structure, their preferred child-rearing practices, and their socioeconomic, linguistic, racial, religious, and cultural backgrounds.

- To better understand the cultural backgrounds of children, families, and the community, program staff (as a part of program activities or as individuals) participates in community cultural events, concerts, storytelling activities, or other events and performances geared to children and their families.

- Program staff ensures that all families—regardless of family structure, socioeconomic, racial, religious, and cultural backgrounds, gender, abilities, or preferred language—are included in all aspects of the program, including volunteer opportunities. These opportunities consider families' interests and skills and the needs of program staff.

- Program staff uses a variety of mechanisms, such as family conferences or home visits, to promote dialogue with families. Program staff asks adults to translate or interpret communications as needed.

- The program compiles and provides information about the program to families in a language the family can understand. This information includes program policies and operating procedures.

Accreditation guidelines that relate to community relationships and diversity program standard are:

- Program staff is familiar with family support services and specialized consultants who are able to provide culturally and linguistically appropriate services. Staff uses this knowledge to suggest and guide families to these services as appropriate.

Program staff connects with and uses the community's urban, suburban, rural, or tribal cultural resources. **naeyc** 2

"Multicultural Lessons: Embracing Similarities and Differences in Preschool Education"

Visit the Education CourseMate website at www.CengageBrain.com to view the video case, and then respond to the following items:

- Discuss how lessons for children about similarities and differences help to promote understanding of diversity.
- How might parents and teachers work together to support children's understanding of diversity?

Relating Diversity to Professional Code of Ethical Conduct

naeyc 6 The early childhood professional "recognizes that those who work with young children face many daily decisions that have moral and ethical implications. The NAEYC Code of Ethical Conduct offers guidelines for responsible behavior and sets forth a common basis for resolving the principal ethical dilemmas encountered in early childhood care and education" (NAEYC, *Code of Ethical Conduct and Statement of Commitment,* http://www.naeyc.org/about/positions/PSETHOS.asp, p. 1). (See Appendix B for complete document.) Three of the seven core values of this code relate specifically to family diversity:

- Recognize that children are best understood and supported in the context of family, culture, community, and society.
- Respect the dignity, worth, and uniqueness of each individual (child, family member, and colleague).
- Respect diversity in children, families, and colleagues.

In addition to the seven broad categories defined as core values, the Code of Ethical Conduct also includes *ideals* and *principles.* It is intended that the ideals reflect the aspirations or desired outcomes of ethical practice, whereas principles are statements to guide ethical conduct.

The following ethical *ideals* are particularly related to working with diverse families:

- To develop relationships of mutual trust and create partnerships with the families we serve.
- To welcome all family members and encourage them to participate in the program.
- To respect the dignity and preferences of each family and to make an effort to learn about its structure, culture, language, customs, and beliefs.

Ethical *principles* that are especially relevant to working with diverse families include:

- We shall not participate in practices that discriminate against children by denying benefits, giving special advantages, or excluding them from programs or activities on the basis of their sex, race, national origin, religious beliefs, medical condition, disability, or the marital status/family structure, sexual orientation, or religious beliefs or other affiliations of their families. (Aspects of this principle do not apply in programs that have a lawful mandate to provide services to a particular population of children.)
- We shall make every effort to communicate effectively with all families in a language that they understand.
- We shall use community resources for translation and interpretation when we do not have sufficient resources in our own programs. **naeyc** 6

Relating Diversity to Family Support Principles

Seven premises of the family support movement are described in Chapter 1. When reviewing these premises, it is evident that each one is stated in a way that is inclusive of all families. Basic understanding of these premises must lead to a respect for diversity and to the implication that early childhood educators must consider all families in decision making regarding instruction, assessment, policies, and other aspects of educational programs.

Reflect on This

Return to Chapter 1 and review the seven evidence-based premises from Family Support America. Choose two of these premises and reflect on how they relate specifically to work with diverse families and their children.

Early childhood education staff should respect, encourage, and foster cultural diversity in the classroom

Summary and Conclusions

Families differ in many ways. It is crucial that early childhood teachers work to increase their understanding of the differences among families and to interact sensitively with all families, bearing these differences in mind. Lifelong learning is a requirement for teachers in this regard, for as society changes, so families change.

Celebration of diversity leads to inclusive practices in early childhood education. Teachers' acceptance of differences among families is essential for each child to feel a sense of belonging in early education programs. Welcoming all families is a prerequisite for effective family involvement. Family members who view themselves as very different from teachers and other school personnel are less likely than other families to be involved in their children's education. It is the responsibility of early childhood teachers to foster a climate that encourages various types of family involvement so that all children may reap the benefits known to occur from home and school partnerships.

Theory into Practice (TIPS)

- Review all of the Web sites found in this chapter. Bookmark them for easy access when you have questions about culture, teaching tolerance, and promoting diversity in your classroom and program.
- Make it a point to get to know individuals and families who are different from you in various ways.
- Begin to collect resources to support diverse families (Examples: English Language Learners, holiday celebration policies, differences in values and goals, etc.).
- "Regardless of children's culture, ethnicity, gender, race, or social class, their learning is profoundly social. It happens within relationships" (Genishi and Dyson 2009).
- Reflect on ways that culture influences knowledge.
- As you learn about variations in culture to increase your cultural competence, consider what you do not know as well as what you do know about each culture.
- Celebrate diversity.
- Family and child perceptions of inclusiveness matter more than school and teacher policies or procedures.
- Never assume that you know all there is to know about differences in families.
- Increase your understanding about causes of poverty by examining factors from the microsystem,

mesosystem, exosystem, macrosystem, and chronosystem.
- Be aware of the multiple ill effects for which young children living in poverty are at risk.
- Participate as a lifelong learner in regard to diversity.
- Diversity must be viewed as the norm.
- Teach tolerance and acceptance through direct and indirect means.
- Visit schools and early education centers that are successful in work with diverse families.
- Reflect on how your own attitudes, beliefs and values influence your perspective of inclusive classroom practice.
- Be aware of your biases and how they influence your relationships and professionalism.

Applications

1. A colleague, a primary grade teacher, tells you that because she has only one child in her classroom who does not celebrate Christmas and 23 who do, she goes with the majority. So, for most of December, the class is involved in projects related to Christmas. How do you respond?
2. What are the key principles that you will incorporate when teaching English language learners?
3. A mother of one of your kindergarten children tells you that you must not celebrate her son's birthday, nor may he attend any birthday celebrations for others because of the family's religious beliefs. What do you do about your tradition of celebrating each child's birthday?
4. When you request photos of each of your preschoolers' families for your bulletin board project, one child brings a picture of herself and two men. The child tells you that this is her with Daddy and Daddy's roommate, Ron, when they were on vacation at the beach. What do you do with the picture?

Questions for Reflection and Discussion

1. Consider the various forms of diversity discussed in this chapter. Discuss your experiences with each type of diversity.
2. Give an example of an experience from your past when you did not feel a sense of belonging or included in the situation. What do you think were

the factors related to your feeling excluded? What were your feelings and how did you manage them?

3. Recall some common celebrations that you have observed in early childhood settings, either when you were a child or more recently. Identify some situations that were not inclusive. What are some ideas that you have for making the celebrations more inclusive?

Field Assignments

1. Interview a Head Start director or family coordinator about the benefits that quality early education has for low-income families.

2. Observe a child care center, preschool program, kindergarten, or primary grade classroom. Note situations that you feel were examples of a good understanding of diversity in families as well as situations that excluded some children or families.

3. Interview a staff member of a religious community. Ask about programs that are offered that support families.

References

Banks, J.A. 1997. *Teaching strategies for ethnic studies,* 6th ed. Needham Heights, MA: Allyn & Bacon.

Boethel, M. 2003. *Diversity: School, family, & community connections.* Austin, TX: National Center for Family & Community Connections with Schools, Southwest Educational Development Laboratory.

Bolger, K.E., C.J. Patterson, and W.W. Thompson. 1995. Psychosocial adjustment among children experiencing persistent and intermittent family economic hardship. *Child Development* 66: 1107–29.

Bredekamp, S., and C. Copple 1997. *Developmentally appropriate practice in early childhood programs,* rev. ed. Washington, DC: National Association for the Education of Young Children.

Bronfenbrenner, U. 1979. *The ecology of human development: Experiments by nature and design.* Cambridge, MA: Harvard University Press.

Brooks-Gunn, J., P. K. Klebanov, and G. J. Duncan. 1996. Ethnic differences in children's intelligence test scores: Role of economic deprivation, home environment, and maternal characteristics. *Child Development* 67: 396–408.

Burns, A., and C. Scott. 1994. *Mother-headed families and why they have increased.* Hillsdale, NJ: Lawrence Erlbaum Associates.

Caldwell, C.H., A.D. Greene, and A. Billingsley. 1994. Family support programs in black churches: A new look at old functions. In *Putting families first: America's family support movement and the challenge of change,* ed. S.L. Kagan and B. Weissbourd. San Francisco: Jossey-Bass.

Cheal, D. 1996. *New poverty: Families in postmodern society.* Westport, CT: Greenwood.

Children's Defense Fund. 2005. Children in the Nation. http://www.childrensdefense.org (accessed November 16, 2005).

Children's Defense Fund. 2005. The State of America's Children 2005. http://www.childrensdefense.org (accessed November 16, 2005).

Children's Defense Fund. 2002. Every child deserves a fair start. http://www.childrensdefense.org/fairstart-faqs .htm.

Clark, L., S. DeWolf, and C. Clark. 1992. Teaching teachers to avoid having culturally assaultive classrooms. *Young Children* 47: 4–9.

Derman-Sparks, L. and J.O. Edwards. 2010. *Anti-bias education for young children and ourselves.* Washington, DC: National Association for the Education of Young Children.

Division for Early Childhood. Mission of DEC. http://www .dec-sped.org.

Elkind, D. 1987. *Miseducation: Preschoolers at risk.* New York: Knopf.

Family Pride Coalition. 2004. Myths and facts. http:// www.familypride.org/site/ (accessed November 18, 2005).

Farver, J., and Howes, C. 2004. Cultural differences in American and Mexican mother-child pretend play. In M. Gauvain and M. Cole (Eds.) *Readings on the Development of Children, 4e.* New York: Worth.

Fernandez Diaz, M. J. 2006. Working with Latin American couples in therapy: migration and acculturation. Unpublished Master's report, Kansas State University, Manhattan, KS.

Furman, E. 1992. Thinking about fathers. *Young Children* 47: 36–37.

Furstenberg, F. F., Jr. 1988. Good dads—bad dads: Two faces of fatherhood. In *The changing American family and public policy,* ed. A. J. Cherlin, 193–218. Washington, DC: Urban Institute Press.

Garbarino, J., and B. Ganzel. 2000. The human ecology of early risk. In *Handbook of early childhood intervention,* ed. J. P. Shonkoff and S. J. Meisels, 2nd ed. New York: Cambridge University Press.

Garfinkel, I., and S. McLanahan. 1989. *Single mothers and their children: A new American dilemma.* Washington, DC: Urban Institute Press.

Genishi, C., and A.H. Dyson. 2009. Children, language and literacy: Diverse learners in diverse times. New York: Teachers College Press.

Hale, J. 1986. *Black children: Their roots, culture, and learning styles,* rev. ed. Baltimore: Johns Hopkins University Press.

Hamner, T.J., and P.H. Turner. 1996. *Parenting in contemporary society.* Needham Heights, MA: Allyn & Bacon.

Hasson, D. J., and G. J. Price. 2008. Parents + Schools = Successful children. National Center on Family Literacy. www.famlit.org/pdf/teacher-guide.pdf. Accessed May 26, 2012.

Hidalgo, N. 1993. Multicultural teacher introspection. In Perry, T. and J.W. Fraser. *Freedom's plow: Teaching in the multicultural classroom.* New York: Routledge.

Howe, L.K. 1972. *The future of the family.* New York: Simon & Schuster.

Hyson, M., ed. 2003. *Preparing early childhood professionals: NAEYC's standards for programs.* Washington, DC: National Association for the Education of Young Children.

Internet Public Library. 2008. Say hello to the world. www.ipl.org/div/hello/ (accessed May 29, 2009).

Johnson, T.W., and P. Colucci. 1999. Lesbians, gay men, and the family life cycle. In *The expanded family life cycle: Individual, family, and social perspectives,* eds. B. Carter and McGoldrick, 3rd ed. Boston: Allyn & Bacon.

Klein, H.A. 1995. Urban Appalachian children in northern schools: A study in diversity. *Young Children* 50: 10–16.

Magida, A., ed. 1996. *How to be a perfect stranger: A guide to etiquette in other people's religious ceremonies.* Woodstock, VT: Jewish Lights.

Many languages, many cultures: Respecting and responding to diversity. 2005. Where we stand. National Association for the Education of Young Children. www.naeyc.org/about/positions/pdf/diversity.pdf (accessed May 29, 2009).

McDade, K. 1995. How we parent: Race and ethnic differences. In *American families: Issues in race and ethnicity,* ed. C. K. Jacobson. New York: Garland.

McGoldrick, M. 1989. Ethnicity and the family life cycle. In *The changing family life cycle,* eds. B. Carter and M. McGoldrick, 2nd ed. Needham Heights, MA: Allyn & Bacon.

McGuire, M., and N.J. Alexander. 1985. Artificial insemination of single women. *Fertility and Sterility* 43: 182–184.

Mellman, M., E. Lazarus, and A. Rivlin. 1990. Family time, family values. In *Rebuilding the nest: A new commitment to the American family,* eds. D. Blankenhorn, S. Bayme, and B. Elshtain. Milwaukee, WI: Family Service America.

Modern Language Association. 2006. MLA Language Map. www.mla.org/map_single (accessed May 29, 2009).

National Academy of Early Childhood Programs. 1991. *Accreditation criteria and procedures.* Washington, DC: National Association for the Education of Young Children.

National Association for the Education of Young Children. 2005. Code of ethical conduct. http://www.naeyc.org/about/positions/PSETHOS.asp (accessed November 19, 2005).

National Association for the Education of Young Children. Program accreditation. http://www.naeyc.org/accreditation/academy.asp (accessed November 18, 2005).

Neugebauer, B. 1990. Going one step further—no traditional holidays. *Child Care Information Exchange* 74.

Olsen, C. S., L. Skogrand, and W. J. DuPree. n.d. Long live the healthy family! Manhattan, KS: Kansas State University Agricultural Experiment Station and Cooperative Extension Service. www.ksre.ksu.edu/library/famlf2/s154.pdf. Accessed May 26, 2012.

Papalia, D.E., D. Gross, and R.D. Feldman. 2003. *Child development: A topical approach.* New York: McGraw-Hill.

Parke, R. 1995. Fathers and families. In Vol. 3 of *Handbook of parenting: Status and social conditions of parenting,* ed. M.H. Bornstein, 27–63. Mahwah, NJ: Erlbaum.

Patterson, C. J. 1995. Lesbian and gay parenthood. In Vol. 3 of *Handbook of parenting: Status and social conditions of parenting,* ed. M. H. Bornstein, 255–274. Mahwah, NJ: Erlbaum.

Patterson, C. 1995. Lesbian and gay parenting. APA Online Public Interest. http://www.apa.org/pi/parent.html (accessed November 18, 2005).

Phillips, C.B. 1995. Culture: A process that empowers. In *Infant/toddler caregiving: A guide to culturally sensitive care,* ed. P.L. Mangione, 2–9. Sacramento, CA: California Department of Education.

Prieto, H.V. 2009. One language, two languages, three languages...more? *Young Children Beyond the Journal.* National Association for the Education of Young Children. http://journal.naeyc.org/btj/200901/pdf/BTJRockingRolling.pdf (accessed May 29, 2009).

Rank, M.R. 1994. *Living on the edge: The realities of welfare in America.* New York: Columbia University Press.

Ribbens, J. 1994. *Mothers and their children: A feminist sociology of childrearing.* Thousand Oaks, CA: Sage.

Santrock, J.W. 1994. *Child development.* Madison, WI: Brown & Benchmark.

Search Institute. n.d. Developmental assets. http://www.search-institute.org (accessed November 18, 2005).

Stauss, J.H. 1995. Reframing and refocusing American Indian family strengths. In *American families: Issues in race and ethnicity,* ed, C.K. Jacobson. New York: Garland.

Trawick-Smith, J. 1997. *Early childhood development.* Upper Saddle River, NJ: Merrill-Prentice Hall.

Triest, R.K. 1997. Regional differences in family poverty. *New England Economic Review* (January-February): 3–18.

Wardle, F. 1987. Are you sensitive to interracial children's special identity needs? *Young Children* 42: 53–59.

Zinn, M.B., and D.S. Eitzen. 1987. *Diversity in American families.* New York: Harper & Row.

 Additional resources for this chapter, including TeachSource videos, can be found on the Education CourseMate. Go to CengageBrain.com.

Developmental Issues in Families with Young Children

OUTLINE

- **Objectives Aligned with NAEYC Standards**
- **Key Terms**
- **Theoretical Foundations**
  Bioecological Theory
  Family Systems Theory
- **Developmental Issues in Families**
  Transition to Parenthood
  Child Care
  Technology
  Sibling Relationships
  Work and Family
  Extended Family Relationships

- **Practical and Ethical Considerations**
  Family Support Principles
  Code of Ethical Conduct
- **Summary and Conclusions**
- **Theory into Practice Suggestions (TIPS)**
- **Applications**
- **Questions for Reflection and Discussion**
- **Field Assignments**
- **References**

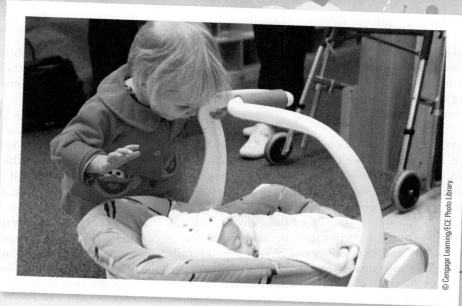
© Cengage Learning/ECE Photo Library.

After reading and reflecting on this chapter, you should be able to:

- Understand developmental issues and transitions facing families with young children **naeyc** 2

- Consider variations in families related to culture, ethnicity, language, socio-economic status, religion, gender, and geographic region even as they attend to developmental issues that face most families with young children **naeyc** 2

- Relate the importance and effects of various social groups to young families **naeyc** 2

- Apply principles of family support and information from the code of ethical conduct to your work as an early childhood educator when working with families with young children **naeyc** 6

Key Terms

downsizing
extended family relationships
family-friendly work policies

family size
high-quality, affordable child care
maternal employment

sibling relationships
transition to parenthood
trilemma

THEORETICAL FOUNDATIONS

Bioecological Theory

naeyc 1 Bronfenbrenner (2001) defines development "as the phenomenon of continuity and change in the biopsychological characteristics of human beings both as individuals and as groups." Using this understanding of development, early educators will note both individual differences and commonalities of family members. This chapter emphasizes changes that typically occur in families as they have children. Even though variations are likely to exist in the manner that families approach the developmental issues discussed in this chapter, most families will be required to consider how best to meet challenges and celebrate joys as they transition to parenthood, support and intervene in **sibling relationships**, make decisions about employment, select child care arrangements, and relate to their extended families. Examining the particular issues that face families with young children in our society can help early childhood teachers increase their awareness of and sensitivity to these developmental transitions, keeping in mind the complexities of everyday family life.

Considering the concentric circle model posed by Bronfenbrenner (explained in Chapter 1), some additional information from this theory provides greater detail through 10 propositions (Bronfenbrenner 2001).

Seven of the propositions most relevant to the content of this chapter are presented here. These propositions offer insights into the application of the theory, enabling teachers to better understand multiple and complex influences on development.

Proposition I A critical element of this theory is experience. Experience is both objective and subjective. This means that objective aspects of one's experience can be observed or assessed by another person. However, this theory posits a comparable influence on subjective aspects of experience, such as an individual's feelings, beliefs, and values. In order for early childhood teachers to understand experiences of children and family members, not only must they engage in objective observation, but also in reciprocal communication in order to understand others' views of their own experiences. According to this proposition of bioecological theory, teachers will better understand family's experiences when partnerships are authentic and strong.

Proposition II Individuals develop in relation to reciprocal interactions with other people and objects in their environment. Over time, these interactions must be more complex in order to support children's developmental progress. "[T]he informal education that takes place in the family is…a powerful prerequisite for success in formal education from the primary grades onward" (Bronfenbrenner 1990). Early educators are in a position to understand the powerful influence that families have on children's learning. Advocating for local and universal policies that support strong families with knowledge about infant and child development is a vital role for professionals.

Proposition III All of development is influenced by the characteristics of the individual and by all the systems (microsystem, mesosystem, exosystem, macrosystem, and chronosystem). Any of these determinants, whether biological or environmental, may be interacting with one or more other determinants at any given time.

Considering mesosystem effects, children are influenced by ongoing patterns of open, effective communication that build trust between and among the systems where children spend most of their time: home and early education settings. Parental workplace stress is a major factor in what happens at home, demonstrating an aspect of exosystem influences. The premise of an extensive study conducted by Parcel and Menaghan (1994) is that conditions in parents' workplaces affect the home environments that adults create for their young children. And, home environments affect children's cognitive and social development. (Findings that support this premise are discussed further in the "Work and Family" section of this chapter.) Macrosystem

effects include public policies that influence child-rearing, including the availability of high-quality early education opportunities for all children.

Proposition IV For all areas of a child's development (physical, cognitive, social, and emotional), it is necessary for children to interact with one or more individuals (especially adults who are in the parenting role) with whom the child develops a strong emotional attachment. Over time, these interactions not only build strong emotional ties, but they also must involve more complex interests for those involved in the relationship. In the busyness of family life, adults who are parenting young children may overlook their own importance in their children's development. Early childhood educators are in a position to support positive parent-child relationships by offering both ideas and appreciation for parents.

Proposition V Strong feelings of attachment between children and those who are parenting them lead to children's motivation and curiosity. When children have this strong emotional foundation, they then express their interest in the world around them. Emotional attachment between parents and children is a powerful phenomenon. Caring communities will emphasize the necessity of this bond through programs for families. Early education programs will benefit from such community efforts in that children's academic progress will be positively influenced by their motivation and curiosity.

Proposition VI In addition to strong, positive emotional bonds, children proceed to their optimal levels of development when their attachment figure has the involvement of another adult "who assists, encourages, spells off, gives status to, and expresses admiration and affection for the person caring for…the child.…Where there is an attachment to two or more parent figures, each can serve as a third party to the other" (Bronfenbrenner 2001). This level of support seems to be essential to adults in parenting roles in order for child outcomes to be most favorable. Families that have support, caring, and outlets for frustration can provide more positive experiences for their children. And, the reverse is also to be understood. Parents who are lacking physical or emotional support will not be able to provide in an optimal way for their children. Creating family involvement programs that offer social support for parents and connecting parents with existing community programs are ways that schools might address this need.

Proposition VII Children influence their parents. Both child behavior and development affect the well-being of parents. Children with "easier" temperaments and a variety of interests and abilities may sway parental psychological development in a positive direction. Parents who are rearing children who display more challenges to the parents may exhibit a lower feeling of well-being. Some parents who appear to be "supermom" or "superdad" may in fact have children who are much more easily parented. That same parent may look very different if challenged by children with more difficult temperaments, disabilities, or dispositions. It is essential that early childhood educators understand this reciprocal nature of development and not assume only a unidirectional effect of parents to children. **naeyc** 1

Family Systems Theory

❝ [B]ecoming a parent is one of the most definitive stages of life, a crossing of the Rubicon. ❞

—B. Carter, 1999

Family systems theory notes that "becoming a parent shares the common characteristic of a change of membership and a change of function of its members" (Bradt 1989). The changes necessary in the family system with the birth of a first child are immense. For both new mothers and new fathers, balance between work and home undergoes an immediate and dramatic shift, as have their expectations regarding their responsibilities in these environments. Also, new parents feel continuously challenged about whether they have the capacity to live up to the responsibility for nurturing this new generation (Bradt 1989). New parents may meet these challenges in very different ways, along a continuum of responses. Some parents insist that there is "nothing to" rearing children, and others become increasingly focused on their children. Most likely, there is middle ground between these perspectives that provides for a healthy response to meeting the new and demanding challenges for parents. However, the middle ground may look very different depending on the parenting skills and characteristics of the particular children.

Challenges abound in families with young children. Changes in roles for parenting adults, changes in relationships with the other parent and extended family members, and changes in expectations regarding work and home responsibilities all work together to increase the difficulty of adjusting to even a joyous occasion. And yet, forming families and having children remains a popular option. Ninety percent of all couples who can have children do have children. About 3,000 couples each year become parents (Belsky and Kelly, as cited in Carter and McGoldrick, 1999).

❝ Being a parent, whether father or mother, is the most difficult task humans have to perform. For people, unlike other animals, are not born knowing how to be parents. Most of us struggle through. ❞

—Karl Menninger, 1959

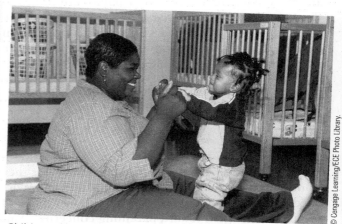

Children are influenced by ongoing patterns of open communication and trust at their school.

DEVELOPMENTAL ISSUES IN FAMILIES

Transition to Parenthood

naeyc 2 The theoretical perspectives previously discussed confirm that huge changes occur in families when individuals become parents. Thus, this transition is characterized by the changes that occur between parenting partners. Many of a couple's established patterns of behavior that have become routine for the couple will be changed with the arrival of a child. These changes in a couple's routine typically change the relationships with each other, as well as with other family members, friends, and coworkers. Some research exists to inform our understanding of what happens in the **transition to parenthood**.

A study in 1957 (LeMasters) revealed that 83 percent of new parents had experienced a serious amount of family distress following the birth of their first baby. The ideal of American family life is that a baby celebrates a couple's love, but this idealism quickly turns to exhaustion as parents expend the effort required to meet the nonnegotiable needs of a baby (La Rossa and La Rossa 1981). Few new parents feel well prepared to meet the constant needs of newborns. Further, most new parents are surprised by the stress that is added to their lives. This indicates that little support is available for couples as they become parents.

Men and women report some differences in their transition to parenthood. Although both clearly feel the loss of nearly all free time, women are more likely to value their relationships with their babies. Fathers are more likely to act as if their babies are things to show to others, and they see babies as being less competent than do mothers. Even egalitarian couples begin to split family responsibilities in the direction of more traditional gender roles (LaRossa and LaRossa 1981).

66 The context of family relationships is continually in flux in the early months of parenthood. 99

—**Laurie Van Egeren, 2004**

Van Egeren (2004) found differences in coparenting relationships between mothers and fathers as they made the transition to parenthood. Coparenting is defined as "that part of the relationship between caregivers specifically directed toward parenting concerns" (Van Egeren 2004). For example, this study (which examined only heterosexual married couples) found that in the first six months of parenting, fathers were more satisfied than mothers. Also, this study found that a major transition exists when new mothers who have taken on most of the child care and a significant amount of home and family responsibilities, return to employment outside the home. New roles for both parents commonly require negotiating the definition and assignment of existing tasks, as well as ways to share the added child care responsibilities. Further, fathers, but not mothers, reported more positive coparenting when their babies had easy temperaments. This study also supports Bronfenbrenner's Proposition VI, the presence of a supportive third party. When husbands were warm and caring, both parents experienced coparenting more positively.

New mothers report that they see it as their responsibility to create a family, "to produce a different sort of social unit" (Ribbens 1994) when the first child is born. Having a family, to most people, means having and caring for children. Even at this point in history, with so much emphasis on gender equality, it seems that both society and individual mothers perceive the mother's role as being that of ensuring the formation and integration of the family unit.

One reason for this move toward "traditionalization" is that larger systems in society—that is, the exosystem and macrosystem—do not support gender equity in parenting (LaRossa and LaRossa 1981). So, even when couples attempt to fully share parenting, the workplace, extended families, and other social institutions often do not provide the necessary support for coparenting. With so many parenting tasks to complete, tired new parents often do not see gender equity as a battle that they have the energy to fight or even can afford to fight. Thus, they give in to the system.

Fathers' and mothers' self-reports on their success with infant care also differ (Hudson, Elek, and Fleck 2001). For the couples in this study, fathers scored lower than did mothers at all three points of the study: when babies were two months, three months,

and four months of age. However, mothers and fathers both scored increasingly higher on a measure of parental satisfaction over the same three time periods. One difference in the satisfaction results, though, was that fathers demonstrated higher scores in their parenting satisfaction with male infants.

It is believed that the differences found between fathers and mothers is at least partly a function of what it means to be a mother and what it means to be a father. As noted previously, even in this era of less stereotypical gender roles, strongly held traditional views of mothering seem to endure. It is only recently that fathers have attended the births of their babies and have been expected to be engaged in infant and child care.

Woollett and Parr (1997) analyzed psychological tasks for women and men in their transitions to parenthood. Some interesting results from this research indicate that the men both looked forward to the birth more than the women and enjoyed childbirth more than the women. These researchers explain women's sometimes ambivalent feelings about parenthood as a reaction to the major transition inherent in becoming a parent. On the other hand, even though males are now expected to become parents who are enthusiastically engaged with their children, their role continues to be less defined by society and their transition to parenthood is less abrupt.

The women in Woollett and Parr's (1997) study also commonly expressed depressive feelings as a postpartum reality. More information about postpartum depression is needed, but existing evidence suggests that 8 to 15 percent of new mothers are affected by it, and an even greater percentage (25 to 50 percent) experience depressive symptoms that are milder or of shorter duration (O'Hara 1997, as cited in Feeney, Alexander, Noller, and Hohaus 2003). The news media are now giving greater attention to postpartum depression, due in part to celebrity mothers who have shared their stories. Depression has been connected to relationship anxiety coupled with the major life change of transition to parenthood (Feeney et al. 2003). Other factors that were related to depressive symptoms included mothers' negative reactions to the news that they were pregnant and mothers' perceptions of their infants as difficult. Thus, couple adjustment in the transition to parenthood is seen as crucial for infant nurturance and positive developmental outcomes.

Another study found that common changes in emotional functioning during the transition to parenthood included depressive symptoms and stress (Perren, von Wyl, Burgin, Simoni, and von Klitzing 2005). In this research, both mothers and fathers reported depressive symptoms during pregnancy as well as postpartum. For parents with prior mental health challenges, stress increased continuously to one year after birth. On the other hand, mentally healthy mothers had a decrease in depressive symptoms from pregnancy until infants were three months old, but then the symptoms increased again.

This longitudinal study explained that additional stress for both parents occurred when mothers returned to employment outside the home. For many of the parents in this study, that shift happened when the baby reached one year of age. Although stress around employment existed for all families, those with psychological dysfunction were believed to be at greater risk.

One point of concern related to research on the transition to parenthood is that most studies have used middle-class or upper-middle-class families. If these families are noting this much stress, what happens in families with fewer resources, human or material? Based on ecological theory, we can only hypothesize that a single mother with a low income will face even greater crises in this transition.

> 66 The transition to parenthood is a major life event that affects all aspects of psychosocial functioning. 99

—Condon, Boyce, and Corkindale, 2004

The Cowans (1995) make an important point: it is clear that families need interventions to assist them during this critical transition. When parents adjust more easily, their relationships with their children are of higher quality. This relationship is a critical factor in the child's development and central to the child's success as a preschooler and an elementary student. It is primarily for this reason that early childhood educators must be aware of the importance of various forms of support for all new parents in their transition to parenthood. Parents face a tremendous challenge especially with their first babies, but each new birth changes the family system and requires added support. As we celebrate births, we must be prepared to offer families the support, help, and care they need to reduce the negative outcomes associated with the transitions of becoming a family.

The trend of looking specifically at fathers' adjustment in the transition to parenthood is relatively recent. There is some evidence that pregnancy, rather than birth or infancy, is the most stressful time for new fathers (Condon, Boyce, and Corkindale 2004; Woollett and Parr 1997). A study that examined the adjustment of first-time fathers found that the men were "ill-prepared for the impact of fatherhood on their lives" (Condon, Boyce, and Corkindale 2004). Some of the explanations for this lack of preparedness include having few or no social support networks for fathering, feeling increased financial responsibilities and thus increased stress about work, having a lack of good role models for fathering, being confronted with idealized media and cultural images of childbirth and parenting, and feeling a reluctance to seek help for emotional problems.

Some efforts are being made to address the need to increase fathers' effectiveness and satisfaction during the transition to parenthood. One such effort is the New Fathers Network, an Internet-based program that offers a library of relevant information, a discussion forum, and e-mail access to advanced-practice nurses (Hudson, Campbell-Grossman, Fleck, Elek, and Shipman 2003). The response from program participants was generally positive. The researchers believe that this program or similar Internet interventions provide social support in a form that made fathers willing to use it. However, it is not known whether such a program would be effective with fathers in high-risk, adolescent, or diverse ethnic or socioeconomic populations. **naeyc** 2

Another Web-based program for first-time fathers is Boot Camp for New Dads (http://www.NewDads.com). This program bills itself as "a guy thing." In addition to the Web site, this intervention program includes parenting classes, at medical or other community centers, on topics such as diapering, when and how to feed your baby, soothing a crying baby, becoming your baby's burping buddy, introducing baby to pets, and helping mom cope. The program also includes a system for connecting with other dads. As with the New Fathers Network, this program seems to take seriously the task of increasing the social network about parenting for new fathers.

All of the research discussed previously can be useful in helping early childhood educators understand the difficulties and stressors affecting women's and men's transitions to parenthood. This research, however, is limited in some important ways because much of it has sampled only middle-class or upper-middle-class, white, married or partnered adults. Recently, however, some attention has been given to the transition as experienced by single, low-income mothers, adolescent fathers, and psychologically depressed mothers and fathers.

The members of nearly half of all female-headed households in the United States, or approximately 6.5 million such households, live below the poverty level. Many low-income women endure both mental health challenges and parenting difficulties. Another correlate to the high risk for this group of women is low social support. With this number of risks, it is clear that low-income, single mothers face greater difficulties with the transition to parenthood than more affluent, healthy, partnered mothers. One study (Keating-Lefler, Hudson, Campbell-Grossman, Fleck, and Westfall 2004) found that many low-income, single mothers had "an array of emotions and mixed feelings," feeling both excited and overwhelmed. Further, the primary source of stress for these women seemed to stem from the loss of their earlier dreams for themselves as well as the loss of relationships with the babies' fathers and sometimes with their own families of origin. In addition, the women reported that having sole responsibility for an infant and few resources to meet those responsibilities caused great stress. Many of the women lacked transportation, did not have enough money to make ends meet, and were uncertain about how they were going to continue to provide for their children. A sense of isolation and sometimes hopelessness about the ability to succeed in the future led to growing negative feelings in these women.

naeyc 2 Given all of these concerns and their overall lack of support, low-income, single women have great difficulty in making a smooth transition to parenthood. This places both the mother and the child in the high-risk category. Thus, it is in the best interest of families, schools, and communities to ensure that alternative sources of support and resources are available for these families.

Information also is lacking about the transition to parenthood for adolescent mothers and fathers. When it comes to adolescent mothers, however, it seems safe to assume that when they are low-income and single, their youth and lack of employment skills add still more risk factors to the outcomes discussed previously. An examination of the transition among adolescent fathers and their partners has shed some light on the details of the challenges that adapting to parenthood poses for these young men. Florsheim, Moore, Zollinger, MacDonald, and Sumida (1999) found that the same risk factors associated with the likelihood of becoming an adolescent father are also related to difficulties in adjusting to fatherhood. One of the most prevalent of these factors is antisocial-hostile behavior. Further findings, leading to concern for infant development, show that when the antisocial-hostile father is living with the infant's mother, her nurturing skills are negatively affected. This result did not occur when the parents were not living together. That is, the mothers' parenting did not seem to be as adversely affected by the father's behavior when he was not living with the mother.

An ongoing concern in these difficult adolescent relationships is that when fathers do not transition to their role as parents during the infancy period, they are more likely to become absent fathers and that "risk begets risk, laying the groundwork for the intergenerational transmission of psychological dysfunction" (Florsheim, Moore, Zollinger, MacDonald, and Sumida 1999).

Research focusing on parental adjustment to new responsibilities with the birth of a child strongly indicates a sense of ongoing and overwhelming exhaustion and stress. Although these findings are based on actual experience, one wonders about the positive aspects of becoming parents. In an essay that includes related research findings, Lorraine Ali concludes that having children may not make one happy. A view beyond the day to day indicates that becoming a parent provides a greater sense of purpose and meaning to life. In addition, one aspect of parenting that may be difficult to quantify is the amazing and deep love that parents feel for their children (Ali 2008). **naeyc** 2

> ### Reflect on This
> What has been your experience in relation to the transition to parenthood? How has the information in this chapter influenced your thinking about this developmental issue?

Child Care

High-quality, affordable child care is not readily accessible to many families. The most common form of out-of-home child care used by families that need it is provided by friends or relatives in their home. In 1982, this was true for 63 percent of families needing out-of-home care (Hofferth, as cited in Greenman 1984). But the number of child care centers and family day homes has increased dramatically in the past three decades. By 2002, of the 63 percent of children who were reported to have a regular arrangement for child care, 40 percent were in relative care and 14 percent were in nonrelative care either in the home of the child's family or of the provider. About 35 percent of children under the age of five who had a child care arrangement in 2002 were enrolled in some type of center or preschool facility. Approximately 6 percent of children in care were placed in licensed family home care. Also, 37 percent of children under five had no regular child care arrangement (Johnson 2005).

By 2007, 55 percent of all preschool aged children (three to six years) were enrolled in center-based care. Demographic differences of families enrolling children in child care centers exist related to income level, ethnicity, and maternal levels of education. Children enrolled in center care were most likely to come from families as follows: income at least 200 percent of poverty level versus those with less income; Asian, Black, or White versus Hispanic; and, mothers who had at least a bachelor's degree versus a high school diploma. In 2010, nearly half of children from newborns through age four years with employed mothers received their primary care from another relative (Childstats 2011).

> 66 We have to ask whether this nurturance is possible in settings where caregivers are caring for four or more babies (and later six or more toddlers), are paid minimal wage, and given little training and little incentive to avoid staff turnover (among those who can get better jobs). 99
>
> —**Brazelton and Greenspan, 2000**

naeyc 2 A variety of nonparental or out-of-home care are possible. For many families, coming up with the best child care arrangement is a huge challenge. Families often decide from among the following choices: care by another family member, employing someone to come into the home (a nanny or au pair), family home child care, center care, or many combinations of these. States require child care centers to be licensed, and many require family home caregivers to be registered or licensed. To best advocate for children, parents must understand the importance of licensed care. Essentially, state licenses demand only minimum requirements for conditions that maintain the health and safety of children. All children deserve at least this amount of protection. naeyc 2

A lot of attention has been given to the child care **trilemma**. How can we balance quality of care, compensate child caregivers fairly, and keep quality care affordable for families?

Let's begin with the first point of the trilemma. The importance of good quality care for children was mentioned previously in the section on families and work. Parents are more productive when they feel good about their children's care. A great deal of research on the outcomes of child care for children shows that when the care is of high quality, children flourish; when the care is not good, it may be harmful to children's development. For example, children in high-quality care have been found to have higher mathematical ability, better thinking and attention skills, fewer behavioral problems, better work habits, and better relationships with peers than children in lower-quality child care situations. On the other hand, children in low-quality care have been found to have language and reading delays and to display more problematic aggression toward other children (Children's Defense Fund, 2005).

What is high-quality child care? Evidence from numerous studies of high-quality child care suggests that multiple components are necessary for positive outcomes in children's development. These components include:

- Responsive adult-child interaction, including positive strategies for guiding children's behavior
- Developmentally appropriate and effective curriculum that includes considerations for the academic integrity of curriculum selected
- Authentic assessment that provides information to caregivers for planning curriculum as well as to share children's development, progress, and concerns with children's families
- Family involvement in children's learning and development, both in and out of child care

- Early education professionals who are well-prepared in child development and early childhood education
- Small group sizes and good ratios of adults to children in the classroom

Some states have considered some or all of these components in their licensing requirements for child care homes and centers. However, given the still large number of centers that provide minimal or poor-quality care for young children, concerns in regard to increasing quality of child care continue. Since 1987, the National Association for the Education of Young Children (NAEYC) has administered a voluntary national early childhood program accreditation system. This accreditation requires that programs meet all of the criteria for providing high-quality care and education for young children and their families. Accreditation is one way for families to judge whether a child care center will provide good care for their child or children. (See Appendix C for NAEYC accreditation criteria.)

66 High quality child care and early education are critical to the success of two national priorities: helping families work and ensuring that every child enters school ready to succeed. 99

—Children's Defense Fund, April 2005

The second point in the child care trilemma is that quality care is not cheap. In our society, parents are generally required to pay tuition. To make child care affordable for families, quality is too often compromised. One of the most serious problems with maintaining quality care is the high staff turnover. Turnover is high primarily because wages are low. It is not uncommon for child caregivers to earn minimum wage and to be employed part-time without benefits. It is not an exaggeration to state that parking lot attendants are usually paid better than child caregivers.

The Children's Defense Fund recently surveyed child care centers in cities and rural areas across the country (Schulman 2000). This survey found a typical tuition range per year for child care for a four-year-old was $4,000 to $6,000, or more than $300 to $500 per month. Some child care costs over $14,000 per year for a four-year-old. Infant care is much more expensive than care for a preschooler, due in part to the smaller ratios of caregiver to child. Infant care was found to cost as much as $4,150 more per year than care for a four-year-old, or more than $300 per month. Cost for child care is lower in rural areas, at about $4,000 per year for a four-year-old. The average cost for infant care in rural areas was more than $4,500 per year. In many cities around the country, four years of child care cost more than four years of public college tuition (National Association of Child Care Resource and Referral Agencies, n.d.). Consider the cost of child care in relation to the fact that many families with young children earn less than $25,000 per year. Further, a family with two parents working full-time at minimum wage jobs earns a little more than $21,000 per year. Clearly, the reality of child care costs hits working families' budgets quite hard—many families who live above the poverty level spend about 7 percent of their income for child care for one child.

Center for the Child Care Workforce
http://www.ccw.org/home/

Child Care Aware
http://www.childcareaware.org/

National Association for Child Care Resource and Referral Agencies (NACCRRA)
http://www.naccrra.org

National Association for Family Child Care (NAFCC)
http://www.nafcc.org

National Association for the Education of Young Children—Accreditation
http://www.naeyc.org/
Click on "Accreditation"

National Child Care Information Center
http://nccic.org/

National Network for Child Care
http://www.nncc.org/

Wheelock College Institute for Leadership and Career Initiatives
http://institute.wheelock.edu

"The Quality of Child Care"
Visit the Education CourseMate website at www.CengageBrain.com to view the video case, and then respond to the following items:

- How does the video demonstrate criteria for quality child care as discussed in this chapter?

- How might all early childhood educators contribute to societal understanding about the importance of quality in child care?

> **Do This**
> Survey several centers in your region to calculate costs of child care for one year for a four-year-old child and a 12-month-old child. Compare your results with others in your class or with online partners in other areas of the country.

Several sources exist for helping families with low incomes to fund child care. The federal government provides such funding for families through the Child Care and Development Block Grant (CCDBG). These funds are limited, however, and it has been estimated that only one in seven of the children who are eligible for funding actually receives it. Further, most states' funding guidelines are such that families making $25,000 per year are not eligible for these funds. A small amount of child care funding also is available through various state programs, the Temporary Assistance to Needy Families (TANF) program, and the Social Services Block Grant (SSBG) (Children's Defense Fund 2005). Even with these sources, however, "the current funding level for child care assistance does not come close to meeting the needs of low-income working families" (Children's Defense Fund 2005).

As noted earlier, a critical component of high-quality child care is well-prepared early childhood education professionals. At this time, child care staff is not compensated in a manner that keeps them in the field. Low wages and the lack of benefits are related to the high turnover of child care staff, leading to another obstacle in maintaining quality programs for young children. Due to a lack of rigorous requirements for these positions, coupled with low pay and the absence of benefits, many caregivers of young children have little or no preparation for understanding children's development. Yet, they are entrusted to care for our youngest children.

In 2002, median hourly earnings for child care workers was less than $8, with the lowest 10 percent earning less than $6 per hour and the highest 10 percent earning more than $11 per hour. While benefits vary by place of employment, they are typically negligible (Bureau of Labor Statistics 2004–2005). By 2010, median hourly earnings for child care workers had risen to $9.28, yielding an annual salary of $19,300 (Bureau of Labor Statistics 2010).

> 66 There's a strong link between staff pay and the quality of the care children receive. Centers that are able to retain highly-trained staff are more likely to sustain high-quality care over time. 99
>
> **—Wages and Quality, 2001**

Reflect on This

What has been your experience in relation to child care? How has the information in this chapter influenced your thinking about this developmental issue?

66 Technology and interactive media should not replace other beneficial educational activities such as creative play, outdoor experiences, and social interactions with peers and adults in early childhood settings.... Educators must emphasize active engagement rather than passive, non-interactive uses 99

(NAEYC 2012, p. 12).

Technology

Digital technology is here to stay. It has worked its way well into the everyday lives of most children and families in our society. To use technology or not to use technology is no longer a relevant question. Instead, early childhood educators and families must educate themselves so that they are able to provide developmentally appropriate and effective learning opportunities through technology in the most optimal ways for each child.

NAEYC issued a position statement in January 2012 in regard to the significance of digital literacy in reference to both technology and various forms of media (NAEYC 2012). The issues surrounding technology and young children as noted in this position are:

- Technology and interactive media are here to stay. Technological tools are used by nearly everyone almost every day. This is true for both family life and education.

- Concerns exist about young children's use of technology and screen media in early childhood education. Screen time for children two years of age and younger should not be included in education programs. Recommended screen time for children between ages two and five years should be kept to a maximum of two hours total, counting both home and school or child care.

- All screens are not created equal. Screens include television, computers, tablets, smart phones, handheld games, portable video recorders, digital cameras, and more. Professionals must make informed decisions about which platforms offer optimal learning experiences based on developmentally appropriate practices for young children.

- A lack of agreement exists about the value of technology in young children's development. Generally, the content, not the format, is what matters most.

- Technology is appealing to both children and adults and thus, can lead to inappropriate uses in early education. Passive technology is of particular concern and should not replace children's active engagement in learning.

- Issues of equity and access are unresolved. Early childhood education professionals must ensure that all children and families have access to technology tools that enhance learning.

 Teaching Technology Skills: An Elementary School Lesson on Power Point

Visit the Education CourseMate website at www.CengageBrain.com to view the video case, and then respond to the following items:

- How does the video demonstrate positive contributions that digital technology might make to young children's learning?

- Discuss ways that early childhood teachers might discuss the pros and cons of young children's technology use with families.

Consider This

Think back throughout your childhood about the technology devices that you had available to you and at about what age you began to use each one. Did your family place restrictions about how and when each device could be used? What technology was used by your schools? Discuss how changes in technology might have affected family interactions and expectations.

Just as with other types of activity, young children need to have limits and expectations placed on their use of various types of technology. Because of the rapid change in available technological gadgets, parents are often uncertain about how to regulate children's time with any given device. For children two and younger, the American Academy of Pediatrics recommends no access to screen media. Authors of a study published in 2010 (Tomopoulos, Dreyer, Berkule, Fierman, Brochmeyer and Mendelsohn) concluded that media exposure at six months of age was related to cognitive and language development at 14 months of age in at-risk, low income families. The average daily media exposure for six month olds in this study was a little over 2.5 hours. At 14 months, lower cognitive and language scores were associated with media exposure. Based on these results, the authors call for advocacy efforts and interventions to reduce media exposure for infants so that developmental outcomes might be optimized.

Children are spending an average of seven hours a day with various technological devices. The pediatric medical community notes that this is a concern since "excessive media use can lead to attention problems, school difficulties, sleep and eating disorders, and obesity" (American Academy of Pediatrics 2011).

In addition to health issues, media concerns include children's level of understanding and social influences. An advocacy organization, Children Now, notes that children under the age of eight years tend to accept programming and advertisements as accurate and unbiased. Cognitively, young children are not able to consider the intent of advertisers to sell products. Portrayals of race, economic class, and gender that do not accurately reflect society may also lead to children's misunderstanding (Children Now 2011).

Interventions by families and teachers can help children to understand the role of advertising and programming that is not an accurate or fair reflection of race, economic class, or gender. Carlsson-Paige and Levin (1990) have addressed such concerns through teaching children to become activist consumers. When adults discuss with children that advertisers attempt to sell and some programming is biased, awareness levels may increase so that children begin to think more critically about what they view. Without such interventions, however, young children tend to rely on their concrete thinking and trust what they view.

Television and video game violence has been a topic that researchers have examined for decades. Although evidence from research is inconsistent, a conservative approach calls for protecting children from exposure to violence and overtly sexual content. Even the researchers who have found little effects on children's behavior from experiences with media violence note that it is likely a factor that does influence aggression.

The rapid evolution of digital media creates a challenge for families and teachers as they strive to provide the best uses of technology for young children. The Joan Ganz Cooney Center at Sesame Workshop and Stanford University has published what they term "a blueprint" for effectively teaching young children with digital technologies. Authors of this statement note research that supports intentional use of a variety of digital media leads to positive learning outcomes for young children. In order for educators to provide optimal learning for young children, these goals must be considered:

- Creation of communities of teachers for collaboration and planning the use of technology with children
- Provide professional preparation for teachers of young children to incorporate technology in developmentally appropriate ways
- Extend the use of public media as a resource for teachers

- Integrate supports for technology into standards and curriculum that includes addressing access equity issues for all schools and children
- Creation of better mechanisms for research and development initiatives to meet the above four goals (Barron, Cayton-Hodges, Bofferding, Copple, Darling-Hammond, and Levine 2011).

Recommendations for families in regard to their children's use of digital media shared by the Australian Psychological Society include:

- Know what your children are watching
- Know when your children are on the Internet
- Communicate clear restrictions on what and when children may use various forms of technology
- Require children to be open with you and use technology in common family spaces
- Discuss content of what children view and participate in and help them to analyze the meaning
- Encourage participation in active and creative experiences (Australian Psychological Society 2000).

While parents and other family members have primary responsibility for children's viewing and using digital media, early childhood educators play a role in supporting families. Discussions with children at school about positive uses and dangers is appropriate during computer-based projects. Further, sharing information with families through newsletters, Web sites, and family meetings can be helpful as families may feel some confusion about the bombardment of technology in their lives.

Sibling Relationships

As families grow, new relationships must be negotiated. As the first child becomes the big brother or big sister, parental roles also change. Attention to **sibling relationships** becomes a new challenge for parents who are often just beginning to feel more confident of their abilities. Young children typically react to the announcement about the coming of a new baby in a variety of ways that are influenced by individual differences in development and temperament. Chelsea, at age two and a half, responded to her parents' announcement about a new baby by stating, "No baby. Doggie." For young preschoolers, this may seem like a reasonable, desirable, and logical variation to the family composition. Others insist that they want to specify the gender of the new baby; for example, "I want a baby sister," or "The new baby will be my brother."

Young children have a great deal to understand when a new sibling is added to the family constellation. Early childhood teachers frequently experience changes in children's behaviors at school when a new baby is expected or has arrived at home. In the previous example, Chelsea seemed resistant to having a new baby in the family. By the time baby Christopher was born, however, she was three years old and seemed to have adapted to the notion: she commented frequently, "He's so nice." One day, however, Chelsea heard her mother refer to herself as "Christopher's mommy, too." The mother was surprised to realize that although Chelsea had gotten used to the idea of the baby living in their house, she had not necessarily understood that the baby also was her mother's child—and she was not prepared to share her mother! Adele Faber and Elaine Mazlish (1987), in their book, *Siblings without Rivalry*, provide a useful analogy to help parents understand some of the feelings of rivalry children may experience with the introduction of new siblings. The researchers suggest that parents try to imagine how they would feel if their spouse added a new spouse into the family!

naeyc 1 Child developmentalists believe that sibling rivalry is common. However, when siblings do not get along well and engage in frequent conflict, the negative relationship affects family accord as well as individual children's development. So, it may be necessary to intervene when the conflict is especially often, harsh, or physical. Research indicates that siblings contribute both directly and indirectly to a child's development (Brody 2004). Further, siblings can affect one another in positive ways as well as in negative ways. From a family systems perspective, the behavior of any one member of a family affects all the members of the family and their relationships with one another (Brody 2004).

Direct ways in which siblings influence one another include:

- Older siblings teach new concepts and language skills to younger siblings.

Understanding and appreciating sibling relationships helps teachers understand families and children.

- Older siblings become better teachers, gain confidence, increase their school achievement, and learn to balance their own needs with others.

- A balance of conflict and nurturance between or among siblings helps children to understand others' emotions and viewpoints as well as how to resolve conflict.

- Younger siblings who have aggressive older siblings are at risk for problems with conduct, academics, and peers.

- Older siblings can serve as a buffer for younger siblings in times of family upheaval (Brody 2004).

Some of the indirect ways in which siblings influence one another include the following:

- Older siblings influence their parents' expectations for younger children.

- Older children also influence teachers' perceptions about younger siblings in relation to academic ability and behavioral expectations.

- Older children who have difficult temperaments or special needs may influence parental ability to provide appropriate nurturance to younger siblings.

- When older siblings do well in school and with peers, parents use more positive parenting strategies with younger children (Brody 2004).

Sibling influences are also noted when parents or parenting figures treat siblings differently. In order to be a responsive parent, children's differences must be noted and cared for. However, when the differential treatment is seen as unfair by siblings, issues may arise.

- Poor emotional and behavioral functioning may occur when children perceive that siblings receive more warmth from parents than they do.

- Low self-esteem in children is related to perceptions of unfair treatment from parents.

Parents can mitigate these negative effects, however, by explaining to children the basis for differential treatment so that children understand the need to individualize parenting for developmental differences or special needs.

Family size, of course, influences family systems, especially the dynamics of sibling relationships. Hernandez (1993) discusses details related to growing up in larger families versus smaller families. The median family size had decreased from 6.6 in the 1890s to 2.9 in the 1940s. During the baby boom (1946–1964), the median family size rose to 3.4. Most recently, during the "baby bust," median family size has decreased to 2.1. Figure 3–1 demonstrates changes in average family size over time. Fewer siblings in the house mean a marked change in the typical family's microsystem. Generally, young children today have fewer relationships within

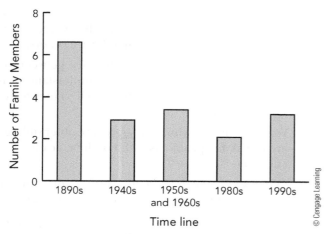

Figure 3–1   Changes in family size.

the family and a greater number of people with whom they interact in additional microsystems. naeyc 1

naeyc 2 Hernandez's analysis indicates that the reasons for declines in family size are related to social, economic, and political changes. The first issue Hernandez (1993) addresses is that having many siblings is a mixed blessing: it creates the opportunity for caring sibling relationships, but less attention is available for each child from parents. Hernandez indicates that children from larger families receive less education, and thus enter lower-status occupations and earn less income. Further, a great deal of research has pointed to the fact that increased interactions with parents leads to gains in children's verbal ability and school success. Smaller families provide greater possibility for parents to interact with children. This is likely one reason that young children currently have higher levels of language development when they enter preschool or kindergarten than was true of children in the past. naeyc 2

Children with Disabilities: Understanding Sibling Issues

http://nichcy.org
Helping Children Adapt to a New Sibling

http://www.nncc.org
Click "Articles and Resources"

How Foster Children Impact Sibling Relationships

http://www.fostercare.net/

Siblings in Adoption—Expanded Families

http://www.pactadopt.org/
Click "Articles of Interest"; click "siblings"

naeyc 1 Many studies regarding the characteristics of only children have demonstrated that they are very similar to those of other children or that only children are even somewhat advantaged (Falbo 1992). Conventional wisdom in U.S. society points to a desire for two or three children, down from a generation or two ago. And conventional wisdom opposes planning for having only one child. Even adults who were reared as only children note that they wish they had grown up with brothers and sisters. Falbo notes that it is rare for an only child to have "strong positive feelings about his or her status because it is and continues to be nonnormative."

In her review of literature regarding only children, Falbo (1992) notes that only children scored higher than others on achievement motivation and self-esteem. They were not unique from other children in many personality traits, including dominance, generosity, autonomy, anxiety, and popularity. In childhood, the home lives of only children have been more likely to encourage intellectual activities such as reading, music, dance, and travel outside the country. In school, only children were not more likely than others to cause trouble or have special needs, but they were less inclined than others to demonstrate antisocial behavior, hyperactivity, dependency, or social withdrawal. naeyc 1

66 Sensitive parenting…often requires that children in the same family be treated differently. 99

—Brody, 1998

naeyc 2 The primary reason for the decline in family size is a desire of individuals and couples to increase their social and economic standing or to keep from falling behind in their economic standing (Hernandez 1993). The cost of having children has increased, and the economic benefit of having children has all but disappeared. As society has shifted from an agrarian emphasis to an industrial and technological one, each child's needs for housing, food, and clothing was no longer provided directly by the family; rather, families had to pay for goods and services. Not only was child labor restricted, but also school attendance became mandatory. During the twentieth century, quality of living has become tied to the increased consumption of goods and services that are produced outside of the home. In addition, parents' expectations about their own lives changed, and they perceived a need for more time for their own careers and recreation. Thus, many parents feel that their resources are too stretched for them to consider having more than one or two children. Essentially, changes in the exosystem, macrosystem, and chronosystem have affected decisions about the size of the family in the microsystem. Childhood within the family context has experienced a "revolutionary shift" (Hernandez 1993) from large to small families within the past 100 years. The downside of this shift from larger to smaller families is that children have fewer siblings who are potential companions throughout childhood and adulthood; the benefit is that children today receive more attention and resources from their parents. naeyc 2

Sibling relationships often challenge parents. Faber and Mazlish (1987) provide many examples from parents of such challenges. It seems that some degree of sibling rivalry may be inescapable within the family context. Parents claim not only that it is hard for them to understand why their children express such dislike for one another, but also that it is difficult to live with the sibling conflicts. Parents believe in the same paradigm used by researchers: that siblings are companions, friends for life. But children's actions rarely support this view.

Researchers interested in studying sibling relationships note that these interactions and emotions cannot be meaningfully studied outside the context of family and peer relationships. Further, research into sibling relationships may dispel the notion that parent-child relationships are the only significant ones in the processes of socialization (Buhrmester 1992).

The causes of sibling rivalry or unity are not completely clear. Some of the factors influencing the quality of sibling relationships that researchers have examined include child temperament, parental depression, parent relationship with a spouse or partner, parenting strategies, and the interaction among any or all of these variables (Brody 1998).

Children with more difficult temperaments, particularly those who were less adaptable, more likely to withdraw from new situations, or emotionally intense, have displayed more troubled attitudes and behaviors with the birth of a new sibling. Further, highly active and siblings with different temperamental qualities have been found to engage in more conflict. Outside influences, including parenting style and family harmony, can assist siblings with these qualities to have more positive relationships with one another. For example, when parents have positive relationships with their children, the sibling relationship typically is more positive as well. However, when parents are negative and overcontrolling, sibling relationships may be affected in a negative manner (Brody 1998).

Evidence indicates that it is important for parenting adults to guide children's behavior and to set positive behavioral expectations. This might best be accomplished in the context of everyday problem-solving discussions with children rather than in the heat of disagreement. Conversely, when parents are aloof from sibling disputes, older siblings may take over, leaving younger siblings to be victims or, at least, to be negatively influenced both socially and emotionally. "Parental intervention in escalating conflict can

Sibling rivalry is to be expected.

© Cengage Learning/ECE Photo Library.

reassure children that their parents are available to help and protect them when they are upset or in danger" (Brody 1998).

In any analysis of sibling relationships, it is important to keep in mind that there is a complex mix of influential factors. Considering only one or two possibilities will most likely lead to oversimplification of the relationship. Still, continuous positive family interactions that emphasize problem solving and conflict resolution seem to provide a strong basis for more positive sibling relationships.

naeyc 1 Children with siblings who have developmental disabilities may face unique challenges in their relationships. It is not unusual for children to be taunted or teased about a sibling with a disability. Gath (1992) notes that a useful strategy for parents of children with disabilities is to provide an understandable explanation to children regarding their sibling's disability. There is some evidence that "life may be easier for a brother or sister when there is another normal [sic] child in the family" (p. 103). Also, "the presence of other normal [sic] children in the family is a great comfort to the majority of parents, but conversely, the arrival of a second handicapped child in the same family increases the grief many times over and the presence of two children with mental retardation or other long standing disability in one family adds up to very much more than twice the burden of one." Other challenges to families who are rearing siblings with and without disabilities include issues of fairness in terms of expectations about behavior and opportunities, as well as overcoming sadness and distress about a child's disability.

"Generally, researchers have hypothesized that when one child has a disability, the sibling relationship would be less warm and positive. Surprisingly, the majority of studies have found the opposite pattern" (Stoneman 2001). Variability in these relationships exists in that when a child's disability is more severe, the interaction between siblings is reduced. Physical or cognitive impairment may hinder children from playing together in ways that are mutually enjoyable. Stoneman's (2001) analysis of differences in sibling relationships of typically developing siblings and of those where one sibling has a disability makes a critical point. Just because the two types of sibling relationships differ does not mean that one trend is the best for all. "Relationship differences can be adaptive and can allow love and friendship to develop in the face of the obstacles imposed by disability" (Stoneman 2001).

Some concerns about sibling relationships would lead one to consider how differences in family structure might influence those relationships. For instance, how do marital transitions affect sibling relationships? Are biological siblings emotionally closer to one another than half- or stepsiblings? What is the impact of sibling relationships in a single-parent family?

Anderson and Rice (1992), in their study of sibling relationships in nondivorced, divorced, and remarried families, found that some personality traits of siblings differed by gender. Girls demonstrated more positive behavior, such as empathy and support, toward brothers and sisters than did boys, but they also showed equal amounts of aggression and hostility as boys. Generally, the findings in this study supported the family systems notion that increased family transitions contributed to conflict or ambivalence in sibling relationships. Negative sibling relationships were more common in stepfamilies and divorced families than in nondivorced families. These researchers emphasize that despite the conflicts among siblings, children in all types of families demonstrated a great deal of positive behavior toward their siblings. **naeyc** 1

Although earlier studies have shown differences in the quality of sibling relationships between "intact" and repartnered families, the work of Deater-Deckard, Dunn, and Lussier (2002) found greater similarities with siblings of both types of families in England. In addition to intact and repartnered families, these researchers also included siblings from single mothers. The results demonstrated that siblings in the single mother families were more negative than those in the other families, but that they engaged in just as much positivity as siblings in the other types of families. Interestingly, in terms of understanding family context, the single mothers in this study also were found to engage in more negativity than the parents in intact or repartnered families. Although most of the research on families in transition has emphasized parent-child interaction, it is important to gain additional information about sibling relationships, since it is well documented that these relationships do have a strong influence on child development.

Even though it is advantageous to be aware of the positive relationships and influences that exist among siblings, parents continue to be frustrated and sometimes overwhelmed by sibling rivalries. In a laboratory study of young siblings, Ram and Ross (2001) found that even very young children are capable of using positive negotiating strategies in order to settle conflicts. Some of the strategies that children used included turn-taking, sharing information about their own points of view, and asking questions of each other. As might be expected, when siblings had ongoing positive relationships with one another and seemed to like and care for one another, contention was reduced. It is possible that the family context (even though not studied in this research) provided siblings with ways to engage one another positively.

Another finding in this study was that the children seemed to be concerned about issues of equality as they played together. As they negotiated situations with one another, they seemed to emphasize that certain toys or playthings were equally desirable and thus would take turns with that toy. Further, the researchers noted that a good selection of playthings probably works to reduce contentious interactions (Ram and Ross 2001).

Parents who have shared their stories in workshops with Faber and Mazlish make it clear that sibling rivalry is difficult to live with. Hetherington (1992) notes that "sibling relationships are unique because they combine the affective intensity and reciprocity of peer relationships with many of the complementary processes associated with parent-child relationships." She goes on to say that sibling relationships have both an intense emotional component and high levels of supportive and antagonistic behavior.

Faber and Mazlish, basing their suggestions on the work of Haim Ginott (1965), offer the following strategies:

- Communicating feelings in acceptable ways
- Knowing when and how to stop children's hurtful actions toward each other
- Avoiding negative and positive comparisons of children
- Understanding the differences between equal treatment and meeting each child's legitimate needs
- Intervening in rivalries when one sibling has a disability
- Setting limits on fighting
- Managing tattling
- Viewing sibling relationships as important across the life span

The last chapter of Faber and Mazlish's book contains stories from parents who are trying to impact their children's relationships in a positive way. Some of the stories that are particularly moving are ones in which parents discuss contacting their own siblings and using the strategies they apply to their children to repair or rebuild their adult sibling relationships.

Reflect on This

What has been your experience in relation to sibling relationships? How has the information in this chapter influenced your thinking about this developmental issue?

Work and Family

Contemporary discussions about work and family focus on adult employment patterns. In contrast, historically, children were viewed as economic assets with the family farm or to be hired out to add to the family income. For the most part, this perspective ceased to exist in the mid-twentieth century.

naeyc 2 Work and family patterns for families with young children have undergone seismic shifts since the 1960s. In 2002, more than half of all new mothers with a child under 12 months of age were in the labor force (Overturf-Johnson and Downs 2005). Between 1961 and 1965, this figure was a little less than 17 percent. The increase in new mothers who are employed by the time their babies are a year old has been steady. See Figure 3–2 for details.

As might be expected, the percentages increased for mothers employed outside the home as their children got older. Figure 3–3 provides information about percentages of mothers in the labor force when their children were two and five years of age.

Families and Work Institute

http://www.familiesandwork.org

Institute for Child and Family Policy

http://www.childpolicy.org/

Today, early in the twenty-first century, the state of the economy is such that many families perceive a need for two full-time incomes. When both parents in two-parent families are working full-time, the result is a dramatic change in the functions that families can and do perform. Many who are concerned about children and families have called on employers to incorporate **family-friendly work policies** for their employees. **naeyc** 2

Along with other members of contemporary society, many early childhood professionals have strong opinions about when and whether mothers of young children should be in the workforce. Each family,

Figure 3–2	Percentages of employed mothers 12 months after first baby.
1961–65	16.8
1966–70	23.9
1971–75	27.9
1976–80	38.8
1981–85	56.3
1986–90	60.8
1991–95	62.0
1996–99	64.6

© Cengage Learning

Figure 3–3	Percentages of employed mothers 24 and 60 months after first baby.	
Time Period	**24 Months**	**60 Months**
1961–65	22.5	33.5
1966–70	29.8	41.1
1971–75	37.0	50.0
1976–80	48.0	64.3
1981–85	63.0	69.9
1986–90	66.6	72.7
1991–95	70.2	78.6
1996–99	Not available	Not available

© Cengage Learning

however, must decide this issue for itself—and only each family can. For some families, this decision is a matter of simple arithmetic (earning the amount of income necessary to keep them solvent); for others, it is a matter of career building. Today, we are more accepting of "Mr. Moms" but still tend to think that women should be willing to consider various work options. Many see this issue as being more political than economic, however.

Although no expert expects a rapid turnaround regarding maternal employment, there has been some recent movement toward the notion of women having flex-careers as well as being more family-centric and less work-centric (Galinsky 2004). Women with flex-careers plan to take time out of the labor force while their children are young. Recently, a survey showed that 28 percent of women who do not yet have children plan to do precisely this in order to spend time with their children.

Contemporary new moms may be making this decision for many reasons, but one has to do with the phenomenon that many Americans are feeling overworked (Galinsky, Bond, Kim, Backon, Brownfield, and Sakai 2004): about 44 percent of respondents indicated that they feel overworked on a regular basis. There are indications that this chronic sense of being over-whelmed in the workplace will lead to greater amounts of depressive disorders. Clinical depression related to work stress is predicted to take over from cancer as the number one cause of death and disability worldwide by 2020 (World Health Organization, as cited in Galinsky et al. 2004). In this context, the movement toward flex-careers by women with young children can be seen as an act of self-preservation.

Despite the enormous changes in work-family patterns experienced by married-couple families in the United States over the past generation, dual-career couples are still the most common type, while couples consisting of the wife as breadwinner and the husband as homemaker remain the least common type, as the following list indicates (Cheal 1996).

Dual-career couples 30 percent

Husband provider, wife coprovider 24 percent

Husband breadwinner, wife homemaker 19 percent

One partially employed 8 percent

Both partially employed 6 percent

Wife provider, husband coprovider 5 percent

Nonworking 5 percent

Wife breadwinner, husband homemaker 2 percent

Stress in the workplace is on the rise. **Downsizing** often means that each employee is required to do all the work previously done by at least two people. Both men and women report working longer hours than they would like. Emotionally, they are torn: they are grateful to have a job, but stressed by the workload and expectations. Workers who have children report even greater levels of stress and are coping less effectively than those without children. Fifteen percent of employed parents say they rarely or never do anything for fun with their children (Galinsky 1994).

Many people believe that **maternal employment** (that is, mothers working outside the home) is always negative for both the women and their families. These people believe that if women would return to caring for their young children, both families and the economy would be better off. Ellen Galinsky points out that this is not always the case. In many dual-earner families, women bring home 40 percent of the total income. This is a significant proportion of household income, and it can be assumed that families would suffer a much lower quality of life without it. Further, researchers since the early 1970s have examined the effects of maternal employment, and the conclusions are that other variables are more important for children's welfare than whether the mother is working outside the home. Some of these variables include variations in home life, effects from the specific work environment, and the availability of quality child care. So, employed moms who have a satisfying family life, a supportive

work environment, and access to quality care for their children provide positive outcomes for children. Segments from both the exosystem and macrosystem can affect families in either positive or negative ways.

In a study of the relation of maternal employment to mothers' and teachers' ratings of children's temperament and social behavior, Farver, Couchenour, and Chrisman (1998) found that young children's mothers who were dissatisfied with their work status, whether they worked outside the home or stayed at home, rated their children as more problematic in terms of difficult temperament. Also, mothers who were younger and had less education and lower incomes were more likely to rate their children as difficult than did older, more educated, higher-income mothers. Further, teacher ratings of the children's behavior yielded some important results.

Teacher ratings of preschool children's behaviors by the categories in Figure 3–4 were examined in relation to mothers working full-time, part-time, or not working outside the home. Each of the high-end scores is marked with an asterisk. Keep in mind that high scores indicate difficulty relating to the characteristics of the preschool children. For mothers not working outside the home, only the "Hesitant" category was noted as significantly troublesome by preschool teachers. It is possible that children whose mothers are not employed outside the home have had fewer external social experiences, and thus demonstrated hesitancy in social encounters in preschool. For mothers who worked part-time, only "Sociable" was noted as a troublesome factor. This may be because some children experience inconsistency in their caregiving arrangements and other aspects of the daily schedule when mothers work part-time, thus leading to the possibility of difficulties in getting along with others. Teachers

Figure 3–4	Mothers' work status by teachers' ratings of children's behavior.		
Not Working		**Working Part Time**	**Working Full Time**
Sociable		*	
Difficult			*
Hesitant		*	
Aggressive			*
Prosocial			*
Asocial			*
Hyperactive/ Distracted			*
Anxious/ Fearful		(No significant findings)	
Excluded		(No significant findings)	

© Cengage Learning

noted more areas of difficulty in children whose mothers worked full-time: difficult temperament, including slower to accept new experiences and a greater frequency of negative emotional responses to others; higher levels of aggression; fewer prosocial interactions and more asocial behaviors; and greater levels of hyperactive/distracted behaviors.

One of the important concepts demonstrated in this study is the complexity of children's behavior and the outcomes of maternal employment. It is important to use information such as this in ways that positively affect all children and families in children's school experiences. For example, early childhood teachers can plan ways to support children who are socially hesitant in preschool. Another example is to redirect aggressive behaviors so that these children can have more successful social experiences.

It is important to note that this study does not show causal relationships between children's social characteristics and maternal employment. That is, one cannot stipulate from this study that maternal employment causes preschoolers to be aggressive or asocial. It is possible that families sometimes choose for children to attend various types of preschools (including full-day child care) because they have assessed that their children would benefit from more social experiences with other children. This view might lead parents to make the choice for mothers to be employed outside the home. Additionally, there are other external factors that were not examined in this study, such as presence or lack of family-friendly characteristics in the workplace, extended family or other social supports for the family, special needs of children or siblings, marital satisfaction, and many others. More research needs to be conducted using a variety of factors before one can conclude that maternal employment causes particular social characteristics, positive or negative, in children. This is an important caveat because the media often publicize studies such as this one to suggest causal results that are not, in fact, supported by the research.

naeyc 2 A primary stressor for working parents is a breakdown in their child care arrangements. Often, this happens when children are ill or their caregiver has an emergency. Further, a lack of empathy and negativism from the child's caregiver has a negative effect on both the mother's and the child's well-being. One of the most severe causes of distress for employed mothers and their children is inconsistency of caregivers.

In addition to child care worries, a variety of other workplace characteristics take a toll on employed moms. Those most notably affecting both marriage and children's development are overly demanding jobs, heavy workloads, job insecurity, long hours with no flexibility, lack of autonomy and lack of control over work schedules, unsupportive supervisors and coworkers, an unsupportive social atmosphere, and the perception of discriminatory practices. While long hours and demanding jobs are typically problematic, many fathers and mothers with complex, challenging jobs that they like have been found to be warmer, more responsive, and firmer with their children (Galinsky 1994). **naeyc** 2

Parcel and Menaghan (1994) note the importance of examining information regarding both parents' employment rather than studying maternal employment alone. The title of their book, *Parents' Jobs and Children's Lives,* represents their primary research question: how does parental employment affect children's cognitive and social development? Results of this study show complex ways in which children are affected by employment of their parents. Some of the more remarkable conclusions follow.

naeyc 1 At ages three to six years, children's verbal facility, including vocabulary development, was related to both maternal and paternal characteristics as well as to the home environment. Verbal facility was higher when the mother's work was complex and she received a good salary; verbal skill was also higher when the father had higher hourly wages. When either or both parents clocked overtime work, children's verbal ability was likely to be hindered. Married mothers with fewer children were likely to have preschoolers who had greater verbal skills.

Later reading and math achievement of children ages six to eight years was also related to some parental characteristics and the home environment. Parents' levels of education, as well as their hourly wages, were positively related to children's reading ability. Children who had higher reading achievement scores were likely to have mothers who were employed in more complex work. One exception to this, however, was when mothers had complex jobs and family size was increasing. In these cases, reading skills of young children were negatively affected. Children whose fathers worked less than full-time were negatively affected in their reading ability. Math skills were positively related to mothers' age and education but had no relation to fathers' age or education.

As with reading skill, math achievement was higher for children whose parents had higher hourly wages and when mothers' work had greater complexity. Some additional characteristics were noted for families of children who had higher math skill: one level of maternal part-time employment (21 to 34 hours per week) showed a positive association, while another level of part-time employment (35 to 40 hours per week) showed a negative association. The researchers speculate that when mothers work 21 to 34 hours per week, they may actually have less spousal support for home and family responsibilities, and/or inconsistent childcare arrangements. Both of these circumstances may increase stress and cause a less positive home environment for children. (It is not clear why these employment patterns did not affect reading achievement in the same way.) Finally, math achievement was also higher in stable marriages and lower when a marriage ended or the family head was stably single. It seems that young children's math skill is more dependent on various home and family characteristics than is reading achievement.

Behavior problems were also examined in relation to parental characteristics, employment, and the home environment (Parcel and Menaghan 1994). Mothers with positive self-concepts and higher levels of education were less likely to have children who manifested behavioral problems. Further, higher maternal wages, stable marriages, and stronger home environments were negatively associated with children's behavior problems. **naeyc** 1

Over and over again, this research points to the fact that maternal employment alone is not responsible for children's academic achievement or social development. Rather, complex interactions help to explain the child outcomes. In summary, when parents' time and energy are overwhelmed, often due to both work and family situations, then children's development is likely to be hindered. However, when employment provides satisfaction and an increase in resources for the family without overburdening parents, children are likely to benefit.

Companies are increasingly providing more work-family assistance to help families balance job and home responsibilities. Even though more worksite programs, such as child care assistance, flexible time, and part-time and leave policies, are offered, it is typically those with higher job status who have more choices and greater access to these programs. Thus, white, upper-middle-class employees are receiving the bulk of these forms of support from employers. Although families that receive such support from employers find them to be extremely helpful, this is yet another example of ways in which the gap between the haves and have-nots is increasing in today's society (Galinsky 1994).

Much of Galinsky's research at the Families and Work Institute confirms the increasing incidence of family support programs in the workplace. It seems that corporations go through stages in their understanding of what types of family support programs are good for families and good for companies. Two areas of current interest are greater training for supervisors about how to support employees' family needs and creation of a family-friendly culture in the workplace.

Galinsky (1994) notes that our societal beliefs about work need to change if we are going to support families to a greater degree. Some of the traditional deep-seated beliefs that she says must change include the following:

- Time equals commitment.
- Presence equals productivity.
- People have to sink or swim.

- People issues and work issues are different.
- If it isn't unpleasant, it isn't work.
- If you give employees an inch, they'll take a mile.
- Employees must sacrifice their personal needs to get ahead.
- There is no connection between the work-family problems of employees and the company's productivity.

Some beliefs that should replace these are the following:

- It is better to focus on work tasks than work time.
- People perform better when they are not hampered by personal pressures.
- Flexibility is a competitive issue and a management tool.
- Manage by empowering, rather than controlling.

When workplaces provide more support to families, children reap the benefits. When children have greater opportunities for optimal development, all of society benefits.

Galinsky (1999) has more recently turned her research endeavors to asking children what they think about parental employment. One aspect of this research was concerned with children's views of the parenting they were receiving and measured this factor by using descriptor phrases such as "good values," "someone I can talk with," "appreciates me," and "is involved with my school." No differences were found in responses from children whose mothers were or were not employed outside the home. Other areas that this study examined included amount of time spent with parents, child care, and the effects of parents' jobs on children and child development. Results included the finding that children who spend more time with their parents when their parents were relaxed and calm saw them in a more positive way. Both quantity and quality of time matter to children. More children reported too little time with their fathers than reported too little time with their mothers.

Only half of the children in the study believed that their child care experiences were positive. Those children generally also felt that child care was good for their development. The problem here, however, is that too little high-quality child care exists to meet the needs of all children (Galinsky 1999).

When children see that their parents are tired and stressed from their jobs, they often worry about their parents. Even though parents in this study seemed to be out of sync with their children's feelings, the children reported that the one thing they would change if they could is that their parents would be less stressed and less tired. Further, it was found that parents often do not share much information about their jobs with their children; they seem to see work as competing with children. This observation led some children to believe that parents did not like their jobs, when in fact, those parents reported liking their jobs (Galinsky 1999).

This study broke new ground regarding the assumptions that adults make about work and children. Understanding the views of children can lead adults to behaviors that will yield more positive outcomes for children. These behaviors include spending a good amount of high-quality time with children, finding ways to reduce job stress, getting enough rest, understanding how to choose high-quality child care, and talking with children about some of the joys and challenges in their work.

Reflect on This

What has been your experience in relation to work and family? How has the information in this chapter influenced your thinking about this developmental issue?

Extended Family Relationships

naeyc 2 With the prevalence of the nuclear family image as the ideal for today's society, **extended family relationships**, especially those with grandparents, are frequently overlooked in early education programs. "The separation of families into generational subsystems, referred to as the 'nuclear' and the 'extended' family, creates artificial separation of parts of a family" (Carter and McGoldrick 1999). However, it is true that unlike the common family configuration of two generations ago in the United States, most children do not live in homes with both their parents and grandparents. During the postwar, mid-twentieth century, the quality of living rose quickly for young families, and so it was expected that they would form their own households. This trend, however, has resulted in "vital connections" (Kornhaber and Woodward 1981) between grandparents and grandchildren going unrealized. These researchers note that the missed connections are a detriment to both the children and the aging members of families. It should be noted, however, that many children have close emotional connections with their grandparents even if they do not share a residence with them. And, some grandparents intentionally forge these relationships even when geographic distance separates them from their grandchildren. **naeyc** 2

In their study of about 300 grandchildren ages 5 to 18 years, Kornhaber and Woodward (1981) noted that only about 5% of them had an intimate connection with at least one grandparent. This emotional closeness was fostered mostly by spending time together; no other factor was as critical to forming vital connections. Grandchildren who are given the gift of grandparents form emotional bonds second only to those they have with their parents. Because the parent-child relationship can be overcome by conflict at various times in the family life cycle, the grandchild-grandparent bond can serve a stabilizing purpose in the emotional life of children. With grandparents, children often feel unconditional acceptance and warmth. This study noted that when children do not have a grandparent-like relationship, they may suffer an emotional loss: "grandparents and grandchildren are naturally at ease with each other while both have intense emotional relationships with the middle generation…grandparents and grandchildren do not have to do anything to make each other happy. Their happiness comes from being together."

The emphasis on the nuclear family often generates a perception of grandparents as "meddlers" or "child spoilers" rather than as people who can help to support the family (Kornhaber and Woodward 1981). Given this view and the accompanying feeling of being unneeded, many grandparents move away from their grandchildren when the grandparents retire. Approximately 90 percent of grandchildren in this study had only sporadic contact with their grandparents, and the children and grandparents did not really know much about each other. Divorce also threatens grandparent-grandchild relationships. The divorce of children's parents often means that the children do not have intimate contact with at least some of their grandparents. Grandparents, parents, and grandchildren all seem to believe that a lack of grandparenting relationships in children's lives is not a tremendous loss. But today's families are overlooking history: "For the 40,000 years that humankind has been known to exist, children have typically been raised in tribes, clans, and variously extended networks of kin."

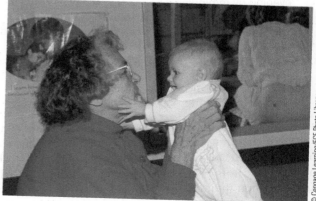

Extended family relationships, especially those of grandparents, are frequently overlooked.

Foundation for Grandparenting
http://www.grandparenting.org
Grandparents Rights Center
http://www.grandparentsrights.org

If grandparents have lost their social significance in the United States, the research by Kornhaber and Woodward demonstrates that they remain an important emotional attachment for grandchildren. "Society…cannot change what a grandparent means to a grandchild."

> "[T]he real experts on the aged are children. Only children understand what elders are for, and only they can meet the real need of the aged: the need to be needed. Children need grandparents and grandparents need children, whether they are their own flesh and blood kin or surrogate grandchildren. And until these mutual needs are acknowledged and supported, the aged will never achieve more than begrudging respect, much less outright affection, as elders in American society."

Kornhaber (1996) has continued to collect data for the Grandparent Study that he and his associates began in the 1970s. Current results confirm prior findings of the "existence of a unique emotional relationship between grandparent and grandchild." An important positive characteristic of effective grandparent-grandchild relationships is a feeling of joy and fun. The following anecdote is one example of those feelings between a grandmother and her granddaughter.

> Four-year-old Chelsea, who lives next door to her grandmother, frequently calls ahead to schedule play time with her. They play games together as well as engage in some messy play such as fingerpainting. Chelsea's grandmother, Dee, admits to trying to avoid the mess of fingerpainting one evening by reminding Chelsea that the plastic clothing protector that came with the fingerpaints had torn. Knowing the resourcefulness of her grandmother, Chelsea countered with, "You can find something to cover my clothes, Mumma." Sure enough, they found an old towel and the fingerpainting activity was on! Both parties reported having fun.

The Grandparent Study shows, of course, that roles are changing for women and men. Many contemporary women, having experienced the world of work outside the home, are now striving for a better balance between their work lives and home lives. One way many of them are attempting to do this is to reduce the number of hours they work outside of the home and to increase the amount of time they spend with family members. This seems to be good news for grandchildren. Grandfathers who may have had little time to spend with children earlier in their lives also seem to be setting priorities that involve their grandchildren. One grandfather who worked two full-time jobs for many years found a great deal of pleasure in the time he spent with his preschool-aged grandson. As the grandson grew to adulthood, this relationship changed from playful interaction to one of genuine friendship. Other family members noted through the years how this pair seemed to really enjoy being together.

naeyc 1, 2 While role changes in contemporary society seem to contribute positively to grandparenting, some changes in contemporary families complicate the grandparenting role. In instances of divorce and remarriage, for example, the complexity of relationships or the sheer number of children and parents involved may interfere with children spending time with grandparents. The increased variations in family structure also contribute to confusion among family members about roles and identities. Some of these variations include:

- An increase in single-parent families
- Single grandparents
- Blended families
- Grandparents serving as parents
- Gay and lesbian partnerships (Kornhaber 1996)

The research discussed previously and a study by Kivnick (1982) examined the effects that grandchildren have on grandparents. Grandparents noted the following:

- Recall of their own parenthood experiences as they anticipate the birth of their first grandchild
- Feelings of joy about arrival of grandchild, even when the timing of that birth was wrong for social reasons
- Wandering thoughts of immortality, connections, spirituality
- Impulse to see, hold, hear, care for, and indulge baby
- Grandparent role central to their lives
- Enjoying role as valued and esteemed elder in family

Kivnick (1982) found that grandparents attached a great deal of meaning to their roles with grandchildren and that the strength of this value was connected to the mental health of grandparents. The role of grandparent seemed to enhance the quality of life for the aging, thus contributing to positive mental health.

Research makes clear the importance of grandchildren and grandparents in each other's lives. Some attention must be given to the middle generation, the parents, so that they, too, might see the benefits of

Long-Distance Grandparenting (www.grandparenting.org/Long-Distance.htm)

Figure 3–5	Guidelines and ideas for long-distance grandparents.

- Find ways to continuously maintain communication.
- Schedule family conferences to plan for continuous communication.
- Discuss the difficulties of long-distance grandparenting with children's parents.
- Pledge to spend as much time together as possible.
- Create an action plan for ways and times to spend together.
- Determine ways to use financial and material resources in ways that increase time to be together.
- Plan for time for grandparent(s)/grandchild(ren) to spend together without presence of parents.
- Make frequent use of technology. Give grandchildren disposable cameras to take pictures to send to you. Consider giving them a fax machine or a long distance phone card to stay in touch with you.
- E-mail.
- Videoconference.
- Fax.
- Telephone.
- All forms of mail, including "snail" mail.
- Videotapes.
- Audiotapes.

grandparents' presence in their children's lives. The need that young parents have to be independent in this society detracts from the real support that grandparents can give, especially to their grandchildren. Although much of the research emphasizes the biological connection between grandparents and grandchildren, especially from the view of the grandparent, enough information exists to support the value of the grandparent role in children's lives, and of the grandchild role in the lives of the aging, to give credence to programs for surrogate grandparents and grandchildren.

The following factors mentioned by Kornhaber and Woodward (1981) apply to surrogate situations as well as biological ones:

- Young children are in awe of the elderly and can delight them.
- The young and old have more time "to be"; parents are at an age where they must produce.
- Grandparents and grandchildren are relatively free of emotional conflict with each other.
- Grandparents are voices out of other times.
- Grandfathers are especially important as male figures for today's children who are so frequently missing those in their lives.

In order to understand the value that grandparents have for children, observe interactions between young children and their grandparents, reflect on your own experiences with grandparents, and ask people of all ages about their relationships with their grandparents.

> At age 3, Chelsea was given an assignment in her preschool class to draw a picture of something for which she was thankful. She drew someone: her grandmother. Several months after Thanksgiving and that assignment, the drawing still has a special place on the grandmother's refrigerator (Figure 3–6).

Neugarten and Weinstein devised five styles of grandparenting in 1964, a classification that continues to be useful to researchers and practitioners (Smith 1995):

- Formal—Using prescribed roles for differentiating grandparents from parents
- Fun Seeker—Viewing grandchildren as satisfying, and a primary role is to have fun with them
- Surrogate Parent—Providing care for grandchildren
- Reservoir of Family Wisdom—Dispensing guidance, skills, or points of view to grandchildren
- Distant—Little contact with grandchildren, usually only for ritual occasions

It is likely that the style of grandparenting influences the grandparent-grandchild relationship. In addition to grandparents' style, other factors may affect these relationships. For example, grandparents' ages and health status affect their activity levels with grandchildren.

© Cengage Learning

Figure 3–6 "I am thankful for Mumma." Preschooler's drawing.

The most common source of child care for single-parent families is grandparents (Kennedy and Keeney, as cited in Smith 1995). While this is true for all families, African-American grandmothers have long served as surrogate parents, often being more active in the parenting role than fathers who were present in the home (Pearson, Hunter, Ensminger, and Kellam, as cited in Smith 1995). Grandparents who assisted teen mothers with children younger than two years of age were studied by Oyserman, Radin, and Benn (as cited in Smith 1995). Although grandmothers in this study had little measured effect on children, the role of grandfathers as male role models for "nurturance and cooperation" was noted. It is generally seen as a positive for young children to have grandparents assist with parental roles.

Smith (1995) discusses two areas of practical concern related to grandparenting in contemporary society.

1. Workshops for effective grandparenting, with the purpose of helping to strengthen family relationships and communication.

2. Legislation in all 50 states providing grandparents with visitation rights when parents of their grandchildren divorce.

The existence of these two phenomena suggests that grandparents see their roles as relevant to the lives of their grandchildren. And as the research shows, grandchildren and grandparents often benefit. **naeyc** 1, 2

Reflect on This

What has been your experience in relation to extended family relationships? How has the information in this chapter influenced your thinking about this developmental issue?

PRACTICAL AND ETHICAL CONSIDERATIONS

Family Support Principles

Considering the seven evidence-based principles of family support that can be found near the end of Chapter 1 in this book, the following five principles are most relevant to the developmental issues in families with young children. Of particular note is that the last four principles point to the need for society to support families in meeting their responsibilities to their children. In a complex, technological society such as that found in the United States, families cannot meet all of the needs of their children without support from other institutions.

At the same time, such support to families helps them to meet their responsibilities to their children, forming the foundation of strong families for society.

- The developmental processes that make up parenthood and family life create needs that are unique at each stage in the life span. This chapter points out some of the salient and common concerns of families who have young children. Based on current evidence, these issues include: the transition to parenthood, sibling relationships, work and family matters, child care, and extended family members.

- Primary responsibility for the development and well-being of children lies within the family, and for ALL families to succeed, ALL segments of society must support families in a variety of ways to meet various needs of families as they rear their children.

- Ensuring the well-being of all families is the cornerstone of a healthy society and requires universal access to support programs and services. In order to achieve universal access, barriers to services must be addressed so that all families, in reality, have opportunities to participate.

- Enabling families to build on their own strengths and capacities promotes the healthy development of children. Existing programs must assess their practices and policies to ensure that a family strengths perspective is at the core of all plans and implementation.

- Families are empowered when they have access to information and other resources and take action to improve the well-being of children, families, and communities. Openness and trust are keys to empowerment.

Code of Ethical Conduct

naeyc 6 The National Association for the Education of Young Children (NAEYC) has developed a Code of Ethical Conduct for early childhood professionals. (See Appendix B for this code in its entirety.) Noted here are the ideals for early childhood professionals in their work with families. Ethical responsibilities to families are: **DAP**

- To be familiar with the knowledge base related to working effectively with families and to stay informed through continuing education and training.

- To develop relationships of mutual trust and create partnerships with the families we serve.

- To welcome all family members and encourage them to participate in the program.

- To listen to families, acknowledge and build upon their strengths and competencies, and learn from families as we support them in their task of nurturing children.
- To respect the dignity and preferences of each family and to make an effort to learn about its structure, culture, language, customs, and beliefs.
- To acknowledge families' child-rearing values and their right to make decisions for their children.
- To share information about each child's education and development with families and to help them understand and appreciate the current knowledge base of the early childhood profession.
- To help family members enhance their understanding of their children and support the continuing development of their skills as parents.

- To participate in building support networks for families by providing them with opportunities to interact with program staff, other families, community resources, and professional services (http://www.naeyc.org/about/positions/PSET H05.asp). DAP naeyc 6

Consider This

Consider the nine ideals for early childhood professionals' responsibilities to families in relation to each of the developmental issues for families with young children as discussed in this chapter. Discuss the strengths that you possess and challenges you face in regard to these ethical ideals.

Summary and Conclusions

Although families differ in values, beliefs, and practices, families rearing young children in Western societies are likely to face similar situations and transitions. Family systems theorists point to this period in the family life cycle as a pressure cooker because parents with young children often are also in the early stages of their career or work life. Jobs may be less stable and incomes may be inadequate to support the family; novice workers may be trying to prove their worth. Balancing family and work is a complicated and ongoing task. Concerns related to caring for children, both in and out of the home, abound. New parents must establish new identities, seeing themselves as mothers and fathers for the first time. Relating to extended families and in-laws may require new skills that may challenge individuals who already are trying to succeed in multiple new roles.

All families with young children need support. This support may come from other family members, friends, neighbors, and community groups. Families with too little support may require more from their children's early childhood programs. Teachers must be aware of all the demands and pressures made on families as they rear their young children. This knowledge serves as a foundation for incorporating practices into early childhood education that support families at this stage of the life cycle. Thus, when teachers can provide support for their recommendations and expectations for family involvement in children's education, they have a better chance of seeing success.

Theory into Practice Suggestions (TIPS)

- Review and reflect on all of the Web sites and organizations that can provide information about development. Add those sites to your bookmarks so you can access them quickly when you have questions about development.

- Start a collection of resources that you can share with families when they have questions about their children's development. Remember that the most common concern will be "Is this normal?" or "Is this advanced" or "Is this behind?"

- When discussing development with families, be careful not to compare with siblings or other children.

- Adopt a perspective of support for families in relation to involvement in children's education.

- Understand that all families need support, though the form and source of support may vary.

- Avoid judgment about parents' hours of employment. Teachers are typically not privy to family financial priorities or concerns.

- Even though it may not be observable to teachers, realize that many parents feel guilt about not having more time to spend with their young children.

- Provide ways to support and affirm the positives that you observe in families.

- Avoid judgment about families' use of child care facilities.

- Be aware that families' experiences cannot be understood in completely objective terms. Each family's experience is viewed through its own perspectives, beliefs, values, and expectations.

- Act on your understanding that children are not equally easy or difficult to parent. Children influence parents' behaviors just as parents influence children's behaviors.

- Assume that all parents are doing the best they can. When teachers share information in supportive ways, it may lead parents to be more effective.

- Avoid judging families when grandparents or other extended family members seem to have primary parenting roles. In some families, this may be best for children and adults.

- Interview parents about their relationships with extended family members and the roles of grandparents, aunts, uncles and cousins.

- Provide concrete and accurate information about sibling relationships to families.

- Compile and share information about high quality early education.

- Help families understand the positive uses of digital technology with young children and help them encourage children to engage in active and creative experiences with various technology platforms.

- Advocate in multiple contexts for children and families. Affecting change in macrosystems will influence children's microsystems.

- Celebrate family attachments in whatever form they exist.

Applications

1. The societal concern about the negative effects of maternal employment on young children was not echoed in the welfare reform legislation (as discussed in Chapter 2). Comment on why you believe the concerns were ignored in this legislation.

2. Plan and implement a way to disseminate information to parents of young children about the components of quality child care as provided in the National Accreditation Criteria.

3. Review and discuss the Faber and Mazlish model for parents to use in limiting sibling rivalry.

4. Grandparents and other adults in extended families often provide various forms of support to families of young children. Discuss the variations that exist in such relationships and family functions.

Questions for Reflection and Discussion

1. How would you explain the notion of family transitions to someone who has not read this chapter? What do family transitions mean for children in your care?

2. Provide examples from your own life of ways in which the macrosystem and exosystem have affected you.

3. What does the term *trilemma* mean in the child care discussion? Give an example from a real-life or hypothetical family situation.

4. Of what importance to your career in early childhood education is the discussion about grandparents?

Field Assignments

1. Interview some grandparents of young children (birth to eight years) about the role they have in their grandchildren's lives. Ask about their satisfaction with their role; would they change anything about it if they could? Extend interviews to other family members as well: aunts, uncles, cousins, and older siblings.

2. Interview parents of young children about changes they made in their work and family life after the birth of their first child. What factors have facilitated their transition to parenthood? What factors have served as barriers? What work and family situations do these parents suggest would have been helpful?

3. Interview an early childhood educator about the effects she believes that maternal employment might have on the lives of young children. Ask about factors such as part-time employment,

flexibility, children's characteristics, availability of child care, parenting style, and extended family support.

4. Observe an early childhood program that has been accredited by the National Academy of Early Childhood Programs. Using the accreditation criteria highlighted in this chapter, note evidence of the criteria during the time of your observation.

Additional resources for this chapter, including Teach-Source videos, can be found on the Education Course-Mate. Go to CengageBrain.com.

References

Ali, L. July 2008. Having kids makes you happy. *Newsweek*. http://www.newsweek.com/id/143792 (accessed May 18, 2009).

American Academy of Pediatrics. 2011. Media and children. www.aap.org (accessed March 25, 2012).

Anderson, E.R., and A.M. Rice. 1992. Sibling relationships during remarriage. In *Coping with marital transitions: A family systems perspective*, Monographs of the Society for Research in Child Development, ed. E.M. Hetherington and W.G. Clingempeel, 57, 2–3, Serial No. 227, 149–77.

Australian Psychological Society. 2000. The effects of violent media on children. www.psychology.org.au/assets/files/effects_of_violent_media_on_children.pdf. Accessed March 26, 2012.

Barron, B., G. Cayton-Hodges, L. Bofferding, C. Copple, L. Darling-Hammond, and M.H. Levine. 2011. Take a giant step: A blueprint for teaching young children in a digital age. The Joan Ganz Cooney Center at Sesame Workshop and Stanford University. http://joanganzcooney-center.org/upload_kits/takeagiantstep_execsummary.pdf. Accessed March 26, 2012.

Bradt, J.O. 1989. Becoming parents: Families with young children. In *The changing family life cycle*, ed. B. Carter and M. McGoldrick. Boston: Allyn & Bacon.

Brazelton, T.B., and S.I. Greenspan. 2000. *The irreducible needs of children: What every child must have to grow, learn and flourish*. Cambridge, MA: Perseus.

Brody, G.H. 2004. Siblings' direct and indirect contributions to child development. *Current Directions in Psychological Science* 13: 124–26.

Brody, G.H. 1998. Sibling relationship quality: Its causes and consequences. *Annual Review of Psychology* 49: 1–24.

Bronfenbrenner, U. 1990. Discovering what families do. In *Rebuilding the nest: A new commitment to the American family*, ed. D. Blankenhorn, S. Bayme, and J.B. Elshtain. Milwaukee, WI: Family Service America.

Bronfenbrenner, U. 2001. The bioecological theory of human development. In *Making human beings human:*

Bioecological perspectives on human development, ed. U. Bronfenbrenner, 3–15. Thousand Oaks, CA: Sage.

Buhrmester, D. 1992. The developmental courses of sibling and peer relationships. In *Children's sibling relationships: Developmental and clinical issues,* ed. F. Boer and J. Dunn, 19–40. Hillsdale, NJ: Lawrence Erlbaum Associates.

Bureau of Labor Statistics. 2004–2005. *Occupational outlook handbook, 2004–05 Edition, Childcare workers.* Washington, DC: U.S. Department of Labor. http://www.bls.gov/oco/ocos170.htm (accessed December 14, 2005).

Bureau of Labor Statistics. May 2010. Occupational employment and wages. Childcare workers. Washington, DC: US Department of Labor. www.bls.gov/oes/current/oes399011.htm. Accessed March 26, 2012.

Carlsson-Paige, N. and D. E. Levin. 1990. Who's calling the shots: How to respond effectively to children fascination with war play and war toys. Philadelphia, PA: New Society Publishers.

Carter, B. 1999. Becoming parents: The family with young children. In *The expanded family life cycle: Individual, family, and social perspectives,* ed. B. Carter and M. McGoldrick, 3rd ed. Boston: Allyn & Bacon.

Carter, B., and M. McGoldrick. 1999. Overview: The expanded family life cycle: Individual, family and social perspectives. In *The expanded family life cycle: Individual, family, and social perspectives,* ed. B. Carter and M. McGoldrick, 3rd ed. Boston: Allyn & Bacon.

Cheal, D. 1996. *New poverty: Families in postmodern society.* Westport, CT: Greenwood.

Children Now. 2011. Media's impact on children: Understanding media's role in childhood development. www.childrennow.org/index.php/learn/medias_impact/ (accessed March 26, 2012).

Children's Defense Fund. 2005. *Child care basics.* Washington, DC: Children's Defense Fund.

Childstats. 2011. America's children: Key national indicators of well-being 2011. www.childstats.gov/americaschildren/famsoc3.asp. Accessed March 26, 2012.

Condon, J.T., P. Boyce, and C.J. Corkindale. 2004. The first-time fathers study: A prospective study of the mental health and wellbeing of men during the transition to parenthood. *Australian and New Zealand Journal of Psychiatry* 38: 56–64.

Cowan, C.P., and P.A. Cowan. 1995. Interventions to ease the transition to parenthood: Why they are needed and what they can do. *Family Relations* 44: 412–23.

Deater-Deckard, K., J. Dunn, and G. Lussier. 2002. Sibling relationships and social-emotional adjustment in different family contexts. *Social Development* 11: 571–90.

Employment characteristics of families in 2001. Bureau of Labor Statistics. http://www.bls.gov/cps (accessed October 19, 2002).

Faber, A., and E. Mazlish. 1987. *Siblings without rivalry: How to help your children live together so you can live too.* New York: Avon.

Falbo, T. 1992. Social norms and the one-child family. In *Children's sibling relationships: Developmental and clinical issues,*

ed. F. Boer and J. Dunn, 71–82. Hillsdale, NJ: Lawrence Erlbaum Associates.

Farver, J. M., D. Couchenour, and K. Chrisman. July 1998. The relation of maternal employment to mothers' and teachers' ratings of children's temperament and social behavior. Research poster presented at the Biennial Meeting of the International Society for the Study of Behavioural Development. Bern, Switzerland.

Feeney, J., R. Alexander, P. Noller, and L. Hohaus. 2003. Attachment insecurity, depression, and the transition to parenthood. *Personal Relationships* 10: 475–93.

Florsheim, P., D. Moore, L. Zollinger, J. MacDonald, and E. Sumida. 1999. The transition to parenthood among adolescent fathers and their partners: Does antisocial behavior predict problems in parenting? *Applied Developmental Science* 3: 178–92.

Galinsky, E. 1994. Families and work: The importance of the quality of the work environment. In *Putting families first: America's family support movement and the challenge of change,* ed. S.L. Kagan and B. Weissbourd. San Francisco: Jossey-Bass.

Galinsky, E. 1999. *Ask the children: What America's children really think about working parents.* New York: Morrow.

Galinsky, E. 2004. Moms in transition—going back to work. Families and Work Institute. http://www.familiesandwork.org/tips102004.html (accessed November 30, 2005).

Galinsky, E., J.T. Bond, S.S. Kim, L. Backon, E. Brownfield, and K. Sakai. 2004. *Overwork in America: When the way we work becomes too much: Executive summary.* Families and Work Institute. http://www.familiesandwork.org (accessed November 30, 2005).

Gath, A. 1992. The brothers and sisters of mentally retarded children. In *Children's sibling relationships: Developmental and clinical issues,* ed. F. Boer and J. Dunn, 101–8. Hillsdale, NJ: Lawrence Erlbaum Associates.

Ginott, H.G. 1965. *Between parent and child: New solutions to old problems.* New York: Macmillan.

Greenman, J. 1984. Perspectives on quality day care. In *Making day care better: Training, evaluation, and the process of change,* ed. J.T. Greenman and R.W. Fuqua. New York: Teachers College Press.

Hernandez, D.J. 1993. *America's children: Resources from family government and the economy.* New York: Russell Sage Foundation.

Hetherington, E.M. 1992. Coping with marital transitions: A family systems perspective. In *Coping with marital transitions: A family systems perspective,* ed. E. M. Hetherington and W. G. Clingempeel. Monographs of the Society for Research in Child Development 57, 2–3, Serial No. 227, 1–14.

Hudson, D.B., C. Campbell-Grossman, M.O. Fleck, S.M. Elek, and A. Shipman. 2003. Effects of the new fathers network on first-time fathers' parenting self-efficacy and parenting satisfaction during the transition to parenthood. *Issues in Comprehensive Pediatric Nursing* 26: 217–29.

Hudson, D.B., S. M. Elek, and M.O. Fleck. 2001. First-time mothers' and fathers' transition to parenthood: Infant care self-efficacy, parenting satisfaction, and infant sex. *Issues in Comprehensive Pediatric Nursing* 24: 31–43.

Johnson, J.O. 2005. Who's minding the kids? Child care arrangements: Winter 2002. *Current Population Reports, P70-101*. Washington, DC: U.S. Census Bureau.

Keating-Lefler, R., D.B. Hudson, C. Campbell-Grossman, M.O. Fleck, and J. Westfall. 2004. Needs, concerns, and social support of single, low-income mothers. *Issues in Mental Health Nursing* 25: 381–401.

Kivnick, H.Q. 1982. *The meaning of grandparenthood.* Ann Arbor, MI: UMI Research Press.

Kornhaber, A. 1996. *Contemporary grandparenting.* Thousand Oaks, CA: Sage.

Kornhaber, A., and K.L. Woodward. 1981. *Grandparents/grandchildren: The vital connection.* Garden City, NY: Anchor Press.

La Rossa, R., and M.M. La Rossa. 1981. *Transition to parenthood: How infants change families.* Beverly Hills, CA: Sage.

LeMasters, E.E. 1957. Parenthood as crisis. *Marriage and Family Living* 19: 352–55.

Long-Distance Grandparenting. n.d. http://www.grandparenting.org/Long-Distance.htm (accessed December 14, 2005).

National Association of Child Care Resource and Referral Agencies. n.d. Cost of child care. www.naccrra.org/public-policy/cost-of-child-care. Accessed March 26, 2012.

National Association for the Education of Young Children. 2005. Code of ethical conduct and statement of commitment. A position statement of the National Association for the Education of Young Children. Washington, DC: NAEYC.

National Association for the Education of Young Children. 2012. Technology and interactive media as tools in early childhood programs serving children from birth through age 8. A position statement of the National Association for the Education of Young Children. Washington, DC: NAEYC.

Overturf-Johnson, J., and B. Downs. 2005. Maternity leave and employment patterns: 1961–2000. *Current Population Report, P70-103.* Washington, DC: Census Bureau.

Parcel, T.L., and E.G. Menaghan. 1994. *Parents' jobs and children's lives.* New York: Aldine De Gruyter.

Perren, S., A. von Wyl, D. Burgin, H. Simoni and K. von Klitzing. 2005. Depressive symptoms and psychosocial stress across the transition to parenthood: Associations with parental psychopathology and child difficulty. *Journal of Psychosomatic Obstetrics & Gynecology 26*: 173–83.

Ram, A., and H.S. Ross. 2001. Problem solving, contention, and struggle: How siblings resolve a conflict of interests. *Child Development* 72: 1710–22.

Ribbens, J. 1994. *Mothers and their children: A feminist sociology of childrearing.* Thousand Oaks, CA: Sage.

Schulman, K. 2000. The high cost of child care puts quality care out of reach for many families. Children's Defense Fund. http://www.childrensdefense.org/pdf/highcost.pdf.

Smith, P.K. 1995. Grandparenthood. In *Handbook of parenting, volume 3: Status and social conditions of parenting,* ed. M.H. Bornstein, 89–112. Mahwah, NJ: Lawrence Erlbaum Associates.

Stoneman, Z. 2001. Supporting positive sibling relationships during childhood. *Mental Retardation and Developmental Disabilities Research Reviews* 7: 134–42.

Tomopoulos, S., B.P. Dreyer, S. Berkule, A.H. Fierman, C. Brockmeyer, and A.L. Mendelsohn. 2010. Infant media exposure and toddler development. *Arch Pediatr Adolesc Med 164 (12).* Accessed from www.archpediatrics.com on March 25, 2012.

Van Egeren, L.A. 2004. The development of the coparenting relationship over the transition to parenthood. *Infant Mental Health Journal* 25: 453–77.

Wages and quality in the child care industry. 2001. *Jobs, Pay and the Economy.* http://www.uaw.org/publications/jobs_pay/01/0901/jpe04.html. (accessed December 14, 2005).

Woollett, A., and M. Parr. 1997. Psychological tasks for women and men in the post-partum. *Journal of Reproductive & Infant Psychology* 15: 159–84.

CHAPTER 4

Family Strengths, Family Functions, and Family Structure

OUTLINE

- **Objectives Aligned with NAEYC Standards**
- **Key Terms**
- **Introduction**
  Defining Family Strengths, Functions, and Structure
- **Family Strengths**
  What Makes a Family Strong?
  What Factors Support Family Strengths?
  Resilient Children
- **Family Functions**
  Historical and Contemporary Purposes of Families
  Causes of Change in Family Functions
  Family Law

- **Family Structure**
  Variations in Family Form
  The Meaning of Birth Order
- **Application of Chapter Information**
  Family Support
  Early Childhood Programs
- **Summary and Conclusions**
- **Theory into Practice Suggestions (TIPS)**
- **Applications**
- **Questions for Reflection and Discussion**
- **Field Assignments**
- **References**

© Cengage Learning/ECE Photo Library.

After reading and reflecting on this chapter, you should be able to:

- Discuss the meaning of the terms *family strengths*, *family functions*, and *family structure* **naeyc** 2

- Explain the relationship of family accord and family pride to family strengths and functions **naeyc** 2

- Describe the factors that are related to changes in family strengths, family functions, and family structure **naeyc** 2

- Apply understanding about the strengths, functions, and structure of families to practices in early childhood education **naeyc** 2, 6

- Discuss factors associated with family resilience **naeyc** 2

Key Terms

at-risk children	family pride	nuclear family
birth order	family strengths	primacy of parental rights
extended family	family structure	resilient children
family accord	family of orientation	right of family integrity
family functions	family of procreation	

INTRODUCTION

Defining Family Strengths, Functions, and Structure

Scholars in family studies attach a great deal of importance to the concepts of **family strengths**, **family functions**, and **family structure**. It is critical that early childhood educators understand these terms. Thus, the meaning of each of these terms and the research supporting them are discussed in this chapter.

It is important for early childhood teachers to know what makes families strong. A great deal of study

on this topic has occurred over the past three decades, and the research indicates that the factors that seem to be routinely related to strong families include **family pride** and **family accord**. Characteristics of family pride are mutual respect, trust, and loyalty within the family, optimism, and shared values. The critical aspect of family accord is a family's competency in dealing with conflict (Olson, McCubbin, Barnes, Muxen, Larsen, and Wilson 1989). For example, families that have ways of acknowledging and respecting differences among their members often demonstrate higher levels of accord. To create harmony, families may accept differences among members or use strategies for compromise.

1 *Bioecological Theory*   Bronfenbrenner's theory points to the importance of **extended family** members as well as larger social institutions acting in support of families with young children. Individuals are affected, both positively and negatively, by their microsystems, or nuclear families. Larger social units, including the macrosystem, also affect nuclear families and the individuals within them. As society changes, functions of families also change. For example, consider the economic function of the family. As society's emphasis has changed from agrarian to industrial to technological, the family maintains an economic function, but the nature of that function has changed. Most families no longer produce all of their own food; instead, it becomes a function of contemporary families to purchase food from grocery stores, butcher shops, and specialty markets. Today, families are much more likely to pay for food with money rather than with labor.

As the nature of families continues to change, family functions continue to evolve. However, some of these functions change slowly enough that the typical family may not be consciously aware of the ways in which their members meet family responsibilities. Some young families often view such functional change as modern versus old-fashioned. Others cling to family traditions that might provide positive support, such as grandparents participating in child care or negative responses to flexibility in gender roles. Nonetheless, families continue to remain at the heart of children's development. It is still each family that selects, either consciously or unconsciously, how each function or responsibility is managed.

Bronfenbrenner (1988) explains that families and the larger social contexts are clearly interdependent on one another. Strong families help to support society, and effective social systems are necessary to sustain families in meeting all of their obligations, particularly to young children. This proposition may be one of the best ways to understand the reason that "it takes a village to raise a child." And, certainly such villages must be composed of strong families! 1

66 Other settings, such as school, church, or [child] care, are important to a child's development, but none can replace this basic unit of our social system:

the family is the most humane, the most powerful, and by far the most economical system known for making and keeping human beings human. 99

—Bronfenbrenner, 1988

▶︎❙❙ **"Family Interactions, School and Community"**

Visit the Education CourseMate website at www.CengageBrain.com to view the Video Case, and then respond to the following items:

• How does the video demonstrate examples of the importance of traditions that get handed down through generations?

• Discuss ways that early childhood teachers might honor various family traditions.

 2 *Family Systems Theory*   Early childhood teachers work with families who have young children, though, of course, not all families fit neatly into one stage at a time. As discussed in the previous chapter, the structure of families with young children changes dramatically with the birth of each new child. Complex life situations such as loss of family members, either by death, divorce, or separation, may also occur during this stage. When early childhood educators understand how such losses affect family structure, as well as the common dynamics of families with young children, they can be better prepared to create positive partnerships with families.

Family systems theorists emphasize the stressors related to particular points in the family life cycle. Carter and McGoldrick (1989) note that three changes in family status are required of families as they transition to parenthood. These family status changes are written for two-parent families; however, new parents who are single and parents who are blending families may find that they must negotiate similar status changes in their families.

• *First Family Status Change.* In two-parent families, couples typically have to create space for children in the system that they have already established.

• *Second Family Status Change.* Two-parent families must negotiate tasks related to nurturing children, consider new expenses and ways to manage finances, and balance house and family work with employment responsibilities. Figure 4–2 illustrates some of the details regarding the tasks that families need to regulate. Assumptions and expectations that some adults hold about parental roles may lead to conflict. When adults understand that they bring different views and experiences about their roles in a family, neither right nor wrong, they often rely on open communication to resolve how their particular family will manage.

- *Third Family Status Change.* Two-parent families find that they need to have new understanding of themselves as parents and of their own parents as grandparents. As their roles are transformed, parents frequently deal with the issues listed in Figure 4–3. **naeyc** 2

Consider This

Consider the five points in Figure 4–1 to increase your understanding about making space for children in a family. With these points in mind, what examples or issues have you experienced in your own families or observed in other families that illustrate this status change in families? How might this status change vary for single-parent families or for families with other structures?

Figure 4–1   First family status change.

1. Children may be born into a family that has:
   a. No space for them.
   b. Space for them.
   c. A vacuum for children to fill.
2. Contemporary families have an emphasis on work outside the home, and devalue events and situations in the domestic sphere, including child-rearing.
3. Young parents often relocate and children then do not have strong ties to extended family members. Fewer available adults leads to less space for children in families.
4. At the other extreme is the child-focused family in which a child fills a vacuum left by a marital partner or the loss of parents' parents.
5. Changes in women's roles have affected family space for children. Women in the workforce are able to time children with more effective birth control methods than in the past. However, many families ignore the "greater complexity of tasks and relationships" (Carter and McGoldrick) that the new baby brings (Bradt 1989).

Carter and McGoldrick (1989)

Figure 4–2   Second family status change.

NURTURING CHILDREN
- Parents must make an emotional adjustment for others to care for their children.
- Couples arrange work schedules to provide for child care, and rarely see or interact with one another.
- Adjustment if one parent stays home to provide full-time care, leaving the workforce.

FINANCIAL MANAGEMENT
- Cost of child care
- Changes in income related to caring for baby
- Decision making related to new expenses for child

HOUSEWORK
- Balancing work and home responsibilities
- Societal expectations and gender roles for mothers and fathers
- Conflicts about who has each responsibility

© Cengage Learning

Do This

Given the three categories of the second family-status change noted in Figure 4–2, list some ways that families might address the challenges of regulating these tasks. How might single-parent families and two-parent families differ in the way they approach this status change?

Figure 4–3   Third family status change.

PARENTS
- What does it mean to be a mother? A father?
- How do past experiences influence these views?
- What are the roles and responsibilities of adults in the family?
- Who must be available to nurture children?

GRANDPARENTS
- Which set of grandparents is more involved and has more influence with their grandchild?
- How do grandparents affect the marital relationship?
- How much contact do new parents have with their child's grandparents? Has it changed since the birth of the baby?
- How do new grandparents see themselves providing for family continuity over the generations?

© Cengage Learning

Consider This

What factors come into play as mothers and fathers incorporate their new identities as parents into their previous identities? How might the relationship transformation differ for single-parent and two-parent families? Consider the relationships that new parents form with their own parents, who are now in the grandparent role. Will these relationships differ according to family structure? Explain differences that might exist.

naeyc 2 Olson's revised family map model is also useful for understanding family strengths, functions, and structure (Olson and Gorall 2003). Through effective communication, families who are undergoing structural changes may find new ways of maintaining their balanced connectedness with one another. The realization that families are dynamic, continually changing in various ways, underscores why it is important that families learn to adjust their communication strategies. Those families who find that they can successfully balance change in ways that sustain their strengths, either with or without professional intervention, may have the greatest opportunity to fulfill all necessary family functions.

For example, one family with two young children, ages six years and 18 months, invited a newly widowed grandmother to reside with them. This change in family structure led to some changes in how functions were met. The grandmother volunteered to provide child care for the six-year-old when she returned from kindergarten each day as well as provide full-time care for the 18-month-old. This functional change resulted in two additional changes: the parents' communication patterns with the grandmother increased tremendously and their travel time decreased because they no longer needed to stop at the child care center before and after the commute to work. In addition, more time was available each evening for parents and children to increase their interactions. This family must continue to work to maintain flexibility as the kindergartner moves to first grade next school year and as both the toddler and the grandmother get older. Communication and adaptations will be needed on a regular basis. naeyc 2

FAMILY STRENGTHS

What Makes a Family Strong?

naeyc 2, 6 The first studies to examine family strengths occurred during the 1970s. Nick Stinnett (1979) and his associates found the following factors to be present in strong families:

Appreciation. Members of strong families make it a point to express appreciation to other family members. This expression might be through simple "thank you" statements, performing acts of kindness in return, or giving a gift that recognizes the uniqueness of another family member. Demonstrations of appreciation help to maintain positive relationships in the family through feelings of warmth and caring.

Spending time together. Even though quality time is known to be an important factor for building healthy relationships, some quantity of time in shared activities is necessary as well. Many families have rituals or routines of time that they spend together such as eating dinner (or another meal) around a common table, holiday celebrations, game night, or even watching movies or sports events on television.

Open communication. Conversations at meal time, during leisure activities, or during a called family meeting all contribute to openness in communication. In our contemporary technological society, various forms of electronic communication must be considered, for example, e-mail, voice mail, and text messaging. However, face-to-face communication remains important in that it encompasses some of the other family strengths, such as spending time together and commitment to one another.

Commitment. The sense of commitment in strong families flows not only among individual family members, but also establishes a bond to the family unit. Thus, individual members might work together for the well-being of their family. Certainly, a commitment to supporting one another also adds to a family's strength.

Religious orientation or spirituality. For some families, this dimension relates specifically to religiosity and is practiced through church attendance, prayer, and consideration of scriptural lessons. For other families, spirituality is practiced more broadly in that they "see a larger purpose for their family than simply their own maintenance and self-satisfaction" (Ages and Stages n.d.). Community or advocacy activities on a local, state, or national level are examples of ways that families might demonstrate this purpose larger than themselves.

Ability to deal with crises in a positive manner. All families face crises, to a lesser or greater degree than others. Part of dealing with a crisis lies in its very definition. Something that one family deems a crisis, another family may view as more routine. No matter how a family defines a crisis, strong families handle the stressors that they face in a positive way. This often means by coming together and supporting one another. For example, when a family member is diagnosed with a serious illness, others provide comfort and assistance with pressing responsibilities. Strong families deal with crises in ways that maintain their strengths in that they continue to spend time together, albeit the way they spend time might reduce leisure and increase the time spent working together.

The family strengths approach provides information about what makes a family healthy. Olson and DeFrain (1994) note that many of the strengths listed previously can be placed in context with the three dimensions of the family circumplex model. Commitment and spending time together are related to family togetherness or cohesion; ability to deal with crises and spirituality facilitate a family's flexibility; and appreciation for one another and effective interaction are aspects of the communication dimension. Early childhood teachers should note that research supports the presence of all of these characteristics in strong families. Teachers can best use this information by supporting families who engage in activities that exemplify these factors rather than criticizing families for a lack of any of these strengths. In some communities, for example, many families attend religious services on a particular night of the week. When teachers are aware of this, they may choose to assign homework on a schedule that supports this practice.

All research perspectives on family strengths indicate that understanding both family relationships and family interactions or behaviors are essential in understanding strong families. Olson (1989) delineated types of interactions that have been described for functional (versus dysfunctional) families. Figure 4–4 provides a list and explanation of eight kinds of interactions. 2, 6

Figure 4–4   Characteristics of functional families.

Family Pride—Families are unified and loyal; they view their family positively and cooperate with one another.

Family Support—Families spend time together and provide love and support to each member for a growth-producing environment.

Cohesion—In addition to cooperating with each other, members respect one another's individuality. Family members are interdependent without being too dependent or too independent.

Adaptability—In the face of change, families can adapt. Tasks may rotate or are completed by those who have time and skill.

Communication—Both sharing of self and careful listening to others is important.

Social Support—Family members accept responsibility for supporting community endeavors.

Values—Families who function well know their values and they work to practice and live by them.

Joy—Families know how to have fun together.

© Cengage Learning

---

66 Among professionals and scholars who focus on the well-being of children, it is widely recognized that children do not do well unless families do well, and that families do not do well unless communities do well. 99

—**Besaw, Kalt, Lee, Smith, Wilson, and Zemler, 2004**

DIVERSITY IN PRACTICE   Although some recent efforts have been made to include diverse families in research that examines family strengths and functionality, more information is needed about families of different cultures, ethnicities, and structures. One recent report (Besaw, Kalt, Lee, Smith, Wilson and Zemler 2004) provides some insight into "family strengthening in Indian America." Not surprisingly, given the importance of understanding any family in context, recent evidence points to the need to emphasize Native self-determination; that is, a plan for tribes to take control of policies and programs for supporting their families. In this vein, one of the most important aspects for strengthening Native American families is attending to the sheer diversity among the hundreds of existing tribes.

Governmental efforts to create one-size-fits-all policies for Native Americans have failed for decades. For education professionals to understand why these programs have failed and what plans might work for effectively supporting strong Native families, it is vital that they become aware of two factors. First, educators must understand that the U.S. Constitution views each tribe as sovereign, just as each state and the nation is sovereign. Next, it is essential that educators become aware of the tremendous amount of oppression and discrimination faced by Native Americans, both historically and in the present. "Romanticizing tribal spirituality and culture or seeing it as solely historical is dehumanizing and a source of countless missteps in coming to a full understanding of the nuances of the complicated ecological environment of Indian families and communities" (Besaw et al. 2004). Culminating conclusions in this report are:

1. Effective programs and policies for strengthening Native American families are self-determined.
2. Leadership can emerge from multiple levels of tribal society.
3. Family-strengthening programs and policies must have buy-in from both the tribal community and the formal leadership of the tribe.
4. Effective family-strengthening initiatives are institutionalized with the tribal government.
5. Effective family-strengthening initiatives have a spiritual core based on the tribe's spiritual practices and beliefs.
6. Effective family-strengthening initiatives are clearly based on cultural practices of the specific tribe.
7. Effective family-strengthening initiatives focus on multiple systems, including individuals, families, and the tribe.
8. Effective family-strengthening initiatives openly strengthen social networks for both children and families.
9. Effective family-strengthening initiatives purposefully invest in the professional skills of trained tribal staff.

This report provides some greatly needed information about specific concerns related to policies for strengthening Native American families. Clearly, however, more such information is needed to most effectively support all families. Viewing the needs of families through various ecological or systems approaches, such as the authors of this report have done, appears to be a constructive tool for both researchers and practitioners who are in positions to influence family strengths.

What Factors Support Family Strengths?

DAP Because we know that young children are dependent on their families and that families have a tremendous impact on child development, it behooves early childhood professionals to foster ways in which the larger society might support specific factors related to strong families. Further, the family support movement (Kagan and Weissbourd 1994) emphasizes that all families have strengths and all families need support. Looking for and supporting families' strengths, even in troubled families, is a useful strategy for early childhood teachers as they work to establish family-school partnerships.

Viewing the need to support strong families and healthy children as an economic imperative, the Family Strengthening Policy Center has identified three fundamental elements for success:

1. Loving, nurturing relationships
2. Financial stability
3. Positive connections to people and organizations in communities

In their call for national systemic change in human services, including education, a quote from the Annie E. Casey Foundation is acknowledged as a strong summary of existing evidence: "Children do better when their families are strong, and families do better when they live in communities that help them to succeed" (Family Strengthening).

An emphasis on assets that families need in order to provide the three fundamental elements for successful children sheds light on effective approaches for strengthening families. Since lower income children are at risk for not being prepared for kindergarten, lower income children are less likely to have safe schools and neighborhoods and are less likely to meet a variety of measures of academic success. Financial stability is a necessary asset for families. Families who are able to save sufficient finances for unforeseen crises are more likely to be able to care for children's well-being. Related assets that are known to assist families' financial stability include literacy, good employment skills, and reliable transportation. DAP

Consider This

How might national policies best help to strengthen families? Be sure to consider necessary assets.

The Center for the Study of Social Policy (CSSP) recently organized an initiative based on current research and known as "Strengthening Families." This project emphasizes five protective factors that serve as indicators against the likelihood of child abuse and neglect in families. Further, the CSSP has drawn strategies from research utilized by early childhood programs that have been shown to foster these five protective factors. Knowledge that early childhood teachers have an essential role in reducing child abuse and neglect provides strong support for high-quality early care and education programs (www.strengtheningfamilies.net).

The five protective factors noted by CSSP are:

- Parental resilience—how parents cope with challenges
- Social connections—various individuals and groups who provide emotional support and assistance to parents

- Knowledge of parenting and child development—accurate information about how parenting strategies impact children's development

- Concrete support in times of need—financial security

- Social and emotional competence of children—children's ability to get along with others and to express feelings in appropriate ways.

DAP Seven strategies that are incorporated into high quality early care and education have been found to clearly support these protective factors in families: valuing and supporting parenting adults in families; facilitating friendships and support systems; strengthening effective parenting approaches; referring families to services and opportunities provided in communities; responding to families as they face crises; and, finally, responding to early warnings of abuse and neglect as they are observed (www.strengtheningfamilies.net). **DAP**

Do This

Discuss the early childhood program strategies that positively influence family protective factors. List concrete examples of ways that programs practice each of the seven strategies.

Building Family Strengths

http://www.clemson.edu/fyd/bfs.htm

Creating a Strong Family

http://www.extension.unl.edu
Click on "family"; click on "publications"; click on "families"

Family Strengthening Writ Large: On Becoming a Nation That Promotes Strong Families and Successful Youth

http://www.nassembly.org/fspc

Family Support and Children's Mental Health

http://www.rtc.pdx.edu/

From Family Stress to Family Strengths

http://www.cdc.gov
Type in "nasd"; type in "family strengths"

Strengthening Families. Center for the Study of Social Policy

http://www.strengtheningfamilies.net

Resilient Children

naeyc 1 Since the mid-1980s, researchers have concluded that some children, even in the face of great adversity, manage to overcome the odds against them to become relatively healthy, functioning adults. These **resilient children** exhibit "good developmental outcomes despite high-risk status, sustained competence under stress, and recovery from trauma" (Werner 1995). Most of the research in this area consists of studies of children from one or more of the following situations:

- Families of chronic poverty
- Parent(s) suffering from serious psychopathology
- Families that separated in various ways or for various reasons
- Children lacking nurturing (Werner 1995)

Although opinions differ about the definition of at-risk children, a great deal of consensus exists that for many, they are "growing up in families with low incomes, have parent/caregivers with low educational attainment levels, or live in disadvantaged neighborhoods" (Family Strengthening). When more than one of the risk factors is present, children are more likely to lack the support they need to become productive adults.

Center on the Family

http://uhfamily.hawaii.edu

Family Resilience

http://outreach.missouri.edu/
Type "family resilience" into the Search field

Family Works, Inc.

http://www.familyworksinc.com/

Project Resilience

http://www.projectresilience.com/

By reviewing several longitudinal studies, Werner (1995) notes factors that seem to be consistent for **at-risk children** who proved to be resilient. An important element appears in the resilient child's temperamental makeup. They are easy children: active, affectionate, and good-natured. These children seem to bring forth positive responses from the adults who care for them, and they learn early to cope with adversity both by being self-sufficient and asking for help when they need it (Werner 1995).

In addition to the child's temperament, family and community components also offer protection for at-risk children. A child who lives amid a great deal of family discord but still builds a relationship with at least one family member who is emotionally competent, stable, and willing to nurture that child, is more likely to become resilient.

Further, community members, especially teachers, are often seen as a source of support when at-risk children are facing crises. Characteristics of these teachers are that they "listened to the children, challenged them, and rooted for them" (Werner 1995). Early childhood teachers often are in a prime position to assist and support children who live with so much adversity. Note that the teachers who help resilient children listen to them and demonstrate concern in their ongoing role as educators. Best educational practices in early childhood education call for such behaviors in teacher-child relationships. **naeyc** 1

Continuing interest in the study of resilience in children is providing access to more details about how families and schools can support children's inner strength to cope with challenges they face (Brooks and Goldstein 2001). Based on current research, Brooks and Goldstein explain 10 ways adults can help children be more resilient or be "can-do kids":

1. Respond to children empathically. Let them know that you understand their point of view, even when you are attempting to teach them another perspective.

2. Talk with children respectfully. Not only will children give you more attention when you are respectful with them, but they will also experience an excellent model for communicating effectively with others.

3. Be flexible, especially in order to find more effective ways of guiding children's behavior.

4. Provide some time for undivided attention for each child. If this is difficult, build it into your schedule.

5. Be accepting of each child's unique interests and personalities.

6. Create opportunities for children to contribute to the family or classroom. This teaches both helpfulness and responsibility.

7. Call mistakes "learning opportunities." Make it clear that avoiding mistakes also means fewer opportunities to learn something new.

8. Become aware of each child's strengths and help each child to see her own strengths as well as those of others.

9. Encourage children to solve problems and make decisions. Be present to support them in this process as well as afterwards.

10. Use discipline strategies that teach children self-control.

These 10 suggestions might be implemented differently by parents or other family members than by early childhood professionals. Yet, the spirit of each idea can easily be practiced in both home and school settings.

Consider This

How might you, as a teacher, incorporate practices that are reflective of the 10 suggestions for building resilience in children?

FAMILY FUNCTIONS

naeyc 2 The family is the essential unit for meeting several functions. It has been common for family sociologists to refer to seven traditional functions of the family: economic, prestige and status, education, protection, religion, recreation, and affection (Eshelman 1988). Figure 4–5 provides a definition for each of these functions.

These functions have been viewed as important since at least the 1930s. As society changes, the precise view of each family function also changes. (For many, these changes evidence a diminished importance of family functions and, in turn, the demise of the family, and perhaps of all society. However, a long-range view of functional changes actually shows the family as a strong unit.) Today, family science experts still view these seven functions as important for maintaining strong families. Note that descriptions and examples for each of the functions have changed over time. These changes are delineated in Figure 4–6.

Families are able to meet functions in a variety of ways, and a family's structure does not determine its ability to meet functions. For example, specific demonstrations of affection vary from family to family. One family may express its love with words and another with actions. Some families show love through kisses and others through helping with chores. Further, families of a variety of structures can meet the functions as fully as any other family. It is possible for single parents to

| Figure 4–5 | Family functions. |

Economic—Families met their own economic needs; they produced what they needed to consume.

Prestige and Status—The family name was important.

Education—The family provided education, especially in the form of job training and household tasks.

Protection—Adults provided safety for children, and adult children took over this role as parents aged.

Religion—Religious practices in families included grace at meals and daily scripture reading.

Recreation—Home provided relaxation and physical activity for enjoyment.

Affection—Love was shared between spouses and through procreation of children.

© Cengage Learning

Figure 4–6 Family functions, past and present.

ECONOMIC
Past—Provided for all needs, goods, and services
Present—Purchase many goods and services

PRESTIGE AND STATUS
Past—Family name
Present—Profession, job responsibility, promotions, social opportunities in community

EDUCATION
Past—Taught children at home, especially for vocational and household responsibilities
Present—Provide access to education, pay for it, advocate for and attain special services, form partnerships with educators

PROTECTION
Past—Fathers especially were to keep the family physically safe
Present—Choice of neighborhood, related to economic function

RELIGION
Past—Practices in the home
Present—Greater responsibility of religious institutions and society to instill spirituality and morality

RECREATION
Past—Activities and fun planned at home with families
Present—Community-oriented sports, arts, nature, parks, and other activities

AFFECTION
Past—Love shown through nurturance
Present—Love shown by providing of "wants" and through various means of caring

© Cengage Learning

meet all of the functional needs for their families, just as it is possible for a two-parent family or a blended family to do so. Essentially, the structure of the family does not indicate whether family functions are or will be met. However, it is more likely that families with greater resources, whether human or physical, may be able to do so more readily. Family-friendly macrosystems will attempt to address issues so that all families are capable of meeting all functions. **naeyc** 2

Historical and Contemporary Purposes of Families

Beliefs about family functions are often based on history or tradition, but as society changes the ways in which families fulfill functions also change. Consider the function of education. In earlier times, the family was the primary educator, not only for infants and very young children but also frequently for adolescents, who

were taught the family business or trade as well as the tasks of caring for the home and family. Today, more than half of all families rely on out-of-home care for their babies during the first year of life. Many families seek some form of preschool education for children between the ages of three and five years, and nearly every child who is eligible attends kindergarten. Despite the home schooling movement in the United States, the vast majority of school-age children receive their elementary and secondary education at public or private schools. Further, many adolescents and young adults receive their career training outside the home. And, arguably, little attention or priority is given to youth regarding skills needed to care for homes and families.

Children, Youth & Family Consortium
http://www.cyfc.umn.edu
Forum on Child and Family Statistics
http://www.ChildStats.gov

So, even though the specific tasks of the education function have changed over several generations, families still must engage in this function by seeking and providing education for their children. When families need child care services for their infants and toddlers, they must choose from the available options those that best suit the needs of their family and their child. Some families choose to live in particular cities or neighborhoods because of the schools their children would attend there. And, frequently, parents and other family members pay for or assist and support students in their postsecondary education. Thus, many families continue to fulfill their function as their children's educators, but the ways in which they do so are very different from the ways of families in the past.

Galinsky and David (1988) quote Urie Bronfenbrenner regarding the connection among child care, families, and work: "One of the most important elements of good quality, and one that is not usually discussed, is the importance of linkages between the family, the day care, and the world of work. If the child care enhances the power of family, there are excellent results for the child. If the family is undermined, then the outcome is not beneficial for the child." This comment makes it clear that systems of work, family, and child care affect one another and that the outcomes for children are very predictable. When workplaces and educational settings hold families in high regard—and let them know it in a variety of ways—children benefit. Conversely, it is also important to note that children may be harmed when workplaces and educational institutions do not honor families.

Teachers have helped children by listening to them and demonstrating concern.

Causes of Change in Family Functions

As changes occur in the systems beyond the microsystem, families need to accommodate to the larger society. For example, economic changes in the United States have affected many families by creating a need for two incomes. Along with the economic changes, a social change has occurred: young adults expect to have many of the luxuries with which they grew up and credit is readily available. At the same time, child care is more available than it was a generation ago. The complex interaction of these changes has affected the decisions that families make about work as well as decisions relating to the care and education of their children.

Family Law

In *The Rights of Families*, Guggenheim, Lowe, and Curtis (1996) provide current interpretations and details regarding family law. Included in this guidebook are

DAP Many early childhood programs include the idea of empowering parents as a goal in their family involvement plan. The Cornell Empowerment Group defines *empowerment* as "an intentional, ongoing process centered in the local community, involving mutual respect, critical reflection, caring, and group participation, through which people lacking an equal share of valued resources gain greater control over those resources" (Dean 1991). This group led a program for child caregivers and parents of children in child care that instructed participants in effective interpersonal communication, using skills such as active listening, assertiveness, and conflict resolution. Their work supports the conclusion that development of effective interpersonal skills is an important process for empowering parents. More information about interpersonal communication is discussed in Chapter 8. **DAP**

Consider This

- In addition to the economy, availability of credit, and the existence of child care, what other factors can you attribute to recent changes in family functions?

- How have functions changed just since you were a young child? Interview those in the previous two generations to gain firsthand information about how family functions have changed over that period of time.

- Speculate about some of the causes of these changes, especially those that occur beyond the microsystem.

Strong families enjoy one another's company and express affection for one another.

the following topics: divorce and child custody, child support, property division, gay and lesbian families, adoption, and child abuse and neglect. In the introduction, the authors make an important point regarding the unique American viewpoint of those who advocate for public policies that support young children and families. They note that even more critical to the well-being of children and families, both historically and today, is the notion of being "free from unjustified governmental interference." They go on to explain:

66 This is, in essence, a "hands off" view of family law, one that focuses heavily on a family's procedural rights. It is very different from other countries' conception of family rights, which reflect their society's commitment to the well-being of children and their families. Unlike the United States, many countries around the world believe that families need positive support in the form of paid childcare leave, national health insurance, subsidized day care, free universal preschool, child allowances, child support assurance, and free (or low-cost) higher education. The absence of such substantive rights for families in the United States is the subject of ongoing debate. 99

Do This

- Consider both the U.S. "hands-off" perspective on family law and the view that families need positive support as noted by Guggenheim, Lowe, and Curtis (1996).
- Make a list of the pros and cons for each perspective.
- Share and discuss your list with a partner or in a small group.

It is interesting to note that the U.S. Constitution makes no mention of children and families, yet courts have inherently upheld the rights of families. Two concepts that have been held in high esteem by the legal system include the **right of family integrity** and the **primacy of parental rights**. The right of family integrity includes the legal basis for parents to bear and rear children and to guide those children according to their own beliefs. The primacy of parental rights upholds the strict limits of the Constitution to interfere with family life (Guggenheim, Lowe, and Curtis, 1996).

Some of the more common issues that are addressed in the family court system include:

- Marriage, civil unions, domestic partnerships, and prenuptial agreements
- Family issues requiring legal intervention, such as domestic violence, paternity, adoption, child

abduction, adultery, bigamy, polygamy, incest, and orders of protection

- Issues around terminating marriage, such as legal separation, divorce, annulment, child custody and visitation, child support, alimony, and property settlements

Do This

Select one of the three categories of common issues addressed in family court and discuss related current topics that you have heard or read about, including areas of concern that might arise for early childhood professionals.

Family Support America
http://www.familysupportamerica.org

FAMILY STRUCTURE

naeyc 2 Another dimension of understanding families is structure. *Structure* refers to family membership. Some cultures define the family more in terms of the **nuclear family**: parents and their children. Others emphasize the extended family, including additional generations from both parents' families, their families of orientation or origin, as well as siblings and their families of procreation. Figure 4–7 defines these terms. For decades in the United States, family structures have most commonly leaned towards a nuclear model. Economic changes impacting families with young children that have occurred in the late twentieth and early twenty-first centuries have contributed to an increase in families who are living with three generations in their homes. Other factors leading to multiple-generation households include the immigration

Figure 4–7	Terms related to family structure.

Nuclear Family—Any two or more persons of the same or adjoining generation related by blood, marriage, or adoption sharing a common residence.

Extended Family—A family in which two or more generations of the same kin live together (extension beyond the nuclear family).

Family of Orientation—The nuclear family into which one was born and reared (consists of self, siblings, and parents).

Family of Procreation—The nuclear family formed by marriage (consists of self, spouse, and children).

© Cengage Learning

of families whose cultures prefer living together and the longevity of aging parents who move in with their children and grandchildren (Yarett, 2009). It will be interesting to see if this old model is renewed as a more common configuration for families in the coming age.

Family pride is shown in portraits.

Understanding variations in family forms helps teachers plan for children realistically and individually.

Family structure refers to the makeup of a family: who are the members of a particular family? Traditionally, in our culture, when families are depicted, it is common to see a mom, dad, son, daughter, and perhaps a pet or two. The concept of this ideal family structure is, of course, that the family has been stable and that the children are biological offspring of both parents. In reality, a depiction of such a family in the United States may be that of a blended family, with a child brought to this current household by each parent. Of concern to child advocates is not so much a marriage of parents as stability of relationships for children. "The bottom line is that while marriage is good for kids, it's best when it results in a stable home" (Wingert 2009). Current practices of parents re-partnering quickly after splitting with a previous partner raise concerns about children's ability to form long-lasting positive relationships that are necessary for healthy development. "Many of the problems faced by America's children stem not from parents marrying too little but rather too often" (Cherlin, 2009). **naeyc** 2

Variations in Family Form

We tend to assume that Figure 4–8 realistically depicts a traditional family. Consider some other possibilities, however: that the adult male is the mother's brother; that the adult female is the father's sister; that the children are cousins being reared in the same home; that the family is blended. The possibilities are endless. How many more possibilities can you produce? The same is true for the members of families depicted in Figure 4–9.

Figure 4–8 People tend to assume that this is a realistic depiction of a traditional family.

Figure 4–9   Structures of families take many forms.

![Diversity in Practice icon]

DIVERSITY IN PRACTICE   Family structure in the United States has changed considerably, as has been previously noted, and it continues to undergo many changes. The modern realities of diverse family structures, the dynamic nature of all families, and changes in societal trends and values have led scholars to categorize contemporary families as postmodern (Cole, Clark, and Gable, n.d.). Some of the many variations in structure that characterize U.S. families with young children include:

> *Married nuclear families* (spouses and child or children)
> *Cohabiting families* (unmarried partners and child or children)
> *Single-parent families* (unmarried parent and child or children)
> *Joint-custody families* (divorced or never married parents sharing custody of child or children)
> *Blended or stepfamilies* (spouses or unmarried partners with child or children from previous relationships)
> *Same-sex partner families* (lesbian or gay parents and their child or children)

Do This

As you prepare for your career in early childhood education:

- Consider the list of services mentioned in the quote on page 95 (paid child care leave, national health insurance, and so on).
- Note the advantages and disadvantages to families with young children if all services were available to families in the United States.
- Interview a variety of citizens about their viewpoints related to one or more of these services.
- Analyze the responses you receive from your interviews. Do your responses support the notion of individuals wanting to be free from governmental interference?

Multigeneration families (parent or parents reside with their parent(s) and their child or children)

Grandparent-led families (grandparent(s) parenting their grandchildren)

Note that these variations are not mutually exclusive. For example, same-sex parent families might also be blended; grandparent-led families might also be multigenerational, with children's aunts and uncles residing with them.

Despite the tremendous changes to family structure that occurred during the last half of the twentieth century and that continue to evolve into the twenty-first, the traditional family form often is still idealized in our society. The reality, however, is that this form is not, in fact, best for everyone. As early childhood educators, we sometimes forget this truth when making judgments about individual families. A case in point follows. One primary grade teacher had the responsibility to assign children in the first grade among four classrooms. In her own classroom, she placed only children who were living with both of their biological parents. One might say that she was aware of the research indicating that children who live in single-parent families are at greater risk for intellectual problems (National Commission on Children 1993) and that she held an idealized view of traditional families. The surprising point in this story is that this teacher herself had been a single parent and successfully reared a son. Discuss ethical concerns that might exist in regard to this situation.

Less than one decade into the twenty-first century, the U.S. Census Bureau announced a major shift in that fewer than half of households are now made up of married couples. Although this percentage has been marked by many sources, experts note that this decline began in the 1970s and is not indicative of a devaluation of marriage. Rather, society's greater acceptance of cohabitation for engaged or otherwise committed couples is a relevant factor (American Community Survey 2009). Percentages at any given time provide only a snapshot of society. Viewing marriage dynamically, on the other hand, allows us to see that over half of these couples marry within five years of living together (Smock 2000).

naeyc 2 Legal rulings in favor of same-sex marriage in some states may impact marital statistics. In 2004, Massachusetts was the first state to issue marriage licenses to same-sex partners. Since then, several additional states have passed legislation in support of same-sex marriage: Connecticut, California, Iowa, Vermont, Maine, and New Hampshire. California's law is being contested through the court system. (National Conference of State Legislators 2009). More recent additions

to states that now provide for same-sex marriage laws include New York, Washington, and the District of Columbia. Although the New Jersey legislature recently passed a same-sex marriage law, the governor has vetoed the legislation.

Legal issues continue to be raised in light of movements for states to address same-sex marriage. Many states have banned same-sex marriage and have legislated the definition of marriage to focus only on one man and one woman. Some states that have not conceded to same-sex marriage have passed legislation that authorizes civil unions. Although many issues and concerns about same-sex marriage or civil unions are playing out in the political realm, lives of families—parents, children, extended families—are affected by particular laws of each state. Concerns relate to definition of "next of kin" in matters of health care and finances. Legal parentage is influenced by state statutes that authorize or ban same-sex marriage or civil unions.

Do This

Conduct a Web search of current state laws regarding same sex marriage and civil unions. Note that such laws are changing at a rather rapid pace, so information may become dated.

Although it is true that a strong marriage often provides a positive environment for rearing children, it is not the only family structure that accomplishes this goal. While it is true that children in single-parent families are at greater risk, many of them have nurturing parents who are meeting their needs (National Commission on Children 1993). Four important components of family structure have been identified by family researchers, regardless of the presence of a married couple (Ihinger-Tallman and Pasley 1987):

1. **Division of labor.** Who is responsible for each family function?
2. **Rules of behavior.** What are the expectations for interacting with family members in everyday life?

Do This

For each of the four components listed, give examples from your family of origin.

For each of the four components, give examples from your family of procreation or your expectations for your future family.

Share your examples in a small group. Discuss commonalities and differences you find within your group.

3. **Family roles.** What behavior is expected for each position in the family? What does the mother do? The father? Each child? Additional adults?

4. **Power hierarchy.** Adult family members typically have more power than children. What happens when this is not so? How might another generation of adults living together influence the power hierarchy? **naeyc** 2

Essential to understanding family structure is the realization that it is dynamic—frequently changing. Whereas some families maintain the same structure for several years or even a decade or more at a time, all families undergo both loss and gain of members. Losses occur as a result of death, marital dissolution, or relocation. Families gain members through births, adoptions, marriages, and remarriages. **naeyc** 1 Sturgess, Dunn, and Davies (2001) examined young children's (ages four to seven years) perceptions of their relationships with family members and found that some children adjust more easily to changes in their family situations than do others. A key factor in this adjustment is related to children who have high levels of warmth in relationships with their mothers. Comparisons were made among children from non-stepfamilies, the biological children of the father from stepfamilies, and the stepchildren of the father from stepfamilies. A majority of children in non-stepfamilies (71 percent) and in biological children of father stepfamilies (62 percent) felt very close to their fathers. However, only 16 percent of stepchildren in stepfather families felt very close to their stepfathers. This study found further that those children who did not feel close to their resident fathers demonstrated more externalizing problems or acting out behaviors. Thus, even though educators can expect that the structures of postmodern families will continue to be dynamic, we must give attention to children who have difficulty with such transitions.

In addition to this research about the effect of parent-child relationships on children's adjustment during family transitions, sibling relationships also affect children's adjustment (Deater-Deckard, Dunn, and Lussier 2002). Negative sibling relationships in some families were found to be related to difficulties in adjustment, with biological siblings in single-mother families having the most negative relationships. More attention must be given to negative sibling relationships when children demonstrate difficulty with emotional adjustment. **naeyc** 1

Although all families experience changes in structure over time, stability of such changes is a factor that impacts children and their family relationships. When adults enter and exit children's lives at a fairly rapid pace, a lack of stability often poses a greater concern than change itself. When children's living arrangements and nurturing relationships are unstable, they have a higher risk of negative outcomes in all areas of development. Current research is being done in this area so that predictions can be made and family transitions might be better understood.

The Meaning of Birth Order

One segment of family structure that has been of interest to researchers, families, and early childhood educators for many years is that of **birth order** of siblings. "When differences in birth order are found, they usually are explained by variations in interactions with parents and siblings associated with the unique experiences of being in a particular position in the family" (Santrock 1994).

Some behaviors have been found to apply more to firstborn children, regardless of the number of siblings that have followed that child's birth:

- More adult-oriented
- More helpful
- More conforming
- More anxious
- More self-controlled
- Less aggressive

There is general consensus among child developmentalists that the presence of these characteristics is related to the demands and expectations placed on children by their parents. Being in the first position seems to be related to both higher levels of achievement and guilt, probably because the parents have some time to focus only on this firstborn. Research on only children has dispelled the popular myth that they are typically bratty and self-centered and has found instead that, most often, only children have the positive characteristics of firstborns (Santrock 1994).

Although popular notions exist about how middle children and youngest children are expected to behave, many researchers believe that birth order alone is an insufficient cause for behaviors. Following are some factors that are not considered in oversimplified beliefs about the birth-order explanation for behavior:

- Number of siblings
- Age of siblings
- Spacing of siblings
- Gender of siblings
- Temperament of siblings
- Individual characteristics of siblings such as talents, skills, and interests
- Health of siblings such as chronic conditions, disabilities, or life-threatening or terminal illness

Although one frequently hears that firstborns possess characteristics of perfectionism and reliability, that middle children avoid all conflict and are very loyal to friends, and that youngest children are irresponsible and charming, these complex character traits are influenced by much more than the factor of birth order.

naeyc 1 Thus, although it is important to understand family dynamics, including that of birth order, it is best to not blame or credit a child's birth order for a set of behaviors. Sibling relationships, for instance, are an equally important factor in understanding children and their families. Other factors that are known to intervene in any sense of typical birth order effects include the presence of abusive or neglectful parenting, the total number of children in a family, and the spacing of children in the family. Detractors of current birth order theory indicate that research methodology needs to be transformed from comparisons among families to an exhaustive examination within families. Comparisons must be made among each child within a family and then repeated with a multitude of other families (Kluger, 2007). Until such studies are complete, our understanding about effects of birth order remain more anecdotal than empirical.

On the other hand, some situations that we can be sure of are:

1. Living in a family is a unique experience that no two people perceive in exactly the same way.

2. A person is more strongly influenced by his family than any other group or system.

3. A person's birth order is one characteristic that typically has a lifelong effect on who that person becomes.

4. Regardless of one's position in a family, there are many variables that influence a person—both positively and negatively (Graham 2005). **naeyc** 1

Consider This

Consider your own position in your family constellation. Now, reflect on how you might be both similar to and different from others who have the same place in their families. What factors do you believe might contribute to such similarities and differences?

Birth Order Affects Career Interests
http://www.osu.edu
Type "birthorder" into the Search field under Locate

Birth Order and Personality Differences
http://www.encouragingleadership.com/

The Effect of Birth Order on Intelligence
http://www.indiana.edu
Type "intelligence and birth order" in the Search field

APPLICATION OF CHAPTER INFORMATION

Family Support

It is important that we use research on family strengths, family functions, and family structure when planning family support policies and programming. However, we also need to use information to help us keep open minds about the widely diverse structures of families. Being aware of the risk that divorce places on children, for example, we might be tempted to judge parents who divorce as being self-centered and not caring about their children. When we do not take all of the systems into consideration, it is easy to blame individual families for their inability to maintain a marriage or provide the best home for their children. But even if this assignment of blame were appropriate or accurate, early childhood teachers do nothing to help children by judging their families.

© Cengage Learning/ECE Photo Library.

When adults in the family provide loving care to children, it matters little whether they are parents, grandparents, aunts, uncles, or friends.

Thus, it is crucial that we understand the effect of larger systems on families and children. One of the most important of these larger systems is economics. Women with college degrees continue to earn less than men with high school diplomas. As a result, "children in one-parent families are six times more likely to be poor than children who live with two parents" (National Commission on Children 1993). After a divorce, women generally are worse off economically and men generally are significantly better off. Taking all of these facts into consideration, it is clear that divorce alone is not why so many young children are living in poverty. Inequality in the economic system must be factored into our understanding of this gloomy picture.

In the booklet *Strengthening and Supporting Families*, the National Commission on Children (1993) notes, "decisions about marriage, divorce, childbearing, and parenting are intensely personal, but they are also influenced by cultural messages and by friends, family, and social institutions." Consider the bioecological systems in Bronfenbrenner's theory: they indicate, as does the preceding quote, that all segments of society have some responsibility for supporting families. As early childhood educators, we know that the most important reason for this is that all children need and deserve homes filled with love and support.

Early Childhood Programs

When early childhood teachers understand that all families have strengths and all families need support, they realize that family structure is less critical than the accomplishment of family functions. Young children can be nurtured in many variations of family structures, and when adults in a family provide loving care to children, it matters little whether they are parents, grandparents, aunts, uncles, friends, or others.

66 Building and maintaining positive relationships with families must resonate throughout programs—in the physical environment, in activities, in administrative and policy guidelines, and in programmatic features. 99

—Barbara Bowman, 1994

As specifics about how families fulfill the requisite functions evolve, so will the role of early childhood educators. In all early education settings, professionals must provide both care and education. As the saying goes, "We cannot educate young children without caring for them and we cannot care for young children without educating them." In support of this creed, both Bettye Caldwell and Magda Gerber have used the term *educare* for the primary function of early childhood education programs.

 Communicating with Parents Using Technology

Visit the Education CourseMate website at www.CengageBrain.com to view the Video Case, and then respond to the following items:

- Analyze the video examples of technology for communicating with parents in relation to family strengths, functions, and structures. What should teachers consider about each family as technology is implemented for communication?

- Discuss ways that different families might view communicating with teachers through technology.

Summary and Conclusions

Early childhood practitioners must understand both family functions and family structure. Whereas many family functions have remained stable over time, the nature of those functions changes as society changes. It is because of societal changes that many families now seek to enroll their children in quality early childhood programs before their children are of traditional school age. Family structure—the makeup of a family—influences how families manage their responsibilities. Single-parent families, by their nature, manage differently from most two-parent families. Blended families face challenges unfamiliar to original families of procreation.

Research points to certain characteristics that relate to strong families. When early childhood teachers apply their knowledge of these characteristics, the resulting program decisions and policies will then support families. It behooves professionals in early childhood education to provide support for the strengths in all families. Such support increases the likelihood of successful partnerships between home and school.

Theory into Practice Suggestions (TIPS)

- Review the Web sites found in this chapter. Bookmark them for future use.
- Start a collection of resources related to content of this chapter to use with families for designing programs, conducting conferences, and making referrals.
- Work to increase understanding about the importance of strong families and communities. Be sure to consider multiple factors related to family strengths.
- Advocate for local and national policies that will support strong families.
- Communicate with families about the importance of positive relationships with their children.
- Demonstrate that you value and support the parenting adults in families.
- Facilitate friendships and support systems for families.
- Provide mechanisms that contribute to strengthening effective parenting approaches.
- Refer families to services and opportunities provided in communities.
- Respond by providing resources and information to families as they face crises.
- Respond to early warnings of abuse and neglect by referring to appropriate school personnel or community agencies.
- Advocate for child abuse and neglect prevention.

- Act on the understanding that family structure is less critical than meeting functions performed by families. The aspect of family structure that is important to healthy child development is stability.
- Work with families to help them understand the importance of stable relationships in children's lives.
- Avoid judging families with varying structures or legal status.
- Understand the difference between change in structure and instability.
- Seek ways to support families in meeting functions so that children benefit.
- Apply the 10 strategies that help to support resilience in children.
- Be cautious about oversimplifying characteristics often attributed to birth order. Birth order is only one variable among many that influence one's characteristics.
- Create strategies to form partnerships with *all* families of children that you are teaching.

Applications

1. Review the information about family strengths in this chapter. Thinking about a family that is familiar to you, comment on each of the strengths in relation to that family.

2. List 10 families you know. Create a representation of each family's current structure or the structure when you had contact with them. Compare and contrast the families' structures. How do the variations among the structures of these families seem to affect specific functions of the family as discussed in this chapter?

3. How will you, as an early childhood educator, help ensure positive relationships with families (in the words of Barbara Bowman) through the physical environment, in activities, in administrative and policy guidelines, and in programmatic features?

Questions for Reflection and Discussion

1. How is knowledge about family strengths, functions, and structures useful to early childhood teachers?

2. How do you understand families differently after reading this chapter?

3. How will your teaching of children and working with families differ after reading about and reflecting on family strengths, functions, and structure?

Field Assignments

1. Interview five people in your own generation. Ask them questions about how they view recent changes in the family. Note their comments. Critique the comments based on what you have learned about how changes occur in various levels of societal systems.

2. Create at least 10 different representations of various family structures. Ask five adults to speculate about the relationships among the family members. Share your findings in class.

3. Interview an early childhood teacher about variations in family structure she has observed in the past three years. Ask the teacher to give you approximate percentages of the types of family structures currently in her classroom. Request comments from the teacher about any special or unusual circumstances. *Please note:* no names of families should be elicited for this assignment—respect confidentiality.

References

Ages and Stages Ejournal. n.d. Saskatchewan Psychology Portal. Strengths in families: Accentuating the positive. http://www.sesd.sk.ca/psychology/psych30/ejournalchildhood/agesandstages_families.htm (accessed January 5, 2006).

American Community Survey. 2009. U. S. Census Bureau. http://www.census.gov/acs/www/index.html (accessed May 22, 2009).

Besaw, A., J. P. Kalt, A. Lee, J. Smith, J. B. Wilson, and M. Zemler. 2004. The context and meaning of family strengthening in Indian America. A report to the Annie E. Casey Foundation by The Harvard Project on American Indian Economic Development.

Bowman, B. 1994. Home and school: The unresolved relationship. In *Putting families first: America's family support movement and the challenge of change,* ed. S. L. Kaganand, B. Weissbourd. San Francisco: Jossey-Bass.

Bradt, J. O. 1989. Becoming parents: Families with young children. In *The changing family life cycle,* ed. B. Carter and M. McGoldrick. Needham Heights, MA: Allyn & Bacon.

Bronfenbrenner, U. 1988. Strengthening family systems. In *Making human beings human: Bioecological perspectives on human development,* ed. U. Bronfenbrenner. Thousand Oaks, CA: Sage.

Brooks, R., and S. Goldstein. March 2001. Raising resilient children. *Parent's Magazine.*

Carter, B., and M. McGoldrick. 1989. Overview: The changing family life cycle. In *The changing family life cycle: A framework for family therapy,* ed. B. Carter and M. McGoldrick. Needham Heights, MA: Allyn & Bacon.

Cherlin, A. J. (2009). *The marriage-go-round: The state of marriage and the family in America today.* New York: Random House.

Cole, K. A., J. A. Clark, and S. Gable n.d. Promoting family strengths. University of Missouri Extension, University of Missouri. http://muextension.missouri.edu/xplor/hesguide/humanrel/gh6640.htm (accessed January 5, 2006).

Dean, C. 1991. Bringing empowerment theory home: The Cornell parent-caregiver partnership program. *Networking Bulletin: Empowerment & Family Support* 2: 10–13.

Deater-Deckard, K., J. Dunn, and G. Lussier. 2002. Sibling relationships and social-emotional adjustment in different family contexts. *Social Development* 11: 571–90.

Eshleman, J. R. 1988. *The family: An introduction.* Needham Heights, MA: Simon & Schuster.

Family Strengthening Writ Large: On Becoming a Nation that Promotes Strong Families and Successful Youth. Family Strengthening Policy Center Brief No. 24. http://www.nassembly.org/fspc (accessed May 20, 2009).

Galinsky, E., and J. David. 1988. *The preschool years: Family strategies that work from experts and parents.* New York: Times Books.

Graham, J. 2005. Birth order. Family issues facts: A fact sheet for families and people who work with families. University of Maine Cooperative Extension Bulletin #4359. http://www.umext.maine.edu/onlinepubs/htmpubs/4359.htm (accessed January 5, 2006).

Guggenheim, M., A. D. Lowe, and D. Curtis. 1996. *The rights of families: The authoritative ACLU guide to the rights of family members today.* Carbondale: Southern Illinois University Press.

Ihinger-Tallman, M., and K. Pasley. 1987. *Remarriage.* Newbury Park, CA: Sage.

Kagan, S. L., and B. Weissbourd. 1994. *Putting families first: America's family support movement and the challenge of change.* San Francisco: Jossey-Bass.

Kluger, J. (October 2007). The power of birth order. *Time.*

National Commission on Children. 1993. *Strengthening and supporting families.* Washington, DC: National Commission on Children.

National Conference of State Legislatures. 2009. Same sex marriage, civil unions and domestic partnerships. http://www.ncsl.org/programs/cyf/samesex.htm (accessed May 22, 2009).

Olson, D. H. L., and J. D. DeFrain. 1994. *Marriage and the family: Diversity and strengths.* Mountain View, CA: Mayfield.

Olson, D. H., H. I. McCubbin, H. L. Barnes, M. J. Muxen, A. S. Larsen, and M. A. Wilson. 1989. *Families: What makes them work.* Newbury Park, CA: Sage.

Santrock, J. 1994. *Child development.* Madison, WI: Brown & Benchmark.

Smock, P. 2000. Cohabitation in the United States: An appraisal of research themes, findings, and implications. *Annual Review of Sociology* 26: 1–20.

Stinnett, N. 1979. In search of strong families. In *Building family strengths: Blueprints for action,* ed. N. Stinnett, B. Chesser, and J. DeFrain. Lincoln: University of Nebraska Press.

Strengthening Families. Center for the Study of Social Policy. http://www.strengtheningfamilies.net. Accessed September 12, 2009.

Sturgess, W. J., J. Dunn, and L. Davies. 2001. Young children's perceptions of their relationships with family members: Links with family setting, friendships, and adjustments. *International Journal of Behavioral Development* 25: 521–29.

Werner, E. E. 1995. Resilience in development. *Current Directions in Psychological Science* (June): 81–85.

Wingert, P. (August 24 & 31, 2009). *Newsweek,* p. 54.

Yarett, I. (August 24 & 31, 2009). *Newsweek,* p. 64.

Parenting

OUTLINE

© Cengage Learning/ECE Photo Library.

After reading and reflecting on this chapter, you should be able to:

- Discuss parenthood within the context of bioecological theory **naeyc** 2

- Understand the multiple roles of parents **naeyc** 2

- Explain differences in parenting beliefs **naeyc** 2

- Understand that a variety of adults may serve in a parenting role or parenting support role at some

- point in a child's life (grandparents, child care providers, and others) **naeyc** 2

- Understand the critical role that parenting adults have in children's development **naeyc** 1

Key Terms

adoption
attachment
authoritarian parenting
authoritative parenting
blended families
donor insemination

expressive (role)
indulgent
instrumental (role)
nurturance
parenting
permissive parenting

public policies
spirituality
socialization
uninvolved

THEORETICAL PERSPECTIVES

Bioecological Theory

What makes a parent? The most obvious answer is biology. But beyond the biological connection that most parents have to their infants and children, what contributes to a mother's or father's development as a parent? Bioecological theory explains this in terms of the systems surrounding the parent, including both past systems and current systems.

A great deal of research on **parenting** style and skills shows that parents are very likely to parent the

way they were parented. Thus, parents who were given supportive **nurturance**, care, and guidance have had positive models for parenting their own children in that manner. On the flip side, parents who were denied appropriate nurturance and care, as well as effective guidance, will have to work hard to overcome their experiences and learn to provide a more appropriate and nurturing environment for their children.

naeyc 1 *Microsystem Effects* Parental microsystems, both past and present, affect parents' behaviors with their children. Love and support from the other parent, significant others, extended

105

families, and friends enable parents to do their best for their children. Parental self-esteem is likely to be more positive when caring others provide various forms of support, leading to greater effectiveness in child-rearing. Recent research (Dunifon 2005) has shown that when children of single parents also have a grandparent living in the home, the children's reading scores were higher than those of children living in single-parent homes without a grandparent present. This finding is in contrast to the many studies that have shown children from single parents doing worse academically than those who live with married parents.

As mentioned previously, past microsystems experienced by those in parenting roles also influence their current microsystems in terms of interactions, care, and values regarding their children. Many characteristics from a person's childhood are carried into their roles as parents. For example, parents who grew up in large families may be less likely to have strong boundaries about physical space since they might have shared a bedroom and bathroom and experienced a larger number of family members at the dinner table.

Exosystem and Macrosystem Effects The exosystem and macrosystem also affect parenting. Extended families, workplace stresses and pleasures, neighborhoods, and faith communities can contribute to the challenges and successes of parenting. The economy, the government, and the political climate certainly affect much of what parents are able to do for children. A recent report from the Children's Defense Fund (2001) lists the amounts spent on raising a child to age 18 for two-parent households at various income levels (see Figure 5–1).

Public policies set by federal or state governments can affect parenting. Recent trends to cut welfare services for mothers who stay home to rear their children indicates a change in viewpoint about the role of parents. A generation ago, welfare policies were based on the premise that mothers should stay home to rear their young children. As societal expectations have changed about mothers in the workplace, the views about welfare have changed as well.

Figure 5–1	Differing Costs to Raise a Child Born in 2008 to Age 17 (United States Department of Agriculture, 2009)

Income	Spent on Child
Low	$159,870
Middle	$221,190
High	$366,660

© Cengage Learning

Do This
Go to www.cnpp.usda.gov/Publications/CRC/crc2008.pdf to review variations in family costs to raise children. Discuss with a classmate the implications for children in various levels of family incomes.

66 [T]he United States also takes the lead, among developed nations ...with respect to poverty... [T]he data are consistent with the general trend among economically developed nations: children and families in the United States experience greater environmental stress. Further, many of the problems facing American families are not restricted to particular ethnic or economic subgroups. Rather, these conditions are pervasive, applying across the population spectrum. 99

—**Urie Bronfenbrenner**

Chronosystem Effects Clearly, the chronosystem, or era in which one is parenting, affects parents and their children. In the 1950s and 1960s, most mothers with young children not only stayed home with their children but also were expected to do so by society. Currently, 79 percent of mothers with children under six years of age work outside the home (Children's Defense Fund 2005). This change not only makes parenting very different, but it also makes the kinds of support that families need very different. Many functions that once were accomplished in the home now require external support, most notably care for young children, while any and all adults in the home spend most of their days or nights in the workplace.

Another aspect of the chronosystem's effect on parenting relates to the period of time in a child's development that parenting is being assessed. For instance, effects of parental employment outside the home may be different for infants and for preschoolers. So, the chronosystem includes not only the historical era, but also the developmental period of a child's life. **naeyc** 1

Developmental Contextualism

The developmental contextualist perspective notes that both children and their parents are part of a larger world in which both generations have roles in addition to that of parent and offspring. For example, a parent may also be employee/employer, spouse/partner, sister/brother, friend, community volunteer, and daughter/son. Children may have roles as siblings, students, friends, grandchildren, and nieces/nephews. This theoretical orientation is similar to the bioecological perspective in that multiple layers of systems affect and are affected by individuals. Thus, parenting provides a basis for child development "not through their sole, main, or direct effects on children, but instead, through their embeddedness in a dynamic, multilevel system" (Lerner, Rothbaum, Boulos, and Castellino 2002).

naeyc 2 Understanding parenting as a complex system related to variations in relational processes, individuals, contexts, and time (both historical and developmental) will lead to new methods for data collection and analysis, but perhaps more important may also lead to more effective social policies. In other words, parenting is a process whereby "the parent shapes the child, but part of what determines the way in which parents do this is children themselves" (Lerner et al. 2002). When parents and their children have a good match of expectations and behaviors, parents are less challenged than when expectations and behaviors are disparate. Yet, beyond this match or mismatch, other variables, such as cultural expectations and social supports, must all be factored into the larger picture in order to understand the complex process of parenting. One area of study that relates to this theory is child temperament (or behavioral preferences and actions). Active, autonomous preschoolers seem to be a good fit for many U.S. parents. However, some Latino cultures have expectations that children, no matter the age, should be compliant. In either case, multilayered systems influence parenting practices. **naeyc** 2

Consider This

Consider both your thoughts and your feelings about parents and parenting. What do you believe to be the roles, responsibilities, and rights of parents in a family? How are mothering and fathering similar? How are they different? What are some common stereotypes about mothers and fathers? From where do these stereotypes come? How might the stereotypes be useful or damaging in your work with families of young children?

Courtesy Donna Couchenour.

Parents introduce their young children to community activities.

WAYS TO PARENTHOOD

Biological and Fertility Alternatives

The most common way in which people become parents is through sexual intercourse that results in pregnancy. Sometimes, becoming a parent in this way is planned, and sometimes pregnancies are unplanned. Despite advances in the types and effectiveness of contraception, no method is 100 percent reliable. When sexual partners are married and conceive a child, most people assume that a child was planned. When partners are not married, many assume that the child was not planned. Of course, these assumptions may be incorrect.

Advances in medical technology provide an array of options for people who want to become parents but who, for a variety of reasons, cannot or do not do so through traditional means. Current technological advances provide three alternative ways to reproduce: in vitro fertilization (IVF), **donor insemination**, and egg donation (Golombok 2002).

Reproduction through in vitro fertilization continues to be widely referred to as the procedure that results in so-called test-tube babies. In the in vitro procedure, an egg is fertilized with sperm in a laboratory and the resulting embryo is placed in the mother's uterus. Most in vitro procedures at this time use an egg and sperm from the parents-to-be; however, donated eggs and sperm may also be used. About one in four births occurring from this technique are multiples, usually resulting in twins and sometimes in triplets (Golombok 2002).

In the 1970s, test-tube babies were rare and considered amazing. The first successful in vitro fertilization occurred in England in 1978. Since then, more than 500,000 births from this procedure have occurred around the world. The number of births from in vitro fertilization has increased greatly in the United States from 257 in 1985 to 11,342 in 1995; as of 2008, more than 1 million successful conceptions have occurred (Medical News Today, January 2009). Even with an average cost of more than $12,000 per trial, this alternative has become quite popular with couples who experience fertility problems (Miracle Babies 1998).

The popularity of this alternative fertilization procedure has increased with its greater acceptance, and the number of procedures and live births continues to grow.

❝ When Louise Brown was born at Oldham Hospital near Manchester, England, in July 1978, the world reacted as if she were a creature of science fiction. The first child conceived by in vitro fertilization—that is, by uniting sperm and egg in a glass container— she was instantly known as the test-tube baby. Such was her notoriety that after leaving the hospital she had to be fed at midnight in a car on an empty street near the family's home in Bristol, since throngs of reporters made it impossible to reach the front door. For years neither she nor her working-class parents, Lesley and John Brown, could escape the global spotlight. The unrelenting scrutiny once prompted Brown, now a preschool nurse in Bristol, to admit, "Sometimes I wish it wasn't me." Despite the attention, she has emerged as a healthy, happy young woman. 🙶

—**Miracle Babies, 1998**

Donor insemination, previously referred to as artificial insemination, is a procedure whereby sperm are transferred to the vagina with a syringe. Typically, this procedure is used when male partners are infertile. Lesbian partners also may utilize this procedure when they choose to become parents. Most often with sperm insemination, the birth mother has a genetic link to the child, but the father does not (Golombok 2002).

The newest form of reproductive technology allows infertile women to conceive a child through the use of egg donation. Donated eggs are extracted from the donor through a complicated medical procedure and then fertilized in a laboratory, often with the prospective father's sperm. The fertilized egg is then placed in the birth mother's uterus. In the case of donated eggs, the father typically has a genetic connection to the child, but the mother may not (unless, of course, the egg donor is biologically related to the mother).

Early childhood educators probably are not aware of the conception or birth methods of the children who come to them. However, researchers have had some concern about the effects of various reproductive technologies on parenting capabilities (Golombok 2002). Concerned about the stress that individuals or couples may have experienced due to infertility, as well as the stress caused by the possibility of coping with multiple births, researchers have hypothesized that those who use reproductive technology to become parents may exhibit some dysfunctional or ineffective parenting. However, after reviewing existing studies, Golombok (2002) concludes that "parents of children conceived by assisted reproduction appear to have good relationships with their children, even in families in which one parent lacks a genetic link with the child." Further, the research poses no evidence to indicate that children who have been conceived through these technologies are at any developmental risk. The most salient issue seems to center around parents telling their children about their methods of conception and, if they do tell, when and how they should do so (Golombok 2002).

Today, there are more alternative methods to becoming parents than thought possible even a few decades ago. While many ethical questions persist regarding these methods, those whose dreams of becoming a parent have been answered through medical technology remain appreciative. Technological advances often provide hope for those wishing to conceive or bear a child.

Blended Families

With greater frequency, men and women are parenting children that they conceived and those of their new spouse or partner. This is the case in **blended families**. Each partner in a blended family may bring biological children to the new marriage. The parents in that household then attempt to provide care, nurturance, and guidance to children who may until very recently have been parented by someone else. Of course, parents do not always live in the same household with their children; many parents are carrying out their responsibilities with the added challenge of residing elsewhere.

Hanson, McLanahan, and Thomson (1996) note their puzzlement that the existing research regarding children in stepfamily households shows the absence of "a remarriage benefit." That is, that even though financial and other resources are greater than those in single-parent families, children are not better off. This concern led to the speculation that perhaps children in blended families experience higher levels of conflict than children in two-parent biological families. Their study examined eight variables related to the child's well-being: school performance, grade point average, school behavior problems, loss of temper or bullying others, sadness or withdrawing from others, sociability, initiative, and a global measure of quality of life. Children in their original two-parent families scored significantly higher on all areas of well-being except for grade point average. While these results are not surprising, it was unexpected that children in blended families would not be doing better than those in single-parent families, including in the areas of school performance and behavior problems. Children in single-parent families were significantly more sociable than those in reconstituted families. In an attempt to explain these results, the researchers studied parental conflict. Their results indicate that children in blended families experience higher levels of parental conflict than do other children because they encounter more intrahousehold conflict than children in original families as well as interhousehold conflict, thus having two sources of possible family conflict. This is likely to increase their stress levels and lead to concern about the negative outcomes regarding child well-being noted by the researchers. Understanding this reality may lead to more effective forms of support for children in blended families, including conflict resolution and stress reduction strategies.

Adoption

Some individuals who want to be parents choose **adoption**. Adoption is a legal process that creates a nonbirth family. Following the legal procedures, adoptive parents assume all of the rights and responsibilities held by birth parents (Guggenheim, Lowe, and Curtis 1996). This path to parenthood was popular from 1950 to 1970 but has decreased in popularity since then, due, in part, to greater acceptance by society of single women keeping and raising their children. Available statistics show that 2 percent to 4 percent of families include an adopted child (Guggenheim, Lowe, and Curtis 1996; Rosenberg 1992). In the United States, a little over half of all adopted children are parented by adults who are related to them (Stolley 1993).

It has been commonly believed that adoption of children offered perfect solutions for both the relinquishing family and the adoptive family, as well as for the adopted child. Presumably, everyone's needs are met, and family life can proceed with ease, happily ever after. However, Elinor Rosenberg (1992) has shown that differences exist between biological families and those in the adoption circle. Being aware of and paying attention to these differences can facilitate healthy adjustment by all of the members of the adoption circle: the birth parents, the adoptive parents, and the adopted child.

In an earlier time, a greater number of European-American infants were available for adoption. From the mid-1950s through the early 1970s, about 20 percent of infants of European-American single mothers were given up for adoption; in 1995, only 2 percent of this same category of mothers relinquished their infants (Chandra, Abma, Maza, and Bachrach 1999, as cited in Brodzinsky and Pinderhughes 2002). Several societal factors now exist that have reduced this number. Among the more obvious factors are less negative responses to single parenthood, the availability of contraception, and the legalization of abortion (Brodzinsky and Pinderhughes 2002).

With this decrease in European-American infants available for adoption, families wishing to adopt have moved increasingly to transracial (including children in foster care) and intercountry adoption, as well as to adopting children with identified special needs. Another fairly recent change in adoption practices is the trend to openness in all aspects of the process and policies. Although each of these practices is not without critics, many families and children are reaping the benefits of these changes.

It is important to note that birth parents do not typically see their decision to give up their child as an easy one. They often take advice from others or see adoption as their only viable alternative. Further, they have life cycle issues related to this decision throughout their lives. Some of these issues include secrecy; anniversary dates, such as the child's birthday or the day on which the legal process was concluded; relationships with children born either before or after the adoption; intimate relationships; guilt; and lack of an official or social process for mourning the loss of a child given up for adoption. It is certain that birth parents do not simply relinquish their child and then never look back. To the contrary, they may question the decision they made for the rest of their lives. Rosenberg notes that even into old age, such parents may wonder about the existence of unknown grandchildren. Today, we hear beautiful stories about reunions between birth parents and the children they relinquished. Not all of these stories have happy endings, however. Sometimes, lives become so complicated that families are unable to cope with reunions.

Although early childhood teachers may not be aware if parents that they interact with are birth parents who have relinquished children, teachers are likely to be aware of families who have adopted a child. Even though this may be a sensitive issue for families to share with teachers, due to the differences in biological family and adoptive family issues, it is helpful for teachers to have this information. One of the most common situations adoptive parents face is the realization that they were unable to have biological children. (While this is not always the case, it is true for most adoptive parents.) Coming to terms with this loss can be challenging, and the pain it generates may continue to surface from time to time, especially if the parents' adoptive child is having some difficulty.

Rosenberg (1992) has created five phases for adoptive parenting, from the decision to adopt to the time that an adopted child reaches school age. Each phase has one or more developmental tasks associated with it. In the first phase, deciding to adopt, developmental tasks may include accepting the inability to reproduce, deciding to parent children outside of the bloodline, and deciding on the type of adoption that will be undertaken. The second phase is the adoption process. Tasks for this stage involve making both social arrangements (those relating to family and community) and legal arrangements. The third phase is the actual adoption. The primary developmental task for this phase is accepting a new member into an existing family. The fourth phase occurs during the child's preschool years, and parents' developmental tasks in this phase include acknowledging adoption as a fact in their family and deciding who, when, what, and how to tell about the adoption. The child's school-age years constitute the fifth phase, which requires adoptive parents to acknowledge adoption in the larger community.

Considering the family life cycle approach, adoptive families may engage in all of the usual tasks that are observed in the transition to parenthood and families with infants and young children. However, they have additional issues with which to cope. According to Brodzinsky and Pinderhughes (2002), these issues include:

- Making the decision to adopt
- Adjusting to adoptive parenthood
- Discussing adoption with their child
- Encouraging discussion about the child's birth family
- Supporting the child in coping with adoption-related loss
- Fostering a healthy, positive view about the child's birth and birth family
- Cultivating positive self-esteem in the child
- Assisting the child in the search for identity
- As child gets older, preparing for and providing appropriate assistance in contacting the birth family

> **Do This**
>
> Review the typical life-cycle events and tasks for new families from earlier chapters in this text. Create a chart that demonstrates those changes along with additional challenges for adoptive families, as noted in this chapter. Consider ways that early childhood professionals can provide support and sensitivity to adopted children and families.

Adopted children also have issues that differ from those of birth children. Today, it is common to tell children the story of how they came to be a member of their family. These stories vary greatly for birth children, who hear about how they grew inside a special place in their mother's body, and for adopted children, who are told they were so special that their parents selected them. It can be safely said that all adopted children wonder about their birth parents; some adopted children are articulate and curious enough to engage their adoptive parents in discussion about this, while others are less inclined to be open about their questions, concerns, or desire for information.

These issues may vary for both parents and children in cases of racial or ethnic differences between adoptive parents and adopted children. In a newspaper editorial, Julie Higginbotham, a European-American mother of a Chinese-American daughter, commented on the insensitivity shown by strangers who ask questions and make comments about her daughter that are really none of their business. She has fielded questions such as: "Is she adopted?" "Where is she from?" "Was it really expensive?" The last paragraph of this editorial helps teachers and others to understand how adoptive parents feel about questions or comments that demonstrate such a lack of concern for parents' and children's feelings: "Alice was adopted, once upon a time. But now she is simply my child and our hearts are knit as tightly as any parent and child's can be. Alice is not a public exhibit. She deserves to be protected from adult questions that subtly invalidate her family's right to exist" (Higginbotham 1998).

As teachers of young children, it is important to be sensitive to issues of adopted children and their families. Concern about terminology should be noted by teachers. Rosenberg (1992) tells about one preschooler who thought "put up for adoption" meant that all of the children who were available for adoption were placed on a shelf and waited for their adoptive families. Teachers of young children must understand that as adopted children and their families proceed through the life cycle, new issues are likely to arise that will require understanding on the part of professionals who work with them.

Foster Parents

"Foster parents provide care to children who cannot remain with their families by bringing these children into their homes" (Haugaard and Hazan 2002). From the beginning of the foster parent-child relationship, it is known that the relationship is expected to be temporary. **Temporary**, however, might mean a few days or a few years; the average stay of a child in a foster home is 22 months. The indefinite nature of the situation alone is a source of stress for children, foster families, and birth families.

Foster care in the United States has evolved over the centuries from colonial times to the present. At the beginning of the twenty-first century, the foster care system is beleaguered by too many challenges and not enough resources. The number of available foster families is decreasing as the number of children needing such placements is increasing.

A recent trend in some states is to have varying categories of foster families available for a range of children's needs. Examples of these categories include:

- Emergency foster families who take children for very short periods of time on very short notice
- Short-term foster families who take children who are expected to be able to return to their birth homes
- Long-term foster families who care for children who will not return to their birth homes
- Specialized care foster families who care for children with particular needs, such as those having a medical condition (e.g., HIV)
- Treatment foster families who receive training to care for children with behavioral or emotional disorders
- Kinship foster care that involves a family who is related to the child, typically grandparents or aunts or uncles (Haugaard and Hazan 2002)

All categories of foster parents have in common some relationship issues that other parents do not typically have. In addition to their relationship with the child, foster parents also must work on creating productive relationships with both the birth family and the placement agency (Haugaard and Hazan 2002). And, even as foster parents are working to build positive relationships with the child who is placed with them, they also must prepare for the eventual loss of that child. Foster parents must work with placement agencies so that the legal aspects of the relationship with the child for whom they care are handled appropriately. Further, foster parents frequently are in a role that requires them to help the child keep or build positive relationships with their birth families. All of these situations can be fraught with conflict that must be resolved for the good of the children and their relationships with their birth families.

These considerations point to the extraordinary challenges that face foster families on a recurring basis. Early childhood teachers may be aware when one of their students is living in a foster home. To support the child's academic progress and emotional well-being, teachers must have compassion and sensitivity for the challenges faced by everyone in this situation. Keep in mind that despite the difficulties faced by foster families, their efforts are based on the belief that they can help a child and her birth family in a time of dire need. A little affirmation and appreciation from school personnel for this challenging work can go a long way in building partnerships with foster families.

About 4 million children in the United States are living with grandparents or other relatives.

© Cengage Learning/ECE Photo Library.

Grandparents as Parents

An increasing number of grandparents are providing all or most of the parental responsibilities for some children. In the recent past, it was common to have at least one grandparent living in the home with parents and children, in an extended-family living arrangement. Many children, though, now live with one or two grandparents, and the parents are not part of the child's daily life. Since 1980, this number has increased by 40 percent (Doucette-Dudman and LaCure 1996). In 1997, available records indicate that about 4 million children in the United States were living with grandparents or other relatives (Bryson and Casper 1998, as cited in Smith and Drew, 2002).

Parenting grandchildren complicates daily living. In addition to caring for the grandchild, or as often is the case, grandchildren, grandparents frequently work to create or maintain a relationship between the birth parent(s) and the child. Some experts believe that this is a crucial task for the children's healthy development. Legal issues related to grandparents and their grandchildren vary from state to state, and in many cases laws are not clear. Some grandparents seek custody or adoption of their grandchildren, but many believe they are serving only as temporary caregivers and that the birth parent(s) will reassume the parenting responsibilities as soon as they can. The reality, however, is that even when the arrangement is perceived by all involved as temporary, it often stretches into years. When grandparents assume parenting roles, it is frequently because birth parents have been involved in alcohol or drug abuse or they have physically, emotionally, or sexually abused the child(ren). The children may also be HIV positive or have other special needs. These desperate situations are often the catalyst for grandparents to attempt to save their grandchildren (Doucette-Dudman and LaCure 1996).

In our society, some helping professionals and policymakers view it as odd that grandparents would want to parent or adopt their grandchildren. Some seem to be concerned that the relationships will confuse the children. For example, in these situations the children's aunts and uncles, and maybe even their birth parents, take on sibling roles. As a grandmother raising her granddaughter, Doucette-Dudman makes an important point:

This is Sabra's life, she has known no other, she is not confused in any way. We have explained, and will continue to elaborate on, her family connections. We [grandparents] are her parents because we parent. She also has birth parents, just like any other adopted child. Sabra loves them, too, but they do not parent....Biological designations are practically irrelevant.

Not only are grandparents discouraged from seeking full custody or adopting their grandchildren, but also few resources are available to them. In many situations, if grandparents did not assume the care of children, foster care would be necessary. The existing social service system allows for financial payments and medical insurance to those providing foster care, but grandparents are not eligible for these resources. Reverend Eduardo Yarde is quoted in *Raising Our Children's Children* (Doucette-Dudman and LaCure):

> With welfare reform, this is where the churches are going to play a crucial part. That's one sector that's been neglected. My philosophy is that these grandparents have already raised their kids, they are under no obligation to raise more kids. And to me they are doing us, society, a favor. They are doing the State a favor. They should be rewarded for that. If we can't see that, we surely have lost sight of everything. The State really looks the other way, "Oh, that's grandparents." They don't even consider giving them some sort of support, nothing. And it's hard.

As grandparents raise their grandchildren, a number of difficulties have been documented (Kornhaber 1993).

1. Without formal custody, grandparents have difficulty getting either preventive or emergency medical care for children.

2. Typically, insurance companies will not permit grandchildren to be included as dependents on policies.

3. Schools may not admit children who do not live with their parents and often deny authority of grandparents.

4. Social Security benefits for the children are available to grandparents only if they legally adopt.

5. Financial assistance from social service agencies is typically not available, not even resources available to foster families.

6. Housing regulations of grandparent residences may not allow children, or zoning laws may exclude grandchildren in the definition of single-family dwellings.

In their extensive review of grandparenthood, Smith and Drew (2002) conclude that "custodial grand-

parents are conducting a service to their communities as well as their families and need support at a national and community level to continue effectively." As one aspect of their advocacy for those over the age of 50 years, the American Association of Retired Persons (AARP) publishes a newsletter for grandparents raising grandchildren, **The GIC Voice**. This free newsletter contains valuable information, including current medical, legal, and psychological facts. The Fall 2005 issue provides a clear description of federal legislation being proposed by both the House and Senate that, if passed, would provide various forms of support for grandparents and other family members involved in kinship care. That same issue of the newsletter also includes a discussion of methods grandparents have used to help their grandchildren raise their test scores and ways that some schools are providing support for grandparents who are parenting their grandchildren. Early childhood professionals who wish to provide this valuable resource for their centers or schools can find more information at http://www.aarp.org/grandparents.

Having some knowledge about the stress that grandparents deal with in raising their grandchildren can help early childhood teachers be sensitive to the needs of the grandparents and children in these families. It is common for children being raised by grandparents to have special needs because of their biological parents' substance abuse or child abuse. Education systems are in a position to ease grandparents' stress; when educators and social service agency personnel work together, children and families benefit. Doucette-Dudman and LaCure issue a plea for teachers to have some understanding of and concern for grandparents who, out of "love and devotion," are nurturing their grandchildren.

Peggy Tuter Pearl (2000) suggests the following for teachers when grandparents are the primary caregivers:

- Modify language in notes, letters, requests for signatures

- Know who the primary caregivers of their students are

- Allow extra time during conferences

Dianne Rothenberg (1996) includes a list of school strategies intended to help grandchildren in the article, "Grandparents as Parents: A Primer for Schools." The following are excerpts from this list. For a complete version and more information, go to http://www.ed.gov/databases/ERIC_Digests/ed401044.html.

- Anticipate transitional or adjustment difficulties, and act to minimize them.

- Look for children's strengths and build on them.

- Try not to single out children because of their family status.

In addition to giving particular attention to grandparents in parenting roles, it is also necessary to be aware that children in grandparent-headed homes are more likely to have had prenatal drug exposure leading to challenges in physical, cognitive or socio-emotional development. More behavioral and emotional challenges appear in children who are living with grandparents than with biological parents. Some of the challenges may derive from learning disabilities or cognitive deficits (Smith and Dannison, September 2003). So, not only are grandparents facing similar challenges as all parents, but often also of those parenting children with special needs.

Teen Parents

When teens become parents, many family roles are altered in what family systems theorists refer to as "off time." In other words, adolescence is a time in U.S. society that is considered to have some freedom from major responsibility for others so that youth might seek their own identities. Further, in many families, grandparents may be quite young or in a family life cycle period when they are still rearing younger children. Thus, considering teen parenting from a family systems perspective, it can be noted that many family members are affected in ways for which they probably have not planned and are not prepared.

Although teenage pregnancy and childbearing rates are decreasing, the United States has the highest rate among most Western countries (Singh and Darroch 2000, as cited in Moore and Brooks-Gunn 2002). Most adolescents who give birth are not married; in 1998, 79 percent of teen mothers (15–19 years old) were single (Ventura, Mathews, and Curtin 1999, as cited in Moore and Brooks-Gunn 2002). Because neither teen parent is typically self-supporting, teen mothers often need help from their families, including their parents, grandparents, and siblings. Often, families of teen parents help with finances, child care, and transportation.

66 Today, teenage parenthood is almost synonymous with single parenthood. Teenage mothers are disproportionately represented on welfare rolls and as high school dropouts…The declining age of intercourse, the increasing rate of nonmarital births, and the disappearance of teenage marriage means that the young parent finds herself in a different situation today than previously. 99

—Moore and Brooks-Gunn, 2002

While it is clear that single teen mothers face many challenges that involve their own development as well as supporting their child's development,

research shows that some buffers exist. Education is a particularly strong factor for successful results among teen mothers. Among the education-related factors that contribute to positive consequences for single teen mothers are being on expected grade level, having parents with more than a tenth-grade education, attending special schools for pregnant girls, and holding aspirations for continued education (Moore and Brooks-Gunn 2002). Those teen parents who have opportunities to complete high school with special programs that include onsite child care are thus more likely to be able to support themselves and their child or children to a greater extent postgraduation.

How do adolescents parent? It is important to note that many individual differences exist in teen parenting styles and that these differences are related to variations in resources and experience, but some commonalities exist among teen parents based on the challenges these parents face. Many teen mothers are confronted by the common stressor of poverty. In addition to their own very low incomes, they may also come from families and live in communities that are negatively affected by circumstances of poverty. Research has shown that these harsh conditions can have negative effects on children of teen mothers through their adolescence and adulthood (Moore and Brooks-Gunn 2002).

Reviews of existing research on adolescent mothers' parenting skills show that they appear to express warmth to their babies as much as older mothers do. However, teen mothers are neither as verbally responsive nor as emotionally available to their infants as would be beneficial for children (Moore and Brooks-Gunn 2002). It is possible that children of teen mothers who live in multigenerational families may experience and benefit from greater verbal responsiveness and emotional availability from their grandparents. This is most likely to be true when the grandparents have higher levels of education and are not living in poverty.

Minimal information is available about young fathers, especially when they are not married to or living with their child's mother. Although the results from one national survey (Lerman 1993, as cited in Moore and Brooks-Gunn 2002) found that one-fourth of young fathers had daily contact with their children and one-half had weekly contact, the quality of the father-child relationship tends to decline over time. Some of the factors that are related to stronger father-child relationships include a close relationship between the teen parents, frequent visits and scheduled child care expectations, and involvement of the paternal grandmother (Coley and Chase-Lansdale 1999, as cited in Moore and Brooks-Gunn 2002).

Considering the challenges of teen parenthood, it behooves early childhood educators to be conscious of situations that are most supportive of families with young parents. Programs and policies that are geared to assisting teen parents with the challenges they face often lead to benefits for their children. On the other hand, negative influences of teen parenthood can also stay with their offspring for a lifetime.

> ### Reflect on This
>
> This quote from A. A. Campbell (1968) is now viewed as classic: "When a 16-year-old girl has a child…90 percent of her life's script is written for her." Based on available evidence, explain the meaning of this quote. Also, describe existing programs, policies, and practices that might influence changes in the adolescent parent's life script.

RESPONSIBILITIES OF PARENTS

Economic

Parents have the ultimate responsibility for meeting all of their children's needs. Based on data from the Department of Agriculture Center for Nutrition Policy and Promotion, the Children's Defense Fund (2001) notes that a married-couple family earning less than $38,000 per year will spend $121,230 to raise a child to age 18. Those who make $38,000 to $64,000 will spend $165,630, and those making more than $64,000 will spend $241,770.

In the United States, most people believe that parents bear the financial obligation for their children's expenses, which include health care, child care, shelter, food, and clothing (see Figure 5–2). This belief is so strong in our culture that we often ignore societal preferences and biases and assume all parents are capable of providing for their children's basic needs. This is not the case, however. For example, parents who have full-time jobs are more likely to have medical insurance for themselves and their children and, thus, access to both preventive and emergency health care. Parents who work in entry-level, lower-paying jobs, even if they work full time, are less likely to have access to health insurance or to have their insurance paid for by employers.

Concern for the well-being of children who do not have health insurance has led the federal government to provide plans for young children. Specifically, in 1997 the federal government created the Children's Health Insurance Program (CHIP) so that uninsured children from low- and moderate-income families are eligible for regular checkups, immunizations, doctor visits, eyeglasses, prescription drugs, hospital care, dental

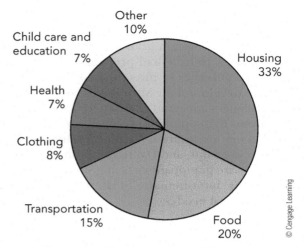

Figure 5–2 Percentages of estimated annual expenditures on a child by husband-wife couples with incomes less than $38,000.

care, and other medical services (Children's Defense Fund, 2004). Although paying for medical expenses is still seen as a parental responsibility, some policymakers have noted that when society helps to pay for healthy children, the cost to society will be less in the future.

Nurturance and Child Care

Another responsibility of parents is to provide care and nurturance for their children. Traditionally, we have referred to this as "mothering" children. Even though many two-parent families currently find that two incomes are required, mothers are still seen as the parent who is responsible for and more capable of caring for children. "The research evidence clearly indicates that husbands share very little of the burden of raising their children and caring for their homes" (Hamburg 1995). Most single parents who are the primary caregivers for their children are mothers. In fact, only about 10 percent of all single-parent families are headed by fathers (U.S. Bureau of the Census, as cited in Hamner and Turner 1996).

Bioecological theory emphasizes the need for parents to have a system of social support in order to do their best at nurturing children. Social support appears to be a strong contributor to parents' ability to care for their children.

> 66 The establishment and maintenance of patterns of progressively more complex interaction and emotional attachment between caregiver and child depend in substantial degree on the availability and involvement of another adult or a third party—spouse, relative, neighbor, or formal service provider—who assists, encourages, spells, gives status to, and expresses admiration and affection for the person caring for and engaging in joint activity with the child. 99

—Bronfenbrenner and Neville, 1994

Note that early childhood teachers may serve as the third party to provide support to parents in their role as nurturers. Thus, it is critical that teachers understand this important role when planning the family involvement component in any program of early childhood education.

Consider This

List and discuss ways that teachers can demonstrate support for parents as nurturers.

Child care outside the home continues to be viewed as a women's issue rather than a family or societal concern. Many policymakers continue to voice the opinion that if mothers stayed home with their young children, there would be no need for child care centers. Oddly enough, these same people often call for mothers receiving welfare assistance to go to work.

It remains the parents' responsibility to choose child care for their young children. Many parents, in reality, have little choice. Accessibility and affordability are two areas of concern. Parents tend to rely on care that is close to home and that costs the least. Often, this means that parents sacrifice quality of care of their children for what they can afford. Current interest and concern for this issue at the federal level and initiated by Hillary Rodham Clinton is welcomed by many child and family advocates. High-quality child care costs more than most families can afford. Further, it is difficult to find.

Early childhood education teachers may serve as the third party to provide support to parents in their role as nurturers.

© Cengage Learning/ECE Photo Library.

Do This

Research child care funding sources at both your state and the federal level.

Attachment and Socialization

The third area of parents' responsibility is related to their children's psychological well-being. Forming emotional attachments is crucial for children's healthy development in all domains. Attachment to parents is necessary for healthy physical, cognitive, social, and emotional development. Figure 5–3 shows the relationship of attachment to all areas of child development.

Parents are the child's link to society. Early **socialization** experiences, including communication, play, and teaching behaviors, all happen within the context of the home. These early attachment and socialization experiences are thought to be a strong influence on children's development. Current research on brain development indicates that social interaction in the first three years of life creates important neuron connections for later learning. Parents are a child's first and foremost teachers, even if they employ other forms of care for their children at very young ages.

Although parents typically understand that they impact their children's social and emotional development, they are often unaware of the timing of milestones (Zero to Three 2009). Early childhood educators may be able to share information about development as well as about the importance of adults' sensitivity and responsiveness to children's feelings. Erik Erikson's psychosocial theory provides global understanding of children's development. (Although this theory addresses lifespan development, only the first four of his eight stages are included in this text.)

Figure 5–3	Relationship of Attachment to the Child's Development: Physical, Cognitive, Social, and Emotional.

Healthy attachments in infancy can lead to the following outcomes for preschool children:

Physical Development—Brain development, physical health

Cognitive Development—Skillful in problem solving, seeking maternal assistance when challenged, curious about new things

Social Development—Leaders with peers, self-confidence, sympathetic to others, competent in peer interactions, well-liked by others, considerate

Emotional Development—Ability to tolerate frustration, expression of positive emotions such as joy

© Cengage Learning

According to Erikson, the stages with approximate ages are:

Birth-1 year: Trust versus mistrust. During the first year of life, infants learn to trust others when their needs are met. When needs are not met in a consistent, responsive manner, babies are likely to mistrust others and have difficulty moving through the remaining stages of social and emotional development.

1–3 years: Autonomy versus shame and doubt. Toddlers who have learned trust in their first year now move on to learning to trust themselves, or to be autonomous. Adults who encourage toddlers to move ahead in this way support their autonomy. A balance of setting limits and encouraging independence is helpful. Unrealistic limits or too little encouragement may lead to toddlers doubting their abilities or being ashamed of their efforts.

3–6 years: Initiative versus guilt: Preschoolers who have developed a sense of autonomy now take initiative in their activities, both in work and play. Adults who encourage children to help them with household or classroom duties help to uphold their sense of initiative. Just as important, though, is the encouragement of play, particularly pretense at this stage. Preschoolers who become good players at this stage are likely to become good workers at school age. A sense of guilt may overcome initiative in preschoolers when adults do not support their efforts in either work or play.

6–12 years: Industry versus inferiority. School age children who have developed a sense of initiative are prepared to develop their industriousness. In U.S. society, children's work is based on school and academic expectations. Adults who recognize children's abilities, efforts, and accomplishments help to support this social-emotional characteristic. When children feel inferior in that they cannot meet expectations that are conveyed, they are more likely to have difficulty in meeting this milestone.

Vygotsky emphasized the importance of social interaction between adults and children in relation to children's learning and thinking. Adults provide social guidance to children so that they might increase their skill or level of competence in a given activity. This view also illuminates the notion that children impact the parent just as the parent impacts them (Vygotsky 1978). Reciprocity of effects is important to consider in socializing children so that one does not make the mistake that the impact of socialization goes only from parent to child. This is clearly observed when parents have children with different temperaments or abilities. Some children are simply easier to parent than others, and parents may have different perspectives on which children are easier or more challenging to parent based on their social interactions.

Building and Maintaining Relationships

Those in the parental role introduce others into the lives of their children. Extended family members, especially grandparents but also aunts, uncles, cousins, neighbors, friends, and siblings, become a part of the child's world. Parents sometimes rely on some people on this list to help with child care or just to socialize with their children. Families include others in varying ways, partly depending on their culture or ethnicity, and partly depending on their individual views. For some families, cousins are almost like siblings, while for others cousins are almost strangers. These individual variations in family relationships are most often decided upon and implemented by parents.

Character Education and Spirituality

Spirituality, in its various forms, is seen as a parental responsibility, and most parents ensure that their spiritual beliefs are shared with their children. For many families, spirituality is defined as and dealt with in the context of organized religion. Many parents count on their church or temple to at least assist with this duty. Religion, along with other factors, influences "the kind of activities the family engages in, the limits set and the controls placed on children's behavior, and the set of expectations that parents hold for their children" (Hamner and Turner 1996).

For other families, morality is of higher value than religiosity. Moral behavior is often related in some way to spirituality or the meaning of life (Coles 1990). Lickona, Schaps, and Lewis (1998) note that school programs of character education should include in the mission statement, "Parents are the first and most important moral educators of their children." In addition to this critical point, Lickona and his associates go on to say,

> [E]ach program should take pains at every stage to communicate with parents. To build trust between home and school, parents should be represented on the character leadership committee that does the planning. The program should actively reach out to "disconnected" subgroups of parents: All parents need to be informed about—and have a chance to contribute, react, and consent to—proposed core values and plans for implementing them. Finally, programs and families will enhance effectiveness of their partnership if they recruit the help of the wider community—business, religious institutions, youth organizations, the government, and the media— in promoting the core ethical values.
> **Clearly we can all agree about the importance of teaching our children, both as individuals and as members of society, the importance of common values such as respect, responsibility, trustworthiness, and citizenship.**

—Richard Riley, Former U.S. Secretary of Education

Collaborating with Societal Institutions

A newer responsibility of parents is that of relating to societal institutions and helping their children to do so, including early childhood settings. This is often a difficult responsibility for parents because they have had no models. This responsibility is related to the very topic of this textbook: how can early childhood education and families form partnerships that benefit not only children but also parents and teachers? For parents, working with their children's teachers often means finding effective means of resolving conflict because parents and teachers may, at times, value different activities or behaviors for children. It is imperative that both parents and early childhood teachers address such conflict in ways that will best help children, while still respecting the family and maintaining the educational program.

> ### Do This
> Consider the responsibilities of parenthood that are discussed in this section of Chapter 5: economic, nurturance and child care, attachment and socialization, building and maintaining relationships, character education and spirituality, and collaborating with societal institutions. Critically assess the resources that parents need to meet each of these responsibilities. Finally, brainstorm ways that early childhood programs and communities might be able to offer various types of support to families in regard to each of the responsibilities.

PARENTING STYLES AND BELIEFS

Diana Baumrind has researched the topic of parenting styles for nearly four decades (1967, 1971, 1977, 1989). Early versions of Baumrind's typology of parenting styles included three variations: **authoritarian parenting**, **authoritative parenting**, and **permissive parenting**. Further work in this area has led Baumrind to descriptions of four types of parenting:

- Authoritarian
- Authoritative
- Indulgent
- Uninvolved

These styles are based on two dimensions: amount of parental control and amount of parental warmth. Authoritative parents are high on both of these elements, whereas authoritarian parents are high on control and lower on warmth. **Indulgent** parents are lower on control and high on warmth, and **uninvolved** parents tend to the low end of both

Figure 5–4 Characteristics of Parenting Styles.

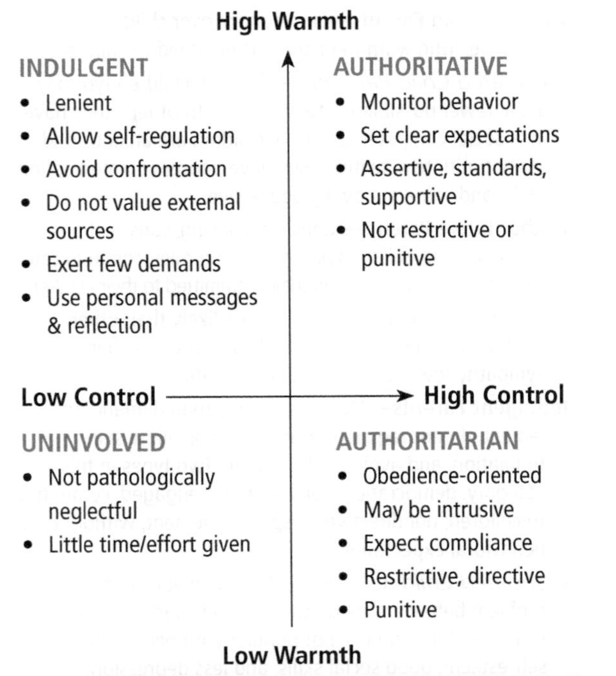

High Warmth

INDULGENT
- Lenient
- Allow self-regulation
- Avoid confrontation
- Do not value external sources
- Exert few demands
- Use personal messages & reflection

AUTHORITATIVE
- Monitor behavior
- Set clear expectations
- Assertive, standards, supportive
- Not restrictive or punitive

Low Control ⟶ **High Control**

UNINVOLVED
- Not pathologically neglectful
- Little time/effort given

AUTHORITARIAN
- Obedience-oriented
- May be intrusive
- Expect compliance
- Restrictive, directive
- Punitive

Low Warmth

© Cengage Learning

control and warmth. See Figure 5–4 for characteristics of parenting styles.

In addition to defining differences in parenting style, Baumrind has shown that variation in parenting is predictive of children's behaviors and characteristics. "Authoritative parenting, which balances clear, high parental demands with emotional responsiveness and recognition of child autonomy, is one of the most consistent family predictors of competence from early childhood through adolescence" (Darling 1999). See Figure 5–5 for descriptions of child behaviors for each parenting style.

In the previous descriptions of parenting style, control refers to children's behavior. Thus, parents demonstrating those styles that emphasize greater control (e.g., authoritarian and authoritative) are concerned with employing strategies that lead to children doing what their parents expect of them. Another aspect of control that has been studied in regard to parenting is psychological control. This factor is what differentiates the notion of control for authoritarian versus authoritative parenting. Authoritarian parenting emphasizes high psychological control as well as behavioral control in that these parents expect their children to accept the parental values and goals without question. On the other hand, authoritative parents are likely to discuss children's views and to sometimes arrive at decisions based on input from the child (Darling 1999).

| Figure 5–5 | Child Behaviors Associated with Varying Parenting Styles. |

Authoritarian Parents—Firm control over children, punitive, little warmth or support provided to children.

Associated Child Behaviors—Because children typically have fewer possibilities to interact with others, they have less social competence. Often, children are anxious and do not initiate activities. They have poorer communication skills and some are overly aggressive.

Authoritative Parents—Consistent, loving, conscientious, secure in their ability to parent, set firm rules, communicate clearly, warm and unconditionally committed to their children.

Associated Child Behaviors—More likely than other children to exhibit prosocial behavior such as sharing, sympathy toward others, and cooperation.

Indulgent Parents—More responsive than demanding, lenient, do not require mature behavior, allow self-regulation, and avoid confrontation. Two types in this category: democratic—conscientious, engaged, committed to children; nondirective—especially lenient, without clear behavioral expectations.

Associated Child Behaviors—May be involved in problem behaviors, mediocre academic performance, disrespectful to others, not popular with peers, higher self-esteem, good social skills, and less depression.

Uninvolved Parents—Low in both control and warmth, bordering on pathologically neglecting, but in normal range, little time or energy given to parenting, low commitment to children.

Associated Child Behaviors—Perform most poorly in academic, social competence, self-esteem, self-regulation, do not handle independence productively.

© Cengage Learning

Trends in Beliefs about Discipline Strategies

Even as existing research shows support for authoritative parenting—that is, for stating expectations and providing explanations to children about reasons for expected behavior—there is a current trend in parental beliefs and behaviors that ignores the importance of balance between "guiding limits and loving compassionate care" for young children (Brazelton and Greenspan 2000). Families who are overwhelmed by responsibility are often attracted to simplistic discipline techniques that rely on punishments and rewards to control children's behavior. When used as a primary disciplinary method, these outdated approaches often lead children to either aggressive behavior or fearful, withdrawn behavior, neither of which supports children's optimal development. This discipline ethic does not consider children's need for sensitive nurturance and developmentally appropriate experiences (Brazelton and Greenspan 2000).

Evidence regarding the harmful long-term effects of physical punishment related to personality and mental health has recently been established through research on a nationally representative sample in the United States (Afifi, Mota, Dasiewicz, MacMillan and Sareen 2012). One noteworthy conclusion of this research is that individuals may suffer long-term negative consequences, such as depression, anxiety, and substance abuse, when parents employ harsh physical punishment, including hitting, pushing, and slapping, that is not legally identified as maltreatment or abuse. One explanation for such results is explained by psychiatrist Michele Knox: "Physical punishment is a chronic and sometimes repeated stressor for young people, and we know that chronic and repeated stressors have a negative impact on the brain…. spanking and other forms of corporal punishment have a huge variety of negative outcomes, and almost no positive outcomes" (Pittman 2012).

Evidence of additional negative effects of spanking and other forms of corporal or physical punishment have been established through numerous prior studies. Higher levels of aggressive behaviors, delinquency, and lower levels of moral internalization are often associated with this mode of discipline. Although many factors contribute to such outcomes, the risk of adding physical punishment to a mix of environmental and biological factors is one that parents and educators can avoid by establishing other methods of child discipline that foster mutual respect. Educational efforts to help parents understand the negative outcomes of physical punishment are necessary since one result of such discipline is immediate compliance from the child. This observable and often desirable outcome often influences parents to continue using such methods. Aforementioned long-term effects are not immediately observable and thus must be shared by educators and other helping professionals.

Center for Effective Discipline
http://www.stophitting.com

Committee to Repeal Section 43 of the Criminal Code of Canada
http://www.repeal43.org

Parenting without Punishing
http://www.nopunish.net

"Early Childhood: Parenting"

Visit the Education CourseMate website at www.CengageBrain.com to view Video Case, and then respond to the following items:

- Discuss the challenges and joys of parenting young children.

- How might teachers of young children support parents in any or all of their roles as described above?

MOTHERHOOD AND FATHERHOOD

Even though we have come to accept the term **parenting** in place of **mothering**, most families and teachers are aware that we have different expectations for mothers and fathers. One single mother reports an occasion when her mother commented on what a good job a particular single father who had custody of his son was doing. The conversation between the single mother and her mother went like this:

Mother: "John works so hard at his job and still is such a good father for Joshua."

Daughter: "I work hard, too. And, I think I'm a good mother."

Mother: "Of course you're a good mother. Women know how to take care of young children. It's natural for them."

Daughter: "Working full time and being a mother is not easy."

Mother: "Women have been having children and taking care of them for generations. It's not new for women your age."

It is safe to say that many people in our society still believe that any woman who has a child knows automatically how to be a mother, but that not all men with children know how to be fathers. This belief sets quite a double standard for our expectations about parental responsibilities.

Generally, women experience greater fulfillment in their parental roles than men do, but they also see being a parent as more of a burden. Mothers feel restricted in other aspects of their lives due to their parenting duties (Goetting 1986). Both of these feelings that are held by many mothers of young children are easily traced to societal expectations. At very early ages, many girls play with dolls, and when asked what they want to be when they grow up, they say "a mommy." Boys, on the other hand, play with toys that are symbolic of the world beyond the home and, consequently, they want to be pilots, police officers, or firefighters. They are expected to and expect to be employed outside of the home, not to be restricted in their occupations by parenting duties. Interestingly, these play themes continue even with the high rate of mothers in the labor force and increasing involvement of fathers in caring for children and household tasks.

In the 1950s, Parsons and Bales (1955) classified the role of mothers as **expressive** and the role of fathers as **instrumental**. By this, they meant that mothers provided children with care and love, while fathers' direct role in caring for children was minimal. A father's position allowed him to be the tie the family had with the outside world. Although times have changed and more mothers of children under six work outside the home, we still observe tenacious vestiges of this perspective. When one parent does stay home to care for children, it is still most often the mother. And when parents divorce, mothers are still more likely to get custody of children.

Current research has examined how mothers and fathers interact with their babies and young children. Many studies have found that mothers are more likely to provide the physical care such as feeding, bathing, and diapering, and fathers are more likely to play with their children. Also, mothers, whether they work outside the home or not, spend a great deal more time with their children than do fathers. Perhaps this accounts for why mothers find parenting more fulfilling and more restrictive.

It is interesting to ask children (if they are old enough to respond) who takes care of them in various ways such as who prepares their food, washes their clothes, makes doctor appointments, and plays with them. Children's perceptions are often quite accurate in terms of understanding which parent performs which duties. One school principal tells of waiting in the deli line at a grocery store when a four-year-old boy asked him, "Where is the girl who lives with you? Why isn't she doing the shopping?"

> ## Do This
> To check this information with families that you know, interview several families with young children and ask the following questions:
> 1. Who provides physical care of your children, including preparing meals, bathing, making certain of clean clothes, and so on?
> 2. If a child is ill, who stays home from work with the child? How is this decided?
> 3. Who makes medical appointments?
> 4. Who plays with the children?

Mothering

Preparation for the role of mothering includes the process that women go through to achieve a maternal identity as well as competency in this identity (Barnard and Solchany 2002). This preparation continues throughout the pregnancy and into the postpartum period. Four maternal tasks have been distinguished as common in this preparation (Rubin 1984, as cited in Barnard and Solchany 2002). These tasks are:

Seeking safe passage. In preparation for her mothering role, a pregnant woman begins to take special care of her own health to keep her child safe through pregnancy, labor, and delivery.

Ensuring acceptance of baby by important others. As an aspect of her maternal role, a pregnant woman begins to adjust her own life and relationships with others in ways that will accommodate the child's needs.

"Binding-in." This process relates to the pregnant woman's psychological attachment to the developing fetus and her future child. "The child begins to be real for the mother long before the child becomes real for family members and friends."

Learning to give of oneself. Expectant mothers consider what they will be giving up to care for a dependent child as well as what they will gain from motherhood. Many mothers-to-be are concerned with their competency, especially when this is a new role for them.

Once women have become mothers, it is generally seen that they have three primary functions in this role (Winnicott 1990, as cited in Barnard and Solchany 2002):

Monitoring-surveillance. Infants and young children must be constantly monitored and supervised in order to keep them safe. Beyond this, mothers also monitor their child's growth, development, health, and behavior. As children grow and develop, mothers accommodate their surveillance to the changing needs of children.

Expectant nurturing. Mothers are typically children's primary caregivers. In this role, they expect to provide nutrition, a safe environment, health care, appropriate climate controls, and meeting all of children's dependency needs. Again, as children grow and develop, mothers accommodate their nurturing to meet children's changing needs.

Responsive caregiving-social partner role. In order to assist children in developing a sense of trust, mothers respond in a timely way to meet children's needs. This responsivity is crucial in teaching children that someone is always there to meet their dependency needs. "It is in the response of others that the child develops meaning of her or his behavior." Thus, responsiveness from mothers helps to support the social partner role with their infants and young children.

> 66 [T]he goal of mothering is to develop an underlying, internal strength that fuels a healthy ego, supports a working conscience, and constructs strong internal working models consistent with individuality; and that the ultimate mothering goal is a child, who can enter adulthood as an autonomous, individuated, responsible person secure in her or his relationships. 99

—Barnard and Solchany, 2002

Expectations of the mothering role change throughout infancy and early childhood. From a child's birth to three years of age, maternal responsibilities include providing food, safety, stimulation, and security; being emotionally available; and developing routines. From three to five years of age, mothers are responsible for setting consistent and reasonable limits and routines; modeling appropriate expression of feelings; and encouraging appropriate forms of autonomy. When children are five to eight years old, important tasks for mothers include providing discipline and limits; supporting emotional development; and creating awareness of values and beliefs of others (Barnard and Solchany 2002).

Although many, perhaps most, mothers rise to the occasion and become warm, nurturing parents, it is known that for some women this capacity is reduced or difficult to attain. Such high-risk women seem to be too consumed with other issues to deal with the psychological tasks of preparing for motherhood. Some women are in abusive relationships, are addicted to various substances, are physically or mentally ill, or are in dire poverty. Some of the greatest risk factors for decreased competency in the maternal role include a childhood that lacked basic needs being met or that included abuse, past or current mental illness, ambivalence about the pregnancy and the birth of a child, and little ability to care for herself (Gabinet 1986, as cited in Barnard and Solchany 2002).

In their research with mothers of young children enrolled in Early Head Start, Barnard and Solchany (2002) found that when mothers had earlier trauma that had not been resolved, it was extremely difficult for them to make psychological space for their babies. These researchers propose that about 25 percent of new mothers have such unresolved trauma and for this reason they are not able to consider the needs of their babies. "When a baby is never taken into a mother's mind, the child becomes an emotional orphan whether or not a mother is physically present." This situation raises serious concerns about the development of a large number of young children in our society. These researchers recommend practices and policies that take into account the critical needs of children to be nurtured. One consideration is referred to as allomothering. This view of nurturing children allows for the constant responsibility of child care to be spread out among several primary caregivers, such as child care providers, extended family members, community agencies, and so on. They also point to the need for greater availability of high-quality child care services as well as the importance of supporting parental involvement with child care providers. High-quality early childhood education may be a good source for prevention of childhood difficulties based on a lack of ability to nurture that traumatized mothers experience.

Fathering

Changes in either women's roles or men's roles in families lead naturally to changes in roles for the other. As mothers with young children are now more likely to spend more time in the workforce, one might expect that roles and responsibilities of fathers have also been adapted. Existing research points to the value of examining both quantity and quality of time that fathers spend with their young children. Typically, differences between mothers and fathers are noted in both of these ways.

Center for Successful Fathering
http://www.fathering.com

National Center for Fathering
http://www.fathers.com

National Fatherhood Initiative
http://www.fatherhood.com

Michael Lamb and his associates (as cited in Parke 2002) have proposed three dimensions that are most relevant for studying father involvement:

1. *Interaction.* This refers to fathers' direct contact with their children. Various types of activities, including playing and caregiving, are included in this dimension. Gradual increases in father interaction in two-parent families have been noted. One study (Yeung, Sandberg, Davis-Kean, and Hofferth 2001, as cited in Parke 2002) found that fathers interacted with their children 67 percent of the time of maternal involvement on weekdays and 87 percent on weekends. Most experts agree that mothers continue to spend more time with their children than do fathers. Generally speaking, qualitative differences in mother-child and father-child interaction exist as well. "Fathers are tactile and physical, and mothers tend to be verbal, didactic and toy mediated in their play" (Parke 2002). While these qualitative differences hold steadily in the United States, more recent cross-cultural evidence leads to the speculation that these differences most likely have cultural roots and so they are not purely based on biological gender differences of parents.

   Some research provides support for the notion of maternal gatekeeping. It has been noted that fathers engage in less interaction with their infants and young children when mothers are unwilling to yield responsibility of child care to fathers. Further, attitudes of mothers who engage in gatekeeping are more likely to be judgmental and lead to criticism of fathers' ways of interacting with their children (Allen and Hawkins 1999, as cited in Parke 2002). On the other hand, Bonney, Kelley, and Levant (1999, as cited in Parke 2002) point out that when fathers are more highly involved with their children, maternal attitudes become more positive and this can lead to greater levels of father participation with their children.

2. *Availability.* This dimension relates to fathers' accessibility for their children. Availability, of course, may vary for those fathers who reside with their children when compared with those who do not live with

their children. Also, as might be expected, when fathers work a greater number of hours, they are less available for, and less involved with, their children than those who work fewer hours. Fathers who hold high-stress jobs tend to be withdrawn from their children, whereas fathers who have positive work experiences demonstrate more supportive interactions with their children (Repetti 1994, and Grossman, Pollack, and Golding 1988, as cited in Parke 2002).

In terms of father-child relationships, both father presence and quality of the relationship matters. Even when fathers do not live with their children, however, it is possible for them to positively influence both the relationship and the child. Children have been found to do better academically and psychologically when nonresident fathers use an authoritative parenting style. Another predictor of positive outcomes for children is related to the amount of child support paid by the nonresident father (Amato and Gilbreth 1999, as cited in Parke 2002).

3. *Responsibility.* Fathers typically have different levels of responsibility than mothers in making sure that children are cared for as well as for arranging that resources are available to meet children's needs. In fact, evidence indicates that even though both mothers and fathers are capable of obtaining child care and medical care, planning schedules, and supervising children, through the middle childhood years mothers are much more likely to bear primary responsibility for their children (Parke 2002). Those fathers who identified nurturance as an important part of their parenting not only had greater interaction time with their children, but also assumed more responsibility than did fathers who rated nurturance as less important to their roles (Rane and McBride 2000, as cited in Parke 2002).

> " In most families, husbands notice less about what needs to be done, wait to be asked to do various chores and require explicit directions if they are to complete the tasks successfully... [M]ost couples continue to characterize husbands' contributions to housework or child care as "helping" their wives. "
>
> **—Coltrane, 1996**

As of 1996, it was estimated that there were approximately 2 million stay-at-home fathers in the United States. Frank and Livingston (2000) state that "Stay at home fathers recognize that caring for children and family is not emasculating; as their children become older they are likely to remain intimately involved with their children, aware of their friends, schoolwork, and activities, and active as the on-call parent who responds when the child is sick at school." If this description is accurate, then teachers need to become aware of the role(s) fathers play

Stay-at-home fathers recognize that caring for children and family is not emasculating.

© Cengage Learning/ECE Photo Library.

in the lives of their children and actively invite and welcome fathers at school. This awareness also helps teachers understand the family's caregiving arrangements.

An important point to be made when examining parenting behaviors is that fathers' roles are less "culturally scripted and determined" (Parke 2002) than are maternal roles. Whereas monitoring, nurturing, and caregiving are all universal expectations for mothers of infants and young children, social expectations for fathers seem to be more flexible and diverse. Some of the sources of these differences include fathers' experiences with their own fathers and families, early practice with caring for children, timing in the life cycle for becoming a father, attitudes about masculine roles, spouse or partner attitudes about paternal competence, and both positive and negative employment experiences.

Much of the research on child effects from paternal behaviors and attitudes has not been conducted so that clear cause can be related to fathering only. In reality, there is most likely a great deal of overlap on children's development from the effects of both mothers and fathers (and even other factors). "Although there is overlap between the effects of mothers and fathers on their children's academic, emotional and social development, evidence is emerging that fathers make a unique contribution to their children's development" (Parke 2002). At this time, several studies using different methodologies have concluded that high-quality relationships with fathers are correlated with higher amounts of empathy, both in childhood and adulthood.

In addition to research on fathering generally, more research is needed that looks at individual differences of fathers. One such study (Jain, Belsky, and Crnic 1996, as cited in Parke 2002) led to a typology of four kinds of fathers: (1) caretakers, (2) playmates-teachers, (3) disciplinarians, and (4) disengaged. Characteristics of the first two types of fathers included more highly educated, more prestigious employment, less neurotic, and less consumed with daily hassles than the other two types. Clearly, more information about variations in fatherhood and their effects on children will be helpful in understanding ways that professionals might intervene to foster more positive outcomes for all.

PARENTING BELIEFS

naeyc 2 Parenting is one of the most important roles a person can perform. Yet, little preparation is required or offered, and it is expected that parenting skills will come naturally. Because so many people do become parents in one way or another, this role is different from many others. Five differences for individuals who parent versus those who do not have been noted (Bigner, as cited in Hamner and Turner 1996).

1. Women receive more pressure to become mothers than men do to become fathers.
2. Parenthood is not always voluntary.
3. Parenthood is irrevocable.
4. Parents receive very little preparation or guidance.
5. Parents develop and accommodate their parenting strategies as their children develop. **naeyc** 2

Consider This

Consider the five parental roles. State your agreement or disagreement with each belief. Give real-life examples to support your view.

Parents' Understanding of Child Development and Current Issues

The Zero to Three National Center for Infants, Toddlers and Families conducted a public opinion survey of parents who had at least one child from birth to three years of age. The representative sample included White, African-American and Hispanic parents. Objectives included discovering issues and challenges currently faced by parents, developing an understanding of factors that influence approaches to parenting, and gaining knowledge about how parents interpret and respond to their children's behavior. Results of this study are reported as seven key points.

1. Parents understand the importance of a number of experiences that are critical to young children's development, such as reading to children, having their children play with other children, comforting children when they are upset, and enforcing rules.

2. Parents lack a clear understanding of when young children are capable of reaching certain developmental milestones, leading to frustration from inaccurate expectations. Areas that parents are lacking in understanding include tantrums, crying, and children not being able to control their emotions.

3. Parents do not understand how deeply children's social-emotional development is affected by certain early experiences. Many are generally unaware that between one and two years of age children are capable of feeling good or bad about themselves and are influenced by parents' moods.

4. Parents trust family members as a source of information and support about parenting, with the child's grandmothers being the most common source.

5. Parenting approaches are strongly influenced by faith, more so than input from professionals or parenting books or magazines.

6. Parents have difficulty finding balance with work, family, and other responsibilities in their lives.

7. The economy has negatively influenced child care arrangements for many families. Both the cost of child care and unemployment of one or both parents have impacted child care provisions (Zero to Three 2009).

Reflect on This

What are the implications for early childhood teachers related to the seven points found in the Zero to Three study?

Do This

Go to the website for the Center on the Social and Emotional Foundations for Early Learning, http://csefel.vanderbilt.edu/. Click "Family Tools" on the left-side menu. Select at least one of the parent training modules, read it, and share ways that you could use the information with families. (Topics include: teaching your child to identify and express emotions; responding to your child's bite; tips on nurturing your child's social emotional development; and, understanding your child's behavior.)

Interactions with Early Childhood Educators

This study leads to many implications for early childhood teachers. One realization is that parents need greater understanding about the importance of experiences that foster healthy development, including talking to babies and, more specifically, supporting early social and emotional development. Further, parents need more information about when young children reach some milestones, especially those related to social and emotional development. Many are under the impression that early trauma has little or no effect on very young children (Zero to Three 2009).

The National Association for the Education of Young Children (NAEYC) has assembled a "Message in a Backpack" series with accurate, high quality, ready-to-go messages to families of preschoolers about a variety of topics, including: sun safety, social and emotional skills at home, fine motor skills, family fun and fitness and rough-and-tumble play. Notes are prepared in both English and Spanish and are available at www.naeyc.org/tyc/backpack. Although these messages cannot replace interpersonal communication with parents, teachers are able to share this information in a way that is supportive of families in caring for their children.

Since many parents trust their family members for advice over professionals or print materials, communication about parenting must take different paths. Additionally, since many parents rely on religious organizations for support and understanding, professionals should partner with faith-based associations so that accurate information might be shared in context (Zero to Three 2009).

naeyc 2 Based on an earlier Zero to Three study, Melmed (1997) suggests two parental needs that early childhood educators can help meet:

- Information for understanding their particular children's feelings or needs, especially for difficult situations

It is important that early education addresses all aspects of the child's development: physical, cognitive, social, and emotional.

- Creative ways that they can spend more quality time with their children 2

"Family history and culture are powerful influences on the approach many parents take to childrearing" (Zero to Three 2009, p. 35). Trawick-Smith (1997) outlines differences in beliefs about children related to culture, poverty, and oppression. Culture affects beliefs about childhood through daily life and expectations; some see childhood as a carefree time to play and explore, and others see it as a time to teach serious responsibility. Often, families and cultures who have endured great adversity in their lives have quite different belief systems than those who were fortunate to receive advantage and privilege.

Consider This

DAP As you review the seven points from the Zero to Three study, consider how these statements might guide parent-teacher conferences and discussions. Understanding and appreciating parents' beliefs and knowledge of child development can help teachers and caregivers plan effective communications and interactions. Providing clearly worded statements about program goals and expectations can also help parents match their beliefs with the program's goals and expectations. Listening to parents can also help programs change and evolve to meet different expectations while still being grounded in developmentally appropriate practice. DAP

The Touchpoints Center (www.brazeltontouchpoints.org) provides a model for early development that describes *touchpoints* as "periods during the first years of life during which children's spurts in development result in disruption in the family system" (Brazelton & Sparrow 2003). With attention to the identified 13 touchpoints that occur within the first three years, a system for supporting parents in their caregiving has been devised. Guiding principles for the Touchpoints model include a focus on the parent-child relationship and a willingness of practitioners to discuss topics that may go beyond their traditional role. The Center considers the view that parents know their children best and that all parents have strengths. Further, it is noted that practitioners want to be competent and need support and respect in their work. Additional useful information for early childhood educators is available at this site.

▶❚❚ "Parental Involvement in School Culture: A Literacy Project"

Visit the Education CourseMate website at www.CengageBrain.com to view the Video Case, and then respond to the following items:

- Discuss ways in which teachers might use ideas from this video case to support parental roles related to their children's education.

- How might parental engagement in a school project support parenting skills?

Summary and Conclusions

Many parents have children through biological means. Others become parents in various ways. No matter how one becomes a parent, there are many responsibilities involved in this family role. All parents need support in providing the best for their children. Traditional mother and father roles continue to be common in today's society, but many children can and do thrive in alternative family forms, including single-parent families, gay and lesbian families, and families headed by grandparents. An authoritative parenting style is most effective in fostering children's optimal development.

Parents have legal rights as well as responsibilities for their children. It is very important that early childhood teachers understand the primacy of the family in the lives of young children. This understanding lends support for active family involvement in early childhood education. Teachers must initiate partnerships with family members because, whether the role of a child's parents is traditional or nontraditional, early childhood professionals increase children's opportunities for academic success by involving adults who parent the young children in their programs.

Theory into Practice Suggestions (TIPS)

- Understand the constant challenges of parenthood.
- Celebrate joys and children's successes with their parents or parent figures.
- Be sensitive to differences in expectations and values.
- Avoid judging parental styles.
- Provide support for parenting in a variety of formats and topics.
- Support parents' involvement in children's education.
- Understand that your work with a family is a snapshot in their total history.
- Share child development information on a regular basis.
- Express appreciation to parents.
- Accommodate both mothers and fathers in their diversity.
- Find ways to support parents' multiple roles as necessary.
- Do not expect that all parents hold the same views, values, and expectations that you do.
- Expect that some grandparents will be parenting children that you teach.

- Facilitate families' support and encouragement of one another.
- Provide for specific needs of family variations, e.g., grandparents, foster parents, and others.
- Demonstrate understanding that some children are easier to parent than others.
- Help parents to secure resources necessary for effective nurturing.
- Provide information for parents about how school might have changed since they were the age of their children.

Applications

1. Consider the results of the Zero to Three study. Discuss the significance of each of the nine findings. How might early childhood teachers or administrators support families in each of these areas?

2. How might the way in which parents come to their parenting role affect their parenting philosophy and strategies? For example, how might adoptive parents differ from biological parents, and so on?

3. Discuss how specifics about each of the parenting roles have changed in the past generation or two. Also, discuss ways in which parents vary in carrying out each of the roles.

Questions for Reflection and Discussion

1. How will you involve all members of a family in your classroom? Will you differentiate requests for fathers and mothers?

2. How will you implement content from this chapter in your interactions with parents?

3. In what way is it helpful to understand variations in parenting styles and behaviors?

Field Assignments

1. Interview three mothers and three fathers about their interactions with their children. Compare the responses to research findings in this chapter.

2. Interview a parent from a blended family who is parenting both her biological child(ren) and a child or children of her spouse. Ask about both challenges and joys.

3. Interview two early childhood professionals about ideas they have for creative ways parents can spend more quality time with their children. Share these ideas in class. Compose a class list of the best ideas to keep for a resource.

4. Interview grandparents who are parenting their grandchildren. Ask them about challenges and joys. Also, invite them to share ways that schools have been helpful to them and additional ways that schools might help.

Additional resources for this chapter, including TeachSource videos, can be found on the Education CourseMate. Go to CengageBrain.com.

References

Afifi, T.A., N. P. Mota, P. Dasiewicz, H. L. MacMillen, and J. Sareen. 2012. Physical punishment and mental disorders: Results from a nationally representative U.S. sample. *Pediatrics*, published online July 2, 2012. http://pediatrics.aappublications.org/content/early/2012/06/27/peds.2011–2947. Accessed August 6, 2012.

Barnard, K. E., and J. E. Solchany. 2002. Mothering. In Vol. 3 of *Handbook of Parenting*, ed. M. H. Bornstein, 2nd ed., 3–25. Mahwah, NJ: Lawrence Erlbaum Associates.

Baumrind, D. 1966. Effects of authoritative parental control on child behavior. *Child Development* 37: 887–906.

Baumrind, D. 1967. Child care practices anteceding three patterns of preschool behavior. *Genetic Psychology Monographs* 75: 43–88.

Baumrind, D. 1971. Current patterns of parental authority. *Developmental Psychology Monographs* 4, 1, Pt. 2, 1–103.

Baumrind, D. 1977. Some thoughts about childrearing. In *Child development: Contemporary perspectives*, ed. S. Cohen and T. J. Comiskey. Itasca, IL: F. E. Peacock.

Baumrind, D. 1989. Rearing competent children. In *Child Development Today and Tomorrow*, ed. W. Damon, pp. 349–78. San Francisco: Jossey-Bass.

Brazelton, T. B., and S. I. Greenspan.2000. *The irreducible needs of children: What every child must have to grow, learn and flourish*. Cambridge, MA: Perseus.

Brazelton, T. B. and J. Sparrow. 2003. The Touchpoints model of development. www.brazeltontouchpoints.org/wp-content/uploads/2011/09/Touchpoints_Model_of_Development_Aug_2007.pdf Accessed April 15, 2012.

Brodzinsky, D. M., and E. Pinderhughes.2002. Parenting and child development in adoptive families. In Vol. 1 of *Handbook of Parenting*, ed. M. H. Bornstein, 2nd ed., 279–311. Mahwah, NJ: Lawrence Erlbaum Associates.

Bronfenbrenner, U., and P. R. Neville. 1994. America's children and families: An international perspective. In *Putting families first: America's family support movement and the challenge of change*, ed. S. L. Kagan and B. Weissbourd. San Francisco: Jossey-Bass.

Children's Defense Fund.1998. What it costs to raise a child. *CDF Reports* 19. http://www.childrensdefense.org/facts-figures—costchild.htm.

Children's Defense Fund.2001. *What it costs to raise a child to age 18*. Washington, DC: Children's Defense Fund. http://www.childrensdefense.org/data/whatitcosts.aspx (accessed December 22, 2005).

Children's Defense Fund. 2004. Child Health, CHIP, Frequently Asked Questions. http://www.childrensdefense.org/childhealth/chip/faqs.aspx (accessed December 22, 2005).

Children's Defense Fund. April 2005. *Child care basics*. Washington, DC: Children's Defense Fund.

Coles, R. 1990. *The spiritual life of children*. Boston: Houghton Mifflin.

Coltrane, S. 1996. *Family man*. New York: Oxford.

Darling, N. 1999. Parenting style and its correlates. Champaign, IL. ERIC Clearinghouse on Elementary and Early Childhood Education, Eric Digest. (ERIC Document Reproduction No. ED 427896.)

Doucette-Dudman, D., and J. R.LaCure.1996. *Raising our children's children*. Minneapolis, MN: Fairview Press.

Dunifon, R., and L. Kowaleski-Jones. 2005. The influence of grandparents in single-mother families. Unpublished manuscript. http://www.cpr.maxwell.syr.edu/seminar/fall05/Dunifon_Kowaleski-Jones.pdf (accessed December 18, 2005).

Goetting, A. 1986. Parental satisfaction. *Journal of Family Issues* 7: 83–109.

Golombok, S. 2002. Parenting and contemporary reproductive technologies. In vol. 3 of *Handbook of Parenting*, ed. M. H. Bornstein, 2nd ed., 339–60. Mahwah, NJ: Lawrence Erlbaum Associates.

Guggenheim, M., A. D. Lowe, and D. Curtis.1996. *The rights of families: The authoritative ACLU guide to the rights of family members today*. Carbondale: Southern Illinois University Press.

Hamburg, D. 1995.The challenge of parenthood. *The challenge of parenting in the '90's*. Queenstown, MD: The Aspen Institute.

Hamner, T. J., and P. H. Turner. 1996. *Parenting in contemporary society*. Boston: Allyn & Bacon.

Hanson, T. L., S. S. McLanahan, and E. Thomson. 1996. Double jeopardy: Parental conflict and stepfamily outcomes for children. *Journal of Marriage and the Family* 58: 141–54.

Haugaard, J., and C. Hazan. 2002. Foster parenting. In Vol. 1 of *Handbook of Parenting*, ed. M. H. Bornstein, 2nd ed., 313–27. Mahwah, NJ: Lawrence Erlbaum Associates.

Higginbotham, J. S. November 12, 1998. *Adoption and privacy*. Harrisburg Patriot-News.

Kornhaber, A. 1993. Raising grandchildren. *Vital Connections* 14: 1–4.

Kostelnik, M. J., L. L. Stein, A. P. Whiren, and A. K.Soderman. 1998. *Guiding children's social development.* Clifton Park, NY: Delmar Learning.

Lerner, R. M., F. Rothbaum, S. Boulos, D. R.Castellino. 2002. Developmental systems perspective on parenting. In Vol. 2 of *Handbook of Parenting*, ed. M. H. Bornstein, 2nd ed., 315–44. Mahwah, NJ: Lawrence Erlbaum Associates.

Lickona, T. E. Schaps, and C. Lewis.1998. Eleven principles of effective character education. *Scholastic Early Childhood Today* (November/December): 53–55.

Maccoby, E. E., and J. A. Martin. 1983. Socialization in the context of the family: Parent-child interaction. In Vol. 4 of *Handbook of child psychology*, ed. P. H. Mussen, 4th ed. New York: Wiley.

Medical News Today (January 2009). Success rate of live births following in vitro fertilization. http://www .medicalnewstoday.com/articles/135583.php. Accessed September 12, 2009.

Melmed, M. 1997. Parents speak: Zero to Three's findings from research on parents' views of early childhood development. *Young Children* 52: 46–49.

Miracle babies. October 12, 1998. *People.*

Moore, M. R., and J. Brooks-Gunn. 2002. Adolescent parenthood. In Vol. 3 of *Handbook of Parenting*, ed. M. H. Bornstein, 2nd ed., 173–213. Mahwah, NJ: Lawrence Erlbaum Associates.

Parke, R. D. 2002. Fathers and families. In Vol. 3 of *Handbook of Parenting*, ed. M. H. Bornstein, 2nd ed., 27–73. Mahwah, NJ: Lawrence Erlbaum Associates.

Parsons, T., and R. Bales. 1955. *Family, socialization, and interaction process.* Glencoe, IL: Free Press.

Pearl, P. T. 2000. Grandparenting. In *Parenthood in America: An encyclopedia*, ed. L. Balter.Denver: ABC– CLIO.

Pittman, G. 2012. Hitting, slapping tied to later mental disorders. Reuters Health. http://www.reuters.com /article/2012/07/02/us-hitting-slapping-mentaldisord-idUSBRE8610N020120702. Accessed August 6, 2012.

Rosenberg, E. B. 1992. *The adoption life cycle: The children and their families through the years.* New York: Free Press.

Rothenberg, D. 1999. Grandparents as parents: A primer for schools. (Report: EDO-PS-96-8). Urbana, IL. ERIC Clearinghouse on Elementary and Early Childhood Education, ERIC Digest (073). (ERIC Document Reproduction No. ED 401044).

Smith, A. B., and L. Dannison. (September 2003). Custodial grandparents and schools: Building successful partnerships. www.wmich.edu/grs/forms/GP%20%20Custodial%20GPs%20and%20Schools.pdf. Accessed September 12, 2009.

Smith, P. K., and L. M. Drew. 2002. Grandparenthood. In Vol.3 of *Handbook of Parenting*, ed. M. H. Bornstein, 2nd ed., 141–72. Mahwah, NJ: Lawrence Erlbaum Associates.

Stolley, K. 1993. Statistics on adoption in the United States. *The Future of Children: Adoption* 3: 26–42.

Trawick-Smith, J. 1997. *Early childhood development: A multicultural perspective.* Upper Saddle River, NJ: Prentice Hall.

United States Department of Agriculture. (2009). Center for Nutrition Policy and Promotion.Expenditures on Children by Families, 2008. http://www.cnpp.usda.gov/Publications/CRC/crc2008.pdf. Accessed September 12, 2009.

Vygotsky, L. S. 1978. *Mind in society: The development of higher psychological processes.* Cambridge, MA: Harvard University Press.

Zero to Three. 2009. Parenting infants and toddlers today research findings. www.zerotothree.org/about-us /funded-projects/parenting-resources/final_survey _report_3-11-2010.pdf Accessed April 15, 2012.

Family Stress

OUTLINE

© Cengage Learning/ECE Photo Library.

OBJECTIVES ALIGNED WITH NAEYC STANDARDS

After reading and reflecting on this chapter, you should be able to:

- Relate the effects of various unpredictable stressors in the lives of families with young children **naeyc** 2

- Understand some of the societal beliefs that are at the root of various forms of family violence **naeyc** 2

- Explain the grief process involved in a family's loss **naeyc** 2

- Explain factors that relate to adaptation, adjustment, and family buoyancy and elasticity **naeyc** 2

- Describe family protective and recovery factors **naeyc** 2

- Understand the role that early childhood educators have in regard to establishing trust in their work with all families **naeyc** 6

Key Terms

adaptation
adjustment
balanced families
buoyancy
child abuse and neglect
crises
disability
elasticity

extreme families
family coping
family protective factors
family recovery factors
family violence
gender inequality
homeless
incarcerated

immigrant families
marital transitions
midrange families
migrant families
resilience
serious illness
substance abuse
vulnerability

FAMILY SYSTEMS THEORY

66 Family stress can be defined as a real or imagined imbalance between the demands on the family and the family's ability to meet those demands. 99

—Clemson Extension, 2002

naeyc 2 Some families are better able to cope with stress than others. Olson and his associates (Olson, Russell, and Sprenkle 1989) found that of the three

types of families categorized by the circumplex model (**balanced**, **midrange**, and **extreme**), balanced families have, and use, more resources for coping with stress. Some of these resources include good financial management skills, an appreciation for the personalities of other family members, strong support from family and friends, and satisfaction with their quality of life. Further, balanced families are more likely to deal with stressors rather than deny them; they are more effective communicators, and they have better problem-solving strategies.

Boss (1988) defines **family coping** as "the management of a stressful event or situation by the family as a unit with no detrimental effects on any individual in that family. Family coping is the cognitive, affective, and behavioral process by which individuals and their family system as a whole manage rather than eradicate stressful events or situations." This definition implies that passively coping with traumatic situations may be detrimental to family functioning. Sometimes, however, giving up is required for a family to change. Boss (1988) notes that "even though it looks like failure when a family fails to cope, the failure itself can be positive." Thus, when families place too heavy an emphasis on coping, they may not adapt or change in ways that could increase their quality of life.

More recently, efforts have been made to study family stress and coping together in terms of family resiliency (McCubbin, McCubbin, Thompson, Han, and Allen 1997). Family **resilience** is defined as "the property of the family system that enables it to maintain its established patterns of functioning after being challenged and confronted by risk factors (**elasticity**)... and the family's ability to recover quickly from a misfortune, trauma, or transitional event causing or calling for changes in the family's patterns of functioning (**buoyancy**)" (McCubbin et al. 1997). Research has led to the identification of family protective factors, which protect against various risks, thus increasing a family's elasticity. Additionally, family recovery factors have been identified; these phenomena support a family's buoyancy.

Family protective factors (FPF) and **family recovery factors (FRF)** comprise the positive side of families' ability to cope with their **vulnerability** and **crises**. *Vulnerability* refers to the family's possibility of being faced with risk factors that have a negative impact on functions, whereas the term *crisis* refers to the possibility for a family's ongoing instability or dysfunction (McCubbin et al. 1997).

The two family processes that have been found to be related to resilience are **adjustment** and **adaptation**. The process of adjustment engages a given family's protective factors in continuing to perform necessary functions even as they are faced with various risks. On the other hand, adaptation engages a family's recovery factors inasmuch as the family has the ability to bounce back or recover after dealing with crises. Although both protective and recovery factors are likely to be based on a given family's strengths, there is evidence that at various points in the family life cycle, particular forms of crises may be related to some common resources. For example, families of preschool children typically find community support and religious programs to be protective, while families of adolescents find family cohesiveness to be especially important (McCubbin et al. 1997). Thus, it behooves early childhood teachers to

attend to current evidence about protective and recovery factors for families of young children.

The previous paragraphs provide terminology in order to understand the evidence regarding family resilience. However, they do not address the specific factors included in adjustment and adaptation, in recovery and protection. Figure 6–1 provides a list of general protective and recovery factors that are known to support family resilience. **naeyc** 2

> ### Consider This
> Consider the 10 factors that support family resiliency in Figure 6-1. Using your personal and professional experience, provide anecdotal evidence for at least three of these factors.

Horizontal Stressors

Chapter 3 addresses the developmental issues typical for young families or families with young children. These horizontal stressors are specifically referred to in family systems theory as developmental stressors. Another type of horizontal stressor in this theory is the unpredictable stressor, affecting families regardless of the stage of the family life cycle (Carter and McGoldrick 1989). The very nature of these stressors—their unpredictability—makes them difficult to cope with and to resolve.

FAMILIES AND UNPREDICTABLE STRESSORS

Examples of unpredictable events include family violence, effects of **substance abuse**, homelessness, disabilities, various illnesses, immigration, military deployment, and the incarceration of a parent.

> ### Do This
> As you read and reflect on each of the stressors in this chapter, consider how economic factors may ease or intensify family issues. Review the economic diversity section, paying special attention to effects of poverty, in Chapter 2.

Family Violence

naeyc 2 Violence is prevalent in the lives of families in the United States. The very institution that should be providing love and nurturance is also the one in which violence is too often perpetrated. It is important that early childhood teachers have some understanding of

McCubbin, McCubbin, Thompson, Han, and Allen (1997)

Figure 6–1	General Family Resiliency Factors.

1. *Family Problem-Solving Communication.* Families are challenged during times of risk or crises to use forms of communication that are affirming of one another. However, those families who are able to use such constructive means of communicating demonstrate an important component of family resilience.

2. *Equality.* Resilience is increased when all family members are empowered to be self-reliant and independent. Stereotypic gender roles that decrease women's authority or power can be a negative factor in terms of resilience. Of course, young children must be supported as they learn to become responsible members of the family.

3. *Spirituality.* Family spiritual beliefs and practices often provide comfort and support as families deal with unexpected, harsh realities.

4. *Flexibility.* Because crises often require families to change in at least some way, those families who are able to alter their roles, expectations, and even traditions have greater resiliency in the face of shifting circumstances.

5. *Truthfulness.* In order to move to helpful changes, families must operate in a realm of truth. Honesty within the family system as well as from external sources (e.g., medical, social services, legal) is necessary for healthy coping and recovery.

6. *Hope.* Families who can optimistically look forward to their future typically have greater resilience. This can be difficult in times of chronic **disability** or terminal illness. Yet, resilient families often find hope through a new generation as they lose members of older ones.

7. *Family Hardiness.* Hardy families pull together with strong resolve to get through crises. One factor in hardiness is commitment to working together, another is a family's belief that it can overcome difficulties.

8. *Family Time and Routine.* Family members build relationships with one another through time together, especially in common routines. When family members are dealing with crises, some semblance of normalcy tends to increase harmony and balance.

9. *Social Support.* Participation in existing networks of support including extended family, friends, and community all contribute to a family's resiliency. Sometimes, adding new social support systems, such as a single-parents network when coping with divorce, increases the ability to cope.

10. *Health.* Both physical and psychological health of family members increases protective and recovery factors for coping with crises. Because so many family crises relate to one or more members' ill health, an emphasis on healthy habits can support resiliency.

the rate of violence as well as ideas about why it is so common. Women and children are at greater risk of being victims of abuse than are men. ⬛naeyc 2

Straus (1991) discusses five social causes of **family violence**:

- High level of conflict inherent to family life
- **Gender inequality**
- Norms that allow violence in the family
- Early training in violence within the family
- Multiple risk factors, such as alcoholism, poverty, and societal violence

High Level of Conflict Inherent in Family Life Some of the inherent conflicts in families arise from gender and age differences, involuntary membership in the family, family insulation or privacy, and the relationship of violence to conflict. These factors are considered to play at least some role in family violence. Any of these factors by itself is not viewed as the sole cause or reason for violence. Understanding the complexity of causes of family violence is important; one cannot predict that violence will exist in a given family based on the presence of one or more of these factors.

Gender and Age Differences Most families are made up of both males and females, and have members of various ages. A great deal of research points to gender differences in values, priorities, interests, and notions about power. These differences lead to male-female differences in families. Some areas of difference include amount of income, activities and interests, and even television programming. In most families, these differences do not lead to violence, but when other factors are present, such differences seem to result in harm against females, younger children, or older family members. Although abuse can be committed against males, it occurs much less frequently, and they are less likely to be physically hurt by it. The generation gap also creates areas of conflict. Different generations have different preferences for music, clothing styles, and how to spend their leisure time.

Involuntary Membership Family members did not necessarily choose each other. Even though marriage partners in the United States are likely to have at one time chosen each other, many factors influence these choices, including the belief that they had many areas in common with one another. Marriage and parenthood often squelch some of those common interests. Responsibilities tend to take over each person, sometimes decreasing the sense of commitment to one another.

Children and parents do not typically choose each other. Rather, they get the luck of the draw. Some children are fortunate to have parents who nurture and understand their needs without reverting to violent methods of child-rearing. Others are less fortunate. The very fact that many family members are put together by circumstance rather than choice can cause tension among members. The old adage "You can choose your friends, but not your relatives" has more meaning than many people realize. This factor carries over to relationships with in-laws and stepchildren.

Preservation and Child Welfare Network
http://www.childwelfare.com

Family Violence Prevention Fund
http://endabuse.org

National Clearinghouse on Child Abuse and Neglect Information
http://ncadi.samhsa.gov

National Coalition Against Domestic Violence
http://www.ncadv.org/

National Council on Child Abuse and Family Violence
http://www.nccafv.org/

National Domestic Violence Hotline
http://www.ndvh.org/

Family Privacy Families are often insulated and have strong beliefs about being self-sufficient. The notion of privacy in the family can often be taken to an extreme. Spouses may speak to each other and their children in ways they would not want anyone else to hear. Behavior that is not observed by outsiders is less likely to be civil or humane, especially in the face of conflict. It is this factor—family privacy—that is overlooked by many when a pillar of the community is accused of spousal or child abuse. Family privacy, while of tremendous value, can also lead to harmful family secrets: "It's nobody's business."

Increasing Conflict Leads to Violence As the amount of conflict increases in a variety of areas within a family, violence becomes more likely. Family privacy, sexism, and disparities in physical power increase the likelihood that a person believes that he is right—and has the right—to use his fists to settle conflict. This belief is accompanied by little chance of getting caught

and the belief that "a good beating" will stop the behavior that is causing conflict.

Gender Inequality Many people continue to believe that husbands are and should be the heads of households. This belief is supported in many informal ways throughout our society. Legal documents often list male names first, even in the case of co-ownership or joint income tax returns. Sometimes, this leads to a belief in male dominance and in the related belief that men have ultimate responsibility for all decisions and practices in their families. Research shows that "the greater the departure from gender equality, the greater the risk that physical force will be used to maintain the power of the dominant person" (Straus 1991). This is true even when females agree that males should be dominant. Even though male dominance is a factor in family violence, it is important to understand that most male-dominant marriages are not violent. Rather, gender inequality is one factor that makes violence more likely.

Society's Sanction of Violence Parents are permitted, and in some communities expected, to use physical punishment on their children. When child abuse laws were passed in the 1970s, most laws indicated that the intent was not to take away parental authority or the rights of parents to use physical punishment. A vast majority of parents use physical punishment, especially with young children. Fully 90 percent of parents support the use of such methods as necessary for child-rearing.

Just as our cultural norms support spanking and other forms of physical punishment of children, they also frequently support hitting in marriage. Even though many say they oppose violence generally, large numbers of adults still note that there are some instances when spouses can and should be hit, especially those related to extramarital sexual affairs. It is never permissible to strike a colleague in the heat of disagreement, nor is it socially acceptable to use violence in any other social setting.

Early Training in Family Violence In families, violence is carried out by loving parents who are genuinely concerned about their children. The use of physical punishment for even small infractions teaches children that hitting within families is okay. "The problem is that these actions also teach the child the principle that those who love you are those who hit you" (Straus 1991). Research has shown that the more adults were physically punished as children, the greater the chance that they will hit their spouses as adults (Straus 1983).

Multiple Causes In addition to the factors already mentioned, other factors that increase the probability of violence in families include alcoholism and other forms of substance abuse, poverty, and other types of stress on families. Again, however, none of these factors necessarily predicts family violence. Even though violence occurs in families at an alarmingly high rate, there are more nonviolent families than violent ones, even when several predictive factors for violence are in place. However, families that possess several of these factors are at much higher risk for violence. One study showed that when factors were placed in a checklist format, as the scores on the checklist increased, so did violence increase (Straus, Gelles, and Steinmetz 1980).

Research indicates that family violence is not committed by only a few very sick individuals. It is much more widespread than many people believe. Early childhood teachers must take seriously any indication that children in their care may have been abused or observed family violence. This is true even when the teacher tends to doubt the possibility of abuse because the child comes from a "good family."

A Particular Form of Family Violence: Child Abuse

The Child Abuse Prevention and Treatment Act of 1974, PL 93–247, defined **child abuse and neglect**. This law described abuse and neglect as "the physical or mental injury, sexual abuse, negligent treatment, or maltreatment of a child under the age of 18 by a person who is responsible for the child's welfare under the circumstances which indicate that the child's health or welfare is harmed or threatened thereby" (U.S. Department of Health, Education, and Welfare 1975). Individual state statutes are based on this federal law and are available from county courthouses, state legislators, or state legislative libraries (Iverson and Segal 1990).

Early childhood educators and child advocates often question the causes of child abuse. They wonder about the type of person who could hurt small children. Also, teachers are commonly concerned about safety and the best placement for children whose family members have abused them. Although many people believe that only someone with a severe mental disorder would harm a small child, reality does not bear this out. Historically, children have been viewed as the property of their parents, and thus they could be legally harmed or killed by parents. This perspective affected, and continues to affect, attitudes and behaviors toward children.

Until the 1974 law was passed, there were few safeguards for children whose parents maltreated them. In contrast, cruelty to animals was outlawed at least a century earlier. It was the Society for the Prevention of Cruelty to Animals (SPCA) that advocated for Mary Ellen in a widely publicized case of severe child abuse in 1874. This astonishing fact demonstrates that abuse of children has been an acceptable practice based in part on the low status of children in families and in society (Iverson and Segal 1990).

naeyc 2 Research over the past 30 years has demonstrated the ill effects of abuse and neglect on children. Early childhood educators are aware that these effects on children ultimately affect classroom dynamics. Based on ecological theory, Garbarino (as cited in Iverson and Segal 1990) notes two primary causes of abuse as parental psychopathology and societal approval of physical punishment of children. It follows that preventive efforts must focus on both of these causes. Thus, family support services must include attention to families' mental health needs as well as to teaching parents alternative methods of discipline to physical punishment.

Some family characteristics have been shown to be related to abuse of children. In their review of literature, Iverson and Segal (1990) note the following factors:

- Parental experience includes models parents have for child-rearing, especially from their own families and in their own cultures; skills for parenting; and understanding of child development.
- High levels of stress caused either by children or environment; poverty is especially stressful.
- Some characteristics of parents who abuse their children include physical or medical problems, intellectual deficits, the lack of ability to form healthy parent-child relationship, marital problems, low self-esteem, immaturity, neuroses, dependency, and depression.
- Teen parents are more likely to possess the characteristics of parents who abuse because of their developmental levels. Because of their developmental stage, teens are consumed with themselves and are typically financially dependent.

These characteristics place them at higher risk for abusing their children.

Although the characteristics listed previously indicate those families that are at higher risk for child abuse, not all teen parents or those with intellectual deficits, for example, will harm their children. Understanding the risk factors should help professionals provide appropriate resources for preventing neglect and abuse of children. For example, parenting programs for those at risk might include not only information about what is best for their children but also child care for teen parents so that they are able to complete their education. Those living in poverty benefit from high-quality child care that provides sufficient time away from childcare responsibilities to enable them to finish school or take advantage of job training opportunities. **naeyc** 2

Figure 6–2	Effects of Abuse and Neglect on Children.

Infants and Toddlers
attachment disorders
aggressive toward peers and caregivers
not responsive to friendly overtures

Preschoolers
physically and/or verbally aggressive
destructive behavior
angry outbursts
less socially mature than nonmaltreated children
play alone or watch others from a distance

School-agers
angry
aggressive
less impulsive than maltreated preschool children

© Cengage Learning

The effects of abuse and neglect on children are listed in Figures 6–2 and 6–3 (Iverson and Segal 1990). **naeyc** 6 Early childhood teachers have a legal responsibility to report any suspected case of child abuse. For this reason, it is important that professionals be familiar with the indicators of physical, sexual, and emotional abuse and neglect of children because this knowledge must be applied when teachers document the reasons they suspect abuse. Reporting an instance of possible child abuse is not intended to punish families, but rather to help them receive the interventions they need to help them manage their children and their lives.

Many states have telephone hotlines for reports of child abuse. If you do not know your state's hotline or who to call, contact your State Department of Human Services. These departments have a variety of other names, including Public Welfare, Human Resources, Family Services, and Child and Youth Services. Check the social service agency listings in your local telephone directory for help. Please note that even though schools and child care centers often create procedures for teachers to report suspected cases of abuse or neglect through principals or directors, many states list teachers as those who are required to report to state officials.

When you call to report a case of suspected child abuse, it is likely that the individual taking your call will ask the following:

- From where are you calling?
- What is your name? (You may choose to remain anonymous, depending on circumstances.)
- What have you observed that led to this call?
- What is the child's name?
- How old is the child?

- What are the child's parents' names?
- Where does the child go to school?
- Can you provide a description of the child?
- What is the child's address?
- Have you discussed your observations with the child or family members? **naeyc** 6

It is important for educators to understand that reports are made to child protective service workers, but that, ultimately, it is the legal system—the courts—that decides the outcome for abused children and their families. Although agencies and courts have critical roles in attacking the problem of child abuse in our society, teachers of young children have an increasingly important role.

When the 1988 reauthorization of funding bill for the National Center on Child Abuse and Neglect was legislated, the importance of increased school involvement in the prevention, identification, and treatment of child abuse and neglect was noted (Cicchetti, Toth, and Hennessy 1993). This recommendation arose from the research evidence that maltreated children's learning processes are interrupted or otherwise negatively affected. To optimize learning for children who have been abused and neglected, Cicchetti and his associates offer several suggestions for educators, details of which can be found in Figure 6–4.

66 Children have neither power nor property. Voices other than their own must speak for them. If those voices are silent, then children who have been abused may lean their heads against windowpanes and taste the bitter emptiness of violated childhoods. Badger every legislator from every county ... let no editor or reporter sleep, until the remedy you want is granted. For you are the only voices of the violated child. If you do not speak, there is silence. 99

**—Justice Francis T. Murphy, cited in
Doucette-Dudman and LaCure, 1996**

Consider This

Consider all eight of the recommendations for schools regarding maltreated children in Figure 6-4. Which items have you observed in practice? Which items do you believe are not commonly practiced? What are some barriers to putting these policies into practice? How might collaboration among schools and agencies increase positive outcomes for maltreated children?

Substance Abuse in Families

naeyc 1 When family members use illegal drugs, or misuse alcohol or prescription drugs, children often suffer great difficulties. Parents who are addicted

Figure 6–3   Indicators of Abuse and Neglect.

PHYSICAL CHARACTERISTICS OF MALTREATED CHILDREN

Physical Abuse

Bruises, lacerations, welts, abrasions, fractures, or burns as follows:

Unusual location:

- Cheeks, lips, mouth, earlobes
- Back, buttocks, back of legs
- External genitalia
- Burns on soles of feet, palms of hands, back or buttocks

Unusual appearance:

- Clustered or patterned
- Resembling the shape of an instrument
- On several different surface areas
- Cigar or cigarette burns
- Immersion (glove- or sock-like burns)
- Rope burns (especially on neck)

Suspicious circumstances:

- No explanation
- Explanation does not fit injury
- Patterns to the occurrence of injuries (e.g., after absences from school)
- Repeated injuries, or injuries in various stages of healing
- Nonorganic failure to thrive

Neglect

Underweight, malnourished

Poor hygiene

Fatigue, constantly falling asleep

Bald spot on infant's head

Unattended physical problems or medical needs:

- Chronic anemia
- Severe diaper rash
- Skin rashes
- Tooth decay/gum disease
- Head/body lice
- Ringworm
- Nonorganic failure to thrive

Sexual Abuse

Swelling, bruising or irritation around:

- Genital areas
- Anal areas
- Mouth

Torn, stained, or bloody underclothing

Vaginal discharge

Pain/discomfort in walking or sitting

Anal ulcers

Genital pain or itching

Venereal diseases

Difficulty in urination

Pregnancy

Emotional Abuse

Physical symptoms of anxiety:

- Psychogenic skin disorders
- Pain with no physical basis
- Ulcers
- Unexplained vomiting

COMMON DESCRIPTIONS OF THE INTERPERSONAL BEHAVIOR OF MALTREATED CHILDREN

Physical Abuse	Neglect	Sexual Abuse	Emotional Abuse
Aggressive	Aggressive	Sexually aggressive or preoccupied with sex	Aggressive
Withdrawal	Withdrawal	Overly compliant	Suspicious
Avoidance	Suspicious/distrustful of others	Seductive	Avoids eye contact
Fearful of others	Unresponsive	Distrustful	Unable to make friends
Angry	Hostility	Fearful of opposite sex	Overly compliant
"Frozen watchfulness"		"Role reversal"	Overly noncompliant
Hostility		Withdrawn	Bizarre or inappropriate interpersonal behavior
		Isolated	

Continues

From Iverson, T. J., and Segal M. (1990). *Child Abuse and Neglect: An Information and Reference Guide*. Table 4.1, p. 72; Table 4.4, p. 95; and Table 4.6, p. 106. Reprinted by permission of Garland Publishing, Inc.

Figure 6–3	Indicators of Abuse and Neglect *(Continued)*

BEHAVIOR SEQUELAE OF MALTREATMENT

Physical Abuse	Neglect	Sexual Abuse	Emotional Abuse
Self-abusive behavior	Irregular school attendance	Excessive daydreaming/ fantasizing	Self-abusive behavior
Lying	Begging, stealing, or hoarding food	Excessive sexual play/ masturbation	Hoarding food
Stealing	Lying	Self-abusive behavior	Referral to self in the third person
Truancy	Theft	Truancy	Thumb-sucking
Tics	Vandalism	Running away	Nail biting
Stuttering	Running away	Regressive/infantile behavior	Habit disorders—sucking, biting, rocking
Unpredictable	Daydreaming	Suicidal gestures	Obsessive or compulsive behaviors
	Bizarre eating habits	Insomnia	Insomnia
	Nail biting		Enuresis
	Tics		Truancy
	Stuttering		Running away
	Unpredictable		Destructive behavior

to drugs or alcohol typically cannot provide consistent nurturing for their children. Further, a family's economic well-being is compromised when adults lose their jobs because of behavior related to substance abuse.

Resources for Information about Child Abuse and Neglect

National Center on Child Abuse and Neglect (NCCAN) 63 Inverness Drive East Englewood, Colorado 80112-5117; (303) 792–9900
http://www.ncadi.samsha.gov
National Committee to Prevent Child Abuse 332 S. Michigan Avenue, Suite 1600 Chicago, Illinois 60604; (312) 663-3520
http://www.casanet.org/
Click "advocate's library;" click "abuse" National Association of Counsel for Children 205 Oneida Street Denver, Colorado 80822; (303) 322-2260
http://naccchildlaw.org/

Mothers' prenatal use of alcohol and drugs may have dire consequences for newborns that last throughout life. Drinking alcohol during pregnancy may lead to babies having Fetal Alcohol Syndrome (FAS); the safe level of alcohol intake during pregnancy is not known. The characteristics of FAS include central nervous system disorders, growth lags,

and facial deformity (Olson 1994). Effects of maternal drug use on infants and young children include neurological immaturity, which is manifested in poor sleeping and eating patterns, poor self-control, inconsolability, hypersensitivity to the environment, and decreased ability to interact with others (Poulsen 1994).

Center for Interventions, Treatment and Addiction Research
http://www.med.wright.edu/
Search for Center for Intervention, Treatment and Addictions Research (CITAR)

Center for Substance Abuse Treatment
http://www.samhsa.gov/centers/csat2002

Center on Addiction and Substance Abuse
http://www.casacolumbia.org/

Addiction to any substance (or condition) points to personality characteristics, disabilities, or impairments, each of which may have significant implications for an adult's ability to parent a child and may predispose an adult to adopt an authoritarian, overcontrolling, or underinvolved style of parenting. Moreover, all abused substances alter to varying degrees an individual's state of consciousness, memory, affect regulation, and impulse control, and may become so addictive that the adult's

Figure 6–4	Policy Implications for Schools Educating Maltreated Children.

Cicchetti, D., S. L. Toth, and K. Hennessy (1993). Child Maltreatment and School Adaptation: Problems and Promises. In *Child Abuse, Child Development, and Social Policy*, ed. D. Cicchetti and S. L. Toth, 301–30. Norwood, NJ: Ablex.

The following recommendations are from the work of Cicchetti, Toth, and Hennessy (1993).

1. Assessments of maltreated children must include not only those for cognitive development and academic achievement but also those for the social and emotional domains. Because many abused children act out in school, too often the emphasis is on the behavior only and not on the emotional disturbance caused by abusive situations.

2. Intervention efforts must begin as soon as identification of maltreatment occurs. Schools may be the only setting in which such interventions can occur. Thus, courts and agencies must work with educators for positive outcomes. At this time, often interpretations of confidentiality procedures exclude educators and schools from appropriate levels of participation in intervention.

   Educators must increase their understanding of the importance of confidentiality in instances of abuse so that they can share appropriately in intervention efforts.

3. Early childhood teachers who are involved in intervention efforts should include parents and other relevant family members. This creates the greatest possibility of continuity between environments.

4. The curriculum for maltreated children must be developmentally appropriate. Including all areas of child development in curriculum goals is essential so that these children have a greater chance for adjustment throughout their lives. Special planning and instructional support may be necessary for children to gain abilities and attitudes for cognitive, social, and emotional growth.

5. Specific training for teachers is necessary in regard to styles and strategies that are conducive to optimizing development of maltreated children. Teachers must recognize and avoid "any physically or

emotionally abusive interchanges with children." The use of physical punishment must be forbidden. Too few teachers are trained in early childhood special education, especially in the area of emotional support.

   Research suggests that an extrinsic, behaviorally focused system for these children may interfere with their motivation. Thus, behavior modification programs should not be used with abused and neglected children. Instead, plans should include strategies for increasing the children's internal motivation while dealing with their emotional distress.

6. Teachers of young children are very important figures in children's lives. A positive relationship based on trust is important. Some current practices such as multiage grouping and looping are useful for abused children in that they may continue to build positive relationships with the same teacher or teachers for longer than one school term.

7. Because identification of abuse and neglect must come before any educational intervention can be offered, teachers and schools must improve their knowledge regarding recognizing and reporting instances of maltreatment. Having the attitude that reporting is required to help the child, not to punish the family, is also valuable.

8. Training must be provided so that child protective services workers and educators can work together effectively. Little progress has been made in this area and unfortunately these groups of professionals often see the other group as problematic instead of working collegially toward more effective interventions. To be fair to individuals, the human services system and the educational system have not typically fostered these working relationships.

---

primary goal is to supply her addiction to the exclusion of all else and all others in her life. These alterations likely have a marked influence, at any given moment, on the adult's capacity to sustain contingent, responsive interactions with an infant or young child (Mayes 1995).

Children who are growing up in homes in which one or more adults are addicted to drugs or alcohol are likely to be affected in one or more of the following ways:

- Reverse roles with parent
- Are fearful, angry, mistrusting, guilty, and sad
- Are either over-responsible or under-responsible
- Suffer chronic grief or depression
- Are isolated from others
- Have academic problems
- Have learning disabilities (Krestan and Bepko 1989) **naeyc** 1

DAP Children living in families with alcoholism or drug abuse frequently need more support than classroom teachers can provide. Referring children to guidance counselors or other mental health professionals may be helpful. **DAP**

66 Numerous barriers stand between women, especially mothers, and drug treatment. For example, women often resist entering treatment programs because they must release their children to someone else's care and fear never seeing them again. Despite this reality, only a handful of residential drug-treatment programs accept women with their children. Treatment programs need to be developed that treat parents, especially mothers, in the context of their families. 99

—Zuckerman and Brazelton, 1994

Marital Transitions and Single Parenting

Divorce and remarriage have become so common in our society that some family experts believe they may be developmental stressors rather than unexpected ones. However, because the consequences of divorce and remarriage for young children are often stressful, and because teachers and parents may disregard or discount the significance of these occurrences in the lives of children, we address these transitions here. Children may benefit from knowing other children and families in similar circumstances, but by and large the changes in family structure are likely to generate concern for all family members.

In the United States, the divorce rate began to rise in the 1960s. Currently, almost 50 percent of marriages end in divorce. Most people who divorce eventually remarry. Remarriages in which children from previous relationships are present have a 50 percent higher rate of dissolution than those without children from previous relationships (Fields and Casper 2001).

The number of single-parent families has also increased since 1970. In 2000, there were 10 million single-mother families, compared to 3 million in 1970. The number of single-father families also increased during that period, from 393,000 to 2 million. Compared to single-father families, single-mother families are more likely to have more than one child, to live below the poverty level, and to have never married. As the proportion of married couples has decreased, the proportion of U.S. families that are led by single mothers has increased. Single-parent families have increased both as a result of the divorce rate and a rise in the number of births among single women. Birth rates among single women continued to increase throughout the 1990s even as the divorce rate began to level off. Some experts predict that the divorce rate may soon fall to 40 percent (Emery 1999; Fields and Casper 2001).

naeyc 1 Disagreement persists among scholars about the effects of divorce on children. Even though many studies have been completed in this area, families' experiences include so many variables that this has impeded researchers from declaring conclusive results. Robert Emery (1999), in his extensive review of research literature, has compiled "four global facts about consequences of divorce for children," as follows:

1. Divorce causes stress for children. Such stress is often related to the loss of frequent contact with one parent. Another common cause of stress has to do with the economic hardship that families face as they divide one household into two.

2. Children whose parents divorce are at an increased risk for psychological difficulties, both internalized (depression, anxiety) and externalized (behavioral, conduct) problems.

3. Despite children's increased risk for psychological problems when their parents divorce, they are resilient in their coping.

4. Even with this ability to cope, children remain emotionally vulnerable when parents divorce. Even well-adjusted adults whose parents divorced when they were children report the existence of painful feelings, unhappy memories, and ongoing distress.

One of the many perplexing topics regarding divorce and children is cause and effect. It might be that children who display serious consequences seemingly from parental divorce may actually have suffered some distress or difficulties before the divorce, and that the source of those difficulties may be troubled parents, relationship issues, parents who lack parenting skills, or parents who have mental health-related issues. Of course, it is possible that parents in these situations are more likely to divorce and to have troubled children (Emery 1999). In such cases, divorce may exacerbate children's behaviors, or it may cause family members or educators to notice these behaviors.

The resilience of children has been documented in research about divorce. Even though children from divorced families have more difficulties than children from married families, "time does appear to help divorced families to heal" (Emery 1999). Support and concern from caring adults are helpful to children experiencing divorce; however, the passing of time also is an important consideration. Researchers have found that most children show significant improvement in their adjustment two years after a divorce (Emery 1999). **naeyc** 1

66 Perhaps what is most insensitive and unjust is to arrive at the conclusions about divorce and its effects on children without carefully considering what we know, not just what we believe. 99

—Robert Emery, 1999

A key question for early childhood teachers when examining the effects of divorce on young children is "What factors help children reach a healthy adjustment as their family structure changes?" First, parents can implement some strategies to support children's adjustment to the new family structure. Galinsky and David (1988) share this advice for parents:

Explain the separation to the children and provide as much consistency as possible. Tell them where they will live, who will care for them, and when and how they will visit the noncustodial parent. Keep them updated on changes in advance of new situations.

Explain that the separation is not the child's fault and that it might take a while to feel better about it. Young children often believe that they caused the separation or divorce because of inappropriate behavior or a onetime wish. Parents most likely will need to frequently remind children that they were not the cause. Sharing feelings, both sad and optimistic, will be important for the healing process.

Encourage children to continue the discussion when they have concerns or questions. In addition to authentic conversations, children's books and media can provide a basis for discussion. Invite children to have conversations with you.

Provide support for children and yourself. Children and adults need various forms of social, emotional, and sometimes physical support as they adjust to new circumstances involved in divorce. Both personal (family and friends) and professional support is helpful.

Avoid promises, uncertain assurances, surprises, and extravagances led by guilt. Focus on what is real. Have fun together. Delight in the joys that exist in the relationship with your child.

DAP Second, teachers and other community members can be excellent sources of support for children and parents as they adjust to their new living arrangements. Early childhood teachers can share the previous advice for parents through newsletters or the establishment of special-interest parent groups. Further, school-wide groups for children have been found to be effective in supporting their adjustment to divorce. Such groups provide a place for children to share their feelings and experiences and to discuss their changing family relationships. In these discussions, strategies can be offered to help children through various **marital transitions** such as separation, divorce, remarriage, or other blended living arrangements. Effective programs teach children specific appropriate skills for problem solving, communication, and expression of emotions, including fear and anger (Emery 1999). **DAP**

"Divorce and Children"

Visit the Education CourseMate website at www.CengageBrain.com to view the Video Case, and then respond to the following items:

- Discuss what is known about the effects of divorce on young children.

- How might parents and teachers work together to best meet the needs of young children whose families are experiencing divorce?

Consider This

Consider the information shared about marital transitions. Have you observed or experienced any of the situations related to this topic? How might teachers best support children and families in such circumstances?

Adjustment Tasks for Stepfamilies

http://www.stepfamilyinfo.org/

Divorce Education and Mediation Program

http://www.hamiltontn.gov/
Click "courts information;" click "circuit court clerk;" click "divorce education seminars"

Helping Children to Understand Divorce

http://www.muextension.missouri.edu/
Type in "Helping children understand divorce"

Primary Project

http://www.childrensinstitute.net
Click "programs for children"

Homeless Families

The number of **homeless** individuals in the United States is increasing. Precise statistics are difficult to come by because of the elusive nature of homelessness; one estimate from 1990 indicates that 500,000 to 750,000 school-age children are homeless and that this number is growing (National Coalition for the Homeless, as cited in Kling, Dunn, and Oakley 1996). Children's advocates agree that all young children have the right to a safe space to live. Much of our understanding about the optimal development of the whole child assumes physical and emotional safety. "The average homeless family includes two to three children under age five." It is believed that a common reason for homelessness is an inadequate supply of affordable housing combined with declining family incomes, even when the adults in the household are employed. In short, there is too little money to pay for available housing.

naeyc 1 The effects on children of being homeless are vast. Among the difficulties are language and motor delays and unmet health needs. Behavioral problems and emotional disabilities are frequently found in children who live in shelters. In addition, many of the children's parents also are plagued with mental health problems (Hamner and Turner 1996). **naeyc** 1

naeyc 2 Living conditions among homeless families vary: some live in a shelter, some have lived in several shelters over a period of months, and others live with friends or extended families. When homeless families move in with another family, conditions are frequently overcrowded and offer no privacy. Stays may last for a few weeks or a few months, and the family may then move in with other friends or family members. For children in early childhood programs, these relocations often mean that they either drop out of the program (before mandatory school age) or change schools. These disruptions may be sudden and create difficult transitions for young children. naeyc 2

Education of Homeless Children and Youth
http://www.naehcy.org

Futures for Children
http://www.futuresforchildren.com/

Homeless Children's Network
http://www.hcnkids.org/

Homes for the Homeless
http://www.homesforthehomeless.com/

The Reading Connection
http://www.thereadingconnection.org/

Following are some characteristics of homeless children:

- Sleep disturbances
- Nighttime anxieties about possessions, even wearing their shoes to prevent theft
- Lethargy and inattention at school
- May hoard food at school
- Nutritional deficiencies
- Delays in immunizations
- Insecurity
- Trouble playing with other children and making friends
- Aggression
- Anxiety
- Language and other developmental delays (Kling, Dunn, and Oakley 1996)

When parents are not able to provide shelter or security for their children, they often feel guilty and helpless: if they are not even competent enough to provide their children's basic needs, how can they possibly assist their children academically? Thus, the self-esteem of parents in homeless families is likely to be very low. Understanding these characteristics of homeless families and children can help early childhood teachers act sensitively toward them.

DAP Early childhood educators must look for the strengths in homeless families, just as they look for strengths in other families. Research shows that although these families have almost no material possessions, they do have "the desire and the will to maintain the family unit regardless of continual changes in their life circumstances" (Kling, Dunn, and Oakley 1996). All children

need consistency in classroom schedules and routines, but children without homes need this consistency even more. They are also likely to need some alone time at school because they often live in crowded situations. DAP

naeyc 2 Parents in homeless families may not be able to participate as active partners in their children's education. Often, just getting their children to school is a huge accomplishment for these parents. So, extending special invitations to homeless parents so that they can be included in school activities in ways they feel comfortable may be a huge boost to their self-esteem. Following are some suggestions for early childhood educators who are working with homeless families:

- Set up a parent lounge where support groups could form and meet regularly.
- Provide reading materials about child development, lists of and contacts for family services available in the community, and free activities for parents and children to do together.
- Set up a toy lending library.
- Formulate a plan for homeless children to borrow toys from school to take to the shelter.
- Provide banks for clothing, food, and first aid materials.
- Maintain appropriate confidentiality while helping families obtain available services. naeyc 2

Do This

Volunteer at a homeless shelter to increase your understanding and experience with children and families who are homeless.

naeyc 6 Early childhood educators also should be aware of the Stewart B. McKinney Homeless Assistance Act of 1987, which provides some funding to states for serving homeless families. Teachers should contact their State Department of Education to find out what programs for homeless families are operating in their state (Kling, Dunn, and Oakley 1996).

The following resources may be helpful in increasing teachers' understanding of working with children from homeless families:

National Alliance to End Homelessness 1518 K Street NW, Suite 206 Washington, DC 20005
(202) 638-1526
http://www.neh.org/

National Coalition for the Homeless
1439 Rhode Island Avenue, NW
Washington, DC 20005
(202) 659-3310

National Law Center on Homelessness and Poverty
918 F Street, NW, Suite 412
Washington, DC 20004
(202) 638-2535
http://www.nlchp.org/ **naeyc** 6

Families and Children with Disabilities

"Children may be born with one or more disabilities, and they may acquire disabilities later in life because of accident or disease" (Hamner and Turner 1996). When a baby is identified with a disability at birth, parents often react with disbelief. Many parents perceive and experience this news as a loss, certainly the loss of a dream if not of a life (see Figure 6–5), and they must then proceed through the grief process. Although parents grieve in individual ways, some conditions of grieving seem to be common (Moses 1983):

- Denial
- Anxiety
- Guilt
- Depression
- Anger

Reading materials about child development, family services available in the community, and free activities for parents and children to do together can be offered by early childhood educators who are working with homeless families.

Figure 6–5	Explanations for Each of the Conditions of Grief.

Denial—Parents who are informed that their child has a disability are so overwhelmed by shock and fear that denial is one way to cope. They are likely to look for complete cures for their child's condition, even when none exist.

Anxiety—Constant concern for the child, as well as for their entire family, often leads parents to feel extreme pressure and worry. Arrangements for the child's medical care and further testing often overwhelm already busy parents. Sleeplessness, irritability, and other symptoms associated with anxiety may become prevalent.

Guilt—"If only I had eaten better"; "If only I had had earlier prenatal care"; "If only I. . . ." Parents attempt to assess what they did wrong and how they are at fault for the child's condition.

Depression—Parents may feel overwhelming sadness about the loss of what their child might have been. Dreams have been shattered. Parents focus on the disability.

Anger—At whom should parents direct their anger? Not the child, not the medical staff, not each other, not families or friends. Sometimes parents blame others who have no responsibility for their situation because there is no logical place to direct the anger.

Acceptance—With warmth and support from professionals, family, and friends, many parents of children with disabilities come to accept not only their child, but also their situation. They begin to focus on the child's gains instead of their own loss at what might have been.

© Cengage Learning

66 What's supposed to be the best day of your life turns out to be like a funeral. 99

—Robin Simons, 1987

naeyc 2 Some factors are known to affect parental grief over the birth of a child with a disability. These include culture; religion; economic status; the nature of the disability; the family's ability to cope; the stability of the parents' relationship; the number, gender, and age of other children in the family; and the availability of support systems. Consider two or three of these factors and tell how you believe they might affect families who have a new baby that has been identified as having a disability.

Even when parents are coping well, families who have a child with disabilities face greater challenges than other families with young children. All infants and young children have many caregiving needs. Anyone who has cared for one healthy infant knows that it is a full-time job. But children with disabilities have even greater needs, which consume much more time than typically developing children. Further, it is often difficult to find substitute care so that parents can have a much-needed respite. Often, substitute caregivers do not feel that they have the additional knowledge or skills necessary to care for the child's special needs.

In addition to the challenge of caregiving demands, a second difference in families who have a child with disabilities is the level of stress. Hamner and Turner (1996) discuss the following causes of stress in these families:

- The need to feel "normal"
- Lack of information about the child's condition

- Concern about what the future holds for their child
- Increased financial needs
- Lack of sufficient support systems
- Single parenthood 🟦naeyc 2

Children with Disabilities

http://www.childrenwithdisabilities.ncjrs.org/

ERIC Clearinghouse on Disabilities and Gifted Education

http://www.ericec.org

Exceptional Parent **Magazine**

http://www.eparent.com/

Federal Resource Center for Special Education

http://www.rrfcnetwork.org

Free Appropriate Public Education Site

http://www.fapeonline.org/

A Guide to Children's Literature and Disability

http://www.nichcy.org
Click "I;" click "literacy"

Individualizing Inclusion in Child Care

http://www.fpg.unc.edu/
On the Most Requested Pages' pull-down menu,
   click "Partnerships for Inclusion"

National Information Center for Children and Youth with Disabilities

http://www.nichcy.org/

Special Child

http://www.specialchild.com/

---

66 I've heard this period called "nothingness" and that's exactly how you feel. You can't move, can't think, can't do anything but feel—leaden, like a rock. There's nothing there—but that disability. 99

—Robin Simons, 1987

The one factor that seems to make a difference in helping families of children with disabilities to make a positive adjustment is the presence of informal support. Support from one's spouse is especially crucial. Families who share tasks within the family and have formal and informal support external to the family seem to cope best (Trivette and Dunst 1992). Some planned

programs for parents who have a child with a disability can include:

- Helping all children understand and relate to a child who is differently-abled
- Helping parents teach their children how to respond to teasing or comments about his disability
- Helping parents know what and how much to expect from their child's academic and social progress
- Helping parents develop strategies to advocate for their children's optimal education
- Helping parents to know how and when to foster independence in their children with disabilities (Hendrick 1998)

66 I talk to other parents. There's no substitute for that. You find out you're not alone. You're not the only one with those concerns. 99

—Robin Simons, 1987

🟦naeyc 6 Since 1975, federal legislation—the Education for All Handicapped Children Act of 1975 (PL 94-142)—has mandated free public education for children with disabilities between the ages of 3 and 21 years. In 1986, additional legislation required that all states provide preschool programs to all children between three and five years who have been identified as having a disability. Thus, many early childhood teachers are working in education settings that include young children with disabilities (see Figure 6–6). Before the Education for All Handicapped Children Act was passed, most children with identified disabilities were not served by public schools or were served only in special classes. Some children were able to attend special schools for children with similar disabilities such as blindness or deafness, but many children did not receive appropriate education or related services.

One of the major pieces of the 1986 legislation is the emphasis placed on the importance of the whole family of children with disabilities. Instead of requiring an Individual Education Plan (IEP), this law requires an Individualized Family Service Plan (IFSP). Attention is given to the needs of the child's whole family. Given the research on the special challenges felt by families of children who have a disability, this approach is believed to be much more effective than planning only an educational program for the child 🟦naeyc 6 (Figure 6–7).

🟦DAP In addition to the parent involvement requirements for typically developing children and their families, Head Start requires even more of the staff working with families who have children with disabilities. The following standards, included by Head Start, are excellent guidelines for all early childhood educators:

Figure 6–6   PL 94-142 and PL 99-457.

PL 94-142 (1975) The Education for All Handicapped Children Act renamed in 1990 to the Individual with Disabilities Education Act (IDEA)

To assure "that all handicapped children have available to them . . . a free appropriate public education which emphasizes special education and related services designed to meet their unique needs, to assure that the rights of handicapped children and their parents or guardians are protected, to assist states and localities to provide for the education of all handicapped children, and to assess and assure the effectiveness of efforts to educate handicapped children."

Also, this act required states to establish "procedures to assure that to the maximum extent appropriate, handicapped children, including children in public and private institutions or other care facilities, are educated with children who are not handicapped, and that special classes, separate schooling or other removal of handicapped children from the regular educational environment occurs only when the nature or severity of the handicap is such that education in regular classes with the use of supplementary aids and services can be achieved satisfactorily."

PL 99-457 (1986) The Infants and Toddlers with Disabilities Act (ITDA), now in IDEA

"ITDA requires provision of coordinated, multiagency, multidisciplinary services necessary to 'enhance' the development of infants and toddlers with disabilities. In addition to enhanced development, the law seeks to minimize the potential for developmental delay of children; eventually to reduce the need for special education and related services, and thereby reduce the cost of education for these children; to reduce the need for institutionalization and to 'maximize' their potential for independent living in a society; to work with families to assist them in meeting children's needs; and to assist the state and localities in meeting the needs of populations which are often underrepresented, for example, children living in poverty" (Guernsey and Klare 1993).

© Cengage Learning

Figure 6–7   Contents of IEPs and IFSPs.

Each IEP and IFSP must contain:

1. Present levels of child's performance
   a. Academic achievement
   b. Social competence
   c. Prevocational and vocational skills
   d. Psychomotor skill
   e. Self-help skills
2. Annual goals for child to achieve by end of school year
3. Measurable short-term instructional objectives that will assist the child in achieving the stated annual goals
4. Specific educational services needed by child including all special education related services, type of physical education program, and special instructional media and materials
5. Dates for services to begin and length of time to be provided
6. Description of how child will be included in regular education programs
7. Justification for type of educational programs prescribed
8. List of those responsible for various aspects of the IEP or IFSP
9. Objective assessment, at least annually, must be specified for measuring achievement of short-term goals
10. Teachers and parents must work together to decide on goals and how they should be achieved

© Cengage Learning

- Support parents of children with disabilities.
- Provide information to parents on how to foster development of their child with disabilities.
- Provide observation opportunities for parents so that they can see activities described in the child's IEP.
- Provide follow-up assistance to carry program activities over into the home.
- Refer parents to support groups or other parents whose children have similar disabilities.
- Inform parents of their legal rights.

- Inform parents of community resources available to them and help them to access the services.
- Identify needs related to the disability of siblings and other family members.
- Provide information regarding prevention of disabilities for younger siblings.
- Build parent confidence and skill in advocating for their children with special needs (Head Start program performance standards and other regulations). DAP

" Sometimes I feel overwhelmed. How can I evaluate this program? How do I know this is best? Then I remember it's a team approach. I'm not in it alone. It's just my job to get the specialists I trust to talk to each other about it. I remind myself that they know programs, and I know my child. "

—Robin Simons, 1987

"Students with Special Needs: The Importance of Home-School Partnerships"

Visit the Education CourseMate website at www.CengageBrain.com to view the Video Case, and then respond to the following items:

- Discuss a variety of reasons that home-school partnerships are important for children with special needs.

- Consider the Head Start guidelines provided above and information from the video case. How might these guidelines be adapted for use with families of children in kindergarten or primary grades?

Do This

Observe and participate in an inclusive classroom. If possible, assist with a parent meeting or conferences with families of children with disabilities.

Families and Children with Serious Illness

naeyc 2 Just as families with children who have disabilities face a major crisis at the time they are informed of their child's condition, so do families of children with a **serious illness**. Hilton Davis (1993) explains the intense feelings of families as they receive information concerning their child's illness. The diagnosis "brings with it irreversible change. The world is instantly transformed in a nightmarish way. The sudden need to adapt to dreadful circumstances is forced upon the parents, their child, and indeed the whole family. Potentially they have to change their whole way of life, amid the terrible pain or anguish implied by the words above. Their vision of the world, their values, their ambitions, their whole philosophy will be altered by this one event."

Medical advances have made it possible for more children to survive even with serious illnesses or disabilities. Not only are more children surviving, but health care professionals are increasing efforts to enable these children to live as normal a life as possible. Thus, such children appear in greater numbers than ever before in early childhood educational programs. Each child's particular illness or disease will affect her special educational needs. Thus, it is important for early childhood teachers to have some knowledge of a child's illness as well as general information about the child and family members (Figure 6–9). **naeyc** 2

Some serious illnesses cause greater concern than others in early education settings. Currently, children who are infected with HIV or have AIDS are among those who generate the greatest apprehension among teachers, other students, and the parents of other students. Often, children with these conditions are ostracized from society because of fears based on an inaccurate understanding of how the disease is transmitted. Additionally, families of infected children face incredible strains on their resources (Hamner and Turner 1996) (see Figure 6–8).

naeyc 6 Policies among early education programs vary widely on how they accept and deal with children with serious illness and their families. Generally, it is important that administrators and teachers understand the needs of all children and their families, and that they work with families to help them receive appropriate services. Although policies for dealing with seriously ill children vary, confidentiality and the rights of children and their families must be the first priority of any policy. It will be necessary for teachers to comply with policy and to take precautions for their own safety, such as wearing gloves when coming into contact with children's body fluids.

Figure 6–8	HIV/AIDS.

"HIV is a retrovirus that infects white blood cells, the brain, the bowel, the skin, and other tissues.

Transmission of the virus occurs through sexual or parental blood contact, or from an infected mother to her fetus or infant. Infection results in a wide spectrum of illness and a high fatality rate.

The most severe manifestation of HIV infection is acquired immunodeficiency syndrome (AIDS). . . .

AIDS cases among children have increased rapidly since the first reports in 1982" (Simonds and Rogers 1992).

Children contract the virus from their mother in three ways:

1. In utero as a fetus
2. During birth
3. By breastfeeding

Not all children born to HIV mothers contract the virus; estimates are that about 25% to 40% do.

Children with AIDS commonly have other illnesses and disorders including pneumonia, serious bacterial infections, skin disease, diarrhea, developmental delays, and neurological dysfunction. Most children with HIV develop AIDS in 3 years, and for most of these children, the disease is fatal.

Treatment is typically through drugs, and new treatments are evolving.

© Cengage Learning

Perrin, J. M. 1985. Introduction: Severe and chronic illness in childhood. In *Chronically ill children and their families*, ed. N. Hobbs, J. M. Perrin, and H. T. Ireys. San Francisco: Jossey-Bass. Pt. 94–142 and Pl. 99–457.

Figure 6–9   Description of Some Chronic Illnesses of Children.

Juvenile-Onset Diabetes—When too little insulin is secreted by the pancreas, juvenile-onset diabetes results. Needs: precise balance of diet, exercise, and insulin by injection; close monitoring of sugar levels is necessary two to three times daily. Snacks may be required during the school day.

Asthma—A chronic lung disease with bronchial sensitivity to many different stimuli. Wide variation in needs of children with mild cases to those with severe cases. Modifications in environment may be necessary to reduce allergens and irritants. Children with severe cases may have a lot of absences and need home-based educational services.

Spina Bifida—Improper closure of spinal column prenatally leads to spina bifida. Difficulties with movement in the lower body; child may not be able to move legs, and have little or no control of bowel and bladder. May need a wheelchair, braces, or crutches; retardation is possible. Schools must provide accessibility to all educational programs.

Cleft Palate and Other Craniofacial Anomalies—Degree of these problems varies from minimal to great. Disfigurement of a child's face is a difficult issue for the child and family to deal with. Some anomalies are easily corrected by surgery; others are more complicated. Children have a high risk for ear infections and hearing loss.

Congenital Heart Diseases—There is a wide variety of structural anomalies in the development of the heart. Surgery is often helpful; it is very expensive; it may help problems, not typically a total cure. Child has restrictions on daily activities after surgery and must be carefully monitored. Uncertainty about survival.

Leukemia—Most common childhood cancer begins with anemia, weight loss, and sometimes bleeding. An excessive number of white cells are in the blood. Child is frequently hospitalized, receives a large amount of medication, and

radiation therapy with major side effects. Uncertainty regarding remission and survival.

Hemophilia—Genetic disease in which blood clotting factor is absent and leads to uncontrolled bleeding. Nearly all affected are male. Often, bleeding occurs without an injury present. Painful arthritis may accompany disease; may require surgery or strong medication. Some treatment with blood products may now be done at home or school; requires fewer hospitalizations.

End-Stage Renal Disease—Extremely severe complication of variety of conditions affecting kidneys. Treatments include dialysis and transplants. When disease begins in infancy, high rate of failure to grow. Survival rate for these children increasing.

Sickle Cell Anemia—Results from abnormality in structure of hemoglobin. This affects shape of cells, and these cells have trouble passing through veins and smaller blood vessels. Risks include lack of oxygen to any body organ and to certain kinds of bacteria that cause bone infections and meningitis. Symptoms include anemia, diminished growth, and late onset of puberty. Children are hospitalized frequently and need strong pain medication.

Cystic Fibrosis—Children with CF have major chronic lung disease and frequent lung infections. Great strides have been made in treating this disease. Diagnosis is usually made in the first two years of life based on poor weight gain and frequent lung infections. Children need equipment for respiratory care, medications, and special diets.

Muscular Dystrophy—More common in boys, this disease involves progressive weakness of large muscles in legs first, and then extends to other muscles of the body. Diagnosis does not usually happen until about age 5 or 6 years, even though cause is genetic. Treatment is very limited.

Caring for Babies with AIDS
http://www.caring4babieswithAIDS.org/

Children's Memorial Hospital (Chicago)— Neonatology
http://www.childrensmemorial.org/
Click "Specialties and services;" click "departments and programs;" click "Neonatology"

Chronically Ill Children: How Families Adjust
http://www.nurseweek.com/
Click "Education/CE"; type in "chronically ill children"

STARLIGHT Foundation
http://www.starlight.org

Davis (1993) offers four guidelines for those who are working with families of ill children:

1. Respect the parents.
2. Parents have the major role in dealing with their child's illness.
3. Professionals work *with* and *for* families, not *on* or *instead* of them.
4. The most important thing for professionals is to really listen to family members as they confer. **naeyc** 6

Do This
Volunteer on a children's wing at a hospital.

Immigrant Families

Immigrant families often feel divided between two sets of emotions. On one hand, they are sad about losing their country of origin and leaving behind family, friends, familiar ways of doing things, and the ease of communicating in their native language. On the other hand, they are hopeful about the new opportunities that living in the United States brings and look forward to improving the quality of life for themselves and their children (Lieberman 1995).

As teachers welcome immigrant families into their programs, it is important for them to keep these dual emotions in mind. It is usually easier for teachers to understand the joyfulness and excitement about coming to the United States, but the accompanying sense of loss is just as real for these families.

naeyc 2 As immigrant families enter their new country, change is sudden and all-encompassing. One immediate and profound change may be that of language: if the family does not speak English, language barriers may be difficult to overcome. This causes great stress, which may lead to anxiety or depression (Lieberman 1995). Also, as children are immersed in a new culture, families may be concerned about a loss of family values and traditions. Teachers can help reduce some of the stress that these families face by applying the following points.

Health Coverage for Legal Immigrant Children

http://www.cbpp.org
Type in "immigrant children" then search for Health Coverage for Legal Immigrant Children

Identifying and Serving Immigrant Children Who Are Gifted

http://www.ericec.org

Immigrant Children Exceed Expectations

http://www.ilw.com/

- Consider the language difference. Speak and write in ways that the family can understand. Use short sentences and simple words to ensure that they understand.

- Explain the daily schedule and routine activities of the class. Take time to explain what happens in the program and to listen to parents' questions or comments.

- Acknowledge that there may be some tension between the family and the staff. It probably is not personal, but rather is based on cultural differences. Think about what you can do to communicate more effectively with the family and thus overcome as many of these tensions as possible.

- Ask questions about the family and their expectations for their children. Avoid getting too personal and do not give advice. Instead, listen carefully so that you can learn about the family.

- Establish a warm and trusting environment for all families and children. If you have concerns about the child or practices of the family, a trusting relationship will allow you to express concerns and work in partnership with the family (Lieberman 1995). naeyc 6

Migrant Families

naeyc 2 **Migrant families** move from one location to another and from one job to another for financial reasons (Chavkin 1991). And yet, migrant families are among the poorest in the United States (Lopez, Scribner, and Mahitivanichcha 2001). It is difficult to estimate the number of migrant families in the United States, but there may be as many as 1.5 million migrant farmworkers (Shotland 1989). Although little information is available about migrant families, it is known that there is diversity among their lifestyles (Chavkin 1991). Some of this diversity might be related to the three primary geographic migration routes: East Coast, Midcontinent, and West Coast (Shotland 1989).

Early childhood education teachers should speak in short sentences and simple words to help immigrant children understand

Ethnicity and culture also contribute to the diversity of migrant families. Those farmworkers who migrate through the southern states and along the eastern seaboard are most often African Americans, Mexican Americans and Mexican nationals, Anglos, Jamaican and Haitian blacks, and Puerto Ricans. Those who migrate through south Texas and move through the Midwestern and western states are most often Mexican Americans and Mexican nationals, as well as some Native Americans. Migrant workers who travel the West Coast through California to Oregon and Washington are also most often Mexican Americans and Mexican nationals. Some of these farmworkers are also southeast Asians (Shotland 1989).

Many factors may lead to poor health in adults and children in migrant families; these factors include continuous relocation, extremely low wages, hard physical work in the fields, unsafe farm equipment, poor nutrition, and lack of consistent medical care. Huang (1993) discusses health problems related to prenatal care, agriculture as a dangerous occupation, and poverty. Poverty contributes to ill health in numerous ways; among them are malnutrition and poor sanitation in substandard housing that lacks indoor plumbing for toilets or drinking water. These risk factors contribute to health-related problems in many segments of the population, of course, but migrant families are particularly susceptible to an extremely high number of them.

Many people who migrate for economic reasons speak only their native language or have limited use of English. Along with migrants' frequent relocations, language barriers obstruct their access to many human service programs available to others in the United States (Chavkin 1991). These characteristics also impact the children's ability to succeed in school as well as families' involvement in their children's education (Menchaca and Ruiz-Escalante 1995; Martinez and Velazquez 2000). **naeyc** 2

DAP Teachers of young children from migrant families must emphasize the strengths that the children bring from this lifestyle. Because they have lived and traveled in several states and often in at least two countries, children have information and perspectives to share that differ from those of other children (Gonzales, as cited in Menchaca and Ruiz-Escalante 1995). When teachers respect and celebrate all cultures and experiences among children in the classroom, including those of migrant children, all children have a greater chance for success. Further, teachers must make all children feel welcome as members of the classroom community of learners, regardless of the length of their stay (Huggins, as cited in Menchaca and Ruiz-Escalante 1995). Moving from one school to another is a challenge for young migrant children, and early childhood teachers can support them by leading efforts to include them and making the classroom a safe place for all. **DAP**

DIVERSITY IN PRACTICE For all young children, family involvement in education contributes to academic success. It may be necessary for teachers to redefine their views about family involvement beyond a traditional view of participation in parent groups, attendance at school functions, and helping children with homework, into a broader view that will encourage marginalized families "by building on each family's cultural values, beliefs, and economic positionality" (Lopez, Scribner, and Mahiti-vanichcha 2001). Some examples of ways that teachers can support migrant family involvement include:

- Placing needs of families as the number one priority
- Developing meaningful, authentic relationships with parents
- Empowering parents by valuing their essential nature to children's success in school
- Genuinely welcoming family members in a personal way to school functions
- Providing specific educational services to help migrant children and families
- Collaborating with agencies in order to affect families' basic needs as well as their health and academic needs (Lopez, Scribner, and Mahiti-vanichcha 2001)

Do This

Review all the variations of diversity discussed in Chapter 2: ethnicity, race, culture, language, economic, gender roles, religiosity, and geographic region. How might differences in families influence stress and resilience?

Anchor School Project
http://www.anchorschool.org

Migrant Education Program
http://www.ed.gov/
Click programs; type in "Migrant Education Programs"

Migrant Head Start
http://www2.acf.dhhs.gov
Click "Head Start;" click "Head Start Bureau;" click "Programs and Services"

Military Families

In 2000, the Department of Defense statistics showed that the total U.S. military force had 3,324,888 members with about 41 percent serving in active duty; that is, not reserve units. Of the active-duty members, nearly 55 percent were married. Fourteen percent of active-duty service members were female, and 64 percent were 30 years of age or younger (Mancini and Archambault 2000). Recent increases in married military members and in the number of female members have led to changes in expectations for military life, heightening concerns about family issues (Drummet, Coleman, and Cable 2003).

naeyc 2 In addition to reviewing military force statistics, Mancini and Archambault (2000) also noted pressing concerns from service members and families as follows: availability of commissary and selection and cost of items; health care information and issues; poor status of base housing and lack of attention to solving housing problems; tuition assistance for military spouses; rates of pay and cost of living calculations; and the need for affordable child care. A major area of study has been the topic of financial stability of military families. About 47 percent of military families reported financial security, 30 percent reported occasional financial difficulty, and 22 percent reported tough financial circumstances where they were "in over their heads." Most junior enlisted officers reported having less than $1,000 in savings, and 7 percent of active-duty members obtained loans for expenses to make a required relocation.

While some stressors are common to the majority of military families, other stressors may be less common and yet challenging to those families faced with such obstacles. One of these challenges is coping with the stress related to children with disabilities. Along with financial and child care concerns faced by a large majority of military families, it has been reported that supporting children with special needs can increase parents' stress. Evidence also exists, however, that families who have a child with disabilities rise to the occasion and make necessary adjustments when provided with helpful support and services. Researchers recommend that because these families often have unmet needs for community services and parent networks, active coordination of such services must be offered to families (Russo and Fallon 2001).

In addition to financial concerns, three unique stressor events for military families have been documented: mandated relocations, separation from family members, and reuniting with family members (Drummet et al. 2003). An increased sensitivity to these and other military family issues has arisen since the Gulf War during the early 1990s, when dual-career military couples and single parents were among those who were deployed suddenly, forcing them to find long-term care

for their children in a matter of hours. These issues affect approximately 3.36 million children of military families (Ryan-Wenger 2001).

The frequent and mandated moves required of military families also demand a great deal of adjustment and adaptation from them. Not only must the household reorganize for a new living space, but the relocation is likely to involve major geographic distance, sometimes internationally. New climates and cultural change also provide challenges for families. Both positive and negative effects have been documented for children in such relocations. The stress caused by each relocation has generally been found to be relatively short-lived for most children. However, some helping professionals continue to believe in a "military family syndrome" in which children exhibit high degrees of psychopathology. Although LaGrone (1978), as cited in Ryan-Wenger (2001), connected such psychopathology to authoritarian parenting styles, family conflicts, and a lack of permanence in families, no comparisons were done with nonmilitary families having similar characteristics. Presently, the existence of this syndrome does not seem to be grounded in reality. In fact, some researchers have found quite the opposite: relocations sometimes have a positive outcome on children's academic achievement (Drummet et al. 2003).

Adult military family members also have stressors related to frequent and distant relocations. The sheer work and concern for children and other family members can easily lead to both physical and emotional exhaustion (Pollari and Bullock 1988, as cited in Drummet 2003). The loss of social networks— family, friends, coworkers, and community—as well as concern about finding new social networks in the next community is a source of stress for adults as well as children. Adult family members who relocate with the military member often face interruptions in their careers and new job searches after the move is made (Drummet et al. 2003).

The second major stressor that has been documented for military families has to do with separation from family members. "Deployment is uniquely different from relocation because deployment seldom includes the family unit. Therefore, a second unique facet of military life is the ever-present possibility of deployment of one or both adults from the family" (Drummet et al.). "Since 1990, the number of United States military personnel deployed for war and operations other than war has been at an all-time high" (Ryan-Wenger 2001). The most common issues related to these family separations relate to care of the children, maintaining a positive couple relationship, negotiating roles and tasks in the family when one or both adult members are away on duty, reduced social support, and the effects of mass communication information that may provide inaccurate information.

Caring for children when a family member has been deployed is always challenging. However, this challenge might be exacerbated when the military family member is a single parent or when both parents are deployed to active duty. At these times, caregivers may not be aware of children's daily routines or special needs, yet step up to provide care for the children in the best way they can. Children whose parents have been deployed are likely to demonstrate behavioral issues that include anxiety, sleep disturbances, and phobias as well as more frequent physical illness. naeyc 2

naeyc 1 Of course, these symptoms may be greater for children whose family members are in combat situations (Drummet et al., 2003). Very little research has been done to examine children's fears and concerns when a parent is serving in a war zone. It seems that many families prefer to protect their children by not asking them about their perspectives and feelings when one or both parents are at war (Ryan-Wenger 2001). Sensitivity is important, but some evidence exists that whether or not a child is asked about her perspective, children are thinking about war. When asked "What would happen in your family if there was war?" one eight-year-old girl who had a parent serving in active duty replied, "My family would be killed, shot, stabbed, and they might be hurt" (Ryan-Wenger 2001). naeyc 1

While it is clear to many people that military relocations and separations are stressful for families, the reunions of such families are often viewed as a greatly anticipated, joyful event. Frequently, military family reunions are just that—happily anticipated. At the same time, however, reunions require an enormous amount of adaptation from all family members, and this typically creates stress. Figure 6–10 provides a list and brief explanation of six family stress factors related to reunions (Drummet et al. 2003).

Children of Incarcerated Parents

About 2 million children in any given year have at least one parent who is **incarcerated** in a state or federal prison, or in a local jail (Bilchik, Seymour, and Kreisher 2001). Since the rate of incarceration has been growing throughout the 1990s and into the twenty-first century, greater numbers of children will be affected by this in the future. The number of children with incarcerated parents has grown by more than 50 percent since 1991 (Federal Resource Center for Children of Prisoners). Fathers are most likely to be incarcerated, but there has been an increase in female incarcerations. About 8 percent of the 2 million children who have an incarcerated parent have mothers who are incarcerated (Bilchik et al. 2001).

naeyc 1 Little information exists about the specific effects of parental imprisonment on children. However, because it is known that these families

| Figure 6–10 | Factors Related to Military Family Stress at the Time of Reunion. |

Roles and Boundary Issues. When a military family member is deployed, other family members are required to pick up the functions that that person contributed to the family. Adjusting to the change and then adjusting again when the family member returns does not always occur without objections. Also, the returning individual might feel frozen out of family processes.

Household Management. Those who manage the household while the deployed member is away may find new success or may be frustrated by what they view as failure. In either case, management issues will most likely move to at least a more shared responsibility with the returning family member.

Honeymoon Effect. Upon the immediate return of the family member, a tremendous amount of joy and relief may overshadow any concerns about family issues. This period may last for various lengths of time, with some families moving gradually to dealing with such concerns, others avoiding concerns, and still others dealing suddenly with a concern, particularly if it seems like a looming crisis.

Social Support. In the excitement of reunion, families might overlook their existing sources of social support outside the family in order to reestablish familial ties. It seems that families who have a balance between outside social networks and family ties have an easier time adjusting through the reunion period.

Parent Rejection and Anxiety. Very young children may not remember or recognize a returning parent. Adult expectations for children to quickly assume relationships with the parent may cause additional anxiety in children.

Physical and Mental Condition of Military Family Member. When military family members return from deployment, they may not be in the same health status as when they left. Both physical injuries and emotional issues may change the expected nature of the reunion.

Drummet, Coleman, and Cable (2003)

are more likely to be living in poverty or affected by substance abuse and violence, the effects are complicated by a number of negative environmental factors. When parents are taken into custody, children are confused, and their world immediately becomes chaotic. Many children believe that they might be responsible for their parents going to jail. The family separation created by parental imprisonment is traumatic for children, especially if the incarcerated parent is a primary caregiver.

Common responses from children with incarcerated parents include a variety of emotional and behavioral difficulties, such as withdrawal, aggression, anxiety, and depression. These children are likely to do poorly in school, and beyond early childhood they are at risk for abusing illegal substances and committing crimes (Bilchik et al. 2001). Because of the trauma associated with a sudden separation from a parent, children may suffer from posttraumatic stress disorder (PTSD), which includes symptoms such as withdrawal, hyperalertness, sleep disturbances, guilt, and impaired memory and concentration (Jose-Kampfner, as cited in Young and Jefferson-Smith 2000).

In addition to emotional and behavioral risk factors, children with incarcerated parents are likely to feel embarrassed and isolated about having a parent in prison. They may attempt to keep others from knowing about the incarceration, by either remaining silent about the information or covering up the truth. Although the very nature of incarceration in our society is to punish the perpetrators of crime, care must be taken to ensure that children of incarcerated parents are not also punished because of their parents' illegal acts.

A common pattern of dealing with children whose parents are incarcerated has been to support the children without dealing with their concerns about their parents or the issue of incarceration. Often, no one mentions the parent or the imprisonment in conversations with these children. Even incarcerated parents themselves, in reaction to their own guilt, may distance themselves physically and emotionally from their children. However, these responses only cause children to feel isolated and rejected. Children, not understanding that their parents may be acting out of guilt or embarrassment, see the parents' behavior as a lack of love for or interest in them, perhaps caused by something that they did (Young and Jefferson-Smith 2000). **naeyc** 1

naeyc 6 Programs for children whose parents are incarcerated are being created in many cities and states, and with input from organizations that have called attention to the needs of children in this situation. Families in Crisis provides a program for school-age children with both educational and therapeutic interventions. Services are provided to both children and parents in order to support strong family bonds that help children cope successfully (Bilchik et al. 2001). Girl Scouts Beyond Bars is a partnership program between correctional departments and Girl Scout councils that was created to continue relationships between young girls and their incarcerated mothers (http://www.ncjrs.org/txtf les/girlsct.txt).

Although fewer women than men are currently incarcerated, a greater number of programs seem to exist to support them in their parenting role, both as they are imprisoned and on their release. This may be because women are often in the role of primary caregiver. However, Mendez (2000) makes the point, supported by his research, that incarcerated men also have

an interest in their children and in increasing their parenting skills.

Fathers and Children Together (FACT) is another program supported by Families in Crisis. Young fathers between the ages of 18 and 21 who are about to be released from the Manson Youth Institute in Connecticut are provided with services to encourage them to be supportive fathers to their young children (Bilchik et al. 2001).

A Bill of Rights for children of incarcerated parents has been created by the San Francisco Children of Incarcerated Parents Partnership (2005). Figure 6–11 illustrates the eight rights of children as well as sample actions or areas for advocacy relating to incarcerated parents.

> 66 I was nine when my mom got arrested. The police came and took her. I was trying to ask them what was going on and they wouldn't say, and then everything went so fast. I guess they thought someone else was in the house. I don't know. But nobody else was in the house. They arrested her and just left us there. For two or three weeks I took care of my 1-year-old brother and myself. I knew how to change his diapers and feed him and stuff. I tried to make breakfast in the morning and I burnt my hand trying to make toast. I had a blister. I wasn't really afraid. I was just trying to take care of my brother. That was my goal—to take care of him. Sometimes he would cry because he probably would want to see my mom. 99
>
> **—Dave, San Francisco Children of Incarcerated**
> **Parents Partnership, 2005** **naeyc** 6

DAP Caregivers and teachers of young children may find it difficult to know how to support children of incarcerated parents. The first step for those who are working with these young children is to understand the confusion and trauma they have faced. Further, early childhood teachers should be prepared to provide a sense of security at school by listening to children's concerns and by providing unconditional nurturance. Answer children's questions in the best and most honest way possible, respect the significance of family bonds, and seek assistance from the family and other professionals as necessary. Be sure to maintain confidentiality regarding sensitive information (Reilly and Martin n.d.). Finally, early childhood educators should use the knowledge base from existing research and family support programs to advocate for greater numbers of appropriate interventions that will serve to keep family bonds strong, reduce the likelihood that parents will return to prison, or that their children will also go to prison, and decrease severe emotional

Figure 6–11 Rights and Actions/Advocacy for Children of Incarcerated Parents.

RIGHT

I have the right to be kept safe and informed at the time of my parent's arrest.

ACTIONS

Develop arrest protocols that support and protect children. Examples: avoid sirens and lights in nonemergency situations; when possible, allow parent to say good-bye and handcuff out of sight of children or have officers give age-appropriate explanations.

RIGHT

I have the right to be heard when decisions are made about me.

ACTIONS

Train relevant staff to recognize and address children's needs and concerns; be truthful with children; listen to children so that their concerns are heard and understood.

RIGHT

I have the right to be considered when decisions are made about my parent.

ACTIONS

Review current sentencing laws in relation to their impact on children and families; include services and support to families and children during and after an arrest; include family impact statements in pre-sentencing investigation reports.

RIGHT

I have the right to be well cared for in my parent's absence.

ACTIONS

Offer support to new or ongoing caregivers; subsidize guardianship for children whose parents are incarcerated; when a parent is arrested, include agencies such as child welfare to help families deal with the crisis.

RIGHT

I have the right to speak with, see, and touch my parent.

ACTIONS

Provide access to visiting rooms that are childcentered, nonintimidating and conducive to bonding; consider proximity to family when siting prisons and assigning prisoners; encourage child welfare departments to facilitate contact.

RIGHT

I have the right to support as I face my parent's incarceration.

ACTIONS

Provide training to relevant professionals to recognize the needs and concerns of children whose parents are incarcerated; provide access to helping professionals with specialized training in working with children whose parents are incarcerated; each state should include 5% of its corrections budget for family support during and after incarceration.

RIGHT

I have the right not to be judged, blamed, or labeled because my parent is incarcerated.

ACTIONS

Create opportunities for children of incarcerated parents to communicate with and support each other; create support for incarcerated parents so that they can work to become better parents and citizens—and then there would be a truth fit to tell their children.

RIGHT

I have the right to a lifelong relationship with my parent.

ACTIONS

Reexamine the 1997 Adoption and Safe Families Act that requires states to begin proceedings to terminate parental rights when the child has been in foster care for 15 of the past 22 months and for 6 months for children under 3 years; inform incarcerated parents of this law; designate a family services coordinator at prisons and jails; support incarcerated parents upon reentry into society by helping them to find employment and apply for benefits.

San Francisco Children of Incarcerated Parents Partnership (2005)

challenges for children whose parents are, or have been, incarcerated. DAP

Families in Crisis

http://www.Familiesincrisis.org

Child Welfare League of America Center for Children of Prisoners

http://www.cwla.org
Click "Programs;" click "Children with Incarcerated Parents"

ROLE OF EARLY CHILDHOOD EDUCATORS

As early childhood teachers prepare to work with an ever-increasing number of children with serious health concerns, several criteria must be included in their professional preparation:

- Knowledge of legal requirements for each special need

- Knowledge of health requirements for each special need

It is the teacher's ethical oblication to exercise the idea of lifelong learning.

- Understanding of family systems effects on children
- Practicing effective strategies to support families as well as planning high-quality early education for the children

- Advocating for needs of all children and families
- Expansion of capacity to demonstrate compassion

Although it is true that a teacher preparation program for entry-level teachers cannot possibly anticipate every situation novice teachers might encounter, it seems evident that more emphasis should be placed on understanding the various needs and strengths of families in stress. Even under difficult circumstances, many families find ways to cope or adapt. Furthermore, as teachers face a variety of challenging situations, it is their ethical obligation to exercise the idea of lifelong learning to ensure the best early education for each child and appropriate support for each family.

Summary and Conclusions

All families face stressful events. Some forms of stress can be predicted, such as the birth of a new baby or a planned relocation. Other stressors faced by families with young children, however, are unique and may be unexpected. Violence in families causes stress for all members, whether or not they are being abused. Stress also is caused by poverty and related economic factors; in extreme situations, families may lose their homes and all of their possessions. Serious illness or disabilities in young children lead to many chronically stressful situations. Some family stress may be the result of poor planning by or dysfunction in families. Much of this stress, however, is unpredictable and perhaps unavoidable.

Families cope in different ways. Those who have support and resources may find it easier to function at the time of a crisis. Others find it very difficult to adapt.

Early childhood teachers can offer support by listening and showing compassion when families need support. It may be necessary for teachers to refer children or families for additional or alternative services. Guidelines for ethical behavior require that early education practitioners form partnerships with all families based on trust and positive regard.

Theories into Practice Suggestions (TIPS)

- Avoid blaming families for their stressful circumstances.
- Create ways to support families when you are aware of their stressful circumstances.
- Be familiar with the needs of families in stress.
- Do not expect all families to cope in the same manner.
- Understand that a temporary failure to cope with stress is not unusual and may eventually be overcome.
- Do not ignore family stress.
- Teacher support for children and families is always helpful, but even more so when families are stressed.
- Be aware that you may not have information about a given family's stress.
- Be prepared to connect families and community resources.
- Understand legal aspects of child abuse, disabilities, and medical care at school.
- Be proactive with your own professional development regarding family stressors of the children with whom you work.

- Volunteer in a community agency and get to know families who are experiencing stressful conditions.
- Be sensitive to cultural differences in expectations and values.

Applications

1. Review the information on factors related to family violence in the United States. Give an example from your experience that helps to explain or support each of these factors.

2. Consider the information provided in this chapter about various serious illnesses experienced by families with young children. Which of these illnesses do you know something about from experience?

3. When a young child is born with or acquires a disability, it affects the entire family. Considering the information in this chapter along with your own experience, how will you view children with disabilities in your classroom? How will you view parents of children with disabilities as they voice their expectations to you? What challenges and joys do you predict when working with young children with disabilities and their families?

Questions for Reflection and Discussion

1. When you think about working with families of young children who have a major source of family stress, what do you see as your strengths? What areas of concern do you have about your reactions to the various stressors?

2. How will you decide on the extent and limits to which you will be involved in families experiencing stress?

3. How might you best prepare yourself as an early childhood educator to deal with the types of unpredictable family stress discussed in this chapter?

Field Assignments

1. Call the administrator of a homeless shelter or women's shelter in your area. Ask what the needs are, and how you might be able to help young children and families at the shelter. Consider a toy drive, clothing drive, food drive, or collection of supplies such as paper, markers, glue, or other items; tutoring school-age children; or reading to children.

2. Observe an early intervention program. Note the activities, participation, family involvement, and forms of assessment. If possible, ask the administrator about roles for early childhood educators in such programs.

3. Interview a children's protective services agent. Ask about experiences with family members who have been identified as child abusers. Discuss ways in which early childhood teachers and protective services workers might collaborate.

 Additional resources for this chapter, including TeachSource videos, can be found on the Education CourseMate. Go to CengageBrain.com.

References

Bilchik, S., C. Seymour, and K. Kreisher. 2001. Parents in prison. *Corrections Today* 63: 108–11.

Boss, P. 1988. *Family stress management.* Newbury Park, CA: Sage.

Carter, B., and M. McGoldrick. 1989. Overview: The changing family life cycle: A framework for family therapy. In *The changing family life cycle,* ed. B. Carter and M. McGoldrick. Needham Heights, MA: Allyn & Bacon.

Chavkin, N. F. 1991. Family lives and parental involvement in migrant students' education. ERIC Document Reproduction No. ED 335174.

Cicchetti, D., S. L. Toth, and K. Hennessy. 1993. Child maltreatment and school adaptation: Problems and promises. In *Child abuse, child development, and social policy,* eds. D. Cicchetti and S. L. Toth, 301–30. Norwood, NJ: Ablex.

Clemson Extension. 2002. *From family stress to family strengths.* Clemson, SC: Clemson University.

Davis, H. 1993. *Counseling parents of children with chronic illness or disability.* Leicester, England: British Psychological Society.

Doucette-Dudman, D., and J. R. LaCure. 1996. *Raising our children's children.* Minneapolis, MN: Fairview Press.

Drummet, A. R., M. Coleman, and S. Cable. 2003. Military families under stress: Implications for family life education. *Family Relations* 52: 279–87.

Emery, R. E. 1999. *Marriage, divorce, and children's adjustment,* 2nd ed. Thousand Oaks, CA: Sage.

Federal Resource Center for Children of Prisoners. n.d. http://www.cwla.org/programs/incarcerated/frccp-about.htm (accessed September 7, 2002).

Fields, J., and L. M. Casper. 2001. America's families and living arrangements. *Current Population Reports.* Washington, DC: United States Department of Commerce, Economics and Statistics Administration, United States Census Bureau.

Galinsky, E., and J. David. 1988. *The preschool years: Family strategies that work from experts and parents.* New York: Ballantine.

Guernsey, T. F., and K. Klare. 1993. *Special education law.* Durham, NC: Carolina Academic Press.

Hamner, T. J., and P. H. Turner. 1996. *Parenting in contemporary society.* Needham Heights, MA: Allyn & Bacon.

Head Start program performance standards and other regulations. 1993. Washington, DC: U.S. Department of Health and Human Services.

Hendrick, J. 1998. *Total learning.* Columbus, OH: Merrill.

Huang, G. 1993. Health problems among migrant farmworkers' children in the U.S. ERIC Document Reproduction No. ED 357907.

Iverson, T. J., and M. Segal. 1990. *Child abuse and neglect: An information and reference guide.* New York: Garland.

Keeping incarcerated mothers and their daughters together: Girl Scouts beyond bars. October 1995. http://www.ncjrs.org/txtfiles/girlsct.txt (accessed September 7, 2002).

Kling, N., L. Dunn, and J. Oakley. 1996. Homeless families in early childhood programs: What to expect and what to do. *Dimensions of Early Childhood* 24: 3–8.

Krestan, J., and C. Bepko. 1989. Alcohol problems and the family life cycle. In *The changing family life cycle,* eds. B. Carter and M. McGoldrick. Needham Heights, MA: Allyn & Bacon.

Lieberman, A. F. 1995. Concerns of immigrant families. In *Infant/toddler caregiving: A guide to culturally sensitive care,* ed. P. L. Mangione, 28–37. Sacramento: California Department of Education.

Lopez, G. R., J. D. Scribner, and K. Mahitivanichcha. 2001. Redefining parental involvement: Lessons from high-performing migrant-impacted schools. *American Educational Research Journal* 38: 253–88.

Mancini, D. L., and C. Archambault. 2000. What recent research tells us about military families and communities. DoD Family Readiness Conference, Phoenix, AZ.

Martinez, Y. G., and J. A. Velazquez. 2000. Involving migrant families in education. ERIC Document Reproduction No. ED 448010.

Mayes, L. C. 1995. Substance abuse and parenting. In Vol. 4 of *Handbook of parenting: Applied and practical parenting,* ed. M. H. Bornstein, 101–25. Mahwah, NJ: Lawrence Erlbaum Associates.

H. I., M. A. McCubbin, A. I. Thompson, S. Han, and C. T. Allen. 1997. "*Families under stress: What makes them resilient?*" 1997. American Association of Family and Consumer Sciences Commemorative Lecture, Washington, DC.

Menchaca, V D., and J. A. Ruiz-Escalante. 1995. Instructional strategies for migrant students. ERIC Document Reproduction No. ED 388491.

Mendez, Jr., G. A. 2000. Incarcerated African American men and their children: A case study. *Annals of the American Academy of Political and Social Science* 569: 86–101.

Moses, K. 1983. The impact of initial diagnosis: Mobilizing family resources. In *Parent-professional partnerships in developmental disabilities services,* ed. J. Mulick and S. Pueschel, 11–34. Cambridge, MA: Academic Guild.

Olson, D. H. L., C. S. Russell, and D. H. Sprenkle. 1989. *Circumplex model: Systematic assessment and treatment of families.* New York: Haworth Press.

Olson, H. 1994. The effects of prenatal alcohol exposure on child development. *Infants and Young Children* 6: 10–25.

Perrin, J. M. 1985. Introduction: Severe and chronic illness in childhood. In *Chronically ill children and their families,* eds. N. Hobbs, J. M. Perrin, and H. T Ireys. San Francisco: Jossey-Bass.

Poulsen, M. 1994. The development of policy recommendations to address individual and family needs of infants and young children affected by family substance use. *Topics in Early Childhood Special Education* 14: 275–91.

Reilly, J., and S. Martin. n.d. Children of incarcerated parents: What is the caregiver's role? http://www.canr.uconn.edu/ces/child/newsarticles/CCC743.html (accessed September 7, 2002).

Russo, T J., and M. A. Fallon. 2001. Helping military families who have a child with a disability cope with stress. *Early Childhood Education Journal* 29: 3–8.

Ryan-Wenger, N. A. 2001. Impact of the threat of war on children in military families. *American Journal of Orthopsychiatry* 71: 236–44.

San Francisco Children of Incarcerated Parents Partnership. 2005. *Children of incarcerated parents: A bill of rights.* Stockton, CA: Friends Outside.

Shotland J. 1989. Full fields, empty cupboard: The nutritional status of migrant farmworkers in America. Washington, DC. Public Voice for Food and Health Policy. ERIC Document Reproduction No. ED 323076.

Simonds, R. J., and M. F. Rogers. 1992. Epidemiology of HIV in children and other populations. In *HIV infection and developmental disabilities: A resource for service providers,* eds. A. C. Crocker, H. J. Cohen, and T A. Kastner. Baltimore: Paul H. Brookes.

Simons, R. 1987. *After the tears: Parents talk about raising a child with a disability.* Orlando, FL: Harcourt Brace.

Straus, M. A. 1983. Ordinary violence, child abuse, and wife-beating: What do they have in common. In *The dark side of families,* ed. D. Finkelhor. Beverly Hills, CA: Sage.

Straus, M. A. 1991. Physical violence in American families: Incidence, rates, causes, and trends. In *Abused and battered: Social and legal responses to family violence,* eds. D. D. Knudsen and J. L. Miller. New York: Walter de Gruyter.

Straus, M. A., R. J. Gelles, and S. K. Steinmetz. 1980. *Behind closed doors: Violence in the American family.* Garden City, NY: Doubleday.

Trivette, C., and C. Dunst. 1992. Characteristics and influences of role division and social support among mothers of preschool children with disabilities. *Topics in Early Childhood Special Education* 12: 367–85.

U.S. Department of Health, Education, and Welfare, Office of Human Development/Office of Child Development, Children's Bureau/National Center on Child Abuse and Neglect. 1975. Child abuse and neglect: The problem and its management. DHEW Publication No. OHD 75-30073.

Young, D. S., and C. J. Jefferson-Smith. 2000. When moms are incarcerated: The needs of children, mothers, and caregivers. *Families in Society* 81: 130-41.

Zuckerman, B., and T. B. Brazelton. 1994. Strategies for a family supportive child health care system. In *Putting families first: America's family support movement and the challenge of change,* eds. S. L. Kagan and B. Weissbourd. San Francisco: Jossey-Bass.

PRACTICE

A Family-Based Philosophy in Early Childhood Education

© Cengage Learning/ECE Photo Library.

OBJECTIVES

After reading and reflecting on this chapter, you should be able to:

- Explain the role of family support in early childhood education **naeyc** 2

- Discuss the components of a family-based philosophy in early childhood education **naeyc** 2

- Appreciate and be sensitive to differences in families **naeyc** 2

- Plan and implement strategies for involving all families in their children's education **naeyc** 2, 4

- Explain four frameworks for family, school, and community partnerships **naeyc** 1, 2

- Describe several examples of transition practices **naeyc** 1, 2, 4

- Discuss characteristics of professionalism in family-based early education **naeyc** 6

Key Terms

advocacy
congruence
continuity
diversity
empowering

Family Education Rights & Privacy
 Act (FERPA)
home visiting
linkages
NAEYC code of ethical conduct

overlapping spheres of
 influence
parental rights
quality indicators

RATIONALE FOR A FAMILY-BASED PHILOSOPHY IN EARLY CHILDHOOD EDUCATION

Families are children's first teachers. By the time children arrive in early childhood education settings, they have already had many learning experiences with their families and communities. Some home and community settings provide a great many experiences to prepare young children for entry into early education. Alternatively, some home and community environments

provide little preparation for early education so that children from these settings experience a lot of discontinuity in their lives when they enroll in child care or school.

Parents or other adult family members who engage in parenting roles provide early social experiences for their children. Extended families and communities that provide opportunities that support parents in the socialization process also contribute indirectly to child outcomes. All socialization efforts are based on culture, including language, gender roles, celebrations, rituals, and behavioral expectations. All that children learn prior to their formal education experiences must be considered when planning for developmentally appropriate practices. Deliberate attention must be given to both typical developmental expectations as well as individualized cultural and familial circumstances.

naeyc 2 Even after children begin formal early education—child care, preschool, or kindergarten—families continue to be the primary force in their development and learning. With this understanding, it is imperative that programs of early childhood education adopt a family-based philosophy. Positive, reciprocal relationships with all families, although a lofty goal, must be a focus for effective early childhood educators. **naeyc** 2

DAP In order to create effective, meaningful programs of family involvement in early education, teachers must have an understanding of family from both a research and theory perspective. Content from the first section of this textbook, Understanding Families, was intended to provide information about families so that early educators might apply that information to their educational practice. Too little attention is currently given to early childhood teachers having deep knowledge of family systems theory (Christian 2006). Establishing family involvement programs without a scientific understanding of families may lead to shallow or transitory efforts with families. Authentic partnerships are more likely to be developed when early childhood professionals have a categorically strong knowledge base in understanding families. "It is critical to use these explanations to better serve children and families rather than for the purpose of blaming or trying to 'fix' families" (Christian 2006).

As we understand more about families in general as well as the families with whom we work specifically, it is clear that family involvement must be varied and abundant. Opportunities for families to participate with their children in the support of their education should take into consideration the obligations and strengths of each family. **DAP**

naeyc 6 Even though multiple barriers exist for practicing family involvement in children's education, being aware of these obstacles can help teachers overcome their negative impact on outcomes for early childhood programs. While it is true that early childhood education, as a field, has been more inclusive of families and communities than have other levels of education, there are still many ways that early educators can enhance their efforts in this realm. Common barriers to family involvement that have been identified for all levels of education (Shartrand, Weiss, Kreider, and Lopez 1997) include the following:

1. *School environments commonly discourage family involvement.* This is often due to lack of time or preparation of teachers as well as a traditional philosophy of schools having a narrow focus on children's educational needs alone. Consider the history of family involvement in public schools as presented in Chapter 1 for an understanding about the disparate roles for schools and families. Decades of this assumption by educators and parents as well as practices based on a school culture that separates microsystem functions can prove a powerful obstacle.

2. *Families and schools have different preferences and different expectations for the nature of family involvement in children's education.* School staff members are frequently concerned with activities that encourage families to support school programs and participate in PTAs or PTOs. On the other hand, many families also are interested in advocacy and decision-making roles, often less popular variations of family involvement with teachers and other school personnel. This disconnect between parents and teachers in definition or values can lead to stalemates in actual levels of family or community involvement.

3. *It is common for teachers and families to view involvement in a negative light.* Teachers may complain about parental lack of concern, while parents may feel like unwelcome and uninvited participants in their children's education. Effective teachers face labor-intensive situations in today's schools. The thought of planning and implementing a family involvement component is seen as an additional expectation rather than one that is likely to help meet goals for children's learning and academic success. Similarly, adults in families with young children often feel overwhelmed with time commitments and responsibilities. Without clear invitations from schools that emphasize the positive outcomes inherent in family involvement in education for children, parents may choose to leave all of the education function up to educators.

4. *Family diversity as it relates to culture, ethnicity, language, employment patterns, and family structure challenges schools and families working toward increased family involvement, even when both parties value and desire family and community engagement with schools.* In order to establish reciprocal relationships with all families, individualization will be necessary. Specific strategies are required to reach variations in family values, beliefs, and expectations. While majority, middle-class parents may be comfortable in typical school environments, parents who are not English speakers or who work night shifts or swing shifts will find it more difficult to demonstrate their concerns for children's educational outcomes.

5. *Teacher preparation programs are generally lacking in providing pre-service teachers with knowledge, skills, and dispositions needed to work with families.* Increasing

attention to knowledge about families, along with skills and dispositions for forming strong partnerships with families, is key to appreciably increasing the emphasis on the reality of family involvement in their children's education. It is common at this time for teacher preparation programs to encourage family involvement, but many still do not provide specific information to teacher candidates about how to effectively do so. Just as those preparing to be teachers must learn content and pedagogy for teaching children, they must also be provided with knowledge about families, dispositions for including all families, and skills for creating and maintaining relationships. **naeyc** 6

> ### Consider This
>
> Consider the five common barriers to family involvement in their children's education as outlined by Shartrand et al. (1997). Using various contexts or systems (as in Bronfenbrenner's bioecological theory), create at least one solution for each of the five barriers.

The Example Set by Head Start

Since its inception in 1965, family involvement has been a component of Head Start's comprehensive educational plan for working with children of low-income families. Many leaders in early childhood education believe that the success of Head Start would not be so remarkable without the emphasis on families. As a consistent segment of Head Start practices, family engagement has evolved over the years and has led to the current comprehensive, evidence-based Parent, Family, and Community Engagement Framework (http://eclkc.ohs.acf.hhs.gov/hsic/standards/IMs/2011/pfce-framework.pdf). With the ultimate goal of child readiness for school, goals for family engagement outcomes are: **naeyc** 2

- Family well-being: safety, health, and financial security
- Positive parent-child relationships: transition to parenthood, development of warm and nurturing relationships, and support for children's development and learning
- Families as lifelong educators: participation in children's everyday learning in multiple settings
- Families as learners: advance learning and interests through education and/or training; activities that support parenting, careers, and life goals
- Family engagement in transitions: support and advocate for children's learning as they transition to any new learning environment

- Family connections to peers and community: formation of social networks that enhance social well-being and community life
- Families as advocates and leaders: participation in leadership development, decision-making, program policy development; community or state organizations focused on early development and learning.

In supporting parents as the first educators of their children, Head Start teachers are aware that parents have enrolled their children in the program so that their children receive the educational benefits the program provides. Appreciating parents' efforts is important to this goal. Similarly, it is important for teachers to accept that whoever is doing the parenting (mothers, fathers, grandparents, or others) needs support from early childhood teachers for this important role, because such acceptance increases the chances for successful partnerships. **naeyc** 2

DAP Like the descriptions of Head Start's three main goals, the following sample strategies to support parental nurturance have been taken from the *Head Start Handbook of the Parent Involvement Vision and Strategies* (1996):

- Provide opportunities for parents to learn about child development
- Share developmentally appropriate activities that parents and children can do together at home
- Encourage parents to visit and participate in the classroom to observe and later discuss how children learn and develop
- Foster participation in decisions about the classroom
- Involve parents of children with disabilities in developing their child's individualized educational plan **DAP**

The stated Head Start goal for parents' personal development may be surprising to some. This goal is based on an understanding that parental competence and self-esteem are tied to one another. Support for adults' personal development will often lead to job skills that will translate to greater economic benefit to families as well as a sense of success. Parents with positive self-esteem are able to do a better job of nurturing and encouraging their young children's development. The Head Start decision makers who defined this goal understood the importance of the family system to children's development. Some areas for parents' personal development for which Head Start programs may provide assistance or resources are:

- Increasing skills for everyday life, such as planning and preparing nutritious meals
- Planning for family life together

© Cengage Learning/ECE Photo Library.

Head Start programs encourage parents to visit and participate in their child's activities.

- Identifying strengths and skills that they already possess that might help in managing family life or in finding a job

- Working on skills they would like to learn or improve, such as effective and appropriate discipline of their children, or how to use a computer

- Learning how to reduce stress and increase wellness

- Creating opportunities to interact with other parents of young children and to build friendships

- Being involved in a community of others who value their language and culture

- Working with teams of parents and Head Start staff to participate in community activities or to address community issues

- Setting goals for themselves and making progress in the achievement of the goals

The preceding list of strategies offers many possibilities. Variations in programs and communities may restrict or increase these possibilities. Early childhood staff members who are sensitive to and understand the strengths and needs of parents may be able to assist them in choosing one or two of these areas as priorities. It is also possible that parents who are veterans of Head Start may be willing to serve as mentors to new parents as they work to meet their goals.

DAP Forming reciprocal relationships with parents is one step to empowering their decision-making in all realms of family life. This goal is intended to sustain families' involvement with their children beyond the Head Start experience. Head Start has been successful in creating a sense of community among its staff and clients that benefits children, teachers, and

families. One of the keys to this community-building effort is that parents—as partners with Head Start staff—are included in decision making throughout all aspects of the program, including the following:

- The children's curriculum

- Choices of health services available to children

- Planning for parent involvement activities

- Activities to work on at home with their children

- Ways to volunteer for Head Start

- Choices about which committees or groups on which to serve **DAP**

 "Communicating with Families: Best Practices in an Early Childhood Setting"

Visit the Education CourseMate website at www.CengageBrain.com to view the Video Case, and then answer the following questions:

- How does the video demonstrate examples of overcoming the five common barriers to communicating with families?

- Discuss ways that the video incorporates some of the ideas about communicating with families that have been included in Head Start programs.

Families in a Democracy

Powell (1989) notes three premises about the role of families in U.S. society that support an emphasis on family involvement in early education (Figure 7–1).

- The doctrine of **parental rights**
- Family influences on children
- Democratic principles

Rights and Responsibilities of Parents In a democracy, citizens have both rights and responsibilities. The rights and responsibilities related to parenting have legal and cultural roots. Professional educators must understand parental rights just as they understand and insist on parental responsibility. In this light, teachers must respect the primacy of the role that parents have with their children. Exceptions to parental rights are also based in law. Examples include the protections offered to children through child abuse and neglect legislation and custody decisions. It is imperative that educators apply only such legal issues, and not personal values or judgments, when relating to children and families.

Although early childhood teachers have been known to face professional dilemmas in ethical judgment about what is best for children, it is important to

Figure 7–1 Roles of Families in U.S. Society That Provide an Emphasis on Family Involvement in Early Education.

Doctrine of Parental Rights—Parents have legal rights and responsibilities in regard to their children. As educators, we often note parental responsibility, especially when we judge that it is not being fulfilled. However, family involvement in education principles must include the importance of **parental rights** as well.

Family Influences on Children—There is no doubt that parents are children's first teachers. Current brain development research finds the child's first 3 years are critical as a time of learning. Early childhood educators and others in the community must help to support parent efforts even before children come to school.

Democratic Principles—Families living in a democracy have the privilege of choosing how to rear their children. At the same time, with all of these choices come huge responsibilities for meeting children's needs. Early childhood professionals can provide information to parents so that they can make knowledgeable choices as they fulfill their responsibilities.

© Cengage Learning

keep personal or cultural perspectives in check. At the same time, professionals must be aware of legal positions and act accordingly. When educators note that the law does not protect children the way that they believe is necessary, advocacy for change is an acceptable action. After all, it was through such advocacy that child abuse and neglect legislation was passed in the 1970s and that corporal punishment in schools has been outlawed in some states.

Continuity

naeyc 2 *From Home to School* In addition to the critical role families play in the lives of young children, early educators have long been concerned about children's adjustment as they enter a formal educational program. The very nature of moving from home to school causes a great deal of discontinuity in a child's world. Many experts believe that **continuity** of experience is beneficial to children and that some of the discontinuity caused by moving from home to school may be bridged when family members have opportunities to communicate frequently with their children's teachers (Powell 1989).

Carlos entered a part-day preschool program when he was just a little over two-and-a-half years old. Each day, his mother, Gina, walked into the school with him and stayed with him while he explored the block center and sometimes the sand table. As children were invited to the group time rug, Carlos reached for his mother's hand and tears streamed down his face. Gina hugged Carlos and told

him that she would be back to pick him up later. Carlos joined the others for group time, singing and moving and participating fully. Carlos continued to cry each day for almost two weeks when it was time for his mother to leave. The school staff encouraged Gina to stay as long as she wanted. Suddenly, one day, Carlos walked with Gina to the group time rug with a big smile on his face—the moment this parent had been waiting for! As Gina left the school that morning, teachers noticed tears streaming down her face. When Gina returned to pick up Carlos later that morning, she told one of the teachers that she did not realize that she was going to feel sad when Carlos happily left her to join the other children.

Transitions during the Day Continuity refers to both **linkages** and the amount of **congruence** between educational programs and families of the children they serve. Linkages are the types and frequency of communication between home and school; congruence is the amount of similarity that schools and homes have in terms of values and goals for children, use of language, and adult-child interaction patterns (Powell 1989). **naeyc** 2

naeyc 6 In order to increase the continuity that children realize between home and school, it is the professional responsibility of early childhood educators to plan, implement, and evaluate the linkages they have with families. To be considerate of all families, teachers may need to use more than one type of communication; that is, written, verbal, and translations. Increased frequency of communication between home and school also increases continuity for children. Many early childhood education programs state in their policy manuals that they require one parent-teacher conference each year. It is vital that the planned or formal conference be combined with other forms of more frequent informal communication with families. Further, communication must include some method of two-way communication, not just one-way communication from school to home. Teachers must also consider variations in nonverbal communication. Practices related to language and cultural diversity must always be considered by early childhood educators. Suggestions for a variety of strategies can be found in Chapter 8.

Congruence of expectations and values between home and school is an important aspect of continuity. It does not take much experience for an early childhood teacher to realize that his objectives will not always be viewed as equally important by children's families. Variations in families' educational and income levels and culture or ethnicity may lead to an incongruence of expectations for children between home and school. The many other family factors discussed in the first six chapters of this text also are likely to contribute to differences between educators and parents in their goals for young children. Even when incongruent expectations are realized, professionals must demonstrate respect and sensitivity to different perspectives of families. This will become the basis for any effective communication. naeyc 6

One school district superintendent, Dr. Clarke, tells about a conversation he had with a parent of a first grader. Dr. Clarke explained to the parent that by using strategies deemed to be developmentally appropriate for young children, the teacher was encouraging children to think for themselves. He went on to explain that children would grow to love learning. The parent interrupted him by saying, "I don't want my daughter to think for herself. I want her to do what I say." This incongruence between the school's philosophy of encouraging a child's autonomy in learning and the parent's value of compliance is one that educators observe frequently. What family, cultural, and societal factors do you believe might have influenced this mother's viewpoint?

      " Schools have choices. There are two common approaches to involving families in schools and in their children's education. One approach emphasizes conflict and views the school as a battleground. The conditions and relationships in this kind of environment guarantee power struggles and disharmony. The other approach emphasizes partnership and views the school as a homeland. The conditions and relationships in this kind of environment invite power sharing and mutual respect, and allow energies to be directed toward activities that foster student learning and development. Even when conflicts rage, however, peace must be restored sooner or later, and the partners in children's education must work together. **"**

                                      —Joyce Epstein, 1995

DAP Although it has been assumed that young children benefit from greater continuity between home and school, there is little research support for this perspective. However, it is possible that when the discontinuity between the two settings is too great, children may fail at school (Powell 1989). It is possible that there is an optimal level of discontinuity in which children will learn to adapt to a variety of settings and that such adaptation is beneficial to children. Powell discusses Lightfoot's (1978) distinction between creative conflict and negative dissonance. Viewing creative conflict as preferable to negative dissonance, the difference seems to lie in the balance of power or mutual respect between home and school. Some educators have been known to give up on the idea of family involvement when the sources and degree of conflict become too great. However, a balance of power and demonstrations of mutual respect are likely to lead to positive outcomes, even in conflict. Thus, it behooves teachers and other school professionals to make continuous efforts at communication with all families. A willingness to share power may be the best conduit for strong partnerships.

Communication with parents should be face-to-face, and the interaction should occur in a private place where confidentiality is maintained.

It is important for early childhood teachers to understand that family involvement is not just about families helping the school. This perspective assumes that the school or the teacher is the base of power. Establishing a family-based philosophy in early childhood education does not necessarily decrease conflict with families. However, it may generate creative conflict that leads to solutions that are beneficial to children, families, and teachers.

Leah was a five-year-old kindergartner reading on the fifth-grade level. In the beginning of the year, her mother was worried that Leah would learn nothing during the year in the developmentally appropriate kindergarten classroom. After two months of observing the teacher and the class, and having frequent heated discussions with the teacher and the principal, the mother finally confided to another parent that her child was very happy and was gaining many unexpected skills.

It is obvious from this example that creative conflict is not always resolved immediately, but may be a process that takes some time. In fact, teachers may not even be aware of the existence of such conflict, and yet respectful reciprocal interactions may be at the center of such incidents.

When there are discontinuities between settings, Bronfenbrenner (1979) noted some assumptions that early childhood teachers can work toward in order to enhance the development of children and their families as they function in various settings.

1. *Attempt to agree on goals.* Schools can inform parents of goals for children in their early education program. This allows parents, as consumers, to consider the various educational options they have for their child. When choices of programs are limited, educators and families can discuss

differences in their goals for children and work to reach a level of agreement that will benefit children.

2. *Supportive linkages are required between the two settings.* Teachers should radiate support for all children and families in their classrooms because the lack of such support or perceived negative feelings about a child's family may lead to unfavorable outcomes for the child. Support for all families is essential. Keep in mind that perceptions may vary; that is, a teacher may believe that she should support all families in the same way. Such actions are likely to be perceived as negative since families, like children, have variations in needs. For example, not all families will need or welcome translation services, but those families who are able to use such support are likely to contribute more positively to favorable outcomes for their children.

3. *It is helpful to have a parent or other close family member from the home setting accompany the child to school.* This often means spending time with the child in the new setting rather than just dropping the child into it. Teachers will need to invite family members to do this because often it is not what families expect. Issue the invitation before the school year begins so that for the first few days of school family members can plan their day around this practice. Keep in mind that work or other demands may prohibit some families from spending time with their child as they enter school. If possible, plan for some evening or weekend events so that families and their children might spend some time together in classrooms.

4. *Communication strategies should be two-way, especially when the topic of communication is personal to the child or family, rather than serving as an announcement for all children in the class.* It is important for teachers to be sensitive to personal or private family matters. Two-way conversation often provides necessary information and can communicate to families that teachers are concerned about them and their children. On the other hand, a written message from the teacher may feel more like a judgment or criticism, causing the parent to avoid contact with the school. Teachers must make it clear that confidentiality will be maintained so that family members perceive them as trustworthy.

5. *Communication should be face-to-face whenever possible.* This is especially true for sensitive topics, when teachers may be tempted to take the easy way out by sending a note home with the child. If timely face-to-face contact is not possible, a telephone conversation is better than a written message. Whether such contact takes the form of telephone calls or face-to-face discussions, it is imperative that the interaction occur in a private place and that confidentiality is maintained. **DAP**

naeyc 1 *Transitioning to Preschool* Greater numbers of preschool programs now plan for extensive forms of supporting young children and their families with the transition from home to school. This situation holds true for preschools for typically developing children, for inclusive preschools, and for those that are designed specifically for children with identified disabilities. Since family involvement is essential in meeting the educational goals for all young children, early childhood educators and early childhood special educators note the importance of a parent or family component in any transition program design.

Preschool continues to be offered under a variety of auspices in the United States. Preschool programs might:

- Be public or private
- Be part-day or full-day
- Meet five or fewer days a week
- Be church-related or secular
- Practice inclusion or enroll primarily typically developing children or those with identified disabilities
- Be taught by qualified early childhood specialists or by someone who has no or minimal qualifications in early education
- Be developmentally effective or use approaches that do not incorporate an understanding of child development

When preschool staff plans for family involvement in children's transition from home to school, children adjust more readily and the stage is set for parents or other family members to become engaged in their children's early education. Methods that preschools use for transitioning include enrollment visits and observations, information sessions for families, handbooks with details about school policies and programs, and having only small groups of children attend for the first few days of school so that children receive more individualized attention.

Transitioning from Preschool to Kindergarten Some early education programs have created both formal and informal activities for supporting children and their families as children move to kindergarten or first grade. Typically, this transition involves a new location, many new people, and vastly different expectations. Often, the essence of this kind of transitioning program is a scheduled meeting for the parents, with one or more of the kindergarten teachers informing parents about what their children should know and be able to do in order to be ready to succeed in kindergarten. Such informational sessions can be somewhat helpful, but they typically do not provide children or families with support or resources for ensuring future success. It is more helpful to offer comprehensive programs that include opportunities for greater communication.

Many Head Start programs have developed and maintained "networks and collaborative relationships within their communities" to assist children and families as they transition "to the next stage of their lives in their communities, carrying with them the supports and strengths they have developed in Head Start" (*Head Start Handbook* 1996). In the Head Start transitioning program, staff attempt to provide opportunities to experience the next steps, not only to hear from the kindergarten teacher but also perhaps to schedule visits to the classrooms and to observe the teacher and children in action. naeyc 1

A transition activity booklet, *Connecting Head Start Parents to the Public School Setting*, is provided by some Head Start programs to parents as their children prepare to enter kindergarten. Figures 7–2 to 7–4 contain excerpts from this very useful guide.

In Pennsylvania, the Capital Area Intermediate Unit provides the *Transition to School: A Planning Guide for Parents* for families of the preschoolers who are attending their programs and who will be moving to school district kindergartens. These preschool programs are especially for children with identified

---

Figure 7–2	Why Parents Should Get Involved in Their Child's Education.

GUIDING PRINCIPLES IN HEAD START PROGRAMS

1. Parents are the most important teachers their children will ever have.
2. Parents know their children better than anyone else.
3. Parents are responsible for their children.
4. Parents' attitudes affect their children's motivation to learn.
5. Parent involvement increases children's academic achievement and success in life.
6. Parents are in the best position to supervise children's leisure time. They should limit television watching and encourage homework, reading, and conversation.
7. Parents are the strongest advocates for their children.

Epps, W. J. (n.d.). Connecting Head Start parents to the public school setting. Florissant, MO: Southern Research Associates

---

Figure 7–3	What Parents Can Do to Help at Home.

TIPS FOR PARENTS

1. Read aloud to your child every day.
2. Select television and video programs that serve specific purposes.
3. Give your child meaningful tasks/chores around the house that the child will be responsible for carrying out.
4. Correct inappropriate behavior in a calm, meaningful way.
5. Take advantage of all family outings to teach your child something new or reinforce something already learned.
6. Practice identifying road and other safety signs with your child.
7. Make it an ongoing practice to engage your child in conversations about different topics.
8. Set aside a period of quiet time where everybody in the home is involved in silent reading or meditation.

Epps, W. J. (1998). Connecting Head Start parents to the public school setting. Florissant, MO: Southern Research Associates

---

Figure 7–4	A Parent Guide for Parent/teacher Conferences and Conference Tips for Parents.

1. Write down questions and comments you want to make a day or two before the conference.
2. Be sure you let the teacher know that you have come to the conference with some questions or concerns.
3. Share with the teacher your child's feelings about friends at school, school activities, transportation, meals, or other topics.
4. Listen carefully and take notes for the future.
5. Ask questions before accepting recommendations from the teacher about behavioral plans, special services, and other areas.

6. Be sure to let the teacher know if there are words, terms, or phrases that are not familiar to you, or if you are unsure of the meaning.
7. If more time is needed, request another conference.
8. Be sure to thank the teacher for concern about your child.

CONFERENCE TIPS FOR PARENTS

1. Be confident
2. Be on time
3. Be organized
4. Be positive
5. Be open and honest
6. Be assertive, not aggressive
7. Be on topic; discuss your child, not other children or parents

Adapted from Epps, W. J. (1998). Connecting Head Start parents to the public school setting. Florissant, MO: Southern Research Associates

disabilities. Goals stated in the planning guide are to:

- Explain the transition process
- Provide information to help parents plan for their child's programs
- Provide information about public school options for children with disabilities

Topics that are included in this guide are shown in Figure 7–5.

Some transitioning plans are formalized among preschools and public schools and are facilitated by various community engagement organizations. In *Successful Kindergarten Transition*, Robert Pianta and Marcia Kraft-Sayre (2003) note that the skills and abilities children bring to kindergarten are only a small part of their adjustment and success. They assert the following five principles should form the core elements for planning and practice:

 1. *Foster relationships as resources.* When teachers create relationships with other professionals through work with community agencies, greater support can be provided for families. Such relationships can be fostered with child care centers, United Way programs, local colleges and universities, and social services.

2. *Promote continuity from preschool to kindergarten.* Children face a multitude of changes and often little continuity as they move from one program to another. Consider all of the changes that a child will face when attending a child care program on a Friday and a new kindergarten on Monday. Make a list of different experiences and expectations in this transition. Create strategies that will facilitate children's transition and lead to greater school success.

3. *Focus on family strengths.* Always search for what families do well and focus your comments on the positive. Even in conversation with colleagues or others, make a habit of stating the positive. A change in attitude is often key to this change in behavior.

4. *Tailor practices to individual needs.* First, investigate for individual needs. Listen to families and build on

---

Figure 7–5	Content for Families in Transition to School: A Planning Guide for Parents.

Introduction
- Goals for the Guide
- Statement about audience for Guide
- Quick checklist for transition that includes a calendar with dates for meetings from October through May and contact information

Part 1 Questions and Answers about Transition
- What does transition mean?
- Why do parents need to be involved in transition?
- What happens during the transition year?
- How does a multidisciplinary team complete an evaluation of each child?
- What is an Individualized Education Plan (IEP)?
- What is the parent's role in the evaluation report and IEP meeting?
- What do parents need to do to ensure child's eligibility for special education services through the school district?
- What services does the school district offer?
- Should I register my child for kindergarten?
- What is the role of my child's present Early Intervention team in the transition?
- Who should I call for information about services for my child in a private school?
- Who should I call about home school services for my child?

Directory of School District Contacts for Preschool Transition

Part 2 Information To Help Me Discuss My Child's Skills
Section A: Typical developmental expectations for children
  The 3-year-old
  The 4-year-old
  The 5-year-old

Section B: Child Profile

Parent reads a short description for each of the following areas and then responds to "My child is able to . . . " and "My child has not yet learned to . . . "

Cognition	Self-Care
Communication	Social Interaction
Movement	

Ten sentence completions, such as "My child likes _____," "My child's favorite toys are _____," and "My biggest concerns about my child are _____."

Section C: Parent Classroom Observation Form

Instructions for scheduling observation visits are provided.

Guiding questions for parents to consider while observing in a kindergarten classroom as well as kindergarten-level programs for special needs children are provided.

Part 3 Resources
Section A: Glossary of Special Education Terms

Section B: Definitions of Disabilities from Federal and State Regulations

Section C: List of Parent Advocacy and Support Groups and Agencies, with Contact Information

Pennsylvania Capital Area Intermediate Unit Preschool Programs

their concerns to individualize transition practices. One size will not fit all, so it is important to plan for variations from the inception of transition programs.

5. *Form collaborative relationships.* Early education professionals must practice openness and flexibility in order to form effective collaborations. Ongoing communication among families, schools, and communities will lead to optimal outcomes. **DAP**

In an interview that is excerpted on *Reading Rockets* (www.readingrockets.org/podcasts/experts/transcripts/pianta/), Pianta stated this in regard to the importance of transition planning:

"Early childhood education programs and kindergartens often collaborate on what we call transition programs for children and for families....And that often involves lots of communications to parents about expectations, it involves visits that go back and forth. And I like to think of effective transition programs as really a conversation among the early childhood providers, the kindergarten teachers, and the elementary school and the parents.

And at the middle of that conversation is a child and that they're communicating about this child's needs under a set of circumstances that reflect the home environment and the early childhood program and the kindergarten all coming together to a common understanding of this child's readiness to attack what's going to be available to them in kindergarten."

naeyc 2 Home Visiting

Home visiting is one method some early childhood programs have found to be effective in helping children transition from home to school. Goals of home visits vary among early childhood programs, with some having goals only related to child outcomes and others that include parent outcomes. A review of research on the effectiveness of home visiting (Sweet and Applebaum, 2004) noted that the two most common purposes for home visits to families with young children were parent education and child development. Program goals will help to guide activities to be conducted during the home visit. Listed here are reasons to conduct home visits, procedures to follow, cautions to consider, and some guidelines for the visit.

Reasons to Implement Home Visits

- Helps the child feel comfortable with a new adult
- Helps the teacher get to know the child (and family) in their own setting
- Helps build trust and communication between the teacher and the family
- Lets the teacher see the child in her home environment

- Offers a focused time to visit with the family and child
- Provides an effective step in the transition to an educational program setting

Procedures for Home Visits

- Check your school's procedures and policies regarding home visiting
- Confirm the visit with the administrator
- Contact the family in advance to set a time and date, and clarify directions (*Note:* some families may prefer to meet in a public place, such as a library, park, or fast-food restaurant.)
- Let the family know what to expect from the visit in advance—give information about length of time and what might be discussed/observed
- Thank the family for allowing you to visit

Safety Considerations for Home Visits

- Make visits with a coworker
- Take a cell phone
- Leave if the situation appears to be unsafe

What To Do during Home Visits

- Introduce yourself
- Ask about the family. How many children are in the family? How long have they lived at this residence?
- Briefly explain the school day to the children and the family.
- Ask whether there are questions or concerns
- Invite the family to visit you at school and provide ways to contact you

Because home visiting programs are multi-pronged and complex in nature, it is difficult to pinpoint exactly what makes a visit effective. Typically, home visits are one aspect of a service or educational program and not a standalone service. Benefits of establishing relationships through home visits are also both direct and indirect for children. Positive effects on adult family members lead to indirect effects with child outcomes. In general, home visiting does seem to support families with young children and to have a positive influence on child outcomes even though specific factors related to effective home visits remain uncertain. Children whose families participated in programs with home visitation displayed better cognitive and socioemotional outcomes than families who did not have home visits (Sweet and Applebaum, 2005). Research does point to home visiting as effective, but does not specify exactly which practices or characteristics lead to the most positive results.

FAMILY SUPPORT

Responsibilities of Families and Schools

"In the family support movement, families are viewed as the dominant support for children's development. Partnerships between families and helping agencies—including schools—must acknowledge families' primacy" (Bowman 1994). The importance of the child's family to her development and education cannot be overstated. Further, if family needs are met and support is available, children have a much greater chance at success. When families are overburdened with stress from poverty, illness, or violence, they often cannot meet their own needs or those of their children. **naeyc** 2

> **Reflect on This**
>
> With the information that you have about transitioning programs for preschool and kindergarten, reflect on how transitions might be helpful to all entities: children, families, teachers, and communities at other levels of early education.

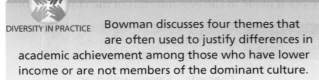

DIVERSITY IN PRACTICE   Bowman discusses four themes that are often used to justify differences in academic achievement among those who have lower income or are not members of the dominant culture.

1. Certain characteristics of the child, such as ethnicity or lack of self-esteem, are barriers to learning.

2. Values from home conflict with school-valued learning and skill development.

3. Discriminatory practices and inequality in the distribution of resources cause disadvantages to poor children and those who are not from the dominant culture.

4. School practices affect individuals and groups differently.

These themes show that, in fact, there is little agreement about why children of color do not do well in school. Teachers need to consider that different children are likely to need different programs to help them succeed (Bowman 1994).

The following are examples of how teachers can plan different programs to meet the needs of more children.

1. Plan activities and projects that are not costly. When the cost of an activity (e.g., field trips) is high, seek external funding.

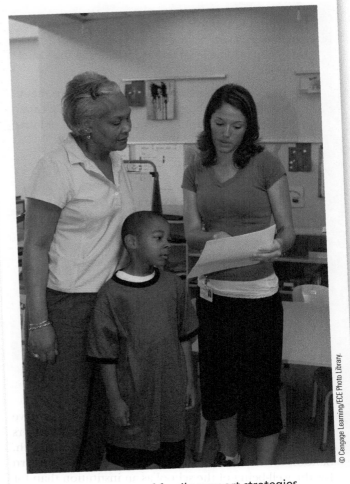

Providing many types of family support strategies meets a wider variety of family needs.

2. Include a variety of resource guests from different careers, income levels, and racial-ethnic groups.

3. Plan for active and passive times each day to meet differing needs. Include music, movement, quiet, and individual and small group choices for various activities throughout the day. Consider multiple modes of learning as well as multiple forms of intelligence as indicated by Howard Gardner (1983, 2000): language, logic and mathematical, musical, kinesthetic, spatial, interpersonal, intrapersonal, and naturalist.

Suggested School Practice Changes

1. When planning school-wide events, include participants from various racial-ethnic and income level groups throughout the year.
2. Invite a variety of racial-ethnic leaders to speak and participate in school activities.

3. When purchasing books and other instructional materials, always consider the racial-ethnic, gender, and income level representations in the visual images.

4. Plan for differing time and space needs to meet unique needs such as before- or after-school care, unique transportation arrangements, and unique language accommodations.

Three excellent resources for ideas to meet unique needs are:

- *Perspectives on Non-Sexist Early Childhood Education* by Barbara Sprung, Teachers College Press, New York, NY.

- *Anti-Bias Education for Children and Ourselves* by Louise Derman-Sparks and Julie Olsen Edwards, NAEYC, Washington, DC.

- *Starting Small* (video and teacher's guide), Teaching Tolerance, Southern Poverty Law Center, Montgomery, Alabama.

Empowering Parents

naeyc 2 Well-educated, affluent parents typically have very different interactions with their children's teachers than do their counterparts with less education or wealth. Schools are often criticized for having greater concern for the well-being of the school as an institution than for individual children and families they serve. It is highly possible that Head Start's successful family involvement model for **empowering** parents is not the model that would best serve other populations. Considering that parents who have higher levels of education and income may already feel empowered and assert themselves easily with teachers and administrators, goals for family involvement with such parents should differ from those of family involvement with low-income or less-well-educated parents. Regardless of the situation, however, authentic communication is necessary to foster growth-producing relationships between parents and teachers. Some family involvement activities that are traditional (such as open houses, conferences, fairs, and so on) may be effective, but it is necessary to assess these activities on an annual basis to make sure they have not become meaningless rituals. Ongoing needs assessment may prevent the "this is the way we've always done it" syndrome.

Empowerment is identified by Coleman and Churchill (1997) as only one theme for guiding a program's philosophy of parent involvement. Additional themes considered by these authors are parenting, identifying and developing family strengths, preparing children for future schooling, providing information about community resources, modeling appropriate learning opportunities for children at home, and improving interpersonal relations between professionals and families. As they assess the needs together, families and teachers may choose one or more of these themes and develop goals together for specific family involvement. New themes are likely to evolve as partnerships are formed and nourished.

LINKING PARENTS AND TEACHERS

Parents as Consumers of Children's Education

In tuition-based early childhood education programs, it is obvious that families are consumers. In public education, the parent's role as consumer is less obvious but no less true (Kostelnik, Stein, Whiren, and Soderman 1993). Parents have made tremendous investments in their children and expect teachers to have some idea of how important their children are (Figure 7–6). To practice a family-based philosophy, early childhood teachers must begin to understand that they are serving both children and their families. In a sense, the role of early childhood teachers and other staff members takes on several new perspectives when this idea is incorporated. This does not necessarily mean that teachers will agree with every request a family member makes, but it does mean that teachers will respect and understand that those requests are often made in the best interests of the child. Further,

Figure 7–6	Concepts for Marketing Family Engagement in Early Education.

Concepts	Sample activities
Family-ready philosophy	Welcome displays, greetings, brochures, Websites; family-friendly forms, policies,
	Teachers, administrators, staff
Professional development	Planned development to understand diverse
	Contemporary family structures, challenges,
	Strengths; practice active listening; knowing when to modify policies, structures and other
	Program aspects to meet diverse needs
Variety of opportunities	Make ALL opportunities relevant to families;
	Provide support for learning at home; use inclusive language; change displays to maintain high
	interest; create transition and readiness activities

© Cengage Learning

when conflict arises between a teacher and a parent, the teacher assumes a professional role in working to resolve the conflict. Chapter 8 includes information about implementing methods of conflict resolution.

With the families-as-consumers paradigm, early education programs may benefit from the notion of "marketing" to families. In the business world, marketing is a process used to identify, satisfy, and keep customers. Engaging all families in children's education in a multitude of ways will assist education programs in their efforts to satisfy and keep families as customers. As always, partnerships with families will serve as key to optimal outcomes for children.

Three major components that are involved in the idea of marketing family engagement in early education are:

- Development of a family-ready philosophy and action plan both for new families and new staff

- Engagement of all staff in professional development that helps them understand diverse family perspectives

- Active creation of a wide variety of possibilities for family engagement

Figure 7–6 provides examples of activities for each of these three major components for marketing family engagement.

Do This

Add some other ideas for themes to the list generated by Coleman and Churchill. Discuss which family characteristics might be more suited to each theme.

Supporting School Policy and Families

It is not impossible to support both school policy and families. Careful listening to parent concerns and reflective responses will often lead to creative problem-solving. When school policies are based on what education professionals believe to be best practices, teachers can explain the purpose of the policy to families (Figure 7–7). Further, information from families may be helpful when modifying school policy. More details about effective interpersonal communication are included in Chapter 8.

naeyc 2

naeyc 4 The National Coalition for Parent Involvement in Education (NCPIE), U.S. Department of Education, has produced posters outlining seven good practices for families. Using the motto "Education is everybody's business!" the Partnership poster includes the following practices.

1. *Take the time.* Moments talking at evening meals and visiting the library, museum, or zoo make a difference.

2. *Read together.* It's the starting point of all learning. Read with your youngsters.

3. *Use TV wisely.* Limit viewing to no more than two hours a school day.

4. *Stay in regular contact with your child's teacher.* Check homework every day.

5. *Meet with your child's teacher and principal.* Compare your school program with standards of excellence so your children can reach their full potential.

6. *Know where your children are.* Support community efforts to start after-school and summer programs.

Figure 7–7	A Parent Looks Back.

As my daughter begins her last semester of college, I am amazed at how quickly the years have flown and how time for both of us seems to be measured by school years. It all seemed so short: preschool, kindergarten, high school graduation, and now I even have lodging reservations for her college graduation weekend!

Brief, almost fleeting, and yet, so many milestones have been accomplished. Overall, I am very pleased and even appreciative of the educational endeavors that she and I chose for her 16+ years of education.

In the beginning, I placed her in a private school.

She was almost four. Her years at the private school led to kindergarten and first and second grades. While there, she was exposed to lots of reading, typing, some Spanish, computers, and her two favorite pastimes to this day: drama and roller skating.

Next came a culture shock for her: public school.

This presented a larger class size, diversity, school spirit, and busing. She barely missed a beat in the adjustment. She was bused to an inner-city school.

She adjusted well and even ran for school president and won! I was pleased with her elementary school experience. I was especially pleased with two teachers who recognized that special creative streak in her and rewarded her for her individuality.

Looking back, there is very little that I would change. I have loved seeing her achieve, stretch, be challenged, and most of all grow into a lovely, well-read, very verbal individual. It was 90 percent education and encouragement and 10 percent community outlets, church, and her mom, grandmother, and beloved uncle.

—Cindy Chrisman

7. *Talk directly to your children.* Share the values you want them to have and about the dangers of drugs, alcohol, and tobacco. It could literally save their lives.

Early childhood teachers can share these practices with families in a variety of ways. Providing parents with information, such as the criteria for quality programs in early education based on guidelines for developmentally appropriate practice or national voluntary accreditation criteria, gives them knowledge so that they can appropriately evaluate their children's education. Many early education programs provide their goals for children and philosophy of teaching and learning in handbooks and orientation sessions for parents. naeyc 4

Consider This

Review the list for families and consider a parallel list for early childhood teachers. Be sure to indicate ways that teachers might be able to support families with these suggestions.

CONCEPTUAL FRAMEWORKS FOR FAMILY, SCHOOL, AND COMMUNITY PARTNERSHIPS

Epstein's Framework

naeyc 2 In her theory-building work, Joyce Epstein (1995) notes the existence of **overlapping spheres of influence** in the lives of children. Her idea that home, school, and community are all important in each child's education has led her to discuss types of involvement as well as examples and practices.

The way schools care about children is reflected in the way schools care about the children's families. If educators view children simply as students, they are likely to see the family as separate from the school. That is, the family is expected to do its job and leave the education of children to the schools. If educators view students as children, they are likely to see both the family and the community as partners with the school in children's education and development. Partners recognize their shared interests in and responsibilities for children, and they work together to create better programs and opportunities for students.

From the preceding quote, one notes that Epstein's framework places children as central. When

families, schools, and communities are truly partners, the possibility of a caring community exists. Epstein identifies the following terms as critical to understanding her framework for partnership:

- Family-like schools
- School-like families
- Community-minded families
- Family-friendly schools and communities

According to Epstein (1995), family-like schools recognize individuality in children and welcome all families; school-like families recognize children as students and learners, and encourage their success; community-minded families (including students) help their neighbors in a variety of ways; and family-friendly schools and communities consider the needs and realities of contemporary families. See Figure 7–8 for a checklist for family friendliness in schools. What items would you place on a similar list regarding school friendliness for families?

Do This

Before reading any further, note some characteristics that you believe to be important to each of the preceding four terms.

Figure 7–8 Examples of School Policies Based on Best Practices.

Best Practice—Teachers work in partnership with parents.
School Policy—A variety of two-way communication strategies are used to meet needs of each family. Schools ask families about useful and preferred means of communication.

Best Practice—Teachers and parents work together to handle differences of opinion as they arise.
School Policy—A plan for conflict resolution is in place and shared with all parents. Family members work with staff to develop the plan.

Best Practice—Teachers solicit and incorporate parents' knowledge about their children.
School Policy—Assessment procedures require conferences with parents. Information is shared appropriately with parents before the time of the conference so that they are prepared to make meaningful use of the time with the teacher. Family members share information about their child that will be used by staff when assessing children.

Best Practice—Parents have opportunities to be involved in ways that are comfortable for them.
School Policy—Parents are informed about a variety of ways in which they can be involved with their children's education, both in and outside the classroom. And families share with staff their skills, interests, and preferences.

© Cengage Learning

Six types of involvement or caring have been recorded by Epstein: parenting, communicating, volunteering, learning at home, decision-making, and collaborating with the community. It is suggested that schools utilize all six types of involvement for balance in their partnerships with families and communities. Figure 7–9 provides a brief explanation of each of the six types.

Epstein and her associates make it clear that creating a comprehensive caring community takes a lot of time and a lot of hard work. Organization and planning are required. They suggest the appointment of an action team and at least a three-year plan. Thus, partnerships are a process, not events. Before beginning the work of the action team, it is important to gather information about the school's existing practices. One way to collect this information is through use of the standards listed in Figure 7–10.

NATIONAL STANDARDS FROM THE PTA

The National Parent Teacher Association (PTA) has had as its primary goal for more than 100 years, "affirming the significance of parent and family involvement… in support of children and their education." With this in mind—and the increasingly powerful evidence from research to support family involvement in education—the PTA, using Epstein's six types of involvement, has created national standards.

Figure 7–9	Checklist for Family Friendliness in Schools.

	Almost always	Most of the time	Sometimes	Rarely	Almost Never
Parent meetings are problem-focused.	5	4	3	2	1
Parents are informed about classroom activities.	5	4	3	2	1
Parents are viewed as a source of information.	5	4	3	2	1
Parental input is valued.	5	4	3	2	1
Parents come to school for positive reasons.	5	4	3	2	1
Parent meetings are held at various times.	5	4	3	2	1
Teachers discuss parents in a positive manner.	5	4	3	2	1
Teachers avoid gossiping about families.	5	4	3	2	1
Parents are informed when their children are doing well.	5	4	3	2	1
Teachers make it a point to invite all parents to school functions.	5	4	3	2	1
Are relationships between parents and teachers generally seen as positive?	5	4	3	2	1
Did most parents of children in the school succeed in school themselves?	5	4	3	2	1

Rosenthal, D. M., & Sawyers, J. Y. (1996, Summer). Building successful home/school partnerships: Strategies for parent support and involvement. *Childhood Education*, pp. 194–200.

Figure 7–10	The Keys to Successful School-Family-Community Partnerships: Six Types of Involvement.

EPSTEIN'S KEYS TO SUCCESSFUL SCHOOL-FAMILY-COMMUNITY PARTNERSHIPS

1. **Parenting**—Assist families with parenting skills and setting home conditions to support children as students, and assist schools to understand families.
2. **Communicating**—Conduct effective communications from school to home and from home to school about school programs and children's progress.
3. **Volunteering**—Organize volunteers to support the school and students.
4. **Learning at home**—Involve families with their children in homework and other activities.
5. **Decision making**—Include families as participants in school decisions and develop parent leaders.
6. **Collaborating with the community**—Coordinate resources and services from the community for families, students, and the school, and provide services to the community.

Epstein, J., L.Coates, K. C. Salinas, M. G. Sanders, & B. S. Simon.1997. *School, family, and community partnerships: Your handbook for action.* Thousand Oaks, CA: Corwin Press.

The purpose for the standards is threefold:

- To promote meaningful parent and family participation
- To raise awareness regarding the components of effective programs
- To provide guidelines for schools that wish to improve their programs (http://www.pta.org/programs/invstand.htm, accessed February 20, 2003)

For each of the six standards for family involvement, the National PTA has provided a quality checklist, including **quality indicators**. Figure 7–11 summarizes the standards. On the Web, go to http://www.pta.org/programs for the entire checklist, including quality indicators.

Although Joyce Epstein's framework for partnerships is, at this time, the most well-developed one with a strong organization, the National Network of Partnership Schools (NNPS), frameworks with alternative perspectives have also been examined. Staff at the Harvard Family Research Project (Shartrand et al. 1997) have identified Epstein's approach as *functional*, referring to its emphasis on specific purposes and roles as noted by the six types of involvement for family, school, and community partnerships. naeyc 2

National Network of Partnership Schools (NNPS)

www.coso.jhu.edu
Click "programs;" click "National Network of Partnership Schools"

The Family Involvement Network of Educators (FINE)

www.gse.harvard.edu
Click "faculty & research;" click "research projects;" click "Harvard family research project;" click "FINE network"

Coleman's Framework

naeyc 2, 4 James Coleman's framework for partnerships is referred to as *social capital*. In his groundbreaking mid-1960s research, "Coleman concluded that a student's home environment had more impact on test scores than any other factor, even school curriculum or student body characteristics" (Lynn 1997). The notion of social capital points to the importance of relationships among individuals and institutions—in our case, families, schools, and communities. Central to this approach is that families are invested in their children's learning, negotiating differences in values in order to best benefit children's education and acquiring skills in communicating with families in ways that demonstrate authentic caring (Shartrand et al. 1997).

In addition to a child's family, social capital emanates from communities. Family interactions in communities may lead to greater access to social capital for children. Coleman (1988) identified three types of social capital:

- Obligations and expectations
- Norms accompanied by sanctions
- Information-flow capability

When teachers have a sense of how families understand their obligations to parenting and the expectations that they have of school staff, a stronger partnership may be formed and greater social capital made available to support children's education. Similar perspective taking is beneficial for variations in norms and related sanctions. Family and community norms often develop through culture and are modified in relation to obligations and expectations. Information flow increases in family, school, and community partnerships when it is two-way and multimodal. Thus, Coleman's social capital model is noted to emphasize cultural expectations and access to information flow or communication. Educator sensitivity to variations in families and communities is necessary for ensuring parity in social capital for all children.

Figure 7–11	Listing of Standards from the National PTA.

NATIONAL PTA STANDARDS FOR FAMILY INVOLVEMENT

Standard I—Communicating
Communication between home and school is regular, two-way, and meaningful.

Standard II—Parenting
Parenting skills are promoted and supported.

Standard III—Student Learning
Parents play an integral role in assisting student learning.

Standard IV—Volunteering
Parents are welcome in the school, and their support and assistance are sought.

Standard V—School Decision-making and Advocacy
Parents are full partners in the decisions that affect children and families.

Standard VI—Collaborating with Community
Community resources are used to strengthen schools, families, and student learning.

Coleman (1991) explains principles that undergird parental involvement in children's education from a social capital perspective. He notes:

- Passivity about family involvement on the part of school staff leads to involvement occurring only when parents perceive a problem, often leading to antagonistic relationships.

- Bringing families together without a specific purpose is generally ineffective. Instead, build on common interests and relationships that have been observed.

- Effective use of technology can help overcome some barriers that exist in family engagement.

- Engaging families' interests and activities at the school leads to stronger relationships that can increase positive outcomes for children's learning.

Cochran's Framework

Parent empowerment best describes Moncrieff Cochran's framework of family involvement in children's education. Because schools have such a central place in U.S. society, they are in a unique and constructive situation to encourage empowerment of parents, families, and communities (Cochran and Dunn 1991). "Empowerment is a process through which people and communities grow toward more equitable, respectful interrelationships with themselves, and their environment....In order for....relationships to become more equitable, the balance of power usually must change" (Dean 2004). Attitudes that are fundamental with this framework include believing that:

- All parents want what is best for their children
- All parents want to be good parents
- Parents are not only children's first, but also their most important teachers (Shartrand et al. 1997)

The term "empowerment" is sometimes hijacked to describe any and all parental involvement in children's education. However, Cochran (1992) notes that the precise definition and application must include the following concepts:

- The process, not the goals, is at the heart of the true meaning of empowerment.

- Mutual respect is defined as sharing power and understanding that all people and family units have strengths.

- Both professionals and family members engage in critical reflection about situational factors and attitudes.

- Caring for one another becomes equally important to protecting individual rights as relationships are established. **naeyc** 2, 4

DIVERSITY IN PRACTICE Further, a knowledge base that provides understanding about societal power structures, oppression, and discrimination is necessary to build partnerships with all families in the school community. Early childhood teachers must work to comprehend the effects of dominant groups and institutions on oppressed people. Thus, skills must be gained in order to communicate respect to all families and to help build confidence in those who need such support (Shartrand et al. 1997). Empowerment skills that are believed to be especially relevant for working with families include: understanding families, effective and sensitive communication, having balance in life, understanding diversity, valuing family strengths, supporting families, engaging families with home visits, facilitating family meetings and conferences, and skills for successful collaboration (Forest n.d.).

Moll's Framework

Luis Moll has defined *cultural competence* as a necessary emphasis for family involvement. This emphasis on cultural competence requires teachers to look beyond what they observe in classrooms. Moll's research found that "many families had abundant knowledge that the schools did not know about—and therefore, did not use in order to teach academic skills" (North Central Regional Educational Laboratory 1994). For example, many rural families knew a great deal about agriculture, farm or ranch management, carpentry, and electricity, and, further, these families shared their knowledge and skills through informal community networks. Moll believes that tapping into these strong networks can be very helpful for schools.

The idea of "funds of knowledge" as described by Moll brings family knowledge into the classroom. Rather than focusing on narrow curricula, teachers who attend to knowledge and skills of children and families in their particular classrooms are able to tap into what is known, instead of a deficit view that attends to what diverse families and children do not know. Teachers must not only take the lead in establishing units of study based on their children's funds of knowledge, but also be willing learn content that may be unfamiliar to them. Examples of such topics include agriculture, construction, and mechanics. Teachers, students and families are able to increase their vocabularies as well as social understanding of contributions to society.

naeyc 2, 4 Relating the cultural competence model to language learning and literacy leads educators to understand the importance of bilingual students taking advantage of their home languages (North Central Regional Educational Laboratory, 1994). Knowledge and skills central to this framework include teachers':

- Awareness of their own beliefs and prejudices that influence building partnerships with all families
- Knowledge about cultural variations in parenting and education
- Skills in gaining translators and creating ways to communicate with all families
- Knowledge of variations in communication styles of various groups of people
- Skills to incorporate family "funds of knowledge" into student learning at home and at school (Shartrand et al. 1997) **naeyc** 2, 4

It is vital that early childhood teachers consider all four of these frameworks as they prepare to work with all families. Many teacher preparation programs place little emphasis, generally, on understanding families and even less emphasis, specifically, on acquiring a deep understanding of, or the skills to work with, families who are culturally different and the systems of power and oppression, and engaging in primary interactions with families to help build their confidence.

PROFESSIONALISM IN FAMILY-BASED EARLY EDUCATION

naeyc 6 Professionalism in early education is enhanced when all staff upholds their responsibilities to children and families. Due to their low pay, early childhood educators are often regarded as having low status in U.S. society. Still, it is imperative that educators view themselves as professionals and see the need to be responsible and to apply the knowledge, skills, and values of the discipline. Although it is true that much is expected of early childhood teachers and that typically they are not compensated fairly for their work, professionalism must be evident in work with children, families, colleagues, and communities.

Following are essential components of professionalism for early childhood educators.

Confidentiality

Early childhood teachers must be able to maintain confidences shared by families. The nature of their work frequently makes early childhood teachers privy to information that may cause embarrassment or harm to a family. Information gleaned through observation, as well as information in formal records, must be kept in confidence. Teachers should make it clear to family members that it is an educator's professional responsibility to maintain confidentiality and that they will not share information unless the family authorizes them to do so.

> **Do This**
> What challenges do you face as you reflect on specifics of the four frameworks for building partnerships? What strengths do you already possess? Develop a plan for your professional progress based on at least one of the frameworks.

Requests to share information should be made only for the purpose of providing assistance to the family or child enrolled in the program. Responsibility for safeguarding confidentiality includes obtaining family consent when sharing information, obtaining family consent when inviting others to team meetings, keeping files secure, never gossiping or talking casually about a family, and respecting confidences that co-workers share with you (*Family Partnerships* 1998). See the **NAEYC Code of Ethical Conduct**, in Appendix B, for statements on written and verbal confidentiality for both children's and families' rights to privacy.

The **Family Education Rights & Privacy Act (FERPA)** is a federal law designed to protect the privacy of a student's education records. Under this act, parents have the right to inspect and review all of the student's education records maintained by the school. Parents have the right to request that a school correct the records believed to be inaccurate or misleading. Generally, schools must have written permission from the parent or eligible student before releasing any information from a student's record. For more information about FERPA, visit http://www.ed.gov/, click policy and then type in FERPA.

Cultural Competence

Advancing understanding and skills related to cultural diversity must be intentional for teachers as they engage in professional development. The National Education Association (NEA) defines cultural competence as "the ability to successfully teach students who come from cultures other than our own" (National Education Association 2008, 1). Further, four skill areas have been identified for all teachers in order to address achievement gaps that continue to exist between various groups of students:

- Teachers must value diversity as demonstrated through acceptance and respect for differences in customs, communication, traditions, and values.
- Teachers must be culturally self-aware by understanding how their own culture and experiences

influence their behavior, values, interests, and expectations.

- Teachers must understand that many factors, including history, affect the dynamics of cross-cultural interactions.

- Teachers must work to institutionalize cultural knowledge and adaptations to diversity by designing programs and services that are sensitive to and effective with diverse children and families.

Advocacy

Advocating for children and families is also a professional responsibility. **Advocacy** can happen within your school or center, in a town or city, in regional or state government, and at the national or international level. Advocacy may be done in person, through e-mail or letters, and by telephone.

Early childhood professionals may advocate within both private and public agencies as well as with elected and nonelected public officials. For a detailed description of advocacy methods and strategies, read *Advocates in Action: Making a Difference for Young Children* (Robinson and Stark 2002).

Evidence-based practice is comprised of applications of research related to child development, families, and effective teaching. Educators must know how to access and interpret current research in the field so that their informed advocacy will best meet the needs of children and families. Information to support these skills for early educators can be found at www.naeyc.org/resources/research/. Additional information about early childhood educators as advocates can be found in Chapter 11.

Collaboration

Professionalism with families also extends into the community through collaboration with other agencies and programs. Collaboration may be minimal (informing parent of opportunities), or more extensive (budgeting time and money for collaborative efforts). Collaboration may be necessary to improve or extend support for families, obtain services for children, or increase knowledge about certain conditions. For further information about family-community collaboration, read "Position Statement on Home-School Collaboration: Partnerships to Enhance Educational Outcomes" by the National Association of School Psychologists (2005) found at www.nasponline.org/about_nasp/pospaper_hsc.aspx.

Understanding Roles and Boundaries

Early childhood teachers should be familiar with the roles and tasks included in their job descriptions. Work with families and children is frequently done on a deeply personal level. Sometimes, some personal disclosure on the part of the professional is effective, but it is critical that teachers are aware of professional boundaries in their relationships with children and families. Demonstration of caring must be balanced with limits in professional relationships. When friendships develop with either families in the program or with colleagues, it is important that professional boundaries be maintained in the interest of fairness and well-being to all. Some strategies that can be helpful in managing professional roles and boundaries include having accurate job descriptions, adhering to policies and procedures, not taking sides in family disputes, skill in assertive communication, knowing how to delegate when a boundary conflict may occur, and respecting professional boundaries with colleagues (*Family Partnerships*, 1998).

Record-Keeping

Having accurate and current records about children as well as relevant family information is useful for the assessment of children. Further, such documentation can be invaluable if referrals for additional or alternative services are necessary. All records must be kept in a locked cabinet so that they are confidential. Keeping notes about informal and formal conferences with family members can serve as a reminder when planning for the group or for individual children. Observations of children in the classroom and in other settings provide meaningful information when compiling evaluations.

66 Programs are only as good as the individuals who staff them. 99

—Head Start Advisory Council on Services for Families with Infants and Toddlers naeyc 6

EMBRACING DIVERSITY

DIVERSITY IN PRACTICE   When early childhood educators attempt to form a family-based philosophy, a willingness to acknowledge and respect family differences is required. Cultural differences in families lead to very different approaches to parenting young children. Some families believe that children are fragile and that families are the protectors of children; other families believe that children are tough and independent, and that families are the trainers of children (Trawick-Smith 1997). **Diversity** in families is part of the richness of our pluralistic culture.

Observing and Appreciating Differences

For any given teacher, one of the parenting approaches just mentioned may be the one they find to be most appropriate. It is important that early

Professionalism in early education is enhanced when all staff members uphold their responsibilities to children and families.

childhood professionals work to understand and respect various parenting approaches. Rather than judging the family, teachers can use the information about parenting approaches to better understand the child in their care. When necessary, differences in practices and expectations between families and schools should be discussed. Open communication can lead to an understanding of the opposing point of view. Teachers can offer to share resources when parents ask questions or seek help with some area of difficulty. Teachers also should realize that a child's family can be the greatest resource for understanding the child.

> 66 We live in an increasingly diverse world. As an early childhood educator you are almost certain to have close contact with people who have different racial, economic, cultural, and linguistic backgrounds and different lifestyles. This diversity offers challenges and opportunities. Although you may have moments of discomfort and self-doubt, you also have the possibility of gaining new appreciation and insights. Each bias and prejudice that you overcome brings you a step closer to helping all children to reach their potential. 99

> —Feeney, Christensen, and Moravcik, 1996

You will teach children who come from a variety of family structures. Encouraging members of a child's family to participate in school functions is an important aspect of early childhood family involvement. Frequently, this might mean inviting a parent (or other family member) who does not live with the child to participate in ways that are comfortable for all family members. Sometimes, parents who do not live together will both attend the same parent-teacher conference, or they may request separate conferences with their child's teacher. Keep in mind that each family defines itself. It is the role of the early childhood teacher to include all family

members, not to judge who is a real mother or real parent. Further, it is important to honor a family's understanding of its own capabilities and preferences.

Some barriers to implementing a multicultural framework in classrooms have been identified by Swick, Boutte, and Van Scoy (1996). The following factors become barriers when early childhood teachers do not engage in ongoing personal and professional development.

Barrier #1: Cultural stereotypes. People are stereotyped when others have minimal or inaccurate information about them. When those in the dominant culture have low self-esteem and are insecure, they tend to foster intergenerational prejudices.

Barrier #2: Social isolation. Having experiences with people from a variety of different cultures often helps to understand those cultures. However, those who have social contact only with others who are similar in culture and beliefs may lack information necessary for understanding differences.

Barrier #3: Tradition. By continuing the same activities in the name of tradition, schools can create exclusionary practices. When traditions are not inclusive, they must be reevaluated and modified, or dropped. All forms of bias must be considered, including racism, sexism, ageism, as well as unfair limits placed on those with disabilities.

Barrier #4: Excessive conformity. Expectations that everyone conform to the majority are sometimes stated as being democratic. This view, however, ignores a crucial aspect of democracy: everyone has a voice and deserves to be represented. While in a vote, majority

It is important that early childhood educators acknowledge and respect cultural diversity

rules, but this is not the case for everyday events in educational settings. Children can learn to celebrate their differences.

> Schools also need to recognize the effect they have on children's multicultural development. Some teachers have limited understanding of their student's cultural backgrounds. The resulting erroneous beliefs must be transcended through staff development, personal reading and enrichment, and through personal growth experiences. Institutional practices of tracking, ability grouping, and rigidly defined graded systems need to be replaced with more inclusionary strategies, such as multiage grouping, cross-cultural peer learning, and more personalized instruction. Unquestioned rituals and policies imprison culturally different children within an inequitable and insensitive environment....Inappropriate and inaccurate labeling has led many children to years of academic failure.
>
> —Kevin J. Swick, Gloria Boutte, and Irma Van Scoy, 1996

Strategies for Overcoming Barriers

1. *Repeatedly invite guests, speakers, and representatives of a variety of cultures into the school program.* Plan education and recreational activities together.
2. *Use various media to show different cultures and promote the celebration of those differences.* For example, display posters depicting many cultures and change them throughout the year; use children's literature with different racial-ethnic and socioeconomic levels represented in positive ways, and use videos depicting a variety of cultures in positive ways.
3. *Plan celebrations throughout the year that involve diverse communities and include food, music, dance, visual, and language traditions.*

Anti-Bias Education

Louise Derman-Sparks and Julie Olsen Edwards (2010) have updated an earlier approach for implementing curriculum goals related to understanding and respect for diversity in early childhood education. In the words of these authors:

> Anti-bias work is essentially optimistic work about the future for our children. Anti-bias teachers are committed to the principle that every child deserves to develop to his or her fullest potential. Anti-bias work provides teachers a way to examine and transform their understanding of children's lives and also do self-reflective work to more deeply understand their *own* lives (p. 2).

Even though the emphasis of the anti-bias curriculum is on teaching and learning in early childhood classrooms, there are ways to consider this philosophy in work with families and communities. Derman-Sparks and Edwards interweave work with

families throughout every chapter of their book. Including work with parents, they say, is vital to the effectiveness of this approach in early childhood education and must be based on "what families wish for their child and what you believe is important for children" (p. 39). In order to create a caring learning community, early childhood professionals will engage in the following ways with families:

- Learn about each family's desires for their child's identity development.
- Approach differences as opportunities to strength-en partnerships. Careful listening to one another is essential to understand family concerns and collaboration.
- Realize and deal with disagreements that are bound to occur with differences in cultural values.
- Facilitate families talking with one another and getting to know one another with events such as potlucks and small group discussions about planned topics of interest.
- Center the curriculum around families by creating spaces for photos and objects of interest and inviting families to participate in a variety of ways in the classroom.

It is clear that carrying out the aforementioned goals challenges most, if not all, early childhood professionals. The value systems held by some families may be on a collision course with the values held by those who believe in an anti-bias approach to education. Various reasons exist for this. Some families have not given these ideas much thought; although they may have some stereotyped ideas based on political or religious ideology, they may also begin to consider the importance of understanding and respecting all people with whom they interact on a regular basis, such as the people in their child's school. Other families agree with the importance of an anti-bias curriculum but have not actively shared their beliefs with their children. Finally, still other families have already embraced, and practice, the philosophy of respect for all people.

For early childhood programs that are serious about implementing an anti-bias approach, the creators of this curriculum offer strong emphasis on fairness as essential to eliminating bias through the following chapters:

1. What is anti-bias education?
2. Children's identity development
3. Becoming an anti-bias teacher: A developmental journey
4. Creating an anti-bias learning community
5. Learning about culture, language, and fairness
6. Learning about racial identity and fairness

7. Learning about gender identity and fairness
8. Learning about economic class and fairness
9. Learning about family structures and fairness
10. Learning about different abilities and fairness
11. Learning about holidays and fairness

Strategies and resources are suggested for each of the previously listed topics. Although this outline is a useful beginning for informing parents about an

anti-bias philosophy in educating young children, it may not be exhaustive. However, it is clearly the intent of this educational philosophy to eliminate all oppression and to advocate for fairness for all people. It requires an attitude of lifelong learning for education professionals.

Figure 7–12 contains suggestions for parents who seem to be reticent about becoming involved in their children's education (Lee 1995).

Figure 7–12	Strategies for Involving Reticent Parents.

Reaching Out to Reticent Parents

The following are suggestions offered by parents who participated in a study about how to reach out to parents who seldom take part in school activities.

1. Encourage active parents to stress the importance of participating in school activities.
2. Urge children to encourage and remind their parents to attend school activities.
3. Invite parents to visit school and observe their children any time, and reassure them that they will be given a friendly welcome when they come to school.
4. Clearly indicate to parents that a language difference need not be a primary concern for those who are interested in getting involved at school.
5. Invite interpreters to come with parents for open house and back-to-school-night activities, or encourage teachers to have interpreters present.
6. If two or more parents belong to the same Asian ethnic group, reassure them that they are free to speak in their own language to each other during parent meetings. This way, Asian parents who are able to communicate in English may help others understand the discussions.
7. Reserve some time to communicate with Asian parents alone after the parent meeting (e.g., on back-to-school night) so that Asian parents do not feel they have been ignored.
8. Visit reticent parents in their homes. In general, Asian parents respect teachers and feel honored when their children's teachers visit. Asian parents also view a teacher's willingness to come forward as a sign of sincerity (Shen and Mo 1993). Parents are more willing to be educational partners when they learn that teachers make an effort to reach out to them.
9. Sometimes, children inhibit parents' participation because they feel embarrassed by their parents' inability to communicate well in English. They sometimes wish their parents would not appear at

school. Convey that a language difference is not a negative trait.
10. Provide an opportunity for parents in the same Asian group, whose children attend the same school, to get acquainted with one another.
11. Schedule parent-teacher conferences to enable parents from the same Asian group, with children in the same class, to visit school at the same time. This way, reluctant parents may not feel as threatened by the unfamiliar school environment and may be encouraged to communicate with the teacher.
12. Asian parents who speak English and are familiar with school procedures can give introductions regarding the following matters to reticent parents from the same Asian group: school registration procedures, immunization, school volunteer programs, parent-teacher conferences, school educational goals, grading and evaluation systems, and so on. Holding meetings about these issues in a parent's home might provide a less threatening environment for the reticent parent. Schools may also conduct seminars in parents' native tongues to help them become familiar with basic features of the school system such as educational services and programs, extracurricular activities, and procedures for assessment and evaluation of children (Yao 1988).
13. Send notes to parents from time to time. The note could be a one- or two-sentence progress report, or it may be something that would make parents smile, such as, "Do you know what your child did today that gave us a good laugh?" or "Would you like to know what interesting thing your child did today?"

From Lee, F. Y., 1995, "Asian Parents as Partners," YOUNG CHILDREN 50 (3): 4–9. Reprinted by permission of the NAEYC.

Figure 7–13	Continuum of Parent Involvement.

HIGH
- Parents, trained by teacher, assist in classroom in such learning activities as reviewing writing samples, assisting at learning centers, or helping with computer use.
- Parents in classrooms reinforce processes and concepts introduced by teachers.
- Parents in classrooms practice with children on vocabulary words, number facts; help them enter answers on computer cards.
- Parents read to children in the classrooms.
- Parents make classroom presentations or present hands-on activities in areas of expertise.
- Parents participate in committees that directly influence school curricula and policies. Committees consist of parents, teachers, and administrator(s).
- PTA parents work on sponsorship and implementation of curriculum-related and family-oriented activities (e.g., cultural arts contests, displays, family fun night).
- Parents make instructional materials for classroom use, as directed by teachers.
- Parents assist in school library, checking out and shelving books.
- Parents participate as room mothers or room fathers.
- Parents supervise on class trips or chaperone at school functions.
- Parents visit classrooms during American Education Week or back-to-school night.
- Parents attend classroom plays, presentations.
- Parents attend school assembly programs.
- Parents attend competitive games, athletic events at school.
- Parents attend promotion ceremonies.
- Parents attend parent-teacher conferences.
- Parents are encouraged to help children with homework at home.
- Parents are involved in PTA fundraising activities.
- Parents are asked to join PTA.
- Parents are encouraged to read school's handbook for parents.
- No parental involvement.

LOW

© Cengage Learning

Understanding That Many Ways of Interacting with Children Can Serve Them Well

Early childhood teachers work with both children and their families. We can best teach children by including their families in a variety of ways. As we provide quality early childhood education programs for young children, we are also supporting and caring for families (Feeney, Christensen, and Moravcik 1996). Adults in families have many ways of nurturing and providing for their children; they have values that may differ from the teacher's values. When early childhood teachers can assess family strengths and not see these differences only as deficits, then it is more likely they will enjoy successful partnerships with families of children in their programs.

EVALUATING THE FAMILY INVOLVEMENT COMPONENT IN EARLY EDUCATION

As with any other component in quality early childhood education, it is important that early childhood teachers and administrators evaluate the success of family involvement. In planning for evaluation, it may be helpful to use the Continuum of Parent Involvement identified by Galen (1991). To evaluate this in a logical and consistent manner, a program must first identify its goals for family involvement. Both short-term and long-term goals may be identified. Examples of goals, strategies, and methods of evaluation are provided in this section. Please note that

Figure 7–14 is a sample and not indicative of a comprehensive family involvement plan for early childhood education.

The results of evaluation of family involvement activities help program staff to be aware of their successes as well as of areas that need attention. Program assessment should lead to new goals that continue to build partnerships with families.

Figure 7–14	Sample Family Involvement Plan for Early Childhood Education.

Goals	Strategies	Evaluation Methods
Providing program information regarding the philosophy of teaching and learning to all new families	Providing written brochures at the time of application, providing handbooks at the time of enrollment	Noting that the program philosophy has been added to the handbook or a brochure
	Personal explanations of program by director or other staff	Having parents sign that they have read and understand the philosophy; Asking parents to submit questions or comments that will be addressed in a parent meeting to increase their understanding of program philosophy
	Teacher-led parent meeting that explains the program early in the year	
Creating an orientation to the program for both children and families	Classroom visits before school starts	Filing the plan for orientation including how and when orientations are conducted
	Making curriculum resources available to families	Ask participants to complete a rating form about the usefulness of the orientation
	Providing explanations or listings of all support services available	Ask family members who have been in the program for at least a year for suggestions for orientation topics and formats
Scheduling home-school conferences at least twice during the school term	Designing flexible schedules to meet family needs	Recording dates and times of conferences
	Including children when appropriate in conferences; Involving other staff, other family members, or advocates when appropriate	Collecting evaluations from family members about the usefulness of conferences and suggestions for improvement
	Giving parents a list of suggested questions they might ask during conferences	Request feedback from volunteers who frequent the classroom
Making family members feel welcome as classroom volunteers	Matching family members' interests or skills with classroom needs; Preparing materials and space in advance for parents	Send questionnaires to those who do not volunteer to request information anonymously about what the program staff can do to increase their comfort level
	Informing parents of daily schedule and exceptions to the schedule	Self-evaluate which families you feel most comfortable having in the classroom and how you might increase comfort level of others
	Consistently welcoming parents throughout the day	
	Personally inviting each parent or family to participate in the classroom	

Summary and Conclusions

To practice a family-based philosophy in early childhood education, teachers must have knowledge of families and value the primacy of families in children's lives. In early childhood education, Head Start has provided a model program for partnerships between programs and families. Since 1965, Head Start has had a primary goal of empowering parents to take responsibility for their lives and for those of their children. High expectations have been coupled with various forms of support for families. Teachers in family-based early education programs see themselves as supports for children and their families.

Policies in early childhood education programs must incorporate current understanding about parents as their children's first teachers. Family involvement must be a priority for early education professionals. As programs for children are planned and implemented, the central role of families must be incorporated in a variety of ways.

Theory into Practice Suggestions (TIPS)

- View your work to understand all families as a lifelong learning opportunity.
- Honor families for the difficult task they have in rearing children.
- Express gratitude frequently to family members as they support children's education.
- Always modify your attitude so that the emphasis is on family strengths rather than how families might be "fixed."
- Be aware of your own strengths and areas for improvement in building reciprocal partnerships with families.
- Acknowledge barriers that exist in collaborations among families, schools, and communities. Create a repertoire of ways to address the barriers so that children are supported to reach their optimal potential.
- Consider that some families may flourish with empowerment strategies and others may respond to a more functional approach to partnership building.
- Be prepared to respond to naysayers regarding the importance of family involvement in early education.
- Understand that advocating for young children also means advocating for their families.
- Be open about your practice of confidentiality. Live up to this professional commitment.
- Plan for a multitude of ways to support the transitions that children and families must make during children's early childhood years.
- Be actively involved in bringing people from various cultural backgrounds into your program.
- Continuously set goals and evaluate progress in your family involvement program.

Applications

1. The most important aspect of family involvement in education is that parents spend time with their children. Describe some ways you can help foster this, even when parents are not volunteering in the classroom.
2. Explain the concept of continuity in children's lives. Give examples of ways early childhood professionals can increase continuity for children.
3. How might a perspective of parents as consumers of early education affect parent-teacher relationships?
4. Consider ways that communities might support families and schools. How might educators influence communities to be more caring?

Questions for Reflection and Discussion

1. Make a list of topics that should be included in a family-based philosophy of early childhood education.
2. Which areas of practicing a family-based philosophy will challenge you? In which areas do you possess experience or strengths?
3. How will particular early education settings (e.g., child care, public school, Head Start, and so on) affect your philosophy about family involvement?
4. Discuss characteristics of the four paradigms of family involvement: functional, social capital, parental empowerment, and cultural competence.
5. Share ideas that you have about activities that might be implemented that would support young children's transition from home to preschool or from preschool to kindergarten.

Field Assignments

1. Ask several parents of young children about daily care and education arrangements they have made for their children. Note the number of transitions some very young children deal with daily.

2. Interview three early childhood teachers about the responsibilities they believe parents have for their children's early education. What suggestions would teachers give to parents of young children related to these responsibilities?

3. Interview three parents of young children about responsibilities they believe early childhood teachers have for their children's early education. What suggestions would parents give to teachers related to these responsibilities?

4. Investigate existing transitioning programs in your local region. Interview local education leaders or community engagement sponsors about transition work in progress.

Additional resources for this chapter, including TeachSource videos, can be found on the Education CourseMate. Go to CengageBrain.com.

References

Bowman, B. 1994. Home and school. In *Putting families first: America's family support movement and the challenge of change,* eds. S. L. Kagan and B. Weissbourd. San Francisco: Jossey-Bass.

Bronfenbrenner, U. 1979. *The ecology of human development: Experiments by nature and design.* Cambridge, MA: Harvard University Press.

Capital Area Intermediate Unit (CAIU) Preschool Program. 2005–2006. *Transition to school: A planning guide for parents.*

Christian, L. G. 2006. Understanding families: Applying family systems theory to early childhood practice. *Young Children* 61: 12–20.

Cochran, M., and C. Dunn. 1991. Home-school relations and the empowerment process. *The Elementary School Journal* 91: 261–69.

Cochran, M. 1992. Parent empowerment: Developing a conceptual framework. *Family Science Review* 5 (1–2): 3–21.

Coleman, J. S. 1988. Social capital in the creation of human capital. *The American Journal of Sociology* 94 Supplement: Organizations and Institutions: Sociological and Economic Approaches to the Analysis of Social Structure, S95–S120.

Coleman, J. S. 1991. Policy perspectives: Parental involvement in education. Washington, DC: Office of Educational Research and Improvement.

Coleman, M., and S. Churchill. 1997. Challenges to family involvement. *Childhood Education* (Spring): 144–48.

Dean, C. 2004. Empowering partnerships with families. *Innovations in community and Rural Development.* Cornell Community and Rural Development Institute. www.cardi.cornell.edu/community_capacity/community_action/000283.php (accessed January 24, 2006).

Derman-Sparks, L., and Edwards, J. O. 2010. *Anti-bias education for young children and ourselves.* Washington, DC: National Association for the Education of Young Children.

Epps, W. J. 1998. *Connecting Head Start parents to the public school setting: A transition activity booklet.* Florissant, MO: Southern Research Associates.

Epstein, J. 1995. School/family/community partnerships: Caring for the children we share. *Phi Delta Kappan* 76: 701–12.

Epstein, J., L. Coates, K. C. Salinas, M. G. Sanders, and B. S. Simon. 1997. *School, family, and community partnerships: Your handbook for action.* Thousand Oaks, CA: Corwin Press.

Family partnerships: A continuous process. Training guides for the Head Start learning community. 1998. Washington, DC: U.S. Department of Health and Human Services.

Feeney, S., D. Christensen, and E. Moravcik. 1996. *Who am I in the lives of children?: An introduction to teaching young children.* Englewood Cliffs, NJ: Prentice Hall.

FERPA. http://www.ed.gov/offices/Om/ferpa.html.

Forest, C. n.d. *Empowerment skills for family workers.* Cornell Empowering Families Project. Cornell University: NYS College of Human Ecology.

Galen, H. 1991. Increasing parental involvement in elementary school: The nitty gritty of one successful program. *Young Children* 46: 19.

Gardner, H. 1983. *Frames of mind: The theory of multiple intelligences.* New York: Basic.

Gardner, H. 2000. *Intelligence reframed: Multiple intelligences for the 21st century.* New York: Basic.

Head Start Handbook of the Parent Involvement Vision and Strategies. 1996. Washington, DC: U.S. Department of Health and Human Services.

Kostelnik, M. J., L. C. Stein, A. P. Whiren, and A. K. Soderman. 1993. *Guiding children's social development.* Clifton Park, NY: Delmar Learning.

Langford, J., and B. Weissbourd. 1997. New directions for parent leadership in a family-support context. In *Leadership in early care and education,* eds. S. L. Kagan and B. T. Bowman. Washington, DC: National Association for the Education of Young Children.

Lee, F. Y. 1995. Asian parents as partners. *Young Children* 50: 4–7.

Lynn, L. 1997. Family involvement in schools: It makes a big difference, but remains rare. Harvard Education Letter. http://www.edletter.org/past/issues/1997-so/family.shtml (accessed January 24, 2006).

National Education Association. 2008. Promoting educators' cultural competence to better serve culturally diverse students: An NEA policy brief. www.nea.org/assets/docs/PB13_CulturalCompetence08.pdf (accessed March 9, 2012).

National PTA. http://www.pta.org/programs/invstand/htm (accessed March 9, 1999).

North Central Regional Educational Laboratory. 1994. Funds of knowledge: A look at Luis Moll's research into hidden family resources. *CITYSCHOOLS* 1: 19–21.

Pianta, R., and M. Kraft-Sayre. 2003. *Successful kindergarten transition: Your guide to connecting children, families, & schools.* Baltimore, MD: Paul H. Brookes.

Powell, D. 1989. *Families and early childhood programs.* Washington, DC: National Association for the Education of Young Children.

Robinson, A., and D. R. Strk. 2002. *Advocates in action.* Washington, DC: National Association for the Education of Young Children.

Rosenthal, D. M., and J. Y. Sawyers. 1996. Building successful home/school partnerships: Strategies for parent support and involvement. *Childhood Education* (Summer): 194–200.

Shartrand, A. M., H. B. Weiss, H. M. Kreider, and M. E. Lopez. 1997. *New skills for new schools: Preparing teachers in family involvement.* Harvard Family Research Project. http://www.ges.harvard.edu/hfrp/pubs/onlinepubs/skills/chptr1.html (accessed January 22, 2006).

Starting Small. Teaching Tolerance Curriculum. Montgomery, AL: Southern Poverty Law Center.

Sweet, M. A. and Applebaum, M. I. 2004. Is home visiting an effective strategy? A meta-analytic review of home visiting programs for families with young children. *Child Development* 75 (5), 1435–1456.

Swick, K. J., G. Boutte, and I. Van Scoy. 1995–1996. Families and schools: Building multicultural values together. *Childhood Education* (Winter): 75–79.

Trawick-Smith, J. 1997. *Early childhood development: A multicultural perspective.* Upper Saddle River, NJ: Prentice Hall.

Family-Staff Relationships

OUTLINE

© Cengage Learning/ECE Photo Library.

OBJECTIVES ALIGNED WITH NAEYC STANDARDS

After reading and reflecting on this chapter, you should be able to:

- Discuss attitudes and practices necessary for effective communication among families, child care, and schools **naeyc** 2, 5

- Understand the most effective communication strategies for specific situations **naeyc** 2, 5

- Apply effective conflict resolution practices in the family involvement component of early education **naeyc** 2, 5

- Familiarize yourself with useful web sites to build and support family-staff relationships **naeyc** 2, 5

- Learn strategies for responding to a variety of interactions with families, including conferencing **naeyc** 2, 5

Key Terms

active listening
conflict resolution
empathy

interpersonal
communication

self-disclosure
two-way communication

BUILDING RELATIONSHIPS

Communication

Family systems theory emphasizes the importance of communication for establishing healthy, functional families. Effective communication also is vital to build relationships among professionals and families. When professionals implement strategies for effectively communicating with families, they serve a twofold purpose: (1) establishing strong partnerships and (2) modeling methods of communication that families have access to and may incorporate in order to strengthen their

familial bonds. Clear communication is an essential professional tool for early childhood teachers and administrators who wish to develop productive partnerships. When we communicate effectively with others, each voice is empowered (Swick 2003).

DIVERSITY IN PRACTICE Communication across cultures sometimes presents challenges to educators. Each of us has been influenced by our culture in our communication style and approaches to understanding. DuPraw and Axner (1997) discuss six patterns of cultural difference in communication:

Figure 8–1	Culturally Different Patterns of Communication.

1. Communication style—(a) meaning of any term as absolute or possibly. Example: Firmness of a "yes" response in any given communication.

   (b) importance placed on nonverbal communication differs

2. Attitudes toward conflict—cultural views toward conflict include viewing it as positive, undesirable and sometimes necessary, or embarrassing.

3. Approaches to completing tasks—some cultures place greater emphasis on establishing relationships and others on task completion. "This does not mean that people from any one of these cultural backgrounds are more or less committed to accomplishing the task, or value relationships more or less; it means that they may pursue them differently" (DuPraw & Axner 1997, 3).

4. Decision-making style—Some cultures prefer majority rule and others focus on building consensus. Some delegate responsibility for specific decisions and others maintain decision-making by authority figures.

5. Disclosure—Variations in the amount and type of information that participants share have cultural bases. Some will openly share emotions and details and others are more reticent. Understanding these differences will help with clear communication.

6. Approaches to Knowing—Gathering data through reading and library research or through observation, interviews, visits with people are both helpful in increasing knowledge. Understanding these differences in cultural variations is a way to increase effective communication.

© Cengage Learning

---

communication styles, attitudes toward conflict, approaches to completing tasks, decision-making styles, attitudes toward disclosure, and approaches to knowing. Figure 8–1 provides information about the meaning of each of these six patterns.

Attitudes A perspective that views teachers and parents as partners in children's education is a very powerful one. The sense of common purpose and mutuality is one of the strengths of the partnership notion (Swick 1991).

Establishing a positive relationship with parents begins with their first phone call to the school or with their first visit, and it involves everyone in the school. For example, the person who answers the phone or greets the family upon arrival may set the tone for the entire visit. Incidental meetings with staff often provide families with useful information.

naeyc 2 What makes a positive or healthy relationship? Clearly, any relationship depends on more than one person's attitudes and behaviors. However, it is also true that one person with certain understandings and skills can help positively impact a relationship. It is the duty of professionals to obtain these understandings and skills and to take the responsibility of directing interactions with students' families and with community members. For example, it is teachers' responsibility to avoid using derogatory terms when describing a family, since using such negative language can degrade or disempower families. In addition, when teachers make such negative statements, it is difficult for them to overcome the negative attitudes and beliefs those statements express and so may make it impossible for that teacher to have an empowering relationship with a given family (Garbarino 1992, as cited in Swick 2003). When

teachers hold negative attitudes about families, their professionalism is likely to be compromised. Thus, it is in their best interest to overcome negativity by searching for positive aspects and strengths.

Some emotional and behavioral characteristics are known to be related to healthy relationships. The following are included by Hanna (1991) in her discussion of this topic:

High Self-Esteem. Teachers who love and accept themselves are more likely to demonstrate caring and acceptance of others. Self-esteem is related to competence, so be aware of what you do well and areas that you wish to strengthen.

Freedom from Codependency. Teachers who are not extremely dependent on others, serving them while not sacrificing personal needs, possess a trait that is important for positive relationships. A healthy way of relating to others is referred to as interdependence. Understand that an ability to work with others is a strength, but consistent self-sacrifice in working relationships may ultimately undermine intended outcomes.

Genuineness. Honest, open, authentic teachers avoid gameplaying in relationships. Teachers who have positive self-esteem and who rely on a recognized professional knowledge base find that genuine interactions produce healthier relationships and better outcomes.

Warmth. Caring for others, despite their faults, helps maintain healthy relationships. Warmth can overcome judgmental positions between teachers and families.

Empathy. Trying to understand the behavior of others and the underlying meaning of that behavior is an important characteristic of building relationships.

An understanding that one cannot be aware of others' experiences and how they have perceived those experiences is helpful in developing empathy for all.

Self-disclosure. Balancing how much and what you disclose about yourself with family and community members can be a challenge. A certain kind and amount of **self-disclosure** is related to other characteristics of healthy relationships such as genuineness, warmth, and **empathy**. Use professional judgment and share personal details only when it may help reach resolution.

Fairness and Dependability. Over time, teachers have the opportunity to demonstrate that others can trust them to be fair-minded and to follow through with commitments. Professionals must be aware that others are observing them in order to evaluate their fairness or dependability.

Energizing Feelings. As teachers build relationships with families and communities, they are likely to feel energized by the possibilities communicated. Experience with such situations is likely to positively influence teachers to work on relationships with parents and other community members. **naeyc** 2

Consider This

Consider characteristics of healthy relationships just mentioned. Think about a teacher you had in the past who seemed to excel in one or two of those areas. Share some examples of teacher behaviors that you believe demonstrate each of these characteristics. Which of these areas do you see as your strengths? In which areas could you use some practice?

The U.S. Department of Education lists seven tips for building partnerships with families. These tips are:

- Work together
- Assess needs
- Survey resources
- Share information
- Seek experienced collaborators
- Set goals
- Decide on measures of success

When these behaviors drive the work that educators and families are participating in together, the results will be not only stronger partnerships, but also greater progress for children's education. A complete description of these tips and more is archived at http://www.ed.gov/pubs/PFIE/families.html.

 "Communicating with Parents about Health in Early Childhood: A Parent-Teacher Meeting"

Visit the Education CourseMate website at www.CengageBrain.com to view the Video Case, and then respond to the following items:

1. How does the video demonstrate examples of the emotional and behavioral characteristics for building healthy relationships as discussed by Hanna?

2. Discuss ways that the video incorporates any of the seven tips for building relationships with families noted by the U.S. Department of Education.

3. Note examples related to cultural differences in communication.

66 The American family is the rock on which a solid education can be built. I have seen examples all over this nation where two-parent families, single parents, stepparents, grandparent, aunts and uncles are providing strong family support for their children to learn. If families teach the love of learning, it can make all the difference in the world to their children. 99

—Richard W. Riley, former U.S. Secretary of Education

Practices

Written Communication One of the initial contacts with parents is usually a letter welcoming their child to the school. Although this letter may be sent by the director or principal, it also should include information and perhaps a greeting from the classroom teacher. The content of all the written information sent home to parents needs to be clear and worded positively. Always proofread for correct spelling and grammar. The initial information should be covered in welcoming, supportive, and inviting ways.

Written communications can include brochures about the early childhood education program that contain a statement of the program's philosophy and goals for children as well as information about school policies and the staff.

Communication in Person When parents visit the school or center for the first time, it is important that both written and human resources are available. Personal communication should include pleasant greetings, a tour of the building and grounds, introductions to teachers and other staff, and an opportunity to ask questions. Figure 8–2 provides one format for interviewing parents or family members who are new to the early childhood program. Be sure to note that this form can be adapted to include additional topics. Currently, a focus of U.S. society is young children's health, nutrition, and fitness. So, item four in Figure 8–2 could include "What are some healthy snack and meal ideas for young children?"

> **Do This**
>
> Considering other current concerns, what would you choose to add (or delete) from this interview form?

DAP Family involvement in early childhood education thrives in programs that practice an open-door policy. Written and personal communication should make clear to parents that they are welcome at the school any time, that they are partners in their child's education, and that their voice is important to the school. Examples of ways in which families are involved in the early childhood program could be shared at this initial visit. Also, be sure to ask family members for their ideas about involvement.

Many early childhood professionals have found it useful to provide parents with a family handbook

Figure 8–2	Parent Interview Form.

1. Would you like to work with the children in the classroom?
2. What would you prefer doing in the classroom if you were to come?
3. Name something special that you can do or make, or something you know about that you would be willing to share with the children.
4. I'm going to read a list of items to you. Tell me if you have ever felt a need to know more about any of these items by answering either yes or no. (Interviewer: Please check appropriate category.)

	Yes	No
a. How to teach my preschool children		
b. Whether my child is developing appropriately		
c. Services provided by community agencies to which I have a right		
d. How to communicate better with my children		
e. How to help my children interact better with others		
f. How to discipline my children		
g. How to make toys and other things for my children		
h. How to tell whether my child is progressing in school		
i. What to do when my children do things that I do not consider proper (temper tantrums, thumbsucking, bad manners)		
j. How to play with my children		
k. Where to take my children so they can have a nice time and learn		
l. How to help my children retain their cultural heritage		
m. How to use and develop the talents and skills that I know I have		
n. How to refrain from hitting my child		
o. How to guarantee that my child will succeed in school		
p. How to talk to teachers		
q. How to help my child learn a second language when I don't speak a second language		
r. How to extend language learning		
s. How to use my home environment as a learning experience for my children		

5. What is your opinion of preschool parents coming together at least once a month to talk and learn more about the areas to which you answered "yes?"
6. If you felt that this parent meeting is a good idea, how can we make sure that the meetings are worthwhile for parents?
7. Would you be willing to help organize the first parent meeting?
8. Are there other ways you might be willing to help with the parent meetings?
9. Name something special that you can do or make, or that you know about that you would be willing to share with other parents.

From Hohman, M., et al (1979). "Parent Interview Form" in Young Children in Action, pp. 328–329. Reprinted by permission of High/Scope Press.

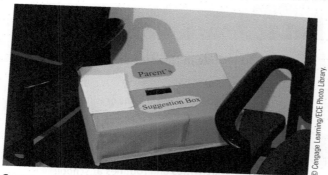
Communication can happen in a variety of ways.

Effective communication takes time and effort to best support families.

during orientation or initial enrollment. These handbooks commonly include a statement of the philosophy of the school's educational program and information about goals or expected outcomes for children, family involvement opportunities, daily schedules, operating policies and procedures, and individual classrooms. Sometimes, individual teachers provide a similar handbook specific to their classroom. DAP

ONGOING COMMUNICATION

One-Way Communication

The following strategies are examples of one-way communication from school to home.

Newsletters   Sending newsletters home from school is one way to help parents stay informed about and connected to school events. Including columns by teachers, children, administrators, and parents allows for a variety of voices and perspectives. This format makes it more likely that a larger number of parents will actually read the newsletter.

Suggestions for topics of interest and concern to families with young children include the following:

- The meaning of developmentally appropriate practice
- The importance of play for young children
- Multiple intelligences
- The meaning of pretend play for young children
- Early literacy
- Nutrition
- Understanding children's physical and motor development
- Understanding children's intellectual development
- Understanding children's social and emotional development

- Appropriate strategies for moving from diapers to potty

Columns about these topics and many others are provided for use by early childhood programs in *Family-Friendly Communication for Early Childhood Programs* (Diffily and Morrison 1996).

> **Do This**
> Considering information about newsletters in this section of the textbook, design an outline or template that you might use as a basis for your newsletters to families. Be sure to demonstrate as many principles as possible from the newsletter segment as well as Figures 8–3 and 8–4, so that your newsletters are relevant to families.

Especially important in a newsletter are dates of upcoming events and brief explanations or descriptions of school activities. Providing both a listing of current activities and those further into the future will remind parents and help them in planning busy schedules. A sample page from a newsletter is found in Figure 8–3. Figure 8–4 suggests content for newsletters to families.

The following ideas were selected from Bob Krech's article, "Improve Parent Communication with a Newsletter" (1995):

- The main goal of the newsletter is to answer parents' questions before they ask them.
- Try to keep the length of the newsletter at one page.
- Always remember to thank parents, at least once, in your newsletter.

Electronic newsletters, or e-newsletters, are being used more frequently by early childhood professionals as a tool for connecting with families. The advantages to sending electronic newsletters include

Figure 8–3	What We Can Do to Help Our Children Learn.

Listen to them and pay attention to their problems.

Read with them.

Tell family stories.

Limit their television watching.

Have books and other reading materials in the house.

Look up words in the dictionary with them.

Encourage them to use an encyclopedia.

Share favorite poems and songs with them.

Take them to the library and get them their own library cards.

Take them to museums and historical sites, when possible.

Discuss the daily news with them.

Go exploring with them and learn about plants, animals, and geography.

Find a quiet place for them to study.

Review their homework.

Meet with their teachers.

Do you have other ideas?

For sale by the U.S. Government Printing Office, Superintendent of Documents, Mail Stop: SSOP, Washington, DC 20402-9328

Figure 8–4	Suggestions for Newsletter Topics.

What To Include in Newsletter Columns

Activities for home:
Those that children would do alone or with siblings or peers
Those that parents would do with children
Those best suited for family outings

Explanations of activities and routines at school:
Upcoming field trips and special events
Importance of play, music, outdoors, etc.

Announcements of child or family-related community activities:
Art, drama, music, films, sports, service

Information about school staff:
Introductions or bios
Recent professional development activities

School changes or announcements:
Those caused by weather conditions
Those due to construction/repairs/maintenance

Articles on parenting, guidance, health, and safety:
Ideas for different seasons
Travel guidelines and activities
Developmentally appropriate toys or gifts for children

Reminders:
Tuition due dates and other fees
Change of clothes, diapers, special dietary needs
Field trips
Closing times and related policies

Parent or family association activity announcements:
Meetings
Fundraising events
Volunteer opportunities

© Cengage Learning

the instant delivery capability and low cost. Of course, because not all families have access to the technology required to enable them to receive e-newsletters, it is important that e-newsletters not replace other forms of communication (Walker 2005). Be sure all families receive some version of the newsletters you are distributing.

The following design tips are offered for either electronic or hard-copy newsletters.

- **Readers experience three stages of relevance:**
  Stage 1: Within three to seven seconds, readers decide whether they are interested by scanning headlines, titles, photos, and captions.
  Stage 2: Readers take from 1 to 90 seconds to decide whether they continue to be interested. Graphic organizers such as short paragraphs, bulleted lists, page borders, and column dividers are useful tools for this stage.
  Stage 3: When readers get to stage 3, they often continue reading the newsletter or put it aside to read at a later time.

- **Layout of document:**
  Readers view a document in a "Z"-shaped path, so that whatever is in the upper-left quarter of the page is seen first. Typically, readers then look across to the upper-right quarter of the page. Thus, the most important and relevant information should be in these two areas. Readers next move their eyes diagonally to the bottom-left portion of the page, which is considered the dead zone. So, it's a good idea to add interest here with a photo, graphic, or picture. Finally, readers move to the page's lower-right quadrant. This is the best place to communicate desired actions from the reader.

- **Typeface/fonts:**
  Most readable—Times New Roman and Courier. Use for text.

Figure 8–5 Sample Daily Information Sheet.

Harrisburg Child Development Center

Daily Information Sheet—Infants

DATE _____   CHILD'S NAME_____

Time of arrival _____   Brought by _____

Supplies brought   Staff signature _____
___ diapers   ___ soft toy for cuddling
___ change of clothing   ___ other _____
___ food/milk

Meals/feedings

Time_____ Description/amount _____
Time_____ Description/amount _____
Time_____ Description/amount _____
Time_____ Description/amount _____

Diapering times and notes

Time_____ Notes _____
Time_____ Notes _____
Time_____ Notes _____
Time_____ Notes _____

Sleep schedule and notes

Activities enjoyed

Developmental milestone(s)

Comments or concerns

An available notebook for parents to jot messages allows teachers to keep up with individual family needs.

Modern and fun—sans serif fonts such as Helvetica and Tahoma. Use for titles, headlines, and captions.

Bolded—slows readers. Use only for five to seven consecutive words.

Underlining—also slows readers.

- **Graphics and color placement:**
  Readers (a) follow direction of movement in any picture and (b) follow the direction of the way a picture is facing. Use directional pictures to move readers toward important content.
  Color is powerful and should be used to establish balance on any page.

- **Alignment:**
  Align text to the left for informality, friendliness, and readability.
  Justified text is more formal and professional, but slightly harder to read.
  Use hyphens sparingly—no more than three in a single column (Walker 2005).

Notes   Notes to families can take a variety of forms and serve a variety of purposes. One form is the standard note sent to all parents in the school or class. This type of note is useful for informing parents about occasions such as field trips or picture days, or about activities for which parents need to either give permission or send items to school (Figure 8–6).

More personal notes include teacher-generated communications regarding a child's academic or behavioral progress. It is important to balance the types of notes and not use them for sending home only negative messages. Incorporating celebratory or congratulatory notes when something has been done well helps parents keep a balanced perspective about their child, the teacher, and even their own parenting. Serious concerns about behavior or school progress are better shared in face-to-face communication. What experiences have you

Figure 8–6 Sample Note Sent Home to All Families in the School or Class.

November 13, 2006

Dear _____ ,

School pictures will be taken on Friday, November 20. Both individual packets of photographs and group photos for each classroom will be available for purchase. We expect all prints to be available by December 11. Individual packets are priced at $12.50 and class pictures are $2.50. All picture money is due by December 16. Please call your child's teacher if you have questions or concerns.

Stacey Blades
School Director

had with personal notes from teachers? What points of consideration do you believe to be important when drafting such notes? Critique the notes sent by teachers to families in Figure 8–7.

Announcements Announcements should be made in a variety of formats over different lengths of time. Providing families with an annual calendar that contains important dates helps to keep everyone informed in a timely way about upcoming events. Sending school-wide announcements home with children is another strategy. Posting signs on doors and at pickup points helps remind families of upcoming events or activities.

Placing emergency announcements on the school's voice-mail system also helps get information to parents. Emergency systems are frequently established that allow family members to subscribe to e-mail or text messages. Some schools have an information line that is updated daily with a new recording that family members can call for information on upcoming events. Placing long-term announcements in newsletters and

Figure 8–7	Sample Personal Notes to Parents or Families.

Note #1:

Dear Mr. Connors,

I just wanted to let you know that the work you've done to help Chris with his spelling words has paid off! He got 100% on his test this week.
Congratulations to both of you!

Sincerely,
Kate Olijiwa

Note #2:

Dear Ms. Lin,

Sara has been having some problems on the playground for the past 3 days. Please call me during my phone hours, Monday through Thursday from 2:45–3:15 p.m., so that we can discuss this.

Steve Elliott

Note #3:

Dear Jackie,

I wanted to let you know how much I appreciate your help in the classroom for the past 3 weeks. You are very good at supervising children during their learning centers time. I hope you will continue to come each week this school term. Thanks for your time and efforts in our classroom.

Martha Douglas

discussing them at parent meetings reinforces dates and other event information.

Daily Information Sheets Some centers and schools use preprinted forms that are completed each day by classroom staff and sent home to families. These sheets contain information that can be useful to parents: what the child ate at each mealtime and snacks, the child's sleep schedule, activities that the child particularly enjoyed, accomplishments or developmental milestones observed, and special comments or concerns.

Two-Way Communication

Frequently, **two-way communication** between home and school is essential. Two-way communication between families and early childhood teachers offers distinct advantages to one-way communication strategies. These methods focus on developing ongoing communication "in which both parties are equals, contributing valuable information to the discussion" (Kagan and Cohen 1997). Two-way communication has the benefit of being able to clarify misconceptions on the spot. Face-to-face communication allows for nonverbal communication such as gesturing and various demonstrations of empathy and warmth to be observed. Useful two-way communication techniques are discussed in the following.

Planned Conferences Planned teacher-family conferences must occur in a quiet place where information can be shared calmly and confidentially. Teachers should have all notes, portfolios, and other necessary materials ready at the time of the conference. It is recommended that the child's strengths be reviewed first, both to begin the meeting on a positive note before discussion of concerns or areas for improvement and to ensure that the conference gives a complete picture of the child's development and progress. Some professionals recommend the use of a "compliment sandwich," in which the early childhood teacher begins and ends the meeting with a positive comment so that these comments "sandwich" the middle of the conference, during which the teacher and family members discuss their concerns. It may also be helpful for the teacher to begin the meeting by mentioning three positive areas before discussing areas of concern. It is important that positive comments be authentic and meaningful, not empty statements whose purpose is only to make three hollow "positive" comments. When teachers need to conference with parents because of a particular concern, the preference for a balance between positive and negative information often is overlooked.

Keep a record of the conference, including brief documentation of the topics discussed. Some early childhood programs have duplicate forms that teachers use when preparing for and holding conferences; one copy of the form stays on file at the school and the other is given to the parents. It is also useful for these forms to include a place for follow-up by the teacher and parents after the conference (Figure 8–8).

Conferences should be planned for times that are convenient for all family members who wish to attend. Many family members have some schedule flexibility if they know conference times and dates in advance. Others' schedules are less flexible, however, and these families may need to schedule conference times that take place before or after the school day, for instance. All

families' schedules must be considered when centers or schools plan for conference times.

Routine conferences are frequently quite short, 15 to 20 minutes, a sufficient time period for a fairly quick overview of a child's progress. More time may be needed, however, if serious concerns are to be shared.

Children may be included and involved in conferences when it is deemed appropriate. Following are some examples of appropriate topics at conferences that include children:

- Reviewing portfolios
- Discussing problem situations

Figure 8–8	Sample Conference Form.

Date _____
Time _____
Location _____

LIST OF TOPICS TO BE DISCUSSED:

_____
_____
_____
_____

Teacher comments
_____
_____
_____
_____

Parent comments
_____
_____
_____
_____

Action to be taken:

Type	By whom	Accomplished by (date)
_____	_____	_____
_____	_____	_____
_____	_____	_____
_____	_____	_____
_____	_____	_____

Signatures:

Teacher(s) _____   Parent(s) _____
_____   _____
_____   _____

- Outlining a new plan of action
- Sharing relevant information

Naturally, children's ages and abilities, as well as any extenuating circumstances, would be considered when deciding whether to include them at conferences. Some programs are experimenting with a variety of formats and measuring positive outcomes related to children leading their conferences. For example, a school in Nebraska had children create PowerPoint presentations that they then used to explain what they had learned and what they needed to learn at school (Young and Behounek 2006).

Involving other teachers and school staff in conferences is recommended when they are involved in the topic of discussion. Following are examples of other staff who might be included:

- Counselors
- Nurse
- Director or principal
- Itinerant teachers or other staff
- Social service coordinator
- Cafeteria or playground supervisor

If parents have not met these people or do not see these staff members on a regular basis, it may be necessary to introduce parents to them. Also, it is a good idea to briefly explain to parents the reason for the additional staff members' attendance at the conference. Be sure to use both effective interpersonal skills and courtesy in all aspects of conferencing.

In turn, invite parents to bring others who are concerned about the child with them to the conference. It can be helpful for parents to have a supportive other person present for several reasons. Sometimes it is not possible for both parents in two-parent families to attend. In addition, single parents are likely to appreciate support from another concerned adult. Parents may want to invite the following:

- A friend
- Grandparent of child
- Child's caregiver
- Significant other
- A medical professional

Figure 8–9 provides a sample of a comprehensive self-assessment form that an early childhood teacher might use in order to increase awareness of the complexity of leading an effective conference.

Unplanned Conferences Sometimes, a conference with parents or other family member needs to be arranged quickly. These conferences are likely to be held

before or after school. Some guiding principles for unscheduled conferences are listed in the following.

1. Move to a quiet area away from other children and families.
2. Ask for someone else to supervise the children in your care, if necessary.
3. If the family member has initiated the conference, listen carefully to the concern before commenting or responding.
4. If you need more time to gather information, tell the family member you will contact him as soon as possible, and then do it.
5. If you have initiated the conference, thank the family member for agreeing to meet with you on such short notice and determine how much time is available.
6. Plan a follow-up meeting to give direction or closure related to the planned resolution.

▶❚❚ **"Home-School Communication: The Parent-Teacher Conference"**

Visit the Education CourseMate website at www.CengageBrain.com to view the Video Case, and then answer the following questions:

1. Discuss examples from the video that demonstrate characteristics for teachers when conducting conferences with family members as identified in Figure 8–8, Self-assessment of a Parent/Family Conference?

2. Using the Self-assessment Figure 8–8, note teacher areas of strength and areas that may benefit from additional attention or practice.

© Cengage Learning/ECE Photo Library.

Telephone calls are a convenient and sometimes necessary way to remain in contact with parents.

| Figure 8–9 | Self-Assessment of a Parent/Family Conference. |

I. Setting

A. Appropriateness of Setting

Meeting setting had distractions and is in a public environment	Meeting setting has some distractions and is in a public environment	Meeting setting contains distraction and is private	Meeting setting is quiet and private
1	2	3	4

II. Level of Preparation

A. Preparation for Family Conference

No records/student work available for family member(s) viewing	Few records/student work available for family member(s) viewing	Some records/student work available for family member(s) viewing	Several records/ student work available for family member(s) viewing
1	2	3	4

III. Greeting

A. Greeting to Family Member(s)

Teacher is not welcoming	Teacher is somewhat welcoming	Teacher is welcoming	Teacher's welcome is warm and genuine
1	2	3	4

IV. Nonverbal Communication

A. Eye Contact

Teacher does not make eye contact	Teacher makes little eye contact	Teacher makes frequent eye contact	Teacher makes appropriate eye contact
1	2	3	4

B. Facial Expression

Teacher's facial expression is not warm or inviting	Teacher uses very little facial expression	Teacher's facial expression occasionally shows warmth	Teacher's facial expression is often warm and inviting
1	2	3	4

C. Head Movements

Teacher does not move head during conference	Teacher occasionally moves head during conference	Teacher frequently moves head during conference	Teacher uses head movements at appropriate times throughout conference
1	2	3	4

V. Body Language

A. Respect for Others' Personal Space

Teacher frequently invades personal space of other(s)	Teacher occasionally invades personal space of other(s)	Teacher invades personal space a little	Teacher demonstrates respect for family members' personal space
1	2	3	4

Continues

Figure 8–9	Self-Assessment of a Parent/Family Conference (Continued)

B. Posture

Teacher's posture is very relaxed or very stiff	Teacher's posture is often very relaxed or very stiff	Teacher's posture is sometimes too relaxed or too stiff	Teacher's posture is appropriately relaxed and professional
1	2	3	4

VI. Verbal Communication

A. Amount of Time Speaking

Teacher speaks less than 10% or more than 90% of the time	Teacher speaks less than 20% or more than 80% of the time	Teacher speaks less than 40% or more than 60% of the time	Teacher speaks about 50% of the time
1	2	3	4

B. Use of Assertive Speech

Teacher uses aggressive or passive speech	Teacher uses occasional aggressive or passive speech	Teacher uses some assertive speech	Teacher uses mostly assertive speech
1	2	3	4

C. Voice Tone/Clarity

Teacher's speech is quiet, muffled or loud	Teacher's speech is low	Teacher's speech is frequently clear and appropriate in tone	Teacher's speech is consistently clear and appropriate in tone
1	2	3	4

VII. Verbal Responses

A. Length of Comments

Teacher's comments are long or terse	Teacher's comments are somewhat long or terse	Teacher's comments are sometimes appropriate in length	Teacher's comments are concise and with meaning
1	2	3	4

B. Use of Open-Ended Comments/Questions

Teacher consistently uses closed (yes/no) comments/questions	Teacher frequently uses closed (yes/no) comments/questions	Teacher sometimes uses closed (yes/no) comments/questions	Teacher typically uses open-ended comments/ questions to encourage family participation
1	2	3	4

VIII. Language

A. Use of Professional Language

Teacher uses inappropriate language/ poor grammar	Teacher uses some inappropriate language/ poor grammar	Teacher mostly uses appropriate language/ good grammar	Teacher typically uses appropriate language/ good grammar
1	2	3	4

Figure 8–9   (Continued)

B. Use of Positive Speech

Teacher phrases comments Negatively	Teacher frequently uses negative comments	Teacher sometimes uses positive comments	Teacher typically phrases comments positively
1	2	3	4

IX. Attitude

A. Avoiding Codependency

Teacher is overly dependent on others	Teacher frequently is too dependent on others	Teacher is sometimes autonomous	Teacher is typically autonomous
1	2	3	4

B. Fairness and Dependability

Teacher does not demonstrate fairness or dependability	Teacher sometimes demonstrates fairness or dependability	Teacher frequently demonstrates fairness and dependability	Teacher consistently demonstrates fairness and dependability
1	2	3	4

C. Self-Disclosure

Teacher frequently discloses personal Information	Teacher occasionally discloses personal information	Teacher discloses a little personal information	Teacher does not disclose inappropriate personal information and sets up reasonable boundaries
1	2	3	4

X. Warmth

A. Genuineness

Teacher is not genuine	Teacher is occasionally genuine	Teacher is frequently genuine	Teacher is consistently genuine in words and actions
1	2	3	4

B. Empathy

Teacher is not empathetic	Teacher is occasionally empathetic	Teacher is frequently empathetic	Teacher is empathetic in words and actions
1	2	3	4

XI. Acceptance

A. Willingness to Accept Others

Teacher demonstrates disapproval of family differences	Teacher does not demonstrate acceptance of family differences	Teacher shows some acceptance of family differences	Teacher is accepting of and accommodating to family differences
1	2	3	4

XII. Active Listening

A. Listening skills

Teacher interrupts family member	Teacher does not listen to family member	Teacher attends to but does not reflect family member's statements	Teacher actively listens and reflects family member's statements
1	2	3	4

Continues

Figure 8–9	Self-Assessment of a Parent/Family Conference (Continued)

B. Use of "I" messages

Teacher uses blaming words and attitude 1	Teacher does not use "I" messages 2	Teacher occasionally uses "I" messages 3	Teacher frequently uses "I" messages and explains her viewpoint as appropriate 4

XIII. Criticism

A. Receiving Feedback

Teacher reacts aggressively or passively 1	Teacher responds with obvious irritation or does not acknowledge feedback 2	Teacher acknowledges feedback 3	Teacher responds appropriately with words and actions 4

B. Giving Feedback

Teacher is aggressive with criticism 1	Teacher uses blame when criticizing 2	Teacher criticizes without offering help or support 3	Teacher sandwiches constructive criticism with compliments and offers support 4

XIV. Conflict Resolution

A. Identifying the Issue/Problem

Teacher is a little unclear in defining issue or problem 1	Teacher is somewhat unclear in defining issue or problem 2	Teacher does not clearly define issue or problem 3	Teacher clearly defines issue or problem and checks to see if family member has common understanding of issue or problem 4

B. Consideration of Family Member's Ideas

Teacher does not get information from families about their ideas 1	Teacher gets little information from families about their ideas 2	Teacher gets some information from families about their ideas 3	Teacher considers ideas of families in an active way 4

C. Consideration of Family Member's Concerns

Teacher does not get information from families about their concerns 1	Teacher gets little information from families about their concerns 2	Teacher gets some information from families about their concerns 3	Teacher considers concerns of families in an active way 4

Figure 8–9   (Continued)

XV. Goal Setting

A. Focusing on the Future

Teacher consistently dwells on past situations	Teacher frequently dwells on past situations	Teacher sometimes looks to the future	Teacher consistently looks to the future
1	2	3	4

B. Identifying Goals

Teacher does not identify goals	Teacher unilaterally identifies goals	Teacher and family create common goals	Teacher and family create common goals and a plan for achieving them
1	2	3	4

XVI. Use of Appropriate Content

A. Knowledge of Evidence of Developmentally Appropriate Practice

Teacher shows no evidence of knowledge of DAP	Teacher shows little evidence of knowledge of DAP	Teacher shows some evidence of knowledge of DAP	Teacher shows consistent evidence of knowledge of DAP
1	2	3	4

B. Use of Bias

Teacher consistently expresses bias	Teacher expresses some bias	Teacher does not express bias	Teacher consistently expresses respect
1	2	3	4

XVII. One-Way Communication

A. Newsletters, E-mail, Phone Calls

Teacher does not use any one-way communication	Teacher rarely uses one-way communication	Teacher frequently uses one-way communication	Teacher consistently uses forms of one-way communication in effective ways
1	2	3	4

XVIII. Two-Way Communication

A. Face-to-Face Communication

Teacher avoids face-to-face communication	Teacher rarely engages in face-to-face communication with families	Teacher sometimes engages in face-to-face communication	Teacher consistently invites families to engage in forms of two-way communication
1	2	3	4

XIX. Resources

A. Appropriate Resources

Teacher does not provide family members with resources or suggests inappropriate resources	Teacher rarely provides or suggests resources	Teacher sometimes provides or suggests resources	Teacher consistently provides and suggests appropriate resources for families
1	2	3	4

Continues

| Figure 8–9 | Self-Assessment of a Parent/Family Conference (Continued) |

XX. Closure

A. Summary

Teacher does not summarize meeting	Teacher summarizes only part of meeting	Teacher summarizes meeting	Teacher and family member together provide summary of meeting
1	2	3	4

B. Plan for Future Contact

Teacher does not plan future contact	Teacher mentions need for future contact, but no plan or action is addressed	Teacher suggests definite plan for the future	Teacher and family member agree on a future date and agenda for next conference
1	2	3	4

© Cengage Learning

Phone Calls Telephone calls are a convenient and sometimes necessary way to remain in contact with parents. Some teachers call families at a prearranged time each week that is convenient for the family. Other teachers set a weekly time to make short calls as follow-up related to concerns noted earlier in the week. As always when communicating with parents, be sure to share positive comments during calls with families as well as using calls to quickly check on any concerns you might have. When planning to call families, however, keep in mind that some families are not accessible by phone, and that there are situations for which phoning is not a reasonable communication alternative, such as when the teacher and family speak different languages or when too many distractions are in the environment. Some suggestions and guidelines for contacting families by phone follow. Before phoning a family:

- Determine whether it is agreeable to call a work number for a conference. Always provide an alternative time choice for parents who do not have flexibility for a phone call at their place of employment.
- Consider advance scheduling for a phone conference.
- Send information home ahead of time so that parents can prepare for the conference.

During the call:

- Maintain confidentiality when making the phone call and after the phone call is completed (central offices or teacher work areas are not the best place for privacy).

- Be polite and calm.
- Try to maintain the time limit agreed on in advance.
- Conclude the call with a follow-up plan.

After the call:

- Make notes about the call.
- Send a follow-up note to families. Include a positive, optimistic, or encouraging statement, such as "I'm glad that we're able to work on this together."

Journaling Maintaining a journal that is sent back and forth between parents and teachers is an increasingly popular method of communication (Figure 8–10). Journaling with a parent is an excellent communication mechanism under the following conditions:

- Both the teacher and the family agree to and are committed to this type of communication
- Confidentiality is maintained
- The families are literate and comfortable writing their comments
- Frequency of writing has been established and agreed upon by both parties; frequency should be assessed occasionally during the school term and modified as deemed necessary
- A reliable courier process has been established, such as use of children's backpacks or wire notebooks, and routine days have been planned for sending and returning journals

Figure 8–10	Excerpts from a Journaling Experience.

A Concern about Four-Year-Old Nicole's Withdrawn and Passive Approach to Activities at Preschool.

Journal for: Nicole Williams

From Teacher(s)

10/2 Nicole joined in play with other children a little more quickly than usual today. After scanning the room briefly, she walked to the art center and joined two others in their work on a mural for our farm theme.

10/4 I didn't realize Nicole had so much farm experience. She has been more enthusiastic than ever with this topic. What other interests or experiences has Nicole had that we might use to build on this positive experience?

From Parent(s)

10/2 I'm glad to hear about Nicole's artwork with the others. She actually seemed excited about the farm mural. Her grandparents live on a farm, and she has always enjoyed the animals and the machinery.

10/5 She likes babies; a new cousin visits us often. She also likes to watch the construction crew working at the end of our street. This summer, she started to be interested in various insects. Thanks for using information from us to help Nicole at school.

Electronic Mail As computer networking becomes accessible to more people in our society, e-mail may become a very useful tool for maintaining communication with families of children in early childhood programs. A few guidelines and concerns about this type of communication are listed here.

- Be aware that e-mail communication may not be private. Avoid sharing highly sensitive information by this method.

- Employers may not want family members to receive personal e-mail at work. Be sure to check with parents about this before sending e-mail to their workplace.

- Many families still do not have access to e-mail. This communication method should not be used in a way that would exclude families without access.

Social Media Varying perspectives on the usefulness or problematic nature of social media websites currently exist in the field of early childhood education. Some institutions place firm restrictions about not using social media with families and others count on professional educators to make ethical decisions

about how they incorporate such technology into their practice. As the novelty wears off and both educators and families increase their comfort with ways to effectively use social media, a movement can be observed within education that is supportive of such sites that may help to increase effective communication.

> **Do This**
>
> Conduct a web search about the use of social media for family involvement in education. Share your findings with classmates. Analyze and summarize the benefits and concerns about the use of social media for family involvement.

Home Visits Early childhood programs with very strong family involvement components often include home visiting as one aspect of their efforts to create strong partnerships between families and teachers. For example, the Head Start performance standards require that teachers make at least two visits to homes of all enrolled children, unless the parents decline the visits. Reasons given for requiring home visits are:

- Making connections between the home and program settings

- Learning more about parent-child interactions

- Developing positive relationships, which allow parents and staff to get to know one another

- Identifying learning opportunities in home environments

- Identifying techniques that can be generalized to other children in the family

- Focusing individualized attention on family strengths, interests, and goals (Head Start Program Performance Standards and Other Regulations, 1993)

Head Start regulations offer alternatives to families who prefer not to have a home visit. Visits may take place at the Head Start site or another place that is deemed to be both safe and private. When safety concerns arise for staff members who are required to make home visits, Head Start regulations provide some precautions. Staff members who make home visits are highly trained, well-supervised, and have access to support services such as monitoring systems or having another staff member make the home visit with the teacher.

These guidelines are useful for other early childhood programs implementing a home visit component. It is important that early childhood professionals be polite and respectful when arranging for and during the visit. Selecting a mutually acceptable time for the appointment and arriving on time are important factors. It is often helpful to define the visit's ending time when making the appointment. During the visit, teachers must use effective interpersonal skills and keep in mind that their role changes when in the context of interactions in a family's home. In home settings, the teacher is the guest and must take the lead from the family. Typically, teachers are in the comfort of their own classroom when they meet with family members. Thus, during home visits, the balance of power is shifted somewhat. While it is true that home visits take a huge time and energy commitment from early childhood teachers, such visits often make the family feel valued and cared about, thus generating an increased level of partnership between families and schools.

Meyer and Mann (2006) examined kindergarten through second grade teacher perceptions about home visits that they made early in the school year and again near the end of the year. Teachers reported multiple benefits, including stronger partnerships with families, better relationships with children and families, improved communication with parents, better understanding of children, and better understanding of impact of home environments on children's learning and behavior.

Effective Interpersonal Communication

When any two people attempt to communicate, they may misunderstand one another: Clarity may be lacking. Emotions may be heated. Vocabulary may differ. Effective strategies for clear communication can be learned, and practicing these strategies leads to a more natural approach for both speaker and listener.

naeyc 2 As you contemplate the following approaches to communication, be cognizant that "cultural learning needs to extend to our daily interactions and the way we see each other as learners" (Swick et al. 1995/96, as cited in Swick 2003). Some multicultural learning strategies that are known to be effective include the following (Comer 1997; Powell 1998; Swick 1993, as cited in Swick 2003):

- Early childhood teachers must acquire accurate information about children and families from cultures other than their own.
- Families and teachers/staff can work together to have relevant, constructive exchanges and joint activities to assist in understanding cultural differences.
- Families and teachers/staff can work together to plan interesting, enjoyable classroom activities that relate to authentic cultural learning.

- Partnership events should have multiple emphases, such as food, music, talents, ideas, and concerns shared in warm, sensitive ways.
- Education programs should be planned through partnerships to increase everyone's understanding of various cultures and groups in the community.
- Programs should include representatives of families and communities to ensure that cultural content in the school curriculum is accurate, meaningful, and inclusive.

Active Listening **Active listening** is a process whereby the listener communicates to the speaker that she values what the speaker is saying. An important criterion for active listening is that the listener is not evaluating the content or the speaker but is genuinely open to the speaker's point of view (Gordon 1970). It is important for teachers to listen to parents to understand their perspective and to be aware of the issues they believe are important. Some teachers find that truly listening to others poses a challenge because the role of a teacher is often to give instruction to others without entering into an extensive dialogue. Another challenge for teachers involves hearing parents' concerns—or complaints—without becoming defensive. Parents may be emotionally charged about an issue. When this occurs, try to listen for the emotion and understand that it is coming from real concern about their children.

Active listening is more easily accomplished when teachers believe in partnerships with parents and believe that parents have knowledge about their own family system that can be helpful information to teachers. This ability of a teacher to actively listen to family members is an extremely important application of the bioecological model of human development.

Following are some behaviors associated with active listening (Hanna 1991):

- Attentive body position
  - Comfortable distance between the communicators
  - Being on the same level, such as both sitting or both standing
  - Facing the other person as each of you speaks
  - Relaxed body posture, slightly leaning toward the other
  - Hands at sides or in lap
- Eye contact
  - Maintain eye contact by looking at other's face
  - Eye contact is recommended for 50 percent to 75 percent of time in interaction

- Facial expression
  — Facial reaction to what is being said include a smile, frown, or look of surprise at appropriate times
  — Change of expression with content of conversation
- Head and body movements
  — Nodding the head for feedback to speaker
  — Other body movements used as feedback to speaker
- Touching
  — Arm is a neutral area generally okay to touch
  — Consider appropriateness of touch
- Verbal responses
  — Short comments such as "oh" or "I see" offer encouragement
  — Open-ended questions to support the speaker
  — Paraphrasing to be sure you understand the point the speaker is making
  — Expressing your interpretation of the speaker's feelings

These active listening behaviors should be modified to meet the needs of different families and settings. naeyc 2

As teachers attempt to incorporate these skills into their communication with families and other community members, they soon understand why Hanna states that "good listening is not for the lazy." Helping professionals in many fields find it helpful to practice behaviors related to listening.

Do This

Working with a partner, practice the listening skills listed previously. After you have practiced for about 10 minutes, evaluate yourself on each of the skills. Which skills have you already mastered? With which listening behaviors will you need more practice?

Often, early childhood teachers have limited amounts of time for conferencing and other **interpersonal communication** with parents or other family members. Due to these time constraints, teachers may be tempted to bypass the importance of listening to parents and move too quickly to offer solutions or tell parents that their concerns are unfounded. In these situations, it is often true that actively listening to parents' comments may be more satisfying to the parent and thus may provide for ongoing positive communication and more efficient problem solving.

An example of this was shared by a child care center director. Parents of a three-year-old who was slightly

Figure 8–11 Examples of Active Listening in Conversation.

Parent: Emily's mother and I have separated. Emily and her brother are living with me. I just wanted you to know so that if something unusual happens at school, you may be better able to help Emily. She is sometimes very sad at home.

Teacher: You're concerned about how your separation is affecting Emily.

Parent: Yes. We hear so much about the effects of divorce on young children. She has been such a joyful child, and now it's hard to see her be so sad.

Teacher: I know that this has been a difficult time for both you and Emily.

Parent: Thank you for understanding my concerns.

Teacher: Let's stay in close communication about Emily during this difficult time. You can call me at school or at my home phone.

© Cengage Learning

injured on a balance beam requested a conference with the director. The classroom teacher had already notified the director that these parents were upset and wanted to have that piece of equipment removed from the classroom. Because this was the only recorded accident with the balance beam in more than 10 years of that teacher's career, the teacher believed strongly that it should not be removed. The director met with the parents, listened to their concerns, and said he was sorry that their son was hurt. After having a chance to be heard and to realize that school personnel were concerned about their child's injury, the parents withdrew their request to have the balance beam taken from the classroom. Further, they increased their involvement with the center's parent organization and advocated for the center with prospective parents (Figure 8–11).

naeyc 5 *Reflecting* Reflecting families' concerns, issues, feelings, suggestions, and complaints allows the teacher to repeat what she has heard. This method gives parents an opportunity to correct or modify the teacher's understanding of the conversation. Reflecting also gives the teacher an opportunity to fully comprehend the meaning of the message being communicated by the parent. Frequently, reflection becomes an excellent problem-solving tool because it increases clarity in interpersonal communication (Figure 8–11).

I-Messages and We-Messages Using I-messages permits teachers to speak from their own perspectives without offending parents. An I-message clearly places the responsibility and the viewpoint of the message on the speaker. Thus, it does not communicate guilt or accusation, as do statements that begin with "You should…" Many professionals find that although

I-messages are effective in practice, they have not learned to speak that way in their interpersonal conversations. Some find that it feels unnatural. Because this strategy is so effective, however, especially when speakers are in the heat of emotion, it is advantageous for early childhood teachers, whether in training or in service, to practice or role-play using I-messages. Gordon (1970) describes three components of an I-message:

1. State concern about other's behavior from your perspective.
2. Pin down the concrete effect the behavior has on the teacher.
3. State feelings teacher has as a result of the effect.

I-messages are effective, not only in working with families but also in all interpersonal contexts, including work with children (Figure 8–12).

I-messages are useful because they reduce threat from a powerful figure, but there are times when *we-messages* are more effective than I-messages. We-messages identify a problem in a group or in a relationship rather than focus on one individual's problem and another individual's behavior. Examples of we-statements include "We don't have enough affection" or "We ought to have more flexibility" (Burr 1990).

We-messages are used to emphasize the closeness in relationships; thus, such communication should not be used for casual relationships between educators and family members (Burr 1990). In early childhood education, however, some caregiver and family member relationships span several years with a great deal of close contact occurring. Often, the topics discussed in these relationships are personal: children's difficulties, parents' feelings, or a variety of family transitions. In such cases, when teachers want to emphasize the teacher-family partnership in working for children, using we-messages may be helpful.

There may be times when it makes sense to combine we-messages with I-messages. This is especially true when the speaker wishes to emphasize the sense of connectedness between the parties, but also wants to add an element of uncertainty to the comment in

an effort to establish more open communication. An early childhood teacher who has had an ongoing relationship with Calvin's parents stated, "I don't think we want Calvin to forget his work anymore." The parents readily agreed, and together they—teacher, parents, and Calvin—set out to solve the problem.

Here is an example of building communication between teachers and families:

66 My first experience with realizing the importance of communication between myself and my teacher was when my daughter was in first grade. We were fortunate to be placed in the classroom of Mr. M. months after moving to one state from another. Mr. M. had a total open door policy and stressed the fact that his policy meant we were welcome any time and without notice.

Mr. M. had a monthly "Family Night" where the students invited the entire family, even grandparents, to come into the classroom and share their daily activities. Several times during the year he also had "Game Board Night" where the family brought and shared playing games with the class. Not only did "Family Night" and "Game Board Night" help my husband and me support and encourage our daughter's education, but also prepared her younger brother for what it would be like when he started school. He did not have any of the typical first day jitters because he was so familiar with the school.

The class also witnessed the importance of socialization skills between families and friends. Throughout the year, we had parties and activities out of the school setting as well. We actually made some of our closest friends during this period of our lives and they are still involved in our lives today, five years later. 99

—L. B., mother of two

Figure 8–12   Teacher Phrases That Help in Reflective Dialogue.

"Let me restate what I heard you say."

"To help me remember clearly, may I rephrase your concerns?"

"To help me work on these problems, may I write out some of your complaints?"

"Thank you for sharing your suggestions. I will summarize them to our director. This is the list I have made."

Figure 8–13   Examples of Effective I-Messages.

Situation—Parent stops teacher in hallway to discuss a concern about his child's progress.

Teacher—"I must be in the classroom now. I'll be glad to phone you after school to arrange for a time for us to talk. Where should I call you?"

Situation—Parents walk into director's office and begin to yell.

Director—"I can tell you're upset about something. Let me get some information from you so that I can figure out what I can do to help."

Situation—Grandmother complains to teacher about her daughter's lack of attention to her child.

Teacher—"I'm sorry you feel so bad about this. I believe that if someone were to read to Jess every day, it would help her a great deal. Is there any chance we could work on this together?"

Here is an example of ineffective communication between a teacher and a parent:

66 *When my son was in kindergarten, I was not prepared for what was to come. We had had a wonderful experience with our daughter from kindergarten all the way to the third grade, and did not realize how a bad situation could avalanche.*

Our son was very prepared and excited to start school, and up to this point we had felt he was very bright. After only two weeks of school, the teacher escorted my son out of the school at the end of the day to have a discussion with his mom about his behavior. This discussion took place in front of all the students and parents that were walking out of the building at the end of the day. Needless to say, my son was devastated, and I was shocked and appalled. I suggested that we go somewhere and discuss this in private, but the teacher did not have time for that so the conversation continued on the front lawn about how my son yells out answers to questions without raising his hand, can't stay in his seat, and wastes time doodling after assignments are done. I listened to what she had to say but did not make many comments because I felt I needed time to process the information.

After discussing the situation with my husband, I decided to ask her to cooperate with me and keep a behavior journal that I would read each day and, surprisingly, she agreed to do so. My son gave the journal to his teacher for two or three weeks, and she never made an entry so we assumed things were okay until conference time when we heard the same complaints as before. When asked about the journal, she simply said she did not think it would help. Needless to say, this was a long battle that totally turned my son against school and reading.

My son is now in the first grade with a wonderful teacher and is eager to learn. On the first day of school, we were getting dressed and he said, "Mommy, do you remember last year when I kept saying I was dumb and you said I was smart?" I said "Yes" and he said, "Well, I finally figured out what happened. I got yelled at so much last year until my brain just shut down."

As the saying goes, out of the mouths of babes! **naeyc** 5 99

> ### Do This
>
> Consider the differences between the two examples of teacher communication. Give some examples from each of the two situations that relate to how individuals have been empowered or degraded. How do these methods of communication affect the development of partnerships? Examine Swick's four communication behaviors for trust-building (in the following), and explain how they are present in or absent from these examples.

---

naeyc 2 If we are to develop authentic, essential partnerships with families, we must cultivate trust with them. Swick (1993, as cited in Swick 2003) notes that there are four communication behaviors that are most likely to build trust among families, schools, and communities for strong partnerships:

Approachability—Making others feel comfortable and secure

Sensitivity—Understanding others in supportive ways

Flexibility—Adapting to the needs or concerns of others

Dependability—Counting on one another to provide continuity

When early childhood teachers implement these four communication behaviors, they will provide strong leadership for creating necessary partnerships.

Nonverbal Communication   As we have seen, the use of language is critical to effective interpersonal communication. It also is important, however, to examine nonverbal communication practices. Following are some behaviors that are components of nonverbal communication:

- Personal space
- Gestures and posture
- Touching
- Facial expression
- Eye contact
- Vocal cues (Knapp and Hall 1992)

The concept of *personal space* includes physical distance between people who are engaged in conversation. Clearly, individual differences in personality lead to differences in comfort level of personal space. Cultural backgrounds and the nature of the relationship of those in conversation (Knapp and Hall 1992) also are factors related to preferences in personal space. Early childhood teachers who are observant and sensitive to family member's preferences for physical space will be able to demonstrate respect in their interactions.

"Gestures are movements of the body...used to communicate an idea, intention or feeling" (Knapp and Hall 1992). Consider the many gestures that are used to communicate nonverbally throughout the course of a day. How do you gesture for "hello" and "good-bye?" When giving someone directions, gesturing is often as helpful as the words you use. How do teachers use gestures meaningfully in the classroom? Touching when communicating can have many meanings. Knapp and Hall (1992) list the following ways in which touch is used:

- Positive affect
- Negative affect

- Play
- Influence
- Interaction management
- Interpersonal responsiveness
- Accidental
- Task-related
- Healing **naeyc** 2

Reflect on This

Observe at least two people who are conversing. Note the kinds of nonverbal communication strategies that they use. How did nonverbal communication contribute to the meaning and understanding among those you observed? Did you observe individual differences? How might you increase your sensitivity to nonverbal modes of communication in your work with young children and their families?

Individual differences have been observed in both gesturing and touch. Culture and gender play a role in these differences.

Facial expressions can communicate a lot of information or just a little. Because of individual differences and the complexity involved in the interpretation of facial expressions, sensitivity is needed when interacting with others. Some people are very expressive, while others demonstrate little affect. There are times when facial expression alone does not reveal an individual's honest feelings. For example, nervousness can lead one to smile or even giggle at an inappropriate time. Variations are also observable in the nature and amount of eye contact. How do you use eye contact? What is your belief system about those who look others "right in the eye?"

Vocal cues such as hesitating and pausing may be used to emphasize a point or to demonstrate reflective listening. Practices such as saying one word more loudly or softly than others in the sentence and consistent or inconsistent rhythm in a person's speech contribute to the meaning of communication (Knapp and Hall 1992).

66 *[O]ur actions speak louder than our words. Bronfenbrenner (1979) notes that children watch closely what we do with each other more than they listen to what we say to each other. Clearly, our modeling of behavior is more important than almost anything else we do. Yet, the nonverbal aspect of communication has been largely neglected in the education of human service professionals.* 99

—Swick, 2003

Guidelines for Giving and Receiving Criticism

Teachers often find it difficult to deliver criticism to family members—at least, they often find it difficult to do so in an acceptable manner. Is it possible to give negative information in a positive manner? Yes, but the challenge is to do so clearly and honestly. It is often helpful to rehearse what you want to share and how you want to say it, as well as to choose a suitable time and place for the communication. The use of I-messages is recommended. Be sure that you criticize the specific behavior or situation, not the whole person. As stated previously, offering a compliment before giving a criticism may make the situation less uncomfortable for the parent or other person with whom you are talking (Hanna 1991). In other words, attempt to make the criticism as constructive as possible. This permits the other person to work toward a solution.

Consider the following examples of criticism. Using the preceding guidelines, note what is constructive and what may be destructive about each example. How would you change each one to make it more constructive?

1. During a scheduled conference with parents of a kindergartner, the teacher says, "I have some concern about the way you discipline Kate. She says that you hit her when she misbehaves. You should know better than that!"

2. In a note to the family of a preschooler, the teacher writes: "Nicole has been dropped off at school at 7:30 this week. School begins at 8:00. You may not bring her to school before 7:45. Thank you, Ms. Farver."

3. In a newsletter, a first-grade teacher includes the following in her letter to families: "Some parents have questioned our rule about not bringing special playthings from home. After some discussion, the school staff has decided to keep this rule. Please do not permit your child to bring toys to school."

naeyc 6 Teachers must be prepared to receive criticism as well as to deliver it. Teachers may be prepared to hear criticism in some instances, while at other times the criticism may take them by surprise. To maintain positive communication with families, it is helpful for early childhood professionals to have skills in accepting and responding to criticism. If you agree with the criticism, admit your mistake—although this is not easy or comfortable, it is the responsible action and enables continued open communication with families. Let the person who voiced the criticism know that you agree with her and briefly state the reason for your behavior. Finally, indicate to her what you will do to change the situation or your behavior to prevent similar occurrences in the future (Hanna 1991). Using these guidelines, write appropriate responses to the following criticisms from family members (assuming you agree with them).

1. "I thought you only served healthy snacks at this child care center. Jason told me that he had a chocolate cupcake for afternoon snack yesterday."

2. "I got a notice about the parent meeting tonight just two days ago. That's not enough time for me to make all the arrangements that are necessary to come to the meeting."

It may be even more difficult to respond to criticism with which you do not agree because there is greater likelihood of negative emotions arising. You may feel that a criticism is inaccurate or unfair. These feelings often lead to an emotional or out-of-control response. Taking a deep breath or silently counting to three is useful for some people when they are aware of such emotion. Responding in a calm manner gives a better chance of allowing communication to continue. When you disagree with a criticism, use a comment such as "I guess I see this differently from you" or "I have another point of view about what may be the wisest course of action." Give some reasons for your perspective and suggest the possibility of another discussion in the future. naeyc 6

Assertiveness versus Aggression

In efforts to be polite and professional, early childhood teachers often overlook the importance of assertiveness in interpersonal communication. Assertiveness does not rule out flexibility or partnerships; instead, it allows teachers to have a voice about their preferences and feelings. Assertiveness is not the same as aggressiveness. A primary difference is that assertiveness enhances interpersonal communication, and aggressiveness discourages or inhibits communication. Assertiveness is self-focused, not other-focused (Lerner 1989). Thus, an assertive response typically uses an I-message and does not blame or attack others. Blaming and attacking often are aggressive and counterproductive in forming partnerships. For example, "I have some concerns I would like to discuss with you about Kelly being sleepy at school" is more effective than "You need to make sure that Kelly gets enough sleep every night."

Boutte, Keepler, Tyler, and Terry (1992) discuss techniques for involving difficult parents (see Figure 8–14).

CONFLICT RESOLUTION

naeyc 2 When authentic relationships are developed with families, it is inevitable that some conflict will occur. Avoiding conflict is not the best solution to dealing with it. Instead, efforts at resolving conflict peacefully and effectively must be learned and implemented. One difficulty is that people bring their existing ideas and feelings about conflict with them: some people believe it is impolite to share a difference of opinion, while others are shy, and still others may present a different point of view in a hostile, rather than an effective, manner.

Essentially, **conflict resolution** often takes the form of problem solving. Problem solving typically is a process that contains several steps, which are outlined in the following. Problems with, between, and about families are common in the life of a teacher. The following strategies are designed to reduce conflict and increase the chances for healthy resolution of a problem.

1. Clearly define the problem at hand. If there is more than one problem, define each one.

2. Let all participants share their viewpoints.

3. As the teacher, reflect each participant's concern.

4. Review any relevant school policy or procedure.

5. Assure the parents that they have been heard and that their issue will be addressed in one of the following ways:

   a. Changes will be made (specify the changes)
   b. Additional participants will be invited into the discussion, such as the principal, the director, a counselor, or a social worker
   c. Another child or family will be contacted, if necessary, to resolve the problem

Many early childhood programs find it useful to specify guidelines for conflict resolution.

Including these procedures in a parent handbook or newsletter indicates to families that their opinions and views are respected and taken seriously. Such guidelines include the following:

1. First, take your concern to the person directly involved.

2. If the conflict cannot be resolved between the two parties, the guidelines specify who is the next person to be contacted. Typically, this is someone in an administrative or supervisory role.

3. The third person acts as mediator, listening to both perspectives and suggesting a resolution.

4. Some programs will have a process that continues with an appeal or taking the situation to an executive director or board. naeyc 2

Some Ineffective and Inappropriate Practices to Avoid in Interpersonal Communication

In addition to understanding the skills related to effective communication, it is also important to acknowledge that certain behaviors are often detrimental to building

Adapted from: Boutte, G. S., Keepler, D. L., Tyler, V. S., & Terry, B. Z. (1992). Effective techniques for involving "difficult" parents. *Young Children* 47(3), 19–22

Figure 8–14	Selected Techniques for Involving Difficult Parents.			
	The parent who exhibits antagonistic behavior	**The parent who frequently complains or is negative**	**The parent who exhibits shy/ unresponsive behavior**	**The parent who is illiterate or is not skilled in Reading or speaking English**
Encourage attendance at all parent—teacher conferences	X	X	X	X
State and restate purpose(s) of the conference	X	X		
Show or tell concrete and specific examples of child's work or behavior	X	X	X	
Do not argue with a parent or become defensive	X	X		
Seek the assistance of other staff when needed	X			X
Elicit parents' ideas and incorporate them into a plan		X		
Frequently state positive strategies or work accomplished		X	X	
Ask open-ended questions and allow for plenty of discussion time	X			X

relationships. Teachers are advised to consciously avoid the following practices:

1. Becoming defensive, argumentative, or combative closes communication.
2. Accusing the child or family is not productive.
3. Name-calling is never appropriate.
4. Gossiping about families is unprofessional.
5. Belittling or berating a child because of a conflict with his family is unethical.
6. Reacting so emotionally or irrationally that there is no opportunity for reconciliation is detrimental to all concerned.

Helpful Attitudes for Effective Interpersonal Communication

naeyc 6 Behaviors and practices are not the only things that affect positive communication. Attitudes are also important. For some teachers, the following

attitudes may be more natural, and some teachers may find that they need to work to develop these perspectives. Such work, though, will be well worth it when good communication with family members is achieved. Hanna (1991) lists the following attitudes as helpful:

- Valuing mutual respect
- Honesty
- Open to lifelong learning and growing
- Willing to share experiences and ideas
- Able to express feelings in appropriate ways
- Knowing appropriate content for discussing in professional contexts
- Flexibility
- A sense of humor
- Ability to think critically and to problem-solve

Discuss the preceding list of attitudes with a partner. Think of a real-life example for each attitude. Think

- Search for ways to make communication effective rather than blaming others as sources of communication breakdowns.

- Listen actively, respect others, and suspend judgment.

- Cultural norms may not apply to the behavior of any particular individual.

- Be aware of imbalances of power or perceived power.

- Be open for discussions of the past, honestly acknowledge each one's history.

Staff-Staff Communication

This chapter focuses on family-staff communication since the goals of this textbook focus on family involvement in early childhood education. However, it is important to point out that effective communication strategies that are applied to building relationships with families can and should also be applied to relationships with colleagues or co-workers. Effective communication and positive relationships in the workplace may serve as a model for families who spend time in early education settings, much as our caring, supportive interactions with children do.

Many topics in this chapter may be applied to staff-staff communication and relationship-building.

It is important for early childhood education teachers to develop mutually respectful working relationships with families.

of one or two additional attributes to add to this list of helpful attitudes for effective communication.

Examples of successful programs in building family-staff relationships can be found on the Northwest Regional Educational Laboratory web site, www.nwrel.org. Other ideas for supporting parents, including information about the No Child Left Behind Act (NCLB) and the Individuals with Disabilities Education Act (IDEA), can be found at the National Coalition for Parent Involvement in Education web site, http://www.ncpie.org. These sites can help teachers and parents find ideas for building family-school partnerships. **naeyc** 6

DIVERSITY IN PRACTICE When considering variations in communication based on culture, DuPraw and Axner (1997) recommend application of these guidelines:

- Consider and learn about cultures from generalizations, but not to the point of stereotyping or oversimplifying peoples.

- Understand that there are multiple effective (right) ways to communicate and practice variations appropriately.

Reflecting on communication practices helps improve methods and strategies for family support.

Information that is particularly useful include cultural variations, conflict resolution, interpersonal communication, and guidelines for giving and receiving criticism.

Summary and Conclusions

While most teachers receive some preparation in classroom management of children, very few receive extensive instruction in communicating effectively with parents and other family members, especially in conflict situations. Conflicts or confrontations with parents are very difficult and may not be resolved easily or quickly. They often require great amounts of time, effort, energy, and knowledge. The importance of building and maintaining relationships with families cannot be overstated. Relationships built on trust and understanding go a long way in helping both parties in their efforts to resolve conflict.

   Understanding the family is a great action plan for teachers to use if a conflict arises. Having an established, mutually respectful working relationship with families prior to a conflict can be very helpful in proceeding to a resolution. Professional ethics and professional practice give school personnel the guidance to sustain their compassion and conduct as they work with families in sensitive and difficult situations as well as in routine interactions.

Theory into Practice
Suggestions (TIPS)

- Review and reflect on all of the web sites and organizations that can provide information about communication and building relationships. Add those sites to your bookmarks so you can access them quickly when you have questions about development.
- Apply an understanding of cultural variations in various aspects of communication.
- Professionals' use of effective communication provides a model for strategies that might be incorporated by families.
- Overcome negative perceptions of families by replacing such views with positive aspects and strengths of each family.
- Practice active listening and clear communication at all times.
- Be aware that two-way communication is often preferred over one-way strategies.
- Know that conflicts will occur. They are best handled through effective communication and steps for resolution.
- Avoidance of conflict also avoids authentic communication, thus inhibiting the development of relationships.

- Work on your own mental health in order to be an effective communicator with others.
- Be prepared for emotional responses from families who are concerned about their children. Effective communication on your part can help to diffuse emotion, resolve issues, and build relationships.
- Be consciously aware of your nonverbal communication strengths as well as habits that may be distracting.
- Proofread all written communication for correct spelling and grammar.
- Create effective newsletters.
- Work on positive attitudes for skillful interpersonal communication.
- Be aware of your tendencies to apply strategies that derail communication.
- Base your communication with families and community members on current research, theory, and best practice.
- Avoid using personal biases in communication with families.
- Express sensitivity to differences in family values, expectations, and behaviors.
- Expect criticism. When it is shared in ways that are not constructive, ask for clarification.
- Practice constructive criticism.
- Practice the compliment-sandwich approach.

Applications

1. Plan a conference with parents about each of the following situations.
   a. A two-year-old has been biting other children. You meet with the parents of the child who is biting.
   b. A preschooler has become increasingly aggressive during outdoor time.
   c. A second-grader is not making expected progress in reading.
2. At the end of the school day, family members come to you with the following situations. What do you say or do?
   a. A father of a kindergarten child is angry and shouts at you that his daughter was not permitted to check out a library book yesterday at the regularly scheduled library time.
   b. The grandmother of a two-year-old tells you that her grandson has been bitten two days in a row and that she expects you to "throw the biter out of the program."
   c. A mother is late picking up her infant for the third day in a row. She is nearly in tears, saying

that she is not able to leave work on time to pick up her baby by closing.

3. Create a newsletter article that explains to families the importance of each of the following early childhood education practices:

   a. Free play

   b. Developmentally appropriate practice

   c. Authentic assessment

   d. Family involvement

   e. Celebrating diversity

2. Create several newsletter articles about strategies for effective communication using ideas from this chapter.

Questions for Reflection and Discussion

1. List situations that might occur in the early childhood classroom for which two-way communication strategies between home and school would be preferred over one-way communication strategies.

2. Getting some parents to come to regularly scheduled conferences can be difficult. What are some strategies you could try for getting such hard-to-reach parents to have a conference with you about their child's progress?

3. What is your typical response to a situation with conflict? Do you avoid it, respond emotionally, or use effective strategies for resolving conflict? Which strategies will you work on for future use in the early childhood profession?

Field Assignments

1. Interview several parents who have their children enrolled in early childhood programs. Ask them about the kinds of communication they have with their child's teachers or the program's administrator. Ask whether they are satisfied or whether they would prefer more communication. If they would prefer more communication, ask about kinds of communication they would like.

2. Contact a number of early childhood education teachers. Inquire whether they have produced parent newsletters. If so, request copies of the newsletters to place in your file.

3. Contact an administrator of an early childhood program. Ask whether there are policies regarding conflict resolution between home and school. If so, are the policies printed in a parent handbook?

If possible, get a copy of the policy.

Additional resources for this chapter, including Teach-Source videos, can be found on the Education Course-Mate. Go to CengageBrain.com.

References

Boutte, G. S., D. L. Keepler, V. S. Tyler, and B. Z. Terry. 1992. Effective techniques for involving "difficult" parents. *Young Children* 47: 19–22.

Burr, W. R. 1990. Beyond I-statements in family communication. *Family Relations* 39: 266–72.

Diffily, D., and K. Morrison, ed.1996. *Family-friendly communication for early childhood programs*. Washington, DC: National Association for the Education of Young Children.

DuPraw, M.E., and Axner, M. 1997. Working on common cross-cultural communication Challenges. Toward a More Perfect Union in an Age of Diversity. WTTF public broadcasting station. www.pbs.org/ampu/crosscult.html. Accessed March 13, 2012.

Gordon, T. 1970. *P.E.T.: Parent effectiveness training*. New York: Peter H. Wyden.

Hanna, S. L. 1991. *Person to person: Positive relationships don't just happen*. Englewood Cliffs, NJ: Prentice Hall.

Head Start program performance standards and other regulations. 1993. Washington, DC: U.S. Department of Health and Human Services.

Hohmann, M., B. Banet, and D. P.Weikart. 1979. *Young children in action*, 328–29. Ypsilanti, MI: High/Scope Press.

Kagan, S. L., and N. E. Cohen. 1997. Not by chance: *Creating an early care and education system for children*. New Haven, CT: The Quality 2000 Initiative.

Knapp, M. L., and J. A. Hall.1992. *Nonverbal communication in human interaction*. New York: Holt Rinehart and Winston.

Krech, B. 1995. Improve parent communication with a newsletter. *Instructor* 105: 67–73.

Lerner, H. G. 1989. *The dance of intimacy: A woman's guide to courageous acts of change in key relationships*. New York: Harper & Row.

Meyer, J. A., and M. B. Mann. 2006. Teachers' perceptions of the benefits of home visits for early elementary children. *Early Childhood Education Journal* 34: 93–97.

Swick, K. 1991. *Teacher-parent partnerships to enhance school success in early childhood education*. Washington, DC: National Education Association.

Swick, K. J. 2003. Communication concepts for strengthening family-school-community partnerships. *Early Childhood Education Journal* 30: 275–80.

Walker, T. 2005. *The director's link*. Chicago, IL: McCormick Tribune Center for Early Childhood Leadership at National Louis University.

Young, D., and L. M. Behounek. 2006. Kindergarteners use Power Point to lead their own parent-teacher conferences. *Young Children* 61: 24–26.

CHAPTER 9

Supporting Young Children's Learning at Home

OUTLINE

- Objectives Aligned with NAEYC Standards
- Key Terms
- Theoretical Foundations
- Overview
- Families and Literacy
- Families and Science
- Families and Mathematics
- Families and Social Studies
- Families and Health, Safety, Exercise, and Nutrition

- Families and the Arts
- Social and Emotional Foundations of Children's Learning
- Summary and Conclusions
- Theory into Practice Suggestions (TIPS)
- Applications
- Questions for Reflection and Discussion
- Field Assignments
- References

OBJECTIVES
ALIGNED
WITH NAEYC
STANDARDS

After reading and reflecting on this chapter, you should be able to:

- Understand how the subject areas of literacy, math, science, and social studies can be supported by families at home **naeyc** 2, 5

- Understand how teachers form partnerships with families and encourage them to support children's learning at home **naeyc** 2, 4, 5

- Use the resources available in each subject area **naeyc** 4, 5

- Create programs that support families' involvement in each subject area **naeyc** 2, 5

- Apply an understanding of the social and emotional foundations of early learning **naeyc** 1, 2

Key Terms

anti-bias
emotional intelligence

literacy
professional associations

tolerance

THEORETICAL FOUNDATIONS

naeyc 1 Bioecological theory points to specific effects on development that emanate from interactions between and among various microsystems. Bronfenbrenner emphasized this phenomenon with the concept of the mesosystem. Not only will home and school environments independently impact children's development, but the interactions or relationships of these environments with one another create additional influences (Bronfenbrenner 1979). Thus, it is essential that teachers and other early education staff form partnerships with families and communities to support children's learning in all content areas. **naeyc** 1

One way to implement this concept is to consider Joyce Epstein's notion of not only creating family-friendly

schools, but also creating ways to support school-friendly families. The National Network of Partnership Schools has identified "learning at home" as one of the six keys for family involvement in their children's education (Epstein, Coates, Salinas, Sanders, and Simon 1997). This chapter emphasizes what teachers can do to support the essential role that families have in encouraging their children's curiosity and interest in knowing.

DIVERSITY IN PRACTICE As early childhood educators work with families in regard to young children's learning at home, they will do well do keep in mind the importance of Moll's (Moll, Amanti, Neff, and Gonzalez

2001) perspective on funds of knowledge. Family members may not feel confident that they are able to teach their children. So, educators who make it a point to know more about their students' rich cultural heritages often find a great deal of information about each one's fund of knowledge. From there, support for families in relation to children's learning at home will benefit all children's academic success.

OVERVIEW

naeyc 4, 5 Young children understand the content of literacy, science, mathematics, and social studies differently than older children and adults. Thus, family members may need help in understanding how young children think about the concepts related to these subjects or content areas. Piaget's description of children's preoperational thinking generally applies to two- to seven-year-old children. Piaget's theory indicates that both biological development and interactions with the environment are necessary in order for children to move from one cognitive stage to another. A major premise to understanding this theory is that children construct their own knowledge as they interact with the environment. Some educators refer to this as the importance of "hands on, minds on" experiences.

At this stage of cognitive development, children are capable of making increased use of symbols, including language and pretense. The ability to pretend requires thought so that one object may be substituted for another, such as when a child uses a wooden block as a phone. In addition to the use of symbols, Piaget noted that children begin to realize that events have causes and begin to think in terms of cause and effect. Observation and experiences lead to understanding such as puddles forming after a rain storm and warmer temperatures melting a snow castle.

As children move through the preoperational stage of cognition, they are increasingly able to organize experiences and objects into meaningful categories. Three-year olds might readily sort blocks into "big" and "little" whereas six-year-olds will sort blocks by shape, color, size, and texture. Children at this stage of development also begin to establish a theory of mind as they think about thinking and learning. Throughout the preoperational stage, children grow in their understanding about mental processing. A classic example of placing pencils in a candy container has been used to demonstrate children's surprise at the contents. When three-year-olds are asked what their friends may think the container holds, they respond with "pencils," but most four-year-olds understand that their friends will think as they did and will be surprised when the content is not candy.

Preoperational thinkers have some limitations to their thinking. Among these are centration, irreversibility, egocentrism, and transductive reasoning. Attention to these limitations assist adults in their efforts to support children's learning at home. Centration, or an inability to decenter, is seen as children focus on one eminent characteristic of a situation and ignore other characteristics such as noting that her sister has more crackers than she does because two of the sister's crackers are broken in half. Similarly, irreversibility refers to a child's difficulty in understanding that reverse operations can restore an original situation, such as turning off a DVD in progress and not being aware that turning it on again will restore it to the place where it was stopped.

Egocentrism is sometimes misunderstood to mean that children are selfish. In fact, young children do have difficulty in taking another's perspective from a physical standpoint as well as a social one. For example, a child may place his nametag on upside down since from his perspective, he is able to observe it as the letters were printed. In social situations, children may not be aware that their playmates wish to use the same toy at the same time as they do, leading to conflict. Transductive reasoning is seen as illogical thought, not based on deduction or induction since young children have difficulty understanding which events may cause which outcomes. Preoperational thinkers may believe that a sibling became ill because they would not let them join in their play earlier in the day or that eating pizza will make them Italian.

By the age of eight years, many children enter Piaget's concrete operational stage where their thinking becomes qualitatively different from preoperational learners. Concrete operational thinkers are able to decenter and to apply inductive reasoning based on their observations and analyses. The ability to decenter leads to children's ability to conserve matter and number. When a clay ball is rolled into a long shape, and no clay is added or taken away, children understand that both shapes contain the same amount of clay. And, when 10 pennies are placed close together with another row of ten pennies spaced farther apart, they understand that both rows have the same number of pennies, or that 10 is always 10.

 Piaget: Preoperational Stage

Visit the Education CourseMate website at www.CengageBrain.com to view the Video Case, and then respond to the following items:

- Summarize your understanding of the preoperational stage of thinking.

- How might all early childhood educators help families to understand that young children think differently than older children and adults?

Early childhood educators can help families to understand that differences in children's quality of thought based on their levels of cognitive development means that variations in teaching strategies are necessary. The notion of developmentally appropriate practice is based, in part, on such an understanding.

The **professional associations** in **literacy** (International Reading Association), mathematics (National Council for Teachers of Mathematics), science (National Science Teachers Association), and social studies (National Council for the Social Studies) include in their standards and publications statements about the importance of family involvement in helping children understand content from each subject area. These associations do not suggest that families directly teach these subjects, but rather that family members' actions and activities at home can support and enhance learning at school. "Learning at home" refers specifically to "encouraging, listening, reacting, praising, guiding, monitoring, and discussing, not 'teaching' school subjects" (Epstein 2001). The professional associations suggest that early childhood programs involve parents in such activities as family game nights, various activities in their homes, and strategies with their children throughout the day. Through these activities, families can explore these subjects with their children and expand their children's conceptual understandings without resorting to drilling or content memorization.

Children's approaches to learning is known to be an important factor in their academic success. Hyson notes that this phrase has come to be shorthand to educators when referring to "behaviors, tendencies or typical patterns that children use in learning situations—such as curiosity, persistence, and flexibility in solving problems" (10, 11). Multiple factors influence each child's approach to learning, including the child's own interests and temperament. Since a child's

relationship with her family is known to be a significant contributor, educators should be sure to support strong, positive interactions within families in addition to suggestions for ways to support children's learning in content areas.

In summary, as early childhood educators work with families and their children's learning at home, it is essential to consider these areas of focus:

- Cultural influences of families
- Children's developmental stages
- Appropriate levels of content
- Parent-child relationships
- Reciprocal relationships between families and school personnel **naeyc** 4, 5

naeyc 2 Epstein (2001) discusses relevant findings from recent research, including the following:

- Single parents, parents who work outside the home, parents who live far from school, and fathers are typically less involved *unless* the school organizes activities that meet the specific needs of these groups.
- Nearly all families want their children to succeed, so families appreciate information from schools that supports them in helping their children.
- Nearly all children want their families to be active partners in their school experiences.
- Caring communities can be intentionally built through strong partnerships.
- Effective programs are comprised of different components at different schools. Partnership practices must match the needs, interests, time availability, talents, and developmental levels of children and families in specific schools and communities.

The next sections of this chapter delineate the need for partnerships between schools and families to

Figure 9–1	At Home Learning for Young Children.

At home learning is:
Encouraging children's interests and curiosity
Listening to children's ideas and questions
Reacting to children by asking questions such as "What do you think?" and comments such as "Let's find out" as you seek information together
Praising children's motivation to learn
Guiding children as they make discoveries
Monitoring children to help maintain their focus
Discussing children's understanding

At home learning is not:
Expecting families to teach school subjects
Assigning work sheets
Requiring families to purchase materials for assignments
Teacher-directed activities

Caring communities can be intentionally built.

support children's learning in each of the subject areas. Early childhood teachers play a vital role in supporting families in this work with their children. 𝐧𝐚𝐞𝐲𝐜 2

National Network of Partnership Schools
http://www.csos.jhu.edu
Click "programs;" click "National Network of Partnership Schools"

International Reading Association
http://www.reading.org

National Council of Teachers of Mathematics
http://www.nctm.org

National Council for the Social Studies
http://www.ncss.org

National Science Teachers Association
http://www.nsta.org

FAMILIES AND LITERACY

𝐧𝐚𝐞𝐲𝐜 1 Families influence children's language and literacy learning in a variety of ways, both before the child's enrollment in an early education program and after formal education begins. A basic way that families affect literacy development begins in infancy, when families act, react, and interact with babies in conversation and other language exchanges during feeding, diapering, and play activities. When family members respond to a

baby's needs, actions, and expressions with vocalizations of their own, children are provided with opportunities for hearing a wide variety of sounds. As the child's language develops in later infancy, toddlerhood, and the preschool years, families continue to support literacy through a variety of means, including:

1. Having conversations; that is, give-and-take interactions involving and responding to spoken language
2. Regular reading times (e.g., bedtime stories)
3. The availability of books and writing materials
4. Daily opportunities to use and gain understanding about language and symbols in context (such as stop signs, cereal boxes, closed caption during TV shows)
5. Regular trips to libraries and bookstores
6. Regular opportunities to hear and use positional words, such as on/off, up/down, above/below, near/far, and so forth.

Willam Teale (2000, as cited in King and McMaster 2000) has stated that "Children from low income families may have been read aloud to as little as 25 hours total prior to entering first grade while children from middle income families typically have been read to 1,250 hours." 𝐧𝐚𝐞𝐲𝐜 1 Family literacy has been identified as such an important component of school success that over the last decade the federal government has defined it in various pieces of legislation. Current federal definitions of family literacy include the following aspects.

1. Interactive literacy activities between parents and their children
2. Training for parents that regards them as the primary teachers for their children and full partners in the education of their children
3. Parent literacy training that leads to economic self-sufficiency
4. An age-appropriate education to prepare children for success in school and life experiences (based on the Reading Excellence Act 1998; the Workforce Investment Act; Even Start; Head Start; and the Community Service Block Grant Act)

Families can encourage and support language development through the use of formal and informal word play, including peek-a-boo games and pat-a-cake with very young children, "I Spy" games with preschoolers and kindergarteners, and board games such as *Concentration* and *Monopoly* with elementary aged children. All of these types of play

RESOURCES FOR SUPPORTING LITERACY IN FAMILIES

The following resources are helpful in supporting these three dimensions of home language and literacy activities.

General Resources for Supporting Literacy in Families

Booklets

- *Helping Your Child Become a Reader*
  U.S. Department of Education
  Office of Intergovernmental and Interagency Affairs
  400 Maryland Ave. SW
  Washington, DC 20202
  Available online: http://www2.ed.gov/parents/academic/help/reader/index.html

- *A Child Becomes a Reader (Birth through Preschool): Proven Ideas from Research for Parents* (Spring 2003)
  The Partnership for Reading
  RMC Research Corporation
  Portsmouth, New Hampshire

Resources from the International Reading Association (IRA)

Videos

- *Read to Me*—Introduces parents to the importance of reading aloud to their children (13 minutes)
- *Becoming a Family of Readers*—Features parents and their children modeling book sharing (10 minutes)

Brochures for Parents

- *Making the Most of Television: Tips for Parents of Young Viewers*
- *Get Ready to Read! Tips for Parents of Young Children*

Resources from the National Association for the Education of Young Children (NAEYC)

Article

- *Hey! Somebody Read to Me!* by M. C. Ulmer. 2005. *Young Children.* Washington, DC

Brochure

- *Raising a Reader, Raising a Writer*

Position Statement

- *Learning to Read and Write*
  Available online: http://www.naeyc.org/files/naeyc/file/positions/PSREAD98.PDF

Web Sites

- Even Start Family Literacy Program
  http://www.ed.gov/
  Click "Offices"; click "ED structure"; click "Office of Elementary and Secondary Education"; type in "Even Start"

- National Center for Family Literacy
  http://www.famlit.org

- Pennsylvania Center for the Book
  http://www.pabook.libraries.psu.edu
  Click "family literacy activities"

- Zero to Three Early Literacy
  http://www.zerotothree.org
  Click "Behavior and Development"; click "Early Language and Literacy

  Some corporations are now providing materials for supporting children's literacy at home. Among them are:

- General Mills
  In collaboration with Simon and Schuster, Cheerios boxes have appealing books on each box. Among the titles are: *Mostly Monsterly, Hello Baby!, If I Were a Jungle Animal, Noodle & Lou, Peeny Butter Fudge, Can I Just Take a Nap?*

  Related activities are available at: http://pages.simonandschuster.com/spoonfulsofstories/

- PNC Bank
  "Grow Up Great" has a focus on early learning, birth to five years. http://www.pncgrowupgreat.com/about/index.html

- PBS Parents
  http://www.pbs.org/parents/education/

enrich children's vocabulary, help children develop language skills by using contextual clues, and give children valuable experience in practicing literacy in playful situations.

naeyc 4 Owocki (1999) provides information about facilitating literacy learning through play.

This book emphasizes, in addition, the importance of teachers collaborating with families as they implement developmentally appropriate methods for teaching literacy through play. Further, Leong, Bodrova, Hensen, and Henninger (1999) explain relationships between play and literacy in terms of four major literacy skills that are accomplished through play:

1. The ability to learn deliberately through planning, developing, and continuity of play

2. The development of symbolic representation as children imagine that objects can be many different things

3. The practice of oral language as children talk through the pretend scenario, creating a script of what will happen in play

4. The preparation for literacy through the introduction of content-related skills and concepts, including reading and writing, practice with encoding and decoding meaning, matching voice to print, and correspondence of sounds and symbols.

As teachers implement play strategies to support children's literacy learning at school, they will also work with families to provide them with information about ways they can extend children's play at home so that families, too, encourage literacy through play activities.

Families can support language development while engaging in everyday activities, such as watching television or traveling in the car with children. As situations are presented in TV shows, family members can ask questions, expand understanding, listen to children's ideas about what is happening, and simply have conversations about program content. While in the car, family members can encourage children to look at traffic signs, billboards, and license plates; to say and spell town names; to read the numerals on speed limit signs; and to have conversations about landmarks. Car time is also an opportunity to sing songs, chant, and to play word and memory games. **naeyc** 4

DAP Early childhood teachers can help families understand the language and literacy development of their children in a variety of effective ways. These can include, but certainly do not need to be limited to, sending home newsletters that contain nuggets of literacy information, thus informing families over time; hosting school programs for parents and other family members related to language development; and providing brochures, DVDs, and Web site addresses about language and literacy strategies. Discussion during family conferences is another forum for language and literacy information sharing.

Dickinson and Tabors (2002) have written that "teachers must actively reach out to families, building on their strengths while guiding them toward the kinds of home language and literacy activities that will help their children achieve the educational success that families

desire for their children." These researchers found three dimensions of children's experiences during preschool and kindergarten that are related to later literacy success:

• Exposure to varied vocabulary

• Opportunities to be part of conversations that use extended discourse

• Home and classroom environments that are cognitively and linguistically stimulating **DAP**

DIVERSITY IN PRACTICE   Families with English Language Learners (ELL) will most likely need to have some additional encouragement from teachers to become involved in their children's literacy education when a language other than English is their home language. All children do best academically when their families are involved in their education. Even though young children will be learning English at school, it is beneficial for parents to assist in their literacy development in their home language. When children have a strong foundation in their home language through reading, writing, and vocabulary, it helps them to read, write, and speak English well. The role of early childhood teachers is to encourage family members to support their young children's literacy development in their home language since there are many advantages to bilingual or multilingual individuals (Hasson and Price 2008).

FAMILIES AND SCIENCE

DAP Understanding that young children view the world differently than adults means that adults' explanations about the world need to be based on children's current levels of understanding. Crowley and Galco (2006) found that the most important outcome of everyday parent-child scientific thinking "may not be the content children acquire, but the interests, habits, and identity they form as someone who is competent in scientific thinking." Listed in the following are some major points that are useful in working with families to develop and support scientific thinking in their young children:

• Children learn science best when it is active (e.g., exploring magnets, cars on ramps, water play).

• Children learn science best when they have opportunities to talk and work with other people.

• Children learn science best when they are the scientist (not just a science word learner).

• Children learn science best when the topic of exploration is related to their own experiences (e.g., food, plants, wheels, care of animals).

- Children learn science best when adults listen to their ideas and questions and then respond to and expand on children's interests.

Sharing this information with families may be done through newsletters, workshops, e-mail, or display areas of the school that are accessible to families. First, when early childhood educators help families learn how to support children's science learning at home, it is important to provide families with information about how science is addressed at school. When families have this information, early childhood programs can build on it by sharing specific information with families about how they can support scientific explorations at home. The American Association for the Advancement of Science (AAAS 1991) lists as part of its standards for professional teacher preparation the following:

> 66 The importance of the family to the learning of the young child is emphasized by the National Education Goals that were established by Congress and the nation's governors in 1990. A parent's statements that "I was never good in math" or "I never had a scientific mind" are often communicated to young children and can stifle a child's desire to learn those subjects. Partnerships between school and family are essential to overcoming these and other obstacles in early childhood programs. 99 **DAP**

Figure 9–2 outlines several school-family science partnership scenarios.

Once families understand how science is taught at school, early childhood teachers can go on to explain to families that young children view the world differently than adults do, which means that adults' explanations about the world need to be based on children's current levels of understanding. Crowley and Galco (2006) found that the most important outcome of everyday parent-child scientific thinking "may not be the content children acquire, but the interests, habits, and identity they form as someone who is competent in scientific thinking." **naeyc** 2 Listed below are useful ideas for working with families of young children to help them help their children develop and support scientific thinking. **naeyc** 2

naeyc 2, 4, 5 Of course, for school-family science partnerships to be effective, early childhood professionals must be knowledgeable about and comfortable with both teaching science and interacting with families to create partnerships. Chrisman (2006) conducted a four-year project (2002–2006) investigating the effects on early childhood teachers' abilities to teach science and to create partnerships with families when they received professional development both through methods of teaching science to young children and with strategies for implementing family involvement. In the project, science content and activities were based on the Developmental Approaches to Science, Health and Technology (DASH) curriculum, and family strategies were based on the work of Epstein and the National Network of Partnership Schools (Epstein, Sanders, Simon, Salinas, Jansorn, and Van Voorhis 2002). The preliminary results from this research indicate that teacher attitudes about both science with young children (through third grade) and family involvement changed positively with focused professional development in both areas. Further, teachers reported an increase in planned activities for including families in supporting children's learning. **naeyc** 2, 4, 5

DIVERSITY IN PRACTICE   In 2003, the AAAS launched the Partnership for Science Literacy, an initiative to increase public awareness, particularly among parents, families, and caregivers of Latino/Hispanic, African-American, and other minority and underserved students regarding the value and importance of science literacy for their children's futures. This initiative provides information and resources to help families find out more about science and about the kind of science education that helps all children. The partnership, a joint project of AAAS (through its Project 2061 and Education and Human Resource directorates) and TryScience.org, was launched with

---

Figure 9–2   **Science Activities for Families of Young Children.**

Activity	Science Content
Pointing out basic characteristics of objects (e.g., colors, shape, number, size, weight)	Increases children's discrimination abilities to sort and name by categories
Naming objects, plants, body parts, events, weather, processes	Provides language for children's developing classification systems
Discussing and explaining how things around the house work: clocks, pipes, toys, television, CD player	Helps children understand the mechanics of commonly used machines with which they have experience
Investigating questions or interests together (i.e., looking up information in books or on the internet)	Gives children models for learning to investigate questions

funding from the National Science Foundation. The initiative is built around the following key messages:

- Science education is for every child.
- Science is around you in your life every day.
- Parents and families can make a huge difference in their child's science education.
- Science is a lot of fun.

Additional useful information on this subject comes from Koralek and Colker (2003), who emphasize the importance of both families and communities in supporting science learning for young children. The following thought-provoking questions and ideas were adapted from their book, *Reflecting, Discussing, Exploring: Questions and Follow-Up Activities*. This source addresses the importance of both families and communities in supporting science learning of young children. **naeyc** 2

1. What strategies can help communicate to families what their children are doing and learning in the areas of science?

2. Most families are legitimately concerned about developing their children's literacy skills. How might you communicate with families about the important connections between science and literacy, or between mathematics and literacy, in a jargon-free and interesting way?

3. Families love to see photographs of their own children: how can you use photos to help family members experience the wonder of their children's science learning?

4. Every community is different, yet each offers many opportunities for everyday scientific investigations. Identify those in your community and share ideas with families to explore together. **naeyc** 2

Ideas related to science and family involvement are posted regularly on the Early Years Science blog. Visit http://science.nsta.org/earlyyearsblog to read more about science and young children. The following selections were taken from the site.

Houghton Mifflin Education Place
http://www.eduplace.com/
Click "science"

Science for Families Update
http://kidscience.blogspot.com

Try Science
http://www.TryScience.org
Click "parents"

National Science Education Standards
http://www.nap.edu/
Type in "nses"

Science nights provide opportunities for families to see activities firsthand.

" We had a family science night with the theme of "Saving the Wetlands." All the stations had to do with wetlands in danger. We got a lot of information from our Coastal Bend Bays and Estuaries foundation and invited people from the community to bring activities. One person works at our waste water treatment plant and brought in an activity. We also have had a family literacy night that incorporated science and literacy with children's trade books about a certain topic. "NSTA Recommends"* has numerous resources. "

Posted by Marilyn Cook on 1/22/2006 2:52:38 PM. (Reprinted by permission of Marilyn Cook, teacher, H. G. Olsen Elementary School):

" A book of take-home science activities that I'm using suggested sending home little bottles of the primary colors of paint so that students could mix the secondary colors at home. 1) "Little bottles" were very expensive. 2) Red, yellow, and blue colored transparencies were not available at our office supply store for overlapping. 3) Colored tablets were available, but the shipping cost more than the tablets. After racking my brain for weeks, I finally "eureka-ed" that I could put drops of red, blue, and yellow food coloring in separate cups, let them dry, and then send them home for students to "reconstitute" by adding water to make cups of water of the primary colors. In three separate empty cups, students could mix the primary colors to make secondary colors at home in a cost-efficient manner. "

FAMILIES AND MATHEMATICS

naeyc 1 Just as with science, young children understand math concepts differently than adults. So, it is important to help family members understand both these differences and how young children gain mathematical skills and concepts. The National Council of Teachers of Mathematics (NCTM) and the National Association for the Education of Young Children (NAEYC), in a joint position statement (2002), recommend the following for early childhood programs: "Build on children's varying experiences, including their family, linguistic, and cultural background; their individual approaches to learning; and their informal knowledge." **naeyc** 1

naeyc 4, 5 This position statement further indicates that resources are needed to support families as partners in developing their young children's mathematical proficiency. NCTM and NAEYC recommend activities such as family math nights and take-home activities, including math games and manipulative materials tailored to children's ages and developmental levels. Teachers might consider creating a math corollary to the popular literacy packs used by children and families. Math packs could include graph paper; a variety of manipulatives, such as Legos, unit blocks, geometric shapes, and patterning activities; and tools, such as compasses and measuring instruments. Math and literacy skills could be integrated by adding books with mathematical themes.

Copley (2000) has written, "Teachers, schools, and early childhood programs may want to use existing resources to help get families on board with math learning. Among these are materials from NCTM, programs from Family Math (Coates & Thompson) and resources available on the Internet." She further states that such approaches focus parents' attention on children's learning and understanding. **naeyc** 4, 5 Figure 9–3 lists excerpts from Activities for Families with Young Children (http://www.ed.gov/pubs/EarlyMath/activities1.html).

DAP Smith (2006) includes the following ideas for involving parents in a school mathematics program:

- Explain your math program philosophy and methods through multiple means, including at open houses, in letters and notes, and at parent-teacher conferences.

- Make videos about math activities in your classroom and be sure to show children's interest and enthusiasm.

- Start a lending library of children's books with math-related themes

- Koralek (2003) also lists several ideas for involving families and communities in math activities for young children. These include:

- Developing a plan for "Family Mathematics Night" when families can learn about and actively participate in their children's mathematics curriculum.

- Taking photos to help family members experience the wonders of their children's mathematics learning. Some ideas might be adding captions or having children write "thought balloons" to the photos and creating displays or documentation panels. **DAP**

Photos help families experience the wonders of their children's mathematics learning

Figure 9–3	Suggestions for Families to Support Young Children's Mathematical Understandings and Learning at Home.

- In the morning:
  Discuss events of the day: what comes first, next, and last
  Discuss patterns (in clothing, on toys, etc.)
  Encourage estimates (how many bites of cereal in a bowl, etc.)
- Sing songs in the car that have math content:
  "Five Little Monkeys"
  "One, Two, Three, Four, Five (Caught a Fish Alive)"
  "One, Two, Buckle My Shoe"
- Read books with mathematical content:
  The Doorbell Rang, Pat Hutchins
  Moja Means One: Swahili Counting Book, Muriel Feelings
  Read Aloud Rhymes for the Very Young, Jack Prelusky

Additional Family Math Resources and Ideas for Involvement

- *Family Math* by Grace Coates and Jean K. Stenmark
  Available from: Lawrence Hall of Science
  University of California
  Berkeley, CA 94720-5200
  http://www.lhs.berkeley.edu
  (510)642-1823
- Web sites:
  Houghton Mifflin Education Place
  http://www.eduplace.com/
  Click "math"
  National Council of Teachers of Mathematics
  http://www.nctm.org/
  Click "resources for families"

66 [I]t takes a community and a family for real success....We have long known that family members are a child's first teachers. Some of us were fortunate enough to learn counting on our grandfathers' knees and to learn to read similarly, using a daily newspaper....[W]e might be more effective if we capitalized on the education that families and a student's community may have provided before the student came to school....The real message here is that we may be missing opportunities when we do not use family and community members to help students learn. 99

—Johnny Lott, past president of NCTM, 2003

Figure 9–4 recaps some of the guidelines for families that the National Council of Teachers of Mathematics proposes. Consider ways that early childhood teachers might make meaning of these guidelines in their work with families.

FAMILIES AND SOCIAL STUDIES

naeyc 4, 5 Social studies curricula for young children differ from the curricula for history, geography, economics, and government for older children. Activities and lessons are based on the cognitive and social understandings of young children in preschool, kindergarten, and primary grades, and thus look different from the lessons and teaching methods used in the upper elementary levels. Therefore, it is

| Figure 9–4 | National Council of Teachers of Mathematics (NCTM) Guidelines for Families. |

- Be positive! Have a "can do" attitude and relate math to other activities that require hard work and persistence, such as learning to play a sport or musical instrument.
- Link math with daily life. Use examples such as reading a map, creating and following a budget, understanding discounts of sale items, pointing out shapes and patterns.
- Make math fun. Play board games, solve puzzles, and participate in brain teasers with your child.
- Learn about math-related careers by researching careers along with qualifications and expectations in regard to mathematical understanding.
- Have high expectations. Math, like literacy, must be for all children. Be sure to advocate for good math opportunities.
- Support children in doing their homework, but do not do it for them. Serve as a guide or facilitator; ask your child to explain it to you as a review procedure or to check on where help might be needed.

| Figure 9–5 | Guiding Principles for Educational Experiences in Social Studies for Young Children. |

1. Integrity of content and authenticity of instruction must be maintained. Methods of inquiry should be used to gain knowledge.
2. A learning community that incorporates a balance of student-initiated and teacher-initiated experiences is optimal.
3. Use democratic methods that lead to children assuming appropriate levels of responsibility in order to gain confidence.
4. Provide many opportunities for children to interact with others who differ in ability, experiences, ethnicity, gender, and culture.
5. Respect diversity of thought, culture, and language.
6. Support children in the use of a wide variety of informational sources.
7. Use multiple symbol systems such as those used in language, math, music, art, graphs, charts, and tables.
8. Assess both process and outcomes of children's learning

Consortium for Interdisciplinary Teaching and Learning (1994) http://www.socialstudies.org/positions/interdisciplinary/

necessary to plan home- and community-based social studies activities that support early learning. Helping families understand these differences is an important first step in planning family involvement. Figure 9–5 provides a list of guiding principles for interdisciplinary educational experiences in social studies for the early childhood years. **naeyc** 4, 5

DAP As discussed in Chapter 1, fundamental to creating effective family partnerships for any subject area is the early childhood teachers' understanding and appreciation of families' varied histories, cultures, and traditions. Building family social studies activities around this knowledge encourages family involvement in home-based social studies learning. Louise Derman-Sparks (1989) has written extensively about creating **anti-bias** activities. Her work features many examples of how to build inclusive strategies for families that support a social studies curriculum. Another resource for planning social studies activities with families is in the *Starting Small* (1997) series, produced by the Southern Poverty Law Center, which is part of SPLC's *Teaching Tolerance* curriculum and available to teachers and schools at no cost. This curriculum is unique in its emphasis on developmentally appropriate explanations and examples relating to respect and **tolerance**. Both of these resources include activities and suggestions for involving members of the community in classroom activities. **DAP**

Figure 9–6 lists family involvement activities with their corresponding social studies content.

Figure 9–6	Sample Social Studies for Families of Young Children.

Activity	Age Level	Content
Draw a map of your house	Pre-K–K	Map-making (geography)
Draw a map of your neighborhood	K–Primary	Map-making (geography)
Make a chart with two columns indicating "Needs" in one and "Wants" in the other	K–Primary	Beginning understandings of economics
Make a collage of photos of either family members or friends	K–Primary	Family history (historical understandings)
Use a map to find all of the places your family members or family friends live	2nd–3rd grade	Map reading (geography)
Add the dollar amounts of each item of your favorite meal	Primary	Beginning understandings of costs (economics)

© Cengage Learning

FAMILIES AND HEALTH, SAFETY, NUTRITION, AND MOVEMENT

For most families caring for the health and safety of their children is a major concern throughout a lifetime. Having regular doctor and dentist visits is routine in many households and practicing safety while riding in a car, crossing streets, and various other circumstances is consistently practiced. However, practices are not universal and sometimes families need information about basic health and safety. Providing basic nutrition information is also more necessary as observed by the increasing obesity rate in young children. With the rise in passive activities over the last three decades due to access and popularity of television and computer games, there is a growing emphasis at all levels of education to provide more information to families about the need for children to increase their physical activity in order to maintain health and prevent illness.

In addition to physical health, families and schools must act in partnership for children's mental health. Too often overlooked and viewed as a stigma, mental health issues that are addressed early are as important to preventive efforts as physical health issues. In order to succeed academically, children must be psychologically healthy. When teachers and schools help families to understand that psychological health is based on positive relationships with parents and other caregivers and also may have a biological or neurological basis, children are more likely to get the attention and services needed to support their emotional health.

Two types of family involvement related to health, safety, nutrition, and movement are typically offered in early childhood programs and schools. One of these is to design information or activities to be sent home for family use. Another is to plan events for children and families to come to a central place at a planned time, such as an open house or game day, to pick up materials and ideas for activities. Listed in the following sections are resources that can be included for both types of family involvement activities.

Websites Related to Health for Families to Use

Action for Healthy Kids
www.actionforhealthykids.org/
Early Childhood Mental **Health Program**
www.ecmhp.org/
Healthy Child Care America
www.healthychildcare.org
Human Development and Family Science
www.hec.ohiostate.edu/famlife/yc/care.htm
Maternal and Child Health Library
www.mchlibrary.info
Medlineplus Health Information
www.nim.nih.gov/medlineplus/childsafety.html
Mental Health America: Recognizing Mental Health Problems in Children
www.nmha.org/farcry/go/information/get-info/children-s-mental-health/recognizing-mental-health-problems-in-children
National Black Child Development Institute
www.nbcdi.org

Websites for Family Nutrition

Food and Nutrition Information Center
www.nal.usda.gov.fnic
National Network for Child Care (with Spanish resources on nutrition)
www.nncc.org
American Dietetic Association
www.eatright.org/ada/files/gerber.pdf

Websites Related to Accident Prevention and Fire Safety for Families

American Association of Poison Control Center
www.aspcc.org
Child Care Safety Checklist for Parents and Child Care Providers
www.cpsc.gov/cpscpub/pubs/childcare.html
Consumer Product Safety Commission
www.cpsc.gov
Fireproof Children Company
www.playsafebesafe.com
Risk Watch: Make Time for Safety
www.nfpa.org/riskwatch/kids.html
Families and Physical Education and Fitness Connect for Kids—Obesity Resources
www.connectforkids.org/obesity_resources
KidsHealth for Parents
www.kidsheath.org/parent/nutrition_fit /nutrition/pyramid.html
National Clearinghouse for Educational Facilities
www.edfacilities.org
PE Control
www.pecentral.org
National Association for Sport and Physical Education
www.aahperd.org/NASPE/template.cfm? template=peappropriatepractice/index.html
Zero to Three Early Childhood Mental Health
www.zerotothree.org/child-development/early- childhood-mental-health/

DAP Additional resources that may be helpful for planning family involvement activities are found on the NAEYC website: Beyond the Journal. One article, "Children's Literature about Health, Nutrition and Safety" (Renck and Jalongo 2004), includes both fiction and picture books in a variety of categories (child health, infectious disease/sanitation/hygiene, safety, nutrition, and oral health among other topics). This is an excellent resource to share with families looking for health-related stories to communicate with young children.

Another beneficial resource found on the NAEYC Webpage Beyond the Journal is entitled "Tots in Action ON and BEYOND the Playground" (Schilling and McOmber 2006). This article describes a physical education program developed at the University of North Carolina at Greensboro, Tots in Action. A section entitled "Integrating physical activity at home" describes both at-school events and at-home events for family involvement that promotes movement and physical activity. DAP

Using a wide variety of information sources supports children's social studies understanding.

FAMILIES AND THE ARTS

DAP Encouraging the arts with families may be natural for some teachers but may be a new concept to others. If the school has specialists in music or art, they will likely be able to provide strategies for family involvement. As stated in the physical activity section of this chapter, there are two basic options for family involvement: events that bring families into schools, and materials that can be sent to homes. Sending home calendars with suggestions may be one of the most basic ways to encourage families to involve children in drawing, listening to music, and creating craft projects. More ideas for calendars are available at the TIPS section at the end of this chapter. DAP

66 Arts education not only cultivates imagination, self-expression, and creativity, but also plays a vital role in the development of critical thinking and problem-solving skills. It promotes visual literacy, which enables students to analyze and interpret the meaning of complex visual imagery that permeates the media and popular culture. 99

—National Parent Teacher Association

As many education programs are undergoing budget cuts, content related to the arts is endangered. When families serve as advocates for arts education, many times their efforts have success and show in a variety of outcomes. The National PTA indicates that parents can work with teachers and decision-makers in the following ways:

- Research and share facts related to the benefits of arts education.
- Investigate state curriculum standards.
- Organize a parent and community member group to meet with decision-makers.
- Enlist support from your local parent/family education association.

- Gain support of state arts agencies.
- Attend board meetings and advocate for the importance of arts content.
- Be persistent.

A helpful idea from the NAEYC Webpage Beyond the Journal (July 2003) includes suggested children's museum sites for families on vacation. These are listed by region of the country. Some examples from this compilation are:

NORTHEAST

The Crayola Factory, Easton, PA
www.crayola.com/factory
The Eric Carle Museum of Picture Book Art, Amherst, MA
www.picturebookart.org

SOUTHWEST

The Children's Museum of South Carolina, Myrtle Beach
www.bearweb.com/cmsckids/

MIDWEST

Children's Museum of Indianapolis, Indiana
www.childrensmuseum.org/catalog/home.asp

SOUTHWEST

Children's Discovery Museum, San Antonio, TX
www.hotx.com/cm/overview.html

WEST COAST

Adventure Park at the Berkeley Marina, CA
www.cl.berkeley.ca.us/parks/parkspages

Do This

Research museums, parks, and other regional sites that would be interesting for family trips and vacations in your area. Send this information home for families to use in their planning. Be sure to indicate price range and, if possible, include events that are free.

SOCIAL AND EMOTIONAL FOUNDATIONS OF CHILDREN'S LEARNING

naeyc 4, 5 Existing evidence points to the importance of understanding not only children's cognition or ways of knowing, but also social and emotional development in order to provide optimal support for children's academic success. For example, family members influence children's confidence, enthusiasm for learning, relationship building, understanding of temperament, self-control, cooperation, and control of aggressive tendencies (Center on Social and Emotional Foundations 2009). Sharing information with families about their roles in children's development in all areas may increase family understanding about effective ways to interact and build positive relationships with their children, necessities for academic success. **naeyc** 4, 5

One initiative that is described by Jones (2007) refers to engaging young children in "Big Jobs," or real work that needs to be done for classroom functioning. Early childhood teachers may want to implement such a program to support children's social and emotional development. Some of the ideas suggested by this author include weeding a garden, changing water in an aquarium, sweeping the blacktop for tricycle riding, and adding a new bag of sand to the sandbox. Since children benefit from learning how to cooperate with others, extending this idea to family functions through newsletters, online discussions, or face-to-face programming will encourage parents to engage children in developmentally appropriate "Big Jobs" at home. Working together builds trust and necessitates communication as well as gets a big job accomplished.

Information about **emotional intelligence** (Goleman 1997) is more readily available than ever before. Children need support from families and teachers to understand themselves so that they are able to increase their relationship-building skills. Competence and success in life are known to require not only academic progress, but also skills for working with others. Families and schools have tremendous impact in this arena and must understand the importance of a strong sense of self in order to build positive relationships and to apply knowledge and skills.

Planning physical activities for families is another way to develop involvement.

© Cengage Learning/ECE Photo Library.

Planning activities to include families with the arts is another way to support involvement with the program.

Numerous social and emotional learning (SEL) programs have been reviewed and described by the Collaborative for Academic, Social and Emotional Learning (CASEL). Several characteristics of effective and appropriate SEL designs have been identified, including: has a sound basis in research and theory; involves families and communities as partners; applies developmentally and culturally appropriate instruction; and leads to enhanced academic performance through attention to affective and social elements (Guidelines for Social and Emotional Learning 2002).

naeyc 2 Involving families in SEL designs is noted as critical to success. Effective strategies incorporate much of the content of this book with emphasis on creating a respectful and reciprocal relationship with all families. In order to do this, teachers

Including the arts with families helps develop relationships and supports children's growth in all areas.

must have a strong knowledge base about families and family involvement in education as well as cultural competence. In addition, implementing the six keys for effective family and community involvement from the National Network of Partnership Schools—communicating, parenting, learning at home, volunteering, decision-making and advocacy, and collaborating with communities—is necessary. More detail about these six keys based on the work of Joyce Epstein and her associates at Johns Hopkins University is available in Chapter 7. **naeyc** 2

An example of how social and emotional development is connected to early literacy has been demonstrated by Santos, Fettig, and Shaffer (2012). These authors note that early literacy activities that families initiate with their young children are supportive of both academic and social and emotional development. They make the following suggestions for parents:

- Read aloud stories. Be sure to engage children in conversation as you read to them.
- Select books that address areas of social-emotional development, such as sharing and making friends.
- Use common print materials, such as food labels and recipes.

Suggestions provided for teachers to involve families include:

- Sending newsletters with suggestions for family activities that support children's social and emotional development, including recommended books and shared activities.
- Offer themed take home literacy bags for families and children to share.
- Plan and invite families to events such as read alouds, story telling, and age-appropriate dramatics that focus on social and emotional skills.
- Suggest ways that typical errands might be discussed with young children to support both literacy and social and emotional development.

Do This

Go to www.casel.org/programs/selecting.php and review the list of programs included in CASEL's Safe and Sound programs. Investigate at least two programs from the list and share detailed explanations of those programs with either posters or brochures.

Summary and Conclusions

Family and community members can be involved in activities that support understandings of young children. Children's mathematical, literacy, scientific, social studies, physical education, and arts learning can be enriched and expanded without resorting to drilling or memorization. Families can learn about and understand the thought processes of young children, and this, in turn, will enable them to better relate to their children's ideas and conceptual frameworks. When teachers build partnerships with families and community members to support children's learning at home and at school, greater success is inevitable.

Theory into Practice Suggestions (TIPS)

Family activities that may be included in a family calendar:

- Literacy

  Create a calendar of family activities that promote literacy such as:

  a. Sing rhyming songs.
  b. Read books every day with your child. Consider listing some books that are related to class topics that are developmentally appropriate for age levels of children in your class.
  c. Go to the library together to choose books with your child.
  d. Take chalk out and write your child's name on the sidewalk (or other words or letters).
  e. Play "I Spy Letters" while driving in the car, riding on the bus, or walking in the neighborhood.
  f. Help your child find letters in the names of food or stuffed animals that have the same first letters of their names.
  g. Sit with your child and write the names of family members.
  h. Sit with your child and make a grocery list.
  i. Place magnetic letters on the refrigerator door or other metal surface.
  j. Talk about the day of the week each day with your child.
  k. Write cards and mail to friends, relatives, or neighbors.

- Science

  Send home ideas in a calendar that include science ideas to try at home:

  a. Find and name the types of flowers in a garden or park.
  b. Go to the grocery store together and choose some fruit. Discuss its size, shape, color, texture, smell, and taste.
  c. Collect objects that go together (e.g., shoes and socks, comb and brush, hammer and nail).
  d. Read and discuss the weather section in the newspaper or online. Discuss the words related to weather: temperature, cloudy, etc.
  e. Look around the house and map out the types of pipes and where they go.
  f. Go outside on sunny days and make shadows. Talk about their length, size, etc.

- Math

  Create a calendar with ideas for families to use at home. Include the following types of math activities:

  a. Talk about and write together home addresses and phone numbers (as well as other people's phone numbers and addresses).
  b. Make a bank out of a coffee can with a plastic lid and count the coins together.
  c. Count backwards from 10 as you are riding in the car.
  d. Play counting games like "How many windows are in this room?" or ceiling tiles, etc.
  e. Play "I Spy Numbers" as you are driving.
  f. Count the number of items on a food tray or plate (e.g., pieces of bread or cookies).
  g. Read stories together that have math words or ideas (e.g., *Five Little Monkeys*).
  h. Play games together that have math concepts (e.g., dominoes, cards with numbers on them like Go Fish).
  i. Look for patterns and shapes as you are walking (e.g., in floor tiles, on fences or brick walls, on signs).

- Social Studies

  Create a calendar with ideas for families to use at home. Include the following types of social studies activities:

  a. Read stories together about being a friend.
  b. Organize a play group.
  c. Plan together with your child what you would like to do today and give appropriate choices.
  d. Play games together and discuss taking turns.
  e. Create a list of three tasks to complete today.

- Physical Activities

  Create a calendar with ideas for families to use at home. Include the following types of physical activities:

  a. Taking walks together in the neighborhood or at parks.

  b. Planning weekly exercise times for both inside and outside.

  c. Ideas for both large muscle movements and small muscle movements that can be done around the house.

- The Arts

  Create a calendar with ideas for families to use at home. Include the following types of arts-related activities:

  a. Look for colors as you walk or drive.

  b. Look at illustrated books and discuss colors and designs.

  c. Have a variety of art materials in a shoebox for easy access.

  d. Have play dough or clay available.

  e. Have a craft box with empty paper towel rolls, small boxes, packing materials, etc. to create sculptures.

  f. Sing songs with your child.

  g. Move to different rhythms.

  h. Listen to different types of music from a variety of cultures.

  i. Make homemade instruments.

Note: Families have varying beliefs about music and dance.

Listings adapted from: *Getting Ready for Kindergarten: A Calendar of Family Activities.* United Way Success By 6.United Way of Carlisle & Cumberland County. September 2008–August 2009.

- Social and Emotional Learning
- Apply strategies from the entirety of this text in order to build strong relationships with all families.

  a. Demonstrate an understanding that social and emotional dimensions of learning are important to school success.

  b. Be aware that application of the six keys to building partnerships with families and communities are essential for children's school success.

Applications

1. Plan a program for families or the community to introduce one of the subject areas: literacy, math, science, social studies, physical/safety, the arts, and social emotional foundations of early learning.

2. Create newsletters for families that explain each of the subject areas.

3. Collect some of the resources mentioned in the chapter resources and references and organize them as a file for current or future use.

4. Using photos of children at work, create a display or documentation board of math, literacy, science, social studies, physical, and arts activities and invite parents and other family members to review the activities.

Questions for Reflection and Discussion

1. What content area would be the most challenging for you to share with families? Why?

2. What strategies would you prefer to use in involving families in each of the content areas? Describe a plan for implementing the strategies you prefer.

3. Discuss reasons why early childhood teachers are called on to build not only family-friendly schools, but also school-friendly families.

Field Assignments

1. Create materials that early childhood teachers might use to support families in engaging in children's learning at home. Ask an early childhood teacher to review the materials and to make recommendations about changes to your materials or plans that would increase effectiveness.

2. Interview several families of young children about how they support children's learning at home. Ask which resources would be helpful to them in their efforts to do this.

3. Work with several other students in an early childhood education or community setting to plan, implement, and evaluate one of the following events for professionals, families, and children: family literacy, math, science, or social studies.

Additional resources for this chapter, including TeachSource videos, can be found on the Education CourseMate. Go to CengageBrain.com.

References

Bronfenbrenner, U. 1979. *The ecology of human development: Experiments by nature and design.* Cambridge, MA: Harvard University Press.

Center on Social and Emotional Foundations for Early Learning. 2009. www.vanderbilt.edu/csefel/family-tools.html (accessed May 25, 2009).

Chrisman, K. 2006. *Preliminary results of the School Improvement Project: Funded from the Dale Kann Endowment.* Shippensburg University Foundation.

Coates, G. D., and V. Thompson. 1999. Involving parents of 4- and 5-year olds in their children's mathematics education: The FAMILY MATH experience. In *Mathematics in the early years,* ed. J. V. Copley, 205-14. Reston, VA: NCTM; Washington, DC: NAEYC.

Copley, J. V. 2000. *The young child and mathematics.* Reston, VA: NCTM; Washington, DC: NAEYC.

Copley, J., ed. 2004. *Showcasing mathematics for the young child.* Reston, VA: NCTM.

Crowley, K., and J. Galco. 2001. *Everyday activity and the development of scientific thinking.* Museumlearning.com: University of Pittsburgh.

Derman-Sparks, L., and the A.B.C. Task Force. 1989. *Antibiascurriculum: Tools for empowering young children.* Washington, DC: NAEYC.

Dialogue on Early Childhood Science, Mathematics and Technology Education. 1991. *American Association for the Advancement of Science.* Washington, DC.

Developmental approaches to science, health and technology. University of Hawaii: Curriculum Research & Development Group.

Dickinson, D. K., and P. O. Tabors. 2002. Fostering language and literacy in classrooms and homes. *Young Children* 57: 10–18. Washington, DC: NAEYC.

Early childhood mathematics education: Promoting good beginnings. 2002. A joint Position Statement of the National Association for the Education of Young Children and the National Council of Teachers of Mathematics. http://www.nctm.org/about/position_statements/earlychildhood_statement.htm (accessed July 5, 2006).

Early childhood: Where learning begins. *Mathematics.* 1999. http://www.ed.gov/pubs/Early Math (accessed July 5, 2006).

Epstein, J. 2001. *School, family, and community partnerships: Preparing educators and improving schools.* Boulder, CO: Westview Press.

Epstein, J., L. Coates, K. C. Salinas, M. G. Sanders, and B. S. Simon. 1997. *School, family, and community partnerships: Your handbook for action.* Thousand Oaks, CA: Corwin Press.

Epstein, J., J. G. Sanders, B. S. Simon, K. C. Salinas, N. R Jansorn, and F. L. Van Voorhis. 2002. *School, family and community partnerships: Your handbook for action,* 2nd ed. Thousand Oaks, CA: Corwin Press.

Goleman, G. 1997. *Emotional intelligence.* New York: Bantam.

Guidelines for social and emotional learning. 2002. Collaborative for Academic, Social, and Emotional Learning. http://www.casel.org/downloads/Safe%20and%20Sound/2A_Guidelines.pdf (accessed May 26, 2009).

Hasson, D. J. and G. J. Price. 2008. *Parents + Schools = Successful children: Practitioner guide.* Louisville, KY: National Center for Family Literacy.

Hyson, M. 2008. *Enthusiastic and engaged learners: Approaches to learning in the early childhood classroom.* New York: Teachers College Press.

Jones, N. P. 2007. Big jobs. *Teaching Young Children, 1* (1), 10–13.

King, R., and J. McMaster. 2000. *Pathways: A primer for family literacy program design and development.* Louisville, KY: National Center for Family Literacy.

Koralek, D. 2003. *Spotlight on young children and math.* Washington, DC: NAEYC.

Koralek, D., and L. J. Colker, eds. 2003. *Young children and science.* Washington, DC: NAEYC.

Leong, D., E. Bodrova, R. Hensen, and M. Henninger. 1999. *Scaffolding early literacy through play.* Paper presented at the annual conference of the National Association for the Education of Young Children. New Orleans, LA.

Moll, L., C. Amanti, D. Neff, and N. Gonzalez. 2001. Funds of knowledge for teaching: Using a qualitative approach to connect homes and classrooms. *Theory into Practice, XXXI,* 2, 132-141.

National PTA. n.d. Parent involvement in arts education. www.pta.org/topic_parent_involvement_in_arts_education.asp Accessed April 3, 2012.

Owocki, G. 1999. *Literacy through play.* Portsmouth, NH: Heinemann.

Piaget, J. 1952. *The origins of intelligence in children.* New York: International Universities Press. (Original work published 1936)

Project 2061. American Association for the Advancement of Science.http://www.project2061.org/publications (accessed July 5, 2006).

Renck, M. A., and M. R. Jalongo. 2004. Children's literature about health, nutrition, and safety. *Beyond the Journal, Young Children on the Web.* Washington, DC: National Association for the Education of Young Children.

Santos, R. M., A. Fettig and L. Shaffer. 2012. Helping families connect early literacy with social-emotional development. *Young Children* 67 (2), 88-93.

Schilling, T., and K. A. McOmber. 2006. Tots in Action ON and BEYOND the playground. *Beyond the Journal, Young Children on the Web.* Washington, DC: National Association for the Education of Young Children.

Smith, S. S. 2006. *Early childhood mathematics,* 3rd ed. Boston, MA: Allyn & Bacon.

Starting small: Teaching tolerance in preschool and early grades. 1997. Teaching Tolerance Project. Montgomery, AL: Southern Poverty Law Center.

CHAPTER 10

Parent Education and Family Life Education

OUTLINE

OBJECTIVES ALIGNED WITH NAEYC STANDARDS

After reading and reflecting on this chapter, you should be able to:

- Understand the theoretical foundation for parent education and family life education **naeyc** 1, 2

- Discuss and implement a number of strategies for parent and family life education **naeyc** 6

- Relate the role of early childhood teachers in providing parent and family life education **naeyc** 2, 6

Key Terms

family life education

parent education

BIOECOLOGICAL THEORY

naeyc 1 Bronfenbrenner's bioecological model supports the premise of parent education in that there is a need for parents to have access to strategies that support all areas of their children's development—intellectual, social, and moral (Bronfenbrenner and Neville 1994). As children develop, they require "progressively more complex activity," and it is especially important that these interactions exist between the child and parents or parental figures. Central to this model of human development is the special importance of appropriate interactions between children and adults who are committed to the child's well-being over their entire lifetime. This theory stresses the crucial concept of enduring emotional attachment for optimal child development.

Further, this model stipulates the importance of a third party who "assists, encourages, spells, gives status

to, and expresses admiration and affection for the person caring for...the child" (Bronfenbrenner and Neville 1994). Parents should also be aware of or educated about the importance of having someone support them as a parent. Bronfenbrenner notes that ideally this third person would be a spouse and that the context of marriage ideally supports this concept. However, if the marriage is not providing such support for each parent, other mechanisms will be needed to do so. Children's development is enhanced when their parents have support for their caregiving. Often, grandparents carry out this family responsibility.

Bronfenbrenner also notes the relevance of mutual respect and communication "between the principal settings in which children and their parents live their lives." So it is necessary for parents and teachers or caregivers to communicate on a regular basis and to be able to believe in each other. When parents' workplaces provide flexible schedules, part-time jobs with benefits, and other programs that support families, a child's development is likely to be enhanced. **naeyc** 1

Programs of **parent education** and **family life education** should include application of the theoretical premises from bioecological theory. This means that such programs always respect the primacy of the family and are designed with the understanding that the basic purpose of parent education and family life education is to support parents in the important task of child-rearing, not to undermine or judge their efforts.

PHILOSOPHY ABOUT PROGRAMS OF PARENT EDUCATION

An undergraduate student in an early childhood teacher preparation program reported to her instructor that she would not be permitted to hold a parent meeting at the center to which she was assigned for her practicum. The director at the center told the student that parents of children at the center told her that they "do not want to be told how to raise their children." Before one jumps to conclusions about the parents' lack of interest in their children's education, let us hypothesize about what led to such comments. Consider the following:

- Experts on discipline are paid to speak to large audiences in school districts or other early childhood programs, indicating a one-method-fits-all approach.
- Family values (a need to customize information).
- Lack of support given to parents in our society.
- Lack of understanding about the need for communication between home and school for child's optimal development.
- Relative new experience of very young children being in care outside the home.
- Few programs adopting a family support model.

Reflect on each of these possibilities. Can you think of others? While the center director in the story might have concluded that parents in that center did not want or need parent meetings, other conclusions might better reflect best practices in early education. If it seems to be a widespread concern of parents that parent meetings are to indoctrinate them, then attention probably needs to be given to the source of that perspective.

It is also important for early childhood professionals to note differences in parenting that may be related to ethnicity and culture. (Some of these differences are noted in Chapter 2.) Parent education programs have been less successful among ethnic minority groups, however, possibly because they generally are based on and reflect Anglo-American, middle-class values. Service providers have demonstrated that parents from ethnic minority groups and from low socioeconomic groups attend and complete parent education

programs if the setting and the content are compatible with their values and their lifestyles (McDade 1995).

naeyc 6 Thus, it becomes the responsibility of early childhood teachers to understand parenting differences and to find appropriate ways to share information with their particular clientele. This information can be garnered from needs assessments as well as knowledge of existing research and practice related to parenting information. **naeyc** 6

DIVERSITY IN PRACTICE Considerations for both individual differences and cultural differences must be implemented in order to be effective with parent and family life education. An understanding of variations in culture based on independence or interdependence is helpful when planning and implementing programs for families. Families from cultures that value independence are more likely to use authoritative parenting strategies such as explanations and problem-solving, whereas families from cultures that value interdependence may use more authoritarian strategies to exert control so that children come to respect their elders and authority figures. Further, families who live in high-risk environments maintain control to keep children safe when dense traffic or violence-prone communities pose dangers to children (Ontai and Mastergeorge n.d.). Discussions during program sessions are necessary so that leaders and participants might understand differences in values and priorities.

The Center on School, Family and Community Partnerships, led by Dr. Joyce Epstein, notes that families have some basic parenting responsibilities that include providing housing, health care, nutrition, clothing and safety; parenting skills; and home conditions that support children as students. In partnership, schools and communities can take a role in supporting families with these responsibilities through workshops, access to videos, courses that include GED preparation and family literacy as well as those related to fostering children's development, family support to share information about healthy nutrition, food co-ops, or parent-to-parent sessions. Such efforts should have as a goal to increase parental confidence and knowledge of child development.

Assessing Needs and Effects

Programs of parent education should not be provided as a unilateral attempt to tell parents how to rear their children. Instead, the philosophy and the driving goals behind such a program should be to offer support for families. One way to initiate such a program is to conduct a needs assessment with families. Figures 10–1 and 10–2 show two formats of needs assessments.

Figure 10–1 Needs Assessment Part A.

At the Campus Early Learning Center, we offer monthly group meetings for parents and other interested family members. Each school term, we ask parents to rank their top three (3) choices of topics for which we might plan. Please rank your first choice as #1, second choice as #2, and third choice as #3. Also indicate days and times that you prefer and please return this form to the Director's Office by September 10. Thanks for your feedback.

_____ Appropriate and effective discipline

_____ How children learn

_____ New information from brain research

_____ Family involvement in children's education

_____ Preparing your child for kindergarten

_____ Healthy nutrition

_____ The importance of play for children's development

_____ Sibling rivalry

_____ Other: _____

_____ Other: _____

Day of the week that I prefer: (please circle all that apply)
Sunday   Monday   Tuesday   Wednesday
Thursday   Friday   Saturday

Time of day that I prefer: (please circle all that apply)
Morning

Lunch time

Afternoon

Evening

Additional information about scheduling of meetings:

Figure 10–2 Needs Assessment Part B.

As we plan for the parent/family involvement component of our program, your responses to the following questions will help us to determine some program content. We would appreciate your responses to the following questions by September 15. Please place your completed form in the box outside the Director's Office.

1. Age(s) of children in family _____
2. Who lives in your home? _____
3. What are your three biggest parenting challenges?
   a.
   b.
   c.
4. What questions do you have about how children learn and develop?
   a.
   b.
   c.
5. Do you have questions regarding our school curriculum?
   a.
   b.
   c.
6. What television programs does your child watch? About how much time each day does your child watch TV?
7. What kinds of play or activities does your child like?

Figure 10–3 Sample Assessment for a Group Parent Meeting.

Time and date of meeting: _____
Location: _____
Topic: _____

1. What was the best thing that happened at the meeting?
2. What changes should be made for future meetings?
3. Other comments

> It is usually assumed in our society that people have to be trained for difficult roles: most business firms would not consider turning a sales clerk loose on the customers without some formal training; the armed forces would scarcely send a raw recruit into combat without extensive and intensive training; most states now require a course in driver's education before high school students can acquire a driver's license. Even dog owners often go to school to learn how to treat their pets properly. This is not true of American parents.

—LeMasters and DeFrain, 1983

It is typical that information sessions have been held for large groups of parents without any evaluation of what happened in homes after the session. Too often, even immediate feedback from parents regarding the program is not solicited. Professionals in early education cannot overlook the need to assess effects of their family involvement activities. Figures 10–3, 10–4, and 10–5 show examples of evaluation forms to be completed by family members after they have participated in planned school activities.

Format of Programs

Powell (1989, 1994) discusses emerging directions for parent education that are sponsored by early childhood education programs. Following are some recent changes in both content and format for effective parent education.

Figure 10–4	Sample Assessment for a Group Parent Meeting.

Time and date of meeting: _____

Location: _____

Topic: _____

1. The information presented is useful to me.
   Very   Somewhat   A little   Not at all
2. The information was presented in an interesting manner.
   Very   Somewhat   A little   Not at all
3. The date and time were convenient for me.
   Very   Somewhat   A little   Not at all
4. Based on this meeting, how likely are you to attend another meeting?
   Very   Somewhat   A little   Not at all
5. I felt comfortable asking questions or responding to the presenter's questions/comments.
   Very   Somewhat   A little   Not at all
6. I believe that group parent meetings generally are important.
   Very   Somewhat   A little   Not at all
7. Comments:

Figure 10–5	Sample Assessment for a Group Parent Meeting.

Time and date of meeting: _____

Location: _____

Topic: _____

1. The thing I learned that will be most beneficial to me is _____.
2. I wish there had been more information shared about _____.
3. My time and day preferences for future meetings are _____.
4. At a future meeting, I would like to have information shared about _____.
5. Services the school could provide to ensure that I could attend more parent meetings are _____.
6. My suggestions for future parent meetings include _____.

1. Matching designs for parent education to the particular population being served is important. Matching is based on the expressed need of the parents rather than on the perceived needs of those planning the programs. Further, models that individualize programs based on parents'

needs are believed to be more effective than planning group programs to meet each need.

2. Defining the role of the education professional in a way that encourages empowerment of parents is another recent change. The professional who acts as facilitator rather than all-knowing dispenser of knowledge is typically more effective. Understanding of adult learning supports the notion that when parents have a more active role in their education, they are more likely to change their behavior and use strategies that may be more beneficial to their children.

3. Finally, programs of parent education are responding to the notion in bioecological theory that parenting is enhanced when parents have social support and other buffers against stress in their lives. When parents have the support they need, their functioning as parents is strengthened. This idea broadens the notion of parent education for early childhood teachers. Consider not only information about child development, effective guidance strategies, healthy nutrition, and other content traditional in parent education programs but also services that support parents such as parent night out, support groups for single parents, or coordinating the sharing of services such as carpools or children's clothing exchanges.

There is little research to support specific types of parent involvement or parent education practices. Until recently, a belief existed that any kind of parent involvement in early childhood programs, or any content and format for parent education, was certainly preferable to none. This view must be questioned in light of the theoretical basis for the family support movement. Concern about the effects of parent education on both children and families must be emphasized. Family needs and preferences must be identified and implemented in order to provide effective parenting programs with desired outcomes.

When group meetings do not appear to draw parents, formats such as information tables or interactive bulletin boards may be an effective alternative. After conducting needs assessments for topics of interest, teachers and other staff from early childhood programs might select relevant high quality content and display it in a visually appealing format on tables or bulletin boards. Items may be available for parents to either sign out or to take away and keep as needed. Multiple articles or lists of suggestions should be provided in order to meet needs of different age groups and interests. As applicable technology evolves, it is also possible that such formats may be implemented through *Pinterest* or closed groups on *Facebook*.

DAP Current expectations for high-quality early childhood programs universally include the importance of family involvement, but often little detail is given about specific attitudes and strategies that are effective. Based on existing knowledge and theory, Powell (1989) delineates four dimensions that should be incorporated by early childhood teachers into their family involvement plan.

1. Be careful to respond to parents' needs in planning and implementing programs for them. A mismatch, even when the professional believes she is acting in the best interest of children, will not be effective and is likely to subvert the intention.

2. The programs must be managed collaboratively. Using a deficit model that has professionals directly telling clients how to change their parenting is not an effective means of education. Conversations that are respectful and formats that are collaborative are far more effective strategies than those that are based on a perceived expert and amateur.

3. The focus of parent education programs must be balanced on the needs of both children and parents. Using parent education as a way to directly affect child outcomes is risky. Concern for parent needs as well as child needs better serves the entire family. At the same time, sharing details about children's developmental needs should not be overlooked. This balance can be difficult to achieve, and for that reason must be emphasized in planning, implementing, and evaluating the educational program.

4. One aspect of parent education that is frequently sacrificed to time limitations is that of open-ended discussion. Parents' experiences are most often shared and affirmed or disputed with this approach. Open-ended discussion is a strategy that is favored by many participating in adult education; child caregivers who attended training and then participated in focus groups for data collection by a researcher noted that they especially liked the focus groups, even though that strategy was only incidental to the training (Chrisman 1996). The temptation to cut the open-ended discussion in parent meetings is one that leaders should not give into because participants frequently rate this time of the session as one of the most valuable. DAP

METHODS OF PARENT EDUCATION

When early childhood education staff members decide to plan for parenting education for their particular population(s), they may consider several existing programs. Most of these programs have stated objectives so that staff and parent representatives might review several programs and then make choices.

One reliable source of parenting education programs is the federally funded Cooperative Extension programs housed at land grant universities throughout the United States. The University of Michigan has identified over 70 parenting programs that are evidence-based (www.parentinged.msu.edu/Parenting-brCurriculum/tabid/55/Default.aspx). Some of the programs are geared for specific age groups of children, such as 1,2,3,4 Parenting from The Ohio State University and Bright Beginnings from North Dakota State University; others are for situational parenting, such as Grandparents Raising Grandchildren from the University of Illinois and Successful Single Parenting from the University of Missouri.

Parent Education Packages

Two popular parent education packages are based on the theoretical works of Adler (1923) and Dreikurs and Soltz (1964). Both the Systematic Training for Effective Parenting (STEP), created by Dinkmeyer, McKay, and Dinkmeyer (1980), and Active Parenting, created by Popkin (1983), focus on the goal of teaching children responsibility. Strategies for teaching responsibility include the use of natural and logical consequences, reflective listening and I-messages, and democratic family meetings (see Figures 10–6, 10–7, and 10–8).

The Incredible Years is a program not only for parenting education, but also includes skills for teachers and children. It has been widely researched and boasts a strong evidence base for supporting parents in their very important mission with their children. Special attention is given to these populations: high-risk socio-economically disadvantaged families, child protective service required families, and families whose children have conduct disorders, ADHD, and internalizing problems. Viewed as a prevention curriculum, a strong attribute of this program is its attention to child development with four core parenting programs for the following age groups: infants, toddlers, preschoolers, and school-agers. Program materials include DVDs, training manuals, parent books and CDs, and home activities.

In her book, *The Incredible Years: Parents, Teachers, and Children's Training Series,* Carolyn Webster Stratton (2011) notes that the theoretical base for the program includes Piaget's cognitive developmental, Bandura's modeling, Bowlby's attachment, and Patterson's cognitive social learning theories. This program is extraordinary in its emphasis on family and school partnerships, noting that "strong family-school partnerships support children's social, emotional and

Figure 10–6	Summary of STEP.

Reasons parents need training are (1) rapid social change; and (2) increasing social equality for all people. The democratic revolution means adult-centered systems of rewards and punishments no longer fit the needs that humans have to be successful in society. The STEP system, a democratic child-rearing approach, is based on mutual respect between parent and child, and equality in terms of human worth and dignity. That is, children have as much right to be treated with respect as do adults. Two critical components of STEP are communication and encouragement. This system encourages parents to provide opportunities for children to make some decisions and to be responsible for their decisions. The use of natural and logical consequences replaces rewards and punishments.

There are topics for nine group sessions:

1. Understanding Child Behavior and Misbehavior
2. Understanding How Children Use Emotions to Involve Parents and the "Good" Parent
3. Encouragement
4. Communication—Listening
5. Communication—Exploring Alternatives and Expressing Your Ideas and Feelings to Children
6. Developing Responsibility
7. Decision Making for Parents
8. The Family Meeting
9. Developing Confidence and Using Your Potential

Materials in the package include a leader's manual; a parent handbook with problem situations, charts, points to remember, and a personal plan for improving relationships; two video cassettes; a script booklet for videos; a discussion guidelines poster; charts summarizing major concepts and principles; certificates for participants; and publicity aids.

Figure 10–7	Summary of Active Parenting.

Goal—To develop innovative methods of presenting existing effective parenting practices to the millions of parents who can benefit from them.

Based on the Work of—Alfred Adler, Rudolf Dreikurs, Carl Rogers, Robert Carkhuff, and Thomas Gordon.

Two Beliefs about Parenting—(1) Parenting well is extremely important. (2) Parenting well is extremely difficult.

Three Assumptions—(1) Most parents have sufficient love and commitment to parent well. (2) Most parents have not been given sufficient information, skills, or support. (3) This can be disastrous in modern society in which children openly reject traditional parenting methods. "Courage is the greatest gift a parent can give a child." (Alfred Adler)

The following topics are included in six sessions:

1. The Active Parent: concept of equality, styles of parenting, fallacy of reward and punishment, courage, responsibility, cooperation, winning positive relationships
2. Understanding Your Child: how children develop, building blocks of personality, family constellation, understanding behavior, four goals of children's behavior, four mistaken goals of misbehavior, parenting and anger, and helping children use their anger
3. Instilling Courage: what is encouragement?, how parents discipline their own children, turning negatives into positives, how to show confidence, building on strengths, valuing the child as she is, stimulating independence
4. Developing Responsibility: responsibility, freedom and the limits to freedom, the problem-handling method for parents, who owns the problem?, I-messages, natural and logical consequences, mutual respect
5. Winning Cooperation: communication, road to cooperation, avoiding communication blocks, listening actively, listening for feelings, connecting feelings to content, expressing love
6. Democratic Families in Action: family council meeting, six good reasons for regular meetings, how to get started, a word about the agenda, ground rules, emphasizing the family unit

Materials in the package include a leader's manual, a parent handbook, two videocassettes, an action guide (parent workbook), and promotional materials.

academic performance" (p. 24). See Figure 10–9 for details about content for parenting each of the developmental age groups.

Parent Education Books

How to Talk So Kids Will Listen and Listen So Kids Will Talk, created by Faber and Mazlish (1980), is a program of parent education that is intended for parents to use individually. This plan for parents is based on the theoretical work of Haim Ginott (1969) (see Figures 10–10 and 10–11).

Raising Good Children from Birth through the Teenage Years is a parenting resource written by Thomas Lickona (1983). This plan is based on the theoretical work of Kohlberg (1964), emphasizing the importance of child development and how children come to understand the difference between right and wrong (Chrisman and Couchenour 1997) (see Figure 10–12).

Two approaches that are currently being marketed for parents are Assertive Discipline (Canter and Canter 1985) and 1–2–3 Magic (Phelan 1995). Concern about the use of these programs with young children is widespread. Research is not available concerning the effects of either approach; however, best practices in early education generally are in opposition to these plans (see Figures 10–13 and 10–14).

Figure 10–8 Critique of STEP and Active Parenting.

These approaches are very similar and so have similar strengths and areas of concern. Based largely on the work of Alfred Adler, both methods provide excellent information about effectively communicating with children. Family meetings and democratic methods are very good ways to interact respectfully with children.

The notion that children learn responsibility through mutual respect holds up well in existing research. Active Parenting has a broader base and includes ideas from Carl Rogers and others.

A weakness in both packages is that not enough attention is paid to developmental or individual differences in children. Neither do they mention much about cultural differences in families. The strategies seem best for children 6 or older and are likely to be viewed more positively by middle-class or affluent families. Even with these limitations, these packages may be useful to share with parents in your early childhood program. Be sure they understand that this is just one set of useful strategies.

Figure 10–9   The Incredible Years Content for Parenting.

INFANT AND TODDLER PROGRAMS
- Secure attachment with parents
- Language and social expression
- Beginning development of a sense of self

PRESCHOOL PROGRAM
- Encouraging school readiness skills
- Emotional regulation
- Beginning social and friendship skills

SCHOOL AGE PROGRAM
- Encouraging children's independence
- Motivation for academic learning
- Development of family responsibility
- Empathy awareness

Parents as Teachers

Some parent education models for parenting young children are centered on home visitation. The Parents as Teachers (PAT) program, which originated in Missouri (Burkhart 1991), is one such approach. Trained parent educators visit homes soon after the birth of a child. They provide practical details and support to parents concerning the child's needs for optimal development.

Figure 10–10   Highlights of *How to Talk So Kids Will Listen and Listen So Kids Will Talk.*

Based largely on the work of Haim Ginott. Methods of communication affect relationships and children's behavior.

The goals of the authors include finding a way to live with each other so that we can feel good about ourselves and help the people we love feel good about themselves, finding a way to live without blame and recrimination, finding a way to be more sensitive to one another's feelings, finding a way to express our irritation or anger without doing damage, finding a way to be respectful of our children's needs and to be just as respectful of our own needs, finding a way that makes it possible for our children to be caring and responsible, and breaking the cycle of unhelpful talk that has been handed down from generations.

Topics in the book are:

1. **Helping Children Deal with Their Feelings**— Connections between how kids feel and how they behave; when kids feel right, they behave right; adults often deny children's feelings; suggestions provided to help with acknowledging feelings

2. **Engaging Cooperation**—Describe what you see, give information, say it with one word, talk about your feelings, write a note

3. **Alternatives to Punishment**—Point out a way to be helpful, express strong disapproval of inappropriate behavior, state your expectations, show the child how to make amends, give a choice, take action, allow child to experience consequences of misbehavior, problem-solve by talking about child's feelings and needs, brainstorm together, write down all ideas, decide on one and follow through

4. **Encouraging Autonomy**—Let child make choices, show respect for child's struggles, don't ask too many questions, don't rush to answer child's questions, encourage child to use sources outside the home, don't take away hope

5. **Praise**—Praise and self-esteem, describe instead of evaluating, describe what you see and feel, sum up the child's praiseworthy behavior with one word

6. **Freeing Children from Playing Roles**—Look for opportunities to show the child a new picture of herself, put child in situations where she can see herself differently, let child overhear you say something positive about her, model the behavior you want to see, be a storehouse for your child's special moments, state feelings and expectations about child's old behavior

Parents as Teachers is built on two premises.

1. All families have strengths.
2. Parents are the experts on their child.

Home visitors are specially trained and certified through the Parents as Teachers National Center in St. Louis, Missouri. The original program included training for working with families of children from

© Cengage Learning

Figure 10–11	Critique of *How to Talk So Kids Will Listen and Listen So Kids Will Talk.*

This approach offers parents many useful strategies for keeping open communication with their children. These strategies ultimately are likely to help build positive relationships. And positive relationships are an excellent basis for children's developing skill at self-control. The authors of this method are concerned for both parents and children and increasing the quality of family life for each member. Some parents find the strategies a little artificial sounding when they first begin, but that may be because, in general, we lack effective interpersonal capabilities in our society. With practice, many adults feel that the strategies become more natural to them.

Adults place expectations on children, not just for blind compliance to their wishes but also for responsibility in the family. This approach is useful not just for disciplining children, but for all interactions with them. Thus, parents are offered suggestions for their entire relationships with children, not only for disciplining them. This approach is generally viewed as a useful one and is highly recommended.

birth to three years. Additional training is now available for families with three- to five-year-old children. The program is comprised of four components.

1. *Home visits.* Visits by certified home visitors to homes of new parents are individualized. The task of home visitors is to provide child development knowledge and child-rearing information and to support parents in using this material within their family.

2. *Group meetings.* Group meetings are scheduled for times when parents who work outside the home can attend, such as Saturdays or evenings. Often, the focus in a group meeting is on parent-child activities to emphasize the importance of family interaction on the child's development. At meetings, families have opportunities to share successes and concerns about their children and to receive feedback from staff members or outside experts.

3. *Developmental screening.* Parents and parent educators are encouraged to observe and monitor the child's development; these ongoing informal

Figure 10–12	Summary and Critique of *Raising Good Children.*

This approach uses developmental theory and research as a basis for parenting strategies. The underlying theme is noted in this quote, "A child is the only known substance from which a responsible adult can be made."

Lickona assumes that a primary goal for parenting is to foster moral development. He lists 10 big ideas from the moral development approach to parenting:

1. Morality is respect.
2. Kids develop morality slowly and in stages.
3. Respect kids and require respect in return.
4. Teach by example.
5. Teach by telling.
6. Help kids learn to think.
7. Help kids take on real responsibilities.
8. Balance independence and control.
9. Love kids and help them develop a positive self-concept.
10. Foster moral development and a happier family at the same time.

Lickona also offers specific parenting strategies that are supported by child development research for various age groups:

Infancy—Love your baby; provide consistent care; smile and talk to baby often

Toddlerhood—Set reasonable limits; provide space for safe exploration; give choices; only say no when you mean it; ignore undesirable behaviors; use distraction; use logical consequences if necessary

Threes—Teach manners; provide habit of helping; read stories with labels such as "naughty" or "nice," but avoid saying "bad girl"

Fours—Offer choices to give the child practice with making decisions; take time to have fun together; reaffirm old limits and set new ones; require kids to give good reasons; assign chores that give a role in the family

Fives—Be the authority figure children need; fives believe they should obey, so use opportunities to remind them of this belief; reinforce manners and other desirable behavior; begin to teach values about why some things are wrong

Sixes to Eights—Offer explanations and reminders, but be firm; appeal to reciprocity or equal exchange; negotiate and compromise in a spirit of fairness; talk about feelings; help them to know what your expectations are; nurture a loving relationship

Critique—This approach is concerned both with the parent and the outcome to the child. The goal is child centered, in that the short-term and long-term effects of parenting strategies on children are geared toward fostering morality. These approaches are supported by a large body of research literature. Variations by ages of children are helpful to parents. Parents can read short segments of the book related to the particular age of their child. It may be helpful to have a professional who is knowledgeable in child development provide support for parents beginning this approach. This book is highly recommended as an approach to parenting.

Figure 10–13	Summary and Critique of *Assertive Discipline*.

Goal—"To help parents take charge before the problems with their children get out of hand."

The authors state, "Assertive Discipline should be used when your everyday approaches to handling children's behavior haven't worked. If talking with your children, reasoning with them or understanding their feelings doesn't help improve their behavior, then it's time for Assertive Discipline.... Through Assertive Discipline, we will teach you how to take charge in problem situations and let your children know you must be the 'boss.'"

The step-by-step plan for this approach is:

1. Communicate assertively. Avoid arguments and praise children when they behave. This approach attempts to teach parents how to speak assertively, how to use non-verbal messages, how to handle arguing, and how to catch children being good. The authors emphasize the use of praise and "super praise" for desired behavior.

2. Back up your words with actions. Plan how you will respond if they do or do not listen to you. The authors discuss how to use consequences for inappropriate behavior, how to handle "testing," and how to provide positive support.

3. Lay down the law. Set up a systematic Assertive Discipline plan. Use "parent-saver" techniques; conduct a "lay down the law" session with your children. Suggested disciplinary actions for minor behavioral problems:

Separation
Taking away privileges
Physical action to remove child or object
"Do what I want" before you do anything else grounding
Suggested actions for serious behavior problems:
"I am watching you": close monitoring of all behavior, even violating privacy
Tape recording child with sitter or at school
Unannounced visits
Room grounding: no TV, stereo, phone, games or toys; leaving only for school, bathroom, and eating
Out-of-home grounding with a neighbor or relative

Positive consequences for desirable behavior: choosing dessert, extra TV time, a jelly bean, choose a treat, stickers, later curfew, reading a story together, point system, fishing trip with dad

Critique—The field-testing aspect considers only the effects of the approach on parents and children's compliance with parents. No effects on children have been studied. The approach is authoritarian in nature.

Some strategies may be useful for parents, but the Assertive Discipline concept is not recommended by experts in child development. This punishment and reward system does not provide a foundation for children to develop responsibility or respect.

© Cengage Learning

Figure 10–14	Summary and Critique of *1–2–3 Magic*.

Goal—"When you finish with this book, you will know exactly what to do, what not to do, what to say, and what not to say in just about every one of the common everyday problem situations you will run into with your kids."

Phelan states his viewpoint about the role of parents early in the book, "When your kids are little, your house should be a dictatorship where you are the judge and jury." His view of children is stated with a quote from another writer, "'Childhood is a period of transitory psychosis.'" Phelan goes on to explain, "She meant that kids, when they are little, are sort of nuts! They are born unreasonable and selfish, and it is our job—and a teacher's job—to help them become the opposite."

Guidelines for this method:

1. Methods must be used exactly as described in the book.
2. Both parents should use the techniques.
3. Single parents can use the methods effectively by themselves.
4. Grandparents, babysitters, and other caregivers have found the methods helpful.
5. The kids should be in good physical health.

Premises of this approach:

1. To stop behavior, use the 1-2-3 "counting" procedure. "That's 1."

"That's 2."
"That's 3—take 5."

2. To start behavior, choose from six tactics:
Sloppy positive verbal feedback (PVF): praise or reinforcement should be given often.

Kitchen timers: set timer as deadline for starting desired behavior.

Docking system: if you don't do the work, money is docked each time.

Natural consequences.

Charting: give stickers or marks for completing tasks.

Information about active listening, self-esteem, and reflecting feelings is added to chapters near the end of the book. In this section, the author warns parents about the dangers of overusing the 1-2-3 counting approach and suggests the importance of listening to their children. However, when the listening turns into an attack by the child, parents are urged to count.

Critique—In this approach to parenting, adults have all of the responsibility to control children, with children being given very little opportunity to develop self-control.

A great deal of research shows that children who are parented primarily through a punishment and reward system do not develop a sense of responsibility or conscience.

© Cengage Learning

assessments often provide useful information about the child's progress or developmental delays. Formal screenings are conducted annually beginning at one year of age. When problems are identified in children's development, parents are helped with resources for appropriate forms of intervention.

4. *Connections with community resources.* Parent educators assist parents in making connections with resources in their particular communities. Examples of possible resources include libraries, health clinics, and programs for children with identified special needs (http://www.parentsasteachers.org, accessed July 4, 2006).

Evaluation research completed on Parents as Teachers (PAT) over the past 15 years confirms the following:

- At age three, children enrolled in this program were significantly more advanced in language, problem solving, and social development than comparison children.

- Children who participated for at least one year scored higher on the Kindergarten Inventory of Developmental Skills than others.

- At the end of first grade, PAT children scored higher on standardized reading and math tests than others.

- In fourth grade, PAT graduates scored higher than the control group on the Stanford Achievement Test.

- By age three, more than half of PAT children with observed developmental delays were on target for expected typical development.

- Even when PAT children and families have many characteristics associated with high risk for educational failure, the children are placing above national norms (http://www.parentsasteachers.org, retrieved July 4, 2006).

Recently, the Parents as Teachers National Center launched a new initiative in the form of a revision of the curriculum with a neuroscience base. This use of new research on brain development is an exemplary model of an existing program adding new scientific advances. The revised design has been named The Born to Learn Curriculum. Currently, assessments are being conducted to measure results of this approach to Parents as Teachers (http://www.parentsasteachers.org).

For more information:

Parents as Teachers National Center
St. Louis, Missouri
(314) 432-4330
http://www.parentsasteachers.org/

Home Instruction Program for Preschool Youngsters

Home Instruction Program for Preschool Youngsters (HIPPY) was developed by the National Council of Jewish Women in Jerusalem in 1969. HIPPY USA was started in 1984 in Tulsa, Oklahoma. This national network provides training and assists local communities with start-up materials. Funding for HIPPY USA comes mostly from three sources: training service fees, royalties from the sale of curriculum materials, and grants from foundations and corporations (http://www.hippyusa.org/, retrieved July 4, 2006).

In this parent education program, paraprofessionals are trained to provide services to families in their homes. The emphasis is on helping parents prepare their three-, four-, and five-year-old children to succeed in school. Storybooks, creative games, and activity packets are shared by paraprofessionals in home visits and at group meetings. Parents practice the activities with paraprofessionals before using them with their children (http://www.hippyusa.org/, retrieved July 4, 2006).

Starting a HIPPY program in a local community involves the seven following steps:

1. Review HIPPY program requirements.
2. Conduct need assessment in local community.
3. Hold a preliminary meeting with community leaders and other interested parties.
4. Secure funding from local and state sources.
5. Submit application to HIPPY USA.
6. Hire or assign a training coordinator.
7. Sign an agreement with HIPPY USA.

HIPPY USA claims the following benefits for children, parents, and the paraprofessionals involved in the program.

For children:

- Skill development
- Confidence
- Better adapted to the classroom when they begin school

For parents:

- Increased sense of their own abilities
- Satisfaction of teaching their children
- Excitement of seeing children's development
- A time for fun and learning with their children
- A positive relationship with another adult (paraprofessional) who cares about them and their children
- Connection with other agencies in the community

For paraprofessionals, many who have been parents in the program previously:

- An opportunity to help others in a leadership capacity
- Often a first job
- A step to a permanent job elsewhere

For more information:

HIPPY USA
220 East 23rd Street
New York, NY 10010
(212) 532-7730
http://www.hippyusa.org

Evaluation research on HIPPY programs in the United States confirms the following information:

- In second grade, children who had participated in HIPPY were higher on school performance and in teacher ratings of motivation and adaptation to the classroom.
- HIPPY children had fewer absences.
- HIPPY children were perceived by their teachers as better students.
- Through parent training in specific techniques for book reading, HIPPY children had higher involvement and interest in this activity.

HIPPY emphasizes growth for parents and paraprofessionals at least as much as it does for children. There seems to be even greater evidence for the success of the program with adults than with children. HIPPY USA suggests that future research focus on needed improvements in the program as well as details about variations required by local communities (http://www.hippyusa.org/, retrieved July 4, 2006).

FAMILY LIFE EDUCATION

Family life education incorporates a broader view of the needs of families. In addition to support for parenting, family life education includes a broader scope of marriage, family relationships, sex education, and work-family issues (Darling 1987). Family life education is currently driven by ecological theory, emphasizing "wholeness and integration." The family life approach places skills and knowledge about parenting in the context of all of family life, thus making it a broad and diverse approach (see Figures 10–15 and 10–16).

Figure 10–15 Family Life Education Substance Areas for CFLE.

1. Families in Society includes marital choice, minority families, gender roles, work, and family.
2. Internal Dynamics of Families includes family stress and crises, conflict management, violence, special needs in families.
3. Human Growth and Development over the Life Span includes prenatal and infancy through adulthood and aging.
4. Human Sexuality includes biological determinants, sexual values and decision making, sexual response and dysfunction.
5. Interpersonal Relationships including communication skills, romance, intimacy, and responsibility.
6. Family Resource Management includes goal setting, allocation of resources, consumer issues, and decisions.
7. Parent Education and Guidance includes parenting rights, practices, variations, and roles across the life cycle.
8. Family Law and Public Policy includes social services, education, taxes, civil rights, and economic support laws.
9. Ethics includes social attitudes and values, our pluralistic society, social consequences of choices, and technological changes.
10. Family Life Education Methodology includes planning, implementing, and evaluating effective techniques.

© Cengage Learning

Figure 10–16 Griggs' Criteria for Evaluating Family Life Education Material.

Evaluation of a family life education program should consider the following:

- Accuracy of content
- Clear presentation
- Nonjudgmental tone
- Logical organization
- Interesting and challenging material
- Relation to existing goals, objectives, or outcomes
- Appealing format
- Absence of sexism, racism, or cultural bias
- Appropriate level for intended participants
- Active learning
- Reflection of various stages of family life cycle
- Recognition of variations in family structure
- Acknowledgement of changing roles of family members

© Cengage Learning

Family life education, when incorporated into early childhood teacher education, would lead to discussions and the generation of knowledge about the following themes:

- Challenges of families from varying socioeconomic backgrounds and how these situations affect involvement of families in their children's education

- Apprehension of families from differing ethnic, religious, racial, and sexual orientation backgrounds about their place in the culture of the school

- Effects of stressors facing families such as divorce, remarriage, and death as families establish relationships with school officials

- Strategies for sensitively including various family forms, such as foster parents, grandparents, and other extended family members who serve as parents or guardians (Coleman and Churchill 1997)

One example of a focus area for Certified Family Life Educators (CFLEs) is military family relocation, separation and deployment, and reunion (Drummet, Coleman, and Cable 2003). Specific content areas for family life educators to address in their work with military families include the following:

Consider This

Choose 2 of the 10 themes in Figure 10–15 that you believe you might be able to provide information about for families. Select 2 others that you would need to search for information in order to share with families. Where would you search for the information?

A. Culture

1. Military culture requires total commitment from military members as well as their family members. Confidentiality does not apply to doctor-patient or counselor-client relationships, making formal interventions questionable for those in the military. Family life educators could assist with formation of self-help or support groups with proximity to military bases.

2. Military communities are ethnically diverse. Locations of bases and required relocations and deployments make it difficult to stay in close touch with family members. Also, racism, sexism, and other biases may be problematic depending on the region to which military members have been deployed. Family life educators can provide an essential educational service by sharing information

about the local culture, long-distance measures of staying in touch with families as well as ways to make the most of living in an unfamiliar culture.

B. Separation

1. Issues related to separation vary by and are influenced by family structure: single parents, dual military families, one parent military and other civilian, and others. Family life educators must demonstrate sensitivity to these variations by assessing each family's needs and providing assistance to the military in developing surveys to get information that would assist retention efforts.

2. Separations affect finances of military families. Family life educators can assist families to plan ahead with separation plans so that legal (power of attorney), medical (for dependent children), and ongoing financial commitment (housing, food, utilities, credit debts) issues can be handled in their absence. Also, family life educators can assist parents who are separated from their young children to maintain contact with the children and their caregivers.

C. Methods of Communication

1. Reliable communication is necessary for military families to maintain cohesiveness with their military family member. Family life educators sometimes hold workshops for family members about maintaining communication. They encourage methods such as having the deployed family member tape record a number of stories for children to listen to as they desire and creating family scrapbooks of pictures and stories that families can "read" and remember happy times together. Family life educators can also encourage children to keep scrapbooks of their activities so that when the military family member returns, they can share together what might have been missed on a daily basis.

2. Gaining information about the safety and well-being of deployed military members is not always an easy process. Family life educators encourage family members to attend sessions held by the military for pre-deployment.

D. Employment Needs of Military Spouses

1. Because military members are deployed or relocated without much notice, spouses often are faced with career dilemmas that can lead the family to be dissatisfied with military life. Family life educators can provide various forms of assistance in this area, such as helping military spouses link with related Internet sources as well as jobs that are done primarily online. Also, collaboration

with the military decision makers regarding the importance of programs to address issues related to spousal employment would help support families.

E. Assistance with Relocation

1. First, military families need to know choices about housing for their upcoming relocations. Information about types of housing, community resources, and schools can help soften the challenges of forced relocation. Family life educators might help set up networks of families, communities, and military personnel to provide such information.

2. Financial aspects of relocating create challenges for many military families. Family life educators often provide workshops on budgeting and debt management as well as establishing networks of trained peer financial counselors.

F. Programs for Relocated Children

1. As children relocate with their military families, they face frequent adjustments to new communities and especially to new schools. Family life educators might set up a system for supporting children's adjustment that would include family tours of schools and collaborating with school staff to create buddy systems for children new to the community. Buddies might be put into place even before the relocation so that a social connection is made prior to the move.

G. Assistance with Family Adjustment During Reunion Periods

1. Military families, often overcome with joy at the knowledge of an impending reunion, may be surprised at the challenges they face with this transition. Family life educators can make families cognizant of the ups and downs often realized during times of reunion, and they can also establish support groups on a base or in a nearby community to support families in this specific transition (Drummet, Coleman, and Cable 2003).

This example of ways in which family life educators can support military families is only one of the many avenues served by highly qualified CFLEs. Their knowledge base and skills can be applied to many diverse family life circumstances in ways to help families navigate through difficulties to successful outcomes.

The National Council of Family Relations (NCFR) sponsors the only national program to certify family life educators (CFLE). Family life education provides skills and knowledge to enrich individual and family life. For more information about family life education, go to http://www.ncfr.org/ and click "CFLE Certification."

THE ROLE OF EARLY CHILDHOOD EDUCATORS IN PARENT EDUCATION AND FAMILY LIFE EDUCATION

naeyc 6 Early childhood professionals must not presume to know the needs of their particular families in terms of parenting support and family life education. Instead, teachers might suggest possibilities for changes in parenting approaches by having families complete needs assessments. Families should always have a voice in the content and format of educational opportunities made available to them.

It is the responsibility of early childhood teachers to be aware of the pros and cons of any parent or family life education offered to families. If a packaged program is used, discuss the downside of the program as reviewed by experts in the field. An important role for early childhood educators is to be aware of existing research related to parenting support and child development in order to ably critique selected programs or publications. Also, ask parents what they like about and find useful in the program as well as what is less appealing to them. Together, consider ways to adjust programs for best results. **naeyc** 6

Topics for Parenting Support

In this section, 14 topics for parenting support that are recommended for inclusion in most early childhood education settings are discussed. Nine topics deal with play, developmentally appropriate practice, positive guidance, limiting television, homework, early brain development, family literacy, childhood obesity, and financial responsibility. These seem to be frequently requested from parents and staff. The remaining topic, healthy sexuality development, is not one that is often discussed by either parents or staff. However, it is included in this book because recent research (Couchenour and Chrisman 1996; Couchenour, Chrisman, and Gottshall 1997; Chrisman, Gottshall, Koons, and Couchenour 1998) found that early childhood teachers do not believe they have enough preparation in this area or that family involvement is required when this topic is addressed in early childhood education programs.

For each of the topics, a variety of formats may be used for dissemination. Some strategies for educating parents about these topics with the information provided herein include sections of parent handbooks, orientation sessions, workshops, newsletters, brochures, videotapes prepared so that parents can check them out at their convenience, mini-conferences with several speakers, or panel discussions. Use of several formats or strategies for any one topic is likely to increase the effectiveness of supporting parents. Early education staff may also wish to divide any of the topics into smaller segments for any one session or strategy.

Topic One: The Value of Play for Young Children

Purpose   To explain to parents of children enrolled in an early childhood program the value of play to all areas of children's development, including physical, cognitive, social, and emotional. (Placing a list of outcomes for children at each learning center is helpful for parents as they volunteer in the classroom or simply learn about child development.)

Goals for Parents

1. To explain how children learn through play and that play is a child's work.

2. To articulate a definition and list the characteristics of play.

3. To describe what children learn as they play in various learning centers around the classroom and outdoors. Examples are:

   Dramatic play—Vocabulary development, cooperation, role identification, and concept development
   Blocks—Spatial relationships, problem solving, patterning, measurement, creativity, cooperation, and vocabulary development

4. To observe and facilitate play in home settings.

Concepts to Highlight

1. Children learn very effectively through play.

2. Play has the following characteristics:
   a. It is intrinsically motivated.
   b. It is the child's choice.
   c. It is active.
   d. It is child directed.
   e. It is fun.

3. Teachers have the following responsibilities regarding play:
   a. It is planned.
   b. It meets the needs of children.
   c. Space is organized for safety and best educational results.
   d. Ample time is allocated in the daily schedule for effective learning through play.
   e. The teacher interacts with children during play in ways that support the child's choices.

4. Play fosters physical development. Both large muscles and small muscles are used for increased gross motor and fine motor skills.

5. Play fosters cognitive development. Children, who from two to seven years are master players, are likely to become master workers soon after that, often during third grade.

6. Play fosters social development. Cooperation is required to play well with other children. Sometimes, children lead and sometimes they follow when they play. Children take on a variety of different roles when they play.

7. Play fosters emotional development. Children gain the ability to express themselves in a variety of appropriate ways. Self-esteem is enhanced through play.

8. Stages of play related to social development are solitary, parallel, associative, and cooperative.

9. Stages of play related to intellectual development are sensorimotor or practice, constructive, dramatic (or pretend), and games with rules.

10. Effective practice in early childhood education emphasizes play as a useful method for teaching and learning.

11. The teacher's role for fostering children's play includes setting up the environment and interacting in ways that enhance the play.

Resources

Dimidjian, V. J., ed. 1992. *Play's place in public education for young children*. Washington, DC: National Education Association.

IPAUSA.org. *The American Association for the child's right to play*. http://www.ipausa.org/ (accessed January 26, 2006).

Jones, E., and G. Reynolds. 1992. *The play's the thing: Teachers' roles in children's play*. New York: Teachers College Press.

Children learn effectively through play

National Network for Child Care.1994. *Play is the business of kids.* http://www.nncc.org/Curriculum/better.play.html (accessed January 26, 2006).

Rogers, C. S., and J. K. Sawyers.1988. *Play in the lives of children.* Washington, DC: National Association for the Education of Young Children.

Sawyers, J. K., and C. S. Rogers. 1988. *Helping young children develop through play: A practical guide for parents, caregivers, and teachers.* Washington, DC: National Association for the Education of Young Children.

Wasserman, S. 1990. *Serious players in the primary classroom: Empowering children through active learning experiences.* New York: Teachers College Press.

Topic Two: What Is Developmentally Appropriate Practice?

Purpose To provide for parents of children enrolled in an early education program the meaning of the term *developmentally appropriate practice*

Goals for Parents

1. To define and explain the term *developmentally appropriate practice*

2. To understand the role of professionals in planning, implementing, and assessing developmentally appropriate educational practice

3. To discuss the importance of school, family, and community partnerships in fostering high-quality programs for young children

Concepts to Highlight

1. Definition of developmentally appropriate practice in early childhood education is three-pronged:

    a. Understanding of child development and learning

    b. Attention to individual differences in children's strengths, interests, and needs

    c. Knowledge of each child's social and cultural contexts

2. The role of early childhood professionals is expansive:

    a. To create a caring community of learners

    b. To enhance children's development and learning

    c. To construct appropriate curriculum for the group and for individual children

    d. To authentically assess each child's development and learning

    e. To establish reciprocal relationships with families

3. Developmentally appropriate practices consider all areas of children's development: physical, cognitive and language, social, and emotional

4. It is necessary to understand the inaccuracy of common myths about the meaning of developmentally appropriate practice, including:

    a. There is only one way to implement developmentally appropriate programs.

    b. Developmentally appropriate classrooms are unstructured, chaotic.

    c. Teachers do not plan or teach anything in a developmentally appropriate classroom.

    d. Developmentally appropriate practice requires that existing curricula be "watered down" and that children fall behind academically.

    e. Academics have no place in developmentally appropriate programs.

    f. Developmental appropriateness is just a fad, soon to be replaced by another fad.

5. A variety of teaching and learning strategies are used in developmentally appropriate practices, including play, small groups, large groups, cooperative learning, and direct instruction. No one method is relied on exclusively; methods are based on how children learn.

Resources

Bredekamp, S., and C. Copple. 1997. *Developmentally appropriate practice in early childhood programs,* rev. ed. Washington, DC: National Association for the Education of Young Children.

Clemens, S. G. 1983. *The sun's not broken, a cloud's just in the way: On child-centered teaching.* Mt. Ranier, MD: Gryphon House.

The role of the early childhood professional is to enhance children's development and learning

Conant, B. *Answers to commonly asked questions concerning developmentally appropriate practices.* http://www.users.stargate.net/~cokids/dapQnA.html (accessed January 26, 2006).

Developmentally appropriate practice in early childhood programs. 1998. http://www.naeyc.org/about/positions/pdf/PSDAP98.PDF (accessed January 26, 2006).

Dodge, D. T., and T. S. Bickart. 1998. *Preschool for parents: What every parent needs to know about preschool.* Naperville, IL: Sourcebooks.

Kostelnik, M. J. 1992. Myths associated with developmentally appropriate programs. *Young Children* 47: 17–23.

Mr. Rogers talks with parents. [videotape, 43 min.]. Washington, DC: National Association for the Education of Young Children.

National Association for the Education of Young Children. *Ten signs of a great preschool.* http://www.naeyc.org/ece/1996/01.asp (accessed January 26, 2006).

Whole language learning. [videotape, 20 min.]. Washington, DC: National Association for the Education of Young Children.

Topic Three: Positive Guidance

Purpose   To explain to parents that discipline is a tool for children's learning and not only about submitting to adult expectations

Goals for Parents

1. To understand that when they guide or discipline children, they affect the whole child

2. To explain that children learn appropriate behaviors through adult modeling and teaching

3. To describe the effects of various types of discipline on children's development

4. To foster strategies of positive guidance in their own parenting

Concepts to Highlight

1. Positive guidance approaches teach children appropriate behaviors.

2. Positive guidance demonstrates respect to children and models respectful interactions.

3. Positive guidance teaches children to appreciate themselves and others as worthwhile individuals.

4. Positive guidance helps children to use conflict resolution strategies as they interact with other children.

5. Positive guidance considers reasons for children's misbehavior or mistaken behaviors.

6. Positive guidance uses a proactive approach, including creating an environment conducive to learning and less likely to cause children's misbehaviors.

7. Positive guidance creates positive relationships between children and adults as adults model respectful behaviors.

8. Strategies for positive guidance help to build partnerships between parents and teachers.

9. Positive guidance nurtures peacemaking and justice.

10. Positive guidance provides opportunities to resolve conflicts in nonviolent ways.

11. Punishment produces harmful consequences to young children.

12. Punishment does not teach children appropriate behaviors.

Resources

Condon, C., and J. McGinnis. 1988. *Helping kids care.* Oak Park, IL: Meyer-Stone Books and the Institute for Peace and Justice.

Gartrell, D. 2007. *A guidance approach for the encouraging classroom*, 4th ed. Clifton Park, NY: Thomson Delmar Learning.

Gartrell, D. 2003. *The power of guidance: Teaching social-emotional skills in early childhood classrooms.* Clifton Heights, NY: Delmar.

Honig, A. S. 1996. *Behavior guidance for infants and toddlers.* Little Rock, AR: Southern Early Childhood Association.

Kaiser, B., and J. S. Rasminsky. 1999. *Meeting the challenge: Effective strategies for challenging behaviours in early childhood environments.* Ontario, Canada: Canadian Child Care Federation.

McGinnis, K., and B. Oehlberg. 1988. *Starting out right: Nurturing young children as peacemakers.* Oak Park, IL: Meyer-Stone Books and the Institute for Peace and Justice.

Nunnelley, J. C. 2002. *Powerful, positive and practical practices: Behavior guidance strategies.* Little Rock, AR: Southern Early Childhood Association.

Topic Four: Limiting Television

Purpose   To help parents understand that young children are particularly vulnerable to potentially harmful effects of too much television viewing

Goals for Parents

1. To be aware of what the potentially harmful effects of watching too much television are

2. To be sensitized to the effects of television violence on young children

3. To identify high-quality children's programming and videos

4. To create alternatives to television/video viewing

5. To plan for family viewing time

Concepts to Highlight

1. Television has a lot of power to influence children's thinking and behavior.

2. Children may become less caring and more fearful when they view too much television violence.

3. Adults have a responsibility to protect children from possible harmful effects of television. Set clear limits and rules about television watching.

4. Parents should monitor all of children's television viewing. It's okay to ban programs that are unacceptable.

5. There is more violence in programming now than when parents were children.

6. When children watch television, they are missing out on play and social experiences that are important to their development.

7. Schools and families can work together to decrease television viewing and to increase better alternative activities for children.

8. Letter-writing campaigns to stations and companies that advertise can be organized by school, family, and community partnerships.

Resources

Healthy habits for TV, video games, and the Internet. Kids Health for Parents. http://kidshealth.org/parent/positive/family/tv_habits.html (accessed January 26, 2006).

Horton, J., and J. Zimmer. 1994. *Media violence and children: A guide for parents.* [brochure]. Washington, DC: National Association for the Education of Young Children.

Levin, D. E. 1998. *Remote control childhood? Combating the hazards of media culture.* Washington, DC: National Association for the Education of Young Children.

Television and children. Child Development Institute. http://www.childdevelopmentinfo.com/health_safety/television.html (accessed January 26, 2006).

Topic Five: Homework

Purpose To help parents understand reasons and expectations for homework in the primary grades

Goals for Parents

1. To explain the purpose of homework for primary children

2. To understand parents' role in helping with homework

3. To implement effective strategies for assisting children with homework

Concepts to Highlight

1. Two common reasons for homework in primary grades:

   a. To practice skills

   b. To collect information, or observe something at home or out of the school setting

2. Homework teaches responsibility and good work habits.

3. A reasonable amount of homework time for first through third grades is 15 to 30 minutes.

4. Strategies for helping children with homework include:

   a. Reminders

   b. Setting up a quiet place to work

   c. Scheduling time to do homework before other activities

   d. Communicating with teachers about expectations and how homework is used at school

Resources

Bickart, T. S., D. T. Dodge, and J. R. Jablon. 1997. *What every parent needs to know about 1st, 2nd, & 3rd grades: An essential guide to your child's education.* Naperville, IL: Sourcebooks.

Homework. Olney, MD: Association for Childhood Education International. http://www.acei.org/brochure.htm (accessed December 26, 2006).

National Education Association. Help your student get the most out of homework. http://www.nea.org/parents/homework.html?mode=print (accessed January 26, 2006).

National PTA National Standards for Parent/Family Involvement Programs. 1998. http://www.pta.org/programs/ (accessed November 25, 1998).

PBS Parents. Supporting your learner: Helping with homework. http://www.pbs.org/parents/goingtoschool/_helping_homework.html (accessed January 26, 2006).

Topic Six: Healthy Sexuality Development

Purpose To help parents understand that early sexuality development is related to all areas of children's development: physical, cognitive, social, and emotional

Goals for Parents

1. To have an awareness of typical behaviors or questions young children have related to sexuality

2. To relate their own discomfort with discussions of sexuality

3. To use appropriate responses to foster healthy sexuality in their children

Concepts to Highlight

1. Sexuality is about who we are, not just a set of behaviors.

2. Children are curious about sexuality, just as they are about almost everything else they encounter.

3. Some aspects of sexuality relate to physical development:

   a. Body functions

   b. Male/female differences

   c. Body parts

   d. Pleasant sensations

4. Some aspects of sexuality relate to social development:

   a. Gender roles

   b. Identification of gender

   c. Social relationships with those of same and opposite gender

5. Some aspects of sexuality relate to emotional development:

   a. High self-esteem is related to feeling good about who you are.

   b. Affection is learned in early family relationships.

   c. Empathy and respect are required for successful relationships.

6. Some aspects of sexuality relate to cognitive development:

   a. Understanding of facts about reproduction

   b. Understanding of family and cultural values about sexuality

   c. Understanding why one is labeled a boy or a girl

7. Teachers and parents must work together to create appropriate responses for fostering healthy sexuality development in young children.

8. Fostering healthy sexuality can be a barrier to sexual abuse.

Resources

Chrisman, K., and D. Couchenour. 2002. *Healthy sexuality development: A guide for early childhood educators and families*. Washington, DC: National Association for the Education of Young Children.

Couchenour, D., and K. Chrisman. 1996. Healthy sexuality development in young children. *Dimensions of Early Childhood* 24: 30–36.

Lively, V., and E. Lively. 1991. *Sexual development of young children*. Clifton Park, NY: Delmar Learning.

Sexuality and U. The development of sexuality from infancy to puberty: Developmental outcomes, common behaviors, concerns, and learning objectives. http://www.sexualityandu.ca/eng/health/SCD/ (accessed January 26, 2006).

Sexuality Information and Education Council of the United States (SIECUS). Families are talking: SIECUS resources for families. http://www.familiesaretalking.org/resources/rsrc0000.html (accessed January 26, 2006).

Wilson, P. M. 1991. *When sex is the subject: Attitudes and answers for young children*. Santa Cruz, CA: Network Publications.

Topic Seven: Early Brain Development
Purpose   To help parents understand the importance of brain development in the early years of a child's life

Goals for Parents

1. To have an awareness of typical brain development

2. To know some implications of brain development theory for families

Concepts to Highlight

1. The importance of multisensory play in brain development

2. The importance of conversation, singing, and language

3. The negative effects of unmonitored television viewing

4. The relationship between emotional development and healthy brain development

Resources

Good Beginnings Alliance. Early brain development. http://www.goodbeginnings.org/brain.htm (accessed January 26, 2006).

Healy, J. M. 1994. *Your child's growing mind: A practical guide to brain development and learning from birth to adolescence*. New York: Doubleday.

National Association for the Education of Young Children. Early years are learning years. http://www.naeyc.org/ece/eyly (accessed December 26, 2006).

Nebraska's Early Childhood Training Center. Early brain development. http://www.esu3.org/ectc/brain.html (accessed January 26, 2006).

Parents' Action for Children. Brain development. http://www.iamyourchild.org/learn/parenting/development/braindevelopment/ (accessed January 26, 2006).

Topic Eight: Family Literacy
Purpose   To help parents understand ways to support literacy development at home

Goals for Parents

1. To have an awareness of the importance of reading to, with, and being a role model for children

2. To understand the importance of providing books, writing materials, and other literacy supports during early childhood

3. To be able to discern fads or gimmicks from age-appropriate literacy stories

Concepts to Highlight

1. Singing, playing, and reading to and with your children are important literacy strategies.

2. Making time to read together each day is important.

3. Talking with your child and responding to your child's sounds, words, and questions is important for language development.

Resources

Herb, S., and S. Willoughby-Herb. 2002. *Connecting fathers, children, and reading.* New York: Neal-Schuman.

National Association for Education of Young Children and the International Reading Association. 1998. *Raising a reader, raising a writer.* Washington, DC: National Association for the Education of Young Children.

National Center for Family Literacy. http://www.famlit .org/ (accessed January 26, 2006). http://www .pabook.libraries.psu.edu/familylit/defaul.html (accessed January 25, 2006).

Topic Nine: Childhood Obesity

Purpose To help parents understand the long-term health concerns associated with childhood obesity as well as to provide strategies for families to increase children's health and wellness

Goals for Parents

1. To know the definition of obesity in children

2. To gain an awareness of the long-term health risks associated with childhood obesity

3. To be prepared to implement ways to increase children's activity levels.

4. To obtain a variety of healthy meal and snack suggestions

Concepts to Highlight

1. The ability to recognize characteristics of childhood obesity at different developmental stages in children

2. An understanding of serious medical risks associated with childhood obesity

3. How families can implement exercise and fitness regimens

4. Healthy nutrition through the use of the new food pyramid, with emphasis on daily foods such as fruits and vegetables, protein and calcium sources, and fatty snacks as occasional food choices

5. How schools/centers and families can work together to battle childhood obesity

6. Recess and outdoor play during the school day is important for children's overall health and wellness

7. The vital role of educators in teaching children about healthy food choices and physical activity

Resources

American Heart Association. Exercise (physical activity) and children. http://www.americanheart.org/ presenter.jhtml?identifier=4596 (accessed January 26, 2006).

KidsHealth. The food guide pyramid. http://kidshealth .org/kid/stay_healthy/food/pyramid.html (accessed January 26, 2006).

Kid Source. Childhood obesity. http://www.kidsource .com/kidsource/content2/obesity.html (accessed January 26, 2006).

Mayo Clinic. Childhood obesity: What parents can do. http://www.mayoclinic.com/health/child hood-obesity/FL00058 (accessed January 26, 2006).

MyPyramid.gov. Steps to a healthier you. United States Department of Agriculture. http://www.mypyramid .gov/ (accessed January 26, 2006).

Promoting physical activity and exercise among children. 1998. *ERIC Digest.* http://www.ericdigests. org/1998-2/exercise.htm (accessed January 26, 2006).

Topic Ten: Teaching Financial Responsibility

Purpose To help parents understand ways that they can teach their children how to manage money and to make financial decisions

Goals for Parents

1. To increase understanding about how children learn financial responsibility

2. To discuss spending, saving, making financial decisions, and being a wise consumer

Concepts to Highlight

1. The difference between wants and needs

2. Setting good examples for being wise consumers and good financial managers

3. Discussion of family budgets to help children understand how money works

4. Deciding on children's allowances and how to help them spend, save, and share

5. The relationship of work to earning money

6. Planning ahead by budgeting

7. Understanding the role of financial institutions with families

Resources

Children and money. Institute of Consumer Financial Education. http://www.financial-education-icfe.org/children_and_money/index.asp (accessed July 4, 2006).

Managing money: Needs vs. wants. PBS Kids. http://pbskids.org/itsmylife/money/managing/article2.html (accessed July 4, 2006).

McKinnon, S. 2004. Allow an allowance. *Consumer Economics Update*. University of Missouri Extension. http://extension.missouri.edu/ceupdate (accessed July 4, 2006).

Social Studies for Kids. n.d. Want vs. need: Basic economics. http://www.socialstudiesforkids.com/articles/economics/wantsandneeds1.htm (accessed July 4, 2006).

Topic Eleven: Bullying

Purpose   To increase parents' knowledge about bullying and effective intervention strategies when bullying occurs

Goals for Parents

1. To increase knowledge about bullying behavior

2. To be familiar with effective bullying intervention strategies

Concepts to Highlight

1. Definition of bullying behavior

2. Effects of bullying on victims

3. Characteristics of children who bully

4. Effective prevention strategies for children and adults

5. The necessity of intervening in bullying situations

Resources

Committee for Children. www.cfchildren.com (accessed May 26, 2009).

Gartrell, D., and Gartrell, J. J. 2008. Guidance matters: Understand bullying. *Young Children Beyond the Journal*. http://journal.naeyc.org/btj/200805/BTJGuidanceMatters.asp (accessed May 26, 2009).

The Ophelia Project. www.opheliaproject.org/main/index.htm (accessed May 26, 2009).

Stop bullying now! Health Resources and Services Administration. U.S. Department of Health and Human Services. www.stopbullyingnow.hrsa.gov/ (accessed May 26, 2009).

Topic Twelve: Family Involvement in Children's Education

Purpose   To increase parents' knowledge about important outcomes of involvement in their children's education and to provide various methods of involvement

Goals for Parents

1. To increase knowledge about family involvement in children's education

2. To be familiar with a variety of ways that families can be involved

Concepts to Highlight

1. Explain the meaning of family involvement.

2. Share research evidence that supports family involvement.

3. Discuss positive outcomes for children, parents, and teachers related to family involvement.

4. Strong families are important to strong schools.

5. Partnerships among families, schools, and communities benefit children's school and life success.

6. Early childhood educators work to empower family members.

Resources

Couchenour, D., and K. Chrisman. 2008. *Families, schools and communities: Together for young children*. Clifton Park, NY: Delmar Cengage.

Diffily, D., and M. Morrison, ed.1996. *Family-friendly communication for early childhood programs*. Washington, DC: National Association for the Education of Young Children.

Family and community. North Central Regional Education Laboratory. www.ncrel.org (accessed May 26, 2009).

Family involvement in early childhood education. Harvard Family Research Project. www.hfrp.org/publications-resources/browse-our-publications/family-involvement-in-early-childhood-education (accessed May 26, 2009).

National Coalition for Parent Involvement in Education (NCPIE). www.ncpie.org (accessed May 26, 2009).

National Standards Implementation Guide. National PTA. www.pta.org/Documents/National_Standards_Implementation_Guide_2009.pdf (accessed May 26, 2009).

Topic 13: Socialization

Purpose To assist parenting family members in understanding their role in the socialization of children. Socialization includes the relationship of parental behaviors, beliefs, and reactions to children's social behaviors including compliance, moral reasoning, aggression, prosocial skills, gender role development, and achievement.

Goals for Parents

1. To understand the relationship between parental behaviors and children's behaviors

2. To understand developmental differences in social abilities and motivation

3. To recognize positive ways of encouraging children's social behaviors

4. To increase skills in supporting children's positive social behaviors

Concepts to Highlight

1. Developmental sequence of young children's social and emotional progress according to Erikson's theory (trust, autonomy, initiative, industry)

2. Children are born hard-wired to be social

3. Relationship of parental attitudes and behaviors to children's behaviors

4. Phrases that offer encouragement versus praise

5. How emotional development and sense of self contribute to prosocial behaviors

6. Understand and responding to differences in children's temperaments

7. Children's self-worth is based on positive relationships with caregivers and opportunities to increase their own competence

8. Understand the relationship between social and emotional development and children's academic success

Resources

Center on the Social and Emotional Foundations for Early Learning. http://csefel.vanderbilt.edu. Click on "Family Tools". Accessed April 6, 2012.

Darling, N. 1999. Parenting style and its correlates. ERIC Digest. ED427896. www.ericdigests.org/1999-4/parenting.htm Accessed April 6, 2012.

DeBord, K. n.d. Growing together: Preschooler development. North Carolina Cooperative Extension. www.ces.ncsu.edu/depts/fcs/pdfs/fcs454.pdf Accessed April 6, 2012.

Gartrell, D. 2003. *The power of guidance: Teaching social-emotional skills in early childhood classrooms.* Clifton Heights, NY: Delmar.

Hyson, M. 2003. *The Emotional Development of Young Children: Building an Emotion-Centered Curriculum.* New York: Teachers College Press.

Oliver, K. K. 2002. Understanding your child's temperament. Ohio State University Extension. http://ohioline.osu.edu/flm02/FS05.html Accessed April 6, 2012.

Raver, C. C. 2003. Young children's emotional development and school readiness. ERIC Digest. ED477641. www.ericdigests.org/2004-1/young.htm Accessed April 6, 2012.

Zero to Three: Free Parent Brochures and Guides. www.zerotothree.org. Click on "Behavior and Development." See: "Challenging Behaviors," "Early Childhood Mental Health," "Early Development," "Play," "Promoting Social Emotional Development," "Temperament and Behavior." Accessed April 6, 2012.

Topic 14: Technology

Purpose To help parents understand both positive and negative effects of technology on young children

Goals for Parents:

1. To increase awareness of the impact that technology has on young children

2. To understand their roles in both encouraging and limiting technology use by young children

3. To increase knowledge about how a variety of digital media technology may be effectively used for children's learning

Concepts to Highlight

1. Technology is a tool that can be appropriately integrated into children's learning.

2. Children need to have balance in their lives. Along with technology use, they also need to have physical and social experiences.

3. Interactive media is more effective than passive observation.

4. Discussions with adults as they engage with interactive media are necessary for children to have optimal outcomes.

5. Inequity of access to effective technology is a concern for child advocates.

Resources

Barron, B., G. Cayton-Hodges, L. Bofferding, C. Copple, L. Darling-Hammond, M. Levine. 2011. Take a Giant Step: A Blueprint for Teaching

Children in a Digital Age. New York, NY: The Joan Ganz Cooney Center at Sesame Workshop. www .joanganzcooneycenter.org/Reports-31.html

National Association for the Education of Young Children. 2012. Technology and interactive media as tools in early childhood programs serving children from birth through age 8. A position statement of the National Association for the Education of Young Children. Washington, DC: NAEYC.

National Association for the Education of Young Children. Technology & Young Children Interest Forum. Technology at home. www.techandyoung children.org/home.html Accessed April 10, 2012.

PBS Parents. Children and media. www.pbs.org/ parents/childrenandmedia/ Accessed April 10, 2012.

Ribble, M. 2009. *Raising a Digital Child (excerpt)*. International Society for Technology in Education. www .iste.org/images/excerpts/DICIPA-excerpt.pdf. Accessed April 6, 2012.

The Joan Ganz Cooney Center at Sesame Workshop. www.joanganzcooneycenter.org/ Accessed April 6, 2012.

 "Parent Technology Volunteers"

Visit the Education CourseMate website at www.CengageBrain.com to view the Video Case, and then respond to the following items:

- Discuss ways that you might incorporate parents as technology volunteers in your current or future position.

- How might parents and teachers reciprocate their knowledge and expertise about the use of technology with young children?

Do This

Select one of the 14 topics previously described. Plan for a family session using an active learning approach. Also, provide resources for families to take home or share with others. Implement your session. For families who were unable to attend, prepare a packet of information and distribute it to them. Be sure to have family members evaluate the information and session.

Summary and Conclusions

Early childhood teachers can provide much needed support for parents and their caregiving responsibilities. However, it is important that professional personnel provide information that is perceived by family members as necessary and useful. Further, information should be shared in sensitive ways. When parents feel they are being judged, criticized, or degraded, they are not likely to participate in parenting support or family life education sessions. It is essential that teachers respect family strengths and cultural differences in parenting values.

In addition to being sensitive to families, early childhood educators must use their knowledge of child development and parenting styles to critically analyze appropriate topics and strategies for parent and family life education. Several popular parent education packages are analyzed in this chapter. New programs undoubtedly will be developed and marketed, however, and it is the responsibility of early childhood professionals to become aware of them as they are implemented and to promote those that will foster healthy practices for families. Programs that do not consider current understanding of child development and the importance of the early years should be screened and not recommended for use by parents or teaching staff.

Theory into Practice Suggestions (TIPS)

- Although parenting education aims to ultimately provide better outcomes for children, planners must focus on the needs and preferences of adults (parents) by using best adult education practices and active learning strategies.
- Always assess needs and preferences of your target audience prior to offering parenting support or family life education programs. Be flexible in order to optimize outcomes.
- Listen to family members' concerns.
- Respect cultural differences in the implementation of programs.
- Be sure to provide accessible information for *all* families.

- Information must be accurate, based on current research.
- Plan for informal discussion time for parents.
- Use multiple modes of information sharing: meetings, videos, newsletters, and others.
- Avoid a deficit approach that indicates experts should tell parents what to do. Instead, use family support principles in planning and implementing programs.
- Use effective interpersonal communication strategies.
- Invite families with enthusiasm and creativity.
- Increase your cultural competence.

Applications

1. Assess one parent or family life education program using the concepts from bioecological theory as discussed in this chapter.

2. Discuss the concerns held by many early childhood educators about *Assertive Discipline* and *1–2–3 Magic*. Why do you believe these programs, even though they are not based on principles of child development, are popular?

3. What is the difference between parent education and family life education?

Questions for Discussion and Reflection

1. How would you design a parenting education or family life education program based on the guidelines from this chapter?

2. How would children benefit from the use of the guidelines presented in this chapter? How would families benefit? How would early childhood teachers benefit?

3. Discuss the pros and cons of the following strategies for parent education: meetings, newsletters, the Internet, and family resource rooms.

Field Assignments

1. Attend a parent meeting held by an early childhood program. Discuss the content and format of the meeting you attended in relation to information from this chapter. What were the best points about the meeting? What suggestions do you have for change?

2. Interview three parents whose children are enrolled in an early childhood education program about their thoughts related to parent education. Ask questions about content they would be interested in and format they would prefer.

3. Interview an early childhood teacher about perspectives on parent or family life education. Does this teacher feel prepared to provide these kinds of programs? Are they needed? Do families want them? How could children and schools benefit?

Additional resources for this chapter, including TeachSource videos, can be found on the Education CourseMate. Go to CengageBrain.com.

References

Adler, A. 1923. *Practice and theory of individual psychology.* New York: Harcourt, Brace and Company.

Bronfenbrenner, U., and P. R. Neville. 1994. America's children and families: An international perspective. In *Putting families first: America's family support movement and the challenge of change*, eds. S. L. Kagan and B. Weissbourd. San Francisco: Jossey-Bass.

Burkhart, A. D. 1991. *Parents are important teachers.* Kansas City, MO: Westport.

Canter, L., and M. Canter. 1985. *Assertive discipline for parents: A proven, step-by-step approach to solving everyday behavior problems.* New York: Harper & Row.

Chrisman, J. K. 1996. *The effects of training on child care providers' attitudes and practices.* Unpublished doctoral dissertation, University of Louisville.

Chrisman, K., and D. Couchenour. 1997. Comparing faith-based parenting guides: An on-going task for the faith community. *Church and Society* 88: 99–104.

Chrisman, K., A. Gottshall, T. Koons, and D. Couchenour. 1998. *Incorporating early sexuality development into early childhood teacher preparation programs: A qualitative study.* Paper presented at the meeting of the National Association for the Education of Young Children, Toronto, Ontario, Canada.

Coleman, M., and S. Churchill. 1997. Challenges to family involvement. *Childhood Education* (Spring): 144–48.

Couchenour, D., and K. Chrisman. 1996. Healthy sexuality development in young children. *Dimensions of Early Childhood* 24: 30–36.

Couchenour, D., K. Chrisman, and A. Gottshall. 1997. *Teaching about healthy sexuality development in young children.* Paper presented at the meeting of the National Association for the Education of Young Children, Anaheim, California.

Darling, C. 1987. Family life education. In *Handbook of marriage and the family*, eds. M. B. Sussman and S. K. Steinmetz. New York: Plenum Press.

Dinkmeyer, D., G. McKay, and D. Dinkmeyer. 1980. *STEP.* Circle Pines, MN: American Guidance Service.

Dreikurs, R., and V. Soltz. 1964. *Children: The challenge.* New York: Hawthorn Books.

Drummet, A. R., M. Coleman, and S. Cable. 2003. Military families under stress: Implications for Family Life Education. *Family Relations* 52: 279–87.

Faber, A., and E. Mazlish. 1980. *How to talk so kids will listen and listen so kids will talk.* New York: Avon Books.

Ginott, H. G. 1969. *Between parent and child.* New York: Avon Books.

Griggs, M. B. 1981. Criteria for the evaluation of family life education materials. *Family Relations* 30: 549–55.

Kohlberg, L. 1964. Development of moral character and moral ideology. In vol. 1 of *Review of child development research*, eds. M. L. Hoffman and L. W. Hoffman. New York: Russell Sage Foundation.

LeMasters, E., and J. DeFrain. 1983. *Parents in contemporary America.* Homewood, IL: Dorsey.

Lickona, T. 1983. *Raising good children from birth through the teenage years.* New York: Bantam Books.

McDade, K. 1995. How we parent: Race and ethnic differences. In *American families: Issues in race and ethnicity,* ed. C. K. Jacobson. New York: Garland.

Ontai, L. L. and A. M. Mastergeorge. n.d. *Culture and parenting: A guide for delivering parenting curriculums to diverse families.* Davis, CA: University of California, Davis. http://ucce.ucdavis.edu/files/filelibrary/5264/20355.pdf Accessed April 4, 2012.

Phelan, T. W. 1995. *1–2–3 magic: Effective discipline for children 2–12.* Glen Ellyn, IL: Child Management.

Popkin, M. 1983. *Active parenting.* Atlanta, GA: Active Parenting.

Powell, D. 1989. *Families and early childhood programs.* Washington, DC: National Association for the Education of Young Children.

Powell, D. 1994. Evaluating family support programs: Are we making progress? In *Putting families first: America's family support movement and the challenge of change,* eds. S. L. Kagan and B. Weissbourd. San Francisco: Jossey-Bass.

Webster-Stratton, C. 2011. *The incredible years: Parents, teachers, and children's training series.* Seattle, WA: The Incredible Years.

CHAPTER 11

Early Childhood Educators in the Community

© Cengage Learning/ECE Photo Library.

After reading and reflecting on this chapter, you should be able to:

- Understand the reasons for and effectiveness of collaborative efforts for children and families **naeyc** 1, 2, 6

- Acquire information about appropriate strategies for discussing referrals for special services with families **naeyc** 1, 2, 6

- Understand the goals and outcomes of early intervention services **naeyc** 1, 2, 6

- Appreciate the importance of community resources to best meet the needs of all children and families **naeyc** 1, 2, 6

Key Terms

community resources
community school
early intervention

interdisciplinary collaboration
preschool inclusion
professional ethics

professional standards
referral

BIOECOLOGICAL AND SOCIOCULTURAL THEORY

The community for the early childhood teacher is not just a theme for a unit, as in community helpers, but is an ongoing reality each day. Understanding how the community affects children, families, schools, and early childhood teachers helps in planning, reflecting, and organizing the curriculum, as well as other aspects of a developmentally appropriate program. Both bioecological and sociocultural theory emphasize the importance of community in children's development. Young children who are enrolled in early childhood programs have been immersed in their families' and communities' activities and ideals. This means that children and

their families will each help to bring a rich diversity to early childhood programs.

Strong communities that support high-quality early childhood education are intentionally built. Advocacy efforts by individuals, professional associations, service organizations, and businesses are all helpful in the continuing efforts that communities place on high-quality programming for young children.

Do This

Research service organizations in your local community and their efforts related to early childhood education. Create a directory for use by schools and early childhood centers in your area.

naeyc 6 Awareness of **community resources** and lack of resources provides teachers with important information. Knowing what is available and what is not immediately available helps teachers define appropriate action and alternatives for decision making about children's needs. When communities support families and young children, everyone benefits. As community members, early childhood professionals can find many incidental ways of advocating for young children and their families (see Figure 11–1).

Currently, the public education, health, and child welfare systems are working to combine their efforts "especially in addressing the needs of poor children and families. This is occurring in large part because program staffs recognize that the interactive effects of inadequate academic mastery, ill health, poverty, and family dysfunction are toxic for families and neighborhoods" (Massinga 1994). One strategy that will increase effectiveness and reduce stress for families is to provide services "all at once in one place." For more information about such partnerships, see the "Program Models" section that provides a description of several approaches for including various services for children and families in educational settings. **naeyc** 6

Figure 11–1	Typical Community Resources.

Many communities have these resources for families. Check your local telephone directory or chamber of commerce for contact information.

- Hotlines for crisis intervention
- Child care (may be listed as day care)
- Preschool education programs
- Head Start
- Literacy Council
- Early intervention services
- Resource and referral agencies
- Library
- Individual and family counseling agencies
- Employment counseling/training
- Red Cross
- Food banks
- Women, Infants, & Children (WIC)
- Human services or welfare offices
- Health care services
- Hospital
- Mental health/mental retardation services
- Planned Parenthood
- Parenting support groups
- Parents without Partners
- United Way

© Cengage Learning

In *Grassroots Success!* (Washington, Johnson, and McCracken 1995), the authors suggest asking the following questions to be sure that schools and families are prepared for and continue to support each other:

- How well does the primary curriculum reflect current research about developmentally appropriate practice?
- What information do parents of newborns seek?
- Are kindergarten entry requirements fair and appropriate?
- Can all young children receive their immunizations?
- How could neighborhood stability be increased?
- What instills a love of reading in young children?
- How could community awareness about the importance of children's early experiences be raised?

COMMUNITY INVOLVEMENT IN EARLY CHILDHOOD EDUCATION

Public education in the United States has a history and tradition of local control through elected boards of education. Many private or nonprofit early education programs also have voluntary boards, serving either in a policy-making or advisory role.

Local School Boards

Local elected boards of education have a wide variety of responsibilities for educational issues within communities. Following is a list of common responsibilities of school boards:

- Ensuring efficient operation of all schools in jurisdiction
- Establishing local tax rates
- Ensuring that school policies and practices agree with state statutes
- Reviewing and securing contracts for services
- Approving the budget and all purchases
- Appointing superintendent and other personnel
- Reviewing the educational program and student progress
- Approving instructional programs to meet needs of all students (http://www.jefferson.k12.ky.us/; click "About Us;" click "Board of Education")

School board meetings are public events, and the times and dates of meetings are provided in newspapers and other community communications. Parts of school board meetings may be closed to the public, however, when members go into executive session for various items of business.

Because education is the business of the entire community, it is necessary for concerned citizens to become involved. Typically, local boards of education have specific procedures for citizens who wish to make public comments. Phoning the local school district office is a good way to find out these procedures. The following guidelines are recommended as a means of making an effective presentation:

- When called to speak, go to the specified location, speak clearly, and state your name and any group you are representing.
- Make your statement, including supporting evidence or examples. Also, suggest a course of action you are requesting of the board.
- Consider making copies of your comments for board members and school district leaders.
- Limit your comments to one issue.
- Always be polite.
- (http://www.jefferson.k12.ky.us/; click "About Us"; click "Board of Education")

> **Do This**
> Have you ever attended a school board meeting? If so, what was your experience? If not, plan to attend to learn about how local communities affect educational practice.

One current trend that some school districts are following is site-based management and planning. In this approach, family members often play a crucial role in decision making. The degree of parental authority allowed by school boards varies across districts.

Reasons to Encourage Family Involvement with Local School Boards

- To learn about current local issues related to education such as curriculum topics, special education, plans for new or innovative facilities, transportation, and district-wide policies
- To demonstrate support for teachers and programs at school board meetings
- To voice parent and family perspectives during the open discussion segment of a school board meeting

> **Do This**
> Contact an administrator of a private or nonprofit early childhood program in your community. Ask about the existence and responsibilities of board members. How has the program benefited from the existence of a board?

 "Kindergarten Curriculum"

Visit the Education CourseMate website at www.CengageBrain.com to view the Video Case, and then respond to the following items:

- Discuss ways that a local school board might respond to information about kindergarten curriculum.
- How might parents and teachers advocate with school board members about best practices in kindergarten?

Boards of Trustees and Advisory Boards

Early childhood programs that have related policy-making or advisory bodies often find such boards to be helpful in their planning and fund-raising efforts. Having a variety of community members serve on these boards from various professions, including education, health, legal, and business, creates wide-ranging support for the program. Responsibilities allocated to these boards differ greatly depending on whether they have policy-making or advisory capacities.

Some of the responsibilities that are performed by boards include:

- Implementing tuition and fee changes
- Creating programmatic changes, such as dates and times of operation; additional programs offered in summer such as school-age summer camps; increases in enrolled children; and family involvement opportunities
- Defining guidelines for new services that are being proposed, such as offering various classes at child care such as dance, gymnastics, and art
- Implementing program and service evaluation by staff and families
- Writing a mission statement and annual or long-term goals for the center
- Making budget recommendations
- Serving on hiring or personnel committees
- Recruiting volunteers and services from community sources

CARING COMMUNITIES

It is clear by now that not only should community resources be tapped as they are needed for intervention, but also that families need communities to be involved in nurturing all children. The 1991 Report of the National Task Force on School Readiness expounds on

Policy-making or advisory bodies are useful in supporting and planning for early childhood programs.

© Cengage Learning/ECE Photo Library.

66 One of the first things we learned when we all went to education school twenty years ago—to work with the whole child. I don't know how we got away from that. But we have. Once we start meeting the needs of the whole child again, we'll begin to see real academic improvement....We need to attach more social workers to the school who can go into the home and provide more services directly to children and families, taking care of bad teeth and nutrition and abuse. We've got to do this now, in the preschools and elementary schools—and in fact, before the child is born, with good prenatal care for mothers. We can't do it later. There's no way. 99

—Sheila Mae Bender, early childhood teacher, Louv, 1990, p. 343, as cited in The Report of the National Task Force on School Readiness

The Search Institute has identified a framework of 40 developmental assets for children and adolescents based on research regarding healthy child development. Developmental assets for infants, toddlers, preschoolers, and elementary-age children can be found at http://www.search-institute.org. These assets include the child, the family, and the community. More information is detailed in Chapter 1.

the need for comprehensive support for all young children and families in the United States. Included in this call for comprehensive support are the following:

- Health care
- Security in family life
- High-quality early education
- Linkages among services

According to this report, quality early education should not stand alone but, rather, should be integrated with other services in the community. Schools and programs should be visible in communities.

naeyc 2 In *Ready Schools* (1998), the National Education Goals Panel lists important steps that can be taken by communities that care about preparing all children for kindergarten.

- Encourage parents to read to their children.
- Help parents connect with parent education programs such as Parents as Teachers and family literacy programs.
- Urge parents to take children for regular health examinations and immunizations.
- Urge pediatricians to share with parents the importance of reading to their children as well as effective parenting strategies.
- Help parents know how to find quality early education programs.
- Support national accreditation of local child care centers.
- Encourage parents to utilize early intervention services when necessary.
- Support programs that help teen parents to complete their education and learn effective, appropriate parenting skills. naeyc 2

REFERRING CHILDREN FOR ADDITIONAL OR VARYING SERVICES

naeyc 6 Sometimes, it becomes evident to an early childhood teacher that a child needs additional support to succeed academically or socially. When teachers are aware of services available in the community, they are better equipped to refer children to the appropriate agencies, services, and programs to best meet the needs of each child. This becomes critical when the teacher is working in a program or school in which there are few support services (such as guidance counselors, social workers, or child psychologists). Without specialists in other disciplines, the early childhood teacher becomes the only qualified advocate for young children in the education system. When children have special needs, early childhood teachers and families alone cannot meet them. Additional professional advice and services are frequently necessary.

Referral is often required when children have difficulty in the classroom. Such difficulty may be academic, behavioral, or developmental. After efforts to individualize have been attempted and when the teacher believes that more information is needed to best help the child, with family agreement, other appropriate professionals are called in to assist the child. Many referrals are related to the child's physical health, including vision, hearing, or level of activity or inactivity. Other referrals may be related to immediate crises such as family financial difficulty or a death, an illness, or another family transition.

Referrals by the early childhood teacher most often need to be made in coordination with the program administrator. Effective administrators give support to teachers as they proceed through the referral process. Examples of early childhood programs in which services are integrated include Community Schools, Head Start, Comer Schools, the Kentucky Educational Reform Act (KERA), and most early intervention designs.

To recommend special services for a child, it is important that early childhood teachers confer with parents beforehand, and that teachers follow appropriate procedures before, during, and after the conference. Abbott and Gold (1991) note the following procedures:

1. Collect a great deal of objective data about the child's behavior and development. Keeping a file of the child's work can be very useful.

2. Arrange for a conference with the appropriate family members. Be sure to indicate the purpose for the conference. It is likely that this will not be the first conference you will have had with this family.

3. Be well prepared for your conference. Collect all work and notes you want to share. Think through what you will say and how you will say it. Discuss the changes that have been made by school personnel to help the child in your classroom. Be prepared with information about possible referral sources. (See examples in Figure 11–2.)

4. During the conference:
   - Be sure the space is comfortable and private.
   - Check with family members about their perceptions of the child's behavior or development that is of concern to you.
   - Note that you will assist in exploring sources when all information leads to a logical conclusion that additional help would benefit the child. Share resources available to your program or from your community.
   - Avoid using the term *special education* (using it is premature at this point), and *do not, under any circumstances, guess at a diagnosis.*
   - Strive for agreement to have a specialist assess the child based on the data collected by you and the family.
   - Expect some emotion from the family. Keep your anxiety about this difficult topic in check. Use effective interpersonal communication skills.

5. Arrange for the assessment.

6. After the assessment, plan to meet with the family members to discuss the recommendations from the specialist and how you can best facilitate that implementation. In the case of a need for special education services, be sure to review and follow the procedures that have been mandated. **naeyc** 6

PROGRAM MODELS

Head Start

DIVERSITY IN PRACTICE   Started in 1965 with federal funding, Head Start was and remains a model comprehensive early childhood program. As its name indicates, this preschool program was originated because many children from economically distressed families were not doing well in school. The

---

Figure 11–2   Problems and Appropriate Referral Agency/person.

Problem	Appropriate Referral Agency/Person
Child behavior concerns	Child psychologist
Child nutrition concerns	Nutritionist, WIC, food stamp program
Child abuse	Human services agency, family therapist
Speech/language concerns	Speech therapist, speech clinic, health department hearing screening
Concern about vision	Health department vision screening, ophthalmologist
Chemical dependency	Health department, hospital
Domestic violence	Domestic violence shelter hotline, legal aid, family counseling, police
Creditor problems	Credit counselor
Utility payment difficulties	Community Action, United Way
Childhood illness	Health department, pediatrician, support group for specific illness
Developmental delays	Special education office, school district office, early intervention programs
Childhood poisonings	Health department lead screening clinic, poison control center
Family loss	Grief counselor

goal was to counter the effects of poverty for both young children and their families by giving children a head start prior to kindergarten. Head Start programs emphasize the whole child, including educational, medical, dental, nutritional, mental health, and family support services (Feeney, Christensen, and Moravcik 1996) (see Figure 11–3).

Head Start hires staff to coordinate all aspects of the program. It is common to see all Head Start staff, including food-service workers and bus drivers, at professional development workshops that focus on child development. Head Start programs not only serve the children and families enrolled in the programs, but also increase local human resources in their broader communities by offering job training and by reducing the need for remedial programs and placement in correctional facilities (Lazar and Darlington 1983; Schweinhart and Weikart 1980).

Comer Schools

The Comer Schools were instituted in 1968 and led by James Comer in New Haven, Connecticut. Dr. Comer believes that children can learn and succeed only when all of their needs are addressed. Thus, emphasizing the whole child, he implemented successful public school reform in New Haven (Weissbourd 1996).

Figure 11–3	Components of Head Start Programs.

Education—Head Start provides early childhood education through high-quality classroom experiences and regularly scheduled home visits to families.

Health—Head Start programs ensure timely immunizations; health screenings including vision, hearing, dental, and speech and language development; nutritious meals; and nutrition education for families.

Parent Involvement—Head Start empowers parents to be their child's first teacher, achieve leadership skills, join committees, and volunteer in the classroom.

Employment possibilities with Head Start and training and financial support for continued education are additional options for family members.

Social Services—Head Start staff provides services and makes referrals to families that are undergoing crises that may be related to violence, substance abuse, physical or mental health needs, unemployment, and others.

Disabilities—Children with disabilities are included in the early education component. Therapies and services that are needed are coordinated through Head Start.

Family Literacy—Information is shared about general equivalency diplomas, adult basic education, and literacy programs. Parents are encouraged to read daily with their children.

Comer Schools attend to healthy child development by placing six developmental pathways at the center of the educational process: children's needs related to physical, cognitive, psychological, language, social, and ethical development. Also, rather than assessing children in the standard contemporary way—in relation to academic progress—Comer Schools assess children through the six pathways (Comer School Development Program 2001).

The philosophical foundation of Comer Schools is based on key assumptions:

1. When families and communities cannot support children's development, children begin school with impairments to their learning ability.

2. All children will be supported and expected to meet high standards that will lead to preparation for modern employment and citizenship.

3. Tracking and lowered expectations for minority and ELL students are denied in the Comer model.

4. All students are entitled to the opportunity to reach their utmost potentials.

5. The six developmental pathways must be considered in order to provide education that leads to academic learning.

6. Educational experiences must be provided so that children can have developmental opportunities that have been lacking in their lives.

7. Schools need families and communities to work in partnership with them in order to achieve these goals (Comer School Development Program 2001).

This model uses a structure of three teams:

School Planning and Management—Made up of teachers, administrators, support staff, and family members who parent

Student and Staff Support—Made up of the principal and staff members with knowledge of child development and mental health (e.g., psychologist, social worker, counselor, and nurse)

Parent Team—Made up of family members (Comer School Development Program 2001)

The Yale Child Study Center has in place a School Development Program to assist districts that are interested in implementing the Comer model. Essentially, the Comer Schools operate as communities that have been created to support children and their families. Figure 11–6 demonstrates a model of the Comer School Development Program process.

Community Schools

The Coalition for Community Schools defines a **community school** as "both a place and a set of partnerships…. Schools become centers of the community and are open to everyone—all day, every day, evenings and weekends" (Coalition for Community Schools n.d.). Data collected from community schools indicate that four important differences exist in community schools when compared to a more typical school:

1. Student learning is improved by addressing all areas of child development (physical, cognitive, social, and emotional).

2. Family involvement with children and schools is promoted. Family members have opportunities as both leaders and learners.

3. The school functions at a higher degree of effectiveness due to partnerships of families, school, and community.

4. Communities are more vital and have an active presence in schools as hubs for such partnerships (Making the Difference 2003).

Early Intervention

DAP Programs of **early intervention** are those that are designated for children with special needs or are at risk for developmental disabilities from birth to three years of age (see Figure 11–4). Public Law 99–457 requires that comprehensive services be provided for all eligible children. In addition to education for young children with disabilities, a variety of therapies and support services are included for them and their families. Public Law 105–17 (1997 amendments to the Individuals with Disabilities Act) contains information about the evolving nature of legal requirements for early intervention services (Ramey and Ramey 1998).

> Times have changed. We have realized that our old views were too simple and our focus on the child needed to be expanded to include the family and its complex support network. The child-focused recipes have been supplemented or even supplanted by family-centered approaches to service.

—McWilliam and Bailey, 1993

Current recommended practice in early intervention typically concentrates on four areas.

1. *Family Centered Practices*—Recognizes the family as central to each child's development

2. *Practices with Children*—Considers each child's individual needs and strengths, engages children in developmentally appropriate experiences, and uses play as well as incidental experiences in teaching and learning

3. *Inclusive Practices*—Provides opportunities for young children with disabilities to interact and learn with typically developing young children

4. *Collaboration in Delivering Services*—Coordinates an appropriate team of professionals to meet the needs of children and families such as special educators; early childhood educators; pediatricians; social workers; physical, speech, and occupational therapists; psychologists; and others (McWilliam and Bailey 1993)

In order to emphasize a family-centered approach to early intervention services, a family strengths model has been advocated. The family strengths approach in early intervention is viewed as being a significantly different way of working with families than has been typical in the recent past. Using this approach, all professionals who provide services to children and families via early intervention programs acknowledge the existing strengths in individual families and attempt to build on those strengths. Professionals build trusting relationships with families so that families can be viewed as partners in the intervention process. In the family strengths approach, the goal shifts from merely providing families with services to supporting and empowering families as they pursue solutions to whatever problems they are facing (Dunst, Trivette, and Mott 1994). **DAP**

DIVERSITY IN PRACTICE When assessing children for early intervention services, it is important to attend to various aspects of functioning that might be related to cultural, ethnic, religious, or language diversity. The United States' diverse population makes it incumbent on professionals to consider the importance of cultural competence for both children and families. The role of families in early intervention may vary, based on the diverse views and values of families. Professionals, as they work to build trusting relationships with families, will make note of differences. Respect must be given to both differences in families and the need that children and families have to be culturally competent (Guralnick 2000).

Families are often eager to talk to each other.

Figure 11–4	Early Intervention Series—Sample Program.

Developmental Delays

Many children are at risk for developmental delays due to premature births, abnormal muscle tone, seizure disorders, hydrocephalus, or other unidentified factors. Early intervention programs have proven to be highly effective with children who have virtually any type of developmental delays.

Benefits of Early Intervention

- Enhances the development of infants and toddlers with special needs.
- Provides a support network for families of children with developmental disabilities.
- Reduces the effect of developmental disabilities among infants and preschoolers.
- Lowers cost to society through the reduced need for special education programs in schools.

Space Coast Early Intervention Center (SCEIC) Program

The focus of this unique program is an interdisciplinary approach that includes normally developing children in the classroom learning alongside their peers. This interaction allows for role-modeling from peers and prepares the children for the eventual mainstream experience. The team spirit nurtured at SCEIC encourages teachers and therapists to cross boundaries in a cooperative manner using the newest and most developmentally appropriate techniques employed in the field.

Infant Program—Birth to approximately 18 months (Holmes Regional Medical Center provides this component of care.) The infant program concentrates on family involvement. The parents receive home programming suggestions from the therapists. These activities are designed to be implemented by the parents during the child's regular daily routine, such as feeding, diapering, or bathing. An occupational therapist and speech/language pathologist provide 1 to 2 hours of therapy per week for each child and parent on an individual basis. This training is designed to be continued on a daily basis by the family, striving to influence developmental gains through the home environment.

The families in the infant program receive an Individualized Family Support Plan (IFSP). This plan focuses on the needs and goals of the child and the family. The plan is reviewed and updated on a 6-month cycle. Referrals for the infant program come from neonatologists and local area pediatricians.

Therapy is much more effective when parents and other caregivers follow through at home.

Transition Class—18 months to 2 years (provided by SCEIC)

The transition class meets five mornings a week. The class focuses on motor developments, self-feeding skills, and ways to cope with the physical environment.

The teachers, in conjunction with the therapists, aid the children in making choices, developing self-assurance and independence, and improving their language and cognitive skills.

Each family also receives an IFSP. Families, teachers, and therapists review and update each IFSP biannually and redevelop it every year.

Toddler Program—From 2 years to 3 years (provided by SCEIC)

The toddlers come to the center three mornings a week. The program focuses on age-appropriate and developmentally appropriate activities for children to develop cognitive and social skills. This includes gross and fine motor, socialization, communication, cognitive, perceptual, and feeding skills.

An IFSP is also designed and updated for each child.

Preschool Program—From 3 years to 6 years (provided by SCEIC)

The preschoolers attend 5 days a week. The preschool program focuses on pre-reading, pre-writing, and pre-math skills. The staff provides a whole realm of real-life and hands-on experiences that offer the environment to develop pre-readiness skills.

To accurately assess each child's progress, an Individualized Education Plan (IEP) is designed. Here, too, families, teachers, and therapists review and update this plan biannually.

Mainstreaming—A major difference between SCEIC and other programs is the concentration on mainstreaming or inclusion. The center believes that the more children with special needs are involved with their normally developing peers, the more it enhances their opportunities for learning the social skills necessary to help them be truly accepted.

SCEIC's children are fully integrated and share in activities such as story time, art projects, songs, fingerplay, snack time, and playground fun. All children are learning to share, take turns, and make friends in a cooperative environment. This approach helps children learn their own teaching skills and gain more self-confidence, which allows them to build a symbiotic relationship in the process. This is an important point, considering many of our children will be mainstreamed into the public schools. Our typically developing children learn that being different is acceptable and not something to be afraid of or shamed by.

Interacting with children with special needs and learning to accept them is a valuable experience for all children.

Socialization—Our Center gives the children opportunities for social interaction with members of the community. The children attend shows and concerts, and go to pet stores, restaurants, supermarkets, farms, and other real-life destinations. Regular field trips are essential to the growth and development of our children.

Our children have been invited to attend chamber of commerce events and other civic group meetings. Public awareness is crucial in order for all children to be accepted and valued. If the community has an awareness of what the center does, and if children with special needs are able to participate in daily life activities, then people at large will be much more accepting.

Continues

Figure 11–4 *(Continued)*

From Space Coast Early Intervention Center, The Program, November 29, 1998. Reprinted by permission of Space Coast Early Intervention Center.

Family Education and Support—Parent education and support is critical to the families involved at SCEIC.

Mothers, fathers, foster parents, grandparents, and other family support members are viewed as vital to their child's development, as are the teachers and therapists on staff. Parents work with the staff to evaluate their child, set goals and objectives, implement the program to reach these goals, and reassess their child's progress.

SCEIC provides the setting for parental involvement and education through class participation, consultations with staff members, and monthly support meetings where ideas can be shared. Support meetings offer a time for parents to interact with each other as well as with outside presenters and staff members. This networking provides an outlet for discussion of parental concerns specific to the family's needs.

Children deserve a chance to succeed in our society.

We Need Your Help

SCEIC's efforts are made possible through funds received from individuals, organizations, foundations and corporations, as well as tuition and annual fundraising.

More than 80% of our budget directly benefits the children, and less than 10% of our budget comes from state funding. Investments from our community are what allow us to continue our programs.

For more information, call (407) 729-6858.

Space Coast Early Intervention Center

3661 S. Babcock Street, Suite D

Melbourne, FL 32901

(407) 729-6858

http://www.sceic.com

 "Programs for Children with Autism"

Visit the Education CourseMate website at www.CengageBrain.com to view the Video Case, and then respond to the following items:

- Discuss how programs for children with autism might meet the expectations for best practices in early intervention.

- How might parents and teachers work together to best meet the needs of young children with autism?

Do This

Interview a staff member from an early intervention program. Ask about their programs and roles for family members. Request permission to observe various aspects of the programs.

Preschool Inclusion

naeyc 6 Revisions in the Individuals with Disabilities Education Act (PL 105–17, IDEA) mandate that inclusive programs have highest priority for placement of children with special needs. **Preschool inclusion** programs are those classroom settings that enroll children with and without disabilities. Individual programs may describe additional requirements for their philosophies of inclusion, so not all inclusive programs look alike. Some of these programs are found in public school systems, but many districts still do not offer preschool classes for typically developing children. Thus, more common places to find instances of preschool inclusion are in Head Start and community-based programs (Odom 2002).

Successful preschool inclusion programs consider the needs of children and families at all levels of Bronfenbrenner's systems (Odom 2002). Research with families of children in inclusive programs has shown that the most common concern is that individual children's educational needs are met. As with all high-quality early childhood programs, partnerships between teachers (and other staff) and families are of great importance. Families of young children with

For early childhood and early intervention practitioners, the issues of quality and efficacy of early intervention programs must be addressed. What are the characteristics of high-quality early intervention programs? What factors of early intervention programs make them effective for supporting development of young children with disabilities? Ramey and Ramey (1998) have extensively reviewed the existing research in this area and have subsequently put forth six principles "based on studies of children from economically impoverished families, children with biological risk factors, children with combined psychosocial and biological risks, and children with developmental disabilities diagnosed in infancy." See Figure 11–5 for a listing and descriptions of the six principles.

Figure 11–5	Six Evidence-Based Principles for Effectiveness in Early Intervention Programs.

1. *Developmental Timing:* When early intervention begins earlier in a child's life and continues for a longer period of time, benefits are generally greater than for those that begin later and are implemented for a shorter period of time.

2. *Program Intensity:* Those programs that operate the most hours per day, the most days per week, and the most home visits per week have greater positive outcomes than those programs that provide less intensive services. Further, children and families who participate the most demonstrate the greatest developmental gains.

3. *Direct (vs. Intermediary) Provision of Learning Experiences:* Direct educational services provided for children with disabilities provide more effective change toward developmental progress than do those programs that provide parent training or training for other intermediaries alone.

4. *Program Breadth and Flexibility:* When early intervention programs provide a larger number of services with a broad focus, children's gains are greater than when programs are simplistic or narrowly focused. Further, programs that incorporate flexibility to meet various needs of children and families are also shown to be more effective than programs providing only a rigid structure.

5. *Individual Differences in Program Benefits:* Some children benefit more from early intervention programs than do others, based at least in part on the severity of their disability or risk situation.

6. *Ecological Dominion and Environmental Maintenance of Development:* Continuing environmental supports are necessary for children to maintain gains achieved through early intervention. These supports are necessary so that children can maintain positive attitudes and behavioral gains.

© Cengage Learning

disabilities face many decisions in terms of the provision of services for their children. When preschool staff shares information through frequent clear communication, families are able to make the best decisions for their children (Beckman, Hanson, and Horn 2002). 6

 "Including Students with High Incidence Disabilities: Strategies for Success"

Visit the Education CourseMate website at www.CengageBrain.com to view the Video Case, and then respond to the following items:

- Discuss experiences that you have had with children with high incidence disabilities.

- How might parents and teachers partner to successfully meet the needs of children with high incidence disabilities?

Other Models

Other models exist in which teams of professionals from a variety of disciplines collaborate to make joint decisions with families about young children's education and care. Such teams have the advantage of regular meetings to share information and plan incrementally, depending on the needs of the child and family.

Instructional Support Teams   One example of an interdisciplinary model is the Pennsylvania model of team planning in public schools. In this model, the Instructional Support Team (IST) members are typically composed of the child's teacher, the building administrator, parents, counselor, and a certified teacher employed as an IST specialist from the school district. Usually, one of the team members expresses a concern about a child's development in some area and a meeting is called. At the meeting, all team members may express their concern or perspective. The team then arrives at a consensus or plan, which is implemented for a 30-day period. At the end of this period, the team is reconvened to assess and consider further options as needed.

United Way's Focus on Our Future   In York County, Pennsylvania, a successful child care initiative has been in place for several years. In 1995, three primary purposes were identified:

1. To focus attention on quality, affordable, available child care as integral to York County's human and economic infrastructure

2. To assess community needs and develop an action agenda to improve early care and education for children and families

3. To facilitate linkages among business, government, education, families, and others to move forward with a community action agenda

After a great deal of study, the United Way's Focus on Our Future defined three goals based on the national trilemma regarding child care and strategies for achieving the goals.

Goal 1: Advance high-quality child care programs

- Adopt and implement quality standards for York County child care services

- Assist child care programs in achieving national accreditation

- Train providers to achieve necessary competencies for national accreditation

- Develop a model to improve compensation for child care providers

- Provide parent education about quality child care

- Provide community education about the importance of quality child care

Goal 2: Address the needs of unserved and under-served families seeking child care

- Increase the number of affordable quality child care spaces
- Support providers to increase the number of spaces for infants and children with developmental disabilities
- Study the need for child care beyond traditional workdays

Goal 3: Develop and support public and private efforts to make quality child care affordable

- Forge partnerships with public and private entities, including churches and businesses
- Promote employer participation in family-supportive benefits
- Provide funding for tuition assistance for training child care providers
- Assist child care providers with cost-effective strategies
- Advocate for state and federal policies for expanding subsidized child care and support for early education

In its latest brochure, Focus on Our Future creatively used data from current brain research to compare Pennsylvania's spending on children at various stages. In an effort to get state policy makers to understand the importance of providing funding to early care and education programs, the brochure notes that 85 percent of brain development occurs by age three. View Figure 11–6 and note the percentage of state spending on young children compared to later years. What's wrong with this picture?

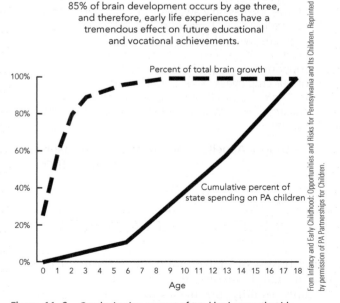

Figure 11–6 Graph viewing percent of total brain growth with cumulative percent of Pennsylvania State spending on children. (Estimates produced by Pennsylvania Partnerships for Children as part of the National Association of Child Advocates Children's Budget Watch Project.)

United Way Success By 6 Based on evidence from research on early brain development, the national United Way originated a community-based partnership model to deliver programs offering demonstrated solutions in early development in order to ensure that children from birth to age six are "healthy, nurtured and ready to succeed" (United Way Success By 6 n.d.). Beginning in Minneapolis in 1988, Success By 6 programs now number more than 350 in the United States and Canada. According to their mission statement, "Success By 6 encourages and facilitates collaborations and partnerships to unite our community's businesses, government, service providers, advocates, educators, and families to ensure that our young children are born healthy, remain healthy, nurtured, and ready to successfully enter school by age 6" (United Way Success by 6 n.d.).

Project Even Start Even Start is a federally funded program with the following components:

- Adult literacy (adult basic education or instruction for English language learners)
- Parenting education
- Early childhood education
- Interactive parent and child literacy activities

Even Start supports family literacy services for parents and children, primarily from birth through age seven, and has three related goals:

1. To help parents improve their literacy or basic educational skills
2. To help parents become full partners in educating their children
3. To assist children in reaching their full potential as learners

INTERDISCIPLINARY COLLABORATION

Benefits

The benefits of **interdisciplinary collaboration** as described in the previous sections of this chapter are as follows:

- Utilization of specialists to best help children and families
- A consensus-building method in which the team recommends a course of action as well as ways to implement it
- Resource availability, including funding, from a variety of sources

Challenges

While the benefits are extremely worthwhile, those who have worked at interdisciplinary collaboration have also met with challenges, some of which follow:

- Coordination of a number of people for scheduling
- Explanation of procedures and language pertinent to each discipline represented
- Conflicting views about the goals of education or understanding of how children learn
- A lack of, or difficulty reaching, a consensus about the best course of action to follow

Although it is important to have an awareness of the difficulties of collaboration, it is even more important to view with optimism the goals that might be reached by working together. Billups (as cited in Bronstein 2003) indicates that consensus among members of the collaborative about goals is necessary in order to be successful. Further, the process of negotiating the plan of action and follow-through must be given attention as the work continues. These processes rely on open communication and commitment to a common end.

FAMILY-CENTERED INTERPROFESSIONAL COLLABORATION

naeyc 6 A human services approach to create partnerships among families and professionals from diverse disciplines such as health, education, and social work is known as family-centered interprofessional collaboration. "Central to the family-centered interprofessional curriculum and practicum experience is the understanding that family empowerment and professional collaboration serve as building blocks to help families...beliefs [that] will lead to effective, skilled, and caring family/professional interactions which will change the plight of children and families in the 21st century" (Davidson, Taba, Yamashita, and Ambrose 1998). Work in this interprofessional collaboration actually calls for a new paradigm for preparing human service workers, including early childhood teachers. "It is the teamwork and care that professionals and families offer to one another that enables all to identify, understand, and reach goals that ultimately benefit children and families." Collaborative efforts are quite complex, and it seems that when such a model is used in professional preparation, it is more likely that teachers, health providers, and social workers will implement interprofessional collaboration into their practice. It is likely that the wave of the future will be to include interprofessional collaboration models in early childhood teacher preparation programs.

The following principles are central to family-centered interdisciplinary collaboration (Davidson et al. 1998):

1. Family members and professionals work together to ensure interagency coordination to provide improved services for children and families.
2. Collaborators recognize and respect the knowledge, skills, and experiences that families and all professionals bring to the effort.
3. The development of trust is integral to the collaboration.
4. Open communication is expected so that all feel free to express themselves.
5. All cultural traditions, values, and family diversity are honored.
6. Negotiation is essential to collaboration.
7. The mutual commitment and shared vision of families, professionals, and communities serve children and families.

Collaboration is a drastically different way of providing services to families than existing methods and systems. It will take time before this revolutionary approach can vastly change ways of working with families. But the effort must begin. If early childhood professionals can, early in their teaching preparation, be provided with understanding of and respect for diversity and the realization that families are children's first teachers and primary nurturers, they will be better prepared for their future careers. Understanding families is necessary for early childhood professionals to succeed in the new millennium. **naeyc** 6

66 We in business, along with all segments of society, are increasingly aware of the vital significance the earliest years have on childhood development. High quality child care is a key component of a positive experience in those formative years. By supporting high quality child care for children of our employees, York County businesses gain in employee loyalty and help ensure that their children will grow to be constructive members of society. 99

—**Louis J. Appell, Jr., president of Susquehanna Pfaltzgraff Co.**

THE BUSINESS COMMUNITY

Some businesses have made a commitment to supporting family involvement in children's education. "'Family-friendly' businesses have at least one of the following policies: allowing time for employees to get involved with schools; initiating, implementing, and funding specific programs that promote family involvement in education; and providing resources to employees on how to become more involved in their own children's education" (Strong Families, Strong Schools 1994).

The Institute for a Competitive Workforce (ICW), a division of the U. S. Chamber of Commerce, notes that:

"Business has a clear economic stake in the future of our nation's children and should be an active partner in promoting policies that help young children succeed." (http://icw.uschamber.com/publication/starting-smart-finishing-strong)

Based on their concern for a highly skilled workforce, ICW advocates for comprehensive early education that includes the delivery of both health and education services to young children from birth through age five years. Further, they point to the need for families to have more accessibility to high quality child care environments and to the alignment of early learning programs with state standards for PK-12 programs. Businesses are encouraged to take the following four steps:

1. Spread the word about the importance of quality, accessible early education in a variety of ways.
2. Include the economic case for quality early education in policy agendas for business organizations.
3. Advocate with local, state, and federal policymakers.
4. Adopt policies in their own environments that support high-quality early education and working families.

In addition, businesses might partner with early childhood programs to offer program support in a variety of ways. Educators work with business leaders in advocacy efforts that may contribute to family involvement in education by providing their employees with the option of working on *flextime*. Several models for flextime exist: Core hours may be required, usually in the middle of the day, such as between 10:00 a.m. and 2:00 p.m. Employees can then choose to arrive at work early or stay late. Some businesses allow for flextime at lunch by allowing employees to either extend or shorten the lunch hour, then make up the difference in an agreed-upon manner. Following are other ways that employers support families:

- Part-time positions
- Job sharing
- Alternative work schedules for full- or part-time employees
- Flexible policies that allow for employee absences on the first day of school, school holidays, or to attend special events at school
- Offering seminars and resources related to parenting and parent involvement in education

- Child care options, such as onsite care or vouchers for discounts at the center parents choose (Strong Families 1994)

Another way that businesses link to education is through direct contributions of money or equipment to schools. Some businesses organize volunteer programs and encourage employees to volunteer in various ways for the schools in their communities. When business, education, and families link their efforts in these and many other ways, communities become more caring and everyone benefits.

PROFESSIONALISM IN EARLY CHILDHOOD EDUCATION

Knowledge Base

naeyc 6 The basis for professionalism stems from a variety of sources. A major source of professional information in early childhood education can be found in the study of child development. Early childhood educators rely on their understanding of children's development when planning educational programs, building or furnishing environments, and making recommendations to families.

In addition to this child development foundation, early childhood teachers depend on pedagogical information from the field of early childhood education. Together, the National Association for the Education of Young Children (NAEYC) and the Division of Early Childhood (DEC) of the Council for Exceptional Children (CEC) have created a professional development document for their members (NAEYC 1994). NAEYC has also developed a statement of **professional ethics** for those in the early childhood field (NAEYC 2005). These can be found in the appendices.

An Ethical Call to Advocacy One of the principles in the Code of Ethical Conduct is related to the early childhood professional's responsibility to participate in child and family advocacy efforts. Advocating for children and families requires both a professional knowledge base and commitment. Skills for advocacy work at the local, state, and federal levels have been widely addressed in a variety of sources. To be effective, early childhood advocates must know how to contact decision makers and to draw from a knowledge base of child development. **naeyc** 6

The following 10 "big ideas" are intended to provide advocates with evidence about children's development (see Figure 11–7).

Big Idea #1. Women's prenatal health is important to a child's optimal development. Optimal health

Figure 11–7   Ten "Big Ideas" for Early Childhood Advocates.

1. Women's prenatal health is important to a child's optimal development.
2. Biological and environmental factors influence the process of development.
3. Families are children's first and most important teachers.
4. Experiences in children's daily lives have profound effects on their development.
5. Individual differences in children must be understood.
6. Discrimination for or against any group of children must be avoided.
7. Infancy is a period of rapid growth and development.
8. Contrary to popular opinion, children ages 1–3 years are not terrible twos, but rather terrific toddlers.
9. Preschool children must have access to high-quality, developmentally effective education.
10. Primary education must be designed to meet the unique development of children of this age.

© Cengage Learning

for babies and children is dependent on pregnant women receiving early and regular prenatal care. When such prenatal care is not available, not affordable, or not accessible, there are great risks for both short-term and long-term physical harm. Healthy maternal nutrition is critical for healthy prenatal development. Existing social programs, especially Women, Infants & Children (WIC) provide healthy foods for pregnant and nursing mothers and their children.

ADVOCACY FACT: Women who receive WIC services have better birth outcomes than their non-WIC peers. Babies are less likely to be born prematurely, mothers are more likely to receive adequate prenatal care, and infant and fetal mortality rates decrease (Women, Infants & Children Program, Office of Nutrition Services, West Virginia Department of Health and Human Resources, http://www.wvdhhr.org/ons/wic.asp, accessed January 4, 2004).

Advocacy issues surrounding prenatal care include costs for medical care and insurance, availability, and affordability of transportation to medical centers or offices, prescription costs for vitamins or other necessary drugs, and employer leave policies. Obstetrician/gynecologists are medical doctors who provide comprehensive prenatal care that includes educational and social services as well as medical and nutritional care. It is not uncommon for low-income women to have difficulty accessing the medical system and, thus, to have trouble obtaining good prenatal care. Advocacy for prenatal care must include informational components that help all citizens understand the necessity of good

prenatal care so that *all* children have the opportunity for optimal development.

Other issues include rehabilitation for intervention services related to drug or alcohol abuse. Infants and young children can pay dearly for the mistakes of their mothers. It is critical that rehabilitation for substance abuse be readily available to women who may conceive. Although some people believe that women who abuse drugs or alcohol should be punished rather than rehabilitated, children need their mothers. Opportunities for overcoming addiction benefit both mothers and children. Rehabilitation services are needed in all areas of the country, urban and rural.

Big Idea #2. Biological and environmental factors influence the process of development. A child's development is influenced by many factors, both biological and environmental. Most child development experts now believe that nature (biology) and nurture (environment) each have nearly equal bearing in developmental outcomes for children. However, it is not accurate to assume that a child is, in effect, half nature and half nurture. A better understanding of this concept informs us that nature and nurture continually interact with each other in the process of development. For example, children who are born with disabilities identified at birth, such as Down syndrome or spina bifida, achieve greater developmental progress when early intervention programs and appropriate medical care are available and accessible. The interaction of nature and nurture is obvious when early educational programs and medical care contribute to the child's development and increasing abilities.

The most crucial area for advocacy efforts related to this principle of development is the availability and accessibility of early intervention services for infants who are born with identified disabilities. Some types of disabilities, such as ADHD and language delays, cannot be identified until children are a little older. Even then, early intervention is more effective than later intervention. Children who do not receive professional assistance with a language delay often are frustrated and act out, leading to behavioral difficulties. When children get therapeutic support as soon as possible, however, the environmental efforts contribute to early successes and more optimal long-term outcomes.

66 Well-designed, well-funded early interventions can have large and significant effects on school readiness and subsequent child outcomes. 99

—Janet Curie

Big Idea #3. Families are children's first and most important teachers. When those who are parenting receive support from extended family or community sources, they are better able to provide for children, economically as well as socially. While it is true that "it takes a village to raise a child," it is children's families who most often connect them to the village.

The bond that exists between infants or young children and their primary caregivers (usually parents) is known as attachment. Many child development experts believe that this bond has both a biological and a social component. It is this powerful bond that leads to the critical relationship that exists between caregiver and child. Strong bonds between parents and their children lead to families being early and influential teachers. Thus, in order for children to develop physically, cognitively (intellectually), socially, and emotionally (including morally), parents need to have experienced healthy relationships in their own families and communities. These relationships offer various forms of support to young parents, including child care, financial assistance, moral support, and social networks.

Head Start is based on the premise that families are children's first and most important teachers. This comprehensive early childhood education program founded in 1965 has family involvement at the heart of all of its components. In addition to providing high-quality preschool education for children of low-income families, various programs are provided to support family involvement in children's education.

One area of advocacy related to this principle of child development is that all families need support. When families have not been able to create these sources of support within their own families or communities, family support programs can be very helpful. Such programs often provide educational programs for parents and for children, as well as preventive medical care for all family members. Other programs may offer financial assistance with home heating bills or other necessities. Advocating for increased funding for Head Start programs is essential for continuing the work of this highly successful early intervention program.

66 If we truly care for our children, we must cherish their parents. 99

—**John Bowlby**

Big Idea #4. Experiences in children's daily lives have profound effects on their development. Child care, whether within or outside the family, must be of high quality in order to best support each child's optimal development. Many adults admit a lack of awareness of the effects that high-quality or low-quality child care programs have on young children. Even when families are providing their children with all possible nurturing and socialization experiences, it is still critical that children's daily experiences outside the home also consider all of the children's needs. More than 80 percent of children four years of age and younger spend at least part of their day in nonparental care. When this care is not high quality, it negatively affects children's development. Research has shown that high-quality child care programs have good adult-child ratios, small

group size, well-qualified teachers, developmentally effective curricula and assessment, as well as support for family involvement. Good care leads to increases in children's cognitive and language development as well as more positive social interactions with peers and adults.

In poor-quality care, staff turnover is often high, and this reduces caregiving consistency for children. Teachers are not well trained, children are expected to behave in ways that are not developmentally appropriate, and family involvement is not encouraged. Such programs can lead to negative effects on children, including behavioral issues and less progress in cognition and language development.

Advocacy for high-quality child care continues to be a high priority. In many cases, tuition or fees paid by parents must pay for all the costs of child care. This often means that four years of child care can cost as much as four years of college. Many families with young children do not have economic resources to afford the high-quality care that all children deserve.

ADVOCACY FACT: The most important aspect of quality early childhood education is the nature of the interaction between teacher and child. Professional development for early childhood teachers must emphasize this.

Children who are victims of maltreatment, whether it is abuse, neglect, or both, suffer long-term negative consequences from such experiences. Even very young children may express anger through aggression toward other children and adults, angry outbursts, and engaging in destructive behaviors. Children who have been abused have great difficulty relating to others. Advocates must work toward preventing child abuse and neglect. Parenting education and quality early education for children can help reduce the rates of child abuse. When children have been abused or neglected, however, it is crucial that intervention strategies consider support for both children and parents. Any suspected case of child abuse can be reported to the State Department of Human Services. Most states have hotline numbers specifically for reporting suspected child abuse.

DIVERSITY IN PRACTICE **Big Idea #5. Individual differences in children must be understood.** Even though children go through similar stages of development, they do so at different rates with individually different qualities. Biological factors in a child's individual makeup must be addressed in order to best meet every child's needs. Some of these factors are related to a child's personality and interests; some to body shape, size, and ability; and some to a child's thinking and learning capabilities. Although biological factors must be considered as we understand children's individual differences, supportive environments may decrease what are believed to be a child's limitations. On the other hand, negative environments may hinder even children possessing biological gifts.

Parents, teachers, and other adults who work with young children must have information about individual differences so that all children feel accepted for who they are. This acceptance is necessary for development of healthy self-esteem. Children's accomplishments should be recognized, whether or not they are part of the adult's value system. For example, a family that holds athletics in high regard must acknowledge a child's musical talent as being as valuable as athletic ability. Teachers must openly value the strengths of all children and provide opportunities for all children to build on their existing strengths and try new challenges.

Advocacy in this arena is related to understanding the social and emotional development of children. At the same time we value the importance of early literacy and numeracy initiatives, we must also know how to support children's sense of self-worth. Advocating for parenting education, teacher education, and staff development to include applications for social and emotional development will lead to a greater emphasis on the whole child.

> 66 Thinking about children as individuals enables adults to adapt programs and strategies appropriately and to be responsive to the variations that exist among children. 99
>
> **—Sue Bredekamp and Carol Copple**

Big Idea #6. Discrimination for or against any group of children must be avoided. All children deserve to have their needs met, regardless of ability, gender, family structure, socioeconomic status, religious affiliation, race, ethnicity, geographic location, or culture. Children who, in any way, are not in a majority group in the United States risk discriminatory policies and oppressive conditions. Thus, advocates for children should be prepared to lobby against discrimination.

> 66 If we are to reach real peace in the world, we have to begin with children. 99
>
> **—Gandhi**

When people are oppressed by others in society, the negative effects are infinite. Although many people prefer to deny the negative effects of discrimination, this is not helpful to children and families who are members of ethnic minority groups in the United States and who suffer from these effects. If we are to celebrate any progress that has been made in the area of civil rights, we must also look to what remains to be accomplished in terms of creating fairness for all citizens. Discriminatory practices in our society often lead to a double disadvantage of being both oppressed and poor.

Babies born into poverty are prone to negative consequences in all areas of their development. They are less likely to receive good nutrition and medical care than other children, thus impeding their optimal physical development. They often live in areas where schools and community services have a lower tax base, and so are poorly funded. Often, parents in low socioeconomic families are overburdened by the number of hours they must work and have little time or energy to foster positive relationships with their young children.

Families living in poverty are often stereotyped as being lazy or shiftless. This often is not the case, however, and advocates must understand the ways that societal economics affects individuals and families. As the national economy has evolved, many blue-collar jobs that paid a sustainable wage have been lost. Further, as the number of households headed by women has increased, household income has decreased because traditionally female jobs tend to pay less. In addition, for the past 30 years a reduction of government benefits to poor families has increased the risk that these families will not have access to health care and other necessities for their children.

ADVOCACY FACT: The United States has the world's second highest rate of children living in poverty—22.4 percent (America's Babies: The ZERO TO THREE Policy Center Data Book Notable Facts).

The remaining four topics relate to specific time periods in children's development. At each period throughout childhood, children have specific needs that *must* be met. Drs. T. Berry Brazelton and Stanley Greenspan refer to these needs as *irreducible*, meaning absolute. Developmental time periods are: infancy, toddlerhood, preschool, and school-age. *Children can't wait.*

> 66 Many things can wait. Children cannot. Today their bones are being formed, their blood is being made, and their senses are being developed. To them we cannot say tomorrow. Their name is today. 99
>
> **—Gabriela Mistral, Chilean poet**

Big Idea #7. Infancy (birth–one year) is a period of rapid growth and development. Infants need nutritionally sound diets for their developing bodies. This involves both a financial issue with the cost of foods for the infant (and the family) but also education of the caregivers about what types of foods are most beneficial for the baby. Information detailing the positive effects from breastfeeding must be shared as well.

> 66 There is no finer investment for any country than putting milk into babies. 99
>
> **—Winston Churchill**

Babies' brains grow very rapidly. Current research about brain development during the first year of life points to the importance of early experiences: all infant experiences can impact brain growth, either positively or negatively. Nurturing environments with responsive caregivers increase a baby's neural connections and eventually lead to a child's more positive behavior. On the other hand, environmental deprivation can decrease brain activity and later lead to less appropriate behavior in children. Infants learn through all five senses and benefit from many things to look at, touch, smell, taste, and hear. Because so much learning and growth takes place in this first year of life, child advocates must work for parenting education and high-quality out-of-home care for infants.

In order to reach optimal levels of development, infants must form healthy attachments with their parents and other primary caregivers. In order to form such bonds, babies need responsive caregiving from consistent adults. Early attachment leads to an ability to trust caregivers and is the foundation for good mental health throughout life. Again, working for more opportunities for parenting education as well as good out-of-home child care will increase the likelihood that all infants will have opportunities to form attachments.

Big Idea #8. Contrary to popular opinion, children ages one to three years are not terrible twos, but, rather, terrific toddlers.

Toddlers need many of the same things that infants do: good nutrition and medical care, responsive caregiving and an interesting, stimulating environment. However, this exciting period is frequently misunderstood by adults who may be challenged by the rapid development that occurs from one to three years of age. Children of this age have gone from being completely dependent on adults to wanting to be able to do things for themselves. And, oh, they can do so many things: walk, talk, feed themselves, take their own clothes off, sometimes put their clothes on, and play.

Brain development continues to be rapid during this stage. At birth, the brain is 25 percent of its adult weight, and by the second birthday it is 75 percent of its adult weight. Play is a critically important contributor to development during this time—as a matter of fact, toddlers learn best as they play. A little before the age of two, most children begin to pretend, so toddlers need many opportunities to play with a variety of toys and objects. Pretend play should be fostered by adults because it is now known to be an important marker for intellectual development.

Caregivers should allow plenty of time to play and also begin to set reasonable limits on the child's behavior. Toddlers need many reminders about what is correct and appropriate behavior; they are, after all, just learning about expected behaviors. It is important

to foster competence at this age by supporting the child's developing skills. Even though some adults want to overprotect or pamper one- and two-year-old children, toddlers interpret such intent as doubt about their abilities and may begin to doubt themselves. All of this can lead to negative self-esteem. Limit setting may not be well received by toddlers, but it is important to teach toddlers how to get along with others. Obviously, it is essential to set limits that prevent children from hurting themselves or others. Reminders and redirecting behaviors are generally more effective than punishment at this age. Because young children think differently than adults, they are unable to connect the consequence that adults see as logical with the mistaken behavior.

Advocacy efforts for this stage of development should continue to emphasize health and nutrition, parenting education, and quality outside-of-home care. Child caregivers who work with children this age need to have specialized training to understand this unique period of development.

ADVOCACY FACT: 39 percent of children from birth through three years are in child care 35 or more hours per week (America's Babies: The ZERO TO THREE Policy Center Data Book; Notable Facts).

Big Idea #9. Preschool children (three to six years) must have access to high-quality, developmentally effective education.

Preschoolers continue to need good medical care and nutrition. Even though brain growth and all types of development are a little less rapid during these years, children still flourish in positive, nurturing environments.

Play remains a crucial activity for children this age. This is actually the age when play is truly a child's work. Safe environments and nurturing adults are prerequisite for children's play. Encouragement and opportunity should be provided for pretend play with other children. High-quality educational programs for children in preschool and kindergarten have play at the center of the curriculum. Excellent early childhood teachers use play as an instructional strategy. Research evidence that links pretend play with early literacy development supports an emphasis on play.

Child care settings, whether in centers or family homes, must be high quality if children are to reach their full potentials. Because welfare reform now requires that low-income mothers must work or be in a job-training program, it is important that all available child care be safe, affordable, and developmentally appropriate for all children. Unfortunately, the United States does not have consistent federal regulation that guarantees safe, affordable, and age-appropriate care for children in out-of-home settings nationwide. Instead, each state legislates its own regulations. The advocacy issues surrounding this issue include increased funding to support quality child care for low-income families and to increase family leave benefits for working parents.

ADVOCACY FACT: 30 percent of preschool children in the United States are cared for in child care centers (Casper 1997).

Most states now partially support preschool programs through public education funding. Advocates must emphasize that an understanding of preschool child development must drive the curriculum in such programs. Teachers must be specially prepared in early childhood education. Family involvement must be a high priority in these programs. Only about one-half of all states include a requirement that family involvement topics be included in teacher preparation programs.

66 Every facet of early learning programs and practices is interrelated with parent and family dynamics....Above all else, families can validate and strengthen schools in ways that enhance the status and functioning of teachers, staff and children alike. 99

—Kevin Swick, 2003

Some children with special needs or disabilities are identified at birth. Many children, though, have needs that are not readily observable. As they begin to spend more time away from their homes in child care, preschool, or kindergarten, teachers or other professionals may observe and refer such children for assessment and additional educational support. According to federal law, all children with disabilities are eligible for early childhood special education. Advocates should lobby for all preschool children with special needs to have access to inclusive education programs. Teachers should be well versed in both early childhood and special education; some states offer specific state certification to early childhood special education teachers.

Federal legislation related to these topics that has been enacted includes: Temporary Assistance for Needy Families (TANF), the Child Care Development Block Grant (CCDBG), and the Individuals with Disabilities Education Act (IDEA). All of these laws require regular reauthorization and are often threatened with reductions.

Big Idea #10. Primary education (six to eight years) must be designed to meet the unique development of children this age.
These young children also need continuous medical care and good nutrition. Currently, childhood obesity has been declared an epidemic in the United States. Children who are obese at this age are at risk for diabetes and heart disease at increasingly younger ages. Obesity is being blamed on several factors: fast food that is high in fat calories, media and computer games that require little activity, and families who are so busy that they are serving their children greater amounts of fast food. Because this is a societal problem and because children this age cannot regulate their own healthy nutrition, the responsibility of solving this situation falls on all of us. Families must have access to adequate information about healthy nutrition, including healthy choices that can be made even at fast-food restaurants. Schools must examine their breakfast and lunch menus, and, maybe more important, consider eliminating soda and sweets from vending machines and celebrations and replacing them with juice, fruits, and vegetables. Further, schools can be very helpful in regard to increasing children's activity levels through physical education, recess, and active outdoor learning experiences.

Early childhood is a unique period in human development and, therefore, requires unique educational experiences. Young children think differently than older children, and this should be reflected in kindergarten and primary grade (first through third) classrooms. Those experiences include having teachers who are specially prepared in early childhood education; safe, active learning environments; language-rich curricula; and support for high levels of family involvement.

Many families use community services for before- and after-school care for their primary age children. Even though children may spend relatively little time in these settings, the quality of this care is important for healthy child development. Young children experience stress as they transition from one setting to another. When staff in before- and after-school programs collaborates with families and schools, children's needs can be met. Choices for children should include homework help, nutritious snacks, active play (inside and outside), and opportunities to interact with friends. It is important to have well-trained staff and a curriculum that is planned with individual children in mind.

Most children with disabilities are now being placed in inclusive classrooms in public schools. It is important that all professionals involved in programs of inclusion have training and support to best meet the needs of all children. Too often, school districts do not have adequate funding for all children with identified disabilities. Some teachers feel they are not encouraged to make referrals for kindergarten children due to such lack of resources in local districts. Advocates can advance the need for greater funding from state and federal governments so that all mandates from these entities are financially supported.

Consider This
How will you use information from the 10 big ideas for advocacy in your professional commitments?

ADVOCACY FACT: Recommended class size for first, second, and third grades is 15 to 18 children (National Association for the Education of Young Children).

Continuing Professional Development

naeyc 6 **Professional standards** and professional ethics are necessary in early childhood education because of the potential for abuse, neglect, or mistreatment of very young children who are given by their families into the care of others. Without such standards, programs and teachers would be left to their own authority as sources for appropriate ethical behavior. Professional conduct must ultimately be embodied in the teacher, caregiver, or administrator, but that does not mean that each early childhood staff member is to create his own standards with each incident or situation.

Applying professional standards and ethics enables early childhood teachers to engage in identified best practices. It is through such a professional community that highest standards can be continuously defined and revised in the best interest of children and their families. Such a professional community is a source of support and guidance for practicing early childhood teachers. According to the systems approach, teachers of young children benefit from such support. In turn, children and families benefit from the work of the early childhood professional community as a whole as well as the work of their children's individual teachers. **naeyc** 6

66 It is everyone's responsibility to be committed to education. And it shouldn't be limited to parents—anyone in the community should be encouraged to think of the local school as 'their' school and should seek active participation in what goes on there. 99

—Lois Jean White, 1998 National PTA president

The Movement to Leave No Child Behind

Under the leadership of Marian Wright Edelman, the Children's Defense Fund has initiated a public awareness campaign. Leave No Child Behind attempts to create a climate that encourages action by policy makers

Children reap the benefits when parents or other family members read to them each day.

on children's agenda. Included in the agenda are the following issues:

- Child care and Head Start
- Education
- Family education
- Nutrition
- Housing
- Child welfare
- Gun safety

The mission of this initiative is "to ensure every child a Healthy Start, a Head Start, a Fair Start, a Safe Start and a Moral Start in life and successful passage to adulthood with the help of caring families and communities." For more details about this child advocacy organization and its leader, Marian Wright Edelman, go to http://www.childrensdefense.org/.

Summary and Conclusions

Early childhood educators must form partnerships, not only with families, but also with members of the larger community. Connections among early childhood program professionals, agency personnel, and the business community serve to increase support and services to young children and their families. The support of the entire community for high-quality early childhood education encourages excellence. Moving beyond home and school partnerships, relationships with the community are needed to provide a caring society for children and families. Knowledge about community resources is essential as early childhood educators attempt to meet the needs of all children and families in their care. Since its inception, early intervention for young children with identified disabilities has used a collaborative model.

Collaborative efforts between education and business have shown to be extremely beneficial to children, families, education, and the community. Although often seen as challenging work, collaboration often leads to positive results for all entities. Educational programs often become more effective with the deep knowledge that is gained when teachers work with other community members. Families, schools, and communities, working together for young children, can support and nurture each other.

Theory into Practice Suggestions (TIPS)

- Gain awareness of community resources available to children and families in your school or center.
- Create ways to involve various individuals, associations, businesses, and agencies from your community with your school.
- Plan ways to implement at least some aspects of community involvement from Head Start, Comer Schools, or community schools.
- Become active with your local school board.
- Consider ways to involve community members as classroom volunteers.
- Practice advocacy on at least a weekly basis.
- Refer children for appropriate services.
- Avoid diagnosing children or families. Instead, collect objective information that might help other professionals to do so.

- Stay informed about best practices for inclusive educational settings.
- Become familiar with and apply principles of the NAEYC Code of Ethical Practice.
- Represent early childhood education research, theory, best practices, and ethical principles in all professional collaborations.

Applications

1. Role-play a conference with family members whose children have demonstrated the following behavior in the early childhood education program:
   a. Nearly always choosing to play alone
   b. Increasingly aggressive behaviors with peers
   c. Frequent negative moods

2. List and describe all of the components of the comprehensive early childhood education program Head Start. What do you see as the benefits to children and families enrolled in this type of program?

3. Explain why early childhood teachers should not label children or guess at a diagnosis.

Questions for Reflection and Discussion

1. What concerns would you have about meeting with family members to discuss referring their child for special services? What are the benefits of such referrals?

2. What are the characteristics of a professional in early childhood education?

3. List and discuss benefits and potential conflicts in collaborative efforts.

4. Select three or four big ideas about advocacy and discuss how you might apply the information.

Field Assignments

1. Visit a Head Start or early intervention program. If possible, ask about the role community members and community agencies play in the program. What agency sponsors the program? Are any volunteers involved?

2. Collect information about resources available in your community (or the one in which you plan to teach) that would be helpful to families of young children. Create a brochure or booklet with the information you locate.

3. Interview an early childhood teacher about her involvement in any interdisciplinary collaboration. Ask about the challenges and the benefits of such work.

Additional resources for this chapter, including TeachSource videos, can be found on the Education CourseMate. Go to CengageBrain.com.

References

Abbott, C. F., and S. Gold. 1991. Conferring with parents when you're concerned that their child needs special services. *Young Children* 46: 10–14.

Beckman, P. J., M. J. Hanson, and E. Horn. 2002. Family perceptions of inclusion. In *Widening the circle: Including children with disabilities in preschool programs,* ed. S. L. Odom. New York: Teachers College Press.

Bronstein, L. R. 2003. A model for interdisciplinary collaboration. *Social Work* 48: 297–306.

Casper, L. M. 1997. Who's minding our preschoolers? *Current Population Reports* (P70–62). Washington, DC: Bureau of the Census.

Coalition for Community Schools. n.d. What is a community school? www.communityschools.org/index.php?option_content&task=view&id=6&Itemid=27#whatCS (accessed May 26, 2009).

Comer School Development Program. 2001. About Comer SDP. http://info.med.yale.edu/comer/about/overview. html (accessed January 26, 2006).

Currie, J. What we know about early childhood interventions. Joint Center for Poverty Research. *JCPR Policy Briefs*, 2. http://www.jcpr.org/policybriefs/vol2num10.html (accessed January 4, 2004).

Davidson, D., S. Taba, L. Yamashita, and A. Ambrose. 1998. *Bridging out: Lessons learned in family-centered interprofessional collaboration.* Honolulu: Health and Education Collaboration Project, Hawaii Medical Association.

Dunst, C. J., C. M. Trivette, and D. W. Mott. 1994. Strengths-based family-centered intervention practices. In vol. 1 of *Supporting and strengthening families: Methods, strategies and practices,* eds. C. J. Dunst, C. M. Trivette, and A. G. Deal. Cambridge, MA: Brookline.

Feeney, S., D. Christensen, and E. Moravcik. 1996. *Who am I in the lives of children?* Englewood Cliffs, NJ: Prentice Hall.

Guidelines for preparation of early childhood professionals. 1996. Washington, DC: National Association for the Education of Young Children.

Guralnick, M. J. 2000. Interdisciplinary team assessment for young children: Purposes and processes. In *Interdisciplinary clinical assessment of young children with developmental disabilities,* ed. M. J. Guralnick. Baltimore: Paul H. Brookes Publishing Co.

Lazar, I., and R. Darlington. 1983. *As the twig is bent: Lasting effects of preschool programs.* Hillsdale, NJ: Lawrence Erlbaum Associates.

Making the difference: Research and practice in community schools. 2003. Coalition for Community Schools. www.communityschools.org/mtdhomepage.html (accessed May 26, 2009).

Massinga, R. 1994. Transforming social services: Family-supportive strategies. In *Putting families first: America's family support movement and the challenge of change,* eds. S. L. Kagan and B. Weissbourd. San Francisco: Jossey-Bass.

McWilliam, P. J., and D. B. Bailey Jr. 1993. *Working together with children & families: Case studies in early intervention.* Baltimore: Paul H. Brookes Publishing Co.

National Association for the Education of Young Children. 2005. Code of ethical conduct and statement of commitment. http://www.naeyc.org/about/position/PSETH05.asp (accessed June 17, 2006).

National Association for the Education of Young Children. 1994. *Personnel standards for early education and early intervention: A position statement of the Association of Teacher Educators, the Division for Early Childhood and the National Association of the Education of Young Children.* Washington, DC: Author.

Odom, S. L. 2002. Learning about the barriers to and facilitators of inclusion for young children with disabilities. In *Widening the circle: Including children with disabilities in preschool programs,* ed. S. L. Odom. New York: Teachers College Press.

Ramey, C. T., and S. L. Ramey. 1998. Early intervention and early experience. *American Psychologist* 53: 109–20.

Ready schools. 1998. Washington, DC: National Education Goals Panel.

Schweinhart, L. J., and D. P. Weikart. 1980. *Young children grow up: The effects of the Perry Preschool on youth through age 15.* Ypsilanti, MI: High/Scope Foundation.

Search Institute. 2000. http://www.search-institute.org.

Stephens, K. 1994. Aiding families with referrals. *First Teacher* (September/October): 34–35.

Strong families, strong schools. 1994. Washington, DC: U.S. Department of Education.

Swick, K. 2003. Working with families of young children. In *Major trends and issues in early childhood education,* eds. J. P. Isenberg and M. R. Jalongo, 69–79. New York: Teachers College Press.

United Way Success By 6.n.d. Success By 6. http://www.uwbg.org/initiatives/successbysix (accessed January 26, 2006).

U.S. Chamber of Commerce. Institute for a Competitive Work-force. 2010. Starting Smart & Finishing Strong: Fixing the Cracks in America's Workforce Pipeline Through Investments in Early Childhood Development. http://icw.uschamber.com/publication/starting-smart-finishing-strong. Accessed April 10, 2012.

Washington, V., V. Johnson, and J. B. McCracken. 1995. *Grass-roots success! Preparing schools and families for each other.* Washington, DC: National Association for the Education of Young Children.

Weissbourd, R. 1996. *The vulnerable child.* New York: Addison-Wesley.

Women, Infants & Children Program, Office of Nutrition Services, West Virginia Department of Health and Human Resources. http://www.wvdhhr.org/ons/wic.asp (accessed January 4, 2004).

CASE STUDIES

The following nine case studies are intended for use in a variety of ways by instructors and students in order to deepen understanding of concepts in *Families, Schools and Communities: Together for Young Children*. The authors believe that the cases provide some situational dilemmas commonly experienced by many early childhood teachers. They can be implemented as one-time discussions or repeated as greater knowledge, skills, and experience lead to students' greater depth of understanding.

Cases may be discussed in two stages. First, analyze the problem presented in the case by reviewing the players and the situation. Questions might include:

- What is the major issue in this case?
- What other issues might be involved?
- What is the perspective of each person?

The second stage focuses on solving the problem. Questions such as:

- How would you advise the teacher in this situation?
- How might this situation be prevented?
- What is the big picture according to best practices in family involvement and early education?

(For further reading, see J. Kleinfeld, 1990, Reference Kleinfeld, J. (1990). The case method in teacher education: Alaskan models. ERIC Digest ED321965.)

Supporting Families in Infant Care Programs

The Teacher

Tricia Clooney graduated two years ago with a bachelor's degree in elementary and early childhood education. She is certified in her state to teach prekindergarten through the eighth grade. In her senior year of college, Tricia was assigned to an infant center for her preprimary field experience. This practicum was a turning point for Tricia, in that now she knew just the age group with which she wanted to work. Being outgoing and independent, Tricia enjoyed the flexible child care environment with some routine and new challenges everyday. She not only enjoyed the infants but also found that she was very competent at working with families.

The Early Childhood Program and the Community

Soon after graduation, Tricia was hired as one of three infant teachers at Grasshopper Hill Child Care Center. She was thrilled. The director, who received her degree in elementary education eight years prior, oversees 60 children and 12 staff members, some of them part time. She has been directing this center for five years; before that, she worked for two years as a kindergarten teacher in another center. Although some of the other teachers in the center have professional preparation as early childhood teachers, Tricia's two colleagues in the infant room, Lil and Roxie, have high school diplomas and regularly attend required training sessions. Roxie is the veteran teacher in this group, with five years' experience with infants at this center. Lil started working in this room just three months before Tricia was hired.

Grasshopper Hill Child Care Center is located in a rural area of southern Indiana. Most of the families who enroll their children at this center are employed in the nearby town of Summitsville. Major employers in Summitsville include a hospital, mall stores, public schools, a textile factory, and several restaurants.

Tricia's Dilemma

Tricia began her work at the center with very high hopes. She carefully studied about developmentally appropriate practices during her early childhood teacher preparation. Understanding the importance of an infant's environment and the necessity of interacting with babies as they are cared for, Tricia approached her work very seriously and enthusiastically. Some of the staff who had been there for a while expected that as Tricia "got her feet wet," her enthusiasm would decline and she would treat her work as a job, not as a calling. Two years later, Tricia is still enthusiastic and serious about caring for infants. At times, Lil has been known to roll her eyes as Tricia shares the latest information about brain development during a child's first three years. Roxie, though, listens and asks questions. Together, Tricia and Roxie work to implement best practices; Lil does her job caring for babies, completing necessary paperwork and interacting with parents as necessary. Having just completed a graduate course that included information about the family support movement, Tricia was eager to add to the center's existing family involvement plan. She had many ideas and lots of energy to work on them.

Tricia discussed with the director the possibility of creating a family resource room in a small storage area that was no longer used by staff. Additionally, she wanted to incorporate both family social events and programs for parent education at Grasshopper Hill. Lil finally spoke up: "How can we give the best care to babies and do all that work required for your family involvement ideas? I think that we'll begin to forget that the babies need us. Some of our babies' families don't even have time for them as it is. We need to pay attention to these babies, not to their parents. That's not our job." Even though Roxie found Tricia's ideas to be interesting, she had to admit that she wasn't sure when they would find the time in their very busy days to do even more. And she had to admit that she liked this job because of the babies; she wasn't sure that she enjoyed working with adult members of their families.

Tricia's Reaction

Although not completely surprised by Lil's and Roxie's concerns, Tricia was disappointed that they did not seem to want to try to provide more support for families at Grasshopper Hill. Tricia empathized with the moms, dads, and grandparents who sometimes seemed to feel guilty as they dropped off their infants, and most often seemed exhausted when they picked them up after the day's work. Tricia sometimes helped her sister, who is a young professional and the single parent of a toddler; she knew firsthand the challenges that working parents face because they want to provide the best care possible for their young children.

Tricia responded to Lil's comments from her own life experiences. She noted that life is difficult for parents as they try to balance their work and family obligations. Lil also responded from her life experiences: "Parents today want it all. They aren't willing to do without new homes, new cars, and vacations. They let us raise their children because

they can't be bothered." These comments did surprise Tricia. She had not realized how different her viewpoint about families was from Lil's.

Tricia had permission from the director to set up a parent resource room and to begin to plan for family events at the center. She intended to conduct a needs assessment of families who had children enrolled in the infant and toddler rooms at Grasshopper Hill. Lil informed Tricia that she was not willing to work on her own time to help with any of these events. Roxie was torn; she did not feel as though she could use her personal time to work on family involvement, but she might be able to help during work hours. Lil warned both Tricia and Roxie that caring for the babies was what they were hired to do.

Questions for Reflection and Discussion

1. Explain the perspective of each of the three teachers: Tricia, Lil, and Roxie. With which do you most identify?

2. Discuss your life experiences that may affect the perspective you take in this situation.

3. Using information from this textbook, explain how incorporating family support programs with early childhood education may benefit families, schools, and communities.

TEXT REFERENCES: Chapter 1 family support and program accreditation, Chapter 7 models of family involvement, Chapter 8 building relationships, Chapter 10 role of early childhood educators in parent and family life education

Case 2

Challenges of Increasing Family Involvement

The Teacher

Amy Gottleib completed her bachelor's degree in early childhood education. She was an honor student all through high school, and she received some criticism from the guidance counselor as well as some of her teachers when she shared her dream of teaching young children. "You're too smart for that," they commented. Her parents and siblings all had graduate degrees and worked as professionals in a variety of fields including engineering and business. However, they supported her desire to teach. During her student teaching experiences, Amy was all the more encouraged to teach in one of the primary grades. She loved being in the classroom with first and second graders. Her cooperating teachers and university supervisors were impressed with Amy's seemingly natural rapport with these young children.

In Amy's teacher preparation program, an emphasis was placed on the importance of family involvement. Many strategies were included for ways to involve families in their children's education. Research was shared that pointed to the importance of family involvement for children's academic success.

The Early Childhood Program and the Community

After graduation in December, Amy was a popular substitute teacher in her home school district. She was called nearly every day before the winter break. At the end of the month, a principal called to ask her to serve as a long-term substitute for a second-grade teacher. She immediately agreed to take this position, even though this school served mostly children from upper-middle-class families. Amy's preference had always been teaching children from less privileged backgrounds because she felt they needed her more than children from other backgrounds.

The South Shore School District is made up of a large area, some of it rural and some of it suburban. Since children attend neighborhood schools in this district, school populations tend to be economically homogeneous. The elementary schools have kindergarten through fifth grades. The school in which Amy is employed, Golden Oaks, has three classrooms of each grade and a fairly traditional approach to education. Many teachers have been employed at this school for 20 or more years. They have a reputation for high expectations and no nonsense. The principal, Mr. Brooks, is in his first year as principal after teaching seventh grade in a neighboring district for five years. Amy, now called Ms. Gottleib, is stepping into a second-grade class that had been taught by Ms. Nan Notting. Ms. Notting had taught for 30 years; she was known as an effective teacher who was firm with children and held high standards.

Family Involvement Traditions at Golden Oaks

Golden Oaks Elementary School has a history of a strong Parent Teacher Association group. The primary function of this group has been fund-raising. The money this group has raised has been used to purchase computers and other technology, as well as to provide for more field trips than the district can financially support. In addition to fund-raising, parents have assisted with holiday parties and other events when teachers felt a need for more adult supervision. Essentially, family involvement at Golden Oaks has centered on parents, especially mothers, supporting teachers and curriculum. Most often, parents initiated the carrying out of this function, not school personnel.

Ms. Gottlieb's Approach

Amy spent a great deal of time planning for and reflecting about her new position before her actual beginning day, January 4. Amy had carefully written lesson plans for the entire first week of school. She had spent time in the classroom arranging the environment and getting acquainted with curriculum materials that were available to her. Amy implemented a hands-on program with several learning centers. She interacted frequently with the large group, as well as small groups and individual children. She greeted the children in the morning and said good-bye to them at dismissal. Her rapport was excellent. The children liked her and were eager to do their work. Ms. Gottlieb challenged her students with projects and supported their interests.

Additionally, Amy drafted a letter to family members, introducing herself and inviting them to participate in the classroom in several different ways. She enclosed an interest survey for parents to complete and sent the letter and survey home with the children on her first day.

By the end of the week, Amy had received only four of the 22 interest surveys she sent to parents. She was surprised and concerned about this, but she was also very busy with other teaching responsibilities. Over the weekend, she decided that she would send a reminder home to the parents on Monday.

Some Reactions to Amy's Ideas

On Tuesday morning, Amy received three completed family interest surveys and a note from an unhappy mother regarding the survey. The note read, "Ms. Gottlieb, I don't understand the reason for this survey. You are the teacher. Ms. Notting did all of the teaching without parental assistance. I hope that you are capable of teaching our children at Golden Oaks. Sincerely, Gloria Noteworthy." At the end of the day, Mr. Brooks called Amy into his office. After some polite conversation, he asked her how things were going. Although she was feeling a little disconcerted about Gloria Noteworthy's comments, she shared her enthusiasm for teaching the second graders. Mr. Brooks gave some positive feedback he had heard from some other teachers about Ms. Gottlieb's attitude. Then he shared with her that Ms. Noteworthy had complained to him about the parent interest survey. She also told him that she had phoned three mothers who had children in the same class and that they all resented receiving this survey from the "new teacher."

Amy's Reaction

Now, Amy was really stunned. It had not occurred to her that inviting parents to participate in their children's education could be seen in any negative way. She absolutely believed that children had more success when teachers formed partnerships with family members. She sent the interest survey for the sole purpose of being the best teacher she could be. It was a surprise to her that a parent would interpret this letter and survey as her inability to teach their children. She was hurt, confused, and a little less confident in herself after this situation.

Questions for Reflection and Discussion

1. Explain the perspectives of Ms. Gottleib, Ms. Notting, Ms. Noteworthy, and Mr. Brooks. With which do you most identify?

2. Discuss your life experiences that may have influenced the way you think about this scenario.

3. Using information from your textbook, discuss why inviting family involvement and collecting information about the interests of family members are often useful strategies for early childhood teachers.

TEXT REFERENCES: Chapter 7 models for family involvement and PTA national standards, Chapter 8 on-going communication, Chapter 9 supporting learning at home

Helping Family Members and Staff to Understand Developmentally Appropriate Practice

The Teacher

Rick Ramirez completed requirements for a state teaching certificate in early childhood education. He had returned to college after working for three years in accounting. Rick received a bachelor's degree in business, and after some experience, decided that he really wanted to teach. He had always appreciated the special characteristics of young children but never really considered a career in education. He and his wife have a 4-year-old daughter and a 6-month-old son. Spending time with his own children influenced his decision to become certified in early childhood education.

Rick excelled in and enjoyed his student teaching experiences. He was placed with a kindergarten teacher, Sally Aysse, who loved her job. Together, they planned and implemented a full-day program based on developmentally appropriate practices. The children learned as they played. The classroom had many print materials and appropriate software for use by the children. Children made choices regarding learning centers and projects. Rick was aware of how effective this active learning environment was for young children.

Ms. Aysse and Mr. Ramirez collected work samples and provided portfolios to share children's progress with their family members. Parents frequently volunteered in the classroom and the teachers had frequent interaction with nearly every family. Having this experience as well as other field experiences associated with his early childhood education coursework, Rick was confident and believed that he was well prepared to teach young children.

The Early Childhood Program and the Community

Rick interviewed for a kindergarten position with a private school, Harmony Academy, in the city of Harmony. The school was well established in this urban setting, providing education for children from kindergarten through twelfth grade for nearly 50 years. Rick felt that he had interviewed well with the principal. Members of the board, including parents and community professionals, also interviewed all prospective teachers for Harmony Academy. Although that proved to be a challenge, Rick thought that he had demonstrated what he knew about teaching young children as best he could.

Three weeks passed before the principal phoned Rick to offer him a job teaching kindergarten at Harmony. Although the salary was somewhat less than that of the suburban public schools in the area, Rick rationalized that the school was close to his urban home and he would save money by using public transportation. Besides, at this time, there were no other kindergarten positions in the area; Rick realized he especially wanted to teach children this age.

Rick's New Job

Two weeks before the start of school, Harmony Academy scheduled professional development for all teachers. In the morning, teachers met in interest groups, and in the afternoon, they worked to prepare their classrooms. Rick decided to join interest groups so that he could get to know the other early childhood teachers at Harmony. It turned out that neither the other kindergarten teacher nor the first- and second-grade teachers had early childhood certification. Both first-grade teachers were elementary certified, the kindergarten teacher had a degree in social work, one second-grade teacher was certified to teach English at the secondary level, and the other second-grade teacher had a business degree and was currently enrolled in a teacher intern program at a nearby college. Rick soon found that his early childhood education vocabulary did not mean much to his colleagues. He became more reticent and listened carefully to the words of his colleagues.

Rick began to really look forward to the afternoons and setting up his kindergarten room. He clustered desks and chairs to make some group arrangements, and he set up six learning centers around the room. On the third afternoon, Sandy Yates came by the classroom and introduced herself as a classroom aide for kindergarten and first grades. She had been assigned to work in Mr. Ramirez's kindergarten every Wednesday. After introducing herself, Sandy volunteered to place the desks and chairs in rows and to make name tags for the back of each child's chair, noting that that is what she typically did to help the kindergarten teachers. Rick was aghast that a classroom aide would suggest changing his room arrangement but responded that he would like to have name tags for each child to wear on the first day of school. After Rick and Sandy decided how to construct the name tags, Sandy worked on them and Rick went back to his desk.

Education at Harmony Academy

By the first day of school for the children, Rick had come to realize that the philosophy of his teacher education preparation and his beliefs about how young children learn best were not common among the teachers at Harmony. The other primary teachers had not been exposed to current best practices in early childhood education; some of them used the same teaching methods their own elementary teachers had used many years ago. Harmony Academy had such a reputation for excellence that Rick could hardly believe these teachers' viewpoints. The principal of the school had experience at the secondary level and concerned herself much more with the curriculum and teachers for tenth, eleventh, and twelfth grades. She was not readily available to any of the primary teachers, so Rick had had little contact with her, even during the 2 weeks of professional development.

Kindergarten children came to school on buses with the older children. Because many families were dual-career, the board had decided several years ago to establish full-day kindergarten programs at Harmony. Because Rick realized that he would not have a ready opportunity to meet his children's parents, he phoned each family before the start of school. He had many short, pleasant conversations with parents, but he also left messages for four families that had not been returned.

The first day of kindergarten brought 18 five-year-olds into Rick's classroom. He greeted them and met with them on the circle rug to inform them about the day's schedule. Each child had a turn to tell about how he or she got ready and came to kindergarten that day. For most of the day, children were actively engaged in learning centers. They spent some time outdoors and had two large group story times. Rick had renewed confidence about his ability to teach by the time the children left for the day.

Rick's First Official Feedback

On Wednesday of the first week of school, Sandy Yates was in Mr. Ramirez's kindergarten to assist him. He had a plan for her to work with individual children at two different learning centers and then to be stationed near the large climbing apparatus during outdoor time. He also asked her to copy some letters he was sending home to parents and to place the letters in the children's cubbies.

Friday morning before the children arrived at school, the principal had left a message for Rick to come by her office at 3:45 p.m., the end of the school day. Surprised by the message, Rick got through the school day with a little anxiety. At 3:45, he met Mrs. Rivers in her office. She apologized for seeing so little of him his first days on the job and then asked how he was doing. Mrs. Rivers was surprised by Rick's enthusiasm for teaching the kindergartners. She was expecting him to state concerns about how best to teach these young children. After she recovered from her surprise, she informed him that Sandy Yates had come to her with some concerns that she and two of the children's parents had about too much playtime in Rick's kindergarten day. It seemed that several people had a lot of concern that children in this kindergarten class would not be learning what they were expected to know as students at Harmony Academy.

Rick's Reaction

Initially, Rick was confused. He had had almost no contact with Mrs. Rivers since he had been hired. Other than some workbooks in the classroom, few curriculum materials existed. Rick had expected that since he had specialized preparation in early childhood education that he might serve as a model for the other teachers, even though they had more experience than he did. Now, he was being criticized because he was applying a model in his classroom consistent with current best practices.

Sometime during the evening, it occurred to Rick that he had plenty of information to share with the principal, the classroom aide, his colleagues, and parents of the kindergarten children. He devised a plan for writing and sending a letter to parents each week that would explain the importance of play and active learning for children in this stage of development. Rick also shared similar information with the others who expressed concern about his methods.

Rick learned from the other kindergarten teacher that they each had a small allowance to purchase books and materials. He decided to purchase information for parents—books and brochures—to help them understand how children think and reasons for their behavior.

Reaction of Others

Principal Rivers' belief was that kindergarten was not really very important and she did not want to invest a lot of her time with the issue of play in kindergarten. She was rarely seen and remote regarding this issue. Sandy Yates remained skeptical about the value of play; however, she did as she was asked in Mr. Ramirez's classroom because she wanted to keep her job. Some parents found the information on play to be not only interesting, but relevant to what they observed in their children. Several of these parents began to actively support Mr. Ramirez's approach to teaching. Other parents continued to question him and state concerns throughout the year. Slowly, a few more parents came to believe that just maybe, Mr. Ramirez knew what he was doing.

Questions for Reflection and Discussion

1. Explain the perspectives of Mrs. Rivers, Ms. Yates, Mr. Ramirez, and the kindergarten parents. With which view do you most easily identify?

2. Discuss your life experiences that may have influenced your perspective on this issue.

3. Using information from the textbook, discuss ways in which teachers might effectively share information regarding children's development and how they learn.

TEXT REFERENCES: Chapter 1 developmentally appropriate practices, Chapter 7 linking parents and teachers, Chapter 8 communication and conflict resolution, Chapter 10 topics for parenting support, Chapter 11 knowledge base

Case 4

Developmentally Appropriate Practices in Head Start

The Teacher

Jenny Kim was just completing an associate degree in early childhood education from her county community college. During her two years of teacher preparation, Jenny had many hours of experience at the campus child care center. She completed the required practicum there and had also been employed as a student assistant to help staff the center in late afternoons. Jenny often had opportunities to interact with parents and other family members when they came to pick up their children. She began to feel quite comfortable chatting with parents, informing them about how their child's day had gone, and taking messages for the morning child care staff.

Jenny had been required to visit other early childhood settings. She spent at least two hours in an early intervention program, a Montessori preschool, Head Start, and a United Way–funded child care center. With the information she gained from her coursework and from these visits, Jenny knew that her goal was to be a lead teacher in a Head Start program in the nearest city, New Rock.

After her graduation in May, she accepted a position with a YWCA summer camp program, leading the prekindergarten group. Later in the summer, she interviewed for a position with Head Start. Jenny was offered a position as assistant teacher. Even though she wanted a lead teacher position, she accepted the offer and began her Head Start work in the middle of August.

The Early Childhood Program and the Community

New Rock has a large Head Start program. Twenty preschool classrooms exist in various parts of the city. Home-based programs are also a part of the New Rock Head Start. With a population of about 100,000, New Rock has a variety of communities, some of them more economically prosperous than others. Also, some neighborhoods are more culturally diverse than others. All of the Head Start preschools are held in churches and agency buildings in the downtown area. Transportation is provided for all of the children enrolled in the program.

Jenny was assigned to be an assistant teacher in Alice Jones' room. Ms. Alice has been a lead teacher for four years. She accepted this position after she worked for two years as an assistant teacher and completed her bachelor's degree in child development. Ms. Alice greeted Jenny at the beginning of their week of professional development meetings before the start of school. Jenny was pleased to hear that the classroom she would be working in was based on developmentally appropriate practices. The campus child care center from which she gained most of her experience had been accredited by the National Academy of Early Childhood Programs, so Jenny had developed many skills that would be useful in her new job.

Jenny in Head Start

The night before the first day for children to come to school, Jenny could hardly sleep. She was thrilled to be working in Head Start. Alice and Jenny worked together to plan for all aspects of the first day. Jenny believed that Alice valued her contribution and that she could make a difference in the lives of the children.

The first week of school was everything that Jenny had hoped it would be. She loved the children, she felt capable, and Alice was an excellent role model. At the end of the week, when Jenny and Alice had their daily planning meeting, Alice mentioned that next week parents would be volunteering in the classroom. One of their tasks was to assign parents to specific days and times, as well as to think through in advance what the parents could do to contribute in the classroom. Alice had already collected information from them about their interests and available times.

Jenny remembered reading about the importance of family involvement to the Head Start program. There had even been a guest speaker from New Rock College during professional development week who had provided innovative strategies for involving families in their children's education. Although she had experience interacting with family members, it was rare at the campus child care center that parents came to the classroom to volunteer. There seemed little need for more adults when staff and students provided very good ratios of adults to children. The child care center did have some meetings and events for family members, but since they were often at the same time as Jenny had a class, she had not attended them.

During the second week of the Head Start year, many parents and other family members volunteered in the classrooms. Each day, there were at least three adult volunteers in the classroom. Alice had organized a chart in advance and directed each volunteer throughout the course of the day. Everything seemed to be well organized and to flow; Alice was as adept at working with the adults as she was with the children. At the beginning of the next week, Alice was ill; the director asked Jenny if she could take over as lead teacher for the few days Alice expected to be out and to have the volunteers as assistants. Jenny agreed to this plan; she was actually pleased to have the opportunity to be in charge for a few days.

As children and parents entered the classroom on Jenny's first day of lead teacher duty, she greeted them all. Most of the children and all of the adults seemed happy to be there. Jenny had carefully planned a group time that would have the children actively involved and then easily transitioned the children into learning center

activities. The parents who were volunteering that day included one mother, Lois LeGrange; one father, Pete Stovall; and one grandmother, Felicia Sanchez. Lois was assigned to the blocks center, Pete to the art center, and Felicia to the dramatic play center. Lois and Pete sat on chairs at the periphery of each of their centers and next to each other. Soon after the children were busy at play, the two parents started talking with one another. This continued, even when children were asking them questions and in need of some direction or redirection. Although Jenny could not be sure, it seemed that they were talking about Felicia. They looked in her direction on occasion and then talked some more. Jenny did not think that she should intervene in this situation in front of the children, so she chose to ignore it. A few minutes later, Felicia raised her voice and threatened to "send you to time out if you don't stop that." Again, although Jenny was uncomfortable with this approach to disciplining children in the classroom, she did not want to correct the adult in the presence of children. She began to feel very nervous and stressed. By the end of the day, Jenny was questioning whether having family volunteers in the classroom was such a good idea. It seemed to work for Alice, but she'd rather have just the teachers in the classroom.

Questions for Reflection and Discussion

1. Explain the perspectives of Alice, Jenny, Lois, Pete, and Felicia. With which of these viewpoints do you most easily identify?

2. Discuss your life experiences that might relate to the perspective you have taken for this scenario.

3. Referring to the textbook, what knowledge and skills might help Jenny feel more prepared to work with family volunteers in the classroom?

TEXT REFERENCES: Chapter 7 Epstein's framework, PTA national standards, and embracing diversity; Chapter 8 communication and conflict resolution

Early Childhood Inclusive Practices

The Teacher

Olivia Ali married right out of high school. She and her husband had three children in eight years. When her youngest child entered first grade, Olivia enrolled in college. In a neighboring town, just 12 miles away, a state university offered a degree in early childhood special education. Olivia knew she wanted to teach; she researched the job market for education majors and found that teachers in this area were likely to be in demand for quite some time. In just six years, Olivia would complete her degree. This meant that she could be employed in a teaching position before their oldest child began college.

During her teacher preparation program, Olivia learned a great deal about children's development, various disabilities and their effects on children and families, and the importance of an interdisciplinary, family-focused philosophy for programs of early intervention. She had opportunities for observation and participatory field experiences in a variety of early childhood settings, some of them inclusive, and others that enrolled only typically developing children or children with identified disabilities. She observed a variety of teaching strategies and teachers with varied kinds of preparation and levels of experience.

Olivia's research paid off. As soon as she graduated, she interviewed for two positions and had offers to teach in both of them. She chose the position that was closest to her home. She would be a member of an interdisciplinary team for an inclusive early intervention program with primary responsibilities for the education component. Most of her work would be planning, implementing, and assessing an educational program for three small groups of children ages 1 to 3 years. She was very excited about teaching and evaluating the children's progress. Olivia also was responsible for a home-based program for infants identified as having a disability and their families. Many hours were also to be spent with an interdisciplinary team, planning and evaluating services for every child and every family.

The Early Childhood Program and the Community

The inclusive early intervention program that hired Olivia is supported by state and federal funds. The local school district is the contact point for the program, with the district's director of special education having a supervisory role over the early intervention coordinator. Twenty children are being served by the center-based program and 12 children are enrolled in the home-based program. Of the 20 center-based children, four are typically developing and 16 have identified disabilities such as pervasive developmental disorder, Asperger's disorder, Down syndrome, and cerebral palsy. All of the home-based children have identified disabilities.

Briarville is a small town with a population of about 22,000 and sparsely populated rural areas nearby. Families do not often migrate from the area, so many families have lived there for several generations. Education is not always as high a priority as most of the local educators would like, but there has been a lot of support for the early intervention program. Concern about children with disabilities and their families is evident in Briarville. Fund-raisers have been successful, and the local newspapers and radio station have provided publicity.

Olivia's Doubt

Before long, Olivia's pleasure about getting the position she wanted turned to concern. She did not enjoy or feel confident in the team meetings. The physical therapist, occupational therapist, speech therapist, psychologist, and family services coordinator all seemed to know exactly what each child needed. Sometimes, one or more of them seemed to dominate the session. When she explained the play-based curriculum that she had been prepared to implement, the others passed it off as fluff. They questioned her about what she was teaching, both in her small group sessions and in her home-based plans. At times, one of the therapists would come to her classroom and pull a child out for therapy that was missed earlier in the week for some reason or other. This would occur without advance planning or notice.

Further, nearly all of the parents (or another family member) stayed with their children during the 2-hour preschool sessions that were held twice each week. So, instead of Olivia teaching four or five children in her classroom, she was coordinating family members and providing assignments for them to complete with their children during the remainder of the week. Often, there would be five or six adults in the classroom and just four children. This role of teacher was very different from the one Olivia had envisioned for herself. She wanted to teach children, not be a family services coordinator. In her frustration, she began to question why families of these young children could not just let them come to preschool for four hours a week. She would be glad to compose newsletters, call families as necessary, and have conferences with them. But she began to resent their presence. Just when she organized the children for a short group time, invariably one or more of the children would go to their parents or look at a parent and cry.

Even though she studied about the importance of interdisciplinary, family-focused models for early intervention, she questioned how this program was being operated. She wished that she had another educator in her workplace to talk with about her doubts and concerns. All she wanted to do was teach; how had she missed what early childhood special educators really do?

Viewpoints of the Others

Parents noted that Olivia was very warm when interacting with their children. She prepared a bright, cheery, appropriately stimulating environment for the children. Olivia planned interesting activities for the babies whose homes she visited. However, several family members commented to the coordinator that Olivia seemed remote to them. They often did not feel welcome during preschool groups.

Other professionals at Briarville's early intervention program either paid little attention to the new teacher or began to feel irritated that she did not seem to come to team meetings with a cooperative attitude. The coordinator overheard two of the others discussing their frustration regarding Olivia's presence at team meetings.

The coordinator decided to move up a meeting that had been planned with Olivia. The meeting was intended to be the regularly scheduled conference after 30 days of employment. However, it seemed that something needed to be done sooner. Olivia was worried when she received a message from the coordinator asking whether they could meet after her afternoon preschool group the next day.

Questions for Reflection and Discussion

1. Explain the perspectives of Olivia, family members, other early intervention professionals, and the coordinator. With which do you most identify?

2. Discuss your life experiences that may affect the perspective you take in this situation.

3. From the textbook, what information might help Olivia see the need for such a family-intensive approach to early intervention? Which skills might help to increase her confidence in this situation?

TEXT REFERENCES: Chapter 1 division for early childhood recommended practices, Chapter 2 relating diversity to professional code of ethical conduct, Chapter 8 ongoing communication, Chapter 11 interdisciplinary collaboration, family centered-interprofessional collaboration, and professionalism in early childhood education

Case 6

Standardized Assessment

The Teacher

Vera Wozniak was a second-grade teacher in a rural school district. She was asked to serve on a district-wide assessment committee. During the third meeting of the committee, the district psychologist recommended that a standardized test be administered to all second-grade students. Vera stated that the test was not age-appropriate and that reading level could be better assessed in other ways. After several discussions, the majority of the committee voted to approve the use of the test in the second grade.

The Early Childhood Program and the Community

As news of the decision was shared at faculty meetings in the district, Vera began to hear from kindergarten, first- and second-grade teachers. Many of them stated that they did not think it was appropriate to give a standardized test in a primary grade. Some parents of first-graders also began to ask questions about the test and asked Vera if they should send their child to a summer school or buy a reading program to get ready for the test.

Viewpoints of Others

After hearing these discussions, Vera decided to go to the principal, Mrs. Vellines. During their discussion, Mrs. Vellines revealed that the superintendent was very pleased that the committee had recommended the test since the district's reading scores were not at the state recommended levels.

Vera left the meeting feeling very frustrated. She knew that second graders were too young for a standardized test. She decided that she would make copies of articles she had read from NAEYC and International Reading Association (IRA) and share those with other teachers and parents. After sharing this information, a group of parents asked to be on the agenda for the next school board meeting. These parents spoke at the meeting and expressed their frustration that children were being pressured simply to get the test scores up. The superintendent agreed to review the plan.

The next day, Vera was asked to meet with the principal and the superintendent.

Questions for Reflection and Discussion

1. Explain the perspectives of Mrs. Vellines, the parents, Vera, and the superintendent.

2. Describe which resources Vera should take to the meeting.

3. How would Vera explain her reasoning in involving parents in this issue?

TEXT REFERENCES: Chapter 1 developmentally appropriate practices, Chapter 5 responsibilities of parents, Chapter 7 linking parents and teachers, Chapter 8 ongoing communication, Chapter 11 community involvement in early childhood education

English Language Learners

The Teacher

Lance Scott was beginning his third year of teaching kindergarten when the suburban school district in which he teaches decided to create a full-day kindergarten program. Lance was informed by the school principal, Dr. Cassidy, that the decision makers believed it had become necessary to provide a full-day program to counteract the effects of families' spoken language on their young children. The emphasis on English as the required language in local and state political arenas was the impetus for this decision. Although Lance had taken several years of Spanish in both high school and college and had learned a little Bosnian from some friends, he was uncertain how to incorporate this knowledge into his teaching of young children. Besides, many teachers and community members were often heard to support immersing ELL into English-only classrooms. So, perhaps, his teaching would not need to change in any way, even with increasing numbers of ELL learners.

In the previous two years, Lance had had little contact with families who did not speak English. Even though some of the children in his kindergarten program were immigrants, their families were bilingual and communicated fairly clearly with him in English. One of his kindergarten colleagues, though, had a child whose family insisted on a translator for the annual conference as well as for newsletters and notes that the teacher sent home. This request was viewed as inappropriate by the teacher and most of the school staff. The result was that written communication essentially was kept to an absolute minimum to avoid any need to translate.

The Early Childhood Program and the Community

Due to an increase in available state funding, the superintendent and the local school board saw the necessity of increasing instructional time for 5-year-olds, especially because there had been a recent change in attendance zone demographics. Just five years ago, the number of children classified as English language learners was less than 1 percent of all kindergartners. The next school year would see this rise to 6.5 percent, and the prediction in the next 10 years is that nearly 10 percent of all kindergartners were likely to be English-language learners. The general attitude about this change in demographics reflected at the school and in the community was that when people came to the United States, they should plan to acculturate and to speak English as quickly as possible. The state legislature had recently begun discussions about requiring schools and other institutions to use English only in all communications.

Viewpoints of Others

Lance was somewhat concerned that there was almost no concern being voiced about how children learn to speak and understand an additional language. Instead, the opinions that were most frequently stated all seemed to reflect political or personal statements about the importance of learning English for U.S. citizenship. Some comments focused on illegal immigration.

Lance approached some of his colleagues and the school principal to request information about professional development for staff that would relate to their responsibilities for English language learning. A common response from colleagues was that the school district should hire specialized personnel to handle these issues. The principal did not seem to think that the superintendent or school board would support funding for such a position.

Lance's Situation

As the new school year was fast approaching, no firm decisions were made or shared with teachers about their specific responsibilities for teaching children in their classrooms who were identified as ELL. However, when Lance received his class list of 20 kindergarten children, four of them were identified as ELL. He was facing the dilemma of moving forward as if full-day programming were his only new challenge, or attempting to find some appropriate information for his professional development related to teaching young ELLs and working with their families.

Questions for Reflection and Discussion

1. Explain the perspectives of Lance, the school principal, other teachers, and the community.

2. What are the professional issues related to best practices in early education that need to be emphasized in this case?

3. Using resources regarding the importance of incorporating children's home language into their learning, what points would you make to support Lance's hunch that seeking professional development related to ELL is valid?

TEXT REFERENCES: Chapter 1 importance of families and communities in children's lives, Chapter 2 language differences among families, relating diversity to developmentally appropriate practice, Chapter 6 immigrant and migrant families, Appendix D responding to linguistic and cultural diversity

A Parenting Grandparent

The Teacher

Tammye Stefano has been teaching third grade in a suburban school district for 20 years. She has seen a number of changes in families during that time period: more mothers working full time, some single-parent families who generally have joint custody of children, and more grandparents becoming involved at school events when parents are unable to attend. This year, though, has brought a new family structure to her classroom. Shalesa Smith lives with her great grandfather, Jerome Heinz. Until last summer, Jerome and his wife, Becca, cared for Shalesa from the time she was 18 months old. Jerome and Becca, grandparents of Shalesa's biological father, legally adopted her when she was 5 years old. After Becca succumbed to a short illness at the end of June, Jerome and Shalesa moved to an apartment, requiring Shalesa to change schools. Shalesa began her third grade year with Ms. Stefano at Rolling Acres primary school.

Tammye met Mr. Heinz at the open house orientation a few days before the school year began. Considering his apparent age, Tammye assumed that Jerome attended the event because Shalesa's parents were unavailable, an increasingly common situation at Rolling Acres. She was surprised when he introduced himself as Shalesa's father and great-grandfather. At this time, Ms. Stefano was not aware of any other aspect of Shalesa's family structure or circumstances, including that Jerome was her adoptive father.

Tammye's Situation

Even though Tammye was quite experienced as a teacher of young children, her experience with male adult family members was minimal. For the past decade, she invited children's parents into the classroom to volunteer for Friday afternoon discovery centers, but in all of that time, all of the volunteers were mothers of the children in her class. It surprised her that she was feeling a little ill at ease about communicating with Jerome as Shalesa's only parental contact. Now, nearly two months into the school year, she had not spoken with Jerome since the open house.

Shalesa seemed to be adapting to her new school fairly well. Academically, she was certainly above average and demonstrated strong ability in math. Although Shalesa worked well in small group activities with her peers, Tammye noticed that she did not seem to be forming friendships that were obvious during choice times or recess. Instead, she engaged in solitary activities or watched other children interact with one another. Also, Shalesa resisted contact with the parent volunteers who came to the classroom on Friday afternoons and for other special occasions.

Tammye reflected on the significance of the concerns that she had about Shalesa's adjustment. Would a little more time take care of her concerns? Did Shalesa prefer her solitary choices? Why hadn't Jerome checked in with her about Shalesa's adjustment to a new school? How would Jerome perceive her concerns if she decided to contact him?

Jerome's Circumstances

Jerome doted on Shalesa from the time she was born. His son had died in an accident and when Shalesa's father, Jerome's grandson, had financial problems, he and Shalesa moved into Jerome's and Becca's modest home. They were happy to help out in this time of need. When Shalesa and her father moved from their home, he found it difficult to provide care for her with employment that required long days and some travel. Shalesa was happiest when she was with Jerome and Becca. Eventually, her father remarried, moved to another state for a promotion, and visited less frequently. He agreed without question to Shalesa's adoption by Jerome and Becca, noticing that she referred to her great-grandparents as Mama and Poppa. When he returned for Becca's memorial service, Shalesa had not seen him in over a year.

Although their mortgage had been paid and Jerome could afford to maintain the home he shared with Becca and Shalesa, he found the memories of Becca to be difficult in his ability to move on. He decided to sell the house and move to an apartment in a nearby suburban neighborhood that was known for its high-quality education system. Since the school district had sent information about the open house before school began, he attended so that he could envision the school and briefly meet Shalesa's teacher. When his biological children had attended school, the only events that he attended were sports and concerts, all held in venues other than the school building. Jerome is so proud of Shalesa and wants to be able to provide all of the care that she needs. Because school and childhood have changed a bit since his earlier experience in a traditional father role, he is unsure at times how he should be interacting with school personnel and other families with young children. In fact, he does not actually give either of these much thought.

Rolling Acres School and Neighborhood

Although Rolling Acres is known in the region for its high-quality educational programs, there has not been much attention paid to supporting families or the community. The expectation has been that families take care of themselves and the community has been, for the most part, separate from school decision-making. Special personnel at the school, such as school counselors, special educators, and subject matter coaches, have placed emphasis on academics and differentiating instruction as necessary to support individual learners to succeed on standardized assessments. The school has been viewed as a wonderful place to work. Teachers feel fortunate to be employed there, thus there has been little staff turnover. In fact, the least senior teacher has now been at the school for

seven years. The school director is beginning her second decade in the position, after having served as a teacher there for 12 years.

A leader in the academic sector, Rolling Acres is a school that is often visited by neighboring district leaders and teachers. The staff continues professional development in academic areas and continuously updates their curricula based on new evidence in literacy, math, science, and social studies. The school even maintains an outstanding arts department and has recently been working on increasing awareness of children's needs for healthy nutrition and exercise.

Tammye and Her Colleagues

Before the beginning of the second staff meeting of the year, Tammye opened up to her colleague, Bess Stanton, a first grade teacher. She briefly stated her concern about Shalesa's timidity and her own lack of certainty about how to communicate with Shalesa's father. Bess related information about variations in family structure that she had studied during a summer institute. She offered to share materials particular to grandparents as parents and Tammye enthusiastically took her up on the offer.

Within just a few days, Tammye found information that increased her understanding of Shalesa's family. The idea that stood out most for Tammye was that while home and school partnerships are essential for all young children, they are even more important for grandparent-headed homes (Smith and Dannison 2003). She decided to meet with the school counselor and director, share the materials and to ask for their support in working with Shalesa's family. This was new ground in many respects for all of the staff since earlier efforts were nearly entirely relegated to academics. The school counselor agreed to invite Mr. Heinz in for a get acquainted meeting. (For more information, see A. B. Smith and L. Dannison, September 2003, Custodial grandparents and schools: Building successful partnerships, www.wmich.edu/grs/forms/GP%20-%20Custodial%20GPs%20and%20Schools.pdf, accessed September 6, 2009.)

Questions for Reflection and Discussion

1. Explain the perspectives of Tammye, Jerome, and other school personnel.
2. What are the professional issues related to best practices in early education that need

to be emphasized in this case? Suggest ideas that the teacher, counselor, and director might consider.

3. Using resources regarding the importance of involving children's families in their education, what points would you make to support the involvement of Shalesa's father?

TEXT REFERENCES: Chapter 1 importance of families and communities in children's lives, Chapter 3 transition to parenthood and extended family relationships, Chapter 4 family structure, Chapter 5 grandparents as parents, Chapter 8 ongoing communication

Case 9

When Parents Deploy

The Teacher

Samuel Vega was beginning his second year of teaching second grade in an urban education center. Samuel had a successful first year of teaching with the support of a mentor who had received a Teacher of the Year award and a principal who was viewed as a regional leader in evidence-based educational practice. As Samuel began his second year at PS 22, he realized that several of the children in his class had parents who were waiting to be deployed to a combat zone by mid-November. Having grown up in a military family, Samuel was keenly aware that this would be a difficult year for those children and their families. He wanted to be proactive by creating a plan so that the school could provide some form of support. The end goal would relate to children's academic success, but also would consider the social and emotional foundations for such achievement.

Samuel took his concern first to the school principal, Dr. Alyssa Demetrius. Alyssa expressed appreciation for his initiative, but felt strongly that any effort should focus on academic achievement and should not interfere with family dynamics. Samuel thanked Alyssa for her consideration and set out to create a plan for the children in his class. When he shared this idea and his conversation with Alyssa with his mentor, Paulo Johnson, Paulo indicated that he would also have some children who will be affected by combat zone deployments and would like to work with Samuel.

PS 22 Families

After the first week of school, Joseph, a parent from a military family, approached Samuel and told him about his wife's imminent deployment. Joseph also indicated to Samuel that it had been estimated that PS 22 would have approximately 25 children facing deployment of family members to a combat zone in November. He noted that the National Military Family Association provided some materials that could help schools in their support of children and families in such circumstances.

Samuel asked Joseph to share materials with him and Paulo. After browsing through the resources, the two teachers met with Alyssa and shared information from their resources that a family emphasis would be more effective than school personnel simply reacting to children's concerns and behaviors. Alyssa would not be swayed. While she had deep concern about the effects of deployment of children at PS 22, she was resistant to becoming involved with families who she observed as having chosen military life.

Questions for Reflection and Discussion

1. Explain the perspectives of Samuel and Paulo, of Alyssa, and of Joseph.

2. What are the professional issues related to best practices in relation to family involvement and early education that need to be emphasized in this case?

3. Using resources regarding the ways in which early education programs might support children and their families when one or more family members deploy to combat, what advice would you give to all of those involved in this scenario?

TEXT REFERENCES: Chapter 1 perspectives on family involvement, Chapter 3 work and family, Chapter 4 family strengths, Chapter 6 military families, Chapter 8 conflict resolution, Chapter 10 family life education

Websites for Professional Development

Family Involvement in Early Childhood Education

(Please note that because Internet resources are time-sensitive and URL addresses may change or be deleted, searches should be conducted by association name or topic.)

A Guide to Children's Literature and Disability
http://www.kidsource.com/NICHCY/literature.html

Action for Healthy Kids
www.actionforhealthykids.org/

Adjustment Tasks for Stepfamilies
http://www.stepfamilyinfo.org/

Alliance for Full Acceptance
http://www.affa-sc.org/

American Association of Poison Control Center
www.aspcc.org

American Dietetic Association
www.eatright.org/ada/files/gerber.pdf

Asian Nation: The Landscape of Asian America
http://www.asian-nation.org

Association for Childhood Education International (ACEI)
http://www.acei.org

Association for Supervision and Curriculum Development (ASCD)
http://www.ascd.org

Birth Order Affects Career Interests
http://www.osu.edu
Type "birthorder" into the Search field under Locate

Birth Order and Intelligence
http://www.indiana.edu
Type in "birth order"

Birth Order and Personality Differences
http://www.encouragingleadership.com/

Building Family Strengths: Research to Application
http://www.clemson.edu
Click "search"; type in "family strengths"

Bureau of Indian Affairs
http://doi.gov/
Click "Bureau of Indian Affairs"

Bureau of Labor Statistics
http://www.bls.gov/

Caring for Babies with AIDS
http://www.caring4babieswithAIDS.org/

Center for Effective Discipline
http://www.stophitting.com

Center for Interventions, Treatment and Addiction Research
http://www.med.wright.edu/
Click "research"
Click "Center for Interventions, Treatment and Addiction Research"

Center for Substance Abuse Treatment
http://www.samhsa.gov/
Click "Center for Substance Abuse Treatment"

Center for Successful Fathering
http://www.fathering.com

Center for the Child Care Workforce
http://www.ccw.org

Center on the Family
http://uhfamily.hawaii.edu/

Character Education Partnership
http://www.character.org

Child Care Aware
http://www.childcareaware.org

Child Care Safety Checklist for Parents and Child Care Providers
www.cpsc.gov/cpscpub/pubs/childcare.html

Children Now
http://www.childrennow.org

Child Welfare and Research on Families
http://www.childwelfare.com/
    Type in "research"

Child Welfare League of America
http://www.cwla.org

Children with Disabilities: Understanding Sibling Issues
http://nichcy.org

Children's Defense Fund
http://www.childrensdefense.org

Children's Memorial Hospital (Chicago)— Neonatology
www.childrensmemorial.org
    Click "departments and programs"; click "neonatology"

Children, Youth & Family Consortium
http://www.cyfc.umn.edu/

Chronically Ill Children: How Families Adjust
http://www.nurseweek.com/
    Click "Education/CE"; type in "chronically ill children"

Clearinghouse on Early Education and Parenting
http://ceep.crc.uiuc.edu

Coalition for Asian American Children and Families
http://www.cacf.org

Committee to Repeal Section 43 of the Criminal Code of Canada
http://www.repeal43.org

Consumer Product Safety Commission
www.cpsc.gov

Council for Exceptional Children
http://www.cec.sped.org/

Creating a Strong Family
http://www.ianrpubs.unl.edu/epublic/
    pages/index.jpg
    Click "publications"; click "families"

Dads and Daughters
http://www.thedadman.com

Department of Health and Human Services Administration on Children and Families
http://www.acf.hhs.gov
    Click "Head Start"; click "Early Childhood Learning and Knowledge Center"

Developmental Assets
www.search-institute.org/
    Click "Developmental Assets"

Divorce Education and Mediation Program
http://www.hamiltontn.gov
    Click "courts information"; click "circuit court clerk"; click "divorce education seminars"

Early Childhood Development
http://www.worldbank.org
    Type in "early childhood"

Early Childhood Mental Health Program
www.ecmhp.org/

Eastern Orthodox Church in America
http://www.oca.org

ERIC Clearinghouse on Disabilities and Gifted Education
http://www.ericec.org/

Exceptional Parent Magazine
http://www.eparent.com/

Facing History and Ourselves
http://www.facinghistory.org/

Families and Physical Education and Fitness Connect for Kids— Obesity Resources
www.connectforkids.org/obesity_resources

Families and Work Institute
http://www.familiesandwork.org

Families in Crisis
http://www.Familiesincrisis.org

Family and Corrections Network
http://www.fcnetwork.org

Family Education Network
http://familyeducation.com/

Family Educational Rights and Privacy Act (FERPA)
http://www.ed.gov/
Type in "FERPA" to search sites

Family Focus
http://www.family-focus.org

Family Literacy
http://www.pabook.libraries.psu.edu
Click "family literacy activities"

Family Preservation and Child Welfare Network
http://www.childwelfare.com
Click "Family Preservation"

Family Resilience
http://extension.missouri.edu
Type in "family resilience"

Family Strengthening Writ Large: On Becoming a Nation That Promotes Strong Families and Successful Youth
http://www.nassembly.org/fspc

Family Support America
http://www.childwelfare.gov/supporting
Search for "Family Support America"

Family Support and Children's Mental Health
http://www.rtc.pdx.edu/

Family Village
http://www.familyvillage.wisc.edu

Family Violence Prevention Fund
http://endabuse.org/

Family Works, Inc.
http://www.familyworksinc.com/

Federal Office of Child Support Enforcement
http://www.acf.dhhs.gov/
Select "Child Support Enforcement" on pull-down menu for ACF Programs

Federal Resource Center for Special Education
http://www.rrfcnetwork.org

Federal Resources for Educational Excellence (FREE)
http://www.ed.gov
Type in "free"

Federation for Children with Special Needs
http://www.fcsn.org

Fireproof Children Company
www.playsafebesafe.com

Food and Nutrition Information Center
www.nal.usda.gov.fnic

Forum on Child and Family Statistics
http://www.childstats.gov/

Foster Care
http://www.fostercare.net

Foundation for Grandparenting
http://www.grandparenting.org

Free Appropriate Public Education Site
http://www.wrightslaw.com
Click "FAPE"

From Family Stress to Family Strengths
http://www.cdc.gov
Type in "family stress"

Futures for Children
http://www.futuresforchildren.org

Grandparents' Rights Center
http://www.grandparentsrights.org

Health Coverage for Legal Immigrant Children
http://www.cbpp.org
Type in "ImmigrantChildren"; click "Health Coverage for Legal Immigrant Children"

Healthy Child Care America
www.healthychildcare.org

Helping Children Adapt to a New Sibling
http://www.nncc.org
Click "Articles and Resources"

Helping Children to Understand Divorce
http://www.muextension.missouri.edu
Type in "divorce"

Home Instruction Program for Preschool Youngsters (HIPPY)
http://www.hippyusa.org

Homeless Children's Network
http://www.hcnkids.org

Homes for the Homeless
http://www.homesforthehomeless.com/

Houghton Mifflin Education Place
http://www.eduplace.com/
Click "science"

How Foster Children Impact Sibling Relationships
http://www.fostercare.net/

Human Development and Family Science
www.hec.ohiostate.edu/famlife/yc/care.htm

Immigrant Children Exceed Expectations
http://www.ilw.com/

Index of Native American Resources on the Internet
http://www.hanksville.org
Click "Index of Native American Resources on the Internet"

Individualizing Inclusion in Child Care
http://www.fpg.unc.edu/~inclusion/

Institute for Child and Family Policy
http://www.childpolicy.org/

International Reading Association
http://www.reading.org

Jewish Holidays
http://www.bnaibrith.org
Click "Jewish Holidays"

Kids Health for Parents
www.kidshealth.org/parent/nutrition_fit/nutrition/pyramid.html

Kwanzaa
http://www.officialkwanzaawebsite.org

Latino Resources
http://latino.sscnet.ucla.edu/

Lev Vygotsky's Theory
http://www.muskingum.edu/~psych/psycweb/history/vygotsky.htm

Maternal and Child Health Library
www.mchlibrary.info

Matthew Shepard Foundation
http://www.matthewsplace.org

Medlineplus Health Information
www.nim.nih.gov/medlineplus/childsafety.html

Mental Health America: Recognizing Mental Health Problems in Children
www.nmha.org/farcry/go/information/getinfo/children-s-mental-health/recognizing-mental-health-problems-in-children

Megaskills from the Home and School Institute
http://www.megaskillshsi.org

Migrant Education Program
http://www.ed.gov
Click "offices"; click "Office of Elementary and Secondary Education home page"; click "programs/initiatives"; click "office of migrant education"

Migrant Head Start
http://www.acf.dhhs.gov
Click "Head Start Bureau" on pull-down menu; click "programs/services"; click "migrant and seasonal program branch"

Multicultural Books Every Child Should Know
http://www.education.wisc.edu
Type in "multicultural"; click "Multicultural Literature Volume 2"

Multicultural Pavilion
www.edchange.org/multicultural

Museum of Tolerance
http://www.wiesenthal.com
Select "Museum of Tolerance" from pull-down menu on top of page

National Association for Family Child Care
http://www.nafcc.org

National Association for Gifted Children
http://www.nagc.org

National Association for Sport and Physical Education
www.aahperd.org/NASPE/template.cfm?template=peappropriatepractice/index.html

National Association for the Education of Homeless Children and Youth
http://www.naehcy.org

National Association for the Education of Young Children (NAEYC)
http://www.naeyc.org

National Association of Child Care Resource and Referral Agencies
http://www.naccrra.org

National Association of School Psychologists
http://www.naspcenter.org

National Black Child Development Institute
http://www.nbcdi.org

National Center for Children in Poverty
http://www.nccp.org

National Center for Education Statistics
http://nces.ed.gov/

National Center for Family Literacy
http://www.famlit.org

National Center for Fathering
http://www.fathers.com

National Center for Policy Analysis: Welfare
http://www.ncpa.org
Type in "welfare"

National Center for Research on Evaluation, Standards and Student Testing
http://cse.ucla.edu/about.htm

National Center on Addiction and Substance Abuse at Columbia University
http://www.casacolumbia.org/

National Center on Child Abuse and Neglect (NCCAN)
63 Inverness Drive East Englewood, Colorado 80112-5117; (303) 792-9900

National Child Care Information Center
http://nccic.org

National Clearinghouse for Educational Facilities
www.edfacilities.org

National Clearinghouse for English Language Acquisition and Language Instruction Educational Programs
http://www.ncela.gwu.edu

National Clearinghouse on Child Abuse and Neglect Information
http://ncadi.samhsa.gov

National Coalition Against Domestic Violence
http://www.ncadv.org/

National Coalition for Parent Involvement in Education
http://www.ncpie.org/

National Council for the Social Studies
http://www.ncss.org

National Council of Teachers of Mathematics
http://www.nctm.org

National Council on Child Abuse and Family Violence
http://www.nccafv.org/

National Council on Family Relations
http://www.ncfr.org

National Dissemination Center for Children with Disabilities
http://www.nichcy.org

National Domestic Violence Hotline
http://www.ndvh.org/

National Dropout Prevention Center/Network
http://www.dropoutprevention.org/effstrat/family_engagement/overview.htm

National Fatherhood Initiative
http://www.fatherhood.com

National Head Start Association
http://www.nhsa.org/

National Network for Child Care
http://www.nncc.org/

National Network of Partnership Schools (NNPS)
www.coso.jhu.edu
Click "programs"; click "National Network of Partnership Schools"

National Parent Information Network
http://www.npin.org/

National Parent Teacher Association (PTA)
http://www.pta.org/

National Science Education Standards
http://www.nap.edu/
Type in "nses"

National Science Teachers Association
http://www.nsta.org

Olson's Circumplex Model
http://www.noeticus.org/uploads/5-OlsonCircumplex_Model.pdf

Parenting without Punishing
http://www.nopunish.net

Parent Teacher Organization (PTO)
http://www.ptotoday.com

Parents Action for Children
http://www.parentsaction.org

Parents Anonymous
http://www.parentsanonymous.org/

Parents as Teachers (PAT) National Center
http://www.parentsasteachers.org

PE Central
www.pecentral.org

Position Statement on Developmentally Appropriate Practice
http://www.naeyc.org/
Click "Resources"; click "Position Statements"

Position Statement on Responding to Linguistic and Cultural Diversity
http://www.naeyc.org/
Click "Resources"; click "Position Statements"

Preservation and Child Welfare Network
http://www.childwelfare.com

Primary Project (School-based Prevention)
http://www.childrensinstitute.net
Click "programs for children"; click "primary project"

Project Resilience
www.projectresilience.com/

Research and Training Center on Family Support and Children's Mental Health
http://www.rtc.pdx.edu

Research Matters
http://www.researchmatters.harvard.edu

Resources for Information about Child Abuse and Neglect
http://www.ncadi.samsha.gov
http://www.casanet.org/
http://naccchildlaw.org/

Risk Watch: Make Time for Safety
www.nfpa.org/riskwatch/kids.html

Science for Families Update
http://kidscience.blogspot.com

Sexual Orientation and Gender Identity
http://www.aclu.org
Click "lesbian and gay rights"

Siblings in Adoption—Expanded Families
http://www.pactadopt.org/
Click "Articles of Interest"; click "siblings"

Special Child
http://www.specialchild.com

Stand for Children
http://www.stand.org

STARLIGHT Foundation for Seriously Ill Children and Their Families
http://www.starlight.org

Strengthening Families. Center for the Study of Social Policy
http://www.strengtheningfamilies.net

Teaching Strategies
http://www.TeachingStrategies.com

Teaching Tolerance
http://www.Tolerance.org

The Division for Early Childhood of the Council on Exceptional Children
http://www.dec-sped.org/

The Effect of Birth Order on Intelligence
http://www.indiana.edu
Type "intelligence and birth order" in the Search field

The Family Involvement Network of Educators (FINE)
www.gse.harvard.edu

The Reading Connection
http://www.thereadingconnection.org/

Try Science
http://www.TryScience.org

Tufts University Child and Family Web Guide
http://www.cfw.tufts.edu

U.S. Census Bureau—Poverty
http://www.census.gov
Type in "poverty"

U.S. Government Publications for Parents
http://www.ed.gov
Click "parents"

Wheelock College Institute for Leadership and Career Initiatives
http://institute.wheelock.edu

ZERO TO THREE
http://www.zerotothree.org/

naeyc®
Code of Ethical Conduct
and Statement of Commitment

Revised April 2005, Reaffirmed and Updated May 2011

A position statement of the National Association for the Education of Young Children

Endorsed by the Association for Childhood Education
International Adopted by the National Association for Family Child Care

Preamble

NAEYC recognizes that those who work with young children face many daily decisions that have moral and ethical implications. The **NAEYC Code of Ethical Conduct** offers guidelines for responsible behavior and sets forth a common basis for resolving the principal ethical dilemmas encountered in early childhood care and education. The **Statement of Commitment** is not part of the Code but is a personal acknowledgement of an individual's willingness to embrace the distinctive values and moral obligations of the field of early childhood care and education.

The primary focus of the Code is on daily practice with children and their families in programs for children from birth through 8 years of age, such as infant/toddler programs, preschool and prekindergarten programs, child care centers, hospital and child life settings, family child care homes, kindergartens, and primary classrooms. When the issues involve young children, then these provisions also apply to specialists who do not work directly with children, including program administrators, parent educators, early childhood adult educators, and officials with responsibility for program monitoring and licensing. (Note: See also the "Code of Ethical Conduct: Supplement for Early Childhood Adult Educators," online at www.naeyc.org/about/positions/pdf/ethics04.pdf and the "Code of Ethical Conduct: Supplement for Early Childhood Program Administrators," online at http://www naeyc.org/files/naeyc/file/positions/PSETH05_supp.pdf)

Core Values

Standards of ethical behavior in early childhood care and education are based on commitment to the following core values that are deeply rooted in the history of the field of early childhood care and education. We have made a commitment to

- Appreciate childhood as a unique and valuable stage of the human life cycle
- Base our work on knowledge of how children develop and learn
- Appreciate and support the bond between the child and family
- Recognize that children are best understood and supported in the context of family, culture,* community, and society

*The term *culture* includes ethnicity, racial identity, economic level, family structure, language, and religious and political beliefs, which profoundly influence each child's development and relationship to the world.

- Respect the dignity, worth, and uniqueness of each individual (child, family member, and colleague)
- Respect diversity in children, families, and colleagues
- Recognize that children and adults achieve their full potential in the context of relationships that are based on trust and respect

Conceptual Framework

The Code sets forth a framework of professional responsibilities in four sections. Each section addresses an area of professional relationships: (1) with children, (2) with families, (3) among colleagues, and (4) with the community and society. Each section includes an introduction to the primary responsibilities of the early childhood practitioner in that context. The introduction is followed by a set of ideals (I) that reflect exemplary professional practice and by a set of principles (P) describing practices that are required, prohibited, or permitted.

The **ideals** reflect the aspirations of practitioners. The **principles** guide conduct and assist practitioners in resolving ethical dilemmas.* Both ideals and principles are intended to direct practitioners to those questions which, when responsibly answered, can provide the basis for conscientious decision making. While the Code provides specific direction for addressing some ethical dilemmas, many others will require the practitioner to combine the guidance of the Code with professional judgment.

The ideals and principles in this Code present a shared framework of professional responsibility that affirms our commitment to the core values of our field. The Code publicly acknowledges the responsibilities that we in the field have assumed, and in so doing supports ethical behavior in our work. Practitioners who face situations with ethical dimensions are urged to seek guidance in the applicable parts of this Code and in the spirit that informs the whole.

Often "the right answer"—the best ethical course of action to take—is not obvious. There may be no readily apparent, positive way to handle a situation. When one important value contradicts another, we face an ethical dilemma. When we face a dilemma, it is our professional responsibility to consult the Code and all relevant parties to find the most ethical resolution.

---

* There is not necessarily a corresponding principle for each ideal.

Section I
Ethical Responsibilities to Children

Childhood is a unique and valuable stage in the human life cycle. Our paramount responsibility is to provide care and education in settings that are safe, healthy, nurturing, and responsive for each child. We are committed to supporting children's development and learning; respecting individual differences; and helping children learn to live, play, and work cooperatively. We are also committed to promoting children's self-awareness, competence, self-worth, resiliency, and physical well-being.

Ideals

I-1.1 To be familiar with the knowledge base of early childhood care and education and to stay informed through continuing education and training.

I-1.2 To base program practices upon current knowledge and research in the field of early childhood education, child development, and related disciplines, as well as on particular knowledge of each child.

I-1.3 To recognize and respect the unique qualities, abilities, and potential of each child.

I-1.4 To appreciate the vulnerability of children and their dependence on adults.

I-1.5 To create and maintain safe and healthy settings that foster children's social, emotional, cognitive, and physical development and that respect their dignity and their contributions.

I-1.6 To use assessment instruments and strategies that are appropriate for the children to be assessed, that are used only for the purposes for which they were designed, and that have the potential to benefit children.

I-1.7 To use assessment information to understand and support children's development and learning, to support instruction, and to identify children who may need additional services.

I-1.8 To support the right of each child to play and learn in an inclusive environment that meets the needs of children with and without disabilities.

I-1.9 To advocate for and ensure that all children, including those with special needs, have access to the support services needed to be successful.

I-1.10 To ensure that each child's culture, language, ethnicity, and family structure are recognized and valued in the program.

I-1.11   To provide all children with experiences in a language that they know, as well as support children in maintaining the use of their home language and in learning English.

I-1.12   To work with families to provide a safe and smooth transition as children and families move from one program to the next.

Principles

P-1.1   Above all, we shall not harm children. We shall not participate in practices that are emotionally damaging, physically harmful, disrespectful, degrading, dangerous, exploitative, or intimidating to children. *This principle has precedence over all others in this Code.*

P-1.2   We shall care for and educate children in positive emotional and social environments that are cognitively stimulating and that support each child's culture, language, ethnicity, and family structure.

P-1.3   We shall not participate in practices that discriminate against children by denying benefits, giving special advantages, or excluding them from programs or activities on the basis of their sex, race, national origin, immigration status, preferred home language, religious beliefs, medical condition, disability, or the marital status/family structure, sexual orientation, or religious beliefs or other affiliations of their families. (Aspects of this principle do not apply in programs that have a lawful mandate to provide services to a particular population of children.)

P-1.4   We shall use two-way communications to involve all those with relevant knowledge (including families and staff) in decisions concerning a child, as appropriate, ensuring confidentiality of sensitive information. (See also P-2.4.)

P-1.5   We shall use appropriate assessment systems, which include multiple sources of information, to provide information on children's learning and development.

P-1.6   We shall strive to ensure that decisions such as those related to enrollment, retention, or assignment to special education services, will be based on multiple sources of information and will never be based on a single assessment, such as a test score or a single observation.

P-1.7   We shall strive to build individual relationships with each child; make individualized adaptations in teaching strategies, learning environments, and curricula; and consult with the family so that each child benefits from the program. If after such efforts have been exhausted, the current placement does not meet a child's needs, or the child is seriously jeopardizing the ability of other children to benefit from the program, we shall collaborate with the child's family and appropriate specialists to determine the additional services needed and/or the placement option(s) most likely to ensure the child's success. (Aspects of this principle may not apply in programs that have a lawful mandate to provide services to a particular population of children.)

P-1.8   We shall be familiar with the risk factors for and symptoms of child abuse and neglect, including physical, sexual, verbal, and emotional abuse and physical, emotional, educational, and medical neglect. We shall know and follow state laws and community procedures that protect children against abuse and neglect.

P-1.9   When we have reasonable cause to suspect child abuse or neglect, we shall report it to the appropriate community agency and follow up to ensure that appropriate action has been taken. When appropriate, parents or guardians will be informed that the referral will be or has been made.

P-1.10   When another person tells us of his or her suspicion that a child is being abused or neglected, we shall assist that person in taking appropriate action in order to protect the child.

P-1.11   When we become aware of a practice or situation that endangers the health, safety, or well-being of children, we have an ethical responsibility to protect children or inform parents and/or others who can.

Section II
Ethical Responsibilities to Families

Families* are of primary importance in children's development. Because the family and the early childhood practitioner have a common interest in the child's well-being, we acknowledge a primary responsibility to bring about communication, cooperation, and collaboration between the home and early childhood program in ways that enhance the child's development.

Ideals

I-2.1   To be familiar with the knowledge base related to working effectively with families and to

---

* The term *family* may include those adults, besides parents, with the responsibility of being involved in educating, nurturing, and advocating for the child.

stay informed through continuing education and training.

I-2.2 To develop relationships of mutual trust and create partnerships with the families we serve.

I-2.3 To welcome all family members and encourage them to participate in the program, including involvement in shared decision making.

I-2.4 To listen to families, acknowledge and build upon their strengths and competencies, and learn from families as we support them in their task of nurturing children.

I-2.5 To respect the dignity and preferences of each family and to make an effort to learn about its structure, culture, language, customs, and beliefs to ensure a culturally consistent environment for all children and families.

I-2.6 To acknowledge families' childrearing values and their right to make decisions for their children.

I-2.7 To share information about each child's education and development with families and to help them understand and appreciate the current knowledge base of the early childhood profession.

I-2.8 To help family members enhance their understanding of their children, as staff are enhancing their understanding of each child through communications with families, and support family members in the continuing development of their skills as parents.

I-2.9 To foster families' efforts to build support networks and, when needed, participate in building networks for families by providing them with opportunities to interact with program staff, other families, community resources, and professional services.

Principles

P-2.1 We shall not deny family members access to their child's classroom or program setting unless access is denied by court order or other legal restriction.

P-2.2 We shall inform families of program philosophy, policies, curriculum, assessment system, cultural practices, and personnel qualifications, and explain why we teach as we do—which should be in accordance with our ethical responsibilities to children (see Section I).

P-2.3 We shall inform families of and, when appropriate, involve them in policy decisions. (See also I-2.3.)

P-2.4 We shall ensure that the family is involved in significant decisions affecting their child. (See also P-1.4.)

P-2.5 We shall make every effort to communicate effectively with all families in a language that they understand. We shall use community resources for translation and interpretation when we do not have sufficient resources in our own programs.

P-2.6 As families share information with us about their children and families, we shall ensure that families' input is an important contribution to the planning and implementation of the program.

P-2-7 We shall inform families about the nature and purpose of the program's child assessments and how data about their child will be used.

P-2.8 We shall treat child assessment information confidentially and share this information only when there is a legitimate need for it.

P-2.9 We shall inform the family of injuries and incidents involving their child, of risks such as exposures to communicable diseases that might result in infection, and of occurrences that might result in emotional stress.

P-2.10 Families shall be fully informed of any proposed research projects involving their children and shall have the opportunity to give or withhold consent without penalty. We shall not permit or participate in research that could in any way hinder the education, development, or well-being of children.

P-2.11 We shall not engage in or support exploitation of families. We shall not use our relationship with a family for private advantage or personal gain, or enter into relationships with family members that might impair our effectiveness working with their children.

P-2.12 We shall develop written policies for the protection of confidentiality and the disclosure of children's records. These policy documents shall be made available to all program personnel and families. Disclosure of children's records beyond family members, program personnel, and consultants having an obligation of confidentiality shall require familial consent (except in cases of abuse or neglect).

P-2.13 We shall maintain confidentiality and shall respect the family's right to privacy, refraining from disclosure of confidential information and intrusion into family life. However, when we have reason to believe that a child's welfare is at risk, it is permissible to share confidential information with agencies, as well as with individuals who have legal responsibility for intervening in the child's interest.

P-2.14 In cases where family members are in conflict with one another, we shall work openly, sharing our observations of the child, to help all parties involved make informed decisions. We shall refrain from becoming an advocate for one party.

P-2.15   We shall be familiar with and appropriately refer families to community resources and professional support services. After a referral has been made, we shall follow up to ensure that services have been appropriately provided.

Section III
Ethical Responsibilities to Colleagues

In a caring, cooperative workplace, human dignity is respected, professional satisfaction is promoted, and positive relationships are developed and sustained. Based upon our core values, our primary responsibility to colleagues is to establish and maintain settings and relationships that support productive work and meet professional needs. The same ideals that apply to children also apply as we interact with adults in the workplace. (Note: Section III includes responsibilities to co-workers and to employers. See the "Code of Ethical Conduct: Supplement for Early Childhood Program Administrators" for responsibilities to personnel (*employees* in the original 2005 Code revision), online at http://www.naeyc.org/files/naeyc/file/positions/PSETH05_supp.pdf.)

A—Responsibilities to Co-workers
Ideals

I-3A.1   To establish and maintain relationships of respect, trust, confidentiality, collaboration, and cooperation with co-workers.

I-3A.2   To share resources with co-workers, collaborating to ensure that the best possible early childhood care and education program is provided.

I-3A.3   To support co-workers in meeting their professional needs and in their professional development.

I-3A.4   To accord co-workers due recognition of professional achievement.

Principles

P-3A.1   We shall recognize the contributions of colleagues to our program and not participate in practices that diminish their reputations or impair their effectiveness in working with children and families.

P-3A.2   When we have concerns about the professional behavior of a co-worker, we shall first let that person know of our concern in a way that shows respect for personal dignity and for the diversity to be found among staff members, and then attempt to resolve the matter collegially and in a confidential manner.

P-3A.3   We shall exercise care in expressing views regarding the personal attributes or professional conduct of co-workers. Statements should be based on firsthand knowledge, not hearsay, and relevant to the interests of children and programs.

P-3A.4   We shall not participate in practices that discriminate against a co-worker because of sex, race, national origin, religious beliefs or other affiliations, age, marital status/family structure, disability, or sexual orientation.

B—Responsibilities to Employers
Ideals

I-3B.1   To assist the program in providing the highest quality of service.

I-3B.2   To do nothing that diminishes the reputation of the program in which we work unless it is violating laws and regulations designed to protect children or is violating the provisions of this Code.

Principles

P-3B.1   We shall follow all program policies. When we do not agree with program policies, we shall attempt to effect change through constructive action within the organization.

P-3B.2   We shall speak or act on behalf of an organization only when authorized. We shall take care to acknowledge when we are speaking for the organization and when we are expressing a personal judgment.

P-3B.3   We shall not violate laws or regulations designed to protect children and shall take appropriate action consistent with this Code when aware of such violations.

P-3B.4   If we have concerns about a colleague's behavior, and children's well-being is not at risk, we may address the concern with that individual. If children are at risk or the situation does not improve after it has been brought to the colleague's attention, we shall report the colleague's unethical or incompetent behavior to an appropriate authority.

P-3B.5   When we have a concern about circumstances or conditions that impact the quality of care and education within the program, we shall inform the program's administration or, when necessary, other appropriate authorities.

Section IV
Ethical Responsibilities to Community and Society

Early childhood programs operate within the context of their immediate community made up of families and other institutions concerned with children's welfare. Our responsibilities to the community are to provide programs that meet the diverse needs of families, to cooperate with agencies and professions that share the responsibility for children, to assist families in gaining access to those agencies and allied professionals, and to assist in the development of community programs that are needed but not currently available.

As individuals, we acknowledge our responsibility to provide the best possible programs of care and education for children and to conduct ourselves with honesty and integrity. Because of our specialized expertise in early childhood development and education and because the larger society shares responsibility for the welfare and protection of young children, we acknowledge a collective obligation to advocate for the best interests of children within early childhood programs and in the larger community and to serve as a voice for young children everywhere.

The ideals and principles in this section are presented to distinguish between those that pertain to the work of the individual early childhood educator and those that more typically are engaged in collectively on behalf of the best interests of children—with the understanding that individual early childhood educators have a shared responsibility for addressing the ideals and principles that are identified as "collective."

Ideal (Individual)

1-4.1 To provide the community with high-quality early childhood care and education programs and services.

Ideals (Collective)

I-4.2 To promote cooperation among professionals and agencies and interdisciplinary collaboration among professions concerned with addressing issues in the health, education, and

well-being of young children, their families, and their early childhood educators.

I-4.3 To work through education, research, and advocacy toward an environmentally safe world in which all children receive health care, food, and shelter; are nurtured; and live free from violence in their home and their communities.

I-4.4 To work through education, research, and advocacy toward a society in which all young children have access to high-quality early care and education programs.

I-4.5 To work to ensure that appropriate assessment systems, which include multiple sources of information, are used for purposes that benefit children.

I-4.6 To promote knowledge and understanding of young children and their needs. To work toward greater societal acknowledgment of children's rights and greater social acceptance of responsibility for the well-being of all children.

I-4.7 To support policies and laws that promote the well-being of children and families, and to work to change those that impair their well-being. To participate in developing policies and laws that are needed, and to cooperate with families and other individuals and groups in these efforts.

I-4.8 To further the professional development of the field of early childhood care and education and to strengthen its commitment to realizing its core values as reflected in this Code.

Principles (Individual)

P-4.1 We shall communicate openly and truthfully about the nature and extent of services that we provide.

P-4.2 We shall apply for, accept, and work in positions for which we are personally well-suited and professionally qualified. We shall not offer services that we do not have the competence, qualifications, or resources to provide.

P-4.3 We shall carefully check references and shall not hire or recommend for employment any person whose competence, qualifications, or character makes him or her unsuited for the position.

P-4.4 We shall be objective and accurate in reporting the knowledge upon which we base our program practices.

P-4.5 We shall be knowledgeable about the appropriate use of assessment strategies and instruments and interpret results accurately to families.

P-4.6   We shall be familiar with laws and regulations that serve to protect the children in our programs and be vigilant in ensuring that these laws and regulations are followed.

P-4.7   When we become aware of a practice or situation that endangers the health, safety, or well-being of children, we have an ethical responsibility to protect children or inform parents and/or others who can.

P-4.8   We shall not participate in practices that are in violation of laws and regulations that protect the children in our programs.

P-4.9   When we have evidence that an early childhood program is violating laws or regulations protecting children, we shall report the violation to appropriate authorities who can be expected to remedy the situation.

P-4.10   When a program violates or requires its employees to violate this Code, it is permissible, after fair assessment of the evidence, to disclose the identity of that program.

Principles (Collective)

P-4.11   When policies are enacted for purposes that do not benefit children, we have a collective responsibility to work to change these policies.

P-4-12   When we have evidence that an agency that provides services intended to ensure children's well-being is failing to meet its obligations, we acknowledge a collective ethical responsibility to report the problem to appropriate authorities or to the public. We shall be vigilant in our follow-up until the situation is resolved.

P-4.13   When a child protection agency fails to provide adequate protection for abused or neglected children, we acknowledge a collective ethical responsibility to work toward the improvement of these services.

Glossary of Terms Related to Ethics

Code of Ethics   Defines the core values of the field and provides guidance for what professionals should do when they encounter conflicting obligations or responsibilities in their work.

Values   Qualities or principles that individuals believe to be desirable or worthwhile and that they prize for themselves, for others, and for the world in which they live.

Core Values   Commitments held by a profession that are consciously and knowingly embraced by its practitioners because they make a contribution to society. There is a difference between personal values and the core values of a profession.

Morality   Peoples' views of what is good, right, and proper; their beliefs about their obligations; and their ideas about how they should behave.

Ethics   The study of right and wrong, or duty and obligation, that involves critical reflection on morality and the ability to make choices between values and the examination of the moral dimensions of relationships.

Professional Ethics   The moral commitments of a profession that involve moral reflection that extends and enhances the personal morality practitioners bring to their work, that concern actions of right and wrong in the workplace, and that help individuals resolve moral dilemmas they encounter in their work.

Ethical Responsibilities   Behaviors that one must or must not engage in. Ethical responsibilities are clear-cut and are spelled out in the Code of Ethical Conduct (for example, early childhood educators should never share confidential information about a child or family with a person who has no legitimate need for knowing).

Ethical Dilemma   A moral conflict that involves determining appropriate conduct when an individual faces conflicting professional values and responsibilities.

Sources for Glossary Terms and Definitions

Feeney, S., & N. Freeman. 2005. *Ethics and the early childhood educator: Using the NAEYC code.* Washington, DC: NAEYC.

Kidder, R.M. 1995. *How good people make tough choices: Resolving the dilemmas of ethical living.* New York: Fireside.

Kipnis, K. 1987. How to discuss professional ethics. *Young Children* 42 (4): 26–30.

The National Association for the Education of Young Children (NAEYC) is a nonprofit corporation, tax exempt under Section 501(c)(3) of the Internal Revenue Code, dedicated to acting on behalf of the needs and interests of young children. The NAEYC Code of Ethical Conduct (Code) has been developed in furtherance of NAEYC's nonprofit and tax exempt purposes. The information contained in the Code is intended to provide early childhood educators with guidelines for working with children from birth through age 8.

An individual's or program's use, reference to, or review of the Code does not guarantee compliance with NAEYC Early Childhood Program Standards and Accreditation Performance Criteria and program accreditation procedures. It is recommended that the Code be used as guidance in connection with implementation of the NAEYC Program Standards, but such use is not a substitute for diligent review and application of the NAEYC Program Standards.

NAEYC has taken reasonable measures to develop the Code in a fair, reasonable, open, unbiased, and objective manner, based on currently available data. However, further research or developments may change the current state of knowledge. Neither NAEYC nor its officers, directors, members, employees, or agents will be liable for any loss, damage, or claim with respect to any liabilities, including direct, special, indirect, or consequential damages incurred in connection with the Code or reliance on the information presented.

NAEYC Code of Ethical Conduct 2005 Revisions Workgroup

Mary Ambery, Ruth Ann Ball, James Clay, Julie Olsen Edwards, Harriet Egertson, Anthony Fair, Stephanie Feeney, Jana Fleming, Nancy Freeman, Marla Israel, Allison McKinnon, Evelyn Wright Moore, Eva Moravcik, Christina Lopez Morgan, Sarah Mulligan, Nila Rinehart, Betty Holston Smith, and Peter Pizzolongo, NAEYC Staff

Statement of Commitment*

As an individual who works with young children, I commit myself to furthering the values of early childhood education as they are reflected in the ideals and principles of the NAEYC Code of Ethical Conduct. To the best of my ability I will

- Never harm children.
- Ensure that programs for young children are based on current knowledge and research of child development and early childhood education.
- Respect and support families in their task of nurturing children.
- Respect colleagues in early childhood care and education and support them in maintaining the NAEYC Code of Ethical Conduct.
- Serve as an advocate for children, their families, and their teachers in community and society.
- Stay informed of and maintain high standards of professional conduct.
- Engage in an ongoing process of self-reflection, realizing that personal characteristics, biases, and beliefs have an impact on children and families.
- Be open to new ideas and be willing to learn from the suggestions of others.
- Continue to learn, grow, and contribute as a professional.
- Honor the ideals and principles of the NAEYC Code of Ethical Conduct.

* This Statement of Commitment is not part of the Code but is a personal acknowledgment of the individual's willingness to embrace the distinctive values and moral obligations of the field of early childhood care and education. It is recognition of the moral obligations that lead to an individual becoming part of the profession.

NAEYC Academy for Early Childhood Program Accreditation Standards and Topic Areas*

Information in Appendix C may be helpful in increasing understanding about NAEYC Program accreditation as discussed in Chapter 1.

Standard 1
NAEYC Accreditation Criteria for Relationships

Program Standard: The program promotes positive relationships among all children and adults to encourage each child's sense of individual worth and belonging as part of a community and to foster each child's ability to contribute as a responsible community member.

Topic Areas

1.A. Building Positive Relationships among Teachers and Families

1.B. Building Positive Relationships between Teachers and Children

1.C. Helping Children Make Friends

1.D. Creating a Predictable, Consistent, and Harmonious Classroom

1.E. Addressing Challenging Behaviors

1.F. Promoting Self-Regulation

Standard 2
NAEYC Accreditation Criteria for Curriculum

Program Standard: The program implements a curriculum that is consistent with its goals for children and promotes learning and development in each of the following areas: social, emotional, physical, language, and cognitive.

Topic Areas

2.A. Essential Characteristics

2.B. Areas of Development: Social-Emotional Development

2.C. Areas of Development: Physical Development

2.D. Areas of Development: Language Development

2.E. Curriculum Content Area for Cognitive Development: Early Literacy

2.F. Curriculum Content Area for Cognitive Development: Early Math

2.G. Curriculum Content Area for Cognitive Development: Science

2.H. Curriculum Content Area for Cognitive Development: Technology

To avoid confusion in the numbering system, there are no criteria labeled 2.I.

2.J. Curriculum Area for Cognitive Development: Creative Expression and Appreciation for the Arts

2.K. Curriculum Content Area for Cognitive Development: Health and Safety

2.L. Curriculum Content Area for Cognitive Development: Social Studies

Standard 3
NAEYC Accreditation Criteria for Teaching

Program Standard: The program uses developmentally, culturally, and linguistically appropriate

*From NAEYC, 2005. NAEYC Early Childhood Program Standards and Accreditation Criteria: The Mark of Quality in Early Childhood Education. Washington DC: Kent Chrisman.

and effective teaching approaches that enhance each child's learning and development in the context of the program's curriculum goals.

Topic Areas

3.A. Designing Enriched Learning Environments
3.B. Creating Caring Communities for Learning
3.C. Supervising Children
3.D. Using Time, Grouping, and Routines to Achieve Learning Goals
3.E. Responding to Children's Interests and Needs
3.F. Making Learning Meaningful for All Children
3.G. Using Instruction to Deepen Children's Understanding and Build Their Skills and Knowledge

Standard 4
NAEYC Accreditation Criteria for Assessment of Child Progress

Program Standard: The program is informed by ongoing systematic, formal, and informal assessment approaches to provide information on children's learning and development. These assessments occur within the context of reciprocal communications with families and with sensitivity to the cultural contexts in which children develop. Assessment results are used to benefit children by informing sound decisions about children, teaching, and program improvement.

Topic Areas

4.A. Creating an Assessment Plan
4.B. Using Appropriate Assessment Methods
4.C. Identifying Children's Interests and Needs and Describing Children's Progress
4.D. Adapting Curriculum, Individualizing Teaching, and Informing Program Development
4.E. Communicating with Families and Involving Families in the Assessment Process

Standard 5
NAEYC Accreditation Criteria for Health Standard

Program Standard: The program promotes the nutrition and health of children and protects children and staff from illness and injury.

Topic Areas

5.A. Promoting and Protecting Children's Health and Controlling Infectious Disease
5.B. Ensuring Children's Nutritional Well-being
5.C. Maintaining a Healthful Environment

Standard 6
NAEYC Accreditation Criteria for Teachers Standard

Program Standard: The program employs and supports a teaching staff that has the educational qualifications, knowledge, and professional commitment necessary to promote children's learning and development and to support families' diverse needs and interests.

Topic Areas

6.A. Preparation, Knowledge, and Skills of Teaching Staff
6.B. Teachers' Dispositions and Professional Commitment

Standard 7
NAEYC Accreditation Criteria for Families Standard

Program Standard: The program establishes and maintains collaborative relationships with each child's family to foster children's development in all settings. These relationships are sensitive to family composition, language, and culture.

Topic Areas

7.A. Knowing and Understanding the Program's Families
7.B. Sharing Information Between Staff and Families
7.C. Nurturing Families as Advocates for Their Children

Standard 8
NAEYC Accreditation Criteria for Community Relationships Standard

Program Standard: The program establishes relationships with and uses the resources of the children's communities to support the achievement of program goals.

Topic Areas

8.A. Linking with the Community
8.B. Accessing Community Resources
8.C. Acting as a Citizen in the Neighborhood and the Early Childhood Community

Standard 9
NAEYC Accreditation Criteria for Physical Environment Standard

Program Standard: The program has a safe and healthful environment that provides appropriate and well-maintained indoor and outdoor physical environments. The environment includes facilities, equipment, and materials to facilitate child and staff learning and development.

Topic Areas

9.A. Indoor and Outdoor Equipment, Materials, and Furnishings
9.B. Outdoor Environmental Design
9.C. Building and Physical Design
9.D. Environmental Health

Standard 10
NAEYC Accreditation Criteria for Leadership and Management Standard

Program Standard: The program effectively implements policies, procedures, and systems that support stable staff and strong personnel, fiscal, and program management so all children, families, and staff have high-quality experiences.

Topic Areas

10.A. Leadership
10.B. Management Policies and Procedures
10.C. Fiscal Accountability Policies and Procedures
10.D. Health, Nutrition, and Safety Policies and Procedures
10.E. Personnel Policies
10.F. Program Evaluation, Accountability, and Continuous Improvement

Responding to Linguistic and Cultural Diversity Recommendations for Effective Early Childhood Education

*A Position Statement of the National Association for the Education of Young Children (1995)**

Information in Appendix D may be helpful in increasing understanding about best practices related to supporting cultural and language diversity as discussed in Chapter 2.

Linguistically and culturally diverse is an educational term used by the U.S. Department of Education to define children enrolled in educational programs who are either non-English-proficient (NEP) or limited-English-proficient (LEP). Educators use this phrase, linguistically and culturally diverse, to identify children from homes and communities where English is not the primary language of communication (García 1991). For the purposes of this statement, the phrase will be used in a similar manner. This document primarily describes linguistically and culturally diverse children who speak languages other than English. However, the recommendations of this position statement can also apply to children who, although they speak only English, are also linguistically and culturally diverse.

Introduction

The children and families served in early childhood programs reflect the ethnic, cultural, and linguistic diversity of the nation. The nation's children all deserve an early childhood education that is responsive to their families, communities, and racial, ethnic, and cultural backgrounds. For young children to develop and learn optimally, the early childhood professional must be prepared to meet their diverse developmental, cultural, linguistic, and educational needs. Early childhood educators face the challenge of how best to respond to these needs.

The acquisition of language is essential to children's cognitive and social development. Regardless of what language children speak, they still develop and learn. Educators recognize that linguistically and culturally diverse children come to early childhood programs with previously acquired knowledge and learning based upon the language used in their home. For young children, the language of the home is the language they have used since birth, the language they use to make and establish meaningful communicative relationships, and the language they use to begin to construct their knowledge and test their learning. The home language is tied to children's culture, and culture and language communicate traditions, values, and attitudes (Chang 1993). Parents should be encouraged to use and develop children's home language; early childhood educators should respect children's linguistic and cultural backgrounds and their diverse learning styles. In so doing, adults will enhance children's learning and development.

Just as children learn and develop at different rates, individual differences exist in how children whose home language is not English acquire English. For example, some children may experience a silent period (of 6 or more months) while they acquire English; other children may practice their

*From Kent Chrisman. Reprinted by permission of the NAEYC

knowledge by mixing or combining languages (for example, "Mi mamá me put on mi coat"); still other children may seem to have acquired English-language skills (appropriate accent, use of vernacular, vocabulary, and grammatical rules) but are not truly proficient; yet some children will quickly acquire English-language proficiency. Each child's way of learning a new language should be viewed as acceptable, logical, and part of the ongoing development and learning of any new language.

Defining the Problem

At younger and younger ages, children are negotiating difficult transitions between their home and educational settings, requiring an adaptation to two or more diverse sets of rules, values, expectations, and behaviors. Educational programs and families must respect and reinforce each other as they work together to achieve the greatest benefit for all children. For some young children, entering any new environment—including early childhood programs—can be intimidating. The lives of many young children today are further complicated by having to communicate and learn in a language that may be unfamiliar. In the past, children entering U.S. schools from families whose home language is not English were expected to immerse themselves in the mainstream of schools, primarily through the use of English (Soto 1991; Wong Fillmore 1991). Sometimes the negative attitudes conveyed or expressed toward certain languages lead children to "give up" their home language. Early childhood professionals must recognize the feeling of loneliness, fear, and abandonment children may feel when they are thrust into settings that isolate them from their home community and language. The loss of children's home language may result **in the disruption of family communication patterns, which may lead to the loss of intergenerational wisdom; damage to individual and community esteem; and children's potential nonmastery of their home language or English.**

NAEYC's Position

NAEYC's goal is to build support for equal access to high-quality educational programs that recognize and promote all aspects of children's development and learning, enabling all children to become competent, successful, and socially responsible adults. Children's educational experiences should afford them the opportunity to learn and to become effective, functioning members of society. Language development is essential for learning, and the development of children's home language does not interfere with their ability to learn English. Because knowing more than one language is a cognitive asset (Hakuta and Garciá 1989), early education programs should encourage the development of children's home language while fostering the acquisition of English.

For the optimal development and learning of all children, educators must **accept** the legitimacy of children's home language, **respect** (hold in high regard) and **value** (esteem, appreciate) the home culture, and promote and **encourage** the active involvement and support of all families, including extended and nontraditional family units.

When early childhood educators acknowledge and respect children's home language and culture, ties between the family and programs are strengthened. This atmosphere provides increased opportunity for learning because young children feel supported, nurtured, and connected not only to their home communities and families but also to teachers and the educational setting.

The Challenges

The United States is a nation of great cultural diversity, and our diversity creates opportunities to learn and share both similar and different experiences. There are opportunities to learn about people from different backgrounds; the opportunity to foster a bilingual citizenry with skills necessary to succeed in a global economy; and opportunities to share one's own cherished heritage and traditions with others.

Historically, our nation has tended to regard differences, especially language differences, as cultural handicaps rather than cultural resources (Meier and Cazden 1982). "Although most Americans are reluctant to say it publicly, many are anxious about the changing racial and ethnic composition of the country" (Sharry 1994). As the early childhood profession transforms its thinking,

The challenge for early childhood educators is to become more knowledgeable about how to relate to children and

families whose linguistic or cultural background is different from their own.

Between 1979 and 1989 the number of children in the United States from culturally and linguistically diverse backgrounds increased considerably (NCES 1993), and, according to a report released by the Center for the Study of Social Policy (1992), that diversity is even more pronounced among children younger than age 6. Contrary to popular belief, many of these children are neither foreign born nor immigrants but were born in the United States (Waggoner 1993). Approximately 9.9 million of the estimated 45 million school-age children, more than one in five, live in households in which languages other than English are spoken (Waggoner 1994). In some communities, however, the number of children living in a family in which a language other than English is spoken is likely to be much larger. Head Start reports that the largest number of linguistically and culturally diverse children served through Head Start are Spanish speakers, with other language groups representing smaller but growing percentages (Head Start Bureau 1995).

The challenge for teachers is to provide high-quality care and education for the increasing number of children who are likely to be linguistically and culturally diverse.

Families and communities are faced with increasingly complex responsibilities. Children used to be cared for by parents and family members who typically spoke the home language of their family, be it English or another language. With the increasing need of family members to work, even while children are very young, more and more children are placed in care and educational settings with adults who may not speak the child's home language or share their cultural background. Even so, children will spend an ever-increasing amount of their waking lives with these teachers. What happens in care will have a tremendous impact on the child's social, emotional, and cognitive development. These interactions will influence the child's values, view of the world, perspectives on family, and connections to community. This places a tremendous responsibility in the hands of the early childhood community.

Responding to linguistic and cultural diversity can be challenging. At times the challenges can be complicated further by the specific needs or issues of the child, the family, or the educational program. Solutions may not be evident. Individual circumstances can affect each situation differently. There are no easy answers, and often myths and misinformation may flourish. The challenges may even seem to be too numerous for any one teacher or provider to manage. Nonetheless, despite the complexity, it is the responsibility of all educators to assume the tasks and meet the challenges. Once a situation occurs, the early childhood educator should enter into a dialogue with colleagues, parents, and others in an effort to arrive at a negotiated agreement that will meet the best interest of the child. For example,

- A mother, father, and primary caregiver each have different cultural and linguistic backgrounds and do not speak English. Should the language of one of these persons be affirmed or respected above the others? How can the teacher affirm and respect the backgrounds of each of these individuals?

- The principal is concerned that all children learn English and, therefore, does not want any language other than English spoken in the early childhood setting. In the interest of the child, how should the educator respond?

- An educator questions whether a child will ever learn English if the home language is used as the primary language in the early childhood setting. How is this concern best addressed?

Solutions exist for each of these linguistic and cultural challenges, just as they do for the many other issues that early childhood educators confront within the early childhood setting. These challenges must be viewed as opportunities for the early childhood educator to reflect, question, and effectively respond to the needs of linguistically and culturally diverse children. Although appropriate responses to every linguistically and culturally diverse situation cannot be addressed through this document, early childhood educators should consider the following recommendations.

Recommendations for a Responsive Learning Environment

Early childhood educators should stop and reflect on the best ways to ensure appropriate educational and developmental experiences for all young children. The unique qualities and characteristics of each individual child must be acknowledged. Just as each child is different, methods and strategies to work with young children must vary.

The issue of home language and its importance to young children is also relevant for children who speak English but come from different cultural backgrounds, for example, speakers of English who have dialects, such as people from Appalachia or other regions having distinct patterns of speech, speakers of Black English, or second- and third-generation speakers of English who maintain the dominant accent of their heritage language. While this position statement basically responds to children who are from homes in which English is not the dominant language, the recommendations provided may be helpful when working with children who come from diverse cultural backgrounds, even when they only speak English. The overall goal for early childhood professionals, however, is to provide every child, including children who are linguistically and culturally diverse, with a responsive learning environment. The following recommendations help achieve this goal.

A. Recommendations for Working with Children

Recognize that all children are cognitively, linguistically, and emotionally connected to the language and culture of their home.

When program settings acknowledge and support children's home language and culture, ties between the family and school are strengthened. In a supportive atmosphere young children's home language is less likely to atrophy (Chang 1993), a situation that could threaten the children's important ties to family and community.

Acknowledge that children can demonstrate their knowledge and capabilities in many ways.

In response to linguistic and cultural diversity, the goal for early childhood educators should be to make the most of children's potential, strengthening and building upon the skills they bring when they enter programs. Education, as Cummins states, implies "drawing out children's potential and making them more than they were" (1989). Educational programs and practices must recognize the strengths that children possess. Whatever language children speak, they should be able to demonstrate their capabilities and also feel the success of being appreciated and valued. Teachers must build upon children's diversity of gifts and skills and provide young children opportunities to exhibit these skills in early childhood programs. The learning environment must focus on the learner and allow opportunities for children to express themselves across the curriculum, including art, music, dramatization, and even block building. By using a nondeficit approach (tapping and recognizing children's strengths rather than focusing the child's home environment on skills yet unlearned) in their teaching, teachers should take the time to observe and engage children in a variety of learning activities. Children's strengths should be celebrated, and they should be given numerous ways to express their interests and talents. In doing this, teachers will provide children an opportunity to display their intellect and knowledge that may far exceed the boundaries of language.

Understand that without comprehensible input, second-language learning can be difficult.

It takes time to become linguistically proficient and competent in any language. Linguistically and culturally diverse children may be able to master basic communication skills; however, mastery of the more cognitively complex language skills needed for academic learning (Cummins 1989) is more dependent on the learning environment. Academic learning relies on significant amounts of information presented in decontextualized learning situations. Success in school becomes more and more difficult as children are required to learn, to be tested and evaluated based on ever-increasing amounts of information, consistently presented in a decontextualized manner. Children learn best when they are given a context in which to learn, and the knowledge that children acquire in "their first language can make second-language input much more comprehensible" (Krashen 1992). Young children can gain knowledge more easily when they obtain quality instruction through their first language. Children can acquire the necessary language and cognitive skills required to succeed in school when given an appropriate learning environment, one that is tailored to meet their needs (NAEYC and NAECS/SDE 1991; Bredekamp and Rosegrant 1992).

Although verbal proficiency in a second language can be accomplished within 2 to 3 years, the skills necessary to achieve the higher level educational skills of understanding academic content through reading and writing may require 4 or more years (Cummins 1981; Collier 1989). Young children may seem to be fluent and at ease with English but may not be capable of understanding or expressing themselves as competently as their English-speaking peers. Although children seem to be speaking a second language with ease, speaking a language does not equate to being proficient in that language. Full proficiency in the first language, including complex uses of the language, contributes to the development of the second language. Children who do not become proficient in their second language after 2 or 3 years of regular use probably are not proficient in their first language either.

Young children may seem to be fluent and at ease speaking a second language, but they may not be fully capable of understanding or expressing themselves in the more complex aspects of language and may demonstrate weaknesses in language-learning skills, including vocabulary skills, auditory memory and discrimination skills, simple problem-solving tasks, and the ability to follow sequenced directions. Language difficulties such as these often can result in the linguistically and culturally diverse child being over referred to special education, classified as learning disabled, or perceived as developmentally delayed.

B. Recommendations for Working with Families

Actively involve parents and families in the early learning program and setting.

Parents and families should be actively involved in the learning and development of their children. Teachers should actively seek parental involvement and pursue establishing a partnership with children's families. When possible, teachers should visit the child's community (for example, shops, churches, and playgrounds); read and learn about the community through the use of books, pictures, observations, and conversations with community members; and visit the home and meet with other family members.

Parents and families should be invited to share, participate, and engage in activities with their children. Parent involvement can be accomplished in a number of ways, including asking parents to share stories, songs, drawings, and experiences of their linguistic and cultural background and asking parents to serve as monitors or field trip organizers. Families and parents should be invited to share activities that are developmentally appropriate and meaningful within their culture. These opportunities demonstrate to the parent what their child is learning; increase the knowledge, information, and understanding of all children regarding people of different cultures and linguistic backgrounds; and establish a meaningful relationship with the parent. The early childhood educator should ensure that parents are informed and engaged with their child in meaningful activities that promote linkages between the home and the early care setting.

Encourage and assist all parents in becoming knowledgeable about the cognitive value for children of knowing more than one language, and provide them with strategies to support, maintain, and preserve home-language learning.

In an early childhood setting and atmosphere in which home language is preserved, acknowledged, and respected, all parents can learn the value of home-language development and the strength it provides children as they add to their existing knowledge and understanding. Parents and teachers can learn how to become advocates regarding the long-term benefits that result from bilingualism.

Parents and teachers recognize the acquisition of English as an intellectual accomplishment, an opportunity for economic growth and development, and a means for achieving academic success. There are even times when parents may wish for the ability, or have been mistakenly encouraged, to speak to their children only in English, a language of which the parents themselves may not have command. The educator should understand the effects that speaking only in English can have upon the child, the family, and the child's learning. The teacher must be able to explain that speaking to the child only in English can often result in communications being significantly hindered and verbal interactions being limited and unnatural between the parent and the child. In using limited English, parents may communicate to children using simple phrases and commands (for example, "Sit down" or "Stop"); modeling grammatically incorrect phrases (for example, "We no go store"); or demonstrating other incorrect usages of language that are common when persons acquire a second language. From these limited and incorrect verbal interactions, the amount of language the child is hearing is reduced, and the child's vocabulary growth is restricted, contributing to an overall decrease in verbal expression. When parents do not master the second language yet use the second language to communicate with their child, there is an increased likelihood that the child will not hear complex ideas or abstract thoughts—important skills needed for cognitive and language development. The teacher must explain that language is developed through natural language interactions. These natural interactions occur within the day-to-day setting, through radio and television, when using public transportation, and in play with children whose dominant language is English. The parent and the teacher must work collaboratively to achieve the goal of children's learning English.

Through the home language and culture, families transmit to their children a sense of identity, an understanding of how to relate to other people, and a sense of belonging. When parents and children cannot communicate with one another, family and community destabilization can occur. Children who are proficient in their home language are able to maintain a connectedness to their histories, their stories, and the day-to-day events shared by parents, grandparents, and other family members who may speak only the home language. Without the ability to communicate, parents are not able to socialize their children, share beliefs and value systems, and directly influence, coach, and model with their children.

Recognize that parents and families must rely on caregivers and educators to honor and support their children in the cultural values and norms of the home.

Parents depend on high-quality early childhood programs to assist them with their children's development and learning. Early childhood programs should make provisions to communicate with families in their home language and to provide parent–teacher encounters that both welcome and accommodate families. Partnerships between the home and the early childhood setting must be developed to ensure that practices of the home and expectations of the program are complementary. Linguistic and cultural continuity between the home and the early childhood program supports children's social and emotional development. By working together, parents and teachers have the opportunity to influence the understanding of language and culture and to encourage multicultural learning and acceptance in a positive way.

C. Recommendations for Professional Preparation

Provide early childhood educators with professional preparation and development in the areas of culture, language, and diversity.

Efforts to understand the languages and cultural backgrounds of young children are essential in helping children to learn. Uncertainty can exist when educators are unsure of how to relate to children and families of linguistic and cultural backgrounds different from their own. Early childhood educators need to understand and appreciate their own cultural and linguistic backgrounds. Adults' cultural background affects how they interact with and/or teach young children. The educator's background influences how children are taught, reinforced, and disciplined. The child's background influences how the child constructs knowledge, responds to discipline and praise, and interacts in the early childhood setting.

Preservice and inservice training opportunities in early childhood education programs assist educators in overcoming some of the linguistic and cultural challenges they may face in working with young children. Training institutions and programs can consider providing specific courses in the following topic areas or include these issues in current courses: language acquisition; second-language learning; use of translators; working with diverse families; sociolinguistics; cross-cultural communication; issues pertaining to the politics of race, language, and culture; and community involvement.

Recruit and support early childhood educators who are trained in languages other than English.

Within the field of early childhood education, there is a need for knowledgeable, trained, competent, and sensitive multilingual/multicultural early childhood educators. Early childhood educators who speak more than one language and are culturally knowledgeable are an invaluable resource in the early childhood setting. In some instances the educator may speak multiple languages or may be able to communicate using various linguistic regionalisms or dialects spoken by the child or the family.

The educator may have an understanding of socio-cultural and economic issues relevant within the local linguistically and culturally diverse community and can help support the family in the use and development of the child's home language and in the acquisition of English. The early childhood teacher who is trained in linguistic and cultural diversity can be a much-needed resource for information about the community and can assist in the inservice cultural orientation and awareness training for the early childhood program. The bilingual educator also can be a strong advocate for family and community members.

Too often, however, bilingual early childhood professionals are called upon to provide numerous other services, some of which they may not be equipped to provide. For example, the bilingual professional, although a fluent speaker, may not have the vocabulary needed to effectively communicate with other adults or, in some instances, may be able to read and write only in English, not in the second language. In addition, bilingual teachers should not be expected to meet the needs of all linguistically and culturally diverse children and families in the program, especially those whose language they do not speak. Bilingual providers should not be asked to translate forms, particularly at a moment's notice, nor should they be required to stop their work in order to serve as interpreters. Bilingual teachers should not serve in roles, such as advising or counseling, in which they may lack professional training. These assignments may seem simple but often can be burdensome and must be viewed as added duties placed upon the bilingual teacher.

Preservice and inservice training programs are needed to support bilingual early childhood educators in furthering educators' knowledge and mastery of the language(s) other than English that they speak, and training should also credit content-based courses offered in languages other than English. Professional preparation instructors must urge all teachers to support multilingual/multicultural professionals in their role as advocates for linguistically and culturally diverse children. Early childhood professionals should be trained to work collaboratively with the bilingual early childhood teacher and should be informed of the vital role of the bilingual educator. Additionally, there is a need for continued research in the area of linguistic and cultural diversity of young children.

D. Recommendations for Programs and Practice

Recognize that children can and will acquire the use of English even when their home language is used and respected.

Children should build upon their current skills as they acquire new skills. While children maintain and build upon their home language skills and culture, children can organize and develop proficiency and knowledge in English. Bilingualism has been associated with higher levels of cognitive attainment (Hakuta and García 1989) and does not interfere with either language proficiency or cognitive development. Consistent learning opportunities to read, be read to, and see print messages should be given to linguistically and culturally diverse children. Literacy developed in the home language will transfer to the second language (Krashen 1992). Bilingualism should be viewed as an asset and an educational achievement.

Support and preserve home language usage.

If the early childhood teacher *speaks* the child's home language, then the teacher can comfortably use this language around the child, thereby providing the child with opportunities to hear and use the home language within the early childhood setting. Use of the language should be clearly evident throughout the learning environment (e.g., in meeting charts, tape recordings, the library corner). Educators should develop a parent information board, using a language and reading level appropriate for the parents. Teachers should involve parents and community members in the early childhood program. Parents and community members can assist children in hearing the home language from many different adults, in addition to the teacher who speaks the home language. Parents and community members can assist other parents who may be unable to read, or they can assist the teacher in communicating with families whose home language may not have a written form.

If the early childhood educator *does not speak* the language, he or she should make efforts to provide visible signs of the home language throughout the learning environment through books and other relevant reading material in the child's language and with a parent bulletin board (get a bilingual colleague to help review for accuracy of written messages). The teacher can learn a few selected words in the child's language, thus demonstrating a willingness to take risks similar to the risks asked of children as they learn a second language. This effort by the teacher also helps to validate and affirm the child's language and culture, further demonstrating the teacher's esteem and respect for the child's linguistic and cultural background. The teacher should model appropriate use of English and provide the child with opportunities to use newly acquired vocabulary and language. The teacher also must actively involve the parent and the community in the program.

If the teacher is *faced with many different languages* in the program or classroom, the suggestions listed above are still relevant. Often teachers feel overwhelmed if more than one language is spoken in the program; however, they should remember that the goal is for children to learn, and that learning is made easier when children can build on knowledge in their home language. The teacher should consider grouping together at specific times during the day children who speak the same or similar languages so that the children can construct knowledge with others who speak their home language. The early childhood educator should ensure that these children do not become socially isolated as efforts are made to optimize their learning. Care should be taken to continually create an environment that provides for high learning expectations.

Develop and provide alternative and creative strategies for young children's learning.

Early childhood educators are encouraged to rely on their creative skills in working with children to infuse cultural and linguistic diversity in their programs. They should provide children with multiple opportunities to learn and ways for them to demonstrate their learning, participate in program activities, and work interactively with other children.

To learn more about working with linguistically and culturally diverse children, early childhood educators should collaborate with each other and with colleagues from other professions. To guide the implementation of a developmentally, linguistically, and culturally appropriate program, collaborative parent and teacher workgroups should be developed. These committees should discuss activities and strategies that would be effective for use with linguistically and culturally diverse children. Such committees promote

good practices for children and shared learning between teachers and parents.

Summary

Early childhood educators can best help linguistic and culturally diverse children and their families by acknowledging and responding to the importance of the child's home language and culture. Administrative support for bilingualism as a goal is necessary within the educational setting. Educational practices should focus on educating children toward the school culture while preserving and respecting the diversity of the home language and culture that each child brings to the early learning setting. Early childhood professionals and families must work together to achieve high-quality care and education for all children.

References

Bredekamp, S., and T. Rosegrant, eds. 1992. *Reaching potentials: Appropriate curriculum and assessment for young children*. Vol. 1. Washington, DC: NAEYC.

Center for the Study of Social Policy. 1992. *The challenge of change: What the 1990 census tells us about children*. Washington, DC: Author.

Chang, H.N.-L. 1993. *Affirming children's roots: Cultural and linguistic diversity in early care and education*. San Francisco: California Tomorrow.

Collier, V. 1989. How long: A synthesis of research on academic achievement in second language. *TESOL Quarterly* 23: 509–31.

Cummins, J. 1981. The role of primary language development in promoting educational success for language minority students. In *Schooling and language minority students: A theoretical framework*, eds. M. Ortiz, D. Parker, and F. Tempes. Office of Bilingual Bicultural Education, California State Department of Education. Los Angeles: Evaluation, Dissemination, and Assessment Center, California State University.

Cummins, J. 1989. *Empowering minority students*. Sacramento: California Association for Bilingual Education.

Garciá, E. 1991. *The education of linguistically and culturally diverse students: Effective instructional practices*. Santa Cruz: National Center for Research on Cultural Diversity and Second Language Learning, University of California.

Hakuta, K., and E. Garciá. 1989. Bilingualism and education. *American Psychologist* 44: 374–79.

Head Start Bureau, Administration on Children, Youth, and Families, Department of Health and Human Services.

1995. Program information report. Washington, DC: Author.

Krashen, S. 1992. *Fundamentals of language education.* Torrance, CA: Laredo Publishing.

Meier, T.R.,and C.B. Cazden. 1982. A focus on oral language and writing from a multicultural perspective. *Language Arts* 59: 504–12.

National Association for the Education of Young Children (NAEYC) and National Association of Early Childhood Specialists in State Departments of Education (NAECS/ SDE). 1991. Guidelines for appropriate curriculum content and assessment in programs serving children ages 3 through 8. *Young Children* 46: 21–38.

National Center for Education Statistics (NCES). 1993. Language characteristics and schooling in the United States, a changing picture: 1979 and 1989. NCES 93-699. Washington, DC: U.S. Department of Education, Office of Educational Research and Improvement.

Sharry, F. 1994. *The rise of nativism in the United States and how to respond to it.* Washington, DC: National Education Forum.

Soto, L.D. 1991. Understanding bilingual/bicultural children. *Young Children* 46: 30–36.

Waggoner, D., ed. 1993. Numbers and needs: Ethnic and linguistic minorities in the United States.

Waggoner, D. 1994. Language minority school age population now totals 9.9 million. *NABE News* 18: 1, 24–26.

Wong Fillmore, L. 1991. When learning a second language means losing the first. *Early Childhood Research Quarterly* 6: 323–46.

Resources

Banks, J. 1993. Multicultural education for young children: Racial and ethnic attitudes and their modification. In *Handbook of research on the education of young children,* ed. B. Spodek, 236–51. New York: Macmillan.

Collier, V. 1989. How long: A synthesis of research on academic achievement in second language. *TESOL Quarterly* 23: 509–31.

Collier, V., and C. Twyford. 1988. The effect of age on acquisition of a second language for school. *National Clearinghouse for Bilingual Education* 2: 1–12.

Derman-Sparks, L., and the A.B.C. Task Force. 1989. *Anti-bias curriculum: Tools for empowering young children.* Washington, DC: NAEYC.

McLaughlin, B. 1992.*Myths and misconceptions about second language learning: What every teacher needs to unlearn.* Santa Cruz: National Center for Research on Cultural Diversity and Second Language Learning, University of California.

Neugebauer, B., ed. 1992. *Alike and different: Exploring our humanity with young children.* Redmond, WA: Exchange Press, 1987. Reprint, Washington, DC: NAEYC.

Ogbu, J.U. 1978. *Minority education and caste: The American system in cross cultural perspective.* New York: Academic.

Phillips, C.B. 1988. Nurturing diversity for today's children and tomorrow's leaders. *Young Children* 43: 42–47.

Tharp, R.G. 1989. Psychocultural variables and constants: Effects on teaching and learning in schools. *American Psychologist* 44: 349–59.

naeyc® NAEYC Standards for Early Childhood Professional Preparation Programs

Position Statement Approved by the NAEYC Governing Board July 2009

A position statement of the National Asssociation for the Education of Young Children

Introduction

The purpose of this position statement

NAEYC Standards for Early Childhood Professional Preparation Programs represents a sustained vision for the early childhood field and more specifically for the programs that prepare the professionals working in the field. This 2009 revision of the standards is responsive to new knowledge, research and conditions while holding true to core values and principles of the founders of the profession. It is designed for use in a variety of ways by different sectors of the field while also supporting specific and critical policy structures, including state and national early childhood teacher credentialing, national accreditation of professional early childhood preparation programs, state approval of early childhood teacher education programs, and articulation agreements between various levels and types of professional development programs.

History

NAEYC has a long-standing commitment to the development and support of strong early childhood degree programs in institutions of higher education. NAEYC standard setting for degree programs in institutions of higher education began more than 25 years ago. This document is the third revision to NAEYC's Early Childhood Teacher Education Guidelines for Four-and Five-Year Programs (1982) and Guidelines for Early Childhood Education Programs in Associate Degree Granting Institutions (1985).

Development and publication of those first standards documents was made possible through the contributions of family and friends of Rose H. Alschuler, a founding member and first Secretary-Treasurer of NAEYC from 1929-1931. During the 1920s, Ms. Alschuler was an early proponent and director of the first public nursery schools in the United States. During the 1930s she directed Works Progress Administration (WPA) public nursery schools in Chicago. During World War II she chaired the National Commission for Young Children. Her life and legacy continue today as our field furthers its work to improve both programs for young children and programs that prepare early childhood professionals.

The Revisions process

The 1985 guidelines for preparation of early childhood professionals were revised in 1996, 2001–2003, and again with this revision in 2009. Each of these sets of guidelines and standards was developed with input from hundreds of early childhood professionals who participated in conference sessions, advisory committees, and work groups. While these are position statements of NAEYC, each was developed with invited input from colleagues in related professional associations, including ACCESS—early childhood educators in associate degree granting institutions, the National Association of Early Childhood Teacher

Educators (NAECTE), the Division for Early Childhood of the Council for Exceptional Children (CEC/DEC), and the National Board for Professional Teaching Standards (NBPTS).

In January 2008, NAEYC's Governing Board appointed a working group to advise staff on the preparation of a revision of the current *Preparing Early Childhood Professionals: NAEYC's Standards for Programs* (2003). This work group was composed of early childhood faculty members from associate, baccalaureate, and graduate degree programs; representatives of NAEYC, ACCESS, and NAECTE; and faculty who use the standards in the National Council for Accreditation of Teacher Education (NCATE) and NAEYC Early Childhood Associate Degree Accreditation (ECADA) systems. Additional input into the standards revision process was gathered during sessions at the 2007 NAEYC Annual Conference, the 2008 NAEYC Public Policy Forum, and the 2008 NAEYC National Institute for Early Childhood Professional Development. Draft revisions were posted on the NAEYC Web site for public comment in Fall 2008. Final revisions were completed in Spring 2009.

What is new?

From all of these perspectives, the feedback indicated that the standards remain strong. Revisions called for are primarily organizational and reflect input from those who are actively implementing the standards in the field. There are *two* significant revisions in this 2009 document.

1. Standard 4 has been separated into two standards, one focuses on early childhood methods and the other on early childhood content. This increases the total number of standards from five to six.

2. The language *all children* is revised to read either *each child* or *every child* to strengthen the integration of inclusion and diversity as threads across all standards. In some cases, the phrase "each child" has been added to a key element of a standard.

Like all NAEYC position statements, the standards for early childhood professional preparation are living documents and as such will be regularly updated and revised.

Standards as a Vision of Excellence

With good reason, many educators have become wary of standards. At times, standards have constricted learning and have encouraged a one-size-fits-all mentality. But standards can also be visionary and empowering for children and professionals alike. NAEYC hopes its standards for professional preparation can provide something more valuable than a list of rules for programs to follow.

The brief standards statements in this document offer a shared vision of early childhood professional preparation. But to make the vision real, the details must be constructed uniquely and personally, within particular communities of learners. Good early childhood settings may look very different from one another. In the same way, good professional preparation programs may find many pathways to help candidates meet high standards, so that they can effectively support young children and their families. (Hyson 2003, p. 28)

Unifying themes for the field

These standards express a national vision of excellence for early childhood professionals. They are deliberately written as statements of core knowledge, understanding, and methods used across multiple settings and in multiple professional roles. The key elements of each standard progress from a theoretical knowledge base to more complex understanding to the application of knowledge in professional practice.

These 2009 NAEYC Standards for Early Childhood Professional Preparation Programs continue to promote the unifying themes that define the early childhood profession. These standards are designed for the early childhood education profession as a whole, to be relevant across a range of roles and settings. These core NAEYC standards are for use across degree levels, from associate to baccalaureate to graduate degree programs. They are used in higher education accreditation systems, in state policy development, and by professional development programs both inside and outside institutions of higher education. These core standards can provide a solid, commonly held foundation of unifying themes from which diverse programs may arise, incorporating the wisdom of local communities, families, and practitioners. These unifying themes include

- **Shared professional values,** including a commitment to diversity and inclusion; respect for family, community, and cultural contexts; respect for evidence as a guide to professional decisions; and reliance on guiding principles of child development and learning.

- **Inclusion of the broad range of ages and settings** encompassed in early childhood professional preparation. NAEYC defines early childhood as the years from birth through age 8. These standards are meant to support professional preparation across diverse work settings, including infants and toddlers, primary grades, family child care, early intervention, government and private agencies, higher education institutions, and organizations that advocate on behalf of young children and their families.

- **A shared set of outcomes** for early childhood professional preparation. These core standards outline a set of common expectations for professional knowledge, skills and dispositions in six core areas. They express what tomorrow's early childhood professionals should know and be able to do.

- **A multidisciplinary approach** with an emphasis on assessment of outcomes and balanced attention to knowledge, skills, and dispositions.

Over time, NAEYC has organized these standards in a variety of ways. In the 1980s, they were organized into two position statements, one for associate degree programs and the other for four-and five-year degree programs. In 1991 one document outlined standards for basic and advanced degree programs. In 1999–2003, three documents outlined standards for associate, initial licensure, and advanced degree programs. In this new position statement, the core standards are presented in *one* NAEYC position statement that emphasizes the essentials of professional preparation for careers in early childhood education, regardless of role, setting, or degree level. This position statement will guide the preparation of supporting materials when these standards are adopted for use in the NCATE and ECADA accreditation systems.

Connecting to accreditation
Many higher education institutions choose to seek NAEYC Early Childhood Associate Degree Accreditation (ECADA) or NAEYC recognition of baccalaureate and graduate degrees as part of the National Council for Accreditation of Teacher Education (NCATE) accreditation for programs leading to initial or advanced teacher licensure. Both accreditation systems use these standards. Note that in these core NAEYC standards, the terms

students and *candidates* are used interchangeably to describe the adults who are prepared by early childhood teacher education programs.

Note that these core standards are student performance standards. Meeting these standards requires evidence that programs (1) offer learning opportunities aligned with the key elements of the standards, (2) design key assessments that measure students' performance on key elements of the standards, (3) collect and aggregate data on student performance related to the standards, and (4) use that data in intentional, responsive ways to improve the quality of teaching and learning in the program.

These core standards are used across both ECADA and NCATE accreditation systems and across associate, baccalaureate, and graduate degree levels. Specific accreditation expectations related to different degree types and levels are published and updated separately for each accreditation system. Indicators of strength in program context and structure—the institutional mission, conceptual framework, field experiences, student characteristics and support services, faculty composition and qualifications, program resources and governance, support for transfer and articulation—are addressed in the guiding materials for programs seeking ECADA and NCATE accreditation.

Defining Professional Preparation in Early Childhood Education

NAEYC continues to use the child development research and evidence base to define the "early childhood" period as spanning the years from birth through age 8. As in past editions of its standards, NAEYC recognizes that within that range, early childhood professionals—and the programs that prepare them—may choose to specialize within the early childhood spectrum (infants/toddlers, preschool/prekindergarten, or early primary grades).

Multiple professional roles and pathways
Specialization can be valuable, but NAEYC believes that all early childhood professionals should have a broad knowledge of development and learning across the birth-through-age-8 range; should be familiar with appropriate curriculum and assessment approaches across that age span; and should have in-depth knowledge and skills in at least two of the three periods: infants/toddlers, preschool/prekindergarten, and early primary grades.

Without knowing about the *past* and the *future* (the precursors to children's current development and learning and the trajectory they will follow in later years), teachers cannot design effective learning opportunities within their specific professional assignment.

In addition, today's inclusive early childhood settings—those that include young children with developmental delays and disabilities—require knowledge of an even wider range of development and learning than was needed in many classrooms of the past. Without understanding a variety of professional settings and roles, as well as current and historical issues and trends that shape those settings and roles, individuals will find career and leadership opportunities in the field limited.

Many early childhood students enter college with a limited view of professional options. While all early childhood professionals should be well grounded in best practices in direct care and education, early childhood degree programs might also prepare students for work in the following roles and settings:

Early childhood educator roles, such as early childhood classroom teacher, family child care provider, Head Start teacher, or paraprofessional in the public schools;

Home-family support roles, such as home visitor, family advocate, child protective services worker, or parent educator; or

Professional support roles, such as early childhood administrator in a child care or Head Start program, staff trainer, peer/program mentor, or advocate at the community, state, or national level.

Core Values in Professional Preparation

NAEYC's standards for professional preparation are derived from the developmental and educational research base found in the resources at the end of this document and in related position statements, including, among others,

- Developmentally Appropriate Practice in Early Childhood Programs Serving Children from Birth through Age 8;
- Early Learning Standards: Creating Conditions for Success;
- Early Childhood Mathematics: Promoting Good Beginnings;
- Learning to Read and Write: Developmentally Appropriate Practices for Young Children;

- Screening and Assessment of Young English-Language Learners;
- Promoting Positive Outcomes for Children with Disabilities: Recommendations for Curriculum, Assessment, and Program Evaluation;
- Responding to Linguistic and Cultural Diversity: Recommendations for Effective Early Childhood Education;
- Still Unacceptable Trends in Kindergarten Entry and Placement; and
- Early Childhood Curriculum, Assessment, and Program Evaluation. www.naeyc.org/positionstatements.

In addition to the common research base and emphasis on the centrality of field experiences, these NAEYC standards affirm the value of, for example: play in children's lives; reciprocal relationships with families; child development knowledge as a foundation for professional practice; practices and curricula that are culturally respectful and responsive; ethical behavior and professional advocacy; and in-depth field experiences in high-quality professional preparation.

To be an excellent teacher: Professional preparation as meaning making

Young children benefit from well-planned, intentionally implemented, culturally relevant curriculum that both supports and challenges them. Research indicates the kinds of experiences that are essential to building later competence in such critical areas as language and literacy, mathematics, and other academic disciplines, as well as in gross motor development, social skills, emotional understanding, and self-regulation. The knowledge base also emphasizes the need for close relationships between young children and adults and between teachers and children's families. Such relationships and the secure base that they create are investments in children's later social, emotional, and academic competence.

Just as curriculum for young children is more than a list of skills to be mastered, professional preparation for early childhood teachers is more than a list of competencies to be assessed or a course list to complete. Early childhood students in well-designed programs develop professional knowledge, skills, and dispositions in a community of learners making sense of readings, observations, field experiences, and group projects through their interactions with others. They make connections between life experiences and new learning. They apply foundational concepts from general education course work to early childhood practice. They learn to self-assess and to advocate for themselves as students and as professionals. They strengthen their skills in written and verbal communication, learn to identify and use professional resources, and make connections between these "college skills" and lifelong professional practice.

Just as children learn best from teachers who use responsive and intentional strategies, adult students learn from instructors who create a caring community of learners, teach to enhance development and learning, plan curriculum aligned with important learning outcomes, assess student growth and development related to those outcomes, and build positive relationships with students and other stakeholders in the program.

Responding to Current Challenges, Needs, and Opportunities

Diversity, inclusion, and inequity

Every sector of the early childhood education community, including professional preparation programs, faces new challenges. Among them is the increased *diversity* of children and families in early childhood programs, from infant/toddler child care through the primary grades. This increased diversity is seen in the large numbers of children from culturally and linguistically diverse communities, as well as in the growing numbers of children with disabilities and other special learning needs who attend early childhood programs. A related challenge is the need to grow a more diverse teaching workforce and a more diverse leadership for the profession as a whole.

Another current challenge is the need to address the *inequities* and gaps in early learning that increase over time, developing into persistent achievement gaps in subgroups of American school children. Differences in academic achievement among ethnic groups, explained largely by socioeconomic differences, are central to the current "standards/accountability" movement in education—from infancy through the early primary grades and again as instructors of adults in early childhood preparation programs. To implement developmentally appropriate practices, early childhood professionals must "apply new knowledge to critical issues" facing the field (Copple & Bredekamp 2009).

One strategy to address these learning gaps and support children is the growth of publicly funded prekindergarten programs. Along with this strategy has come a new focus on preK-3 curriculum alignment; more high-quality professional development for teachers; partnerships between states, universities, community colleges, quality rating systems, and schools; and more highly qualified teachers in prekindergarten and early primary grades—teachers who have completed higher education degree programs with specialized early childhood preparation (Haynes 2009).

Preparation across the birth-through-8 age range

Professional preparation program leaders must make difficult decisions as they work with limited resources to design curriculum, field experiences, and assessment systems to prepare teachers for work across the full spectrum of the early childhood age range. Teacher licensure complicates the picture, since states' definitions of the early childhood age span and its subdivisions vary greatly and are changed frequently. Even programs that emphasize the upper end of the age range may not adequately prepare candidates in the critical content or subject matter areas needed to build children's academic success. Literacy is only one example: National reports (e.g., National Institute of Child Health and Human Development 2000) repeatedly fault teacher education for failing to provide candidates with research-based knowledge about reading and in-depth practical experience. An equally important concern is the tendency for teacher education programs to give inadequate attention to children's critical early years, especially the birth-to-age-3 period. Teachers who take positions in infant/toddler care but whose preparation has slighted that period may fail to support children's learning and development because the curriculum and teaching strategies they were taught to use are more effective with older children.

Programs also make difficult decisions related to *inclusion, diversity, and inequities* in adult education and in the early childhood field. Calls for greater formal education have not been matched by public investments in salaries and working conditions for early childhood staff, especially in early childhood programs in community-based settings that serve the vast majority of children under age 5.

Across all degree levels, NAEYC cautions programs against the superficial "mile wide and inch deep" model of professional preparation. Looking at the standards in this document, program faculty will be challenged to weigh breadth versus depth (standard by standard and element by element) within the context of their own program, student needs (including the need to acquire concepts and skills in general education), and the realities of a degree completion time frame. Every degree program that specializes in early childhood education has a responsibility to address all of the standards, each in its own way and with its own best decisions on breadth and depth. Like houses that start out with the same foundation and framework but look entirely different as rooms are added, combined, altered, and personalized, each professional preparation program may implement these standards in distinctive ways—as long as what is implemented is of uniformly high quality.

Field experiences

A key component of each of NAEYC's standards is hands-on field or clinical experiences, whether this is immersion in applied research for the doctoral student, systematic inquiry into their own classroom practices for the student already working in the field, or field observations for the student considering an early childhood career. Excellence in teaching requires a continuous interplay of theory, research, and practice. Supervised, reflective field experiences are critical to high-quality professional preparation. Rather than a separate standard on field experiences, programs should note that each standard includes a key element focused on application or use of knowledge and skills related to the standard. These key elements are best learned, practiced and assessed in field experiences.

The Professional Development School movement underscores the challenge of identifying and partnering with high-quality sites for education professionals to develop or refine their skills with competent mentorship and supervision. Finding a high-quality field site is a challenge across all early childhood settings—whether primary school, private preschool, child care center, or family child care home.

Many programs are working with states, communities, or local school districts to raise the qualifications of teachers already in the field—students who need to complete degree programs while maintaining current staff positions. These students may be already working in child care, Head Start, or as aides in primary grade classrooms. Other programs

are deliberately providing field experiences in high-need/low-resource schools. In any of these cases, the quality of the site may not be high but the field placement may be selected for other reasons. The strongest indicator of quality is the quality of the student's opportunities to learn and practice, not the quality of the site itself.

Field experiences consistent with outcomes emphasized in NAEYC standards are

- **Well planned and sequenced,** and allow students to integrate theory, research, and practice.

- **Supported by faculty and other supervisors** who help students to make meaning of their experiences in early childhood settings and to evaluate those experiences against standards of quality.

- **Selected to expose students to a variety** of cultural, linguistic, and ethnic settings for early childhood care and education.

- **When the settings used for field experiences** do not reflect standards of quality, students are provided with other models and/or experiences to ensure that they are learning to work with young children and families in ways consistent with the NAEYC standards.

Faculty development

Strong professional preparation programs ensure that faculty members demonstrate the qualifications and characteristics needed to promote students' learning in relation to the NAEYC standards. Both full- and part-time faculty should have the academic and practical expertise to guide students toward mastery of the competencies reflected in NAEYC standards. In many programs, current faculty are aging and do not reflect the diversity of children or of adult college students served.

In 2008, NAEYC and the Society for Research in Child Development (SRCD) convened a meeting to develop recommendations that would advance the field of early childhood and improve outcomes for young children, especially those living in the most vulnerable circumstances. Final recommendations included,

"Create and evaluate a sustainable system of faculty professional development that incorporates adult learning principles and evidence-based practices for improving outcomes for the most vulnerable children" and "Convene

teacher preparation associations (e.g., the American Association of Colleges of Teacher Education [AACTE]) to brainstorm strategies that will increase the total number of future teacher educators, faculty, and researchers, especially from ethnically diverse backgrounds" (NAEYC & SRCD 2008, p. 593).

While strong programs put together a team of full- and part-time faculty members who each make an individual contribution, programs will be best prepared to meet the NAEYC standards when—

- All faculty are academically qualified for their specific professional roles; have had direct, substantial, professional experience; and continue to enhance their expertise in the early childhood profession.

- Faculty hold graduate degrees in early childhood education/child development or substantive early childhood course work at the graduate level and have demonstrated competence in each field of specialization they teach.

- Faculty know about and implement the principles in the position statements, NAEYC Code of Ethical Conduct and Statement of Commitment, in addition to its Supplement for Early Childhood Adult Educators.

- The program uses a variety of strategies to recruit, hire, mentor, and retain a diverse faculty.

The growing role of community colleges in teacher education

The early childhood field is increasingly committed to identifying and supporting a more diverse group of talented leaders. High-quality community college degree programs offer a promising route toward closing that gap. These programs play a critical role in providing access to higher education—and to the positions that require such education—for many groups, especially those currently underrepresented in professional leadership roles.

Cost, location, scheduling, or students' previous educational experiences can impede access to postsecondary education. Community colleges have the explicit mission of increasing access to higher education programs. Consequently, most community colleges offer courses in English as a second language and developmental courses in reading, writing, and mathematics for students who need that additional support.

Almost half of all higher education students in the United States—including 43 percent of African American and the majority of Native American and Hispanic undergraduates—are enrolled in community colleges. Two-thirds of community college students attend part-time. More than 80 percent of community college students work either full- or part-time, and 39 percent are the first in their families to attend college (AACC 2009).

As part of their effort to be responsive to students' varied needs, community colleges offer a variety of educational or degree options. The American Association of Community Colleges (AACC) recommends the following terminology: The Associate of Arts (A.A) degree generally emphasizes the arts, humanities, and social sciences; typically, three-quarters of the work required is general education course work. The Associate of Sciences (AS) degree generally requires one-half of the course work in general education, with substantial mathematics and science. The Associate in Applied Science (A.A.S) degree prepares the student for direct employment, with one third of the course work in general education. While many students who seek A.A.S degrees do not intend to transfer, these degrees are not intended to create barriers to transfer. "The [A.A.S] degree programs must be designed to recognize this dual possibility and to encourage students to recognize the long-term career possibilities that continued academic study will create" (AACC 1998).

According to estimates from Early and Winton's (2001) national sample, more than 700 institutions of higher education offer associate degree programs in early childhood education. The majority of these are in community colleges. The general community college population is more culturally and linguistically diverse than the student populations in other institutions of higher learning. Early childhood students in two-year programs represent greater diversity than do early childhood students in four-year programs.

Increasing numbers of students entering early childhood associate degree programs have been working—most in child care or Head Start programs (Early & Winton 2001). Many of those students continue to work while attending college part-time. These students are taking the lead in their own education, developing long-term career goals as they improve the quality of their current work with young children and families.

The career goals of students in these programs vary. For some, the degree may enhance their current position, build on a prior Child Development Associate (CDA) credential, and perhaps lead to greater responsibilities in the setting where they work. Although these work settings vary widely, Early and Winton's (2001) data suggest that proportionately more associate degree students work or plan to work with infants and toddlers than do students in four-year programs and many entering students have been working in family child care or child care administrative positions.

Transfer and articulation: meeting immediate needs while keeping doors open

Most early childhood associate degree programs focus on preparing students for direct work with young children in settings outside of primary school classrooms—positions that generally do not require baccalaureate degrees or early childhood teacher certification. However, many community college students are planning to transfer into a four-year college, heading toward teacher certification or other work in the early childhood field. A strong general education foundation together with an introduction to early childhood professional issues and skills is often the combination these students seek.

Still other students enter a community college program with a relatively limited set of objectives (e.g., to take one course that meets a child care licensing requirement or to receive college credit for work toward the CDA) but find unexpected pleasure and challenge in higher education. With support, such students often continue through the associate degree toward a baccalaureate degree and beyond.

Students who need time to succeed in developmental reading, writing, and mathematics courses also need time to develop confidence, skills, and career goals before deciding whether to seek transfer into a four-year institution. Early tracking of students into nontransfer or terminal programs can perpetuate the idea that little education is needed to teach our youngest children. In addition, premature tracking may create unnecessary barriers to students' future options—a serious concern given the higher proportions of students of color in community college programs. Tracking students into nontransfer programs deprives the field of opportunities for these students to become part of a more diverse leadership.

The strongest associate and baccalaureate degree programs serving students already in the field are attempting to keep transfer doors open through high-quality professional course work offered concurrently with strong general education and also by designing programs that simultaneously enhance one's current practice while still maintain transfer options from associate to baccalaureate to graduate degree programs. Increasing numbers of associate degree programs are offering distance learning, noncredit to credit course work, courses offered at worksites, and specialized courses that support particular settings and roles such as family child care or infant/toddler teacher.

Institutional and policy supports

Two recent surveys indicate some of the challenges facing early childhood degree programs as they strive to deliver high quality birth-through-age-8 preparation. A 2006 study found that only one-third (266) of accredited early childhood baccalaureate degree programs were designed as four-year programs, were housed in regionally accredited institutions of higher education, and offered both preschool and K–3 preparation. The study examines explicit and embedded preparation for diverse, multicultural, or inclusive classrooms and recommends a more comprehensive developmental theory and pedagogy, "transformation" of faculty, and attention to developing new leaders. The capacity of institutions and faculty to undertake these deep quality improvements is unclear, as are the market constraints posed by competition from alternative certification programs and from teacher specializations that are in more demand in the job market (Ray, Bowman, & Robbins 2006).

Hyson et al. (2009) surveyed 231 of an estimated 1,200 higher education institutions offering a degree in early childhood education. A large majority of programs at all degree levels (72 to 77 percent) relied heavily on NAEYC standards to guide program quality and improvement work. Most frequently, improvement efforts were focused on developing new student assessments, improving field experiences, and redesigning course work. Across degree levels, programs were focused on improvements related to preparation for linguistic and cultural diversity and to appropriate assessment of young children. The study makes a number of recommendations, including (1) invest in more full-time faculty with early childhood backgrounds, (2) expand faculty knowledge about research and evidence-based practices, (3) promote and support accreditation for higher education programs, and (4) strengthen connections between associate, baccalaureate, and graduate programs.

NAEYC's *Workforce Designs: A Public Policy Blueprint for State Early Childhood Professional Development Systems* offers guiding principles for states as they develop policy related to professional standards, career pathways, articulation, advisory structures, data, and financing. These guiding principles promote stronger integration across early childhood systems (teacher licensing, Head Start, prekindergarten, child care); quality improvement beyond minimum requirements; attention to diversity, inclusion and access issues; and building in compensation parity with rising qualifications (LeMoine 2008).

High-quality early childhood programs develop intentional responses to these current challenges. While a number of programs are engaged in quality improvements and innovative initiatives, there is a pressing need for faculty leadership from both current and new faculty as well as for institutional and policy support for efforts to improve early childhood professional preparation (e.g., Bowman 2000; Zaslow 2005; Washington 2008; Lutton 2009).

Components and Organization of the Standards

The standards that follow include a number of interconnected components. Those components, and their organization, are outlined below.

Core standards

There are six core standards, each of which describes in a few sentences what well-prepared students should know and be able to do. It is important to note, then, that the standard is not just that students know something about child development and learning—the expectations are more specific and complex than that.

Supporting explanations

Each standard includes a rationale or "supporting explanation," which offers a general description of why that standard is important.

Key elements

Three to five "key elements" within each standard clarify its most important features. These key elements break out components of each standard, highlighting what students should know, understand, and be able to do.

Examples of opportunities to learn and practice and of learning assessments

Guidance for programs seeking ECADA and NCATE accreditation will include examples of how early childhood degree programs might help students learn and practice the knowledge, skills, and professional dispositions within that aspect of the standard.

Accreditation materials will also include examples of opportunities to learn and practice— examples of ways that faculty might assess or document student growth and development.

Terminology

Assessment In these standards the term *assessment* refers primarily to the methods through which early childhood professionals gain understanding of children's development and learning. Systematic observations and other informal and formal assessments enable candidates to appreciate children's unique qualities, to develop appropriate goals, and to plan, implement, and evaluate effective curriculum (see Standard 3). Secondarily, *assessment*, here, refers to the formal and informal assessments of adult students as required for degree completion. In higher education accreditation systems, these are referred to as "key assessments" and provide evidence that the degree program and its graduates meet the NAEYC standards.

Candidates/students Refers to college students who are candidates for completion of an early childhood professional preparation program. In some cases, these students are also candidates for professional licensure or certification.

Children This term is used throughout the standards rather than *students* to refer to the young children in early childhood classrooms, child care homes, and other early childhood settings. In this document, child/children refers to young children in the period of early childhood development, from birth through age 8.

Culture Includes ethnicity, racial identity, economic class, family structure, language, and religious and political beliefs, which profoundly influence each child's development and relationship to the world.

Developmentally Appropriate Practice Refers to the NAEYC position statement first developed in 1985 and most recently revised in 2009. The term *developmentally appropriate practice*, or DAP for short, refers to a framework of principles and guidelines for practice that promotes young children's optimal learning and development.

Field experiences Includes field observations, fieldwork, practica, and student teaching or other clinical experiences such as home visiting.

Inclusion and diversity Is not a separate standard, but is integrated into each standard. The phrase "each child" or "all children" is used to emphasize that every standard is meant to include all children: children with developmental delays or disabilities, children who are gifted and talented, children whose families are culturally and linguistically diverse, children from diverse socioeconomic groups, and other children with individual learning styles, strengths, and needs.

Technology Is not a separate standard, but is woven throughout the standards. Early childhood teachers understand technology and media as important influences on children's development. They use technology as one way of communicating with families and sharing children's work, while recognizing the importance of using other communication methods for families with limited internet access. Similarly, they use technology in child assessment and as a professional resource with colleagues and for their own professional development.

Young children Refers to children in the developmental period known as early childhood. Although developmental periods do not rigidly correspond to chronological age, early childhood is generally defined as including all children from birth through age 8.

Standards Summary

Standard 1.
Promoting Child Development and Learning

Students prepared in early childhood degree programs are grounded in a child development knowledge base. They use their understanding of young children's characteristics and needs and of the multiple interacting influences on children's development and learning to create environments that are healthy, respectful, supportive, and challenging for each child.

Key elements of Standard 1

1a: Knowing and understanding young children's characteristics and needs

1b: Knowing and understanding the multiple influences on development and learning

1c: Using developmental knowledge to create healthy, respectful, supportive, and challenging learning environments

Supporting explanation

The early childhood field has historically been grounded in a child development knowledge base, and early childhood programs have aimed to support a broad range of positive developmental outcomes for all young children. Although the scope and emphasis of that knowledge base have changed over the years and while early childhood professionals recognize that other sources of knowledge are also important influences on curriculum and programs for young children, early childhood practice continues to be deeply linked with a "sympathetic understanding of the young child" (Elkind 1994).

Well-prepared early childhood degree candidates base their practice on sound **knowledge and understanding of young children's characteristics and needs.** This foundation encompasses multiple, interrelated areas of children's development and learning—including physical, cognitive, social, emotional, language, and aesthetic domains; play, activity, and learning processes; and motivation to learn—and is supported by coherent theoretical perspectives and by current research.

Candidates also understand and apply their understanding of the **multiple influences on young children's development and learning** and of how those influences may interact to affect development in both positive and negative ways. Those influences include the cultural and linguistic contexts for development, children's close relationships with adults and peers, economic conditions of children and families, children's health status and disabilities individual developmental variations and learning styles, opportunities to play and learn, technology and the media, and family and community characteristics. Candidates also understand the potential influence of early childhood programs, including early intervention, on short- and long-term outcomes for children.

Candidates' competence is demonstrated in their ability to **use developmental knowledge to create healthy, respectful, supportive, and challenging learning environments** for all young children (including curriculum, interactions, teaching practices, and learning materials). Such environments reflect *four critical features.*

- First, the environments are *healthy*—that is, candidates possess the knowledge and skills needed to promote young children's physical and psychological health, safety, and sense of security.

- Second, the environments reflect *respect* for each child as a feeling, thinking individual and then for each child's culture, home language, individual abilities or disabilities, family context, and community. In respectful environments, candidates model and affirm antibias perspectives on development and learning.

- Third, the learning environments created by early childhood teacher candidates are supportive. Candidates demonstrate their belief in young children's ability to learn, and they show that they can use their understanding of early childhood development to help each child understand and make meaning from her or his experiences through play, spontaneous activity, and guided investigations.

- Finally, the learning environments that early childhood candidates create are appropriately *challenging.* In other words, candidates apply their knowledge of contemporary theory and research to construct learning environments that provide achievable and stretching experiences for all children—including children with special abilities and children with disabilities or developmental delays.

Standard 2.
Building Family and Community Relationships

Students prepared in early childhood degree programs understand that successful early childhood education depends upon partnerships with children's families and communities. They know about, understand, and value the importance and complex characteristics of children's families and communities. They use this understanding to create respectful, reciprocal relationships that support and empower families and to involve all families in their children's development and learning.

Key elements of Standard 2
2a: Knowing about and understanding diverse family and community characteristics

2b: Supporting and engaging families and communities through respectful, reciprocal relationships

2c: Involving families and communities in their children's development and learning

Supporting explanation
Because young children's lives are so embedded in their families and communities and research indicates that successful early childhood education depends upon partnerships with families and communities, early childhood professionals need to thoroughly understand and apply their knowledge in this area.

First, well-prepared candidates possess **knowledge and understanding of diverse family and community characteristics** and of the many influences on families and communities. Family theory and research provide a knowledge base. Socioeconomic conditions; family structures, relationships, stresses, and supports (including the impact of having a child with special needs); home language; cultural values; ethnicity; community resources, cohesiveness, and organization—knowledge of these and other factors creates a deeper understanding of young children's lives. This knowledge is critical to the candidates' ability to help children learn and develop well.

Second, candidates possess the knowledge and skills needed to **support and engage diverse families through respectful, reciprocal relationships.** Candidates understand how to build positive relationships, taking families' preferences and goals into account and incorporating knowledge of families' languages and cultures. Candidates demonstrate respect for variations across cultures in family strengths, expectations, values, and childrearing practices. Candidates consider family members to be resources for insight into their children, as well as resources for curriculum and program development. Candidates know about and demonstrate a variety of communication skills to foster such relationships, emphasizing informal conversations while also including appropriate uses of conferencing and technology to share children's work and to communicate with families.

In their work, early childhood teacher candidates develop cultural competence as they build relationships with diverse families, including those whose children have disabilities or special characteristics or learning needs; families who are facing multiple challenges in their lives; and families whose languages and cultures may differ from those of the early childhood professional. Candidates also understand that their relationships with families include assisting families in finding needed resources, such as mental health services, health care, adult education, English language instruction, and economic assistance that may contribute directly or indirectly to their children's positive development and learning. Well-prepared early childhood candidates are able to identify such resources and know how to connect families with appropriate services, including help with planning transitions from one educational or service system to another.

Finally, well-prepared candidates possess essential skills to **involve families and communities in many aspects of children's development and learning.** They understand and value the role of parents and other important family members as children's primary teachers. Candidates understand how to go beyond parent conferences to engage families in curriculum planning, assessing children's learning, and planning for children's transitions to new programs. When their approaches to family involvement are not effective, candidates evaluate and modify those approaches rather than assuming that families "are just not interested."

Standard 3.
Observing, Documenting, and Assessing to Support Young Children and Families

Students prepared in early childhood degree programs understand that child observation, documentation, and other forms of assessment are central to the practice of all early childhood professionals. They know about and understand the goals, benefits, and uses of assessment. They know about and use systematic observations, documentation, and other effective assessment strategies in a responsible way, in partnership with families and other professionals, to positively influence the development of every child.

Key elements of Standard 3
3a: Understanding the goals, benefits, and uses of assessment
3b: Knowing about and using observation, documentation, and other appropriate assessment tools and approaches

3c: Understanding and practicing responsible assessment to promote positive outcomes for each child
3d: Knowing about assessment partnerships with families and with professional colleagues

Supporting explanation
Although definitions vary, in these standards the term *assessment* includes all methods through which early childhood professionals gain understanding of children's development and learning. Ongoing, systematic observations and other informal and formal assessments are essential for candidates to appreciate children's unique qualities, to develop appropriate goals, and to plan, implement, and evaluate effective curriculum. Although assessment may take many forms, early childhood candidates demonstrate its central role by embedding assessment-related activities in curriculum and daily routines so that assessment becomes a habitual part of professional life.

Well-prepared early childhood candidates can explain the central **goals, benefits, and uses of assessment.** In considering the goals of assessment, candidates articulate and apply the concept of *alignment*—good assessment is consistent with and connected to appropriate goals, curriculum, and teaching strategies for young children. The candidates know how to use assessment as a positive tool that supports children's development and learning and improves outcomes for young children and families. Candidates are able to explain positive uses of assessment and exemplify these in their own work, while also showing an awareness of the potentially negative uses of assessment in early childhood programs and policies.

Many aspects of effective assessment require collaboration with families and with other professionals. Through **partnerships with families and with professional colleagues,** candidates use positive assessment to identify the strengths of families and children. Through appropriate screening and referral, assessment may also result in identifying children who may benefit from special services. Both family members and, as appropriate, members of interprofessional teams may be involved in assessing children's development, strengths, and needs. As new practitioners, candidates may have had limited opportunities to experience such partnerships, but they demonstrate essential knowledge and core skills in team building and in communicating with families and colleagues from other disciplines.

Early childhood assessment includes **observation and documentation and other appropriate assessment strategies.** Effective teaching of young children begins with thoughtful, appreciative, systematic observation and documentation of each child's unique qualities, strengths, and needs. Observation gives insight into how young children develop and how they respond to opportunities and obstacles in their lives. Observing young children in classrooms, homes, and communities helps candidates develop a broad sense of who children are—as individuals, as group members, as family members, as members of cultural and linguistic communities. Candidates demonstrate skills in conducting systematic observations, interpreting those observations, and reflecting on their significance. Because spontaneous *play* is such a powerful window on all aspects of children's development, well-prepared candidates create opportunities to observe children in playful situations as well as in more formal learning contexts.

Many *young children with disabilities* are included in early childhood programs, and early identification of children with developmental delays or disabilities is very important. All beginning professionals, therefore, need essential knowledge about how to collect relevant information, including appropriate uses of screening tools and play-based assessments, not only for their own planning but also to share with families and with other professionals. Well-prepared candidates are able to choose valid tools that are developmentally, culturally, and linguistically appropriate; use the tools correctly; adapt tools as needed, using assistive technology as a resource; make appropriate referrals; and interpret assessment results, with the goal of obtaining valid, useful information to inform practice and decision making.

Although assessment can be a positive tool for early childhood professionals, it has also been used in inappropriate and harmful ways. Well-prepared candidates understand and practice **responsible assessment.** Candidates understand that responsible assessment is ethically grounded and guided by sound professional standards. It is collaborative and open. Responsible assessment supports children, rather than being used to exclude them or deny them services. Candidates demonstrate understanding of appropriate, responsible assessment practices for culturally and linguistically diverse children and for children with developmental delays, disabilities, or other special characteristics. Finally, candidates demonstrate knowledge of legal and ethical issues, current educational concerns and controversies, and appropriate practices in the assessment of diverse young children.

Standard 4.
Using Developmentally Effective Approaches to Connect with Children and Families

Students prepared in early childhood degree programs understand that teaching and learning with young children is a complex enterprise, and its details vary depending on children's ages, characteristics, and the settings within which teaching and learning occur. They understand and use positive relationships and supportive interactions as the foundation for their work with young children and families. Students know, understand, and use a wide array of developmentally appropriate approaches, instructional strategies, and tools to connect with children and families and positively influence each child's development and learning.

Key elements of Standard 4

4a: Understanding positive relationships and supportive interactions as the foundation of their work with children

4b: Knowing and understanding effective strategies and tools for early education

4c: Using a broad repertoire of developmentally appropriate teaching/learning approaches

4d: Reflecting on their own practice to promote positive outcomes for each child

Supporting explanation

Early childhood candidates demonstrate that they understand the theories and research that support **the importance of relationships and high-quality interactions in early education.** In their practice, they display warm, nurturing interactions with each child, communicating genuine liking for and interest in young children's activities and characteristics. Throughout the years that children spend in early childhood settings, their successful learning is dependent not just on instruction but also on personal connections with important adults. Through these connections children develop not only academic skills but also positive learning dispositions and confidence in themselves as learners. Responsive teaching creates the conditions within which very young children can explore and learn about their world. The close attachments children develop with their teachers/caregivers, the expectations and beliefs that adults have about young children's capacities, and the warmth and responsiveness of adult-child interactions are powerful influences on positive developmental and educational outcomes. How children expect to be treated and how they treat others are significantly shaped in the early childhood setting. Candidates in early childhood programs develop the capacity to build a caring community of learners in the early childhood setting.

Early childhood professionals need **a broad repertoire of effective strategies and tools** to help young children learn and develop well. Candidates must ground their curriculum in a set of core approaches to teaching that are supported by research and are closely linked to the processes of early development and learning. In a sense, those approaches *are* the curriculum for infants and toddlers, although academic content can certainly be embedded in each of them. With preschool and early primary grade children, the relative weight and explicitness of subject matter or academic content become more evident in the curriculum, yet the core approaches or strategies remain as a consistent framework. Engaging conversations, thought-provoking questions, provision of materials, and spontaneous activities are all evident in the candidate's repertoire of teaching skills.

Candidates demonstrate the essential *dispositions* to develop positive, respectful relationships with children whose cultures and languages may differ from their own, as well as with children who may have developmental delays, disabilities, or other learning challenges. In making the transition from family to a group context, very young children need continuity between the practices of family members and those used by professionals in the early childhood setting. Their feelings of safety and confidence depend on that continuity. Candidates know the cultural practices and contexts of the young children they teach, and they adapt practices as they continue to develop *cultural competence*—culturally relevant knowledge and skills.

Well-prepared early childhood professionals make purposeful use of various learning formats based on their understanding of children as individuals and as part of a group, and on alignment with important educational and developmental goals. A flexible, research-based **repertoire of teaching/learning approaches to promote young children's development** includes

- Fostering oral language and communication
- Drawing from a continuum of teaching strategies
- Making the most of the environment, schedule, and routines
- Setting up all aspects of the indoor and outdoor environment
- Focusing on children's individual characteristics, needs, and interests
- Linking children's language and culture to the early childhood program
- Teaching through social interactions
- Creating support for play
- Addressing children's challenging behaviors
- Supporting learning through technology.
- Using integrative approaches to curriculum

All of these teaching approaches are effective across the early childhood age span. From the infant/toddler room to the early grades, young children are developing not only early language and reading skills but also the *desire* to communicate, read, and write. They are developing not only early math and science skills and concepts but also the *motivation* to solve problems. They are developing empathy, sociability, friendships, self-concept and self-esteem. Concept acquisition, reasoning, self-regulation, planning and organization, emotional understanding and empathy, sociability—development of all of these is deeply entwined with early experiences in mathematics, language, literacy, science, and social studies in the early education program.

Early childhood professionals make decisions about their practice based on expertise. They make professional judgments through each day based on knowledge of child development and learning, individual children, and the social and cultural contexts in which children live. From this knowledge base, effective teachers design activities, routines, interactions and curriculum for specific children and groups of children. They consider both what to teach and how to teach, developing the habit of **reflective, responsive and intentional practice** to promote positive outcomes for each child.

Standard 5.
Using Content Knowledge to Build Meaningful Curriculum

Students prepared in early childhood degree programs use their knowledge of academic disciplines to design, implement, and evaluate experiences that promote positive development and learning for each and every young child. Students understand the importance of developmental domains and academic (or content) disciplines in an early childhood curriculum. They know the essential concepts, inquiry tools, and structure of content areas, including academic subjects, and can identify resources to deepen their understanding. Students use their own knowledge and other resources to design, implement, and evaluate meaningful, challenging curricula that promote comprehensive developmental and learning outcomes for every young child.

Key elements of Standard 5

5a: Understanding content knowledge and resources in academic disciplines

5b: Knowing and using the central concepts, inquiry tools, and structures of content areas or academic disciplines

5c: Using their own knowledge, appropriate early learning standards, and other resources to design, implement, and evaluate meaningful, challenging curricula for each child.

Supporting explanation

Strong, effective early childhood curricula do not come out of a box or a teacher-proof manual. Early childhood professionals have an especially challenging task in developing effective curricula. As suggested in Standard 1, well-prepared candidates ground their practice in a thorough, research-based understanding of young children's development and learning processes. In developing curriculum, they recognize that every child constructs knowledge in personally and culturally familiar ways. In addition, in order to make curriculum powerful and accessible to all, well-prepared candidates develop curriculum that is free of biases related to ethnicity, religion, gender, or ability status—and, in fact, the curriculum actively counters such biases.

The teacher of children from birth through age 8 must be well versed in **the essential content knowledge and resources in many academic disciplines.** Because children are encountering those content areas for the first time, early childhood professionals set the foundations for later understanding and success. Going beyond conveying isolated facts, well-prepared early childhood candidates possess the kind of content knowledge that focuses on the "big ideas," methods of investigation and expression, and organization of the major academic disciplines. Thus, the early childhood professional knows not only *what* is important in each content area but also *why* it is important—how it links with earlier and later understandings both within and across areas. Because of its central place in later academic competence, the domain of language and literacy requires in-depth, research-based understanding and skill. Mathematics too is increasingly recognized as an essential foundation.

Teachers of young children demonstrate the understanding of **central concepts, inquiry tools, and structure of content areas** needed to provide appropriate environments that support learning in each content area for all children, beginning in infancy (through foundational developmental experiences) and extending through the primary grades. Candidates demonstrate basic knowledge of the research base underlying each content area and of the core concepts and standards of professional organizations in each content area. They rely on sound resources for that knowledge. Finally, candidates demonstrate that they can analyze and critique early childhood curriculum experiences in terms of the relationship of the experiences to the research base and to professional standards.

Well-prepared candidates choose their approaches to the task depending on the ages and developmental levels of the children they teach. They use their own **knowledge, appropriate early learning standards, and other resources to design, implement, and evaluate meaningful, challenging curriculum for each child.** With the youngest children, early childhood candidates emphasize the key experiences that will support later academic skills and understandings—with reliance on the core approaches and strategies described in substandard 4b and with emphasis on oral language and the development of children's background knowledge. Working with somewhat older or more skilled children, candidates also identify those aspects of each subject area that are critical to children's later academic competence.

With all children, early childhood professionals support later success by modeling engagement in challenging subject matter and by building children's faith in themselves as young learners—young mathematicians, scientists, artists, readers, writers, historians, economists, and geographers (although children may not think of themselves in such categories).

Early Childhood curriculum content/ discipline areas include learning goals, experiences, and assessment in the following academic disciplines or content areas:

- Language and literacy
- The arts—music, creative movement, dance, drama, and visual arts
- Mathematics
- Science
- Physical activity, physical education, health and safety
- Social studies

Designing, implementing, and evaluating meaningful, challenging curriculum requires alignment with appropriate early learning standards and knowledgeable use of the discipline's resources to focus on key experiences for each age group and each individual child.

Early childhood teacher candidates, just like experienced teachers, go beyond their own basic knowledge to identify and use high-quality resources, including books, standards documents, Web resources, and individuals who have specialized content expertise in developing early childhood curriculum. In addition to national or state standards (NAEYC & NAECS/SDE 2002), or several larger goals are also held by all early childhood teachers:

- **Security and self-regulation.** Appropriate, effective curriculum creates a secure base from which young children can explore and tackle challenging problems. Well-implemented curriculum also helps children become better able to manage or regulate their expressions of emotion and, over time, to cope with frustration and manage impulses effectively rather than creating high levels of frustration and anxiety.
- **Problem-solving and thinking skills.** Candidates who have skills in developing

and implementing meaningful, challenging curricula will also support young children's ability—and motivation—to solve problems and think well.

- **Academic and social competence.** Because good early childhood curriculum is aligned with young children's developmental and learning styles, it supports the growth of academic and social skills.

With these goals in mind, candidates develop curriculum to include both planned and spontaneous experiences that are developmentally appropriate, meaningful, and challenging for all young children, including those with developmental delays or disabilities; address cultural and linguistic diversities; lead to positive learning outcomes; and, as children become older, develop positive dispositions toward learning within each content area.

Standard 6. Becoming a Professional

Students prepared in early childhood degree programs identify and conduct themselves as members of the early childhood profession. They know and use ethical guidelines and other professional standards related to early childhood practice. They are continuous, collaborative learners who demonstrate knowledgeable, reflective, and critical perspectives on their work, making informed decisions that integrate knowledge from a variety of sources. They are informed advocates for sound educational practices and policies.

Key elements of Standard 6

6a: Identifying and involving oneself with the early childhood field

6b: Knowing about and upholding ethical standards and other professional guidelines

6c: Engaging in continuous, collaborative learning to inform practice

6d: Integrating knowledgeable, reflective, and critical perspectives on early education

6e: Engaging in informed advocacy for children and the profession

The early childhood field has a distinctive history, values, knowledge base, and mission. Early childhood professionals, including beginning teachers, have a strong **identification and involvement with the early childhood field** to better serve young children and their families. Well-prepared candidates understand the nature of a profession. They know about the many connections between the early childhood field and other related disciplines and professions with which they may collaborate while serving diverse young children and families. Candidates are also aware of the broader contexts and challenges within which early childhood professionals work. They consider current issues and trends that might affect their work in the future.

Because young children are at such a critical point in their development and learning, and because they are vulnerable and cannot articulate their own rights and needs, early childhood professionals have compelling responsibilities to **know about and uphold ethical guidelines and other professional standards.** The profession's code of ethical conduct guides the practice of responsible early childhood educators. Well-prepared candidates are very familiar with NAEYC's Code of Ethical Conduct and are guided by its ideals and principles. This means honoring their responsibilities to uphold high standards of confidentiality, sensitivity, and respect for children, families, and colleagues. Candidates know how to use the Code to analyze and resolve professional ethical dilemmas and are able to give defensible justifications for their resolutions of those dilemmas. Well-prepared candidates also know and obey relevant laws, such as those pertaining to child abuse, the rights of children with disabilities, and school attendance. Finally, candidates are familiar with relevant professional guidelines, such as national, state, or local standards for content and child outcomes; position statements about, for example, early learning standards, linguistic and cultural diversity, early childhood mathematics, technology in early childhood, prevention of child abuse, child care licensing requirements, and other professional standards affecting early childhood practice.

Continuous, collaborative learning to inform practice is a hallmark of a professional in any field. An attitude of inquiry is evident in well-prepared candidates' writing, discussion, and actions. Whether engaging in classroom-based research, investigating ways to improve their own practices, participating in conferences, or finding resources in libraries and on Internet sites, candidates demonstrate self-motivated, purposeful learning that directly influences the quality of their work with young children. Candidates—and professional preparation programs—view graduation or licensure not as the final demonstration of competence but as one milestone among many, including professional development experiences before and beyond successful degree completion.

At its most powerful, learning is socially constructed in interaction with others. Even as beginning teachers, early childhood candidates demonstrate involvement in collaborative learning communities with other candidates, higher education faculty, and experienced early childhood practitioners. By working together on common challenges, with lively exchanges of ideas, members of such communities benefit from one another's perspectives. Candidates also demonstrate understanding of and essential skills in interdisciplinary collaboration. Because many children with disabilities and other special needs are included in early childhood programs, every practitioner needs to understand the role of the other professionals who may be involved in young children's care and education (e.g., special educators, reading specialists, speech and hearing specialists, physical and occupational therapists, school psychologists). Candidates demonstrate that they have the essential communication skills and knowledge base to engage in interdisciplinary team meetings as informed partners and to fulfill their roles as part of Individualized Family Service Plan and Individualized Education Program (IFSP/IEP) teams for children with developmental delays or disabilities. They use technology effectively with children, with peers, and as a professional resource.

Well-prepared candidates' practice is influenced by **knowledgeable, reflective, and critical perspectives.** As professionals, early childhood candidates' decisions and advocacy efforts are grounded in multiple sources of knowledge and multiple perspectives. Even routine decisions about what materials to use for an activity, whether to intervene in a dispute between two children, how to organize nap time, what to say about curriculum in a newsletter, or what to tell families about new video games are informed by a professional context, research-based knowledge, and values. In their work with young children, candidates show that they make and justify decisions on the basis of their *knowledge* of the central issues, professional values and standards, and research findings in their field. They also show evidence of *reflective approaches* to their work, analyzing their own practices in a broader context, and using reflections to modify and improve their work with young children. Finally, well-prepared candidates display a *critical stance*, examining their own work, sources of professional knowledge, and the early childhood field with a questioning attitude. Their work demonstrates that they do not just accept a simplistic source of truth; instead, they recognize that while early childhood educators share the same core professional values, they do not agree on all of the field's central questions. Candidates demonstrate an understanding that through dialogue and attention to differences, early childhood professionals will continue to reach new levels of shared knowledge.

Finally, early childhood candidates demonstrate that they can engage in **informed advocacy for children and families and the profession.** They know about the central policy issues in the field, including professional compensation, financing of the early education system, and standards setting and assessment. They are aware of and engaged in examining ethical issues and societal concerns about program quality and provision of early childhood services and the implications of those issues for advocacy and policy change. Candidates have a basic understanding of how public policies are developed, and they demonstrate essential advocacy skills, including verbal and written communication and collaboration with others around common issues.

References

Introduction

AACC (American Association of Community Colleges). 2009a. AACC statement regarding the Project on Student Loan Debt report on community college loan access. www. aacc. nche.edu/About/Positions/Pages/ps04162008.aspx

AACC. 2009b. Fast facts. www.aacc.nche.edu/AboutCC/Pages/fastfacts.aspx

AACC. 1998. AACC position statement on the associate degree. www.aacc.nche.edu/About/Positions/Pages/ps08011998.aspx

Bogard, K., F. Traylor, & R. Takanishi. 2008. Teacher education and PK outcomes: Are we asking the right questions? *Early Childhood Research Quarterly* 23 (1): 1–6.

Burchinal, M., M. Hyson, & M. Zaslow. 2008. *Competencies and credentials for early childhood educators: What do we know and what do we need to know?* NHSA Dialog Briefs 11 (1).

Curenton, S. 2005. Toward better definition and measurement of early childhood professional development. In *Critical issues in early childhood* professional development, eds. M. Zaslow & I. Martinez-Beck, 17–19. Baltimore:. Brookes.

Darling-Hammond, L. 2007. We need to invest in math and science teachers. *The Chronicle Review* 54 (17): B20.

http://chronicle.com/weekly/v54/i17/17b02001.htm

Early, D., & P. Winton. 2001. Preparing the workforce: early childhood teacher preparation at 2- and 4-year institutions of higher education. *Early Childhood Research Quarterly* 16 (3): 285–306.

Gilliam, W. S. 2008. *Implementing policies to reduce the likelihood of preschool expulsion.* Foundation for Child Development FCD Policy Brief 7. http://ziglercenter.yale. edu/documents/PreKExpulsionBrief2.pdf

Haynes, M., & J. Levin. 2009. *Promoting quality in preK-grade 3 classrooms: findings and results from NASBE's Early Childhood Education Network.* NASBE Issues in Brief. Arlington, VA: National Association of State Boards of Education.

Hyson, M., H.B. Tomlinson, & C.A.S. Morris. 2009. Quality improvement in early childhood teacher education faculty perspectives and recommendations for the future. *Early Childhood Research and Practice* 11 (1). http://ecrp.uiuc. edu/v11n1/hyson.html

Karp, N. 2005. Designing models for professional development at the local, state, and national levels. In *Critical issues in early childhood professional development*, eds. M. Zaslow & I. Martinez-Beck, 225–30. Baltimore: Brookes.

Kelly, P., & G. Camilli. 2007. *The impact of teacher education on outcomes in center-based early childhood education programs: A meta-analysis.* New Brunswick, NJ: National Institute for Early Education Research.

LeMoine, S. 2008 *Workforce designs: A policy blueprint for state early childhood professional development systems.* Washington, DC: NAEYC.

Lima, C., K.L. Maxwell, H. Able-Booneb, & C.R. Zimmer. 2009. Cultural and linguistic diversity in early childhood teacher preparation: The impact of contextual characteristics on coursework and practica. *Early Childhood Research Quarterly* 24 (1): 64–76.

Lutton, A.. 2009. NAEYC early childhood professional preparation standards: A vision for tomorrow's early childhood teachers. 2009. In *Conversations on early childhood teacher education: Voices from the Working Forum for Teacher Educators*, eds. A. Gibbons & C. Gibbs. Redmond, WA: World Forum Foundation and New Zealand Tertiary College.

Martinez-Beck, I., & M. Zaslow. 2005. Introduction: The context for critical issues in early childhood professional development. In *Critical issues in early childhood professional development*, eds. M. Zaslow & I. Martinez-Beck, 1-15. Baltimore: Brookes.

NAEYC & SRCD (Society for Research in Child Development). 2008. Using research to improve outcomes for young children: A call for action. Final report of the Wingspread Conference, September 18–20, 2007. *Early Childhood Research Quarterly* 23 (4): 591–96.

Ray, A.., B. Bowman, & J. Robbins. 2006. *Preparing early childhood teachers to successfully educate* all *children: The contribution of four-year undergraduate teacher preparation programs.* Report to the Foundation for Child Development on the Project on Race, Class, and Culture in Early Childhood. Chicago: Erikson Institute. www.erikson. edu/PageContent/en-us/Documents/pubs/Teachered.pdf

Snow, K.L. 2005. Completing the model: Connecting early child care worker professional development with child outcomes. In *Critical issues in early childhood professional development*, eds. M. Zaslow & I. Martinez-Beck, 137–140). Baltimore: Brookes.

Snyder, T.D., S.A. Dillow, & C.M. Hoffman. 2009. *Digest of education statistics 2008.* NCES #2009-020. Washington, DC: National Center for Education Statistics, Institute of Educational Sciences, U.S. Department of Education. http://nces.ed.gov/pubsearch/pubsinfo. asp?pubid=2009020

Tout, K., M. Zaslow, & D. Berry. 2005. Quality and qualifications: Links between professional development and quality in early care and education settings. In *Critical issues in early childhood professional development*, eds. M. Zaslow & I. Martinez-Beck, 77–110. Baltimore: Brookes.

Washington, V. 2008. *Role, relevance, reinvention: Higher education in the field of early care and education.* Boston: Wheelock College.

Whitebook, M., L. Sakai, F. Kipnis, M. Almaraz, E. Suarez, & D. Bellm. 2008. Learning together: A study of six B.A. completion cohort programs in early care and education. Year I Report. www.irle.berkeley.edu/cscce/pdf/learning_ together08.pdf

Zaslow, M. 2005. Charting a course for improved professional development across varying programs and practices. In *Critical issues in early childhood professional development*, eds. M. Zaslow & I. Martinez-Beck, 351–53. Baltimore: Brookes.

Standard 1: Importance of Knowing Child Development

Bowman, B.T., S. Donovan, & M.S. Burns. 2000. *Eager to learn: Educating our preschoolers.* Washington, DC: National Academies Press. [1, 4]

Bronfenbrenner, U. 2004. *Making human beings human: Bioecological perspectives on human development.* Thousand Oaks, CA: Sage. [1]

Buysse, V., & P.W. Wesley. 2006. *Evidence-based practice in the early childhood field.* Washington, DC: Zero to Three Press. [1]

Copple, C., & S. Bredekamp, eds. 2009. *Developmentally appropriate practice in early childhood programs serving children from birth through age 8.* Washington, DC: NAEYC. [1, 4, 5]

Essa, E.L., M.M. & Burnham, eds.2009. *Informing our practice: Useful research on young children's development.* Washington, DC: NAEYC. [1,4]

Hendrick, J., & P. Weissman. 2009. *The whole child: Developmental education for the early years.* Upper Saddle River, NJ: Prentice Hall. [1]

National Research Council & Institute of Medicine. 2000 *From neurons to neighborhoods: The science of early childhood development.* Jack P. Shonkoff and Deborah A. Phillips, eds.; Committee on Integrating the Science of Early Childhood Development; Board on Children, Youth, and Families of the Commission on Behavioral and Social Sciences and Education. Washington, DC: National Academies Press. [1]

NCATE & NICHD (National Institute of Child Health and Human Development). 2006. *Child and adolescent development research and teacher education: Evidence-based pedagogy, policy, and practice.* Retrieved June 1, 2009 at www. ncate.org/documents/research/ChildAdolDevTeacherEd. pdf [1]

NICHD Early Child Care Research Network. 2005. *Child care and child development: Results from the NICHD Study of Early Child Care and Youth Development.* New York: Guilford. [1]

Rogoff, B. 2003. *The cultural nature of human development.* Oxford, UK: Oxford University Press. [1]

Tabors, P.O. 2008. One child, two languages: A guide for early childhood educators of children learning English as a second language. Baltimore, MD: Brookes. [1, 4]

Standard 2: Building Family and Community Relationships

Bouffard, S., & H. Weiss. 2008. Thinking big: A new framework for family involvement policy, practice, and research. *The Evaluation Exchange* 14 (1&2): 2–5. [2]

DEC (Division for Early Childhood) & NAEYC. 2008. Early childhood inclusion: Joint position statement of the Division for Early Childhood (DEC) and the National Association for the Education of Young Children (NAEYC). www.naeyc.org/about/positions/pdf/DEC_NAEYC_EC.pdf [2]

Epstein, J. 2001. *School, family, and community partnerships: Preparing educators and improving schools.* Boulder, CO: Westview. [2]

Epstein, J. L., & S.B. Sheldon. 2006. *Moving forward: Ideas for research on school, family, and community partnerships.* Retrieved June 1, 2009 at www.csos.jhu.edu/P2000/ pdf/Literature%20Review%20-%20Epstein%20and%20Sheldon%2006.pdf [2]

Henderson, A.T., & K.L. Mapp. 2002. *A new wave of evidence: The impact of school, family, and community connections on student achievement.* Austin, TX: National Center for Family & Community Connections with Schools, Southwest Educational Development Laboratory. Retrieved June 1, 2009 at www.sedl.org/connections/ resources/ evidence.pdf [2]

Lopez, M.E., H. Kreider, & M. Caspe. 2004. Co-constructing family involvement. *Evaluation Exchange* X (4): 2–3. [2]

Lynch, E.W., & M.J. Hanson. 2004. *Developing cross-cultural competence: A guide for working with children and their families.* Baltimore, MD: Brookes. [2]

Ray, A.., B. Bowman, & J. Robbins. 2006. *Preparing early childhood teachers to successfully educate all children: The contribution of four-year undergraduate teacher preparation programs.* Report to the Foundation for Child Development on the Project on Race, Class, and Culture in Early Childhood. Chicago: Erikson Institute. www.erikson. edu/PageContent/en-us/Documents/pubs/Teachered.pdf

Valdés, G. 1999. *Con respeto: Bridging the distances between culturally diverse families and schools. An ethnographic portrait.* New York: Teachers College Press. [2]

Weiss, H.B., M. Caspe, & M.E. Lopez. 2006. *Family involvement in early childhood education.* Cambridge, MA: Harvard Family Research Project. [2]

Xu, Y., & J. Filler. 2008. Facilitating family involvement and support for inclusive education. *The School Community Journal* 18 (2): 53–71. [2]

Standard 3: Observing, Documenting, and Assessing to Support Young Children and Families

Cohen, D.H., V. Stern, N. Balaban, & N. Gropper. 2008. *Observing and recording the behavior of young children.* 5th ed. New York: Teachers College Press. [3]

DEC (Division for Early Childhood). 2007. Promoting positive outcomes for children with disabilities: Recommendations for curriculum, assessment, and program evaluation. Missoula, MT: Author. www.naeyc.org/about/positions/ pdf/PrmtgPositiveOutcomes.pdf [3]

Gonzales-Meña, J. 2005. *Resources for observation and reflection to accompany foundations of early childhood education.* New York: McGraw Hill [3]

Kagan, S.L., C. Scott-Little, & R.M. Clifford. 2003. Assessing young children: What policy makers need to know and do. In *Assessing the state of state assessments: Perspectives on assessing young children,* eds C. Scott-Little, S.L. Kagan, & R.M. Clifford, 25–35. Greensboro, NC: SERVE. [3]

Lynch, E., & M. Hanson. 2004. Family diversity assessment and cultural competence. In *Assessing infants and preschoolers with special needs,* 3rd ed., eds. M. McLean, D.B. Bailey, & M. Wolery, 71–99. Columbus, OH: Merrill/ Pearson. [3]

Meisels, S.J., & S. Atkins-Burnett. 2000. The elements of early childhood assessment. In *Handbook of early childhood intervention,* 2nd ed., eds. J.P. Shonkoff & S.J. Meisels, 387–415. New York: Cambridge University Press. [3]

NAEYC. 2005. Screening and assessment of young English-language learners: Supplement to the NAEYC and NAECS/SDE [National Association of Early Childhood Specialists in State Departments of Education] joint position statement on early childhood curriculum, assessment, and program evaluation. http://208.118.177.216/about/positions/ pdf/ELL_Supplement_Shorter_Version.pdf [3, 4]

NAEYC & NAECS/SDE. 2003. Early childhood curriculum, assessment, and program evaluation: Building an effective, accountable system in programs for children birth through age 8. Joint position statement. http://208.118.177.216/about/`positions/pdf/CAPEexpand. pdf [3]

National Research Council. 2008. *Early childhood assessment: Why, what, and how.* Eds. C.E. Snow & S.B. Van Hemel, Committee on Developmental Outcomes and Assessments for Young Children; Board on Children, Youth, and Families & Board on Testing and Assessment, Division of Behavioral and Social Sciences and Education. Washington, DC: National Academies Press. [3]

Standard 4: Teaching Methods and Strategies

August, D., & T. Shanahan. 2006. *Developing literacy in second-language learners: Report of the National Literacy Panel on Language-Minority Children and Youth.* Mahwah, NJ: Erlbaum. [4, 5]

Burchinal, M., C. Howes, R. Pianta, D. Bryant, D. Early, R. Clifford, & O. Barbarin. 2008. Predicting child outcomes at the end of kindergarten from the quality of pre-kindergarten teacher-child interactions and instructions. *Applied Developmental Science* 12 (3): 140–53. [4]

Harowitz, F.D., F. Darling Hammond, J. Bransford, et al. 2005. Educating teachers for developmentally appropriate practice. In *Preparing teachers for a changing world: What teachers should learn and be able to do,* eds. L. Darling-Hammond & J. Bransford, 88–125. San Francisco: Jossey-Bass. [4]

Hemmeter, M.L., R.M. Santos, & M.M. Ostrosky. 2008. Preparing early childhood educators to address young children's social-emotional development and challenging behaviors. *Journal of Early Intervention* 30 (4): 321–40. [4]

Hirsh-Pasek, K., R.M. Golinkoff, L.E. Berk, & D.G. Singer. 2009. *A mandate for playful learning in preschool: Presenting the evidence.* New York: Oxford University Press. [4]

Howes, C., & S. Ritchie. 2002. *A matter of trust: Connecting teachers and learners in the early childhood classroom.* New York: Teachers College Press. [4]

Hyson, M. 2008. *Enthusiastic and engaged learners: Approaches to learning in the early childhood classroom.* New York: Teachers College. [4]

Mouza, C. 2005. Using technology to enhance early childhood learning: The 100 Days of School project. *Educational Research and Evaluation* 11 (6): 513–28. [4]

Pellegrini, A.D., L. Gada, M. Bartinin, & D. Charak. 1998. Oral language and literacy learning in context: The role of social relationships. *Merrill-Palmer Quarterly* 44 (1): 38–54. [4]

Saracho, O.N., & B. Spodek. 2008. *Contemporary perspectives on science and technology in early childhood education.* Charlotte, NC: Information Age Publishing. [4, 5]

Standard 5: Curriculum

Bae, J. 2004. Learning to teach visual arts in an early childhood classroom: The teacher's role as a guide. *Early Childhood Education Journal* 31 (4): 247–54. [5]

Bodrova, E., & D.L. Leong. 2005. Self-regulation: A foundation for early learning. *Principal* 85 (1): 30–35. [5]

Clements, D.H., J. Sarama, & A.M. DiBiase. 2004. *Engaging young children in mathematics: Standards for early childhood mathematics education.* Mahwah, NJ: Lawrence Erlbaum. [5]

Derman Sparks, L., & J. Olsen Edwards. 2009. *Anti-bias education for young children and ourselves.* Washington, DC: NAEYC. [5]

Dickinson, D.K., & P.O. Tabors. 2001. *Beginning literacy with language: Young children learning at home and school.* Baltimore, MD: Brookes. [4, 5]

Gelman, R., & K. Brenneman. 2004. Science learning pathways for young children. *Early Childhood Research Quarterly* 19 (2): 150–58. [5]

Ginsburg, H.P., J.S. Lee, & J.S. Boyd. 2008. Mathematics education for young children: What it is and how to promote it. *Social Policy Report* 22 (1): 3–11, 14–22. [5]

Hyson, M. 2004. *The emotional development of young children: Building an emotion-centered curriculum.* 2nd ed. New York: Teachers College Press. [5]

Mindes, G. 2005. Social studies in today's early childhood curricula. *Young Children* 60 (5): 12–18. [5]

National Early Literacy Panel. 2008. *Developing early literacy: Report of the National Early Literacy Panel—A scientific synthesis of early literacy development and implications for intervention.* Washington, DC: National Institute for Literacy. [5]

National Mathematics Advisory Panel. 2008. *Foundations for success: The Final Report of the National Mathematics Advisory Panel.* Washington, DC: U.S. Department of Education [5]

Sanders, S.W. 2006. Physical education in kindergarten. In *K today: Teaching and learning in the kindergarten year,* ed. D.F. Gullow, 127–37. Washington, DC: NAEYC. [5]

Singer, M.J. 2008. Accessing the musical intelligence in early childhood education. *Australian Journal of Early Childhood* 33 (2): 49–56. [5]

Standard 6: Becoming a Professional

Baptiste, N.E., & L.C. Reyes. 2008. *What every teacher should know about understanding ethics in early care and education.* 3rd ed. Upper Saddle River, NJ: Prentice Hall. [6]

Division for Early Childhood (DEC). 2009. *Code of ethics.* Retrieved August 27, 2009, at www.dec-sped.org/uploads/docs/about_dec/position_concept_papers/Code%20of%20 Ethics_updated_Aug2009.pdf [6]

Freeman, N.K., & K.J. Swick. 2007. The ethical dimension of working with parents: Using the code of ethics when faced with a difficult decision. *Childhood Education* 83 (3): 163–69. [6]

Hurst, B., & G. Reding. 2009. *Professionalism in teaching. What every teacher should know about.* 2nd ed. Columbus, OH: Merill/Pearson. [6]

Kagan, S.L., K. Kauerz, & K. Tarrant. 2007. *The early care and education teaching workforce at the fulcrum: An agenda for reform.* New York: Teachers College Press. [6]

NAEYC. 2004. Code of ethical conduct: Supplement for early childhood adult educators. A joint position statement of NAEYC, NAECTE (National Association of Early Childhood Teacher Educators), & ACCESS (American Associate Degree Early Childhood Teacher Educators). http://208.118.177.216/about/positions/pdf/ethics04.pdf [6]

NAEYC. 2005. *Code of ethical conduct and statement of commitment. A position statement of the National Association for the Education of Young Children.* Brochure. Washington, DC: Author. [6]

NAEYC. 2006. Code of ethical conduct: Supplement for early childhood program administrators. A position statement. http://208.118.177.216/about/positions/pdf/PSETH05_ supp.pdf [6]

Paige-Smith, A., & A. Craft. 2008. *Developing reflective practice in the early years.* England: Open University Press. [6]

Rust, F., & E. Meyers. 2006. The bright side: Teacher research in the context of educational reform and policy making. *Teachers & Teaching* 12 (1): 69–86. [6]

Wesley, P.W., & V. Buysee. 2006. Ethics and evidence in consultation. *Topics in Early Childhood Special Education* 26 (3): 131–41. [6]

Winton, P.J., J.A. McCollum, & C. Catlett, eds. 2007. *Practical approaches to early childhood professional development: Evidence, strategies, and resources.* Washington, DC: Zero to Three.

Zaslow, M., & I. Martinez-Beck, eds. 2005. *Critical issues in early childhood professional development.* Baltimore, MD: Brookes.

The 2008–2009 Standards Work Group

Becky Brinks
Child Development Program Director, Grand Rapids Community College, Michigan Chair, Commission on NAEYC Early Childhood Associate Degree Accreditation

Julie Bullard
Director, Early Childhood Education, University of Montana–Western, Dillon, Montana
NAEYC Reviewer and Audit Team member, NCATE

Josué Cruz Jr.
President and CEO, Council for Professional Recognition, Washington, D.C.

Sharon Fredericks
Education Division Director/Instructor, College of Menominee Nation, Green Bay, Wisconsin Community College faculty in ECADA Self Study, Head Start Higher Education Grantee

John Johnston
Professor and Director of Assessment, College of Education, University of Memphis, Tennessee NAEYC Reviewer, Audit Team, and Specialty Areas Standards Board member, NCATE

Frances O'Connell Rust
Senior Vice President for Academic Affairs, Dean of Faculty, Erikson Institute, Chicago, Illinois

Ursula Thomas-Fair
Assistant Professor, University of West Georgia, Carrollton, Georgia

NAEYC Position Statement on the Prevention of Child Abuse in Early Childhood Programs and the Responsibilities of Early Childhood Professionals to Prevent Child Abuse*

Information in Appendix F may be helpful in increasing understanding about ethical responsibility of early childhood professionals in relation to prevention of child abuse as discussed in Chapter 6.

Child abuse is any nonaccidental injury or pattern of injuries to a child for which there is no "reasonable" explanation (National Committee to Prevent Child Abuse 1995). It includes physical, emotional, and sexual abuse. As the nation's largest organization of early childhood professionals and others dedicated to improving the quality of early childhood programs in centers, schools, and homes, the National Association for the Education of Young Children (NAEYC) is committed to safeguarding the well-being of children. Child abuse violates children's health and safety and betrays their trust.

Most child abuse is perpetrated by family members; 1994 figures indicate that in 90% of reported cases of abuse, perpetrators were parents or other relatives (U.S. Department of Health and Human Services 1996). Early childhood programs in centers, homes, and schools can help minimize the potential for this type of abuse by working to support families and providing referrals to appropriate helping services as needed. Although much less frequent than abuse by family members, child abuse also occurs in out-of-home settings such as schools, child care, foster care, and organized youth activities. Child abuse by those working with children violates the fundamental principle in NAEYC's *Code of Ethical Conduct* for working with young children: "Above all, we shall not harm children" (Feeney and Kipnis 1992).

Estimates of the proportion of child abuse in out-of-home settings vary, ranging from 1% to 7% of reported rates of abuse (Wells et al. 1995). Fortunately, the majority of employees and volunteers working with young children are caring individuals committed to promoting children's safety, healthy development, and learning. However, because previous and potential abusers may seek opportunities with access to children, those organizing and operating any type of out-of-home setting for children and youth must take proper precautions to minimize the potential for harm to children.

NAEYC deplores child abuse in any form in any setting and believes that all early childhood professionals, families, and communities must be vigilant in protecting children from all forms of abuse. NAEYC offers the following recommendations as strategies to prevent child abuse, including physical, emotional, and sexual abuse, in early childhood programs to the greatest extent possible. These recommendations outline specific roles for early childhood professionals, early childhood programs, family members, and public regulation. Particular attention is given to the role of early childhood programs, focusing on the importance of carefully planned and implemented policies with regard to practices with children, staff screening and recruitment, and partnerships with families. In addition, this statement outlines responsibilities of early childhood professionals to prevent child abuse in other settings. These recommendations focus on children from birth through age 8 attending any type of group program, including child

*Adopted September 1996. From Kent Chrisman. Reprinted by permission of the NAEYC.

care centers and preschools, kindergarten and the primary grades, and family child care homes.

Role of Early Childhood Programs

NAEYC recommends that early childhood programs in centers, homes, and schools adopt policies consistent with the guidelines that follow. In some cases these policies will be set by a larger organizational structure, such as a school district, religious group, corporation, or community agency.

Program Policies

1. Early childhood programs should employ an adequate number of qualified staff to work with children and to provide adequate supervision of program staff and volunteers.

Limiting the number of children for which each adult is responsible and the overall group size helps staff to better meet the individual needs of each child. Teachers are better able to provide supervision of all children and to recognize signs or changes in behavior that may indicate the possibility of abuse. NAEYC's accreditation criteria for centers (NAEYC 1991) recommend group sizes of no more than 6 to 8 infants, 8 to 12 toddlers, 14 to 20 preschoolers, 16 to 20 kindergartners, and 20 to 24 primary grade children, always with at least 2 adults per group. Smaller numbers may be necessary for children with certain emotional or behavioral problems who require more intensive and direct supervision.

2. The program environment (including both indoor and outdoor areas) should be designed to reduce the possibility of private, hidden locations in which abuse may occur.

Young children need opportunities for solitude and quiet play in small groups throughout the day, but all early childhood program spaces should be regarded as public. Both indoor and outdoor areas can be designed and set up in ways that provide opportunities for solitude while also allowing for unobtrusive adult supervision. Likewise, the program environment should be designed to reduce the likelihood that staff members, volunteers, or others have opportunities for hidden interactions with children.

3. All program staff, substitutes, and volunteers should receive preservice orientation and refresher training at regular intervals that include but are not limited to **(a) an understanding of what constitutes child abuse, (b) the program's discipline policy and appropriate guidance of children, (c) means of preventing potential abuse situations in group settings, (d) identification of signs of potential abuse, and (e) individual obligations and procedures for reporting suspected cases of abuse.**

Individuals who work with young children and their families are obligated to report any suspicions of child abuse to the appropriate authorities. Ensuring that staff members and program volunteers understand and keep abreast of (a) strategies to reduce abuse, (b) ways to recognize potential signs of abuse, and (c) appropriate actions for reporting abuse helps reduce risk and meets legal obligations while minimizing the potential for false reports.

4. Centers, schools, and homes should have clear policies and procedures for maintaining a safe, secure environment.

Access to the facility should be controlled, for example, by requiring all visitors to sign in and sign out of the program area or to check in and check out with the administrative office. In the case of family child care homes, parents should be informed prior to the use of a substitute, and children should never be left in the care of an individual without their parents' knowledge.

5. Teachers and caregivers should be supervised by qualified personnel on an ongoing basis, and parents should be encouraged to spend time in the program.

In instances when a teacher or caregiver works primarily alone, periodic, drop-in visits by supervising personnel, parents, or others should be encouraged; such visits can reduce the isolation sometimes experienced by individual providers, thus minimizing the potential for abuse.

6. Programs should not institute "no-touch" policies to reduce the risk of abuse.

In the wake of well-publicized allegations of child abuse in out-of-home settings and increased concerns regarding liability, some programs have instituted such policies, either explicitly or implicitly. No-touch policies are misguided efforts that fail to recognize the importance of touch to children's healthy development. Touch is especially important for infants and toddlers. Warm, responsive touches convey regard and concern for children of any age. Adults should be sensitive to ensuring that their touches (such as pats on the back, hugs, or ruffling a child's hair) are welcomed by the children and appropriate to their individual characteristics and cultural experience. Careful, open communication between the program and families about the value of touch in children's development can help achieve consensus on acceptable ways for adults to show their respect and support for children in the program.

Staff Screening, Recruitment, and Retention Policies   Programs should employ careful screening and recruitment practices to increase the likelihood of selecting appropriate candidates as staff, substitutes, or volunteers to work with children. NAEYC's recommendations reflect the screening decision-making model developed by the American Bar Association's Center for Children and the Law (Wells et al. 1995) that identifies a variety of potential screening mechanisms, including personal interviews, verification of personal and professional references and education qualifications, criminal record checks, and affidavits attesting to history of conviction for abuse or other violent crimes. NAEYC recommends that all early childhood programs in centers, homes, and schools have a comprehensive screening policy in place and that this policy be publicized to existing and potential staff and volunteers, families and other interested policies.

NAEYC recommends the following guidelines be used in developing a screening policy.

1. At a minimum, basic screening should be conducted on all staff members, substitutes, volunteers, and other individuals who may have access to young children but do not have direct responsibility for their care and education.

For example, bus drivers, janitors, cooks, and administrative assistants should be screened in the cases of centers and schools, and all older children and adults present in a family child care provider's home (family members, friends, or employees) should be screened. The basic screening should include a signed, written application, careful review of employment record, checks of personal and professional references, and a personal interview. Additional screening, such as verification of educational status and checks of motor vehicle record, criminal record, and other registries may be appropriate depending upon the duration, frequency, and type of contact between the adult and children and the degree of supervision. In the case of self-employed family child care provid-

ers, public agencies should provide for screening and make the results of the screening available to parents on request.

2. All potential employees, substitutes, and volunteers should be required to attest to any previous convictions, in particular, whether they have ever been convicted of any crime against children or other violent crime.

Factors such as the relevance and recency of any conviction and demonstration of rehabilitation should be weighed in making hiring and placement decisions for individuals who admit to previous convictions. A volunteer's or employee's failure to fully disclose previous convictions should be viewed as automatic grounds for dismissal.

3. All potential employees and volunteers should be required to provide at least three personal references from previous employers, parents of children served, or educators.

Programs should check these references carefully.

4. All new employees and volunteers should be required to complete a mandatory probationary period.

Although new staff members or volunteers should have no unsupervised access to children during the probationary period, they should have supervised interactions with children so that their competencies in working with young children can be assessed.

5. In addition to screening policies designed to ensure that appropriate individuals are engaged in work in the program, early childhood programs should have policies designed to retain competent staff and remove others if necessary.

Programs that provide competitive salaries, good benefits and working conditions, and regular opportunities for advancement are more likely to recruit and retain competent staff who provide better quality care to children. In addition, the provision of employee assistance programs can provide support to staff facing stressful circumstances, thus minimizing the potential for abuse.

Policies also should provide for the removal of individuals whose performance on the job is deemed unacceptable or whose behavior outside the job could affect their performance (such as a bus driver being convicted for driving under the influence).

6. Clear procedures should be in place for responding to an accusation of abuse in the program.

These procedures should address steps to protect children and provide due process for the accused, and they should be publicized in advance to staff as well as parents.

Policies to Promote Close Partnerships with Families Ongoing program policies that strengthen partnerships with families also can help minimize the likelihood of abuse in the program. Examples of such policies follow.

1. Programs should strongly encourage and provide ample opportunity for family participation.

2. Family members should have access to any part of the center, school, or family child care home to which children have access while their children are in care.

3. Field trips should include parents when possible, be approved by the program administrator, be supervised by regular program personnel, and be conducted with written parental permission.

4. Programs should require that children be released only to parents or legal guardians or to those persons authorized in writing by their parents or guardians. Staff should check identification of authorized individuals who are unfamiliar to them.

5. Programs should inform parents about the characteristics of good quality programs and the signs of potential abuse. Parents should be informed also about the child protection practices implemented by the program through (a) written policies shared with parents and family members, (b) access to public records documenting regulatory compliance (when applicable), and (c) publicized mechanisms for registering complaints and the procedures to be followed in response to a complaint.

Close partnerships with families also can help reduce the potential for child abuse by family members. Early childhood programs can provide information to parents and families regarding child development and effective strategies for responding to children's behavior. Teachers and caregivers should be knowledgeable about and alert to signs of family stress and provide support to families. Early childhood professionals can collaborate with state agencies, such as protective services, to promote understanding of child development, support and empower families, and advocate for

children. Working with families in this way may help break cycles of family violence and prevent children from becoming abusers themselves.

Role of Family Members

Parents and other family members can assist in the prevention of child abuse in early childhood programs by

- Increasing their sensitivity to children's communications

- Participating in and observing their children's programs

- Talking regularly with other families who use the program

- Understanding and using child abuse reporting procedures when appropriate

Children have minimal responsibility in the prevention of child abuse. Indeed, many of the child-oriented abuse prevention materials and techniques that have been developed in the wake of highly publicized allegations of abuse do not reflect an understanding of children's development and learning. They can be confusing to children and promote anxiety and fear. Rather than placing the responsibility on children to prevent abuse, NAEYC believes it is the responsibility of parents, early childhood professionals, and other adults to ensure to the greatest degree possible that abuse does not occur by providing safe, well-planned, and well-supervised environments.

Role of Public Regulation

An effective regulation system is an essential component in public efforts to reduce the potential for abuse in early childhood programs. The nature of public regulatory systems governing early childhood programs varies by program auspice. States license or employ other means of regulation for the majority of programs in centers and schools. Nearly all states also have regulatory processes in place for family child care homes, although it is estimated that only a small fraction of family child care providers in the nation is indeed regulated (Willer et al. 1991).

Public regulatory processes help reduce the potential for abuse when

- All settings providing education and care to children of two or more families are subject to regulation.

- Waivers that erode the intent of the regulatory standards are not allowed.

- Funding is sufficient to provide adequate regulatory staff for inspection on at least an annual basis.

- Regulatory personnel are knowledgeable about complaint and law enforcement procedures so that implementation of all regulatory requirements is ensured.

- Regulatory standards require policies regarding parental access to programs, authorization of children's release, and parental notification and approval of children's participation on field trips.

- Parents and the public are provided information about what defines good quality care, regulatory standards and monitoring procedures, and complaint procedures.

Some child care settings, such as in-home care in which families employ someone to care for the child in their home or other private arrangements in which an individual provides care for only one family, are not subject to public regulation. Therefore, public mechanisms to prevent child abuse in out-of-home settings must extend beyond traditional licensing and regulatory processes.

Most states require individuals working in schools, centers, and family child care homes to successfully complete a criminal background check prior to full employment. NAEYC supports the use of such background checks but warns that they are only one of many necessary strategies to reduce risk. Even the most sophisticated system of criminal background checks is limited by the fact that many instances of abuse go unreported and therefore never result in a conviction. Also, no system for such checks can detect first-time or potential abusers. Because many problems exist with the current system of background checks, parents and the community should not be lulled into a false sense of complacency regarding children's safety when such a system is in place. Given this caveat, NAEYC offers these recommendations for the effective use of criminal record checks.

1. The costs of completing a criminal record background check should be kept as low as possible, and the check should be completed in a timely manner.

2. The scope of the check should be clear. State regulations vary as to which records are searched: local, state, and/or federal criminal convictions; child abuse registries; or sex offender registries. With regard to child abuse registries, states employ different standards as to the type of information recorded, resulting in serious shortcomings of these data. For example, some registries include unsubstantiated allegations, and some registries record instances of abuse by the name of the victim rather than the perpetrator, making it difficult to track abusers (Cohen 1985).

3. If convictions are uncovered, clear procedures for action should be in place. Some states require individuals to undergo a background check before they can be hired to work with children but have no clear procedures for action when substantiated convictions are found.

4. Results of background checks should be readily available to families, especially those families using in-home child care, family child care, or other settings exempt from public regulation. Some states have used technology to make information on background checks readily available to families and providers. Colorado has instituted a system that allows access to information at public libraries and child care resource-and-referral programs. California was the first state to institute a Child Care Trustline. This database includes current and potential child care providers who have successfully undergone a criminal record background check. Parents and programs can check potential employees against the database to ensure that their names appear (as opposed to a criminal background check in which being listed is a negative).

Role of Early Childhood Professionals

Monitoring by public agencies helps to ensure basic acceptable levels of quality in early childhood programs. However, it is the responsibility of early childhood professionals to

1. Promote standards of excellence toward which programs may strive. NAEYC encourages centers and eligible schools to pursue NAEYC accreditation. This process requires programs to undertake a rigorous self-study process and provides for an independent external assessment to determine whether high standards are met. Other accreditation systems are available for family child care homes and schools not eligible for NAEYC accreditation.

2. Assist in informing the public about the need for and the ingredients of high-quality early childhood programs.

3. Encourage the continued professional development of all early childhood professionals.

4. Advocate for well-designed, sufficiently funded, and effectively implemented public regulations and programs that reduce the incidence of abuse against children.

5. Understand their ethical obligations to recognize and report suspicions of abuse (see Feeney and Kipnis 1992).

Early childhood professionals can also play an important role in helping to prevent the incidence of child abuse in other settings beyond early childhood programs. The vast majority of child abuse is committed by family members or others who are close to the family. By establishing supporting relationships with families, early childhood professionals may help reduce the likelihood of child abuse by family members. Programs should make readily available to families under stress appropriate information and referrals to community services and provide information and support for families regarding appropriate discipline and guidance of young children. In addition, early childhood professionals should advocate for effective community support services, including child protective services, social services, and mental health services that include sufficient numbers of qualified staff sensitive to meeting the individual needs of children and families.

Conclusion

The National Association for the Education of Young Children is strongly committed to promoting high quality in early childhood programs. Practices that lead to high-quality programs help reduce the likelihood of abuse of children in out-of-home settings, and high-quality programs can provide support to families to reduce instances of abuse in the home. Thus, the members of NAEYC pledge their commitment and expertise to work with other concerned individuals and groups to provide a safe and wholesome environment for all of America's children.

References

Cohen, A. 1985. *Use of statewide central child abuse registries for purposes of screening child care workers: False promises and troubling concerns.* San Francisco: Child Care Law Center.

Feeney, S., and K. Kipnis. 1992. *Code of ethical conduct & statement of professional commitment.* Washington, DC: NAEYC.

NAEYC. 1991. *Accreditation criteria and procedures of the National Academy of Early Childhood Programs,* rev. ed. Washington, DC: Author.

National Committee to Prevent Child Abuse. 1995. *Annual survey of incidence of child abuse.* Chicago: Author.

U.S. Department of Health and Human Services. National Center on Child Abuse and Neglect. 1996. *Child maltreatment 1994: Reports from the states to the National Center on Child Abuse and Neglect.* Washington, DC: GPO.

Wells, S., N. Davis, K. Dennis, R. Chipman, C. Sandt, and M. Liss. 1995. *Effective screening of child care and youth service workers.* Washington, DC: American Bar Association Center on Children and the Law.

Willer, B., S. L. Hofferth, E. E.Ksiker, P. Divine-Hawkins, E. Farquhar, and F. B. Glantz. 1991. *The demand and supply of child care in 1990.* Washington, DC: NAEYC.

Additional Resources

Feeney, S., and K. Kipnis. 1992. *Code of Ethical Conduct and Statement of Commitment.* [Brochure available in English and Spanish editions.] NAEYC.

Kendrick, A. S., R. Kaufmann, and K. P. Messenger, eds. 1995. *Healthy young children: A manual for programs.* Washington, DC: NAEYC.

NAEYC Position Statement on Violence in the Lives of Children. 1993. [Brochure.] Washington, DC: NAEYC.

National Committee to Prevent Child Abuse. 332 S. Michigan Ave., Chicago, IL 60604.

Tower, C. C. 1992. *The role of educators in the prevention and treatment of child abuse and neglect: The user manual series.* U.S. Department of Health and Human Services, National Center on Child Abuse, and Neglect. DHHS Publication No. (ACF) 92-30172.

GLOSSARY

accreditation: A voluntary process with a goal of increasing and maintaining high quality in early childhood programs

active listening: An interpersonal communication strategy that promotes clear and honest exchanges of information

adaptation: In family systems theory, a process that engages a family's recovery factors so that family members are able to bounce back after crises

adjustment: In family systems theory, a process that engages a family's protective factors to help it continue to function even with risks

adoption: A legal process of taking a child into one's family and raising that child as one's own

advocacy: Activities that support and call for support for children and families

anti-bias: An educational approach that fosters fairness, equity, and inclusion in all areas, including culture, ethnicity, gender, language, and more

at-risk children: Children at risk for developmental delays or disabilities due to family situations including poverty, psychopathology, loss of members, or inability to nurture

attachment: The psychological, and probably biological, process by which parents and children create emotional bonds with one another

authoritarian parenting: An approach to child-rearing that emphasizes adult control of children's behavior

authoritative parenting: An approach to child-rearing that includes stating expectations for children and communicating with them in respectful ways

balanced families: According to the circumplex model, families that demonstrate a balance in both cohesion and flexibility

bioecological theory: Theory proposed by Urie Bronfenbrenner that relates ecological systems to human development

birth order: The sequence in which children are born or adopted into families

blended families: Families in which one or both partners bring children from another relationship

buoyancy: In family systems theory, a family's ability to recover quickly from a challenge or transition

child abuse and neglect: Maltreatment of a child and the failure of parents or other responsible adults to provide necessary care and supervision

chronosystem: According to bioecological theory, the sociohistorical context of an individual

circumplex model: A family systems model intended to demonstrate how all family members are interconnected

codependency: When a person sacrifices his or her own needs to serve another person to an unhealthy extreme

cohesion: According to the circumplex model, family togetherness

community resources: Support available to children and families in a particular community

community school: an educational model that places schools in the center of communities, open to all, and created through multiple partnerships

conflict resolution: Strategies for constructively processing differences between individuals or groups

congruence: The degree of similarity between home and school

contextualist theories: Approaches that demonstrate the importance of relationships among children, families, and communities that are crucial to effective family involvement in early childhood education

continuity: Efforts made to support children as they move from home to school or from one school setting to another

crises: In family systems theory, the possibility for a family's ongoing instability or dysfunction

culture: Socially transmitted behavior patterns typical of a population or of a community at a given time

developmental assets: Critical factors necessary for children's healthy development

developmental contextualism: A theoretical approach to understanding human development that considers both a strong biological foundation and family as the central social institution

developmentally appropriate practices (DAP): Those practices in early childhood education that are derived from deep knowledge of individual children and the context in which they develop and learn

disability: Physical, learning, or emotional factors that call for adaptations

diversity: The understanding that family structures, functions, characteristics, and interests are varied

donor insemination: The introduction of semen from a known or anonymous male into the female reproductive organs without sexual contact

downsizing: A phenomenon of corporations reducing number of employees

early childhood education: Any program of care and education for children from birth through 8 years of age

early intervention: Comprehensive educational programs for young children who are at risk or who have been identified as having a disability

elasticity: In family systems theory, a family's capacity to maintain its ability to engage in established patterns of functioning after being challenged by risk factors

emotional intelligence: ability to perceive, understand and control feelings and expressions of emotion

empathy: Understanding another's feelings, situation, values, and goals

empowering: The establishment of a model whereby all families can assert an active role in the education of their children

ethnicity: Identification with or belonging to a religious, racial, national, or cultural group

exosystem: According to bioecological theory, a system that has indirect effects on an individual

expressive role: Traditionally, the role that mothers have in providing the primary care and love for their children

extended family: Family members beyond parents and children, especially grandparents, aunts, uncles, and cousins

extended family relationships: The nature of the connection between an individual and extended family members

extreme families: According to the circumplex model, classification of families that are extreme in both cohesion and flexibility

family accord: Relates to a family's impression of competency in dealing with conflict

family coping: Strategies of families for dealing with stress

family-friendly work policies: Employer policies that consider the primacy of the family

family functions: Primary reasons for existence of the family unit

family life cycle approach: An approach to understanding families that considers how families typically change over time

family life education: A broad understanding of the influences in a child's life including quality of relationships with family members

family of orientation: The family into which one is born

family of procreation: The family that one creates by having children

family pride: Characteristics such as mutual respect, trust, loyalty, optimism, and sharedvalues in a family

family protective factors: In family systems theory, a positive side of families' ability to cope when faced with stressors that lead to increases in a family's elasticity

family recovery factors: In family systems theory, a positive side of families' ability to cope when faced with stressors that lead to supporting a family's buoyancy

family size: The number of family members residing together

family strengths: An approach to understanding families that emphasizes characteristics of healthy family relationships

family structure: The unique ways that families organize

family support movement: A perspective that recognizes that families are responsible for their children's development and that no family can function alone

family systems theory: A framework that emphasizes the notion that everything that happens to any family member affects all other family members

family violence: Abuse or injury within families

FERPA: Family Education Rights and Privacy Act is a federal law designed to protect the privacy of students' academic records

flexibility: According to the circumplex model, a family's ability to deal with change

gender inequality: The phenomenon of males having greater power than females in society

gender role: Expected social behavior relating to being male or female

high-quality, affordable child care: Child care that local families can pay for and meets these criteria: child-centered curriculum, well-trained teachers, and planned family involvement

home visiting: An educational practice whereby early childhood professionals meet with families in their homes

homeless: Having no home or refuge

horizontal stressors: According to family systems theory, stress-producing events that occur over time

ideals: In the NAEYC Code of Ethical Conduct, the aspirations of practitioners.

immigrant families: Families that leave one country to settle in another

incarcerated: Jailed or imprisoned; denied freedom

inclusion: An educational practice whereby programs enroll both typically developing children and children with identified disabilities

inclusiveness: An educational approach that is welcoming to all children and families

indulgent: A parenting style that is lenient, does not require mature behavior and avoids confrontation

instrumental role: Traditionally, the role of fathers with their children that has a minimal role in caring for children

interdisciplinary collaboration: A consensus-building model that uses a variety of perspectives to determine a plan for family involvement in a child's education

interpersonal communication: Effective strategies of human interaction between or among people

irreducible needs: Those needs that are basic to children's survival and optimal development

linkages: The level, type, and frequency of communication between families and schools

literacy: The ability to use language, especially reading, writing, speaking, and listening in order to communicate

macrosystem: According to bioecological theory, the culture in which one lives

marital transition: Process involved in moving into or out of marriage

maternal employment: The number of hours mothers of young children are employed outside the home

mesosystem: According to bioecological theory, relationships between contexts in the microsystem

microsystem: According to bioecological theory, the setting in which one lives or the near environment

midrange families: According to the circumplex model, families that are extreme with either cohesion or flexibility and balanced with either cohesion or flexibility

migrant families: Families who travel from place to place in order to gain employment

NAEYC code of ethical conduct: The early childhood education profession's expectations for appropriate, optimal behavior and practices for its members

nuclear family: Self-contained family unit consisting of parents and children

nurturance: Caring for and providing for children

overlapping spheres of influence: The understanding that families, schools, and communities are intermingled and not discrete

parent education: Providing a variety of sources of support for the parents' role in caring for their children

parental attachment: The strong emotional bond that exists between parents and their children

parental rights: An educational philosophy based on the understanding that parents have the primary role in their children's lives

parenting: Care, love, and guidance provided by parents to their children

permissive parenting: An approach to child-rearing that exercises little control over children and exerts few demands on children's behavior

preschool inclusion: A preschool educational practice that provides planned programs for children with and without identified disabilities

primacy of parental rights: A view that upholds the strict limits of the U.S. Constitution to interfere with family life

principles: In the NAEYC Code of Ethical Conduct, guides to assist practitioners in their conduct for resolving ethical dilemmas.

professional associations: Groups with membership open to specific professions that often provide information about and guide current research, practice, and advocacy

public policies: Federal, state, and local laws

quality indicators: Standards used by the National Parent Teacher Association to assess family involvement in schools

race: A group of people distinguished by more or less distinct genetically transmitted physical characteristics

referral: The process of seeking and acquiring additional or different educational or support services to meet needs of individual children

religiosity: The degree to which a family values or practices religious beliefs

resilience: In family systems theory, the property of the family system that enables it to be elastic and buoyant

resilient children: Children who exhibit good developmental outcomes despite high-risk family situations

right of family integrity: The legal basis for parents to bear and rear children according to their own beliefs

self-disclosure: Sharing information from one's own life situation

serious illness: Health conditions that are chronic or life-threatening

sibling relationships: Connections and interactions between or among children in the same family (sisters and brothers)

socialization: A parental responsibility to teach and support children in how to get along with others

sociocultural theory: Vygotsky's theory that emphasizes the relationship of the social environment, particularly cultural, to cognition and learning

spirituality: The quality of being concerned with the soul, God, and/or a religious institution

substance abuse: Illegal or overuse of drugs or alcohol

Temporary Assistance for Needy Families (TANF): Federal legislation that provides support to families in poverty

tolerance: Acts intended to promote equity, diversity, and inclusiveness, as well as to deter hate

transition to parenthood: Adjustment of an individual to new roles as a parent

trilemma: Issues that arise in concerns for quality, affordability, and accessibility of child care

two-way communication: Various educational practices that foster essential communication between home and school (as opposed to unilateral sharing of information in one direction only)

uninvolved: a parenting style that is low on control and warmth with a low commitment to children

vertical stressors: According to family systems theory, stress-producing events that are embedded in particular families' patterns of relating

vulnerability: In family systems theory, a family's possibility of being faced with risk factors that may negatively affect functioning

zone of proximal development (ZPD): According to Vygotsky, the mechanism by which human development occurs

INDEX

Page numbers followed by f indicate figures.

Families, Schools, and Communities: Together for Young Children
Correlation with the National Association for the Education of Young Children (NAEYC)
Standards for Initial Early Childhood Professional Preparation Programs*

NAEYC Standards	Correlated with Content in *Families, Schools, and Communities: Together for Young Children*
Standard 4. Using Developmentally Effective Approaches	**Chapters and Page Numbers**
4a: Understanding positive relationships and supportive interactions as the foundation of their work with young children	Chapter 1—pages 4, 5, 7, 17, 18, 21, 22 Chapter 2—pages 32, 35, 38, 44, 45, 46, 48 Chapter 3—page 63 Chapter 6—pages 147, 150 Chapter 7—pages 165, 167, 168, 174, 179 Chapter 9—pages 224, 227
4b: Knowing and understanding effective strategies and tools for early education, including appropriate uses of technology	Chapter 1—pages 7, 8, 9, 18, 20, 21, 22 Chapter 2—pages 32, 35, 36, 38, 48, 49, 50, 51, 52 Chapter 4—page 91 Chapter 7—pages 167, 168, 169, 170, 171, 175, 179 Chapter 8—page 203 Chapter 9—pages 217, 219, 220, 221, 223, 224 Chapter 10—pages 238, 239, 240 Chapter 11—pages 267, 268
4c: Using a broad repertoire of developmentally appropriate teaching/learning approaches	Chapter 1—pages 18, 20, 21, 22 Chapter 2—pages 32, 35, 36, 48, 49, 50, 51, 52 Chapter 7—pages 167, 168, 169, 170, 171 Chapter 9—pages 220, 223
4d: Reflecting on own practice to promote positive outcomes for each child	Chapter 2—page 31 Chapter 7—pages 176, 179, 181
Standard 5. Using Content Knowledge to Build Meaningful Curriculum	**Chapters and Page Numbers**
5a: Understanding content knowledge and resources in academic disciplines: language and literacy; the arts—music, creative movement, dance, drama, visual arts; mathematics; science, physical activity, physical education, health and safety; and social studies	Chapter 2—pages 35, 36 Chapter 9—pages 219, 221, 222, 223, 224, 226

Continued

5b: Knowing and using the central concepts, inquiry tools, and structures of content areas or academic disciplines	Chapter 2—pages 35, 36 Chapter 9—pages 217, 224
5c: Using own knowledge, appropriate early learning standards, and other resources to design, implement, and evaluate developmentally meaningful and challenging curriculum for each child	Chapter 1—pages 8, 9, 10, 11, 12, 16, 17, 18, 19, 20, 21, 22, 23, 24 Chapter 2—pages 35, 36, 48, 49, 50, 51, 52 Chapter 9—pages 217, 227, 228
Standard 6. Becoming a Professional	**Chapters and Page Numbers**
6a: Identifying and involving oneself with the early childhood field	Chapter 1—pages 5, 6, 7, 8, 9, 10, 12, 16, 17, 18, 19, 20, 21, 22, 23 Chapter 2—pages 29, 33, 35, 37, 40, 45, 46, 49, 50, 51, 52 Chapter 11—pages 262, 271
6b: Knowing about and upholding ethical standards and other early childhood professional guidelines	Chapter 1—pages 16, 17, 18, 19, 20, 21, 22, 23 Chapter 2—pages 31, 34, 35, 40, 50, 51, 52 Chapter 3—pages 78, 79 Chapter 6—pages 134, 152 Chapter 7—pages 170, 176 Chapter 8—page 204 Chapter 11—pages 271, 277
6c: Engaging in continuous, collaborative learning to inform practice; using technology effectively with young children, with peers, and as a professional resource	Chapter 3—page 58 Chapter 6—pages 137, 140, 145, 150, 151 Chapter 7—pages 173, 176, 177 Chapter 8—pages 196, 209 Chapter 10—page 234 Chapter 11—pages 262, 268, 269, 270
6d: Integrating knowledgeable, reflective, and critical perspectives on early education	Chapter 1—pages 17, 18, 19, 20, 21, 22, 23 Chapter 2—pages 31, 45, 46 Chapter 3—pages 62, 65, 71, 75, 78 Chapter 4—pages 86, 87, 88, 90, 92, 94, 95, 97, 100 Chapter 5—pages 110, 114, 115, 117, 122, 123, 124 Chapter 6—pages 130, 134, 139, 142, 147 Chapter 7—pages 172, 176 Chapter 8—pages 189, 205, 207, 209, 210 Chapter 10—pages 234, 245

Continued